FreeCAD 1.0 Learn by doing

Tutorial Books

FreeCAD 1.0 Learn by doing

For resource files contact us at
freecadtuts@gmail.com

Table of Contents

Table of Contents iv
Introduction 1
Topics covered in this Book 1
Chapter 1: Getting Started with FreeCAD 1.0 2
Introduction to FreeCAD 2
Selecting a Plane 4
Starting FreeCAD 6
User Interface 6
Graphics window 7
File Menu 8
Toolbars 9
File Toolbar 9
Edit Toolbar 9
View toolbar 10
Menu 14
Status bar 14
Mouse Functions 15
FreeCAD Help 18
Questions 18
Chapter 2: Sketch Techniques 20
Creating Sketches 20
Grid and Snap Settings 20
Toggle grid 21
Toggle Snap 22
Sketch Commands 22
The Line command 23
The Polyline command 24
Creating Arcs 26
The Center and end points command 26
The Create arc by 3 points command 27
Creating Circles 27
Center circle by center 27
3 rim points 28
Creating Rectangles 28

Create a 2 Point Rectangle 28

Centered Rectangle 28

Rounded Rectangle 29

Create Slot 29

Create Slot 30

Creating Polygons 30

Triangle 30

Square 31

Pentagon 31

Hexagon 32

Heptagon 32

Octagon 32

Regular Polygon 33

The Create ellipse by center command 33

The Create ellipse by 3 points command 34

Toggle Construction geometry 35

Adding Dimensions 35

The Dimensions command 35

Constrain Horizontal Distance 37

Constrain Vertical Distance 38

Constrain Distance 39

Constrain angle 39

Constrain diameter 39

Adding Dimensions to an Arc 40

Adding a Radius 40

Adding a Linear dimension to the Arc 41

Constrain auto radius/diameter 41

Over-constrained Sketch 42

Geometric Constraints 42

Constrain Coincident 42

Constrain Horizontal 43

Constrain Vertical 44

Constrain horizontal/vertical 45

Contrain equal 45

Constrain tangent or collinear 46
Parallel Constraint 46
Perpendicular Constraint 47
Symmetrical Constraint 47
Block Constraint 48
Toggle driving/reference constraint 48
Activate/deactivate constraint 49
The Create Fillet command 49
The Create Chamfer command 50
Preserve corner 50
The Extend edge command 51
The Trim Edge command 51
The Split Edge command 52
The Select unconstrained DOF command 52
Move/array transform 53
Delete all Constraints 56
Delete all geometry 56
Remove axes alignment 57
Removing Redundant Constraints 57
The Mirror Sketch command 59
Creating Splines 59
Create B-spline 60
Periodic B-spline by control points 61
B-spline by Knots 61
Periodic B-spline by Knots 62
Best Practices 62
Cautions 63
Tips 63
Tutorial 1 (Millimetres) 64
Starting a new part file 64
Starting a sketch 65
Adding Constraints 67
Adding Dimensions 67
Tutorial 2 (Inches) 71
Creating a New document 72

Creating a Sketch 72
Tutorial 3 (Millimetres) 78
Creating a New Document 79
Creating a Sketch 79
Questions 87
Exercises 88
Exercise 1 88
Exercise 2 88
Exercise 3 89
Chapter 3: Pad and Revolve Features 90
Pad Features 90
Extruding the Sketch in the Custom Direction 91
Revolved Features 92
Best Practices: 95
Cautions: 96
Tips: 96
External Geometry 96
Pocket 98
The Groove command 98
Planes 99
Creating a Parallel plane 99
Inertia 2-3 100
Plane at Angle 100
Plane by 3 Points 101
Normal to 3 Points 101
Tangent to Surface 101
Normal to edge 102
Revolution section 102
Best Practices: 103
Cautions: 103
Tip: 103
Datum Line 103
1st principal axis 103
Through Two Points 104
Normal to surface 105

Datum Point ...105
Center of mass ...105
Vertex ...106
Additional options of the Pad and Pocket commands ...106
Extent Type ...106
Adding Taper to the Pad Feature ...109
Best Practices while Extruding Sketches ...110
Cautions to Keep in Mind ...111
Useful Tips ...111
View Modification commands ...112
Tutorial 1 (Millimeters) ...115
Creating a New Document ...115
Creating a Sketch ...115
Creating a Pad Feature ...116
Creating a Pocket Feature ...117
Extruding a sketch up to the Face next to the sketch plane ...118
Extruding a sketch up to a selected face ...121
Tutorial 2 (Inches) ...121
Creating a New document ...122
Creating a Revolved Feature ...122
Creating a Groove feature ...123
Adding a Revolution Feature to the Model ...124
Questions ...125
Exercises ...126
Exercise 1 ...126
Exercise 2 ...127
Exercise 3 ...127
Chapter 4: Dress-up Features ...129
Hole ...129
Simple Hole ...130
Counterbored Hole ...132
Countersink Hole ...133
Counterdrill Hole ...134
Threaded Hole ...134
Best Practices ...136

Cautions 137
Tips 137
Fillet 137
Selection Modes 138
Best Practices 139
Cautions: 139
Chamfer 140
Equal Distance chamfer 140
Distance and Angle chamfer 141
Two Distances chamfer 141
The Draft command 142
General Guidelines 144
Drafting Tips for Different Part Types 144
Cautions: 145
Thickness 145
Best Practices 146
Cautions 147
Tips 147
Tutorial 1 (Millimetres) 148
Creating a New document 148
Creating the Pad Feature 149
Creating the Hole Features 152
Creating Fillets and Chamfers 156
Tutorial 2 (Inches) 158
Creating a New document 158
Creating the Pad features 159
Creating the Rib 162
Creating the Pocket features 164
Creating the Fillet and Hole features 166
Tutorial 3 (Millimeters) 167
Creating a New document 167
Creating the Pad features 168
Creating the Angled Plane 169
Creating the Pad feature 169
Creating the Hole feature 171

- Questions ... 172
- Exercises ... 173
  - Exercise 1 (Inches) ... 173
  - Exercise 2 (Millimeters) ... 174

Chapter 5: Patterned Geometry ... 176

- Mirrored ... 178
  - Mirror Bodies ... 179
  - Best Practices ... 179
  - Cautions ... 180
  - Tips for Specific Part Types ... 180
- Create Patterns ... 180
  - Linear Pattern ... 180
  - Polar Pattern ... 181
  - Multi Transform ... 183
- Tutorial 1 ... 187
  - Creating a New document ... 187
  - Creating the Pad features ... 188
  - Creating the Hole features ... 190
  - Creating the Multi transform feature ... 192
  - Creating the threaded Hole feature ... 193
  - Mirroring the Features ... 194
  - Creating the Hole and Pocket features ... 195
- Tutorial 2 (Millimetres) ... 198
  - Creating a New document ... 199
  - Creating the Pad Feature ... 199
  - Adding a Lip to the model ... 203
  - Creating Bosses ... 204
  - Creating Ribs ... 208
- Tutorial 3 (Millimeters) ... 212
  - Creating a New document ... 212
  - Creating the Pad feature ... 213
  - Creating the Counterbore Hole ... 217
  - Creating the Polar Pattern ... 217
  - Creating a New Body ... 218
  - Creating a Common Body Between the Two Bodies ... 219

Creating Cylindrical Feature and Hole at the center....219
Creating Fillets....221
Tutorial 4 (Millimeters)....221
Creating a New document....222
Creating the Pad feature....222
Adding the Pad feature....223
Creating the Polar Pattern....225
Creating the Pocket Features....225
Creating a Polar Pattern....227
Questions....228
Exercises....228
Exercise 1....228
Chapter 6: Pipe Features....231
Additive Pipe....232
Section Orientation....234
Creating an Additive Pipe between two Cross-sections....235
Subtractive pipe....236
Best Practices for Pipe features....238
General Swept Features:....238
Plastic Parts:....238
Casted Parts:....238
Forged Parts:....238
Machined Parts:....239
3D Printed Parts for Makers:....239
Additive helix....239
Subtractive helix....243
Best Practices....243
Cautions....243
Tips for Different Types of Parts....243
Tutorial 1....244
Creating a New document....245
Creating the Pipe Feature....245
Adding the Pad Feature....250
Creating the Polar pattern....251
Questions....254

Exercises ... 255
Exercise1 ... 255
Chapter 7: Loft Features ... 256
Additive Loft ... 256
Subtractive Loft ... 259
Best Practices ... 259
Cautions: ... 260
Tips for Specific Types of Parts: ... 260
Plastic Parts: ... 260
Casted Parts: ... 260
Forged Parts: ... 260
Machined Parts: ... 260
3D Printed Parts: ... 260
Tutorial 1 ... 260
Creating a New document ... 261
Creating a Loft Feature ... 261
Mirroring the Loft and Pad features ... 264
Questions ... 265
Exercises ... 265
Exercise 1 ... 265
Chapter 8: Modifying Parts ... 267
Edit Sketches ... 267
Edit Feature ... 268
Deleting Sketches ... 269
Attachment Editor ... 269
Best Practices ... 271
Cautions ... 271
Additional Tip ... 271
Tutorial 1 (Inches) ... 272
Creating a New document ... 273
Editing a Feature ... 273
Editing Sketches ... 274
Questions ... 277
Exercises ... 277
Exercise 1 ... 277

Exercise 2 277
Chapter 9: Assemblies 279
Starting an Assembly 279
Inserting Components 280
Moving and Rotating Parts 281
Applying Constraints 282
Coincident Plane Constraint 282
The Opposed direction 282
The Aligned Direction 283
Axis Coincident Constraint 284
Circular Edge Constraint 286
Angled Planes Constraint 286
Planes Parallelism Constraint 288
Sphere to Sphere constraint 288
Editing an Imported Part 289
Edit selected constraint 291
Sub-assemblies 291
Best Practices 292
General Cautions 292
Tutorial 1 (Bottom-Up Assembly) 292
Creating the Assembly file 294
Inserting part files in the Assemblies 295
Defining Constraints 296
Questions 300
Exercises 301
Exercise 1 301
Chapter 10: Drawings 303
Starting a Drawing 303
Inserting the Drawing page 304
Insert View 305
Insert Active View 307
Section View 307
Section View alignment 309
Creating an Offset view 309
Creating a Revolved Section View 312

Detail View 315
Add Centerlines to Faces 317
  Add Centerline between 2 Lines 318
  Add Centerline between 2 Points 318
  Add Circle Centerlines 319
  Add Bolt Circle Centerlines 320
  Add Cosmetic Thread Hole Bottom View 320
  Add Cosmetic Thread Hole Side View 321
  Add Cosmetic Thread Bolt Side View 321
  Add Cosmetic Thread Bolt Bottom View 322
  Add Cosmetic Intersection Vertex 322
Dimensions 323
  Add Axonometric length dimension 328
  Create Coordinate Dimensions 329
  Cascade Dimensions 330
  Chain Dimensions 332
  Position Chain Dimensions 333
  Calculate the area of selected faces 334
Add Leaderline to View 335
Insert Rich Text Annotation 337
Insert Annotation 338
Add Welding Information to Leaderline 339
Create a Surface Finish Symbol 341
Adding hole Fit or Shat Fit 342
Chamfer Dimensions 345
Best Practices for Generating Drawings in FreeCAD 345
  Specific Considerations for Different Types of Parts 346
  Precautions 346
Tutorial 1 346
  Creating a New Drawing 347
  Inserting the Base View 348
  Generating the Section View 349
  Inserting the Isometric View 350
  Adding the center lines to the drawing view 350
  Adding Dimensions 352

Questions 357
Exercises 357
Exercise 1 357
Exercise 2 358
Index 359

Introduction

Welcome to *FreeCAD 1.0 Learn by doing* book. This book is written to assist students, designers, and engineering professionals in designing 3D models. It covers the essential features and functionalities of FreeCAD using relevant tutorials and exercises.

Topics covered in this Book

- Chapter 1, "Getting Started with FreeCAD," gives an introduction to FreeCAD. The user interface and terminology are discussed in this chapter.

- Chapter 2, "Sketch Techniques," explores the sketching commands in FreeCAD. You will learn to create parametric sketches.

- Chapter 3, "Pad and Revolve features," teaches you to create basic 3D geometry using the Pad and Revolve commands.

- Chapter 4, "Dress-up Features," covers the features which can be created without using sketches.

- Chapter 5, "Patterned Geometry," explores the commands to create patterned and mirrored geometry.

- Chapter 6, "Pipe Features," covers the commands to create swept and helical features.

- Chapter 7, "Loft Features," covers the Loft command and its core features.

- Chapter 8, "Modifying Parts," explores the commands and techniques to modify the part geometry.

- Chapter 9, "Assemblies," helps you to create assemblies using the bottom-up and top-down design approaches.

- Chapter 10, "Drawings," covers how to create 2D drawings from 3D parts and assemblies.

Chapter 1: Getting Started with FreeCAD 1.0

Introduction to FreeCAD

FreeCAD is an open-source CAD application. It is a parametric and feature-based system that allows you to create 3D parts, assemblies, and 2D drawings. The design process in FreeCAD is shown below.

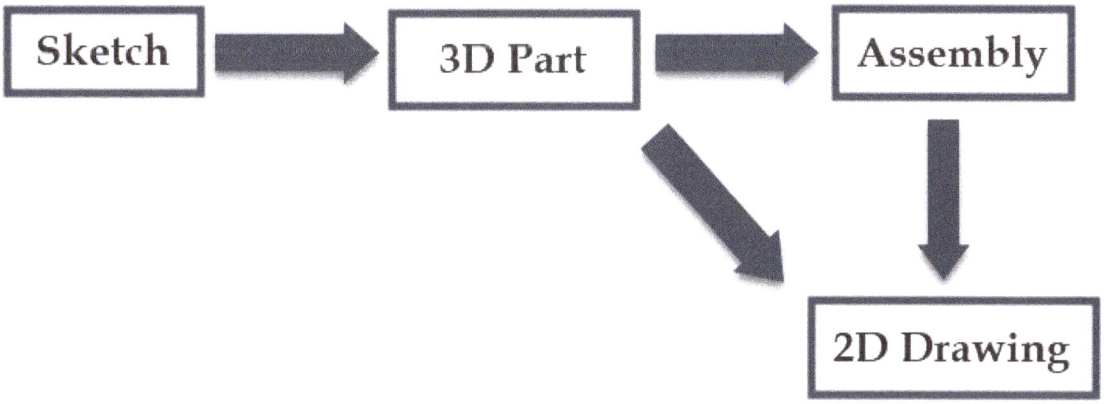

In FreeCAD, everything is controlled by parameters or constraints. For example, if you want to change the position of the hole shown in the figure, you need to change the constraint that controls its position.

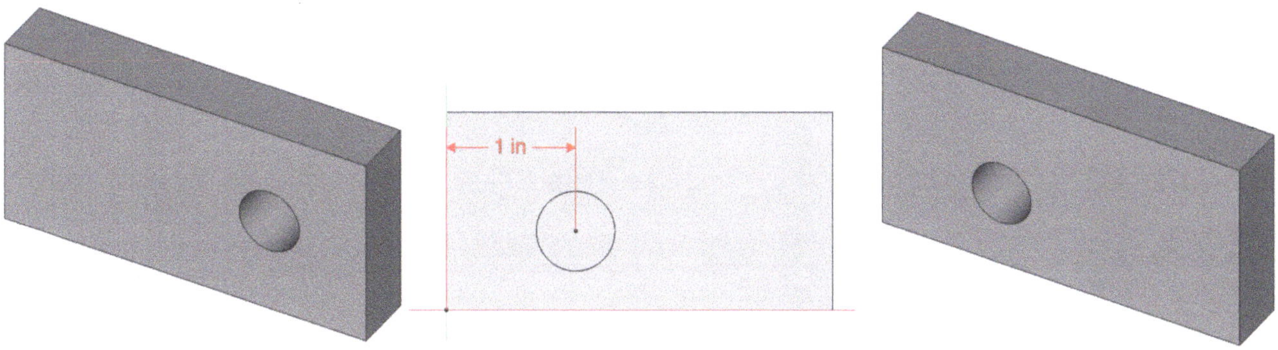

The parameters and constraints that you set up allow you to have control over the design intent. The design intent describes the way your 3D model will behave when you apply constraints to it. For example, if you want to position the hole at the center of the block, one way is to add constraints between the hole and the adjacent edges. However, when you change the size of the block, the hole will not be at the center.

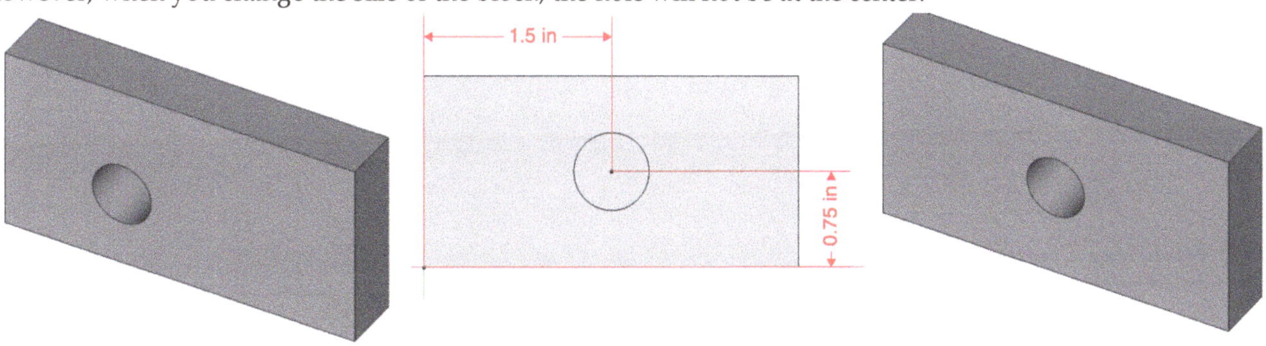

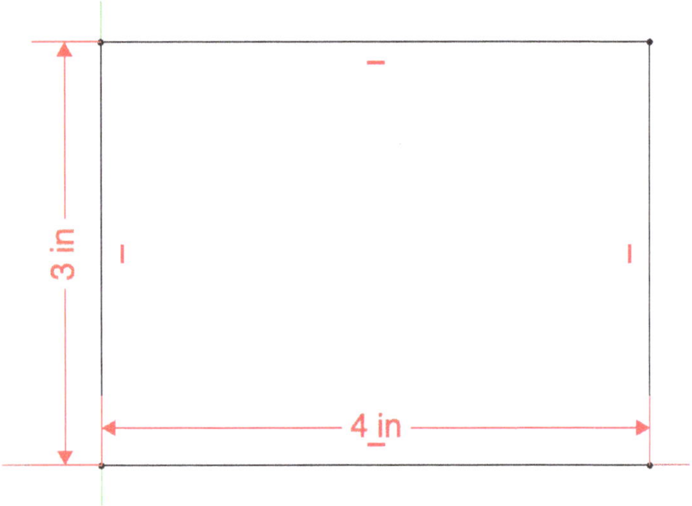

You can make the hole to be at the center, even if the size of the block changes. To do this, right click on the sketch used to create the hole and select **Edit sketch**. Next, delete the constraints and create a diagonal construction line. Apply the **Symmetrical** constraint between the hole centerpoint and the endpoints of the construction line. Next, click **Close** on the **Combo View** panel.

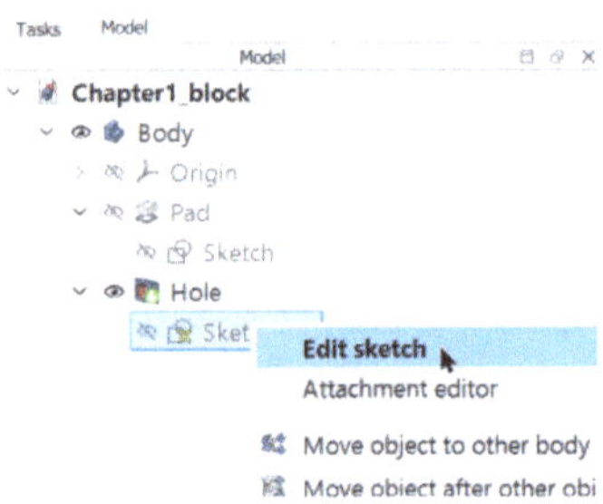

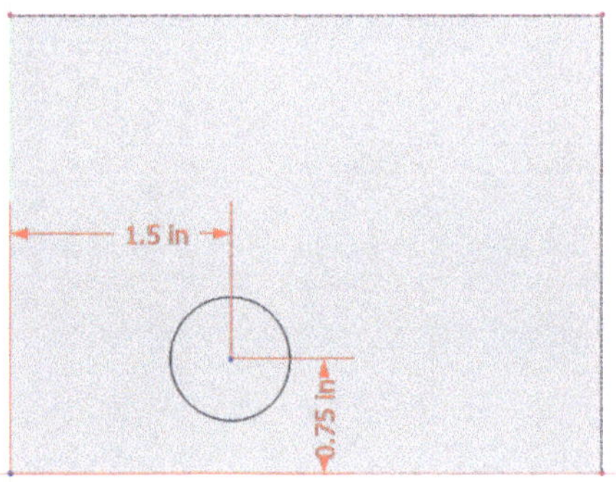

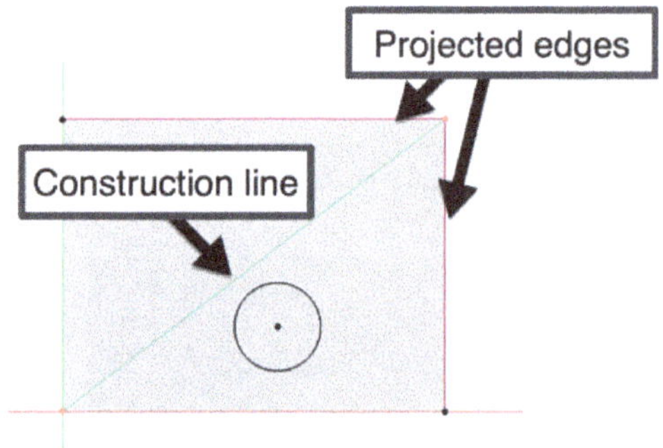

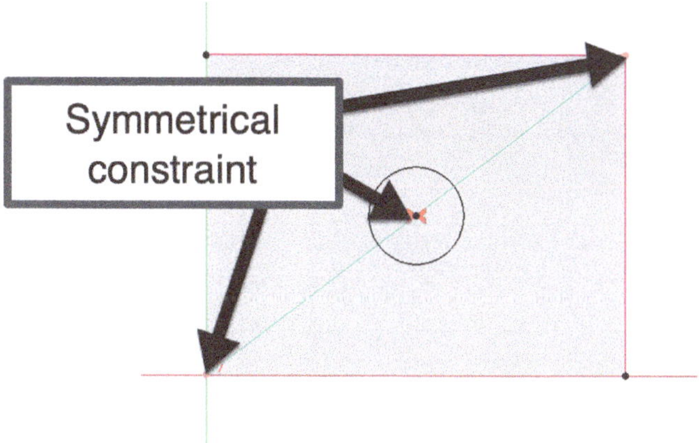

Now, even if you change the size of the block, the hole will always remain at the center.

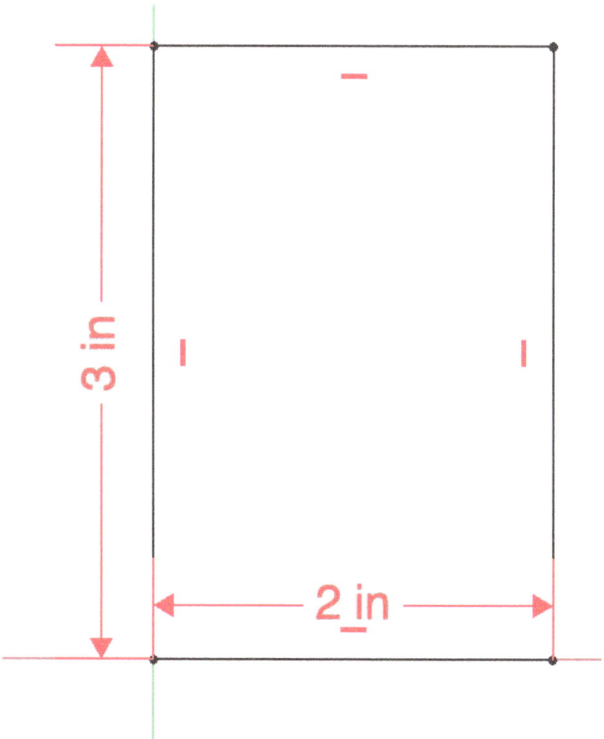

Selecting a Plane

When designing a parametric model, selecting the initial sketch plane sets the stage for how features develop spatially. For example, consider a pad feature of a rectangular profile. If the sketch is drawn on the XZ-plane, the pad will project perpendicularly along the depth axis, creating a 3D block that extends forward or backward.

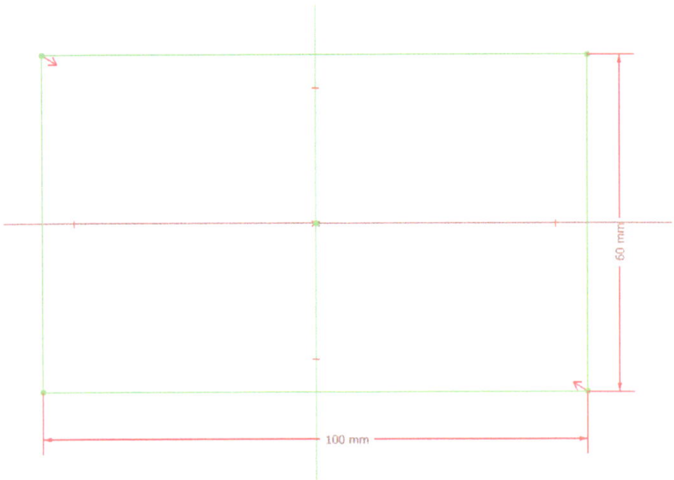

Sketch created on XZ-Plane

However, if the same sketch is placed on the XY-Plane, the pad feature will instead build upward or downward along the vertical axis, resulting in a tower-like structure. This directional dependency means you must choose the plane that aligns with the intended geometry's "growth" direction, such as matching a part's manufacturing orientation (e.g., a vertically cast component starting from the top plane).

For pipe features, the sketch plane governs the path's orientation. Imagine creating a pipe using a Additive pipe feature: if the path is sketched on the YZ-plane, the pipe can still curve forward/backward or upward/downward, bending within that plane's orientation. Conversely, drawing the path on the XZ plane allows the hose to curve left, right, upward, or downward.

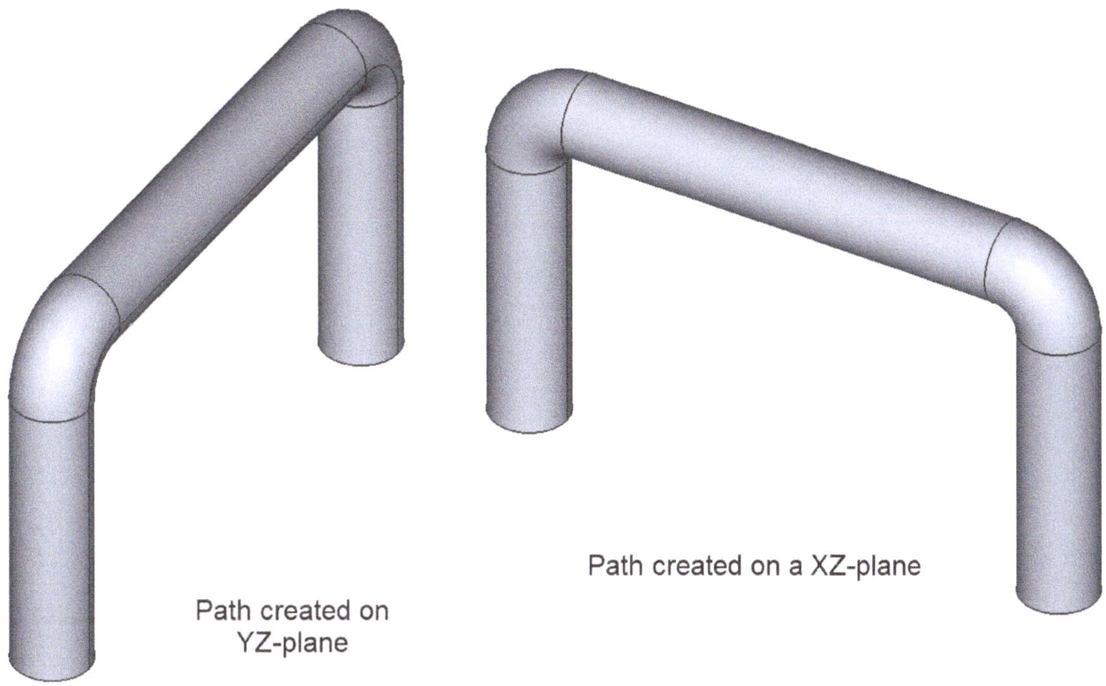

Standard planes work well for simple designs, but complex shapes often need custom planes. Picking the right plane early helps avoid problems, like parts not fitting together correctly. By planning how features align with the plane, you save time fixing errors later.

Starting FreeCAD

To start **FreeCAD**, click the **FreeCAD 1.0** icon on your Desktop. On the menu bar, click **File > New**; a new design file will appear on the screen. You can change the working units of the file. To do this, click the **Edit > Preferences** on the menu bar. Next, click the **General** tab and set the **Default unit System** and click **OK**.

User Interface

The following image shows the **FreeCAD** application window.

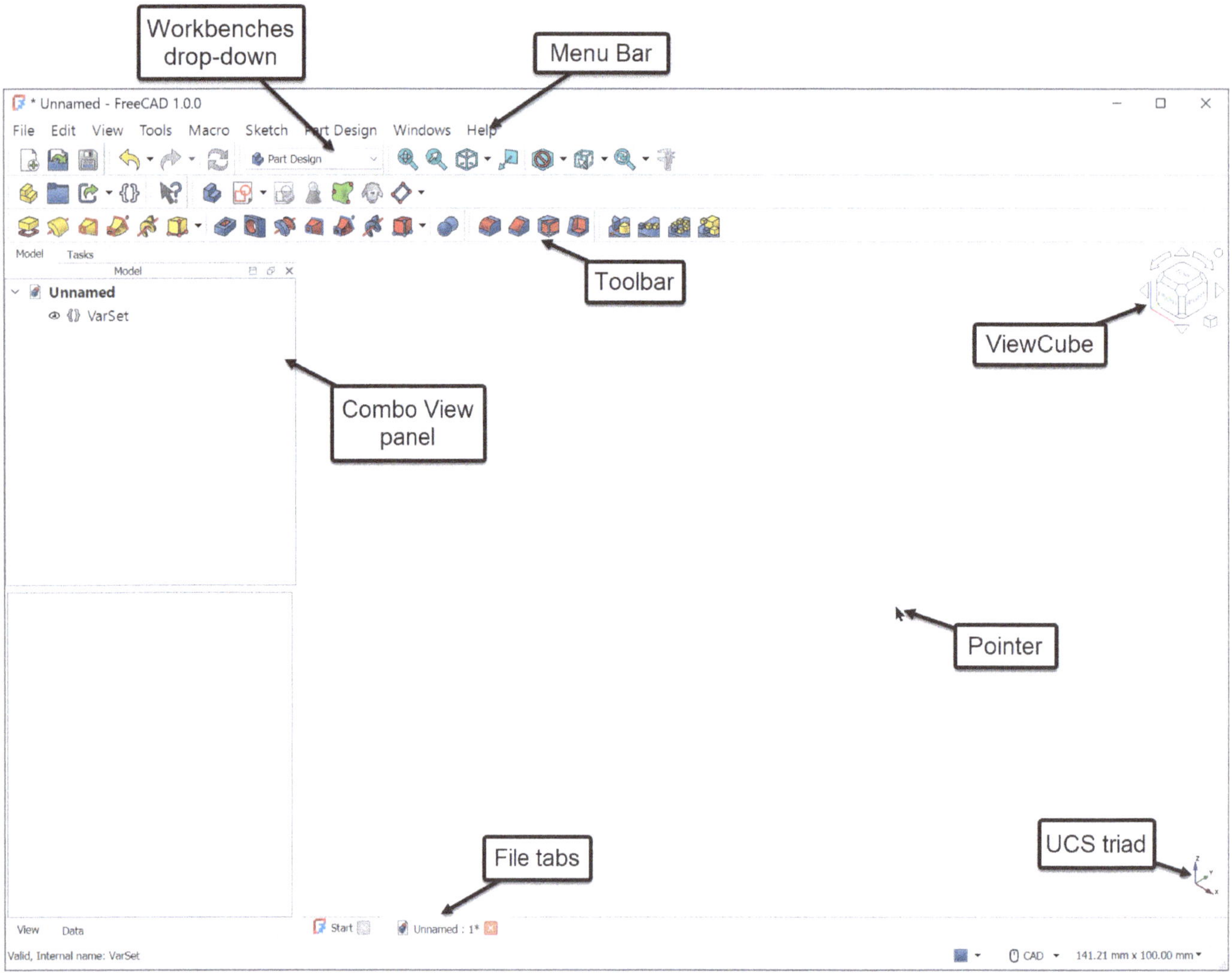

Graphics window

The Graphics window is the blank space located below the toolbars area. You can draw sketches and create 3D geometry in the Graphics window.

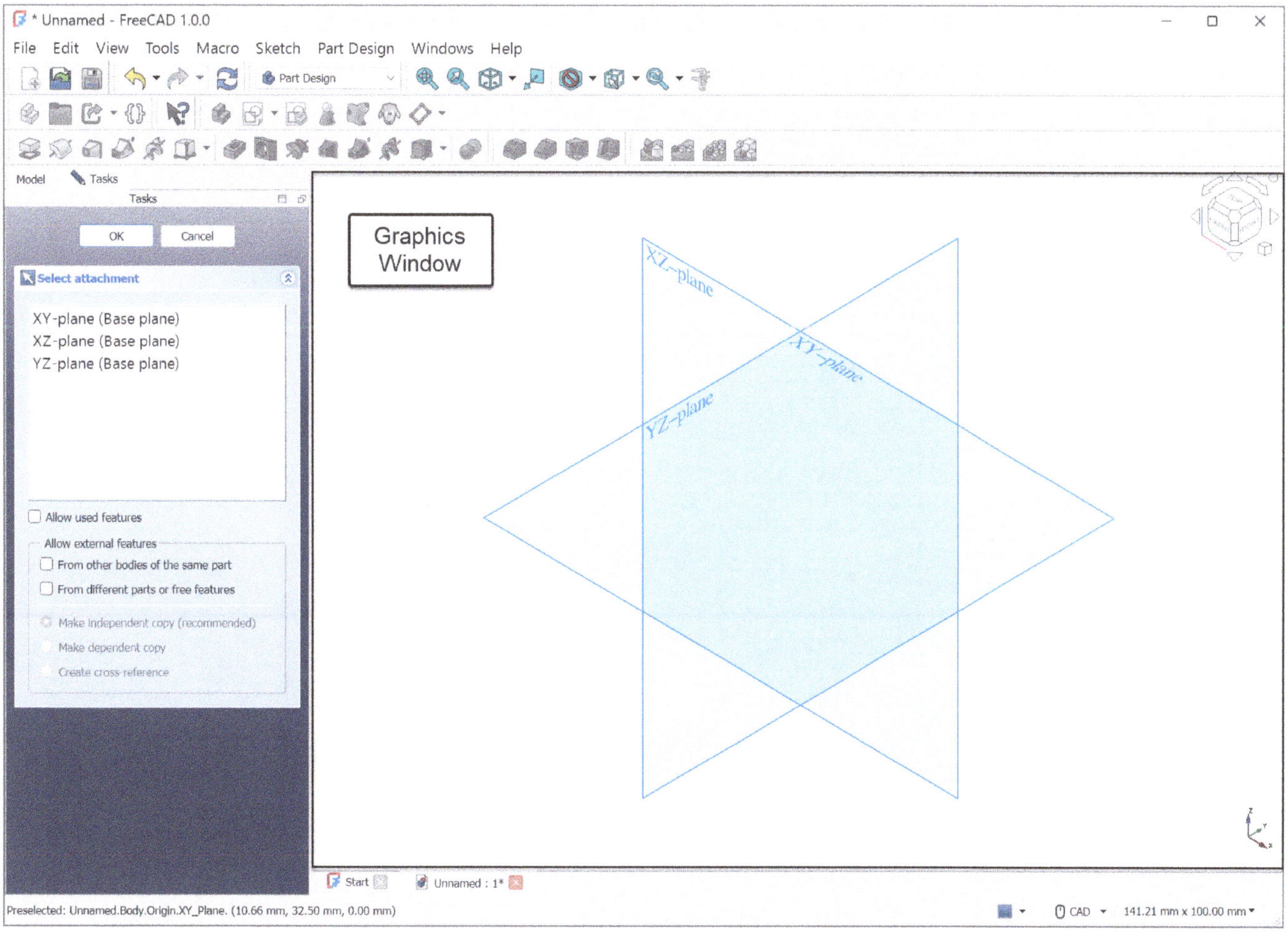

File Menu

The **File** menu appears when you click on the **File** option located at the top left corner of the window. The **File** menu has a list of open menus. You can see a list of recently opened documents under the **Recent Files** sub-menu.

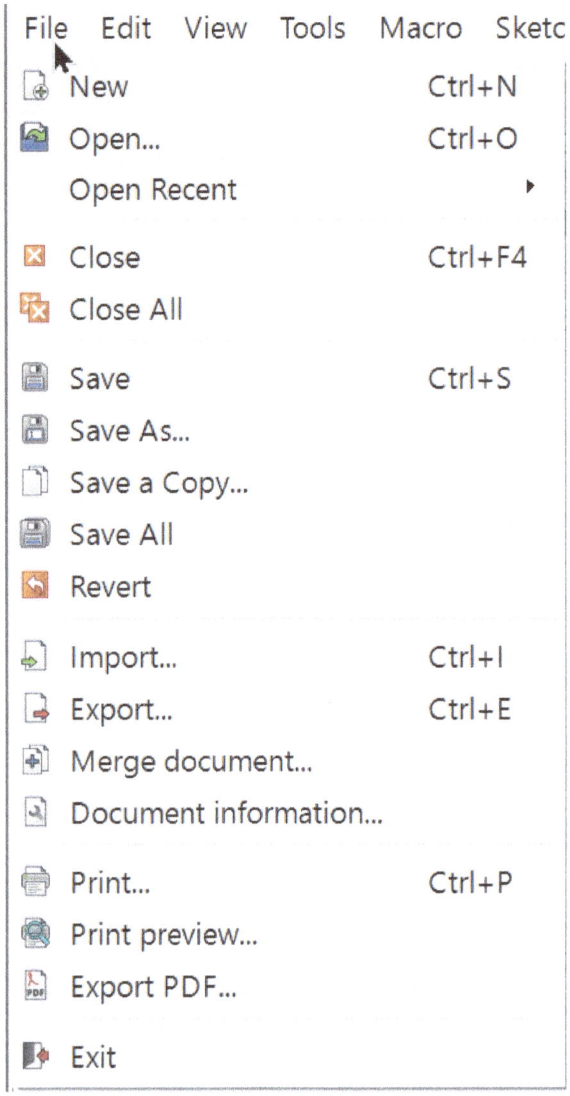

Toolbars

A toolbar is a set of tools, which help you to perform various operations. Various toolbars available in the FreeCAD are:

File Toolbar

This toolbar contains tools such as **New**, **Open**, and **Save**.

Edit Toolbar

This toolbar contains tools such as **Undo**, **Redo**, and **Refresh**.

View toolbar

This toolbar has the tools to modify the display and orientation of the model.

Workbench Toolbar

This toolbar allows you to change the workbench.

Macro

This toolbar has tools to create and execute macros.

Structure

It has tools to create or open part files.

Sketcher Toolbars

Sketcher

This toolbar has tools to start or exit a sketch.

Sketcher edit tools

This toolbar lets you adjust the shape and grid settings. It also allows you to control the order of geometry display.

Sketcher geometries

This toolbar has tools to create sketch elements.

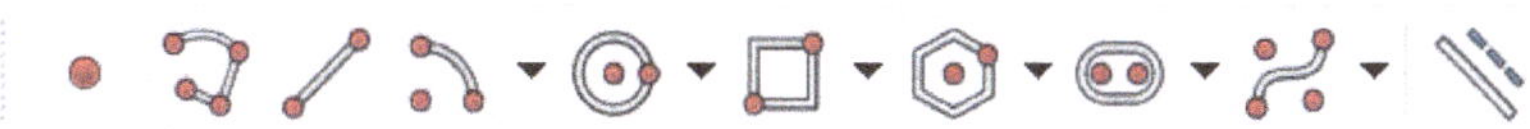

Sketcher constraints

This toolbar has tools to apply constraints between sketch elements.

Sketcher B-spline tools

This toolbar has tools to create and edit B-splines.

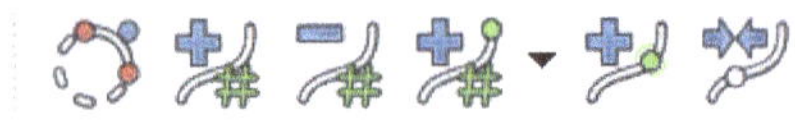

Sketcher Visual

This toolbar helps you to hide or show constraints.

Sketcher tools

This toolbar has various selection tools and options that aid you in creating sketch elements very fast.

Part Design Toolbars

Part Design Helper

This toolbar has tools to create new bodies, datum points, axis, datum planes, and clones. You can also create or leave a sketch.

Part Design Modeling

This toolbar has commands to create solid features based on the sketch geometry.

Part Design Dressup

This toolbar contains tools to add features like fillets and chamfers to the model.

Part Design Pattern

This toolbar has commands to patterns.

Assembly Toolbars

Assembly

This toolbar has tools to create components or insert existing components into an assembly.

Assembly Joints

This toolbar has tools to apply joints between components.

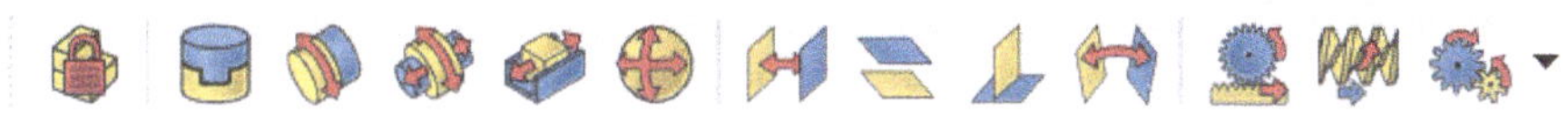

TechDraw Toolbars

TechDraw Views

This toolbar has tools to generate standard views of a 3D geometry.

TechDraw Pages

The tools on this toolbar help you to add a new page and refresh the drawing page.

TechDraw Stacking

This toolbar provides options to adjust the stacking order of elements.

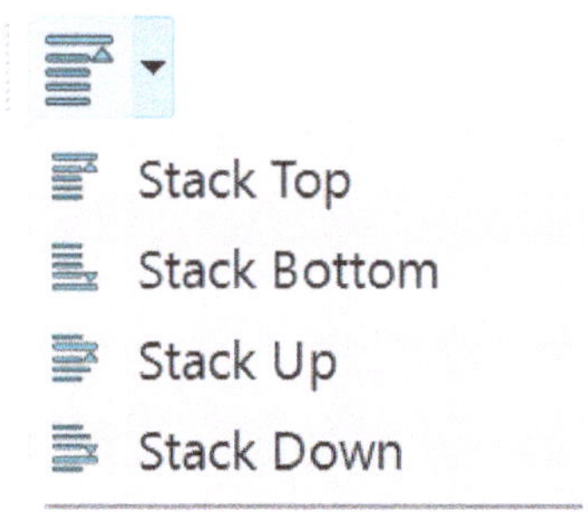

TechDraw Dimensions

The tools on this toolbar help you to add dimensions to the drawing views.

TechDraw File Access

This toolbar helps you to export the drawing page to the SVG format.

TechDraw Decoration

The tools on this toolbar help you to change the hatch patterns and insert images.

TechDraw Attributes

The tools on this toolbar help you edit the attributes of a view, dimension, and lines.

TechDraw Centerlines

The tools on this toolbar help you to add centerlines and cosmetic threads.

TechDraw Extend Dimensions

The tools on this toolbar help you to add or remove prefix to the dimension. Also, you can change the decimal values of the dimensions.

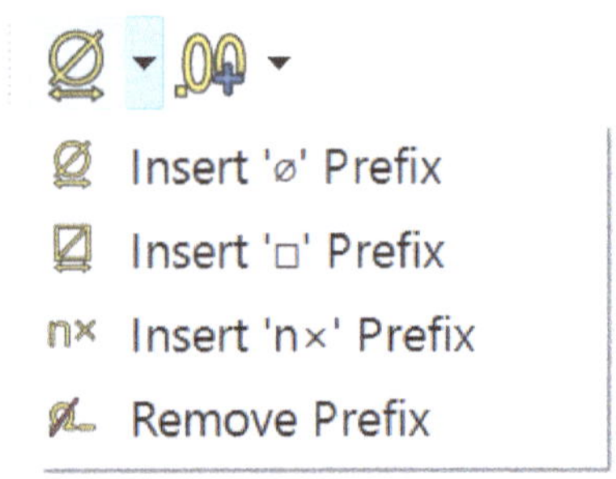

TechDraw Annotations

The tools on this toolbar help you to add annotations such as text, leaders, roughness symbols to the drawing views.

Some toolbars are not visible by default. To display a particular toolbar, click **View > Toolbars** on the menu bar. Next, select the toolbar from the sub-menu.

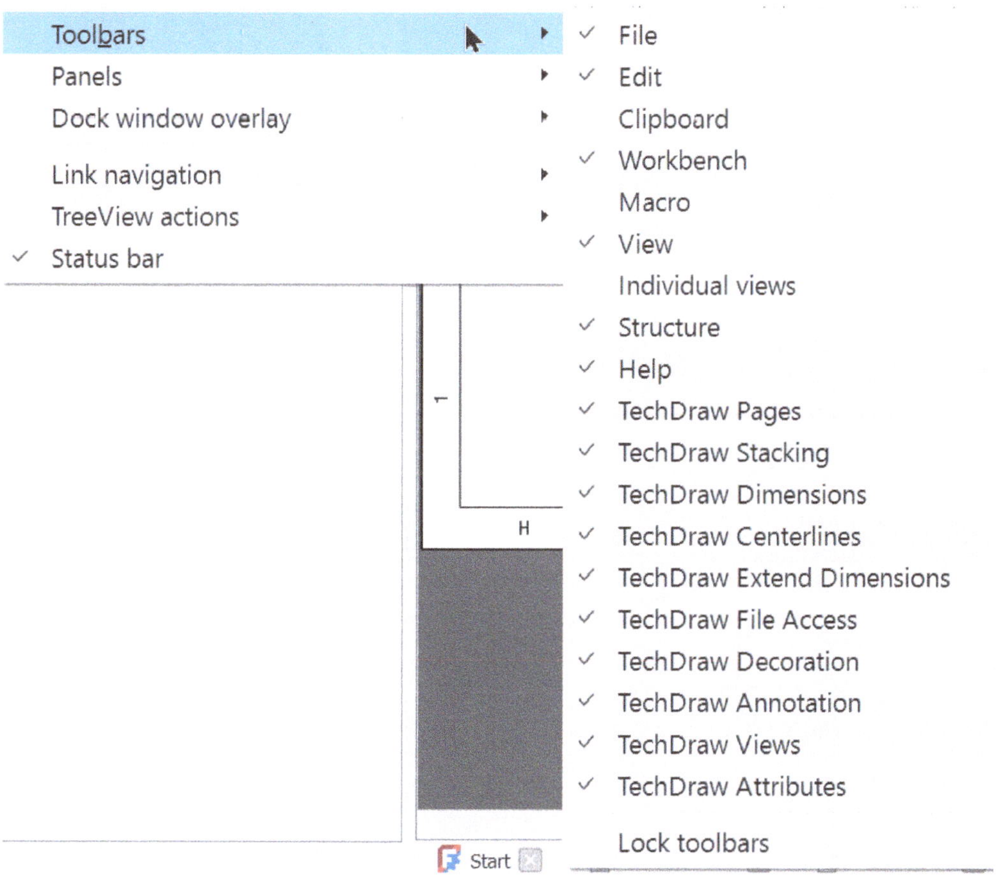

Menu

The menu is located on the top. It has various options (menu titles). When you click on a menu title, a drop-down appears. Select an option from this drop-down.

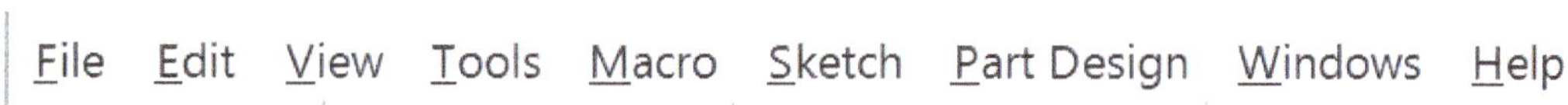

Status bar

The status bar is available below the graphics window. It shows the current status.

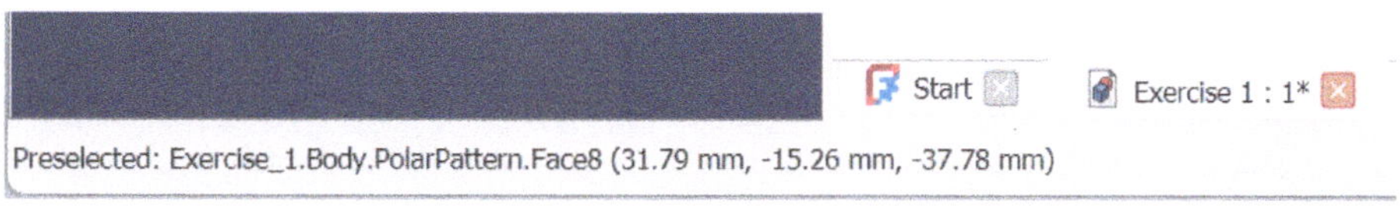

Model panel

It contains the list of operations carried while constructing a part.

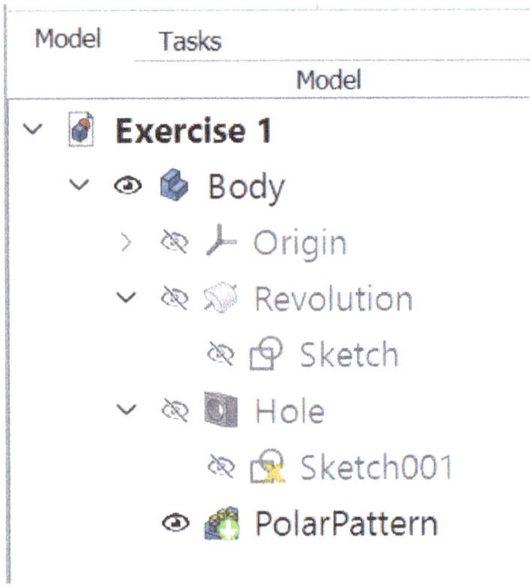

Tasks panel

When you execute any command in FreeCAD, the options related to it appear in the **Tasks** panel. The **Tasks** panel has various options. The following figure shows various components of this tab.

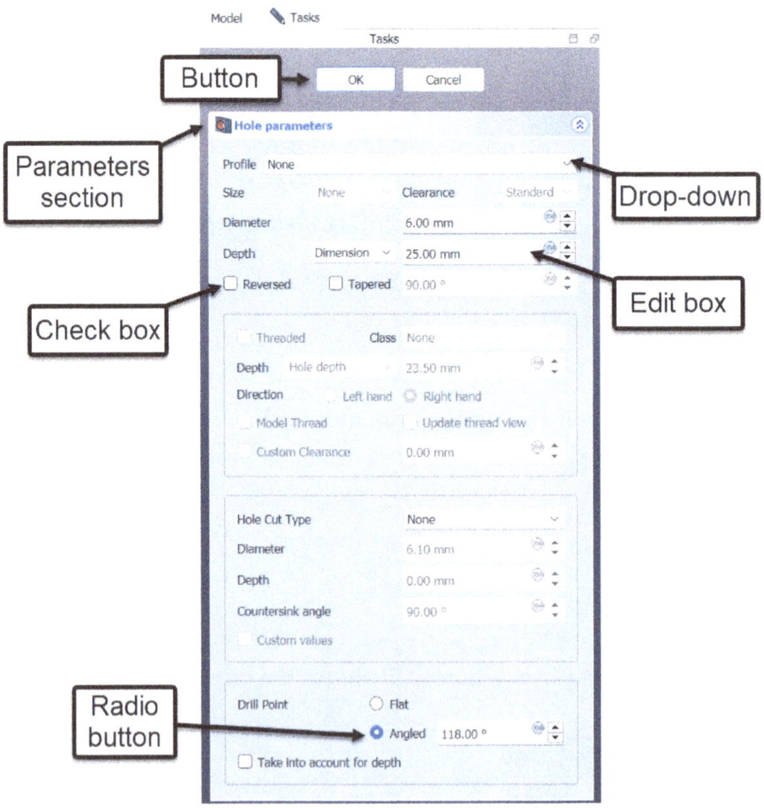

Mouse Functions

Various functions of the mouse buttons are:

Left Mouse button (MB1)

When you double-click the left mouse button (MB1) on an object in the **Model** panel, the parameters section related to the object appears in the Tasks panel. Now, you can edit the parameters of the objects.

Middle Mouse button (MB2)

Click this button to pan the view.

Right Mouse button (MB3)

Click this button to open the shortcut menu. The shortcut menu has some options to modify the display of the model.

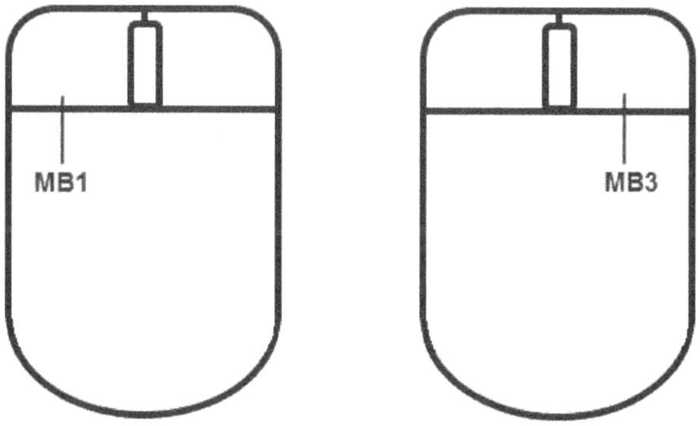

Select　　　　Shortcut Menu

Edit Background

To change the background color of the window, click **Edit > Preferences** on the menu bar (or) click **FreeCAD 1.0 > Preferences** on title bar, if you are working on MacOS. On the **Preferences** dialog, click the **Display** option on the left side. Next, click the **Colors** tab and select **Background color > Simple color**. Click the color swatch next to the **Simple color** option. Select the white color from the **Select Color** dialog and click **OK**.

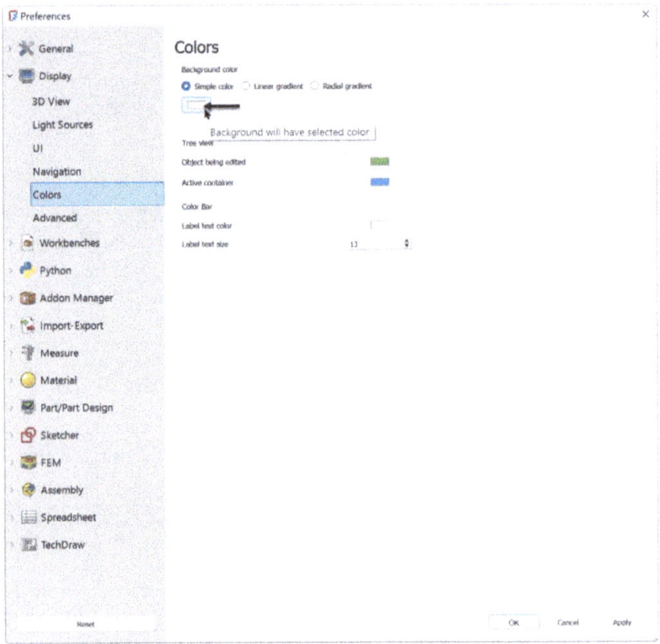

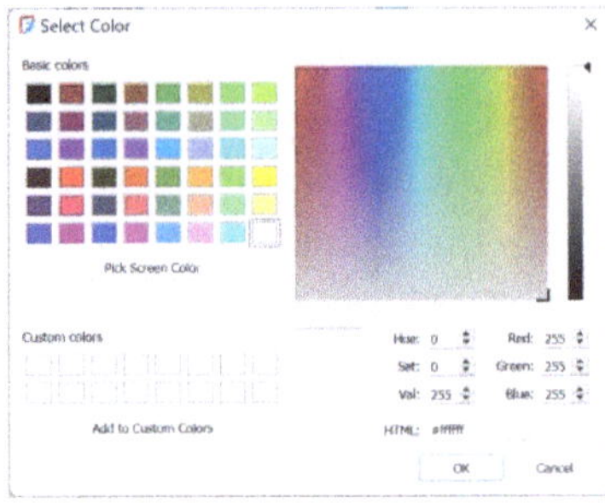

Click the **Sketcher** option on the left side of the Preferences dialog. Next, click the **Appearance** tab and change the **Edge**, **Vertex**, and **Cursor crosshair** to black. Click **OK** to apply the changes.

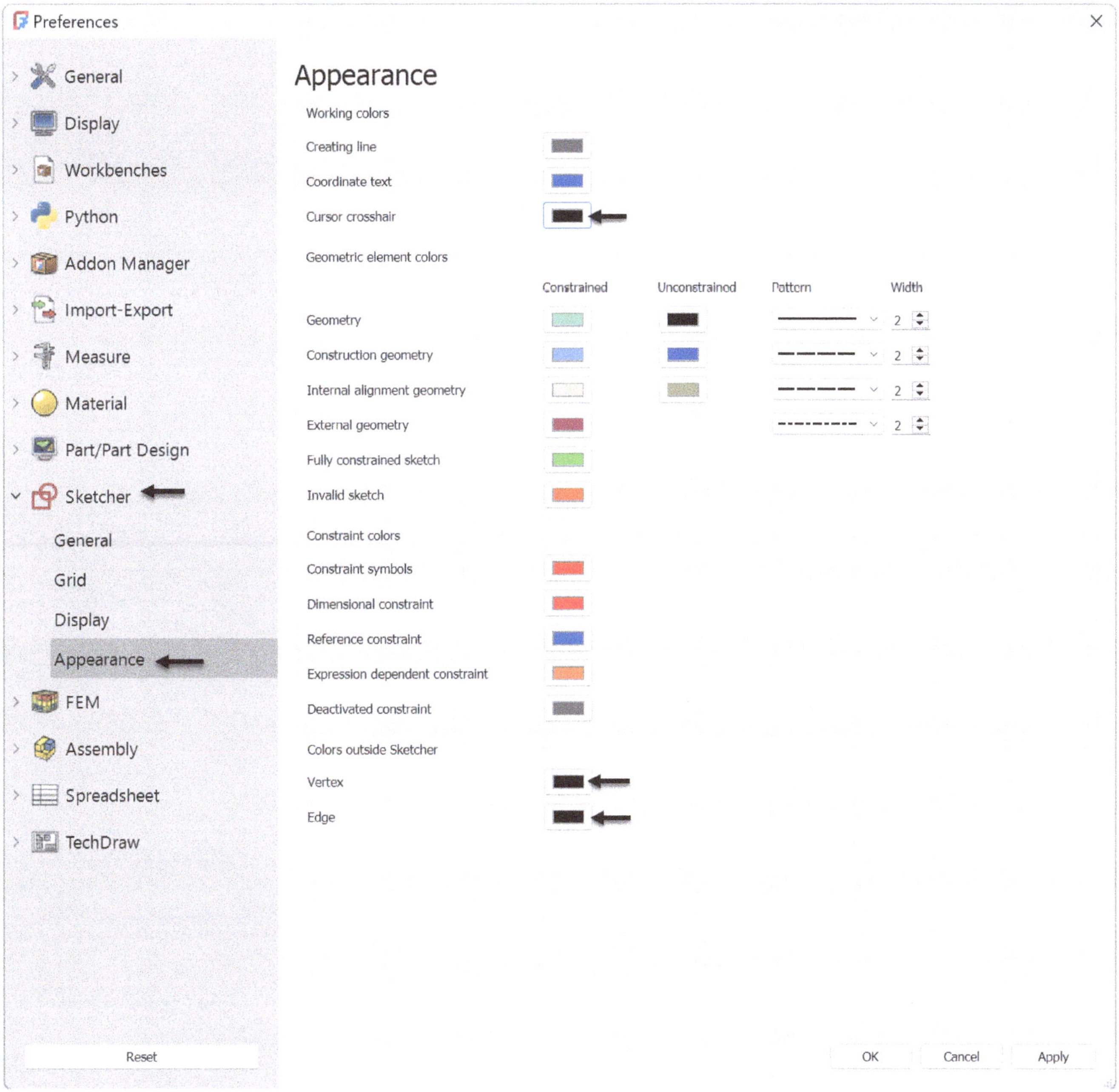

FreeCAD Help

FreeCAD offers you the help system that goes beyond basic command definition. You can access FreeCAD help by using any of the following methods:

- Press the **F1** key.
- Click **Help > Help** on the menu bar.

Questions

1. Explain how to hide or display toolbars.
2. Give one example of where you would establish a constraint between a part's features.

3. List any two procedures to access FreeCAD Help.
4. How to change the background color of the graphics window?
5. How is FreeCAD a parametric modeling application?

Chapter 2: Sketch Techniques

This chapter covers the methods and commands to create sketches in FreeCAD 1.0. In FreeCAD 1.0, you create a rough sketch, and then apply dimensions and constraints that define its shape and size. The dimensions define the length, size, and angle of a sketch element, whereas constraints define the relations between sketch elements.

In this chapter, you will:

- Create sketches
- Use constraints and dimensions to control the shape and size of a sketch
- Learn sketching commands
- Learn commands and options that help you to create sketches easily

Creating Sketches

FreeCAD 1.0 allows you to create sketches directly in the graphics window. To create sketches, click the **Create sketch** icon on the **Part Design Helper** toolbar. Next, click on any of the planes displayed at the center of the graphics window. Click the **OK** button on the **Tasks** panel. You can find different sketch commands on different sketcher toolbars. You can use these commands and start drawing the sketch on the selected plane. After creating the sketch, click **Close** on the **Tasks** panel to finish the sketch.

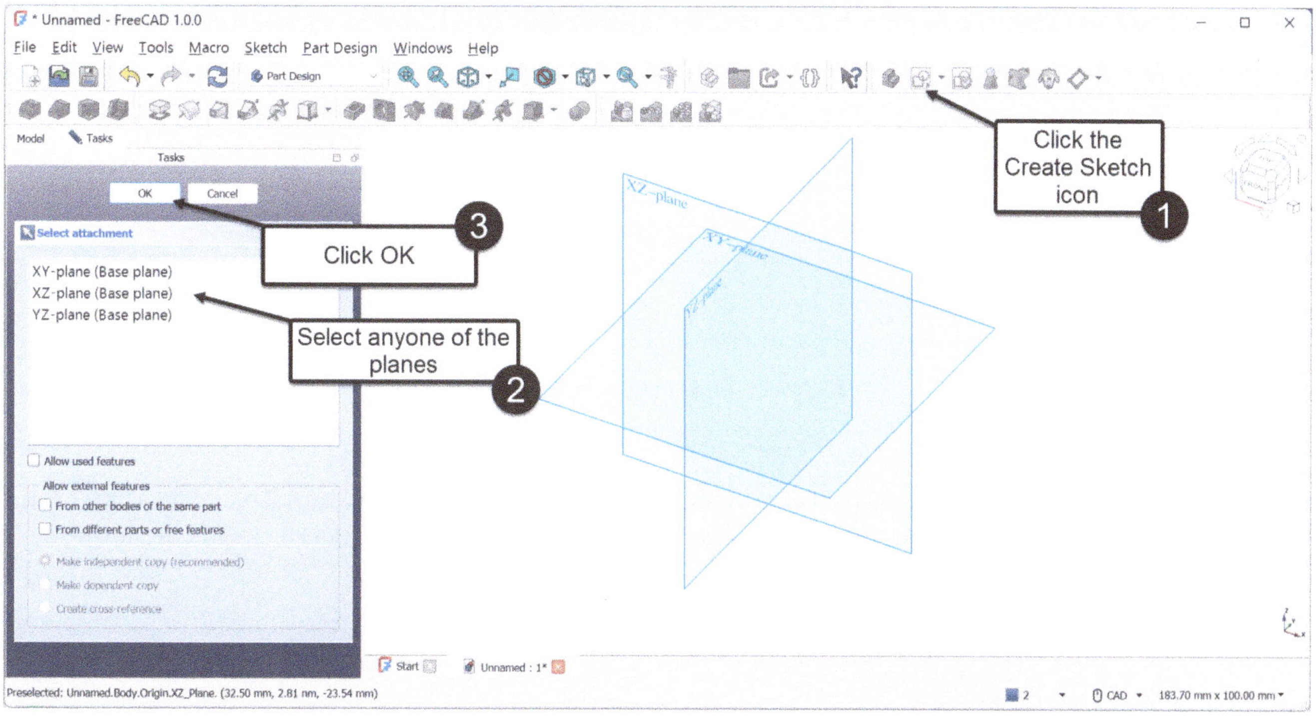

Grid and Snap Settings

In FreeCAD 1.0, you can access grid and snap settings through the **Sketcher edit tools** toolbar, which includes the following options: **Toggle grid**, **Toggle snap**, and **Configure rendering order**.

Toggle grid

In FreeCAD 1.0, you can use the **Toggle Grid** tool to show or hide the grid in the Sketcher workbench. The grid has evenly spaced horizontal and vertical lines to help you draw accurately. You can find this tool in the **Sketch Edit Tools** toolbar. If the grid makes your design hard to see, you can turn it off for a clearer view. When you need precise alignment or measurements, you can turn it back on easily. You can switch the grid on and off as many times as needed while working, making it a simple and useful tool for your sketches.

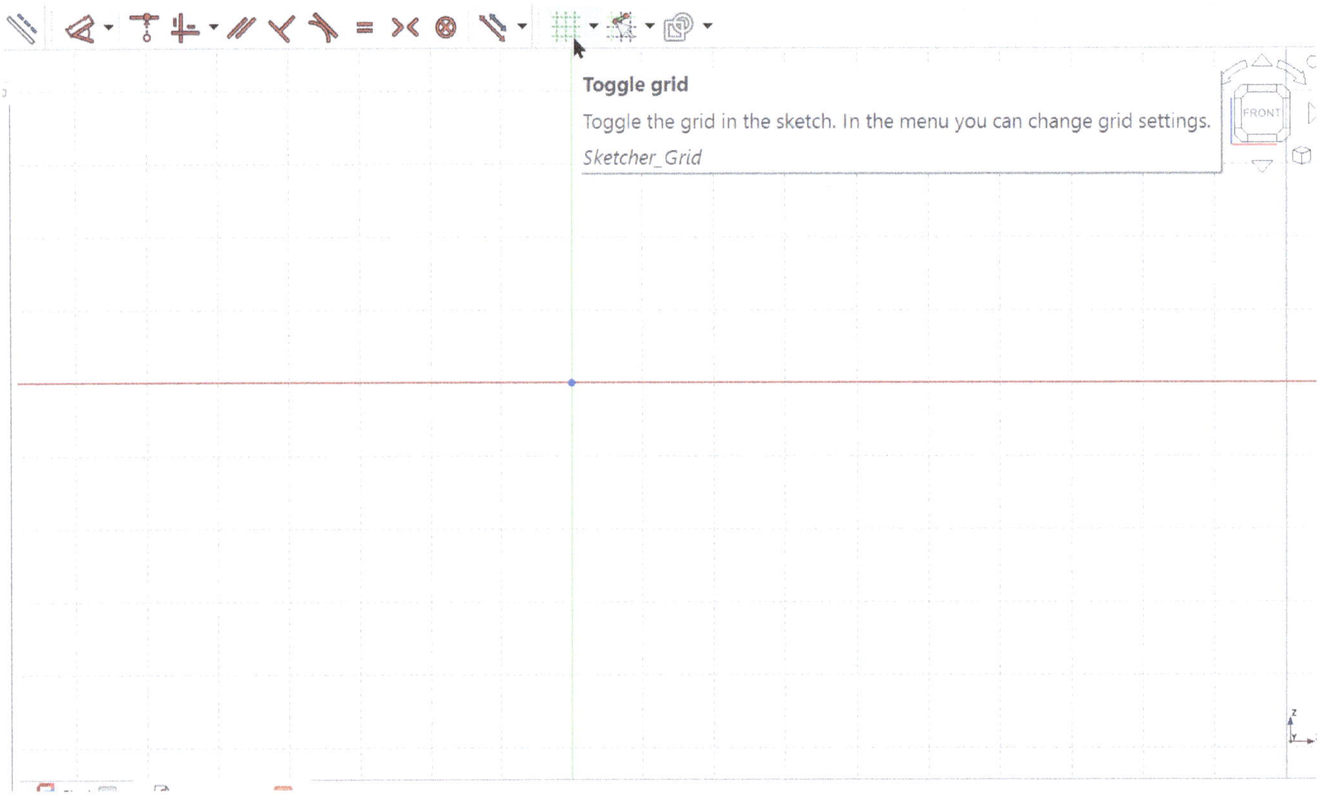

Grid auto spacing and Spacing

Grid Auto Spacing and **Spacing** help you control the gaps between objects in a grid. **Grid Auto Spacing** adjusts gaps automatically based on object sizes, keeping the spacing even. **Spacing** lets you set the exact gap manually, no matter the object sizes.

In the Sketcher Workbench, you can adjust both settings. To use **Grid Auto Spacing**, turn it on in the **Toggle Grid** menu. For manual control, enter your desired gap size in the **Spacing** box. These options help you organize your sketches easily.

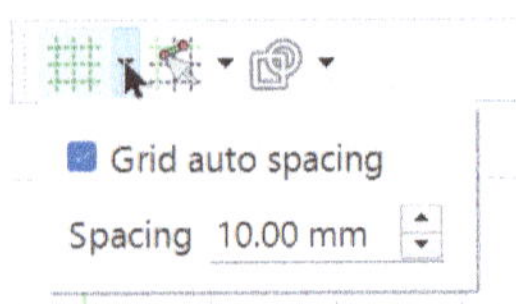

Toggle Snap

The **Toggle Snap** tool lets you turn snapping on or off while drawing or editing. Snapping helps you pick exact points on objects or the grid.

When you turn it on, your cursor sticks to the nearest point on the grid or an object. This makes it easier to draw and edit with precision. It is useful for designs that need accurate measurements and alignments.

To turn **Toggle Snap** on or off, click the **Toggle Snap** icon on the **Sketcher Edit Tools** toolbar. You can also choose snap modes, like **Snap to grid** or **Snap to objects**, from the drop-down menu.

This tool helps you work faster by letting you switch between snapping and freehand drawing whenever needed.

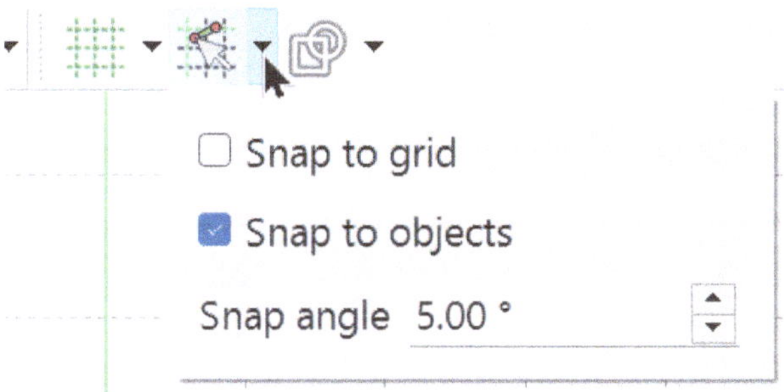

Sketch Commands

FreeCAD 1.0 provides you with a set of commands to create sketches. These commands are available on **Sketch** tab of the menu bar (or) the **Sketcher geometries** toolbar.

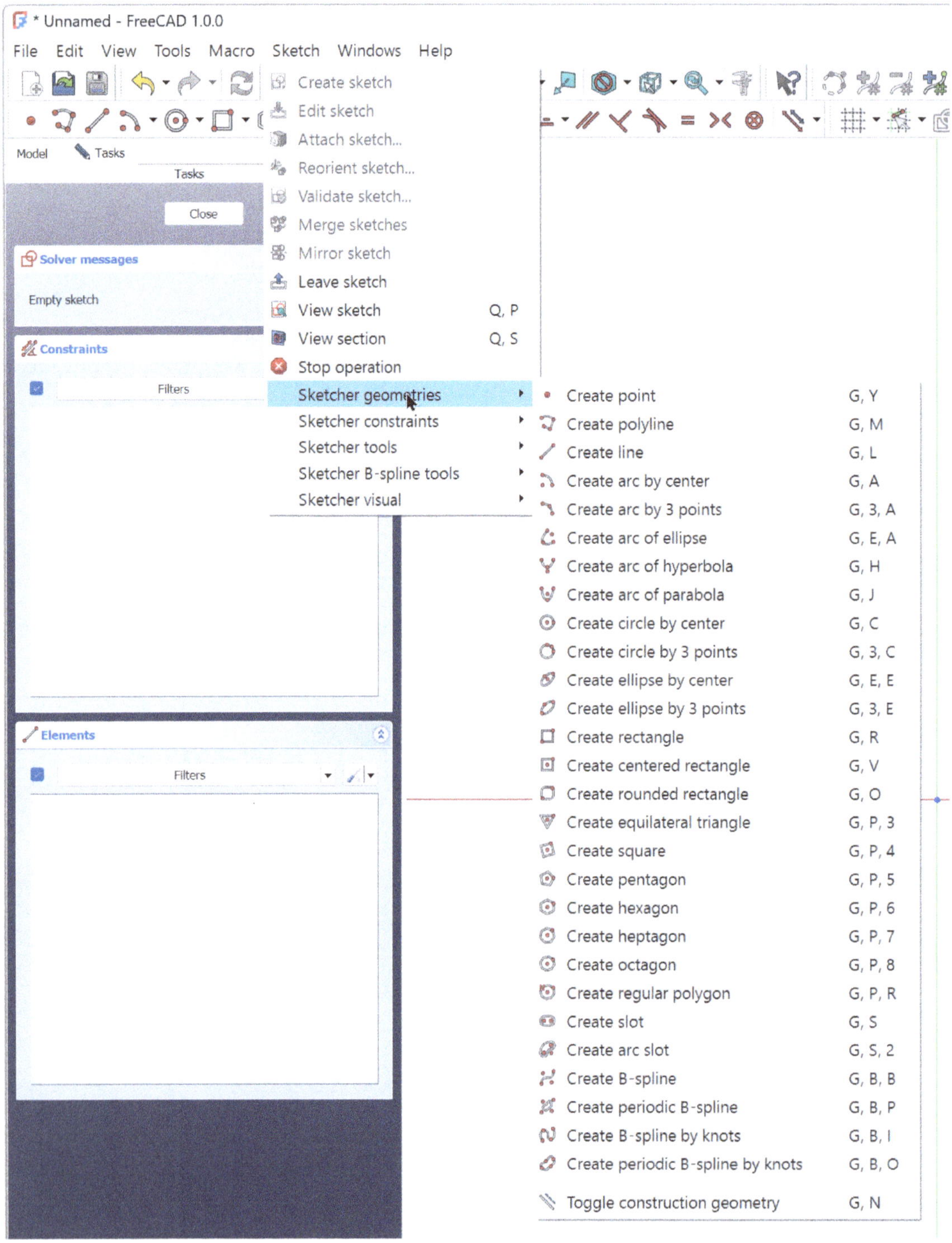

The Line command

The most frequently used command during sketch creation is the Line command. To activate it, you can either click the **Line** 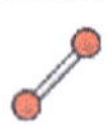 icon located on the **Sketcher geometries** toolbar or access it through the menu bar by clicking **Sketch**, then **Sketcher geometries**, and finally, **Create Line**. To draw a line, click on the graphics window and move the pointer. You'll see that the length and angle dimensions are dynamically attached to the line, showing its measurements. Enter a value in the length dimension box and press the TAB key. Then, input a value in the angle box and press ENTER to create and orient the line at the desired angle. Alternatively, you can simply click to set the start point, move the pointer to the desired end point, and click again to create the line without specifying dimensions.

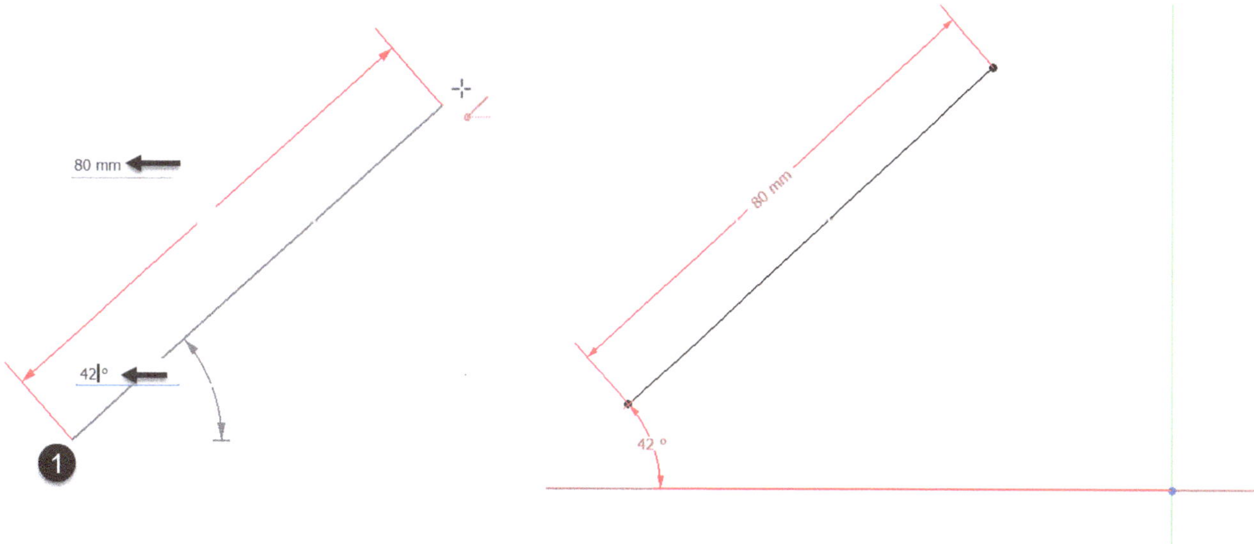

If you wish to create a horizontal line, indicate the starting point of the line and move the pointer horizontally. You'll notice a Horizontal constraint glyph appear beneath the line, which means the line is constrained to be horizontal. Click again to confirm and create the horizontal line with this constraint applied. More details about constraints will be covered in a later part of this chapter. Similarly, a vertical line can be drawn by moving the pointer vertically and clicking at the desired endpoint.

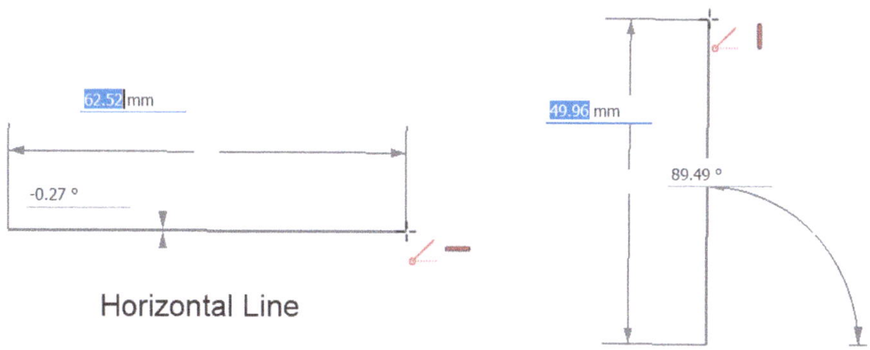

Horizontal Line

Vertical Line

The Polyline command

The **Polyline** command is used to create continuous lines and arc segments connected by their vertices. To activate this command, you can either click the **Polyline** icon on the **Sketcher geometries** toolbar or go to **Sketch > Sketcher geometries > Create Polyline** on the menu bar. Here is a step-by-step explanation of how to use the **Polyline** command after activating it.

1. **Start the polyline:** Click on the graphics window to place the first point of the polyline. Move the pointer and click again to add an endpoint and start another line segment. This allows you to create a chain of lines.

2. **Add more line segments**: Continue clicking on the graphics window to add more line segments to the polyline. The polyline can include straight lines and arc segments, depending on the mode of the Polyline command.

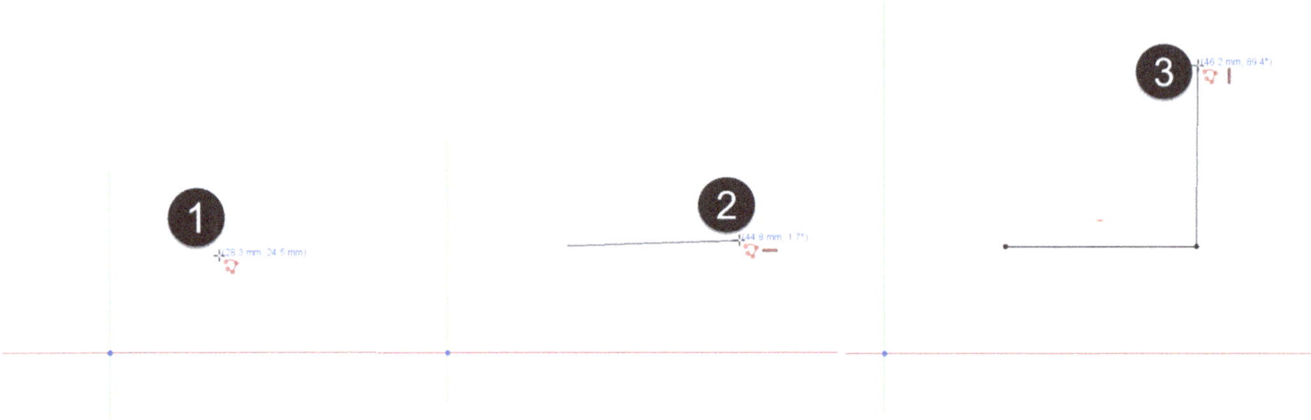

3. **Toggle between different modes:** After placing the first line segment, you can toggle between different modes of the Polyline command by pressing the M key. This allows you to draw tangent or perpendicular arcs following a line or arc segment.

Press the M key once: A line **perpendicular** to the existing line is attached to the cursor. Click to create the perpendicular line.

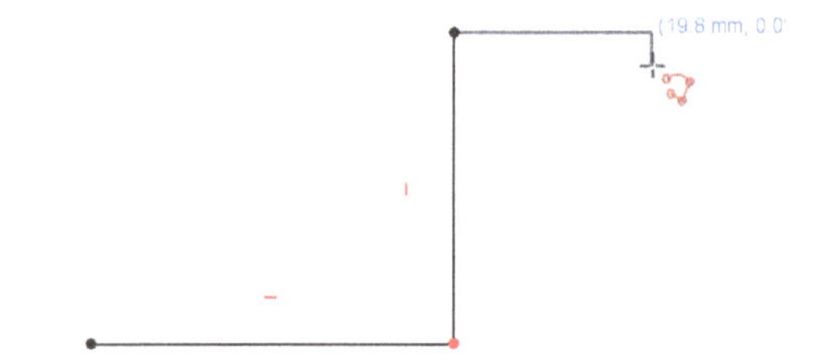

Press the M key twice: A line **collinear** with the existing line is attached to the cursor. Click to create the collinear line.

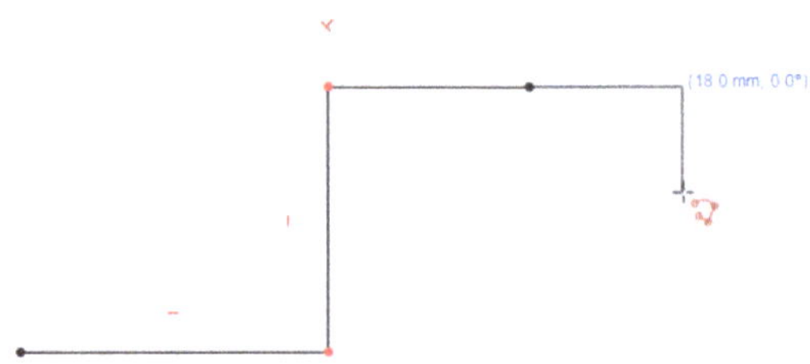

Press the M key three times: An **arc tangent** to the previous line is attached to the cursor. Move the cursor and click to define the radius and arc length of the tangent arc

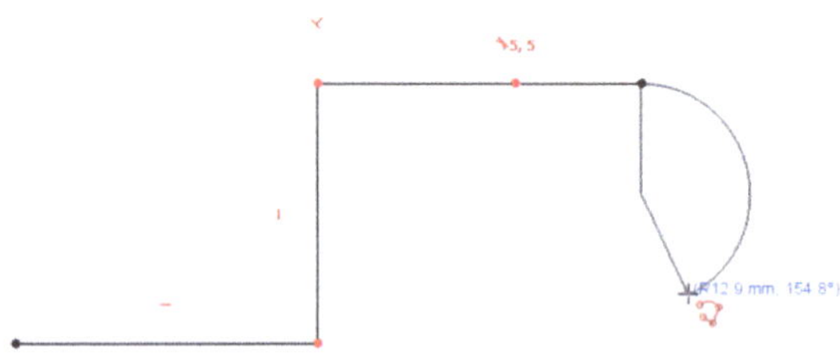

Press the M key four times: An **arc perpendicular** (normal) to the previous line or arc is attached to the cursor. Move the cursor and click to define the radius and arc length of the perpendicular arc.

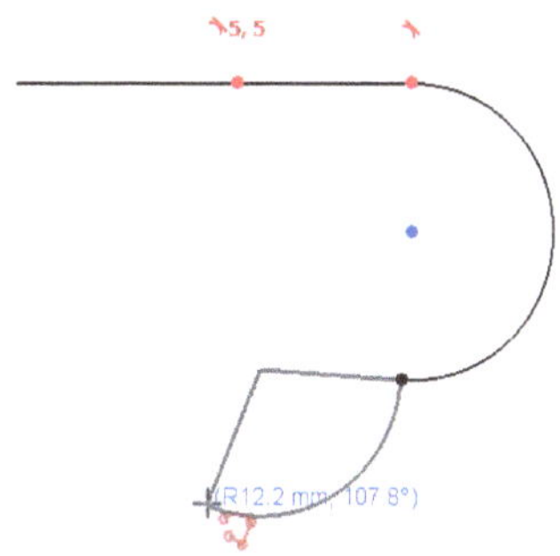

4. **End the line chain:** Right-click on the graphics window to end the line chain and complete the polyline.

5. **Deactivate the Polyline command:** Press the ESC key if you want to deactivate the **Polyline** command.

The **Polyline** command is a useful tool for creating complex shapes and designs in FreeCAD, as it allows you to easily create and modify chains of connected lines and arc segments.

Creating Arcs

FreeCAD 1.0 allows you to create arcs using two commands: **Create arc by center** and **Create arc by 3 points**.

The Center and end points command

This command creates an arc by defining its center, start, and end. Activate the **Center arc by center** 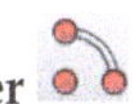 command (Click **Arc** drop-down > **Center arc by center** on the **Sketcher geometries** toolbar). Click on the graphics window to set the center point of the arc. As you move the pointer away from the center, dynamic dimensions for the radius, start angle, and end angle will appear, allowing you to visualize the arc's size and orientation. For precise control, you can input specific values: type the desired radius into its dimension box and press TAB, then enter the start angle, press ENTER. Next, input the end angle before pressing ENTER to finalize the arc. Alternatively, you can create the arc freeform by clicking to set the center, clicking again to define the radius, and dragging the pointer to adjust the sweep angle before clicking a third time to complete the arc. The dynamic dimensions update in real-time as you move the pointer, making it easy to create arcs with either precision or intuitive flexibility.

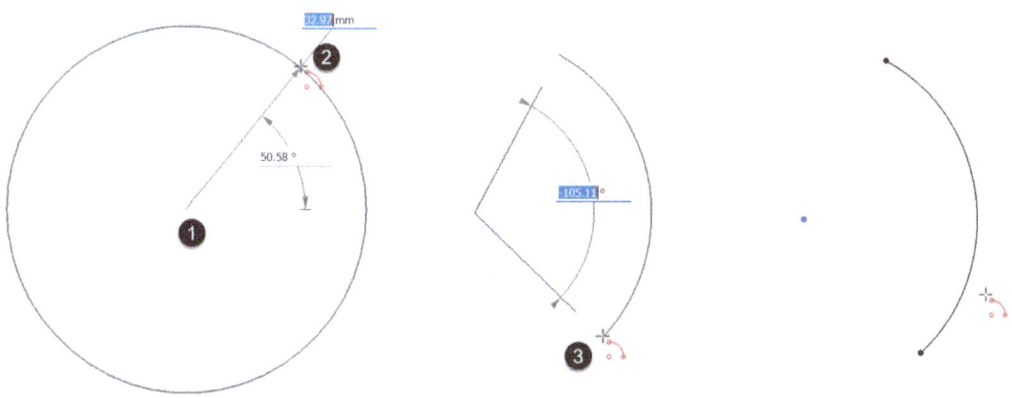

The Create arc by 3 points command

This command creates an arc by defining its start, end, and radius. Click **Arc** drop-down > **Create arc by 3 points** 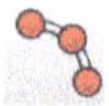 on the **Sketcher geometries** toolbar (or) click **Sketch > Sketch geometries > Create arc by 3 points** on the menu bar. In the graphics window, click to define the start point of the arc. Next, move the pointer and click again to define the endpoint of the arc. After defining the start and end of the arc, you need to define the size and position of the arc. To do this, move the pointer and click to define the radius and position of the arc.

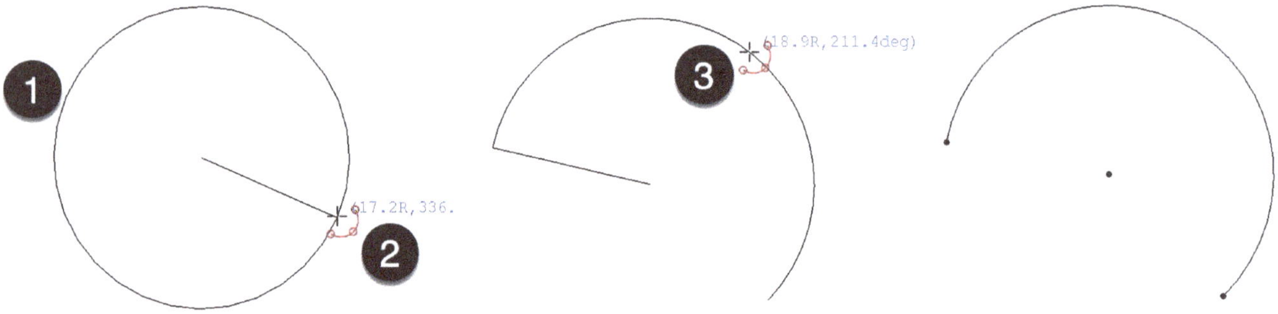

Creating Circles

FreeCAD 1.0 allows you to create circles using two commands: **Center and rim point** and **3 rim point**.

Center circle by center

This is the most common way to draw a circle. Click **Circle** drop-down > **Center circle by center** on the **Sketcher geometries** toolbar (or) click **Sketch > Sketcher geometries > Create circle by center** on the menu bar. Click on the graphics window to set the center point of the circle. As you move the pointer away from the center, a dynamic dimension for the diameter will appear, showing the circle's size in real-time. For precise control, you can type the desired diameter value directly into the dimension box and press ENTER to finalize the circle. Alternatively, you can create the circle freeform by simply clicking to set the center and then clicking again at the desired radius point without entering specific measurements.

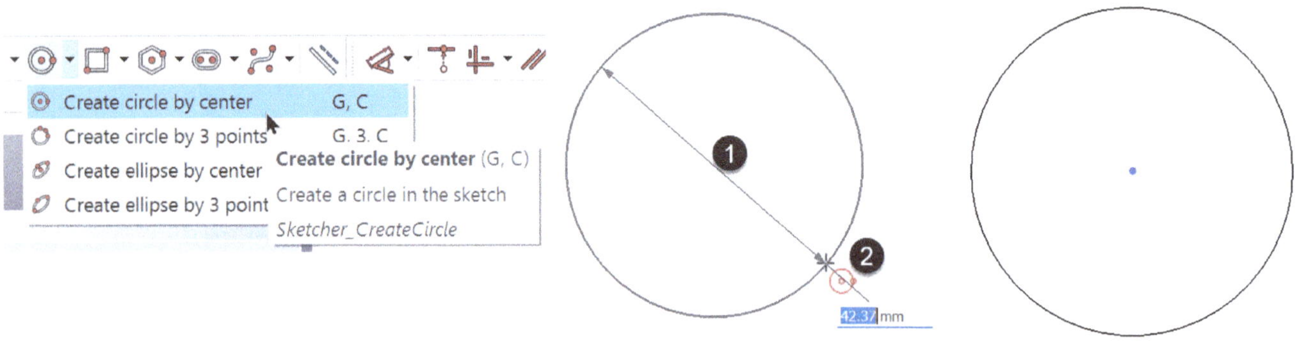

3 rim points

You can create this type of circle by specifying three points or by selecting three existing points. Click **Circle** drop-down > **3 rim points** on the **Sketcher geometries** toolbar (or) click **Sketch > Sketcher geometries > Create circle by three points** on the menu bar. Next, specify the three points of the circle, as shown.

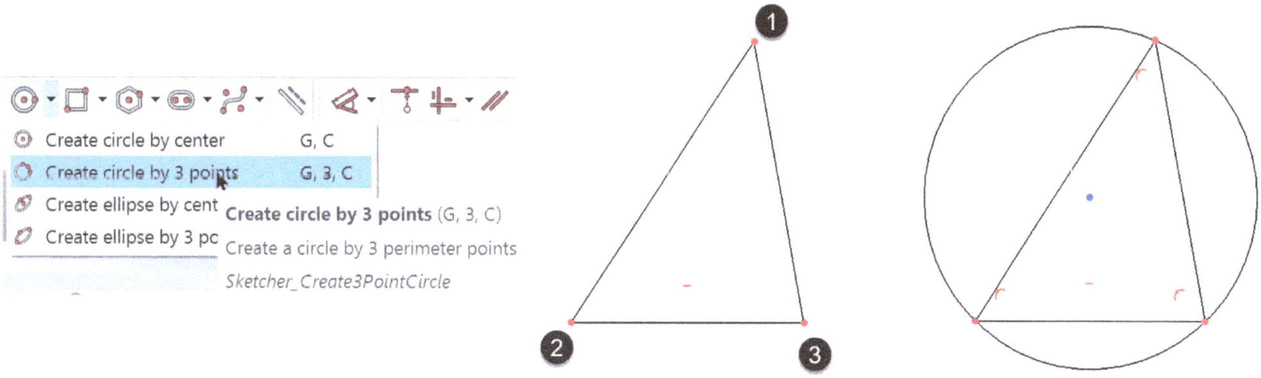

Creating Rectangles

FreeCAD 1.0 allows you to create rectangles using three different commands: **Create Rectangle, Rounded Rectangle,** and **Centered Rectangle**.

Create a 2 Point Rectangle

The **Create Rectangle** creates a rectangle by defining its diagonal corners. Click the **Rectangle** drop-down > **Rectangle** icon on the **Sketcher geometries** toolbar (or) click **Sketch > Sketcher geometries > Create Rectangle** on the menu bar. Click on the graphics window to set the first corner point of the rectangle. As you move the pointer, you'll see a dynamic preview of the rectangle forming, with dimensions for its width and height updating in real-time. For precise control, you can type the desired width value into its dimension box, press TAB, and then enter the height value before pressing ENTER to finalize the rectangle. If you prefer a more freeform approach, simply click to set the first corner, drag the pointer to adjust the size and proportions of the rectangle, and click again to place the opposite corner.

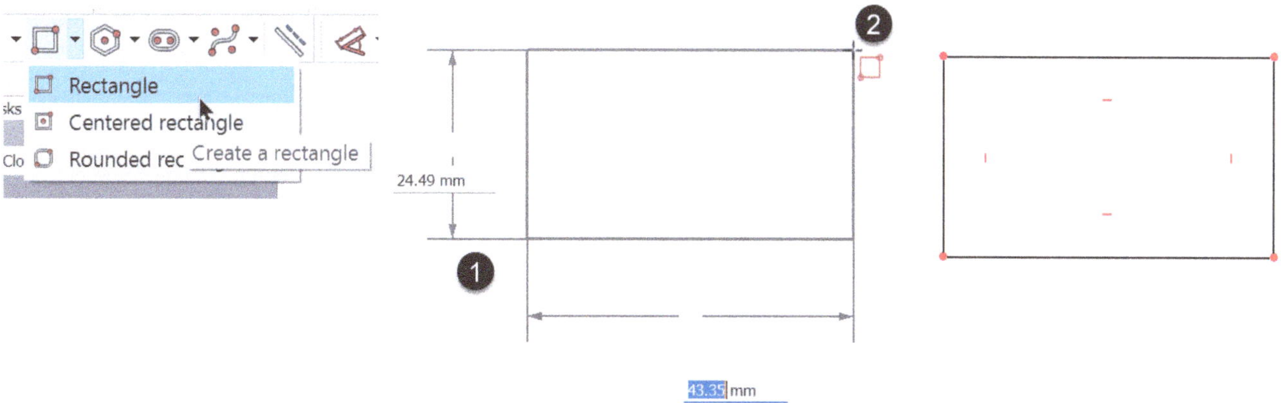

Centered Rectangle

This command creates a rectangle using two points: center and corner points. Click the **Rectangle** drop-down > **Centered Rectangle** icon on the **Sketcher geometries** toolbar (or) click **Sketch > Sketcher geometries > Create centered rectangle** on the menu bar. Click on the graphics window to define the center of the rectangle. Next, specify the corner point to define the width and height of the rectangle. You can also type-in values in the value boxes displayed in the graphics window.

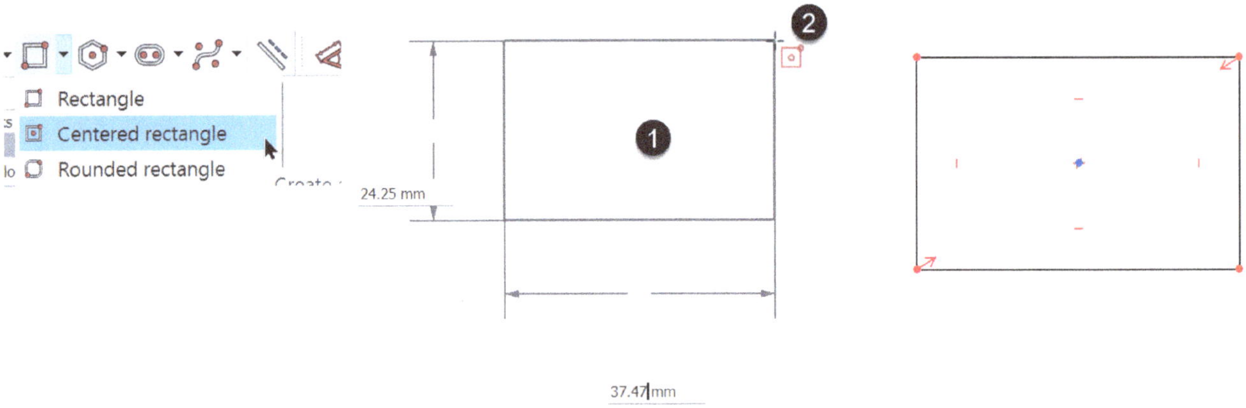

Rounded Rectangle

This command helps you to create a rectangle with rounded corners. Click **Rectangle** drop-down **> Rounded Rectangle** on the **Sketcher Geometries** toolbar, (or) click **Sketch > Sketcher geometries > Create rounded rectangle** on the menu bar. Click on the graphics window to set the starting corner of the rectangle. As you drag the pointer diagonally, you'll see the rectangle take shape, with dynamic dimensions for its width and height appearing on the screen. For precise control, you can input specific values: type the desired width and press TAB, then enter the height and press ENTER. Next, input the corner radius before pressing ENTER to finalize the shape. If you prefer a more freeform approach, simply click to set the starting point, drag to define the size of the rectangle, and adjust the corner radius by moving the pointer until the corners look just right.

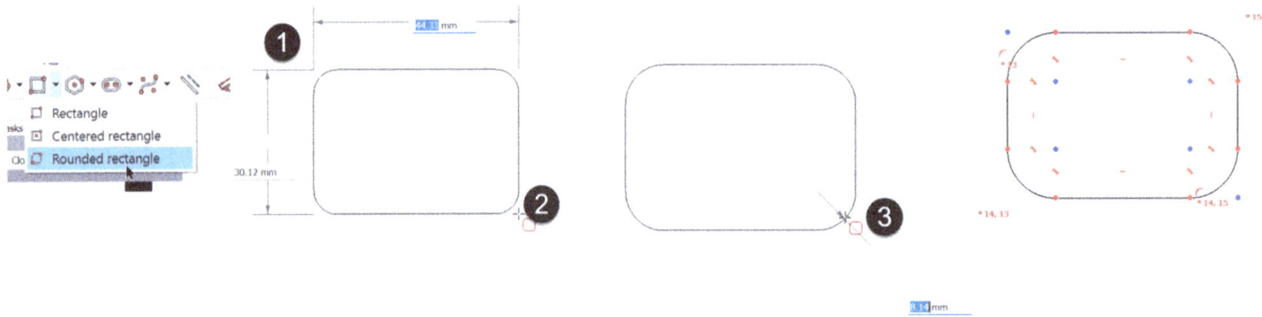

Create Slot

This command creates a straight slot by defining its start and width. Click the **Slot** drop-down > **Create Slot** icon on the **Sketcher geometries** toolbar (or) click **Sketch > Sketcher geometries > Create slot** on the menu bar. Click on the graphics window to set the starting point of the slot. As you move the pointer, you'll notice dynamic dimensions for the length and angle of the slot appearing first, allowing you to visualize its orientation and size in real-time. For precise control, type the desired length into the dimension box and press TAB, then input the angle and press ENTER to lock in the slot's direction. Next, you'll see the slot radius dimension appear dynamically as you adjust the slot's shape. Type-in the slot radius and press ENTER to define the slot with. If you prefer a more freeform approach, simply click to set the start point, drag the pointer to define the length and angle, and click again to complete the slot.

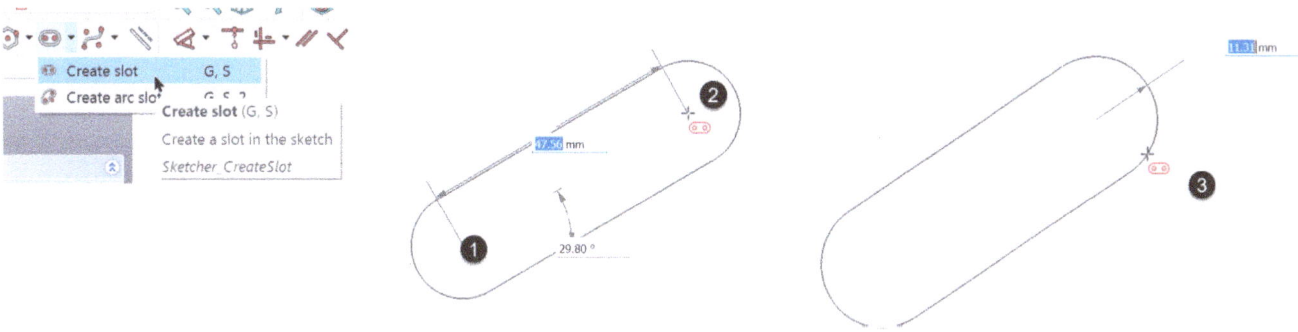

Create Slot

This command creates a straight slot by defining its start and width. Click the **Slot** drop-down > **Create arc slot** icon on the **Sketcher geometries** toolbar (or) click **Sketch > Sketcher geometries > Create arc slot** on the menu bar. Once activated, click on the graphics window to set the center point of the arc slot. As you move the pointer, dynamic dimensions for the radius and angle will appear, giving you real-time feedback on the arc's size and orientation. For precise control, type the desired radius into the dimension box and press TAB, then input the start angle, press ENTER. Next, enter the end angle before pressing ENTER to finalize the arc. You can enter positive or negative end angle value to define the side of the arc slot. Next, you'll see the width dimension appear dynamically as you adjust the slot's shape. If you prefer a more freeform approach, simply click to set the center, drag the pointer to define the radius and sweep of the arc, and click again to complete the slot.

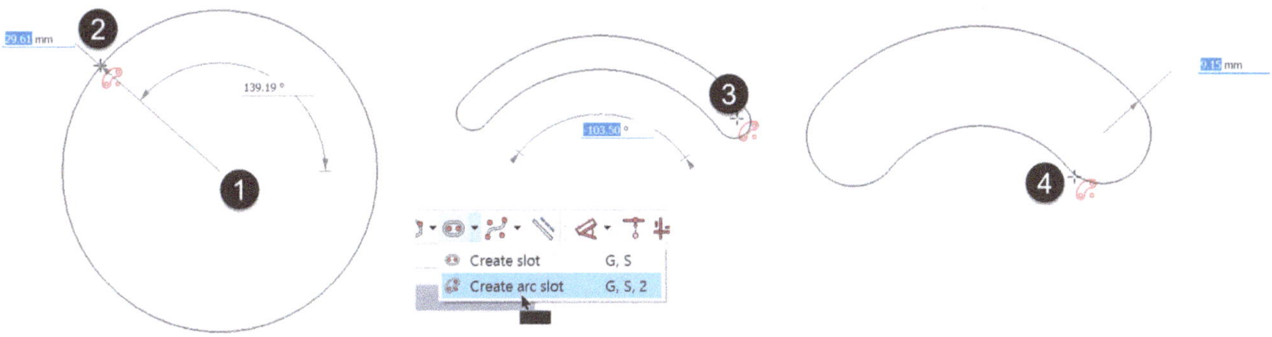

Creating Polygons

In FreeCAD 1.0, you can create a polygon using seven different commands: **Triangle**, **Square**, **Pentagon, Hexagon, Heptagon, Octagon,** and **Regular Polygon**.

Triangle

Click the **Polygon** drop-down > **Triangle** on the **Sketcher geometries** toolbar (or) click **Sketch > Sketcher geometries > Create equilateral triangle** on the menu bar. Click on the graphics window to set the center point of the triangle. As you move the pointer, dynamic dimensions for the radius (distance from the center to a corner) and angle will appear, allowing you to visualize the triangle's size and rotation in real-time. For precise control, type the desired radius into the dimension box and press TAB, then input the angle and press ENTER to lock in the triangle's orientation. If you prefer a more freeform approach, simply click to set the center, drag the pointer to define the radius and rotation, and click again to place the first corner – the other two corners will automatically adjust to form a perfect equilateral triangle.

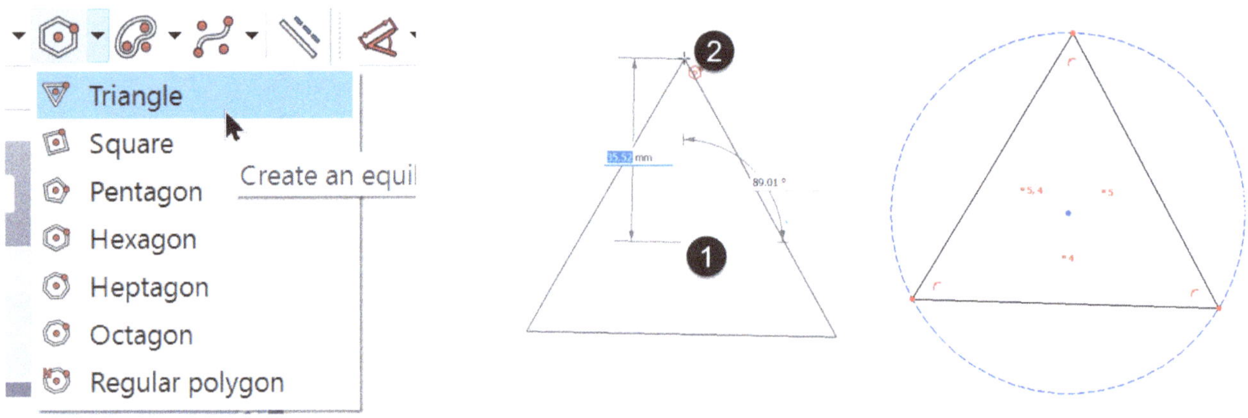

Square

Click the **Polygon** drop-down > **Square** on the **Sketcher geometries** toolbar (or) click **Sketch > Sketcher geometries > Create square** on the menu bar. Specify the center point of the square. Move the pointer outward and click to specify the vertex point of the square.

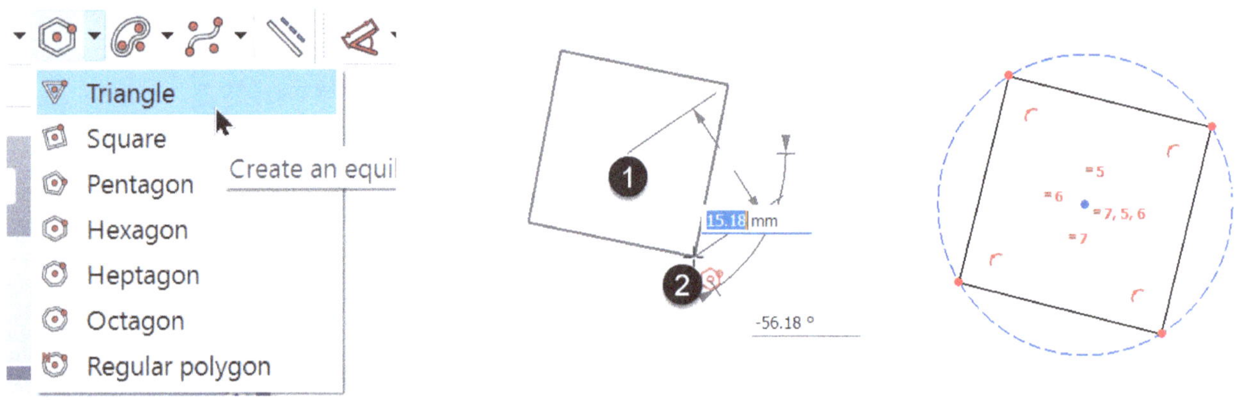

Pentagon

Click the **Polygon** drop-down > **Pentagon** on the **Sketcher geometries** toolbar (or) click **Sketch > Sketcher geometries > Create pentagon** on the menu bar. Specify the center point of the pentagon. Move the pointer outward and click to specify the vertex point of the pentagon.

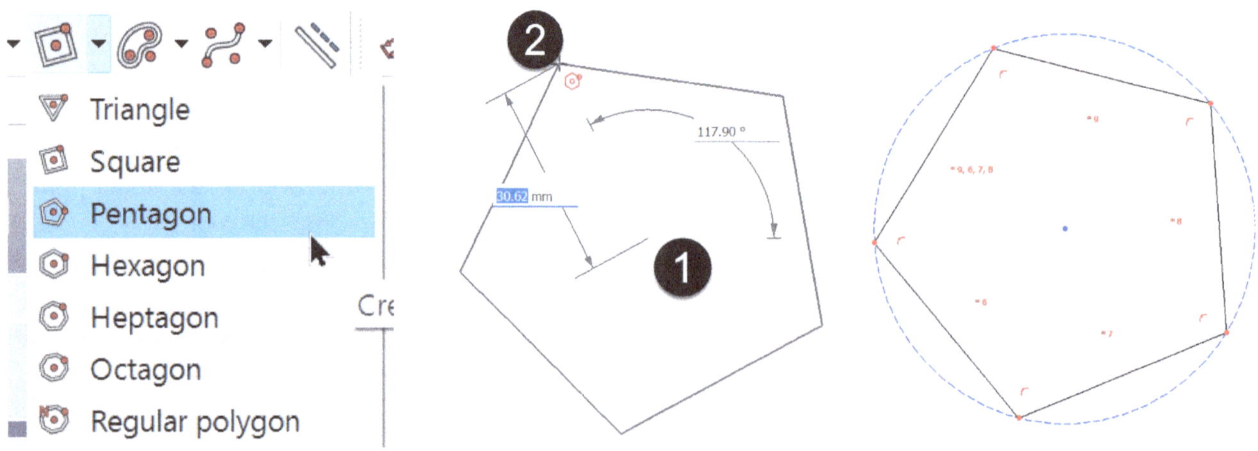

Hexagon

Click the **Polygon** drop-down > **Hexagon** on the **Sketcher geometries** toolbar (or) click **Sketch > Sketcher geometries > Create hexagon** on the menu bar. Specify the center point of the hexagon. Move the pointer outward and click to specify the vertex point of the hexagon.

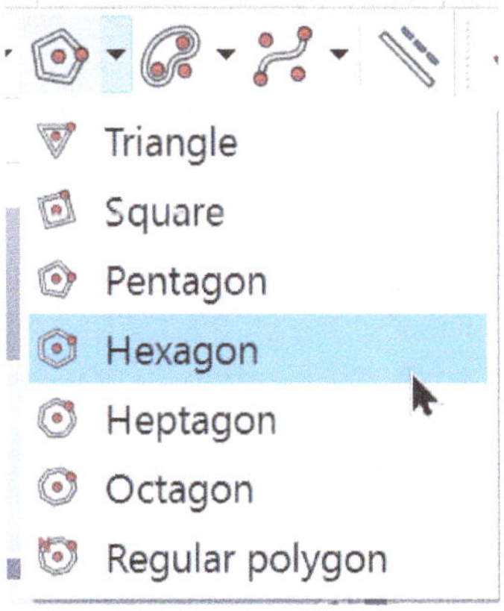

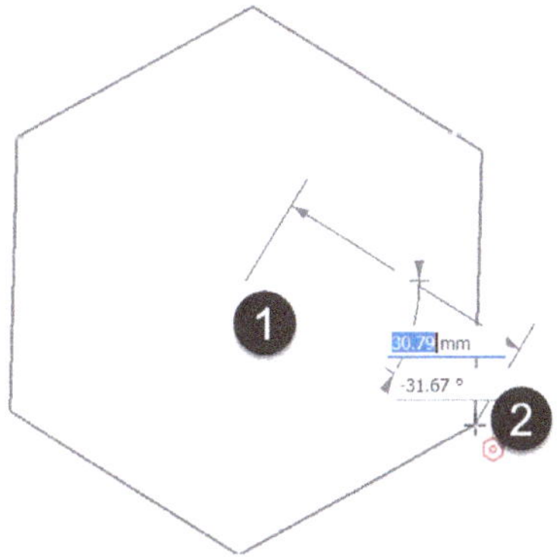

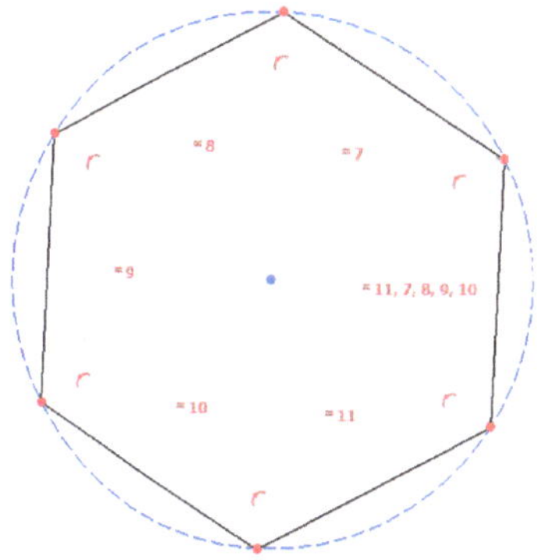

Heptagon

Click the **Polygon** drop-down > **Heptagon** on the **Sketcher geometries** toolbar (or) click **Sketch > Sketcher geometries > Create heptagon** on the menu bar. Specify the center point of the heptagon. Move the pointer outward and click to specify the vertex point of the heptagon.

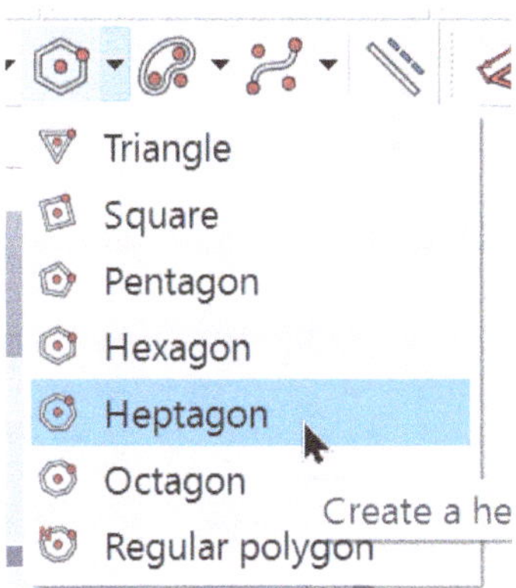

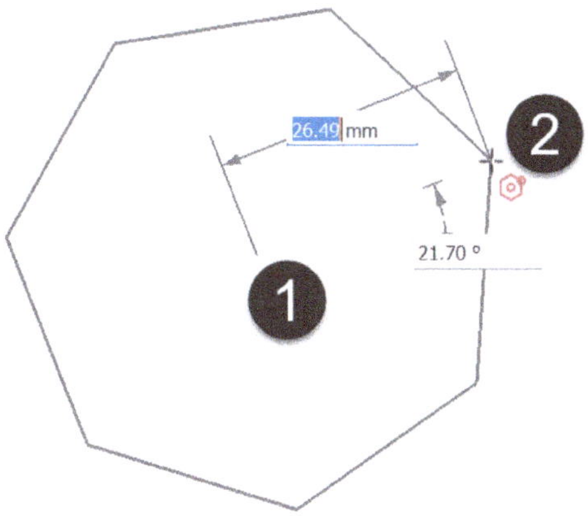

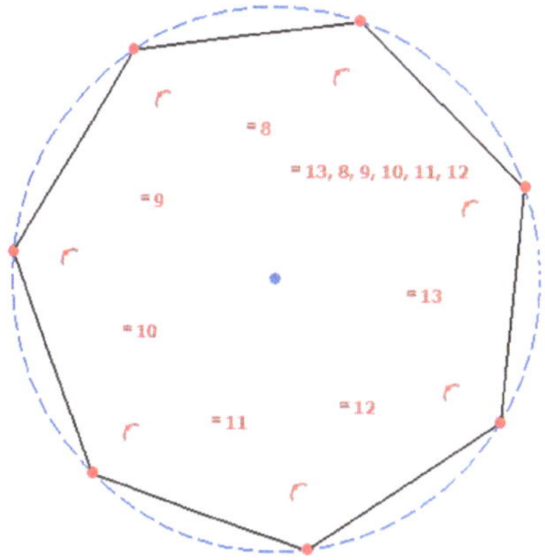

Octagon

Click the **Polygon** drop-down > **Octagon** on the **Sketcher geometries** toolbar (or) click **Sketch > Sketcher geometries > Create octagon** on the menu bar. Specify the center point of the octagon. Move the pointer outward and click to specify the vertex point of the octagon.

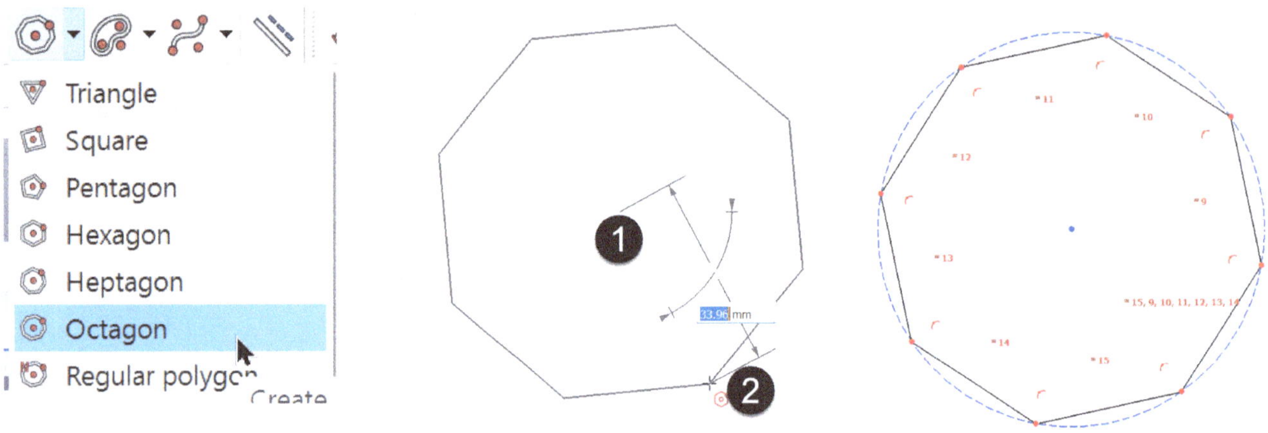

Regular Polygon

This command creates a polygon with the number of sides that you specify. Click the **Polygon** drop-down > **Regular Polygon**  on the **Sketcher geometries** toolbar (or) click **Sketch > Sketcher geometries > Create regular polygon** on the menu bar. Next, specify the number of sides of the polygon in the **Create regular polygon** dialog. Click **OK** and click on the graphics window to define the center of the polygon. Move the pointer outward and click to create the polygon. Notice that a circle is displayed touching the vertices of the polygon.

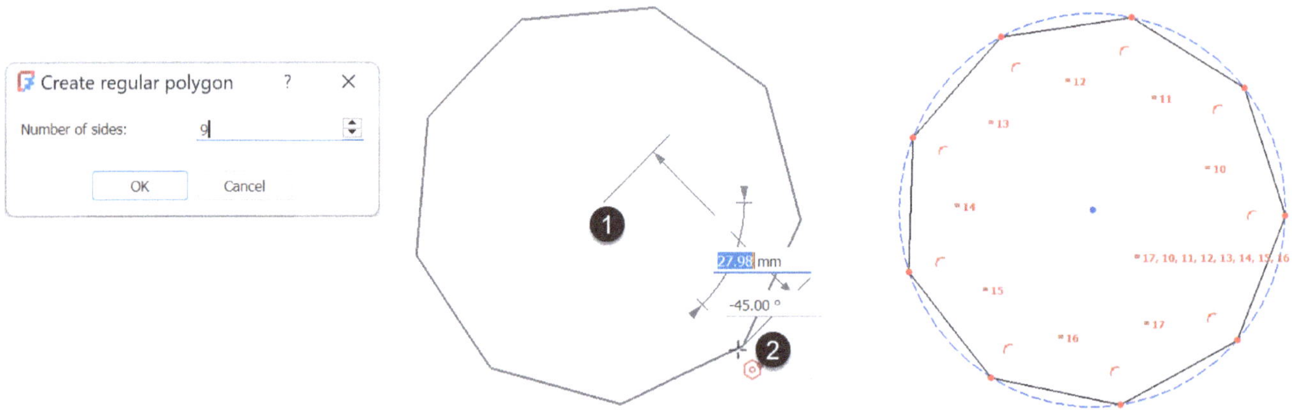

The Create ellipse by center command

This command creates an ellipse using a center point, and major and minor axes. Click the **Circle** drop-down > **Create ellipse by center** on the **Sketcher geometries** toolbar (or) click **Sketch > Sketcher geometries > Create ellipse by center** on the menu bar. In the graphics window, click to define the center point of the ellipse. As you move the pointer, dynamic dimensions for the first axis and angle will appear first, allowing you to visualize the initial orientation and length of the ellipse in real-time. For precise control, type the desired length for the first axis into the dimension box and press TAB, then input the angle and press ENTER to lock in the ellipse's orientation. Next, the second axis dimension will appear dynamically as you adjust the ellipse's shape. Type the desired length for the second axis and press ENTER to finalize the ellipse. If you prefer a more freeform approach, simply click to set the center, drag the pointer to define the first axis and angle, and then adjust the second axis by moving the pointer perpendicularly before clicking again to complete the ellipse.

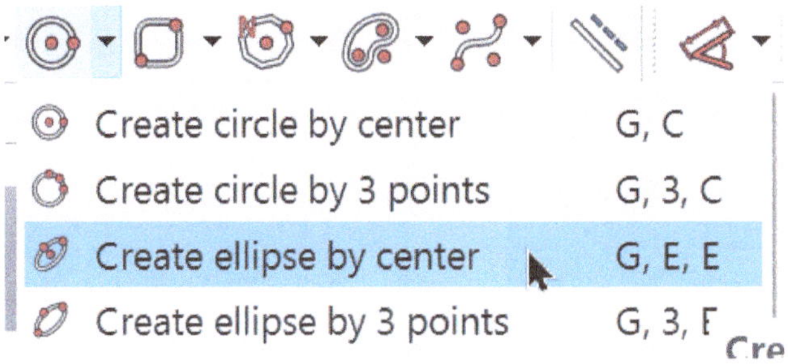

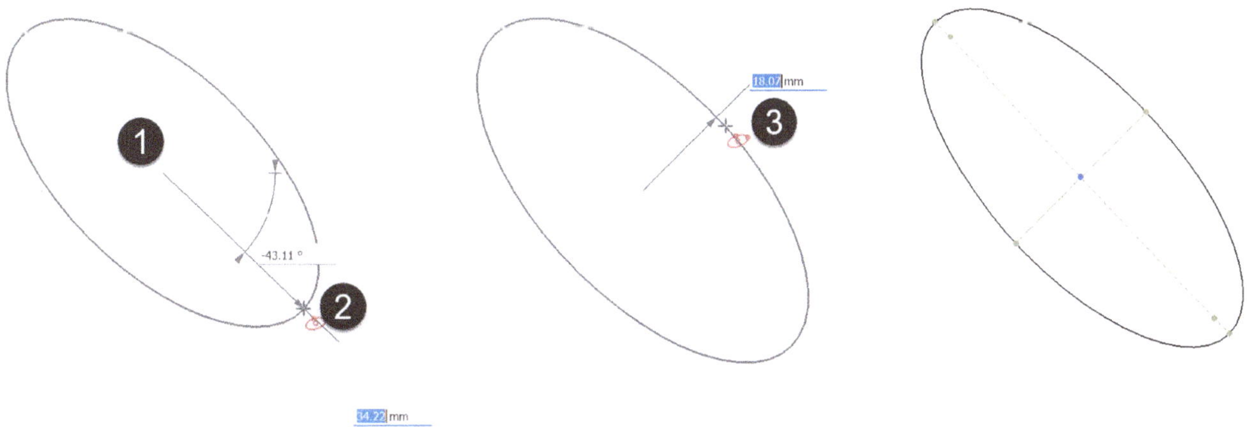

The Create ellipse by 3 points command

This command creates an ellipse by specifying three points. The first two points define the location and length of the first axis. The third point defines the second axis of the ellipse. Click the **Circle** drop-down > **Create ellipse by 3 points** on the **Sketcher geometries** toolbar (or) click **Sketch > Sketcher geometries > Create ellipse by 3 points** on the menu bar. In the graphics window, click to define the start point of the first axis. Move the pointer away and click to define the distance and orientation of the first axis. Next, move the pointer in the direction perpendicular to the first axis and click; the ellipse is created.

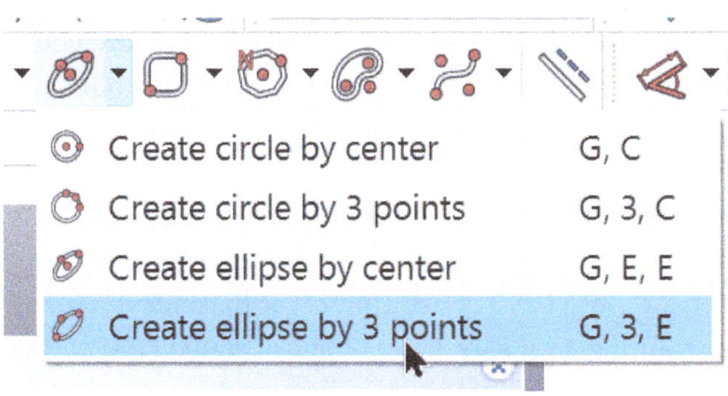

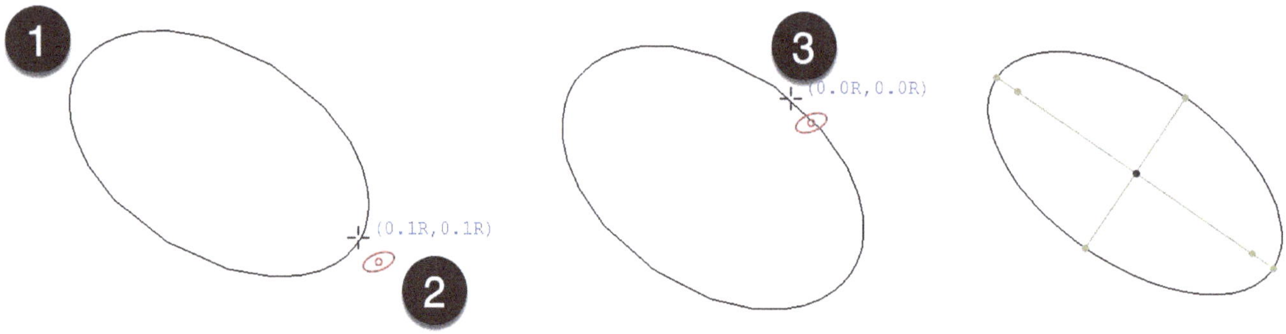

Toggle Construction geometry

This command converts a sketch element into a construction element. The construction elements support you in creating a sketch of the desired shape and size. To convert a sketch element to a construction element, select it and click the **Toggle Construction geometry** icon on the **Sketcher geometries** toolbar.

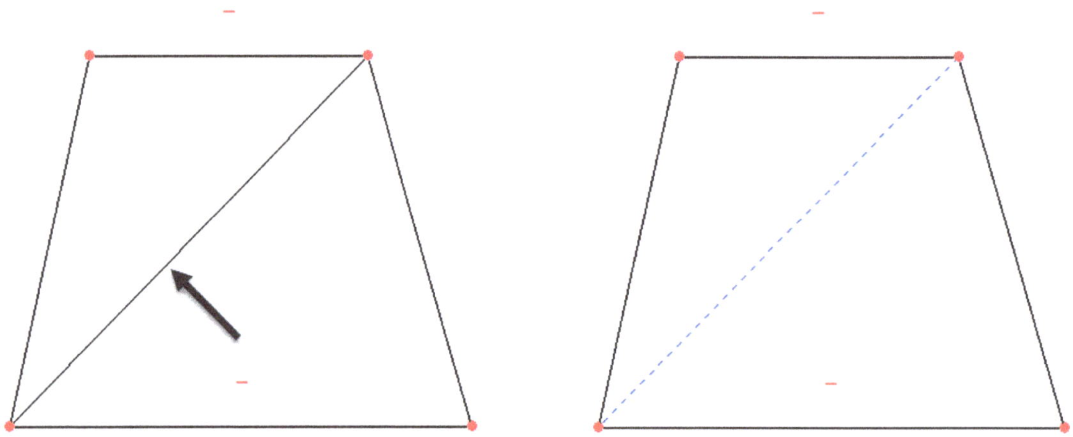

Adding Dimensions

When working with FreeCAD, it's essential to make sure that your 2D sketches are fully constrained before you start creating solid features. So, what does "fully constrained" mean? It simply means that your sketch should have a definite shape and size without any uncertainties. This is achieved by using two types of constraints: geometric and dimensional. Geometric constraints ensure that your 2D shapes follow specific geometric rules related to lengths, angles, and relationships like horizontality and verticality. On the other hand, dimensional constraints help you specify precise measurements. You can apply these constraints using the commands found in the Sketcher constraints toolbar. FreeCAD's Sketcher workbench also has a constraint solver that calculates and maintains the constraints for your 2D geometry. By fully constraining your sketch, you make it stable and predictable, which is quite handy when you're ready to turn it into solid features.

The Dimensions command

It is generally considered good practice to ensure that every sketch you create is fully-constrained before moving on to creating features. You can add dimensions to a sketch by using the **Dimension** command. You can use this command to add all dimensions such as length, angle, and diameter. This command creates a dimension based on the geometry you select. For instance, to dimension, a circle, activate the **Dimension** command and then click on the circle. Next, move the pointer and click again to position the dimension; notice that the **Insert diameter** box pops up. You can type in a value in this box and then press Enter to update the dimension.

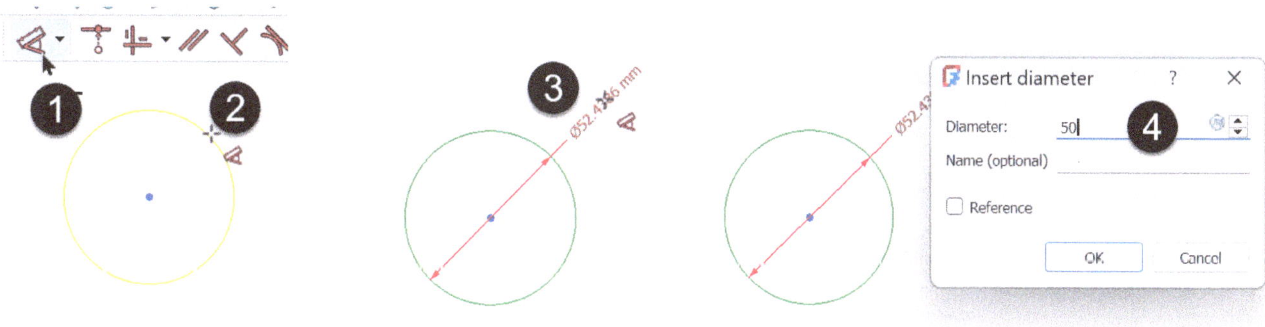

If you select a line, this command automatically creates a linear dimension. Move the pointer and click to position the dimension. Type in a value and press Enter; the dimension will be updated.

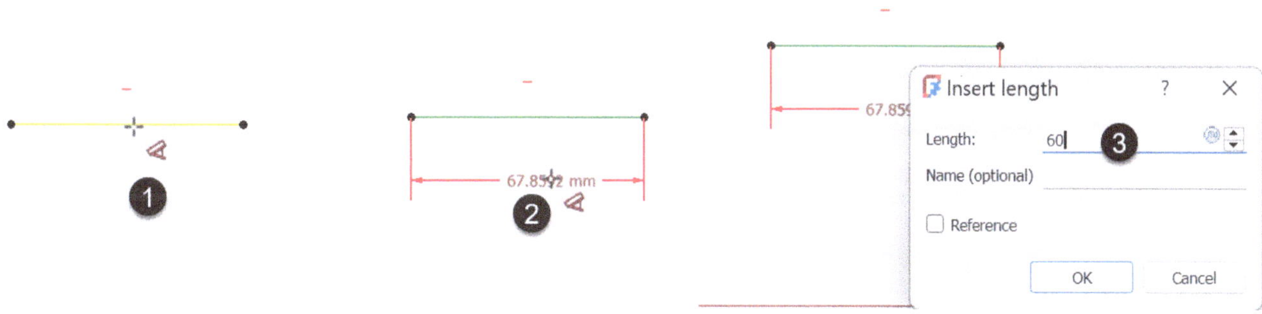

The **Dimension** command can be used to create three different types of linear dimensions between two points. Activate this command and select the center points of the two circles, as shown. Move the pointer vertically downward and notice the horizontal dimension between the two selected points. Move the pointer horizontally and notice the vertical dimension between the selected points.

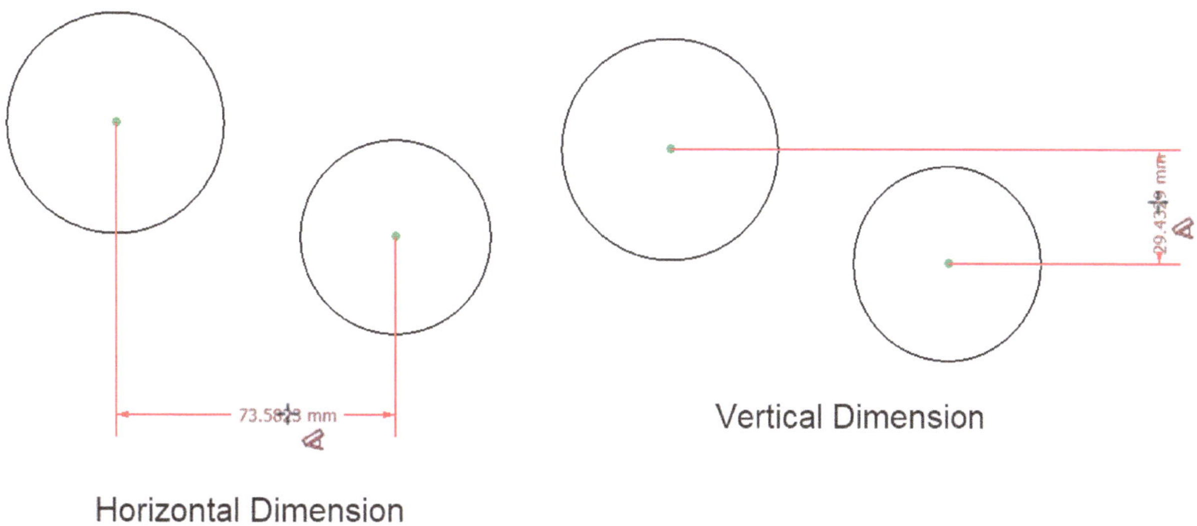

Move the pointer between the two selected points and notice that the dimension is turned into an aligned dimension.

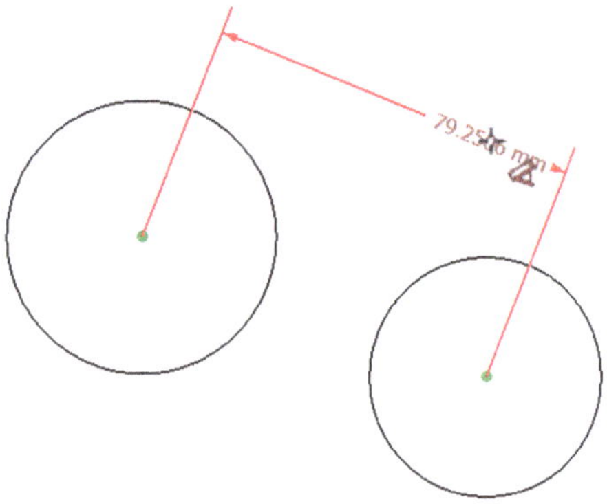

You can also use the **Dimension** command to create an angle dimension. Activate this command and select two lines that are positioned at an angle to each other. Move the pointer between the two lines and click to position the dimension. Type-in a value, and then click the green check on the **Insert angle** box.

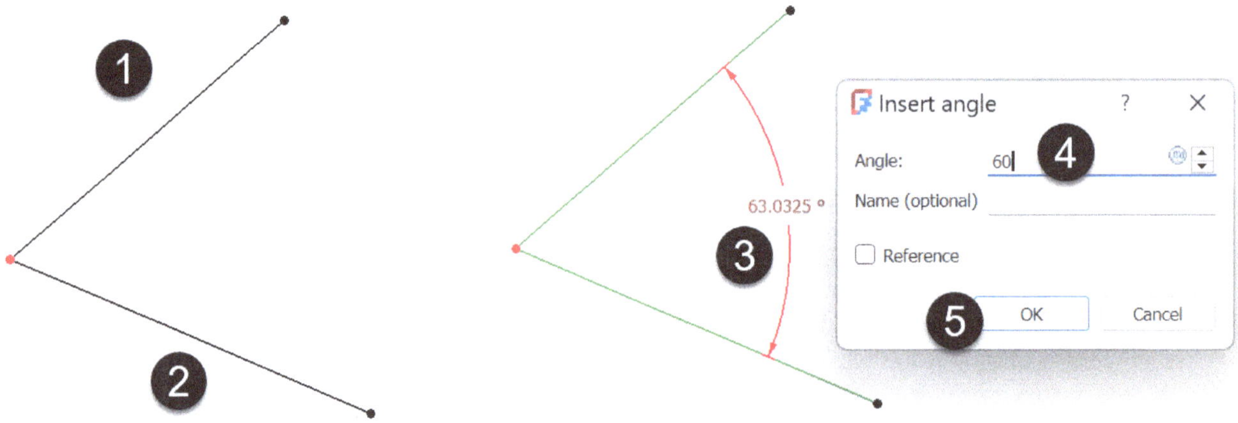

Constrain Horizontal Distance

To add a horizontal distance constraint, click the **Dimension** drop-down > **Constrain horizontal distance** icon on the **Sketcher constraints** toolbar (or) click **Sketch > Sketcher constraints > Constrain horizontal distance** on the menu bar. Select two points (or) a line from the graphics window. Next, type-in a value in the **Insert Length** dialog and click **OK**; the horizontal dimension is created.

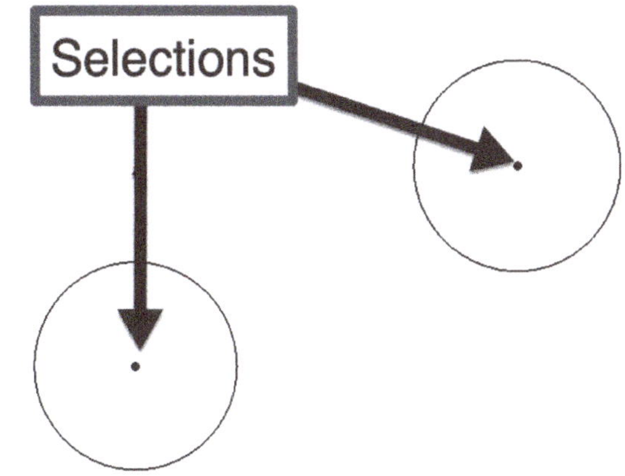

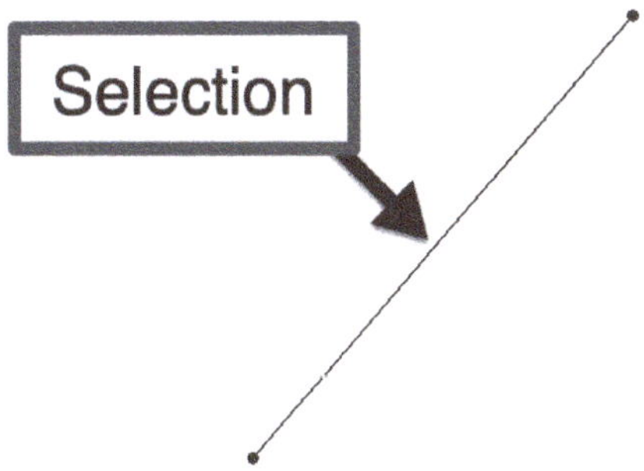

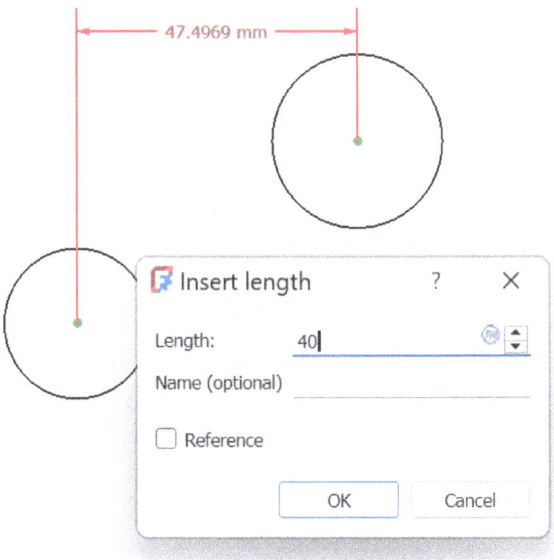

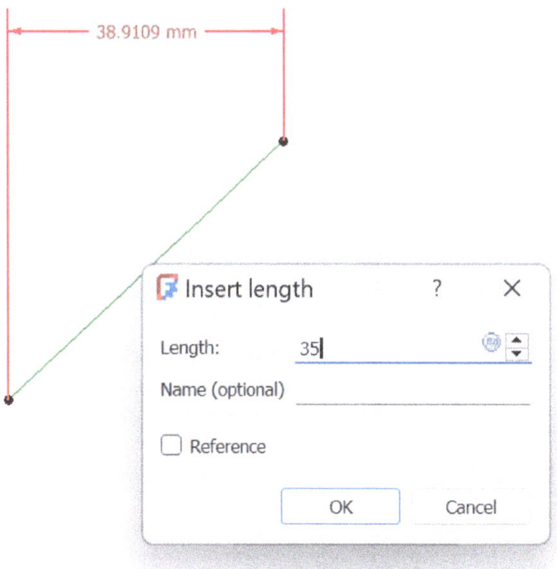

Constrain Vertical Distance

To create a vertical distance constraint, click the **Dimension** drop-down > **Constrain vertical distance** icon on the **Sketcher constraints** toolbar (or) click **Sketch > Sketcher constraints > Constrain vertical distance** on the menu bar. Select two points (or) a line from the graphics window. Next, type-in a value in the **Insert Length** dialog and click **OK**; the vertical distance constraint is created.

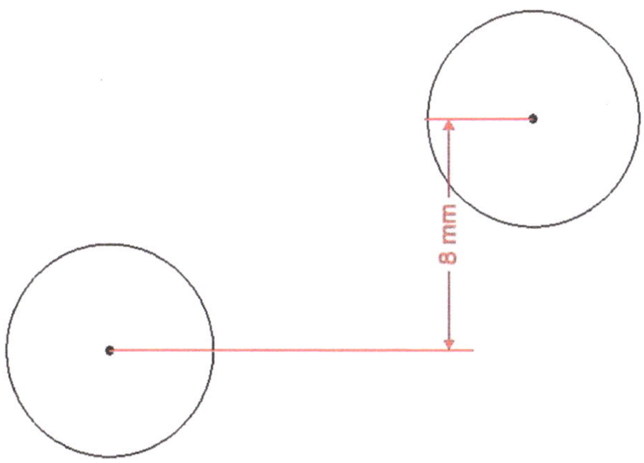

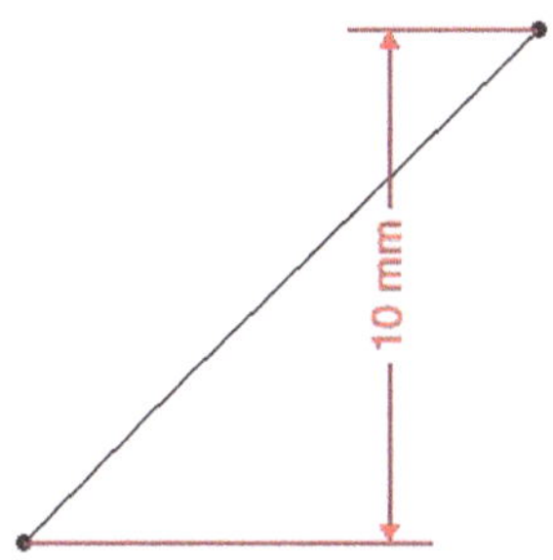

Constrain Distance

To create a dimension aligned between two points or a selected line, click the **Dimension** drop-down > **Constrain distance** icon on the **Sketcher constraints** toolbar (or) click **Sketch > Sketcher constraints > Constrain distance** on the menu bar. Select two points or a line from the graphics window. Next, type-in a value in the **Insert Length** dialog and click **OK**.

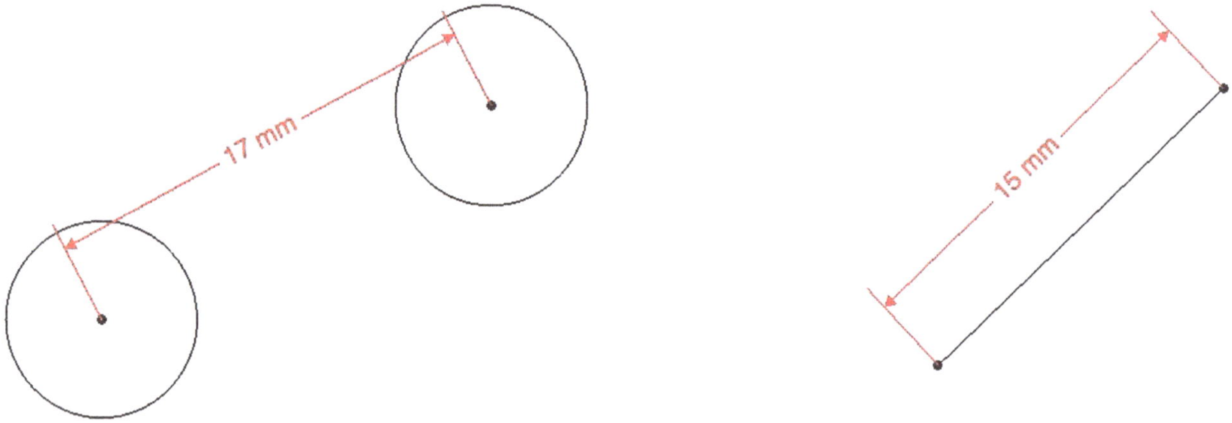

Constrain angle

Click the **Dimension** drop-down > **Constrain angle** icon on the **Sketcher constraints** toolbar (or) click **Sketch > Sketcher constraints > Constrain angle** on the menu bar. Next, select two lines that are positioned at an angle to each other. Move the pointer between the selected lines and click to position the dimension. Next, type in a value and click the **OK** button.

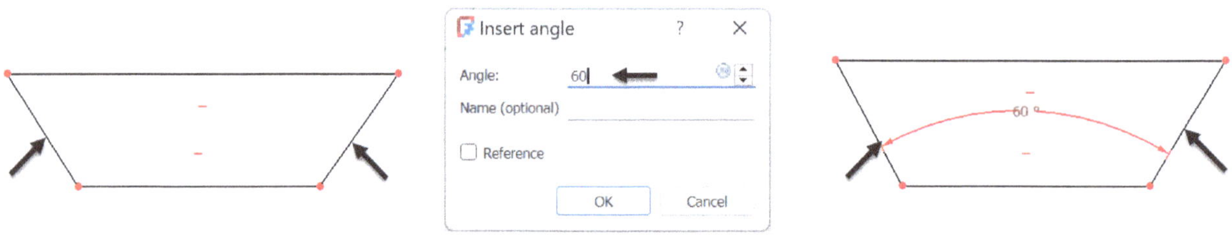

Constrain diameter

This command adds a diameter constraint to a circle or arc. To do this, click the **Dimension** drop-down > **Constrain Diameter** icon on the **Sketcher constraints** toolbar (or) click **Sketch > Sketcher constraints > Constrain diameter** on the menu bar. Next, select a circle or arc; the **Insert diameter** dialog pops up. Type-in a value in this dialog, and then click **OK** to update the dimension.

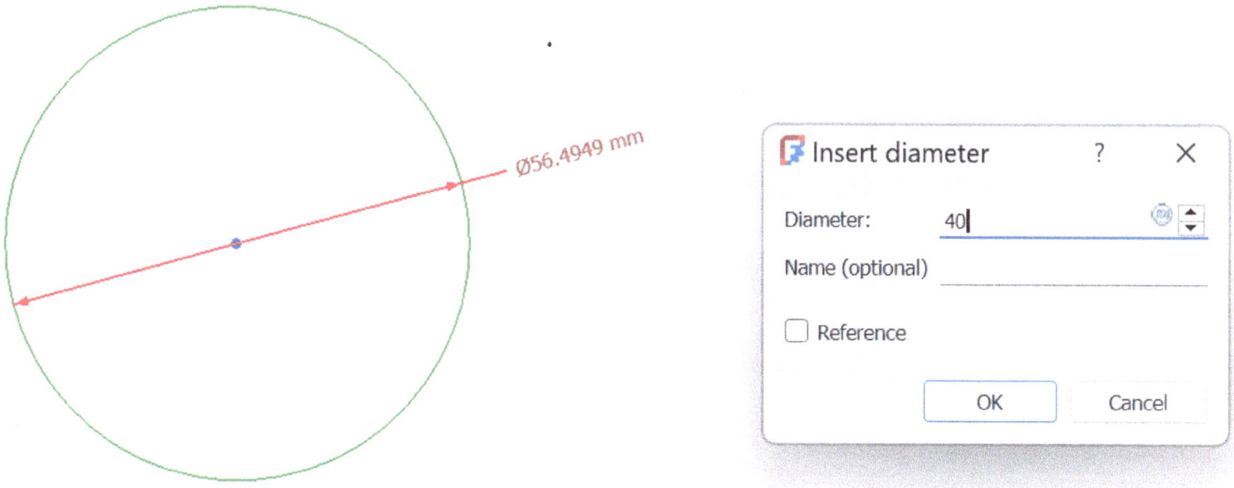

Adding Dimensions to an Arc

FreeCAD 1.0 allows you to add five types of dimensions to an arc: Radius, Diameter, and Linear dimension.

Adding a Radius

To add a radius to an arc, click the **Dimension** drop-down > **Constrain radius**  icon on the **Sketcher constraints** toolbar (or) click **Sketch > Sketcher constraints > Constrain radius** on the menu bar. Next, select the arc and type the radius value in the **Insert radius** dialog. Click **OK** to create the radius dimension.

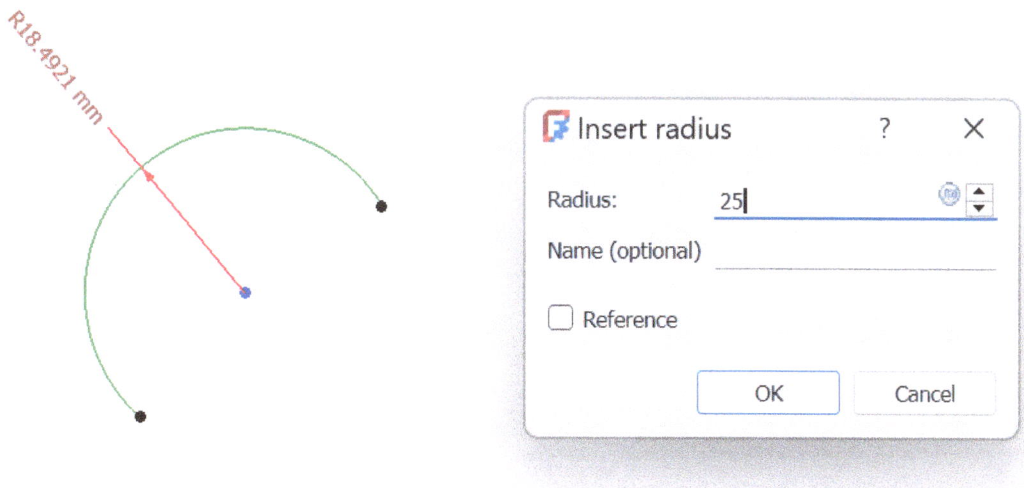

Adding a Linear dimension to the Arc

To add a linear dimension to an arc, activate the **Constrain distance** command and select its endpoints. Type the distance value and click **OK**.

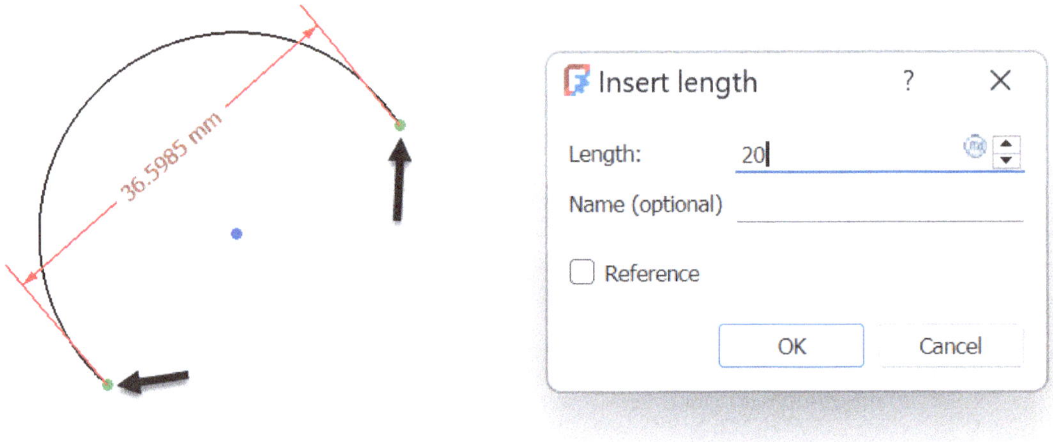

Constrain auto radius/diameter

This command adds a radius constraint to an arc and diameter constraint to a circle. Click the **Dimension** drop-down > **Constrain auto radius/diameter** icon on the **Sketcher constraints** toolbar (or) click **Sketch > Sketcher constraints > Constrain auto radius/diameter** on the menu bar. Next, select a circle; the **Insert diameter** dialog pops up. Type-in a value in this dialog, and then click **OK** to update the dimension. If you select an arc, the **Insert radius** dialog appears. Type-in a value in this dialog and click **OK** to create the radius dimension.

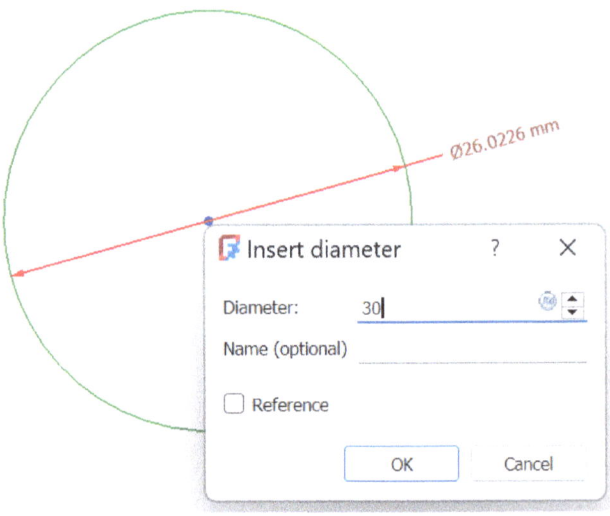

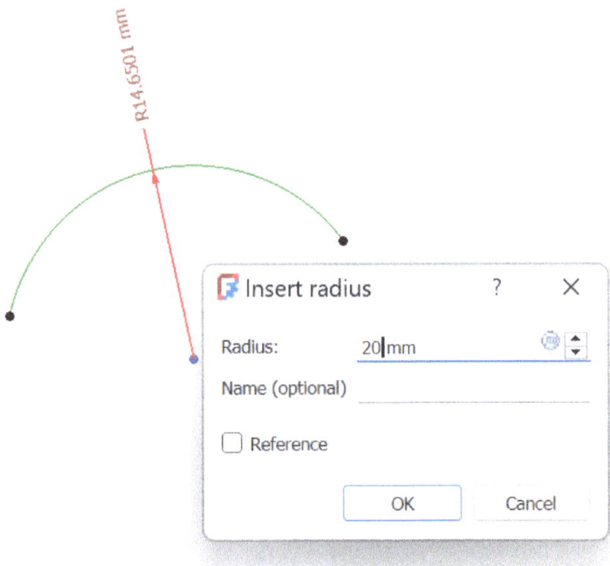

Constrain Lock

This command is used to lock a selected point at its location. Click the **Dimension** drop-down **> Constrain Lock** icon on the **Sketcher constraints** toolbar (or) click **Sketch > Sketcher constraints > Constrain lock** on the menu bar. Select the point to be locked; the dimensions are created between the selected point and the sketch origin.

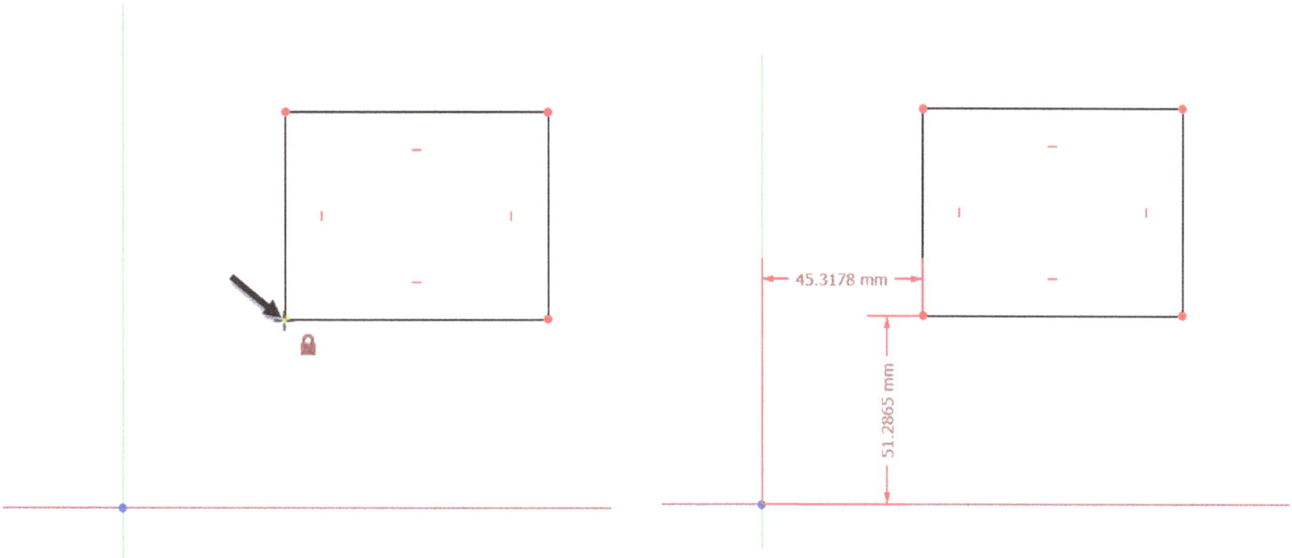

Over-constrained Sketch

When creating sketches for solid or surface features, FreeCAD will not allow you to over-constrain the geometry. The term 'over-constrain' means adding more dimensions than required. The following figure shows a fully constrained sketch. If you add another dimension to this sketch (e.g., diagonal dimension), an error message appears in the Report View panel and the redundant dimension is deleted.

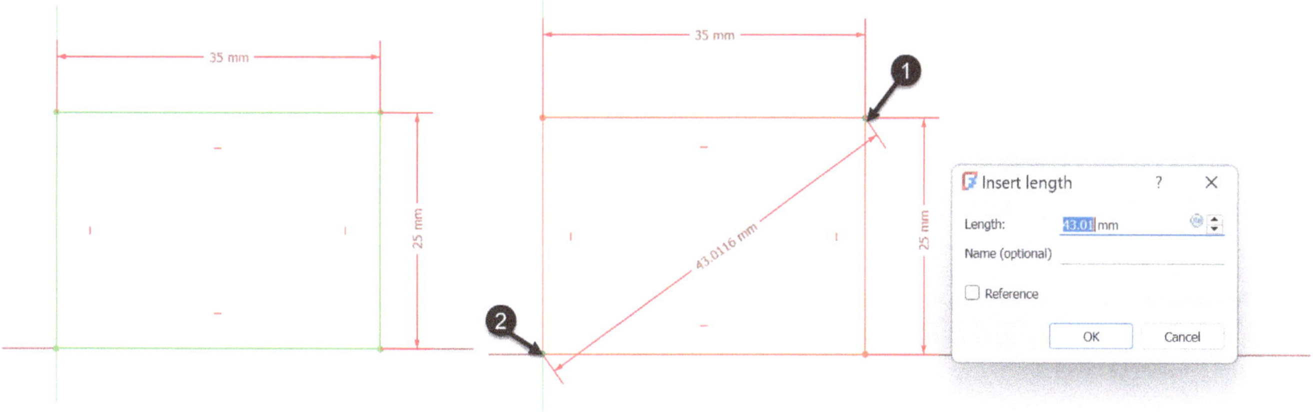

Geometric Constraints

The constraints are used to control the shape of a drawing by establishing relationships between the sketch elements. You can apply constraints to a sketch using the commands displayed on the **Sketcher constraints** toolbar.

Constrain Coincident

This constraint connects a point with another point. On the **Sketcher constraints** toolbar, click **Coincident constraint**  and select the points to be made coincident to each other. The selected points will be connected.

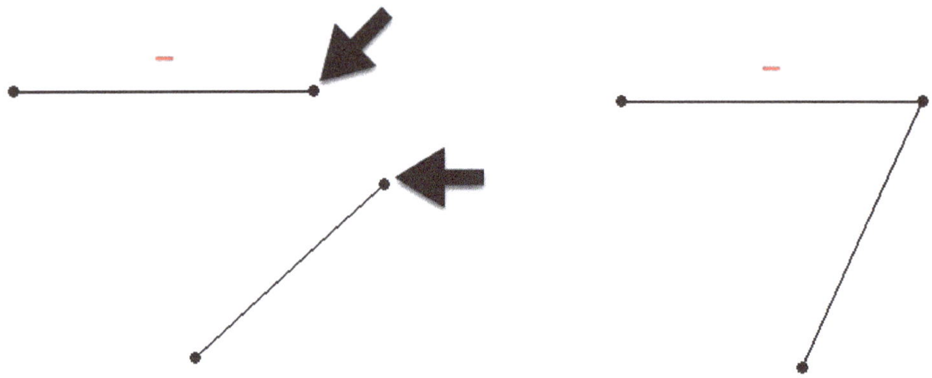

This constraint also makes a vertex or a point to be on a line, curve, arc, or circle. Activate this command and select a line, circle, arc, or curve. Select the point to be made coincident. The point will lie on the selected entity or its extension.

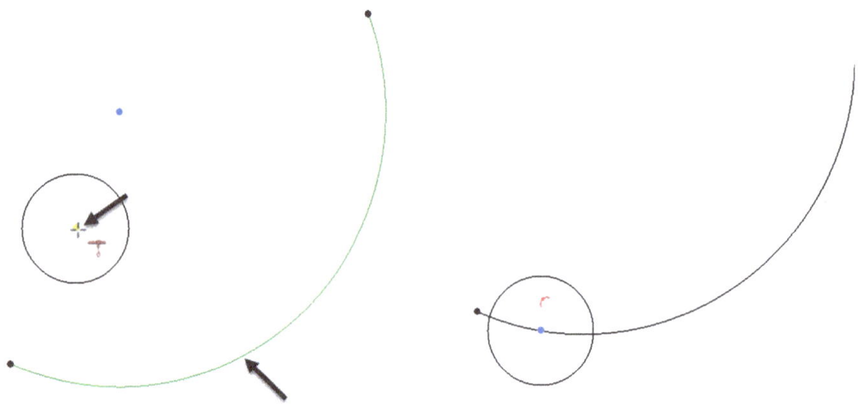

Constrain Horizontal

This constraint makes a line horizontal. Click the **Constrain Horizontal/Vertical** drop-down **> Constrain Horizontal** icon on the **Sketcher constraints** toolbar (or) click **Sketch > Sketcher constraints > Constrain horizontal**. Next, select a line; the line is made horizontal.

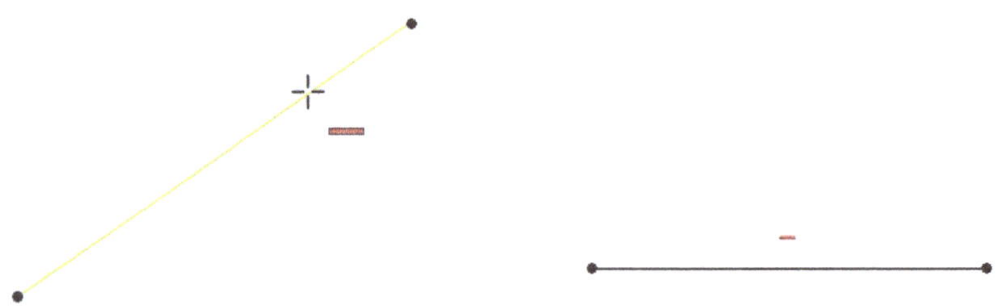

The **Horizontal Constraint** also aligns the two selected points horizontally. Click the **Constrain Horizontal/Vertical** drop-down **> Constrain Horizontal** icon on the **Sketcher constraints** toolbar and select the points to be aligned horizontally.

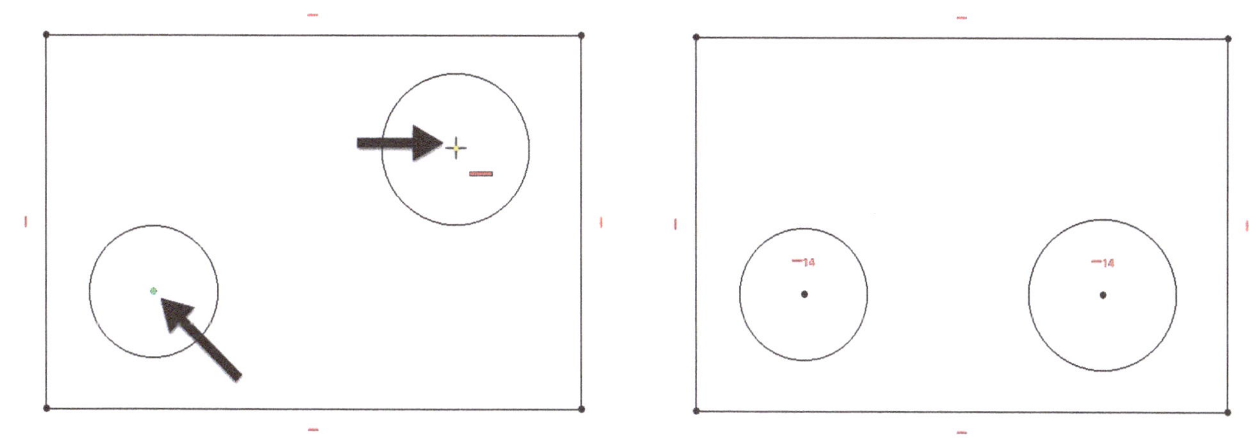

Constrain Vertical

This constraint makes a line vertical. Click the **Constrain Horizontal/Vertical** drop-down **> Constrain Vertical** icon on the **Sketcher constraints** toolbar (or) click **Sketch > Sketcher constraints > Constrain vertical**. Select a line; the line is made vertical.

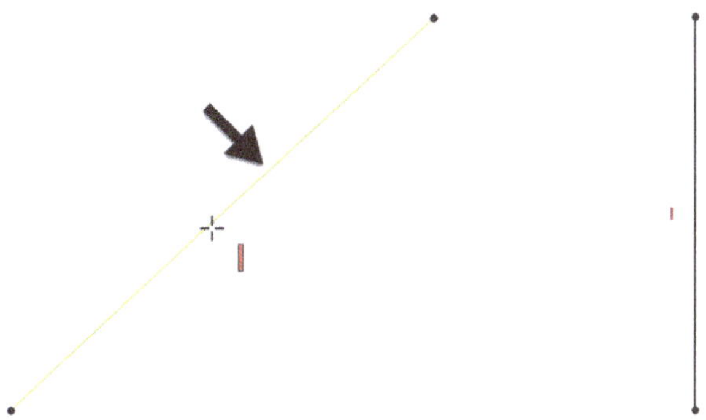

The **Constrain Vertical** also aligns the two selected points vertically. Click the **Constrain Horizontal/Vertical** drop-down **> Constrain Vertical** button on the **Sketcher constraints** toolbar and then select the points to align them vertically.

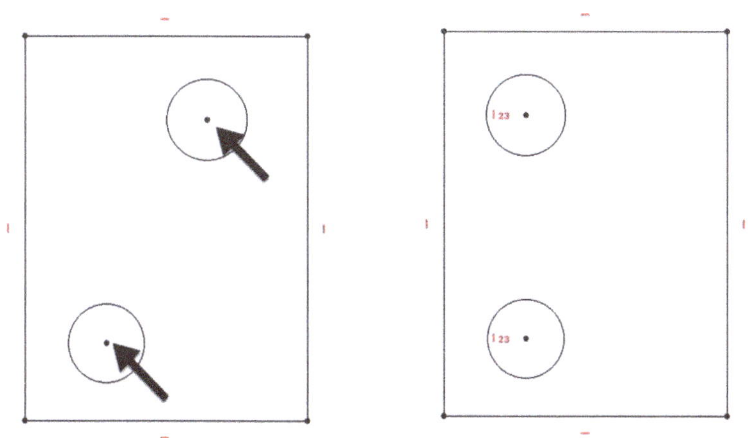

Constrain horizontal/vertical

This constrain makes a line horizontal or vertical. The lines positioned at an angle below 45-degrees will be made horizontal. The lines positioned at an angle above 45-degrees will be made vertical. You can also make two points horizontally or vertically aligned with each other.

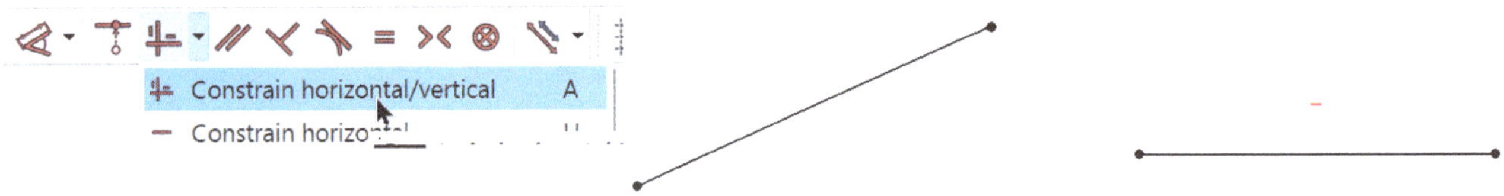

Horizontal

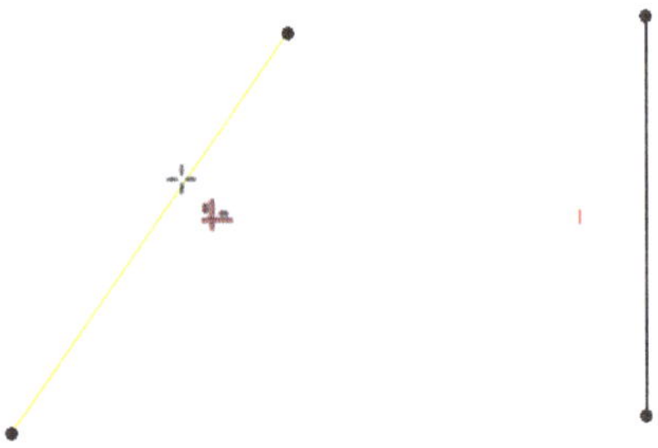

Vertical

Contrain equal

The **Equal**  constraint makes two lines equal in length. Click the **Constrain equal** icon on the **Sketcher constraints** toolbar (or) click **Sketch > Sketcher constraints > Constrain equal**. Select two lines; the two lines are made equal in length.

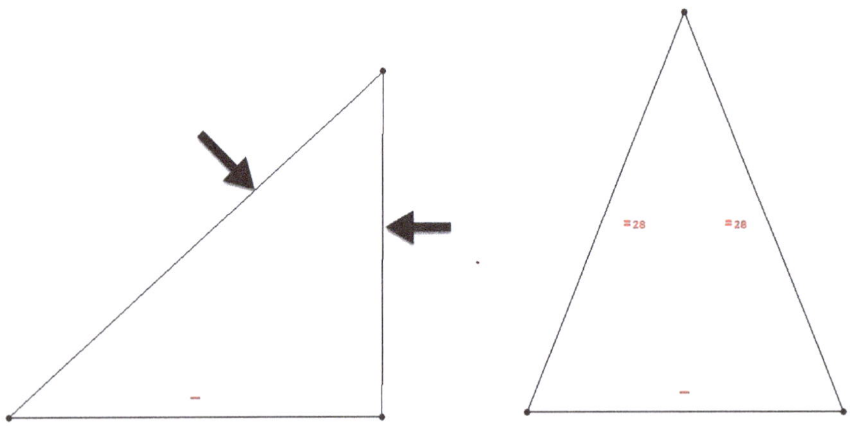

In addition to that, this constraint makes two circles or arcs equal in size.

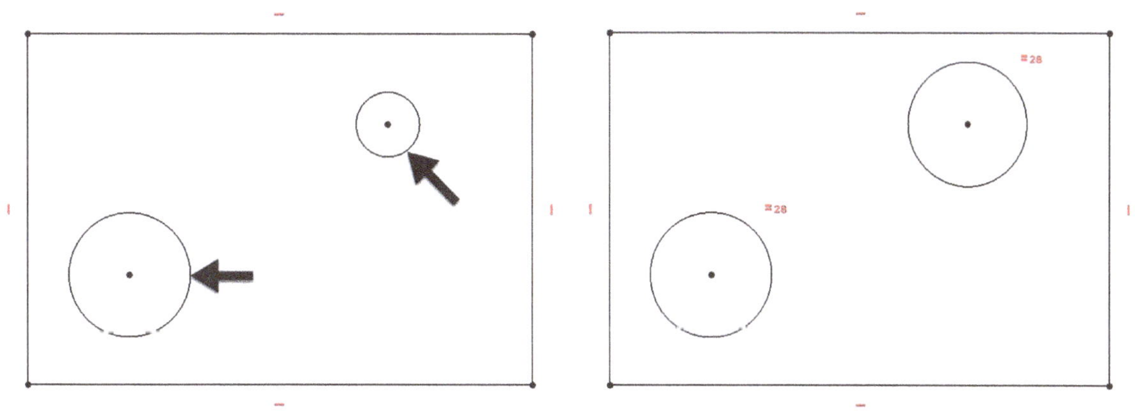

Constrain tangent or collinear

This constraint makes an arc, circle, or line tangent to another arc or circle. Click the **Constrain tangent or collinear** icon on the **Sketcher constraints** toolbar (or) click **Sketch > Sketcher constraints > Constrain tangent or collinear**. Next, select a circle, arc, or line. Select another circle, arc, or line; both the elements become tangent to each other.

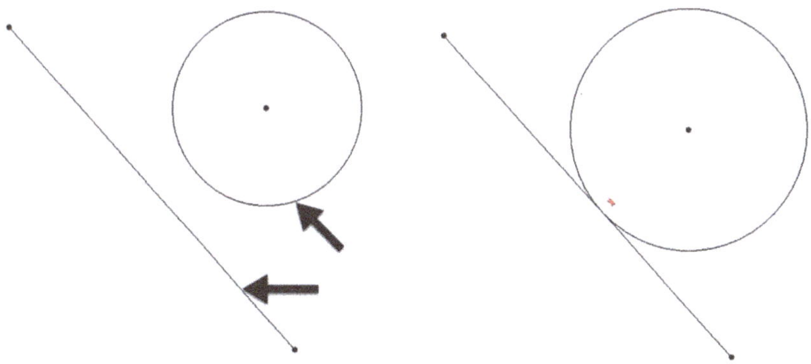

This constraint also forces a line to be collinear to another line. The lines are not required to touch each other.

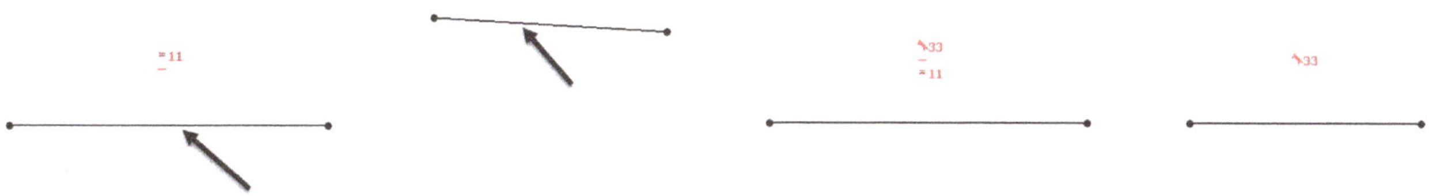

Parallel Constraint

This constraint makes two lines parallel to each other. Click the **Constrain parallel** icon on the **Sketcher constraints** toolbar (or) click **Sketch > Sketcher constraints > Constrain parallel.** Next, select two lines from the sketch. The under-constrained line is made parallel to the constrained line. For example, if you select a line with the **Horizontal** constraint and a free to move line, the free-to-move line becomes parallel to the horizontal line.

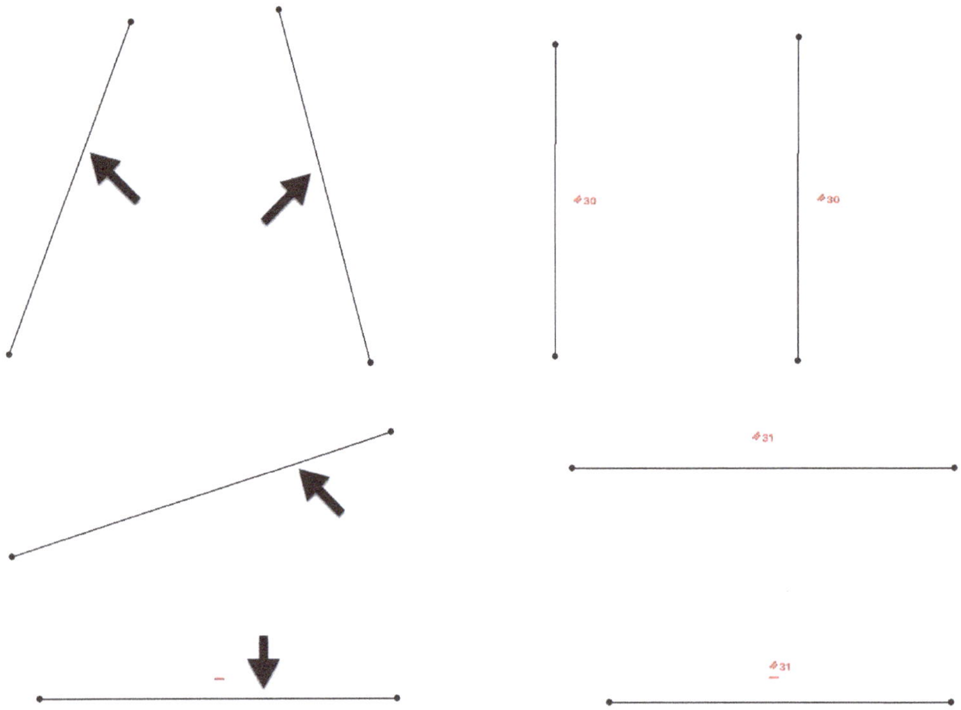

Perpendicular Constraint

This constraint makes two lines perpendicular to each other. Click the **Constrain perpendicular** icon on the **Sketcher constraints** toolbar (or) click **Sketch > Sketcher constraints > Constrain perpendicular**. Next, select two lines from the sketch. The two lines will be made perpendicular to each other.

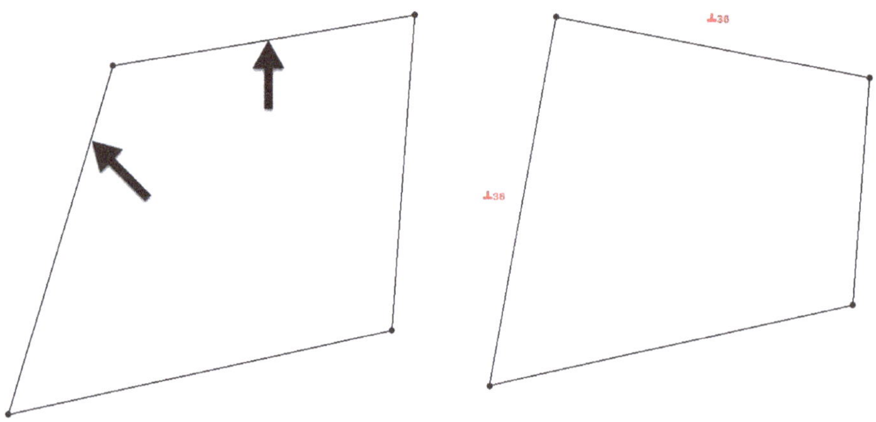

Symmetrical Constraint

This constraint makes two points symmetric about a line or third point. The objects will have the same position about the symmetry line. Click the **Symmetrical constraint** icon on the **Sketcher constraints** toolbar (or) click **Sketch > Sketcher constraints > Constrain symmetrical**, and click on the first point. Next, click on the second point, and then select the symmetry line. The two points will be made symmetric about the symmetry line.

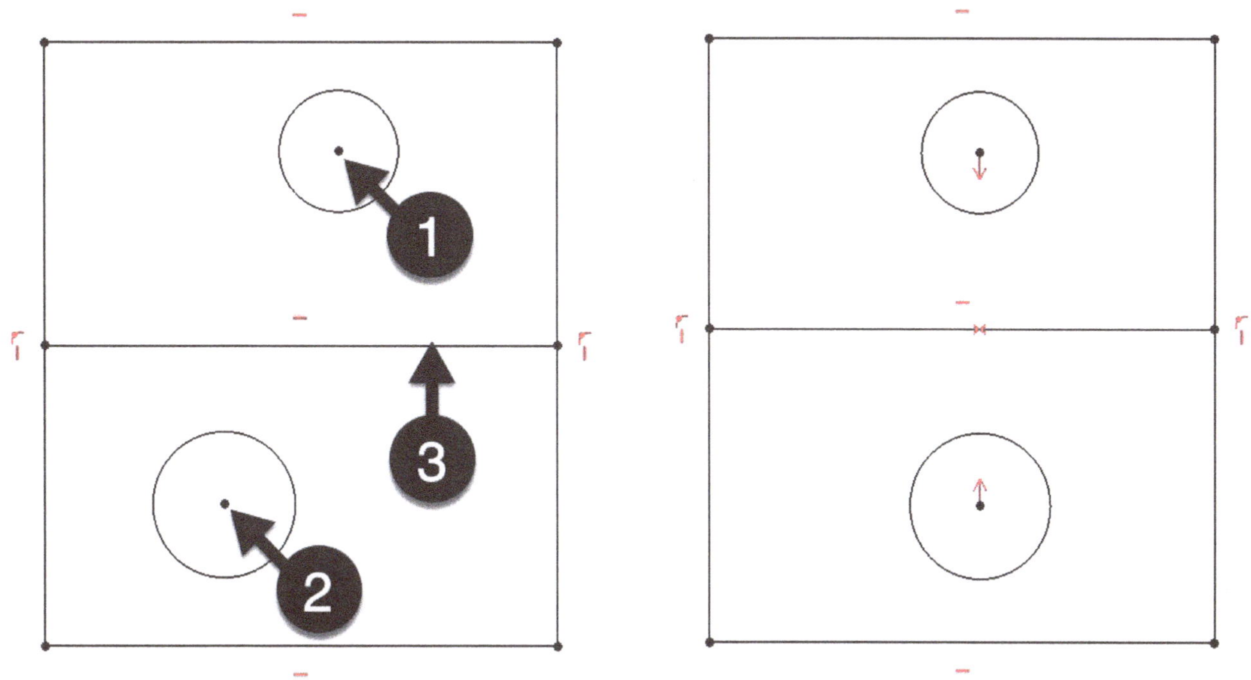

Block Constraint

This constraint fixes the selected objects at their current location. Click the **Constrain block**  icon on the **Sketcher constraints** toolbar (or) click **Sketch > Sketcher constraints > Constrain block** on the menu bar. Next, select single or multiple objects from the graphics window. Now, click on the fixed objects and try to drag them; the objects are unmovable.

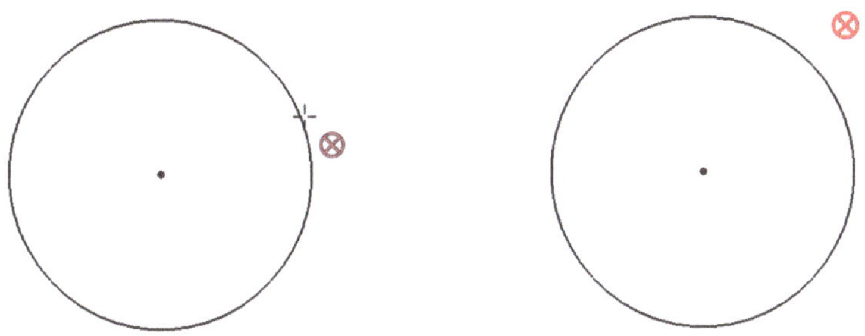

Toggle driving/reference constraint

This command allows you to switch a constraint between two types: driving and reference. A driving constraint directly controls the shape or size of an object. For instance, it can define the exact length of a line. In contrast, a reference constraint only displays information, such as the length of a line, without influencing the design. This feature is useful when you need to check measurements without altering the design. Switching between these two types helps you better manage how your design behaves. If you activate this command before applying any constraints, all subsequent constraints will be set as driven.

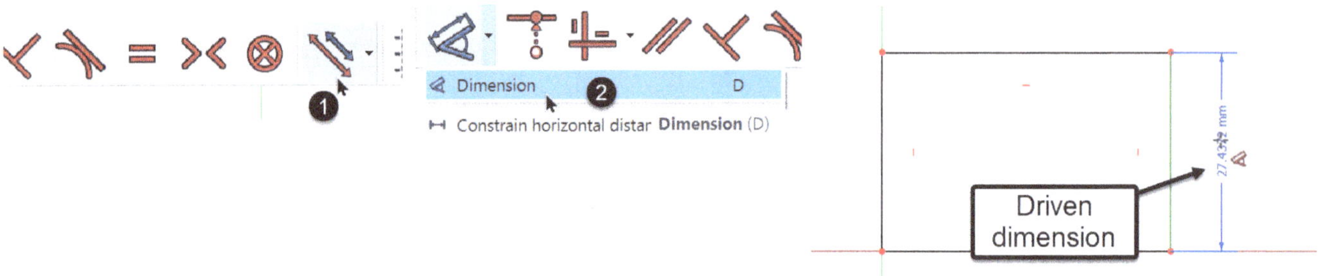

If you select an existing driving constraint and activate this command, the selected constraint will be changed to driven.

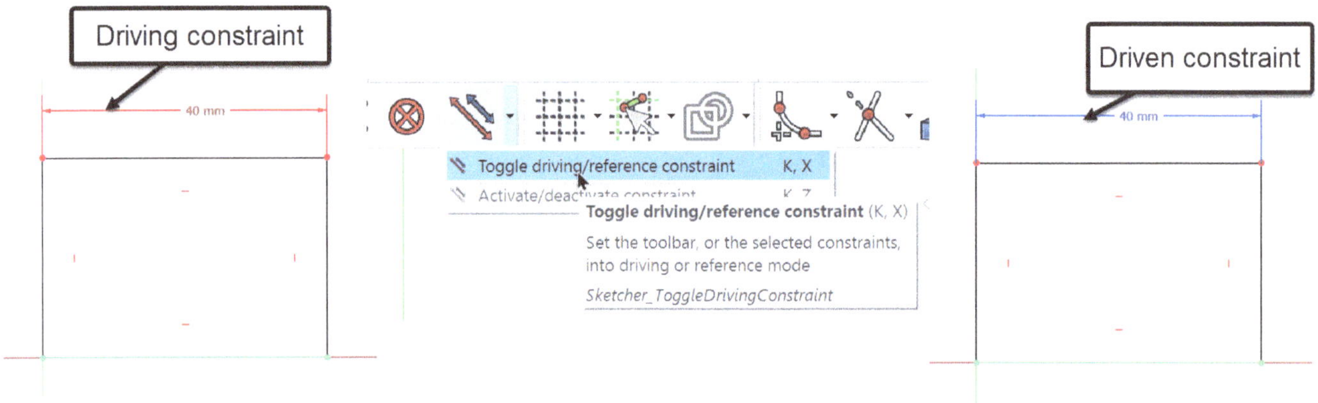

Activate/deactivate constraint

This command enables you to enable or disable a constraint without removing it. To deactivate a constraint, select it and click the **Activate/Deactivate Constraint** icon on the Sketcher constraints toolbar. When a constraint is active, it influences the shape or position of an object. When deactivated, it no longer impacts the design, providing greater flexibility to make adjustments. This functionality is particularly useful when experimenting with different design ideas while preserving the original constraints of your design.

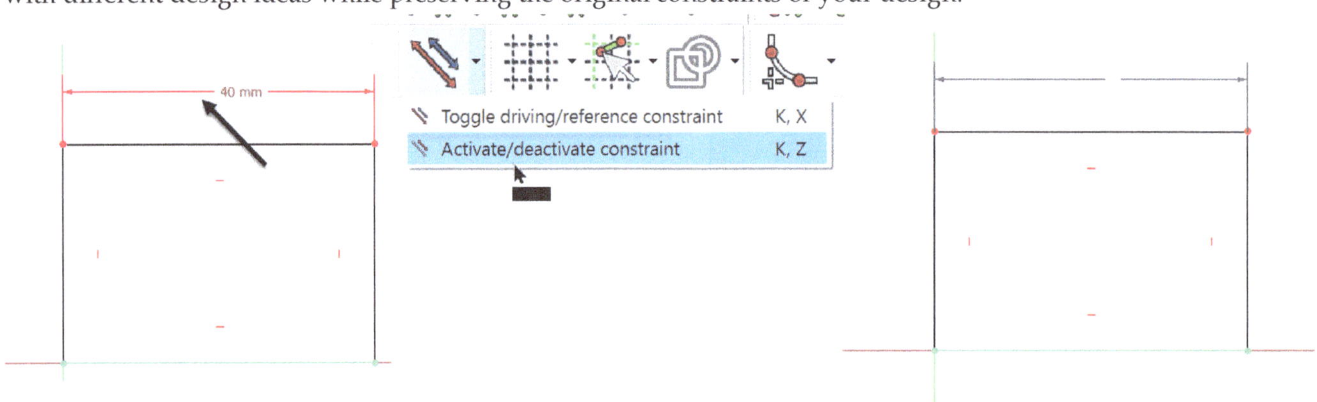

The Create Fillet command

This command rounds a sharp corner created by the intersection of two lines, arcs, circles, and rectangle. Click the **Fillet > Create Fillet** icon on the **Sketcher tools** toolbar (or) click **Sketch > Sketch tools > Create fillet** on the menu bar. Next, select the elements to be filleted. The elements to be filleted are not required to touch each other. Keep on selecting the elements of the sketch; the fillets are added at the corners at which two selected elements intersect. Note that the existing constraints associated with the intersection edges will be deleted.

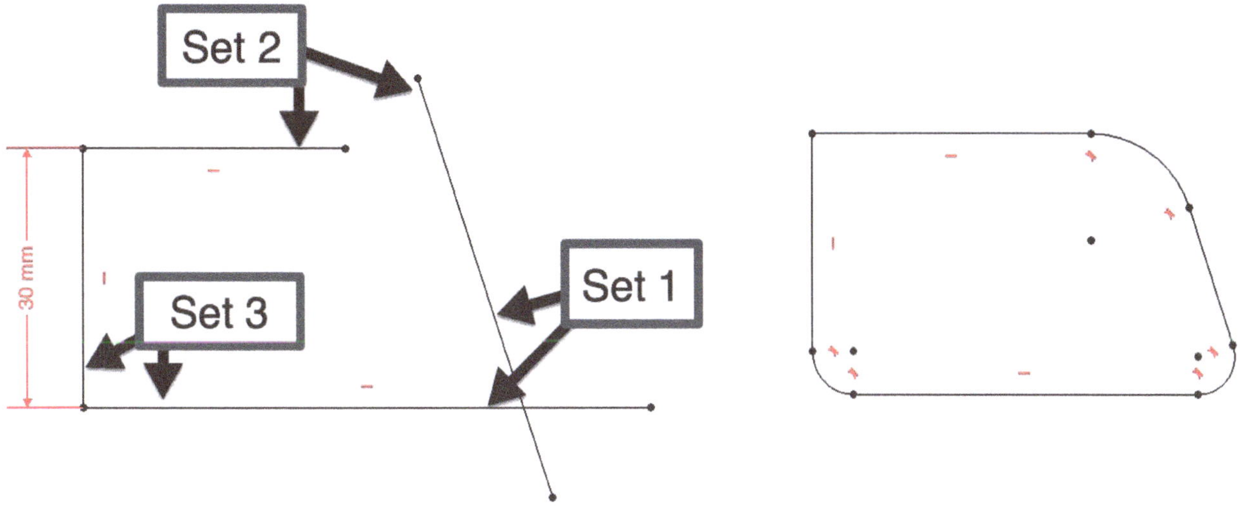

The Create Chamfer command

This command bevels a sharp corner created by the intersection of two lines, arcs, circles, and rectangle. Click the **Fillet > Create Chamfer** icon on the **Sketcher tools** toolbar (or) click **Sketch > Sketch tools > Create chamfer** on the menu bar. Next, select the elements to be chamfered. The elements to be chamfered are not required to touch each other. Continue selecting the elements of the sketch; the chamfers are added at the corners where two selected elements intersect.

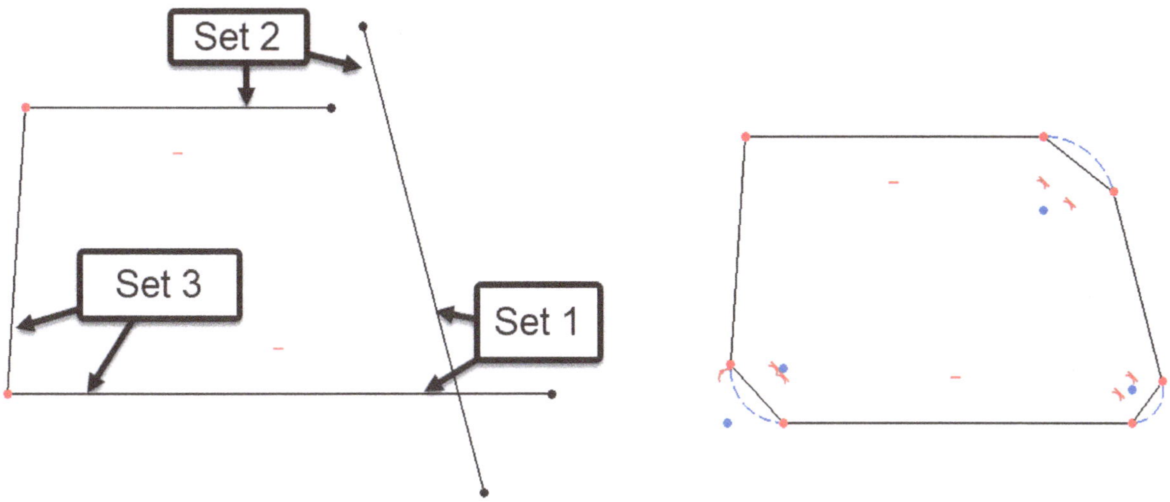

Preserve corner

The **Preserve corner** option available on the **Filler/Chamfer parameters** section of the **Tasks** panel rounds a sharp corner created by the intersection of two elements without deleting the existing constraint.

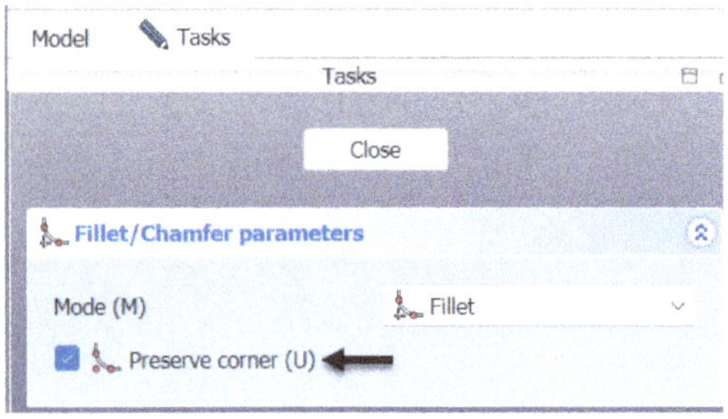

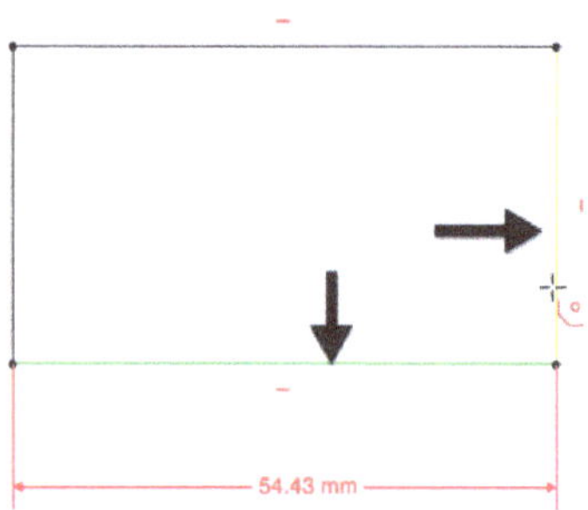

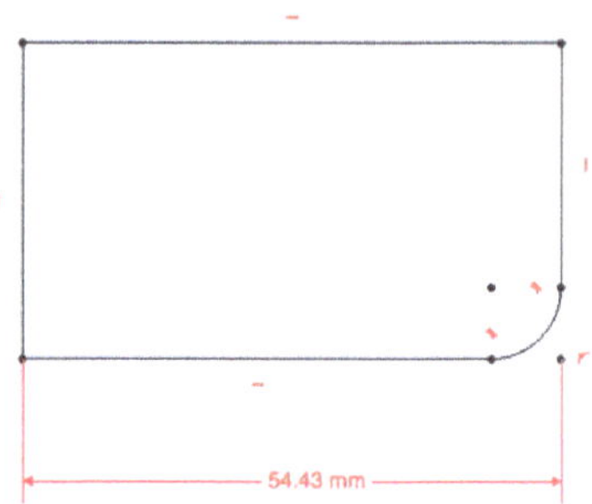

The Extend edge command

This command extends or trims elements such as lines, arcs, and curves until they touch another element called the boundary edge. Click the **Trim** drop-down > **Extend edge** icon on the **Sketcher tools** toolbar (or) click **Sketch > Sketch tools > Extend edge** on the menu bar. Next, click on the element to extend. Select the boundary edge; the element is extended up to the boundary edge.

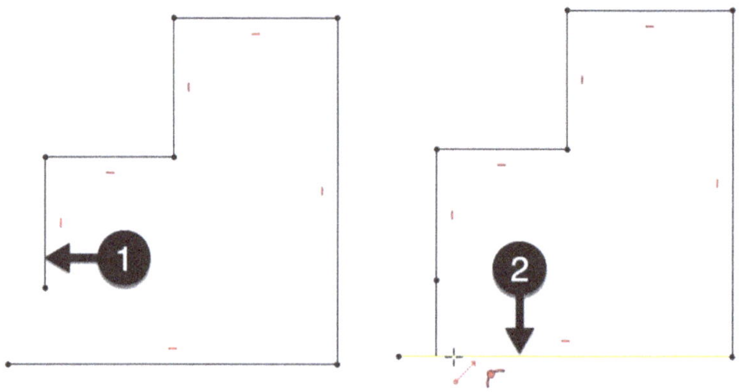

To trim an element up to a boundary element, select the element to be trimmed. Next, select the boundary edge.

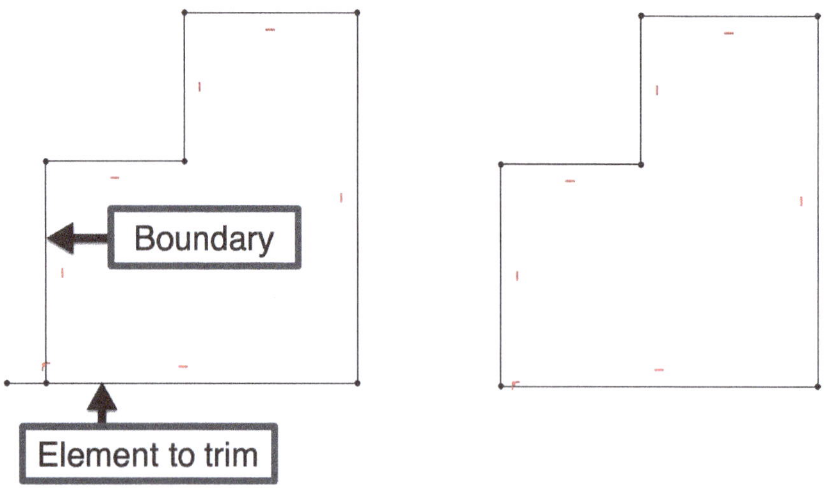

The Trim Edge command

This command trims the end of an element back to the intersection of another element. Click the **Trim** drop-down

> **Trim edge**  icon on the **Sketcher tools** toolbar (or) click **Sketch > Sketch tools > Trim edge** on the menu bar. Click on the element or elements to trim. FreeCAD will trim them where they meet something else. If there are things on both sides of where you clicked, it cuts out the piece you clicked on. When you're done, press Esc or right-click to finish. Just remember, this tool only works where things cross each other. If the thing you clicked on doesn't cross anything, it gets deleted. This tool is handy for changing sketches and making more complicated shapes by trimming edges to create new ones.

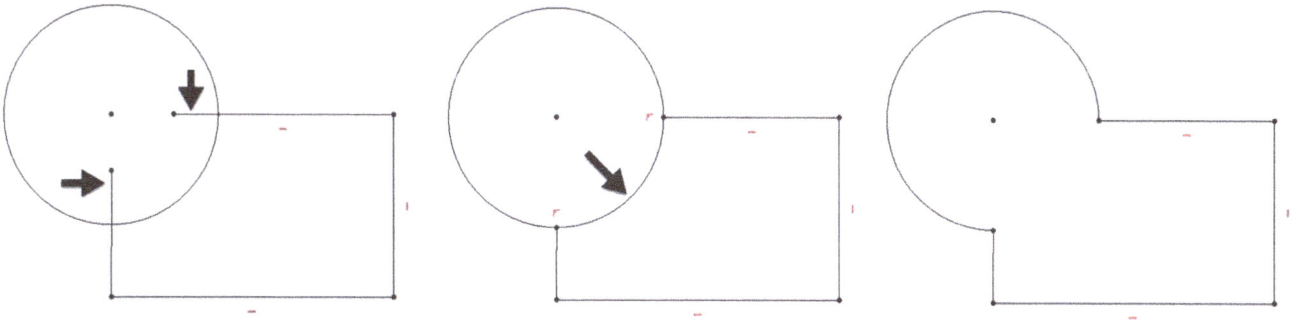

The Split Edge command

This command is useful when you want to divide a sketched object into two separate objects. This can be helpful when you want to modify one part of the object without affecting the other part. Click the **Trim** drop-down > **Split edge**  icon on the **Sketcher tools** toolbar (or) click **Sketch > Sketch tools > Split edge** on the menu bar. Click on the element or elements to split. This will divide the sketched object into two separate objects.

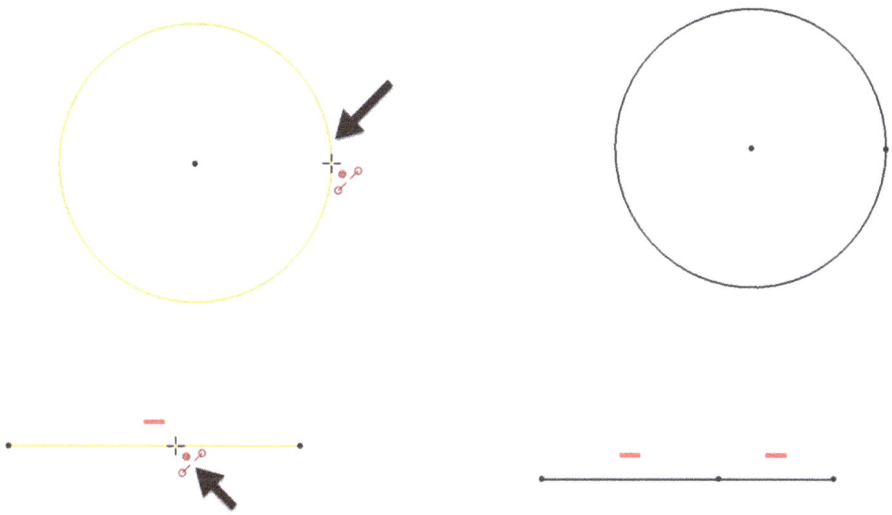

The Select unconstrained DOF command

This command selects the under-constrained element of a sketch. Click **Sketch > Sketcher visual > Select under-constrained elements** on the menu bar. The under-constrained sketch element is selected.

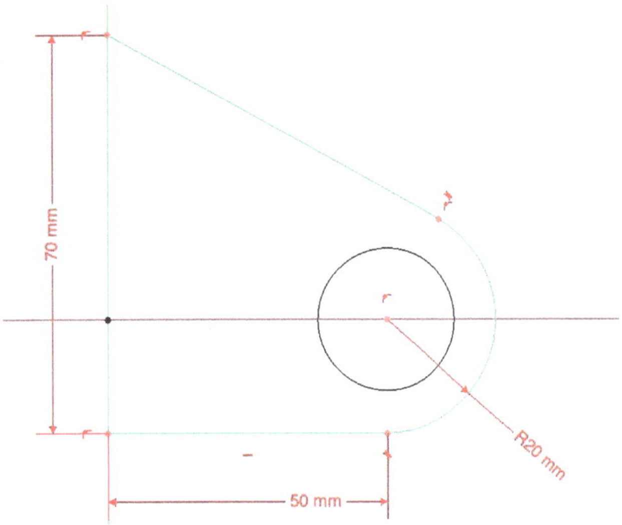

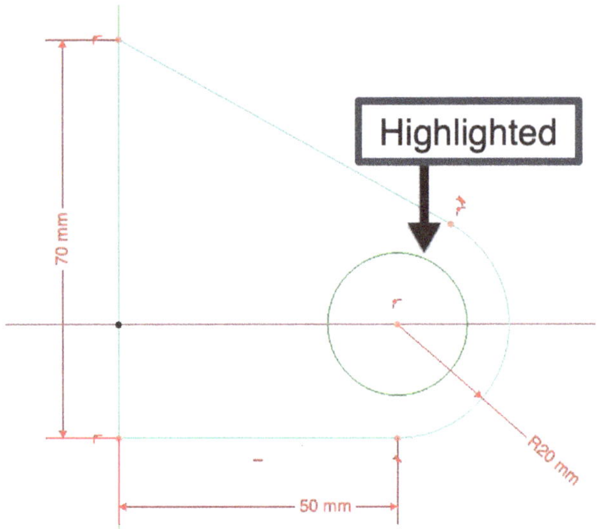

Move/array transform

This command allows you to move, copy, or create patterns (arrays) of selected sketch elements in a precise and controlled manner. Select the sketch elements you want to move or transform. You can select individual elements or multiple elements at once. Next, go to the menu bar and select **Sketch > Sketcher tools > Move/array transform**. Alternatively, you may find this command on the **Sketcher tools** toolbar. After activating the command. You can perform three types of operations: move, copy, or array.

Moving the selected element

To move an element using the **Move/Array Transform** command, set the **Copies** value to **0** in the **Translate parameters** section on the **Tasks** panel. Click to set the **start point**, then move the pointer and click again to specify the **destination point**. Keep in mind that this action may affect existing constraints or dimensions, as FreeCAD will automatically adjust or remove them. After moving, review the sketch to ensure everything is correctly aligned and constrained.

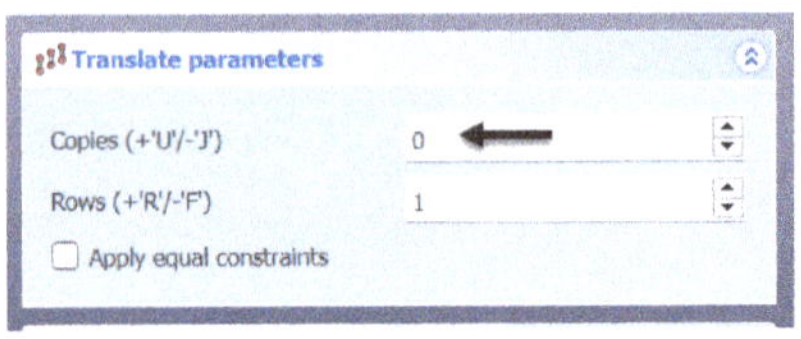

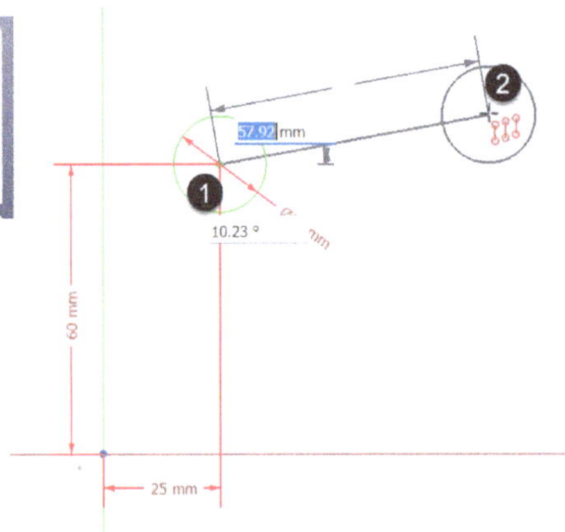

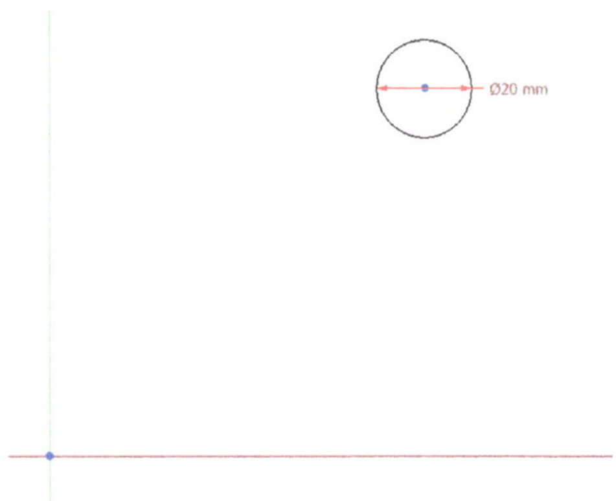

Creating an array copy

To create an array copy, begin by selecting the sketch element you want to duplicate. Next, activate the **Move/Array Transform** command. In the **Translate parameters** section, enter the desired number of copies in the **Copies** box to specify how many duplicates will be created, and enter the number of rows in the **Rows** box to define the number of rows in the array. If you want to apply equal constraints between the array objects, check the **Apply equal constraint** option in the **Translate parameters** section. Click to set the start point, then move the pointer and click again to specify the spacing and orientation along the first direction. You can also enter the spacing and angle values directly in the dynamic dimensions displayed in the graphics window for precision. Similarly, specify the spacing and orientation along the second direction to complete the array setup.

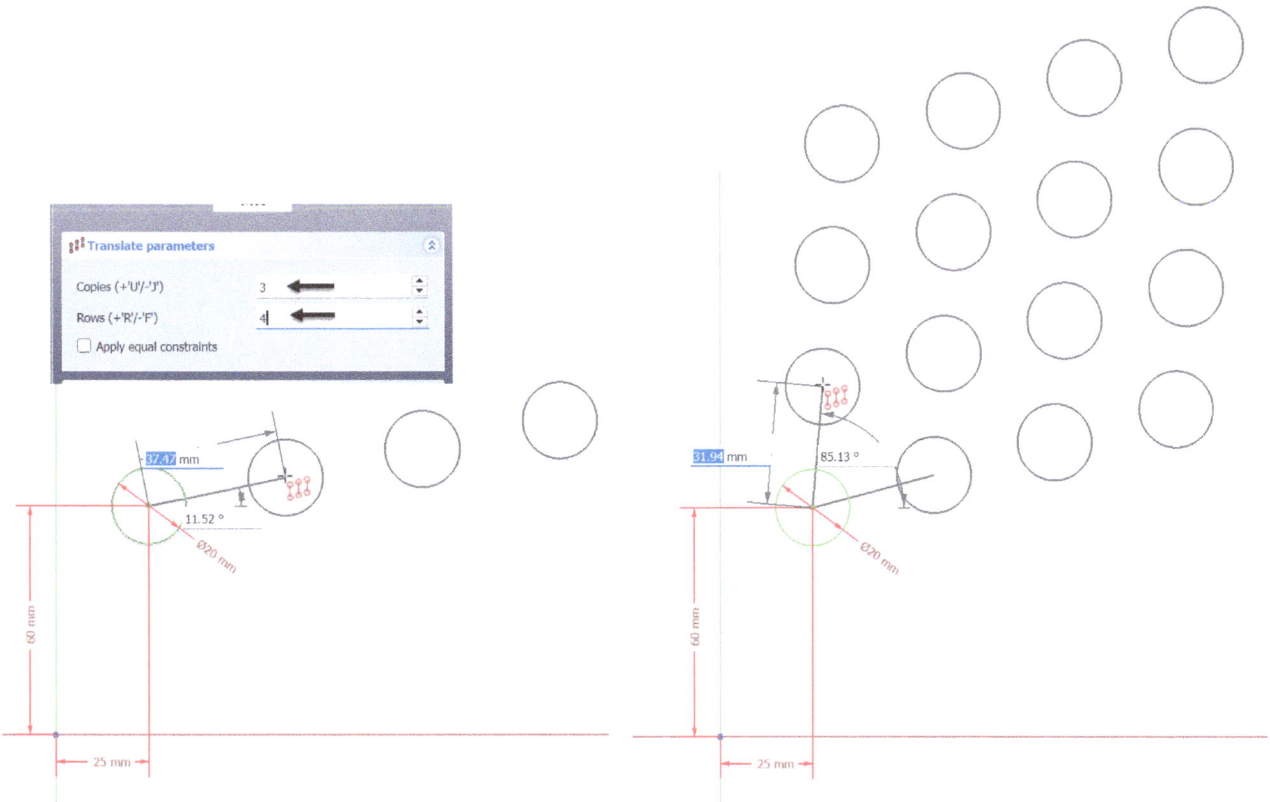

Rotate/Polar Transform

This command allows you to rotate or create circular patterns (polar arrays) of selected sketch elements in a precise and controlled manner. Select the sketch elements you want to rotate or transform. You can select individual elements or multiple elements at once. Next, go to the menu bar and select **Sketch > Sketcher tools > Rotate/Polar Transform**. Alternatively, you may find this command on the **Sketcher tools** toolbar. After activating the command, you can perform two types of operations: rotate or polar array.

Rotating the Selected Element

To rotate an element using the **Rotate/Polar Transform** command, set the **Copies** value to **0** in the **Rotate parameters** section on the **Tasks** panel. Click to specify the **start point** of the rotation axis, then click again to set the **endpoint** of the rotation axis. Move the pointer to define the rotation angle, or enter the angle value directly in the dynamic dimensions displayed in the graphics window. Click to confirm the rotation. Keep in mind that this action may affect existing constraints or dimensions, as FreeCAD will automatically adjust or remove them. After rotating, review the sketch to ensure everything is correctly aligned and constrained.

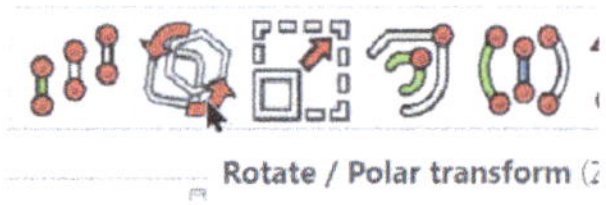

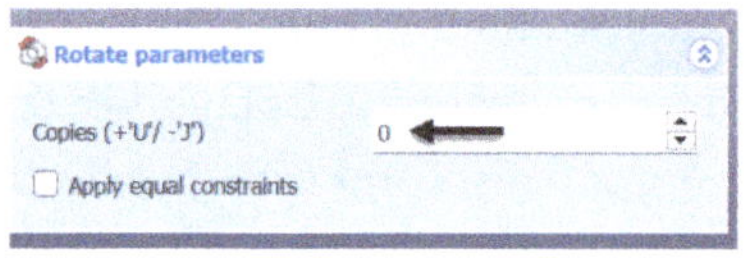

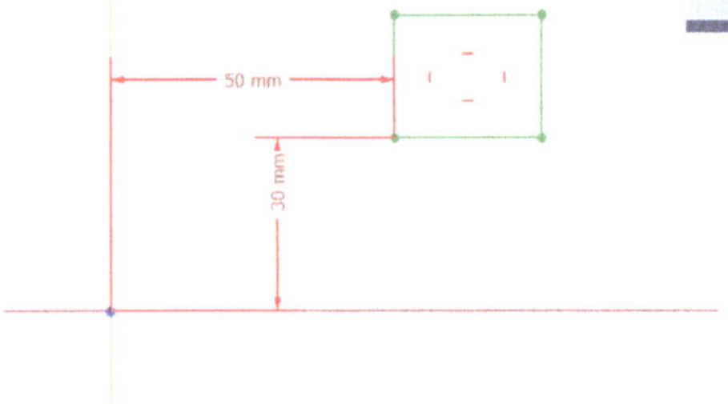

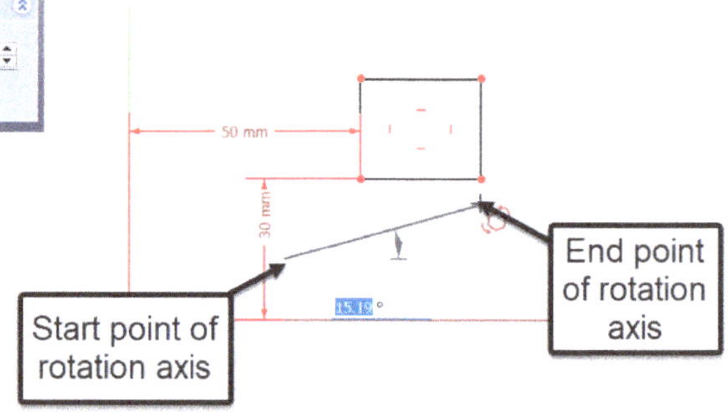

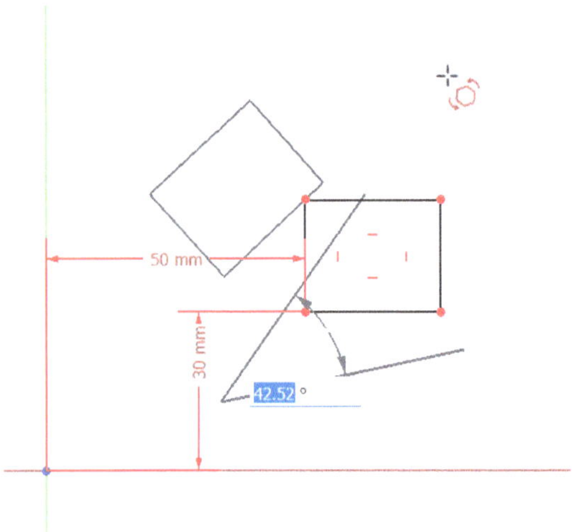

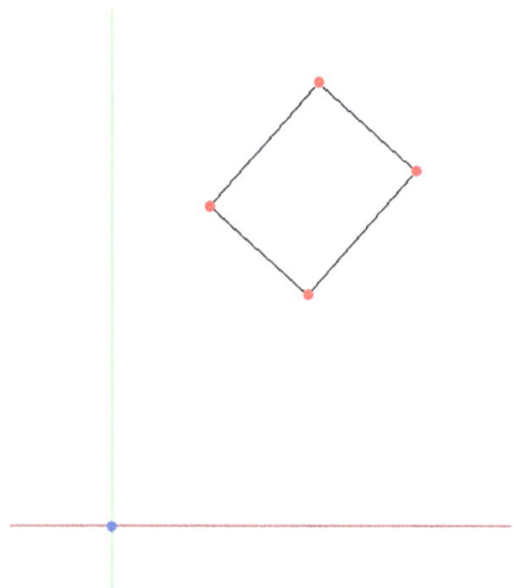

Creating a Polar Array

To create a polar array, begin by selecting the sketch element you want to duplicate. Next, activate the **Rotate/Polar Transform** command. In the **Rotate parameters** section, enter the desired number of copies in the **Copies** box to specify how many duplicates will be created. Click to specify the **start point** of the rotation axis, then click again to set the **endpoint** of the rotation axis. Move the pointer to define the total angle for the array, or enter the angle value directly in the dynamic dimensions displayed in the graphics window. If you want to apply equal constraints between the array objects, check the **Apply equal constraint** option in the **Rotate parameters** section.

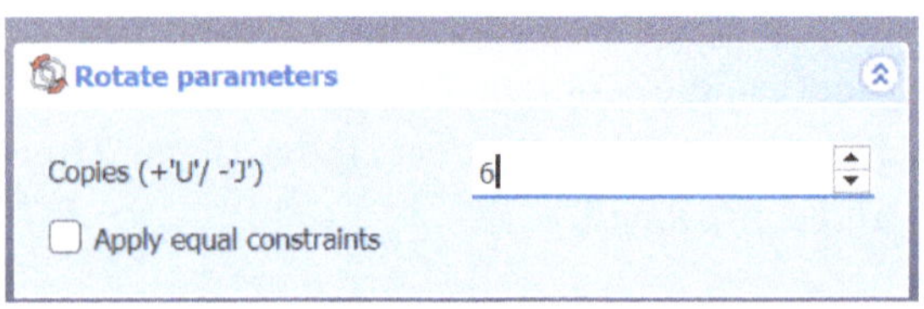

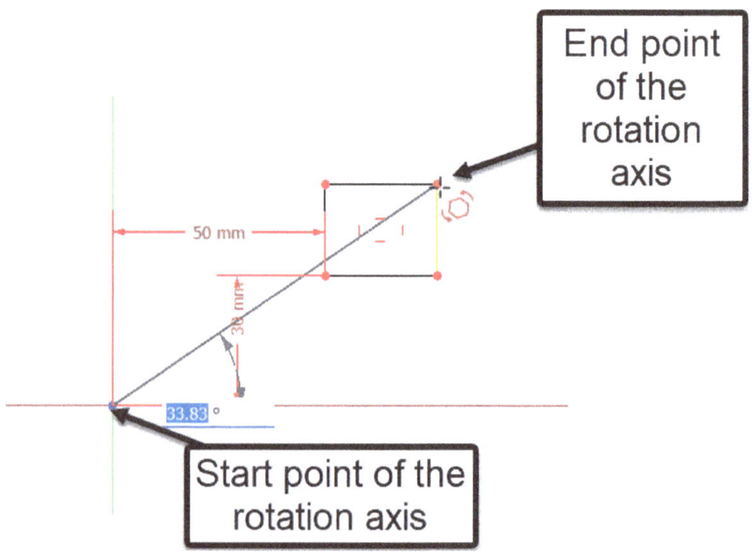

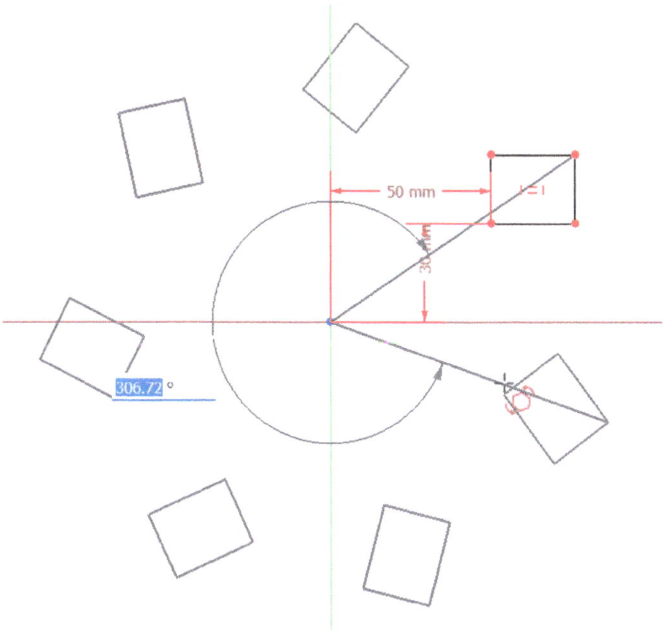

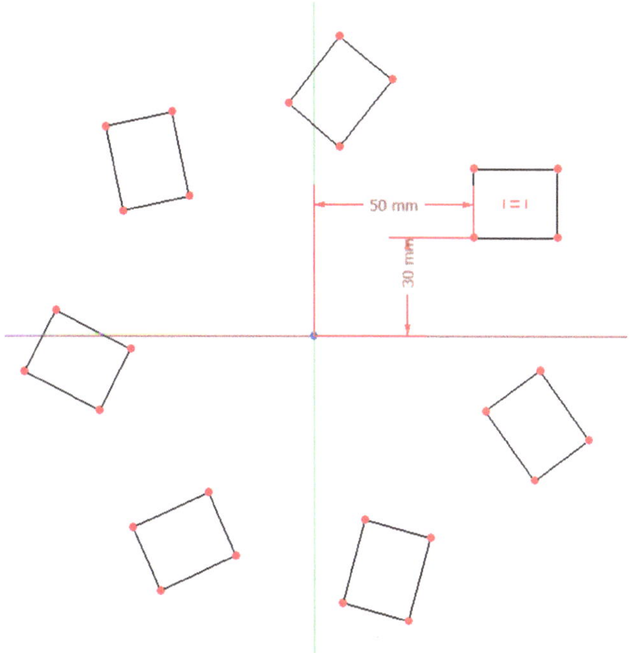

Delete all Constraints

This command is used to delete all constraints of a sketch. To do this, click **Sketch > Sketcher tools > Delete all constraints** on the menu bar. Next, click **Yes** on the message box.

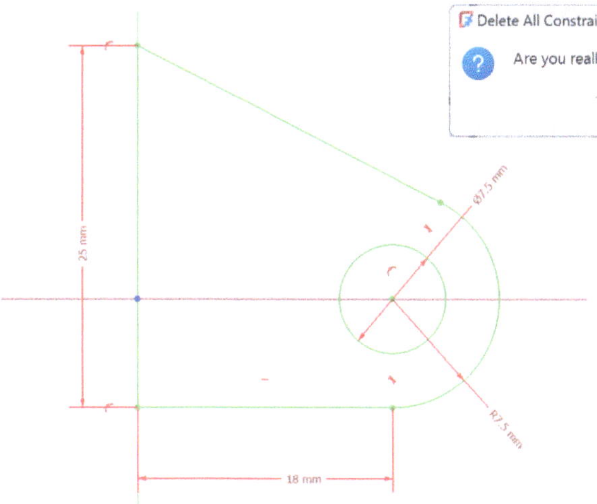

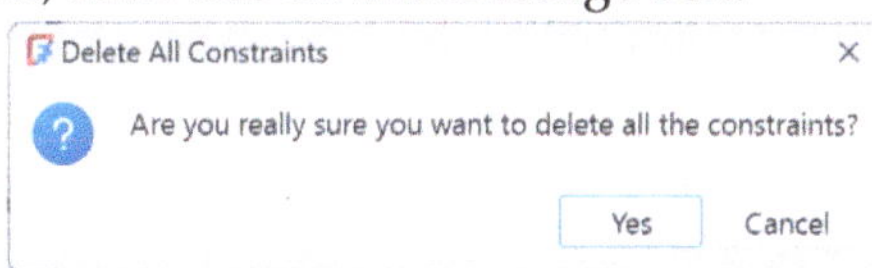

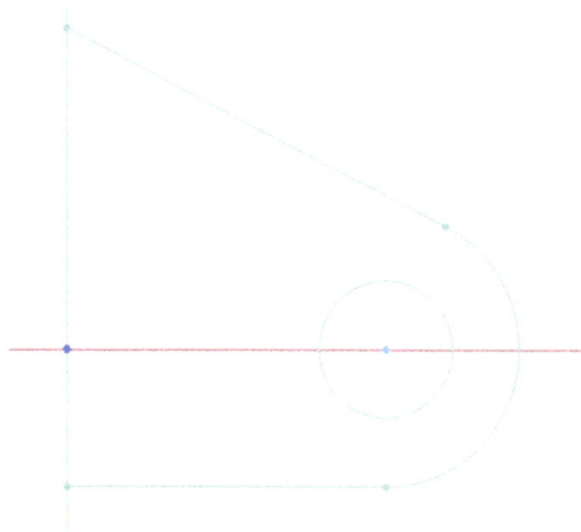

Delete all geometry

This command is used to delete all elements of a sketch. To do this, click **Sketch > Sketcher tools > Delete all geometry** on the menu bar. Next, click **Yes** on the message box.

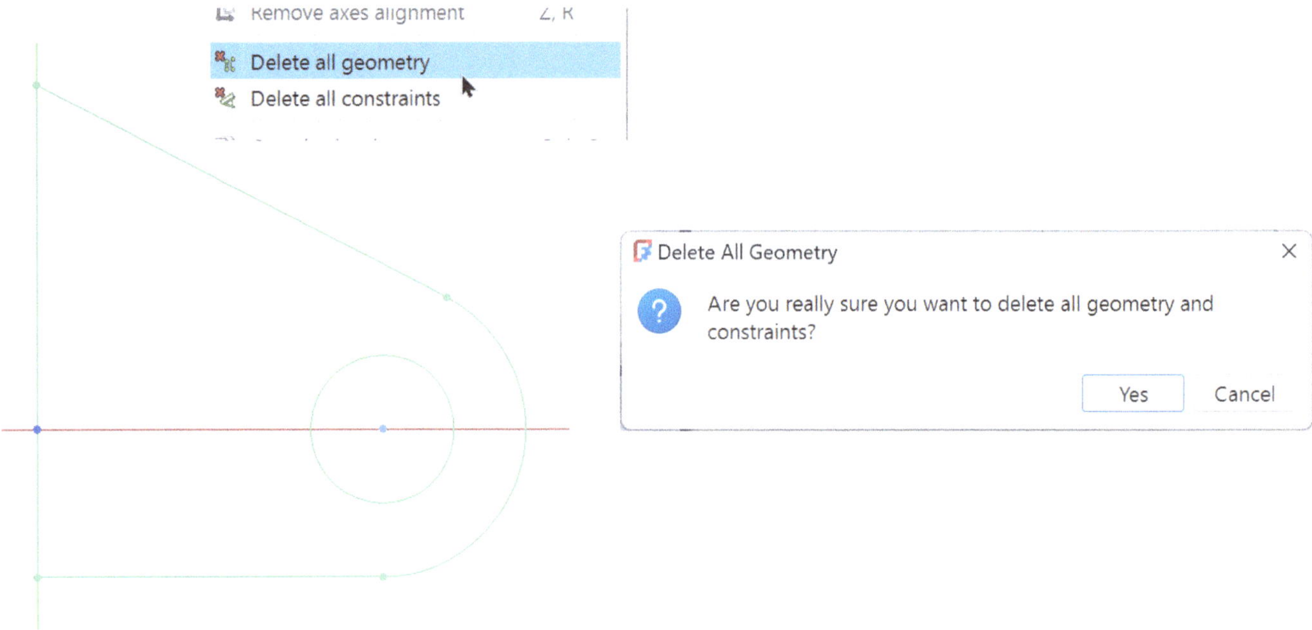

Remove axes alignment

This command deletes the horizontal or vertical constraints of a selected entity. For example, select a vertical line and click **Sketch > Sketcher tools > Remove axes alignment** on the menu bar; the vertical constraint of the selected entity is deleted.

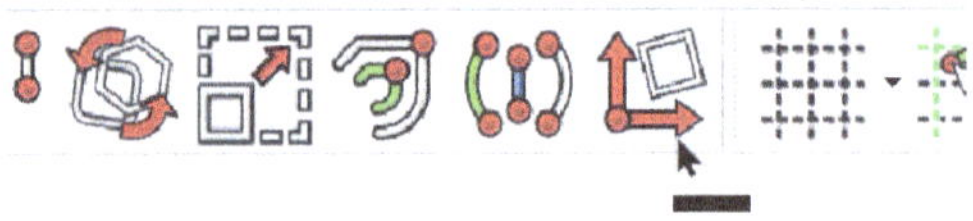

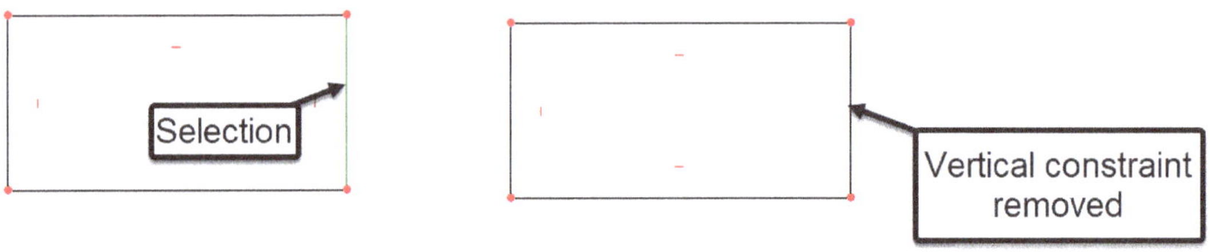

Removing Redundant Constraints

Redundant constraints are unnecessary constraints between two entities of a sketch. For example, activate the **Polyline** command and click on the horizontal axis of the sketch. Next, move the pointer toward the top-right corner and click. Again, click on the horizontal axis of the sketch. Next, click on the start point of the first line. Notice the sketch is turned red. Also, the **Redundant Constraints** message is displayed in the panel.

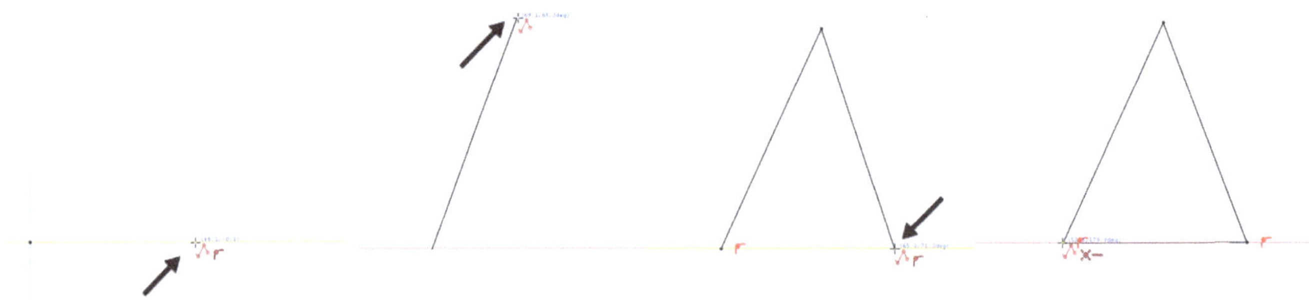

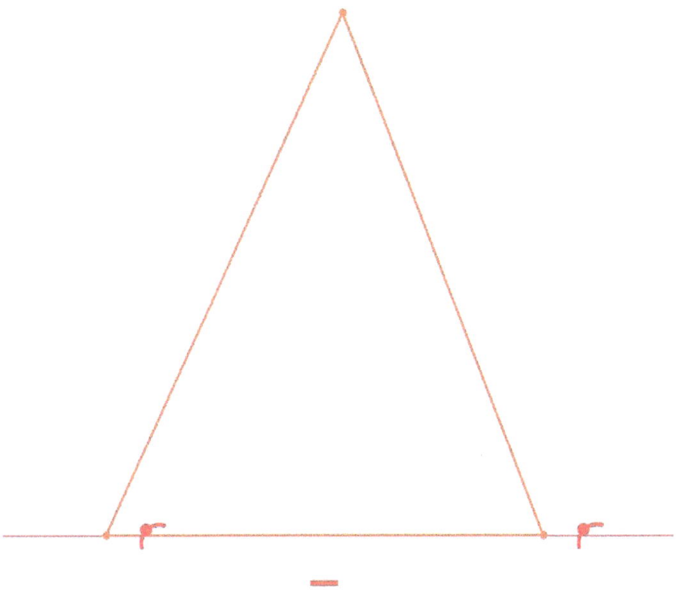

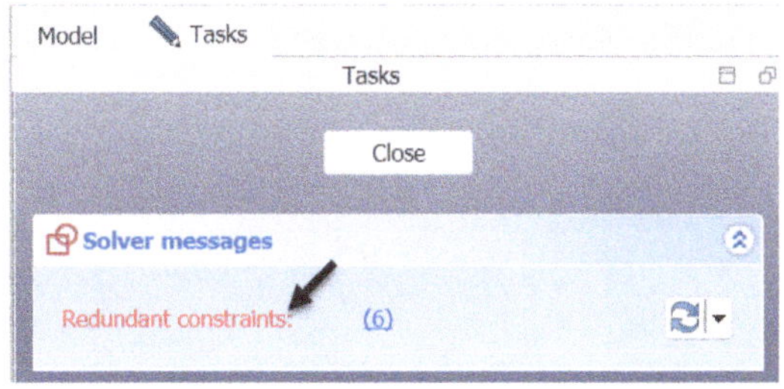

Now, click the **Sketch > Sketcher Visual** > **Select Redundant Constraints** icon menu bar. Next, click **Edit > Delete** on the menu bar; the redundant constraints are deleted.

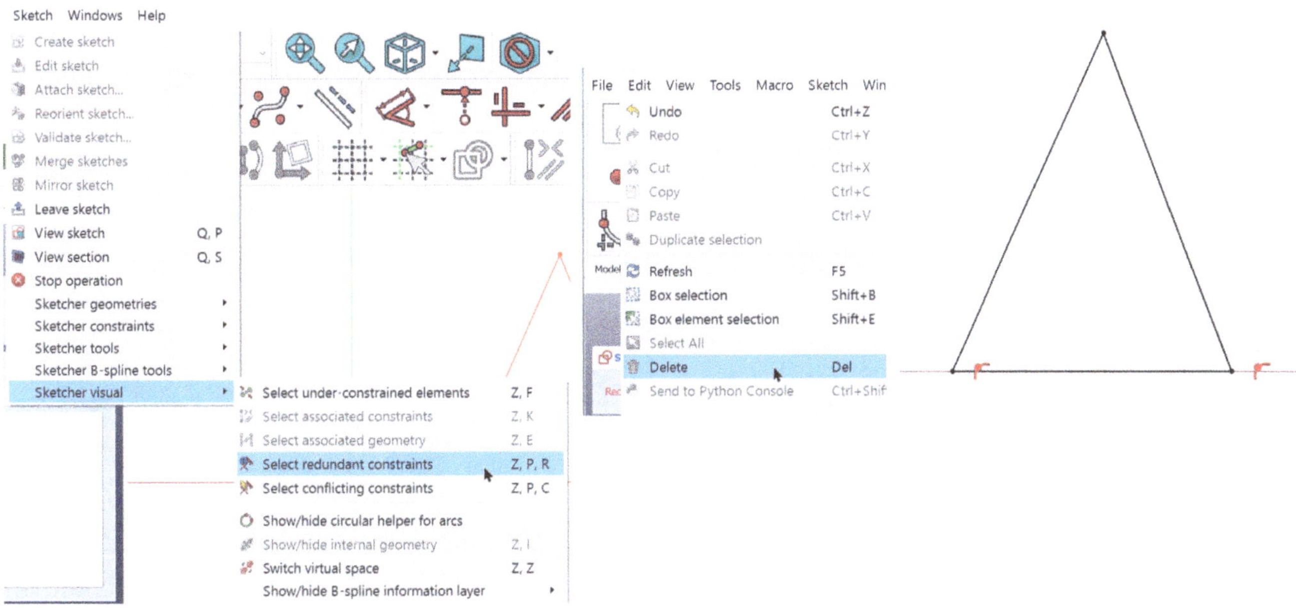

Alternatively, you can click the drop-down available on the **Constraints** section of the **Tasks** panel and check the **Auto remove redundants** option before drawing the sketch; the redundant constraints are automatically deleted.

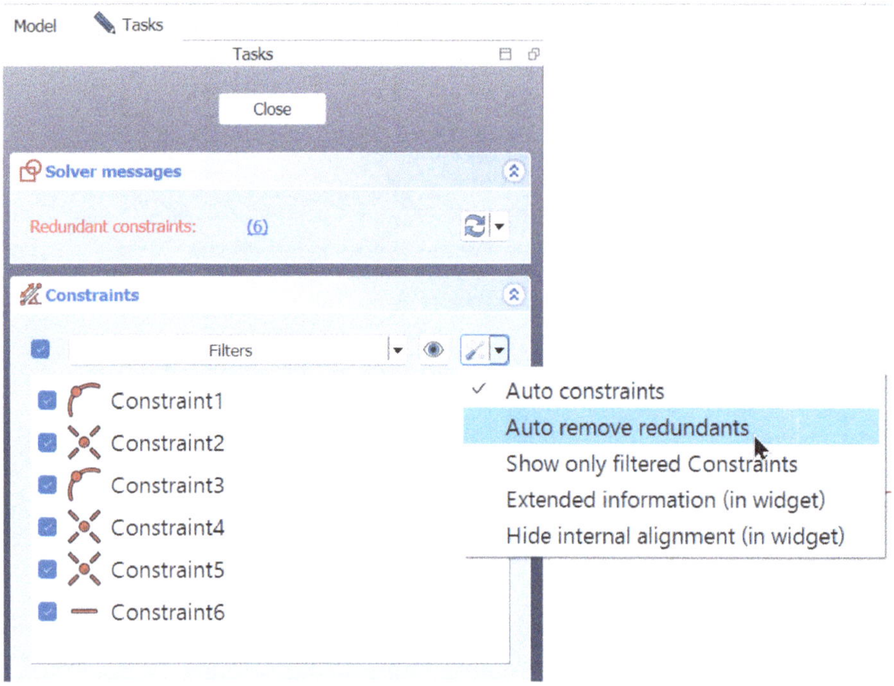

The Mirror Sketch command

This command creates a mirror copy of the selected elements using the X, or Y axes, or origin point. Select the objects to mirror and click **Sketch > Mirror sketch** on the menu bar. Next, select the **X-Axis** option and click **OK** on the **Select Mirror Axis/Point** dialog to mirror the objects about X axes. Click the **Model** panel and notice that a new sketch for the mirror object is created.

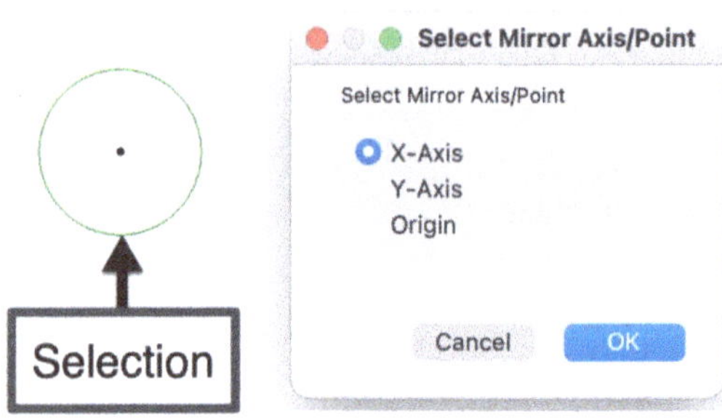

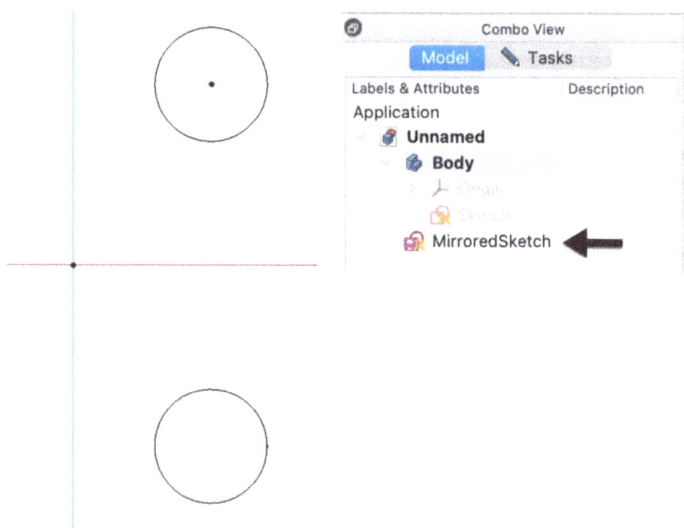

Creating Splines

Splines are non-uniform curves, which are used to create smooth shapes. In FreeCAD 1.0, you can create a smooth spline curve using four commands: **B-spline by control points**, **Periodic B-spline by control points**, **B-spline by knots**, and **Periodic B-spline by knots**.

Create B-spline

A B-spline is a curve that is defined by a set of control points and mathematical functions known as basis functions. These basis functions dictate how each control point influences the shape of the curve. The "B-spline by control points" command allows you to create a spline by specifying these control points, which act as anchor points. By strategically placing these control points, you can shape the curve as desired. The position of each control point plays a crucial role in determining the final form of the curve.

To create a B-spline, click on the **Spline** drop-down menu and select the **Create B-spline** icon from the **Sketcher geometries** toolbar. Alternatively, you can navigate to **Sketch > Sketcher geometries > Create B-spline** in the menu bar.

In the graphics window, click to place the first control point. As you move the cursor, dynamic dimensions will appear, showing the distance and angle between the start point of the spline and the cursor. These real-time measurements provide feedback on the length and orientation of the curve. For more precise control, you can manually enter the desired length in the dimension box, press **TAB**, input the angle, and then press **ENTER** to create the second point. Continue specifying additional control points in this manner.

As you define the control points, the spline will gradually take shape. To complete the spline, right-click. If you prefer a more freeform approach, you can also dynamically click in the graphics window to place the control points without entering specific dimensions.

Once the spline is created, you can further refine its shape by adjusting the control points. You can also apply dimensions and constraints to the control points for greater precision and control over the curve's geometry.

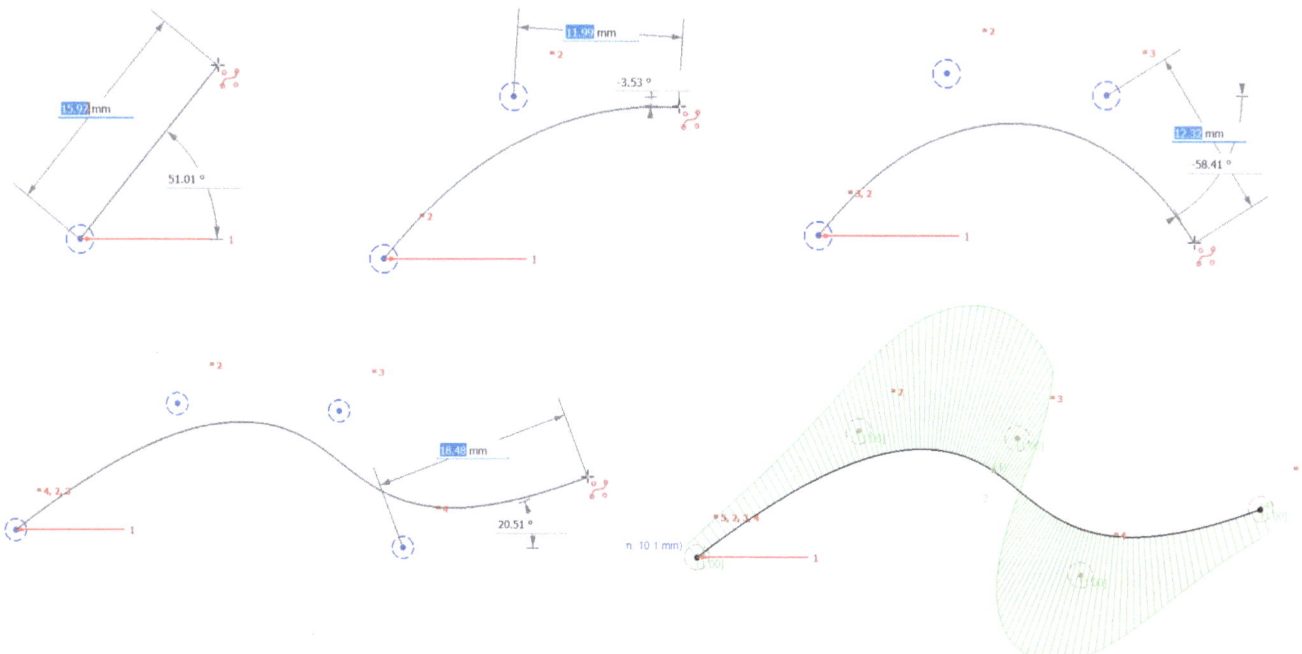

Periodic B-spline by control points

The **Periodic B-spline by control points** command creates a closed B-spline. Click the **Spline** drop-down > **Periodic B-spline by control points** icon on the **Sketcher geometries** toolbar (or) click **Sketch > Sketcher geometries > Create periodic B-spline** on the menu bar. Next, specify the control points and right-click.

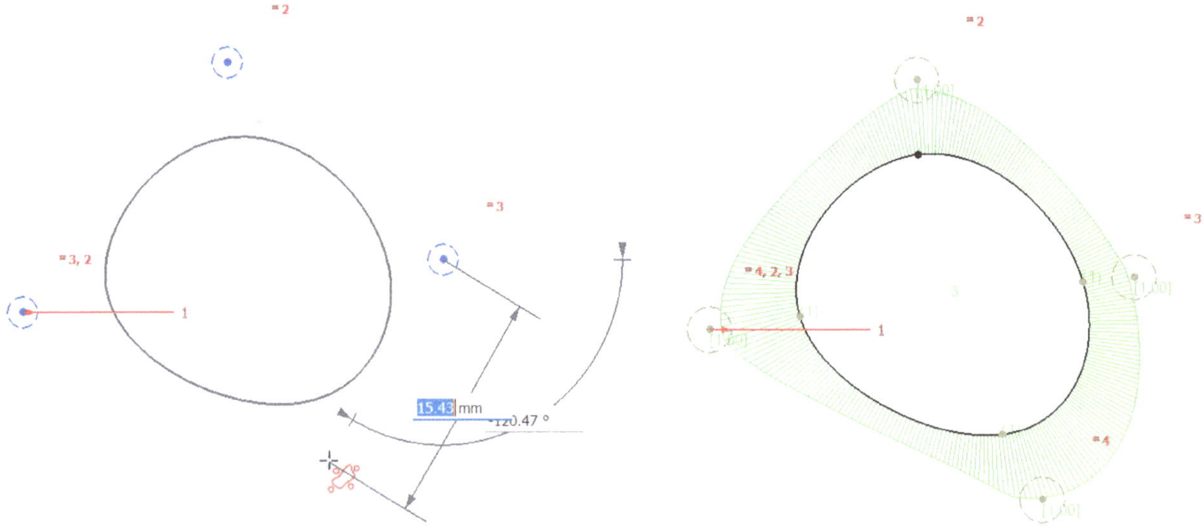

B-spline by Knots

This command creates a smooth B-spline curve along the selected points. B-Splines are non-uniform curves, which are used to create irregular shapes. Click the **B-splines** drop-down **> B-spline by knots** on the **Sketcher geometries** toolbar (or) click **Sketch > Sketcher geometries > Create B-spline by knots** on the menu bar. Next, click to specify points in the graphics window. Next, right click; the spline is created passing through the points.

In the graphics window, click to place the first knot point. As you move the cursor, dynamic dimensions will appear, showing the distance and angle between the start point of the spline and the cursor. These real-time measurements help you visualize the curve's length and orientation. For precise control, you can manually enter the desired length in the dimension box, press **TAB**, input the angle, and then press **ENTER** to place the next knot point. Continue adding knot points in this manner.

As you define the knot points, the spline will gradually take shape. To complete the spline, right-click. If you prefer a more freeform approach, you can dynamically click in the graphics window to place the knot points without entering specific dimensions.

Once the spline is created, you can refine its shape by adjusting the knot points or control points. You can also apply dimensions and constraints to these points for greater precision and control over the curve's geometry.

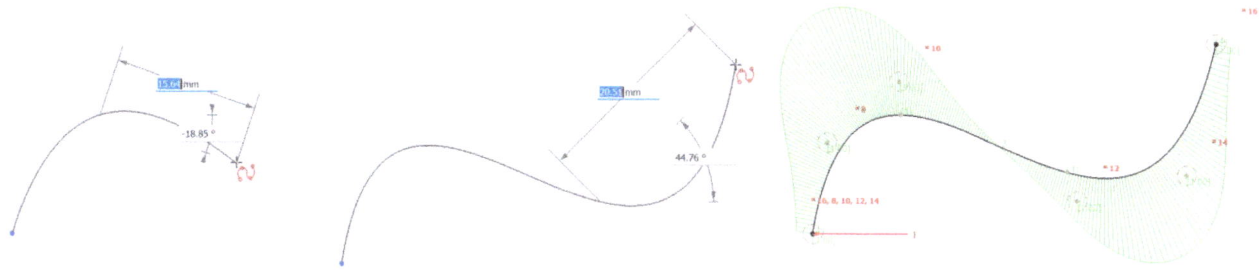

Periodic B-spline by Knots

The **Periodic B-spline by Knots** command creates a closed B-spline passing through the specified knots. Click the **Spline** drop-down > **Periodic B-spline by knots** icon on the **Sketcher geometries** toolbar (or) click **Sketch > Sketcher geometries > Create periodic B-spline by knots** on the menu bar. Next, specify the knots and right-click.

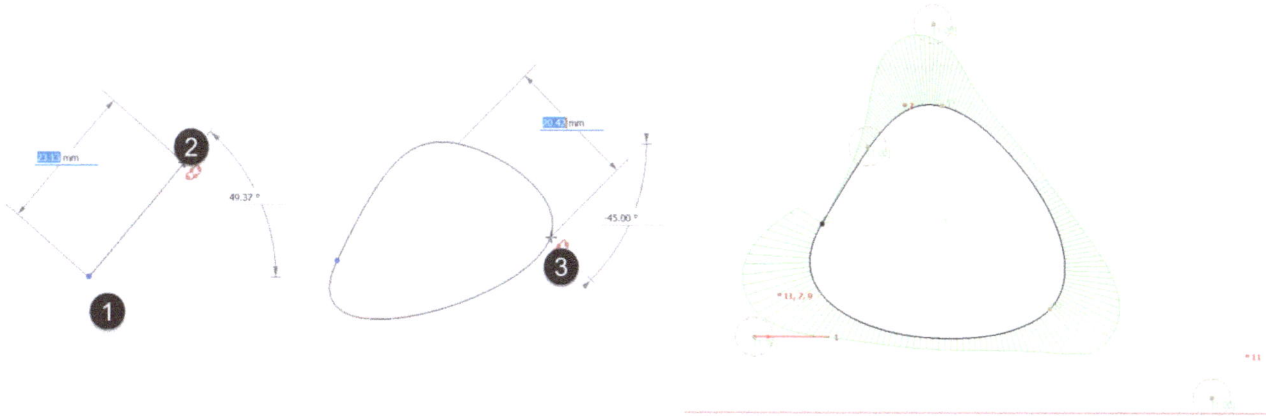

Best Practices

Proper Units: Ensure that your units are correctly set from the beginning, aligning with industry standards such as metric or imperial.

Start with Planes: Most sketches in FreeCAD are created on predefined planes. Begin by defining and naming these planes accurately to maintain an organized design environment.

Fully Define Your Sketch: Industry standards often require fully defined sketches. This means there should be no degrees of freedom left in your sketch, ensuring it is locked in position and accurate.
Avoid Over-Defining: While fully defining is important, be cautious not to over-constrain your sketch. Over-constraining can limit flexibility during design iterations.

Keep It Simple: Simplicity is key. If you can create a sketch with fewer entities and relations without compromising design intent, do so. A clean and straightforward sketch is easier to modify and troubleshoot.

Use Automatic Constraints: Automatic constraints are relationships applied to sketch elements (lines, points, circles, etc.) that maintain their positions relative to one another. They can include horizontal/vertical alignment, parallelism, perpendicularity, equal lengths, and more. When you create a sketch in FreeCAD, the software automatically applies these constraints as you draw, helping you maintain a fully defined sketch. Creating sketches with automatic constraints in FreeCAD is a valuable skill that helps streamline the design process and ensures your models adhere to industry standards for fully defined sketches. Understanding how to use automatic constraints effectively can significantly improve your efficiency and accuracy when using FreeCAD for 3D modeling.

Use Grid Lines: Sketching often becomes more manageable with the use of grid lines or construction geometry. These lines help you align your sketch elements correctly.

Constrain Early, Dimension Later: It's a good practice to apply constraints and relationships as much as possible before introducing specific dimensions. Fully defining your sketch with constraints helps maintain its stability and makes it more robust for modifications.

Avoid Excessive Fillets and Chamfers: It's a good idea not to use too many fillets or chamfers in the sketch. Instead, it's better to add those features directly to the 3D model itself. This way, you won't overcomplicate the sketch, which can slow down the model's performance when it needs to regenerate.

Cautions

Overlapping and Self-Intersecting Geometry: Be mindful of overlapping or self-intersecting lines and curves as they can lead to modeling errors and failed features. Resolve any overlapping entities promptly.

Incorrect Units: Ensure you use the correct units, as working with the wrong units can lead to significant errors, especially when collaborating with others or when adhering to industry-standard dimensions.

Ignoring Warnings and Errors: Pay attention to and resolve any warnings and error messages that FreeCAD provides. Ignoring these messages can lead to issues that affect the integrity of your model.

Inadequate Dimensioning: Proper dimensioning is essential for conveying design intent. Include relevant dimensions and consider adding tolerances and geometric tolerances where needed.

Using Dimensions for Symmetric Rectangle: Rely solely on dimensions to make a rectangle symmetric about the planes. While it may seem like a straightforward option, using dimensions can clutter your sketch and lead to unnecessary complexity when modifications are needed. Instead, use constraints to maintain the symmetry of your sketch, especially when creating rectangles or base features. These constraints help ensure that your sketch elements remain aligned with reference planes, reducing the need for manual dimensioning.

Tips

Shortcut Keys: Learn and utilize shortcut keys for frequently used sketching tools. They can significantly speed up your workflow.

Constraints: Use constraints to control the behavior of your sketch elements. These tools help you maintain design intent and ease modification.

Save Incrementally: Save your work incrementally.

Avoid Underdefined Sketches: Be cautious with underdefined sketches, as they can lead to unstable models. The goal is to fully define your sketches for stability.

Regularly Check for Interference: As you proceed with your modeling, regularly check for interferences between sketch entities, features, and components to prevent issues later in the design process.

By following these best practices, being mindful of cautions, and applying these tips, you can create sketches in FreeCAD that adhere to industry standards, contribute to more efficient modeling, and help you maintain design intent throughout your projects.

Tutorial 1 (Millimetres)

In this example, you will draw the sketch shown below.

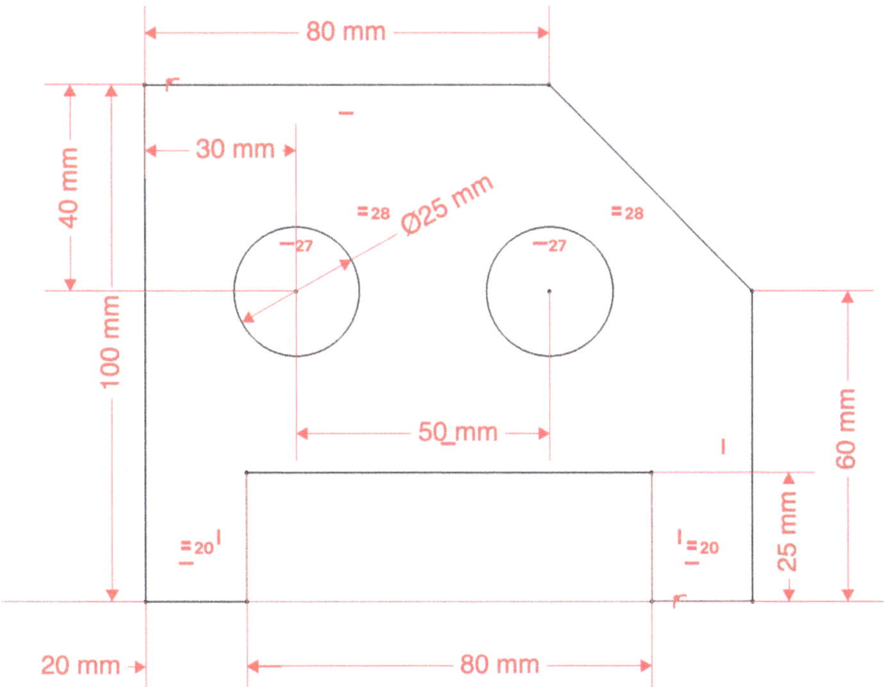

Starting a new part file

1. Click **FreeCAD** on the desktop to start the application.
2. Click the **New** icon on the **File** toolbar; it creates a new document.
3. On the **Workbench** toolbar, select **Workbench** drop-down **> Part Design** (or) select **View > Workbench > Part Design** on the Menu bar.
4. Click **Edit > Preferences** on the Menu bar (or) click **FreeCAD 1.0 > Preferences** on title bar, if you are working on MacOS; the **Preferences** dialog appears on the screen.
5. Click the **General** tab and select **Default unit System > Standard (mm/kg/s/degree)**.
6. Select **Number of decimals > 2** and click **OK** on the **Preferences** dialog.

Starting a sketch

1. To start a new sketch, click **Part Design Helper** toolbar > **Create a new sketch** .
2. Select the XZ-plane from the graphics window.
3. Click the **Toggle grid** button on the **Sketcher edit tools** toolbar.
4. On the **Sketcher geometries** toolbar, click the **Polyline** icon (or) click **Sketch > Sketcher geometries > Create polyline**.
5. Click on the origin point to define the first point of the line.
6. Move the pointer horizontally toward the right and notice that the horizontal constraint symbol appears below the cursor.
7. Click to define the endpoint of the line.
8. Move the pointer vertically upward and notice the vertical constraint symbol below the cursor. Click to draw the vertical line.

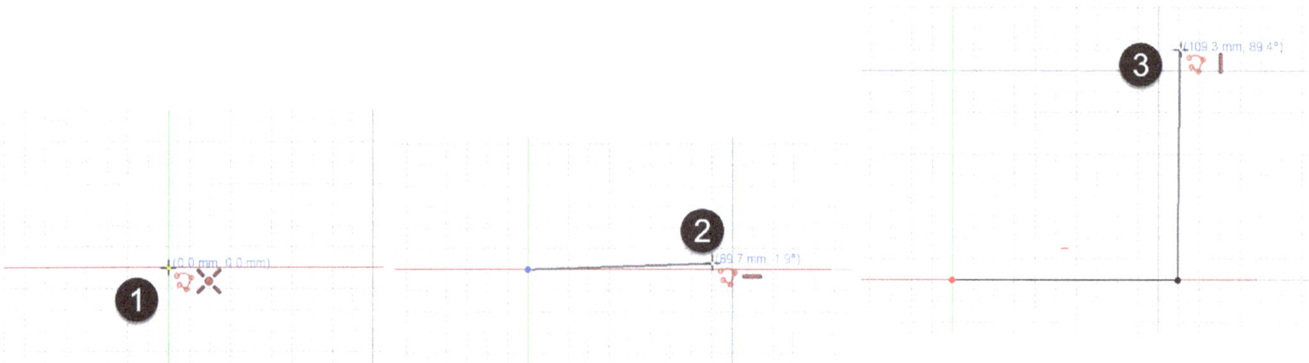

9. Move the pointer horizontally toward the right. Click when the horizontal constraint glyph appears.
10. Move the pointer vertically downward. Click when the vertical constraint and coincident constraint glyphs appear.

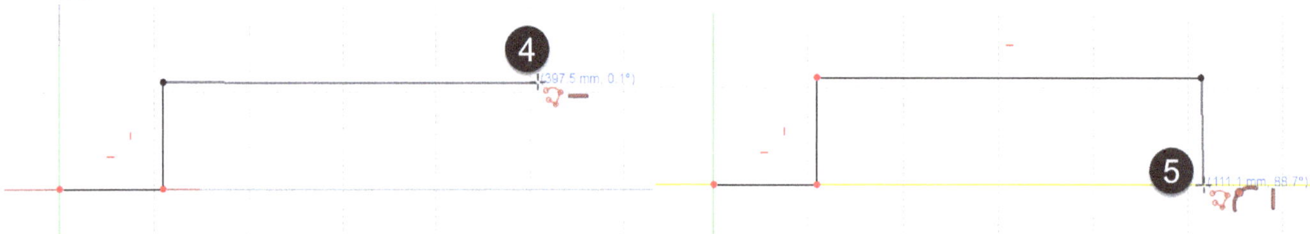

11. Move the pointer horizontally toward right up to a short distance. Click when the horizontal constraint glyph appears.
12. Move the pointer vertically upward and click.

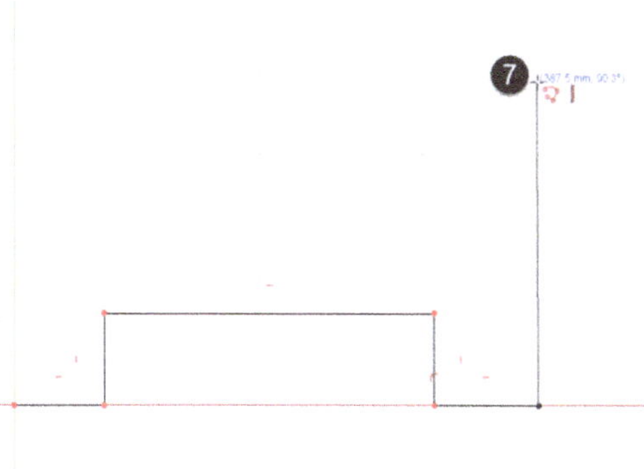

13. Move the pointer in the top-left direction and click to create an inclined line.
14. Move the pointer horizontally towards left and click.

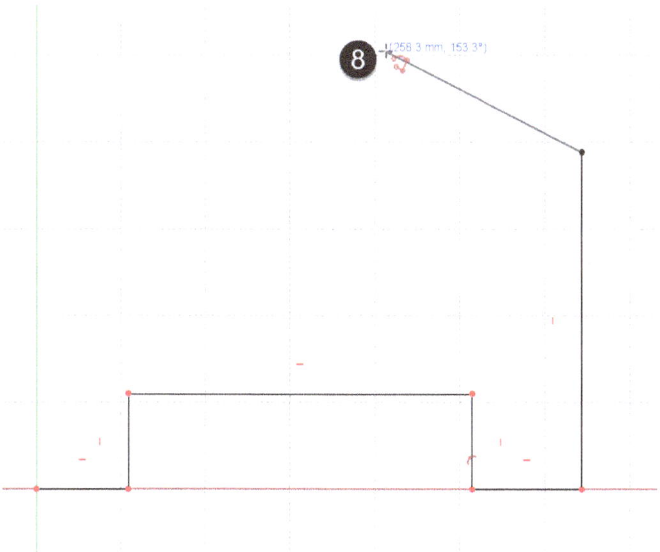

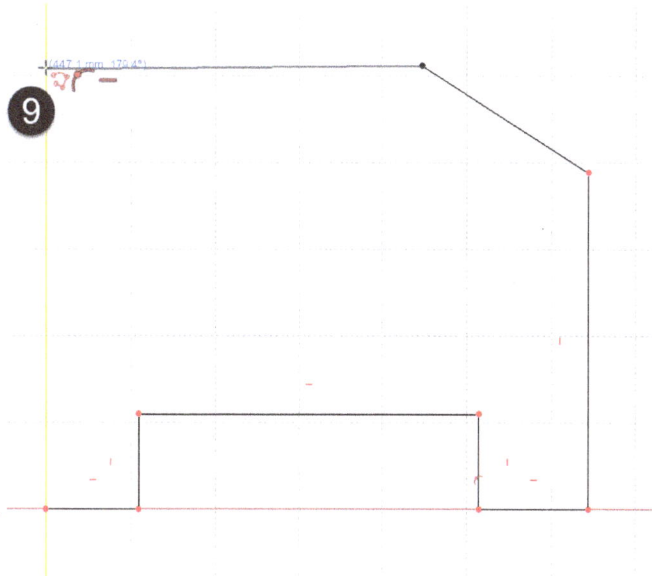

15. Move the pointer vertically downward and click on the origin point.
16. Right-click twice to deactivate the **Polyline** tool.

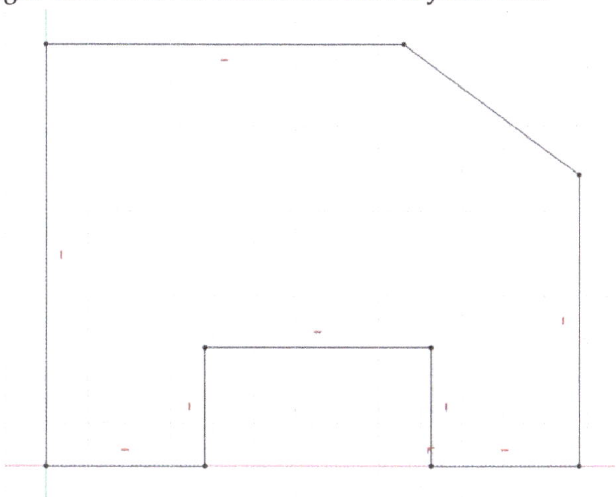

17. Click the **Sketcher visual > Select redundant constraints** on the menu bar.
18. On the Menu bar, click **Edit > Delete**; any redundant constaints will be deleted.

Adding Constraints

1. On the **Sketcher constraints** toolbar, click **Equal** . Next, select the two horizontal lines at the bottom; the selected lines become equal in length.

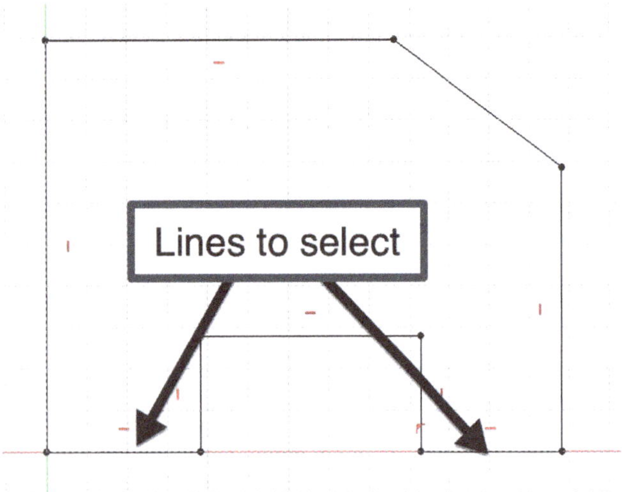

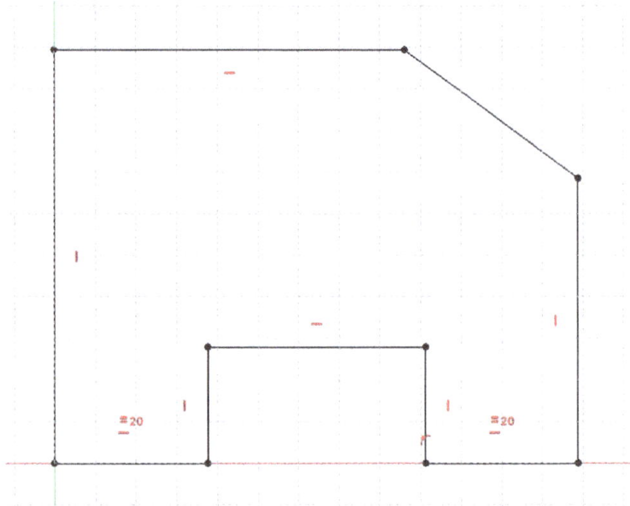

Adding Dimensions

1. On the **Sketcher constraints** toolbar, click the **Dimensions** drop-down **> Constrain horizontal distance** icon (or) click **Sketch > Sketcher constraints > Constrain horizontal distance** on the menu bar.
2. Select the bottom horizontal line of the rectangle.
3. Type-in **20** in the **Length** box of the **Insert Length** dialog and click the **OK** button.

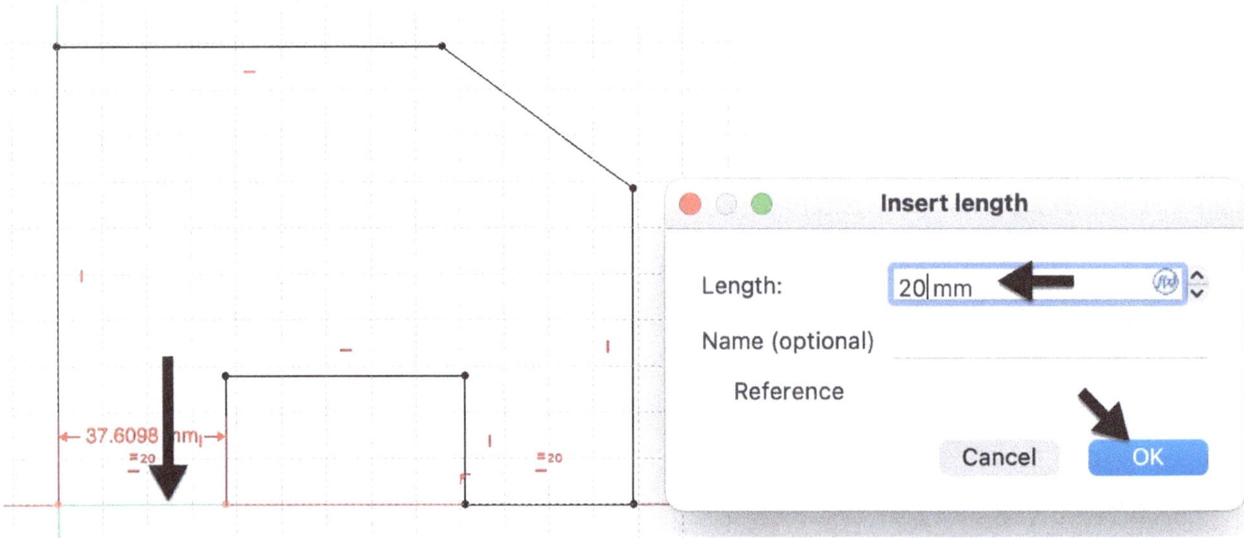

4. On the **Sketcher constraints** toolbar, click the **Dimensions** drop-down > **Constrain vertical distance** icon (or) click **Sketch > Sketcher constraints > Constrain Vertical distance** on the menu bar.
5. Click on the small vertical line located at the right side. Move the mouse pointer towards the left and click to position the dimension.
6. Type-in **25** in the **Length** box of the **Insert Length** dialog and click the **OK** button.

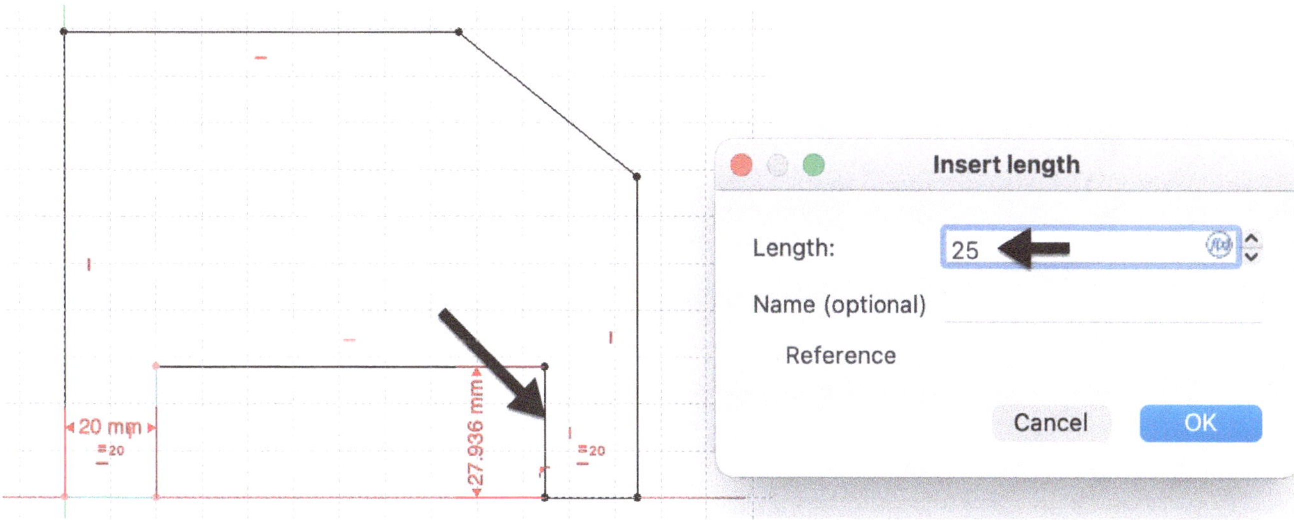

7. Create other distance constraints in the sequence, as shown below. Use the **Constrain horizontal distance** and **Constrain vertical distance** commands.

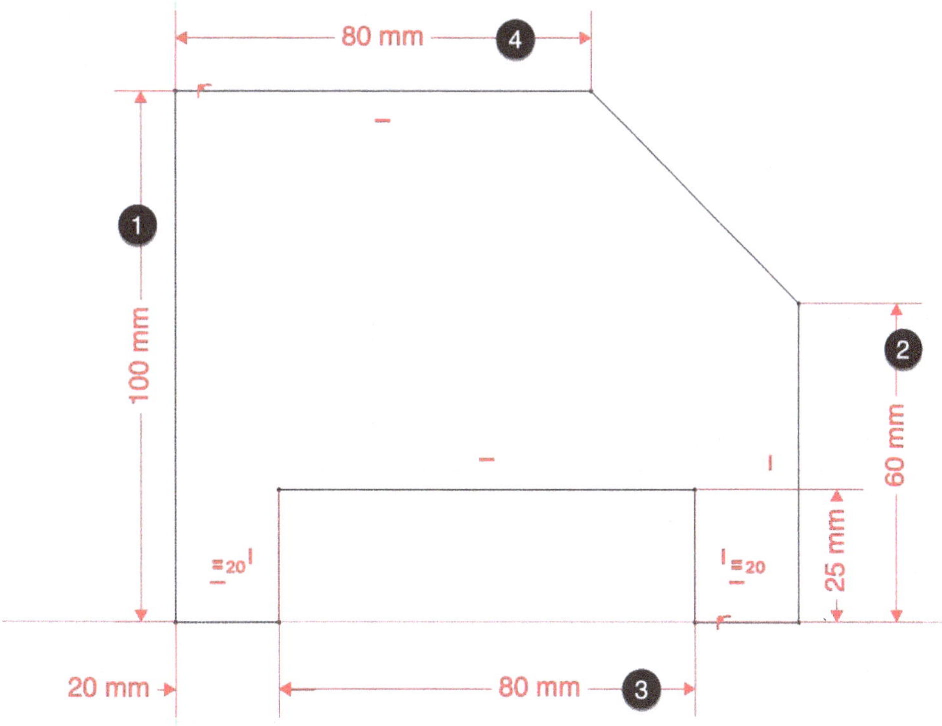

8. On the **Sketcher geometries** toolbar, click the **Create Circle** icon (or) click **Sketch > Sketcher geometries > Create Circle**.
9. Click inside the sketch region to define the center point of the circle. Move the mouse pointer and click to define the diameter. Likewise, create another circle.

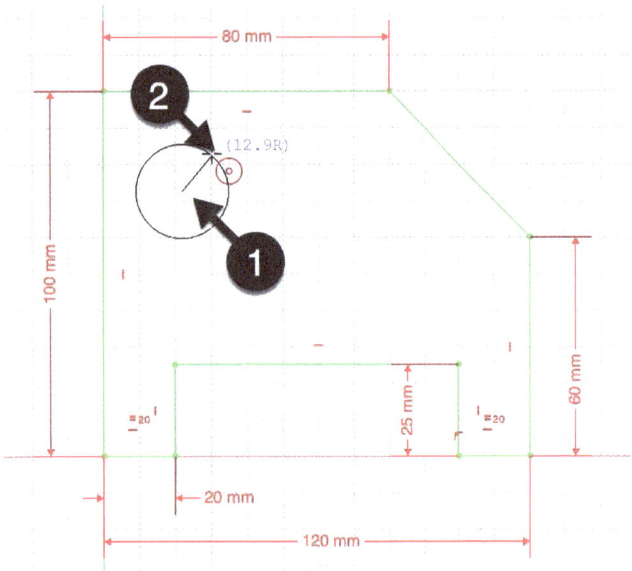

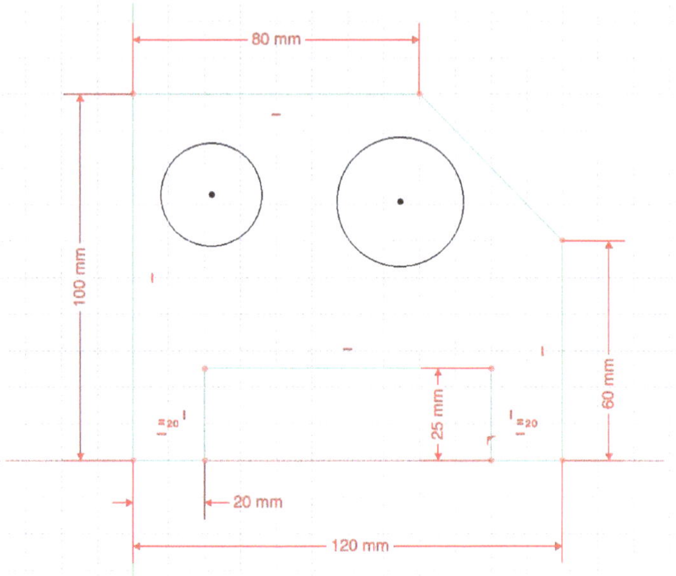

10. Press and hold CTRL key and click on the center points of the two circles. On the **Sketcher constraints** toolbar, click **Constrain horizontally/vertically** drop-down > **Constrain horizontally** ; the centers of the circles are aligned horizontally.

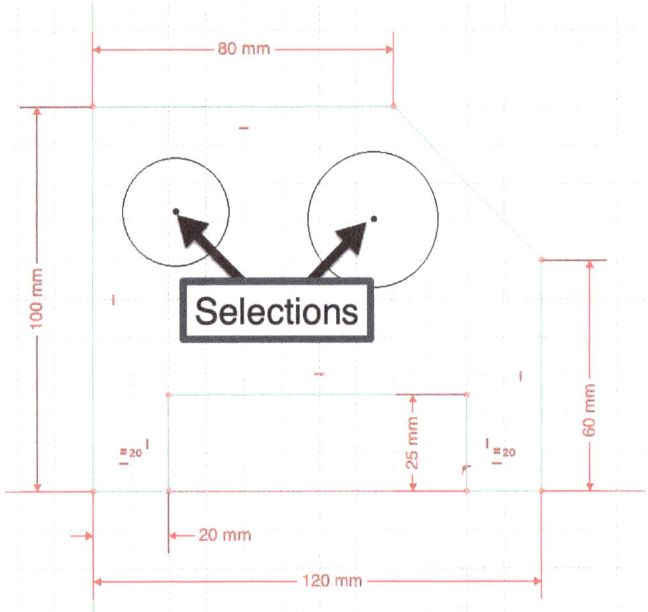

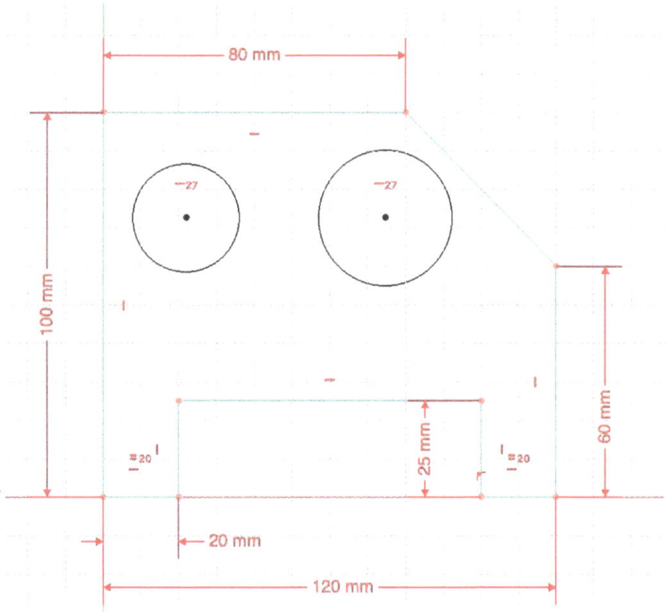

11. On the **Sketcher constraint** toolbar, click the **Constrain equal** icon. Next, click on the two circles; the diameters of the circles become equal.

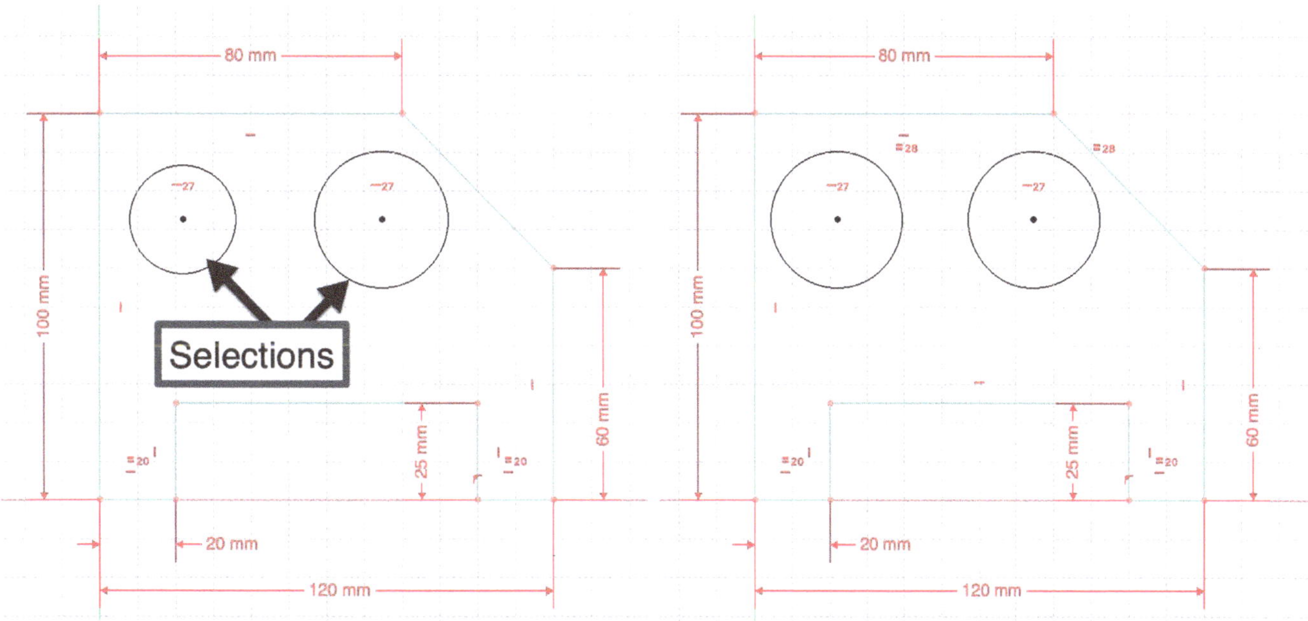

12. On the **Sketcher constraints** toolbar, Click **Dimension** drop-down > **Constrain diameter**.
13. Click on any one of the circles. Move the mouse pointer and click to position the dimension. Type **25** in the **Diameter** box and press Enter.

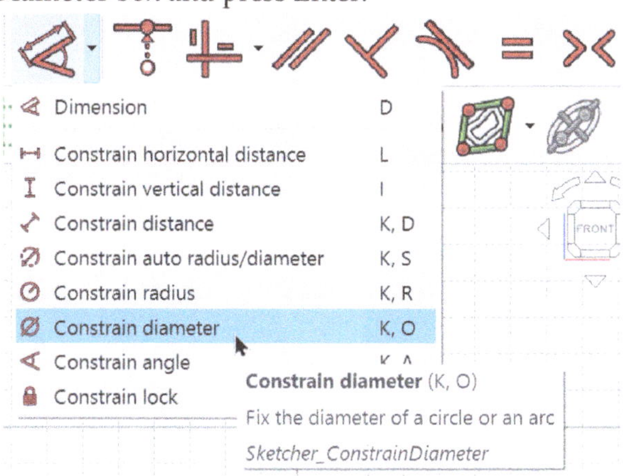

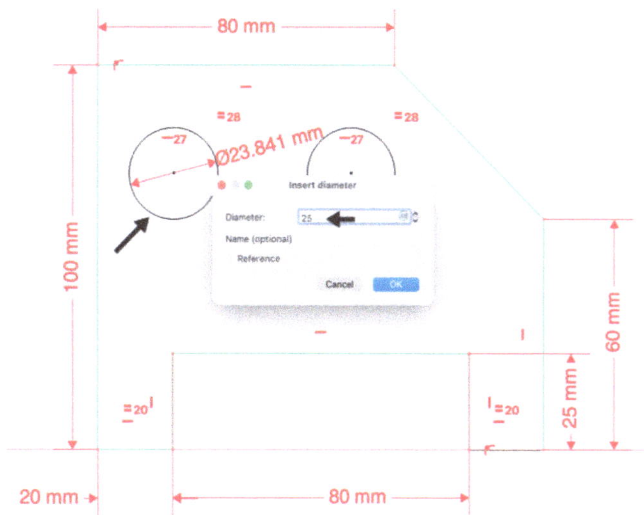

14. On the **Sketcher constraints** toolbar, click the **Dimension** drop-down **> Constrain vertical distance**  icon (or) click **Sketch > Sketcher constraints > Constrain Vertical distance** on the menu bar.
15. Select the center point of the left circle and the top endpoint of the left vertical line. Move the mouse pointer towards the left and click to position the dimension.
16. Type **40** in the **Insert Length** dialog and click **OK**.
17. On the **Sketcher constraints** toolbar, click the **Dimension** drop-down > **Constrain Horizontal distance** icon (or) click **Sketch > Sketcher constraints > Constrain Horizontal distance** on the menu bar.
18. Select the center point of the left circle and the top endpoint of the left vertical line. Move the mouse pointer upward and click to position the dimension.

19. Type **30** in the **Insert Length** dialog and click **OK**.
20. Select the center points of the two circles. Next, move the pointer downward and click.
21. Type **50** in the **Insert Length** dialog and click **OK**.

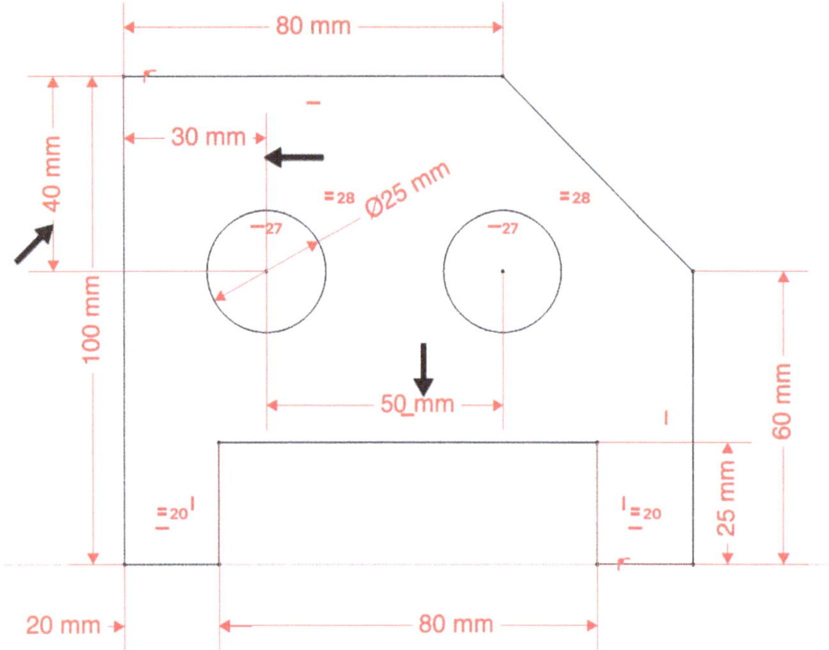

22. Click the **Close** button on the **Tasks** panel.
23. Click **File > Save** on the Menu bar. Next, browse to the required location on your computer and type **C2_example1** in the **File name** box. Click **Save**.
24. Close the file tab on the bottom of the window.

Tutorial 2 (Inches)

In this example, you draw the sketch shown below.

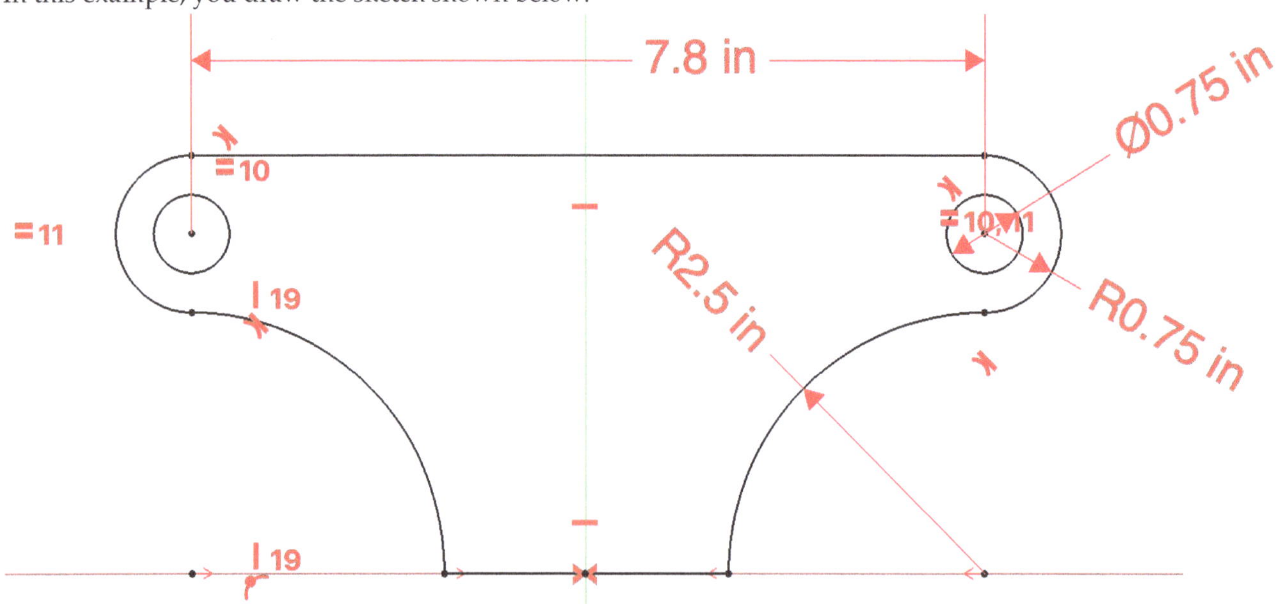

Creating a New document

1. Start FreeCAD 1.0.
2. Click the **New** icon on the **File** toolbar; it creates a new document.
3. Select the **Part Design** option from the **Workbenches** drop-down.
4. On the Menu bar, click **Edit > Preferences**. Next, click the **General** tab on the **Preferences** dialog.
5. Select **Default unit system > Imperial decimal**. Next, check the **Ignore project unit system and use default** option.
6. Type **3** in the **Number of decimals** box, and then click **OK**.

Creating a Sketch

1. Click the **Create sketch** icon on the **Part Design Helper** toolbar.
2. Select the XZ Plane to start the sketch.
3. Deactivate the **Toggle grid** icon on the **Sketcher edit tools** toolbar.
4. On the **Sketcher geometries** toolbar, click the **Create line** icon.
5. Click on the left side of the graphics window.
6. Move the pointer horizontally towards the right and click to draw a line.

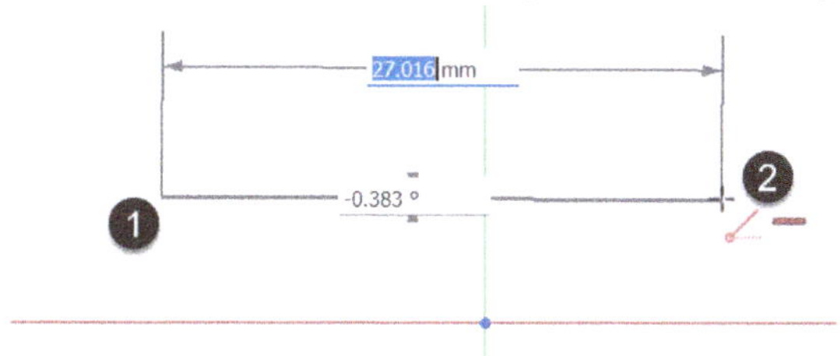

7. Right-click to deactivate the **Create line** tool.
8. Click **Arcs** drop-down **> End points and rim point arc** on the **Sketcher geometries** toolbar and click on the right endpoint of the line.
9. Move the pointer in the top-right direction, and then click to define the endpoint of the arc.
10. Move the pointer and click to define the radius of the arc.

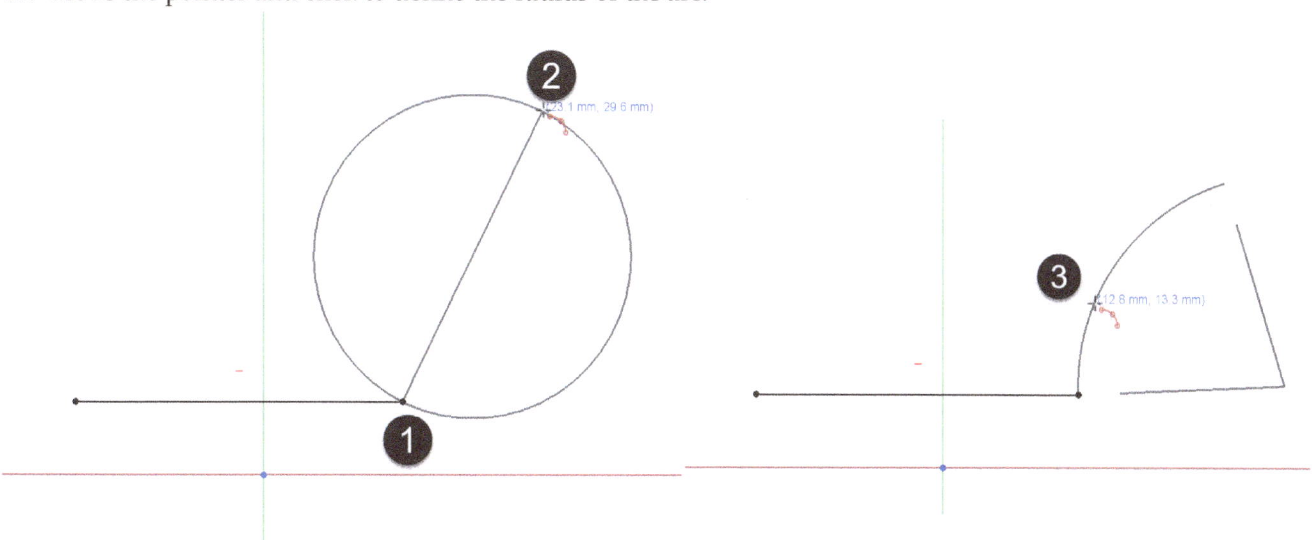

11. Click on the endpoint of the arc. Next, move the pointer upward and click to define the endpoint of the arc.
12. Move the pointer and click to define the radius of the arc.

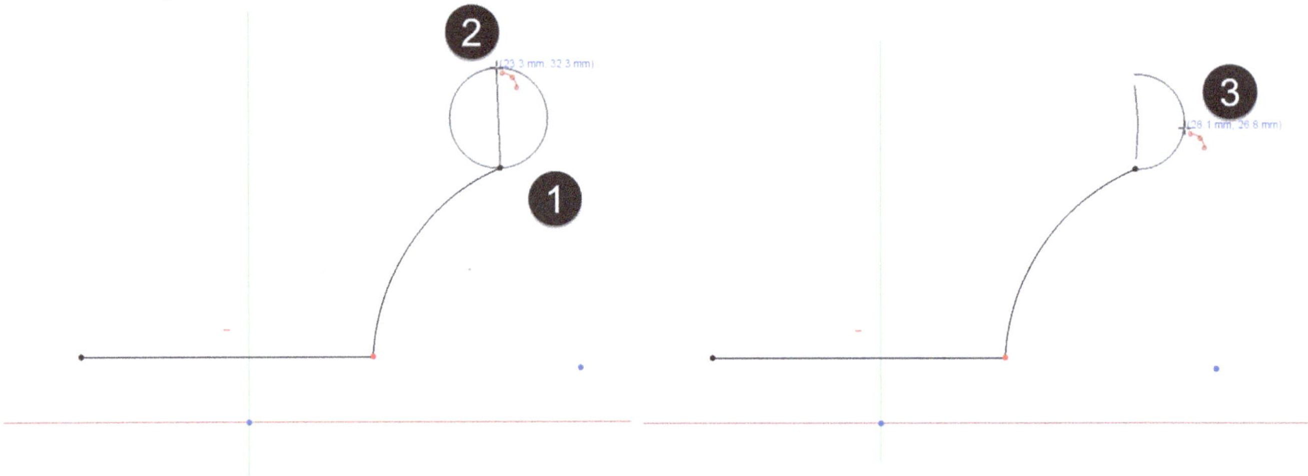

13. Activate the **Create line** tool (click the **Create line** icon on the **Sketcher geometries** Toolbar).
14. Select the endpoint of the arc.
15. Move the mouse pointer towards the left and click to create a horizontal line. Note that the length of the new line should be greater than that of the lower horizontal line.

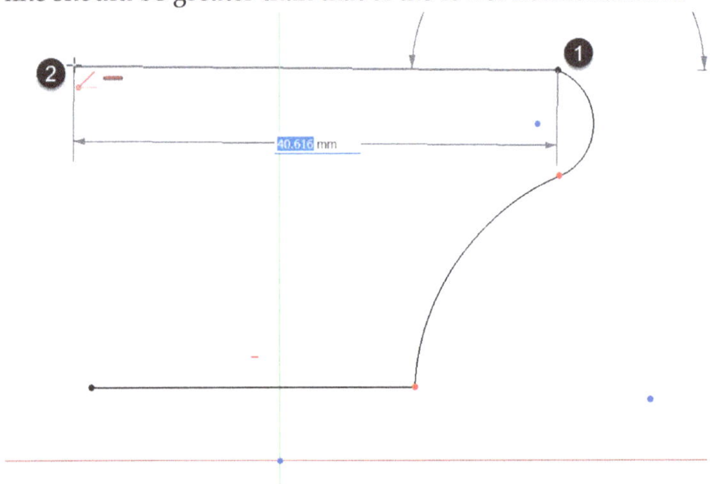

16. Press **Esc** to deactivate the **Create Line** tool.
17. Activate the **End points and rim point arc** tool and click on the endpoint of the line.
18. Move the pointer downwards and click. Next, move the pointer towards the left and click to define the radius of the arc.

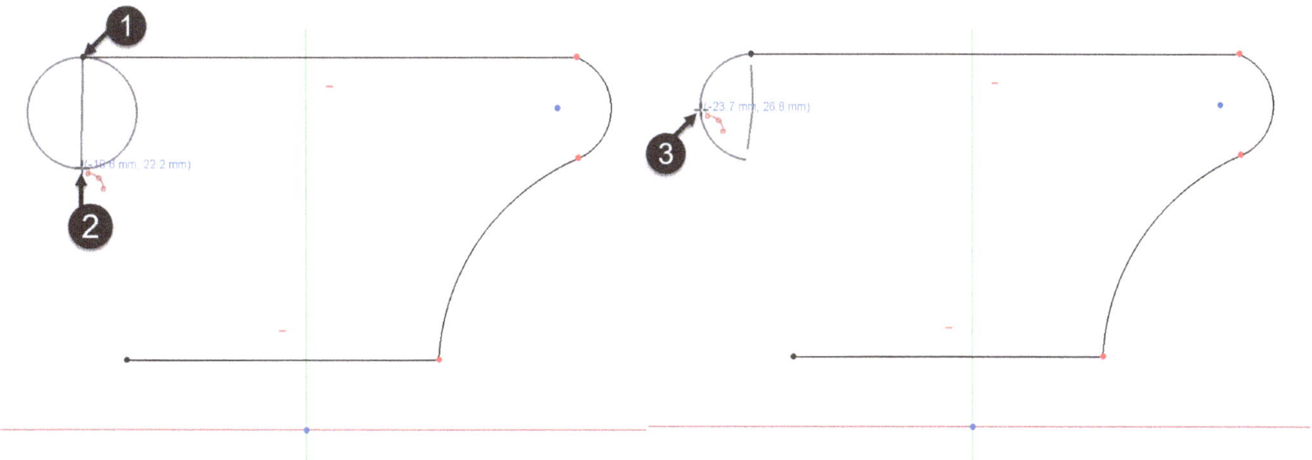

19. Click on the endpoint of the previous arc. Next, select the start point of the sketch.
20. Move the pointer and click to define the radius of the arc.

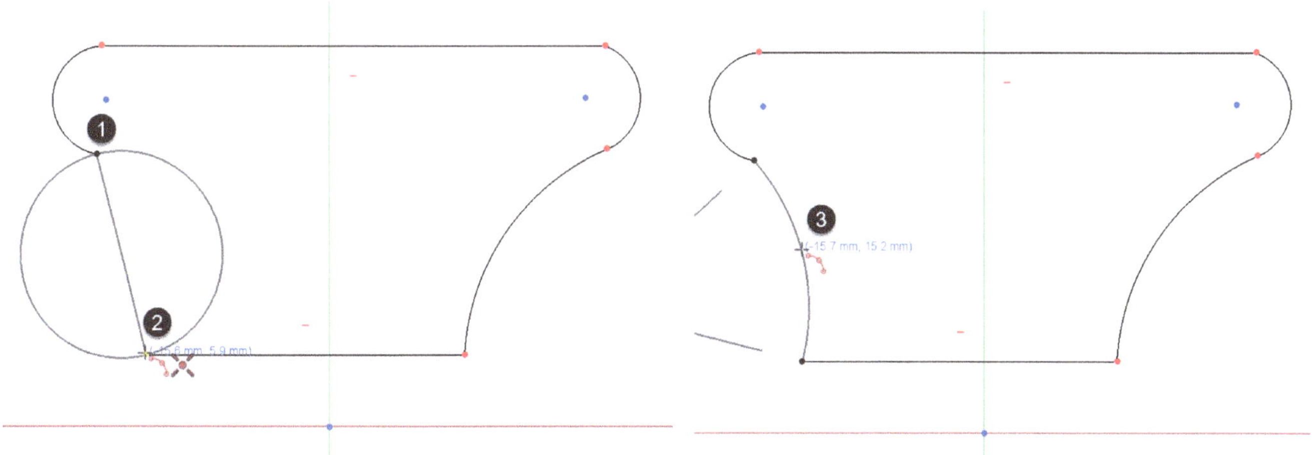

21. Click the **Constrain symmetrical** icon on the **Sketcher constraints** toolbar.
22. Select the left endpoint of the lower horizontal line, the right endpoint of the lower horizontal line, and the origin point. The endpoints of the horizontal line are made symmetric about the origin point.

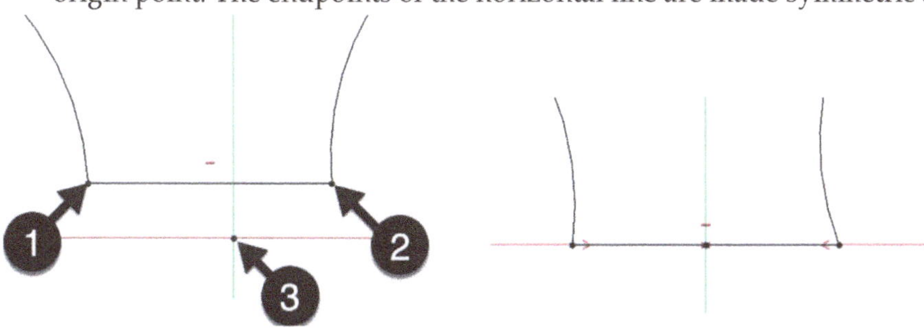

23. Click the **Constrain Coincident** icon on the **Sketcher constraints** toolbar.
24. Select the center point of any one of the large arcs. Next, select the horizontal axis.

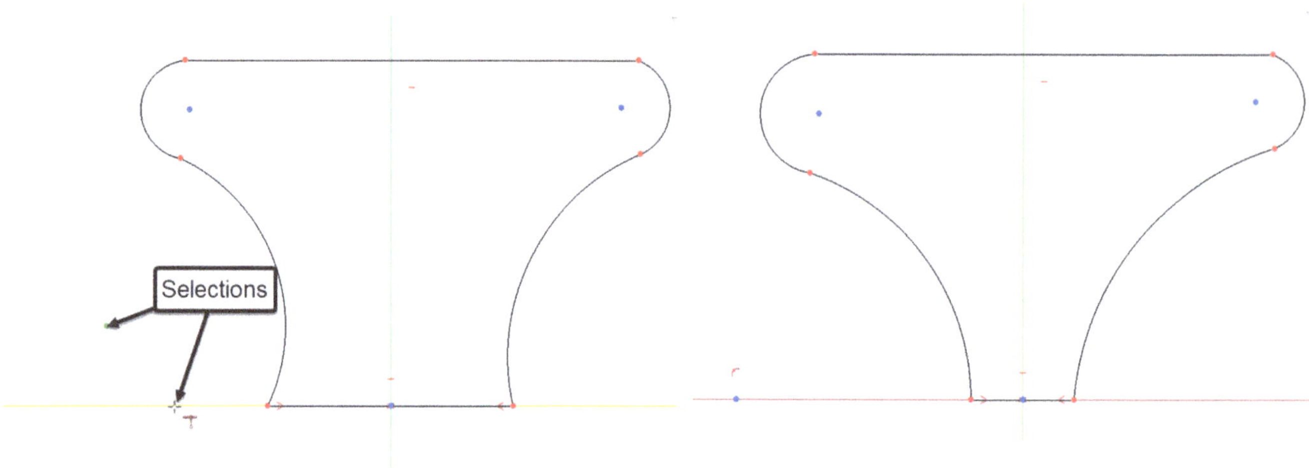

25. Click the **Constrain symmetrical** icon on the **Sketcher constraints** toolbar.
26. Select the center point of the left large arc, the center point of the large right arc, and the origin point. The centerpoints of the arcs are made symmetric about the origin point.

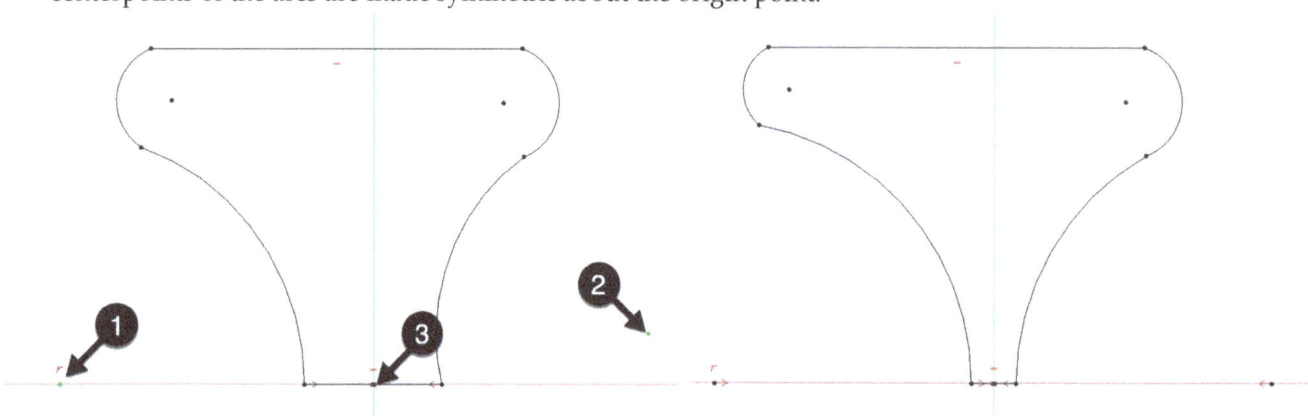

27. On the menu bar, click **Sketch > Sketcher geometries > Circle drop-down > Create circle by center**.
28. Select the center point of any one of the small arcs. Next, move the pointer outward and click to create the circle.
29. Select the center point of another small arc, move the pointer outward, and then click.

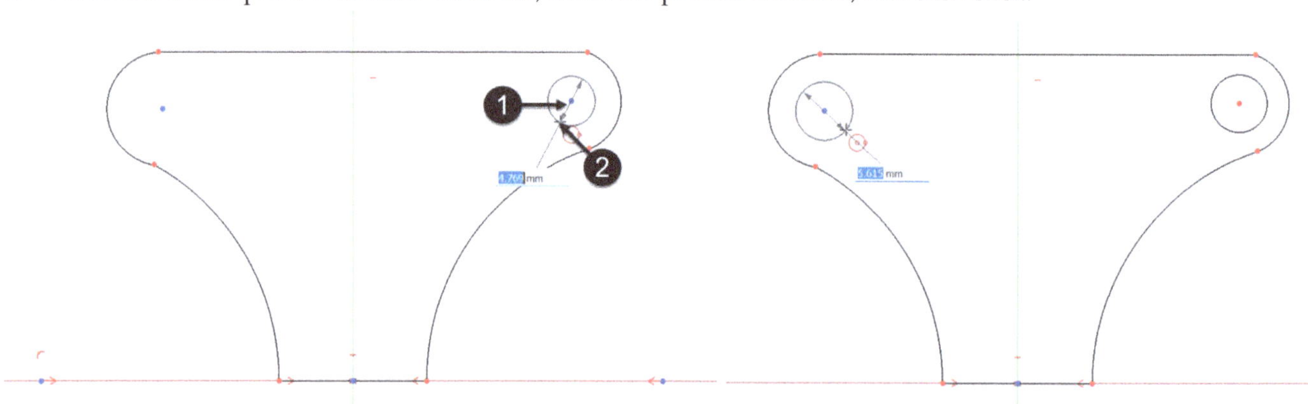

30. Click the **Constrain equal** icon on the **Sketcher constraints** toolbar. Next, select the two circles to make them equal in size.

31. Select the two small arcs to make them equal in radius.

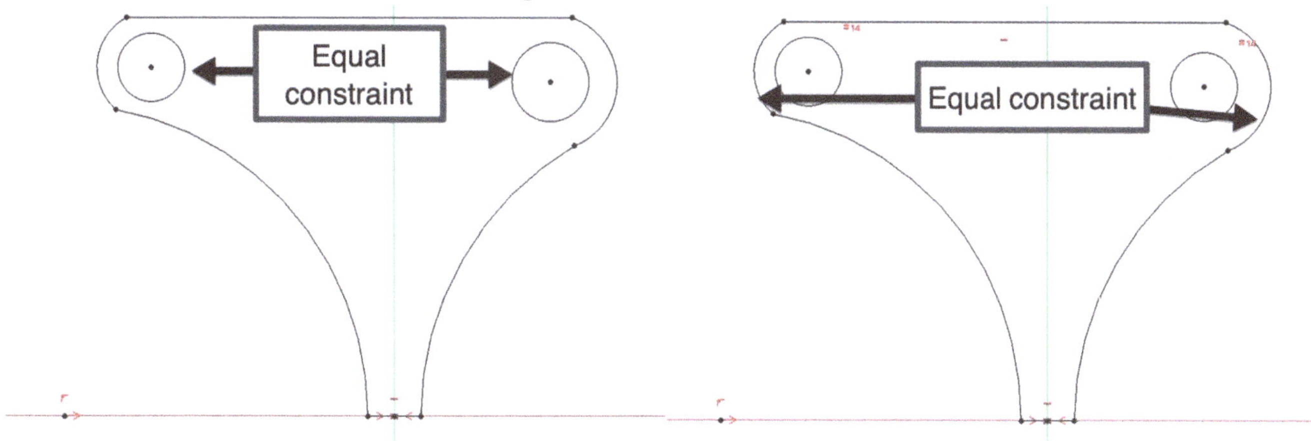

32. Click the **Constrain tangent** icon on the **Sketcher constraints** toolbar. Next, select the large and small arcs on the left side; the **Sketcher Constraint Substitution** message box appears. Click **OK** to delete the Coincident constraint and apply the tangent between the two arcs.
33. Likewise, create the tangent constraints by selecting the other elements, as shown. Press ESC.

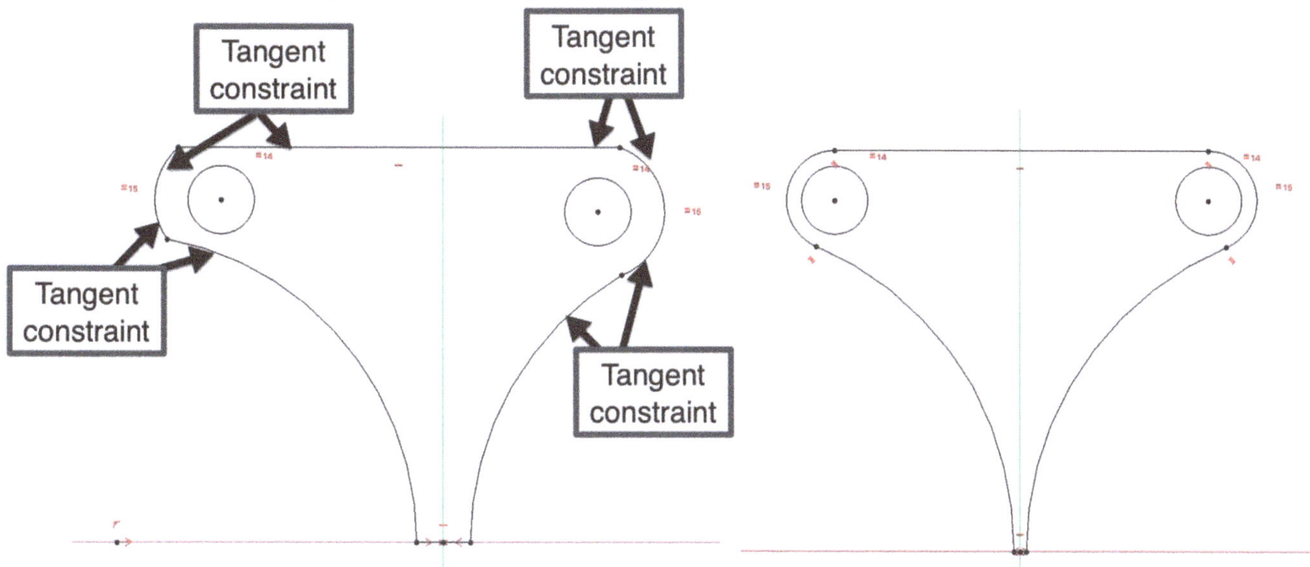

34. Click the **Dimension** drop-down **> Constrain radius** icon on the **Sketcher constraints** toolbar.
35. Select any one of the small arcs. Type **0.75** in the **Radius** box and click **OK**.

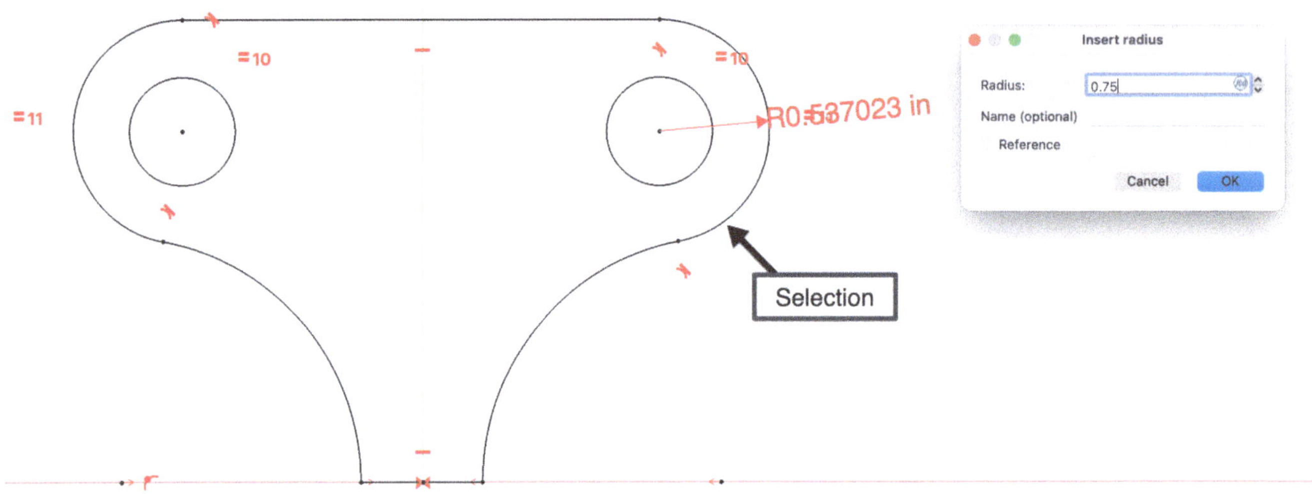

36. On the **Sketcher constraints** toolbar, click **Dimension** drop-down > **Constrain diameter**.
37. Select any one of the circles. Type 0.75 in the **Diameter** box and click **OK**.

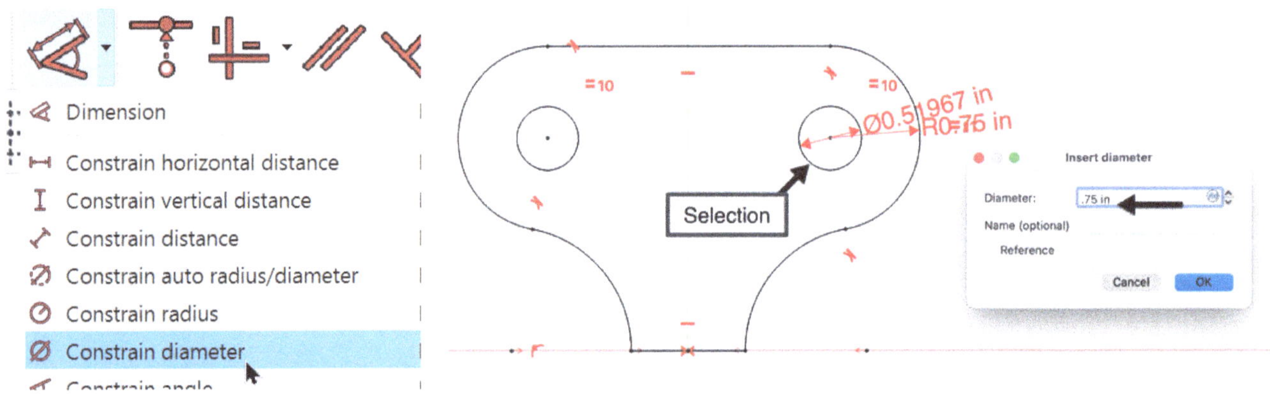

38. Click the **Dimension** drop-down > **Constrain horizontal distance** icon on the **Sketcher constraints** toolbar.
39. Select the centerpoints of the two circles. Type 7.8 in the **Length** box and click **OK**. Right-click to deactivate the **Constrain horizontal distance** tool.

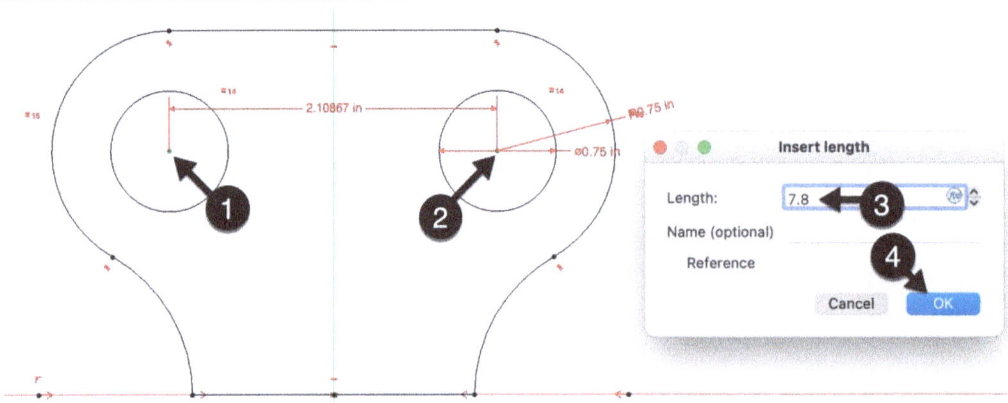

40. Press and hold the Ctrl key and select the centerpoint and endpoint of the left large arc.

41. Click the **Constraint horizontal/vertical** drop-down > **Constrain vertical** icon on the **Sketcher constraints** toolbar; the selected points are aligned vertically.

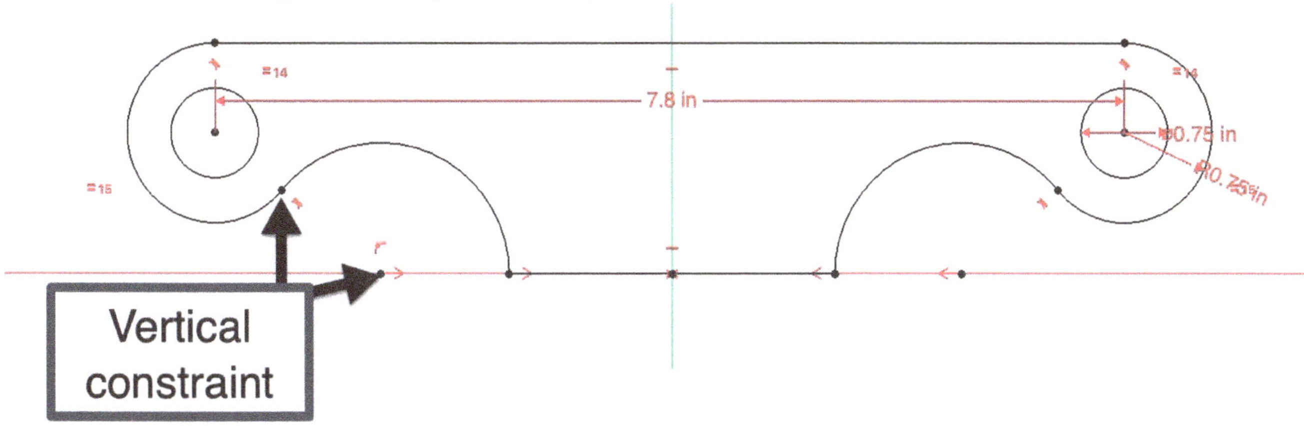

42. Click the **Dimension** drop-down **> Constrain radius** icon on the **Sketcher constraints** toolbar.
43. Select any one of the large arcs. Type **2.5** in the **Radius** box and click **OK**.

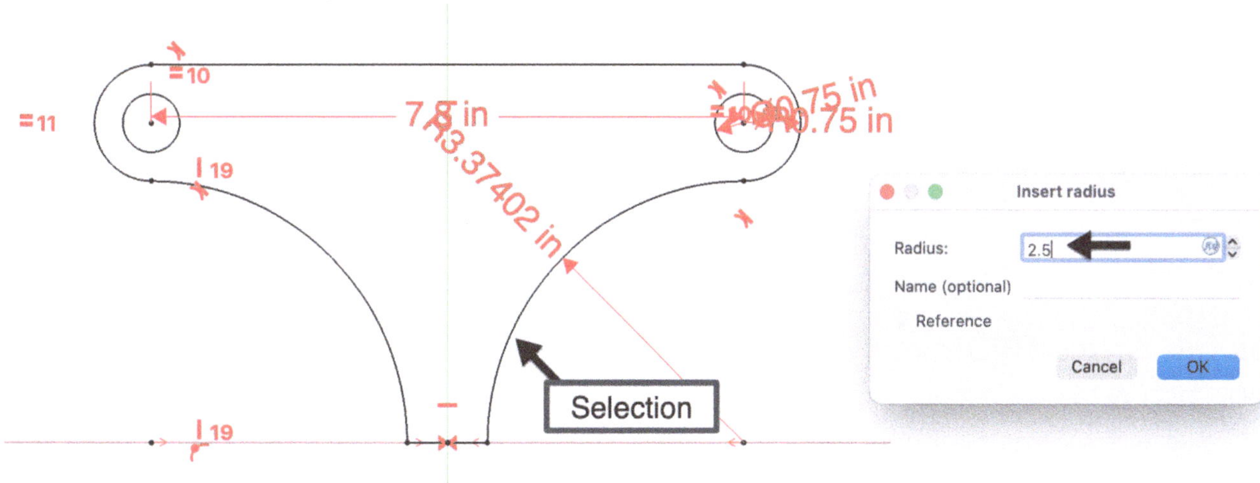

44. Click the **Close** button on the **Tasks** panel.
45. Click **File > Save** on the Menu bar. Next, browse to the required location on your computer and type **C2_example2** in the **File name** box. Click **Save**.
46. Close the file tab on the bottom left corner of the window.

Tutorial 3 (Millimetres)

In this example, you draw the sketch shown below.

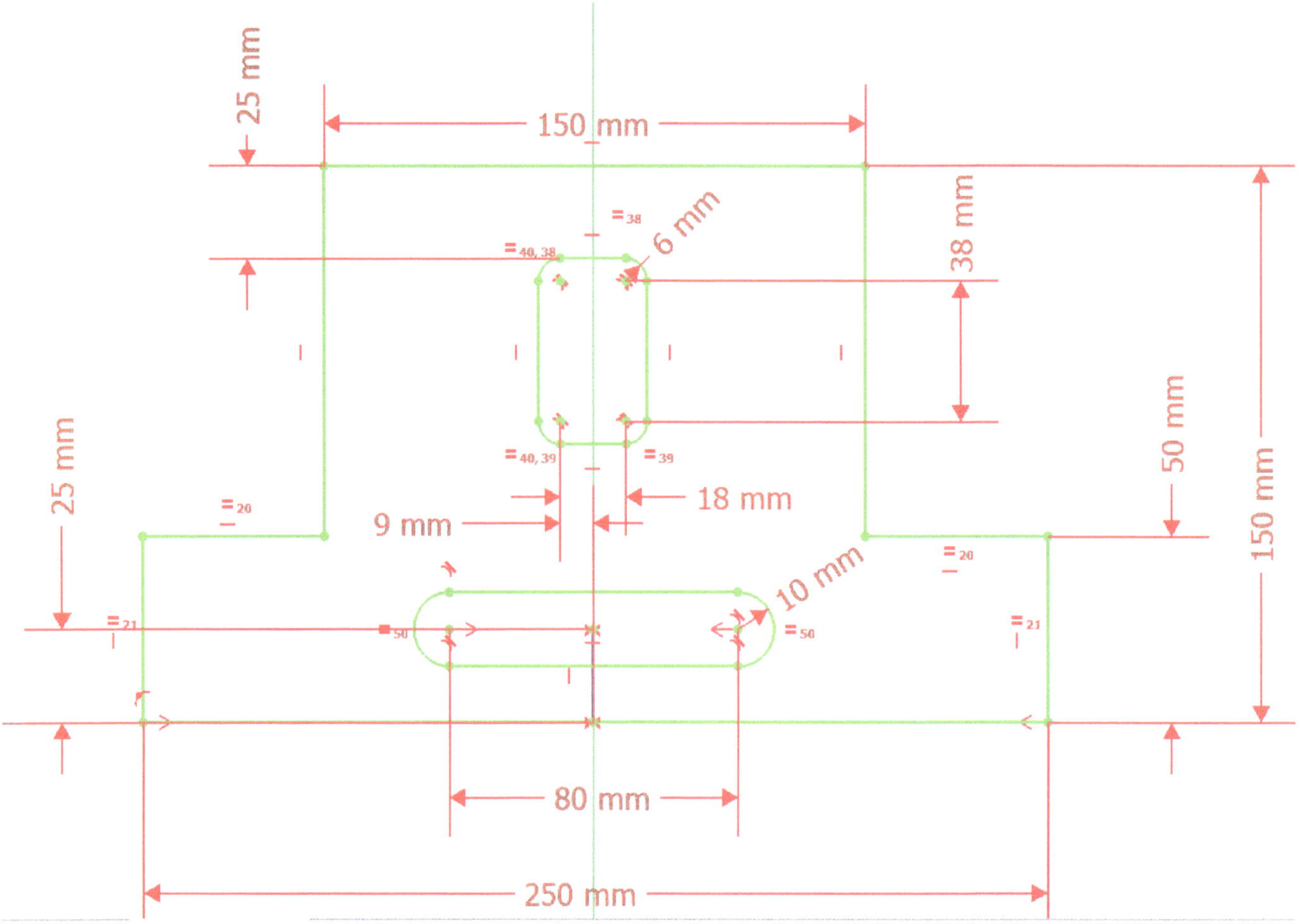

Creating a New Document

1. Start **FreeCAD 1.0**.
2. Click the **New** icon on the **File** toolbar; it creates a new document.
3. Click **Edit > Preferences** on the menu bar (or) click **FreeCAD 1.0 > Preferences** on title bar, if you are working on MacOS; the **Preferences** dialog appears on the screen.
4. Click **General** tab on the dialog and select **Unit System > Standard(mm/kg/s/degree)**.
5. Select **Number of decimals > 2** and click **Apply**.
6. Click **OK** to close the **Preferences** dialog.
7. On the **Workbench** toolbar, select **Workbench** drop-down > **Part Design** (or) select **View > Workbench > Part Design** on the Menu bar.

Creating a Sketch

1. To start a new sketch, click **Create Sketch** tool on the **Part Design Helper** toolbar.
2. Select **XZ_Plane** from the graphics window.
3. Activate the **Create line** tool (click the **Create line** icon on the **Sketcher geometries** toolbar).
4. Click on the origin point and move the pointer vertically up. Next, click to create a vertical line.

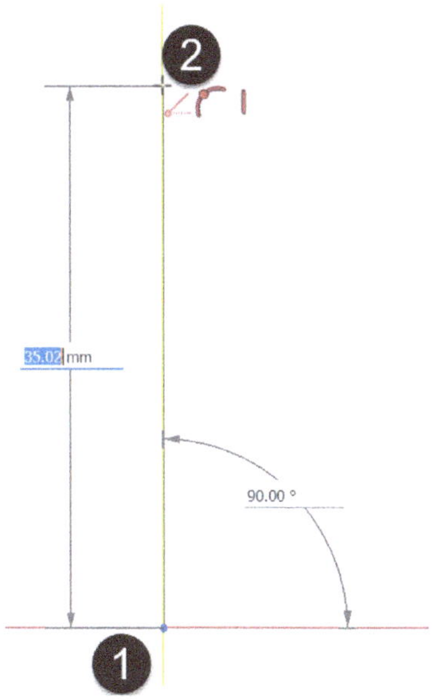

5. Right-click to deactivate the **Create line** tool.
6. Select the vertical line and click the **Toggle Construction geometry**  tool on the **Sketcher geometries** toolbar.
7. Activate the **Create polyline** 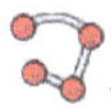 tool and click the horizontal axis of the sketch on the left side of the construction line.
8. Move the mouse pointer vertically up and click to define the second point.
9. Move the pointer horizontally toward the right and click to create a horizontal line.
10. Move the pointer vertically up and click to create a vertical line. Right-click.

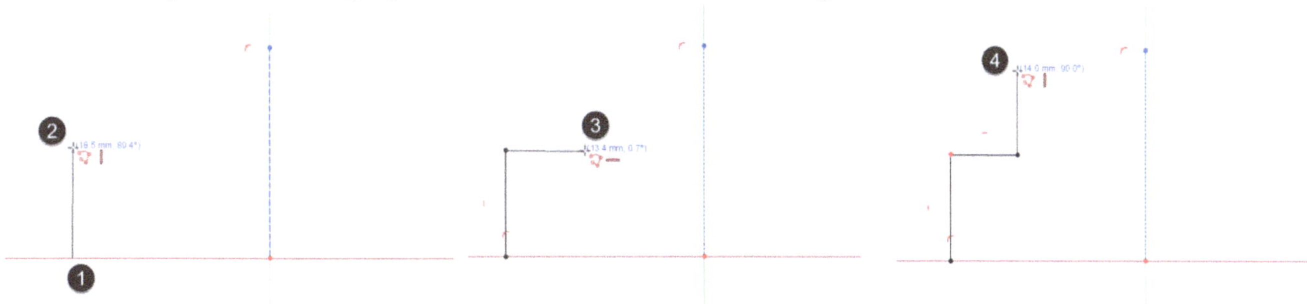

11. Press and hold the Ctrl key and select the lines.
12. Click the **Symmetry** 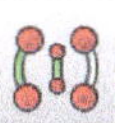 icon on the **Sketcher tools** toolbar (or) click **Sketch > Sketcher tools > Symmetry** on the menu bar.
13. Select the construction line; the lines are mirrored about the construction line.

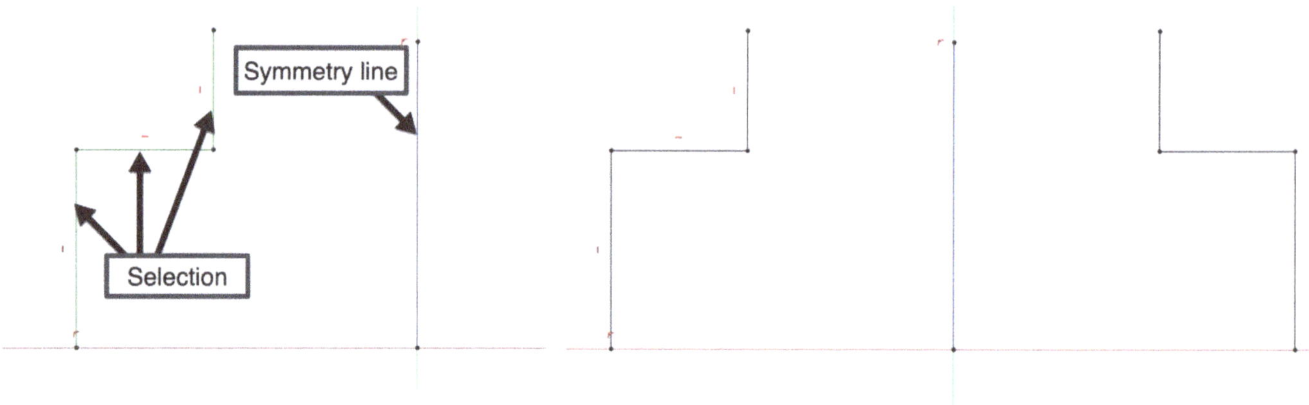

14. Activate the **Create line** tool (click the **Create line** icon on the **Sketcher geometries** toolbar).
15. Select the endpoints of the lower vertical lines displayed on both sides of the construction line.
16. Select the endpoints of the upper vertical lines. Next, press ESC.

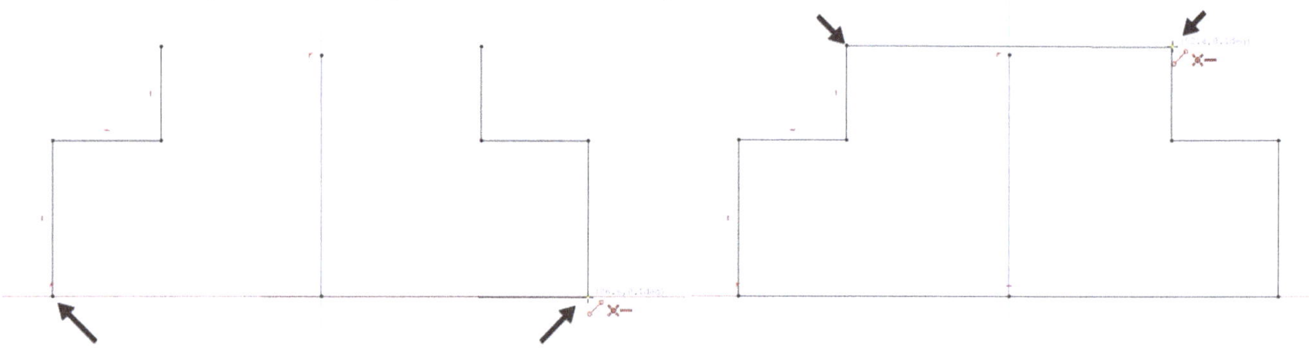

17. Apply Horizontal and Vertical Constraints to the lines, as shown.

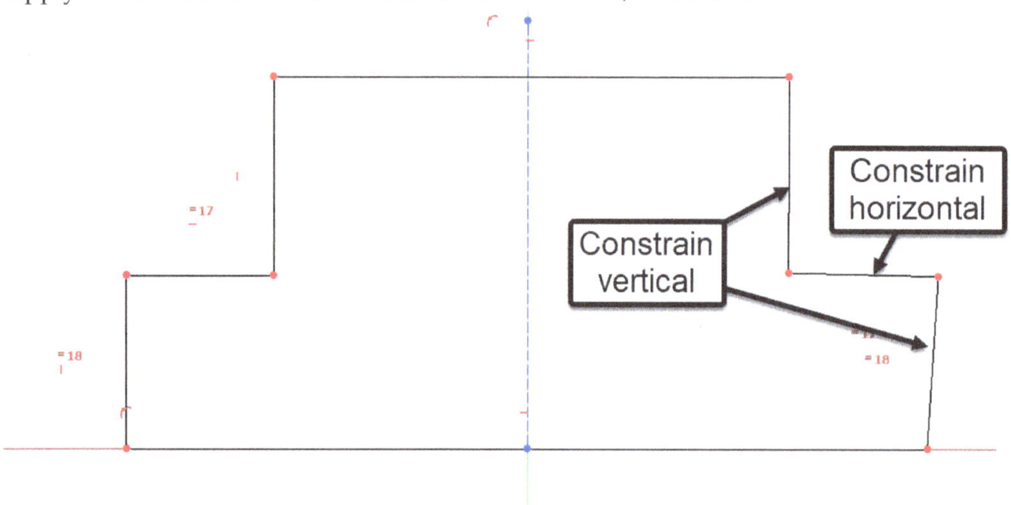

18. On the **Tasks** panel, click the drop-down available on the **Constraints** section and check the **Auto remove redundants** option.
19. Click the **Constrain symmetrical** icon on the **Sketcher constraints** toolbar.
20. Select the horizontal line and origin point, as shown in the figure. The endpoints of the horizontal line are made symmetric about the origin point.

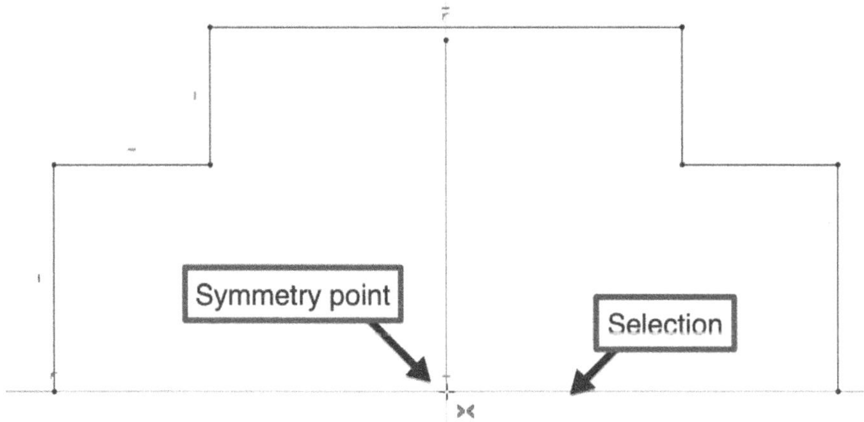

21. Click the **Constrain equal** icon on the **Sketcher constraints** toolbar
22. Select the two horizontal lines, as shown.
23. Select the two vertical lines to make them equal in length.

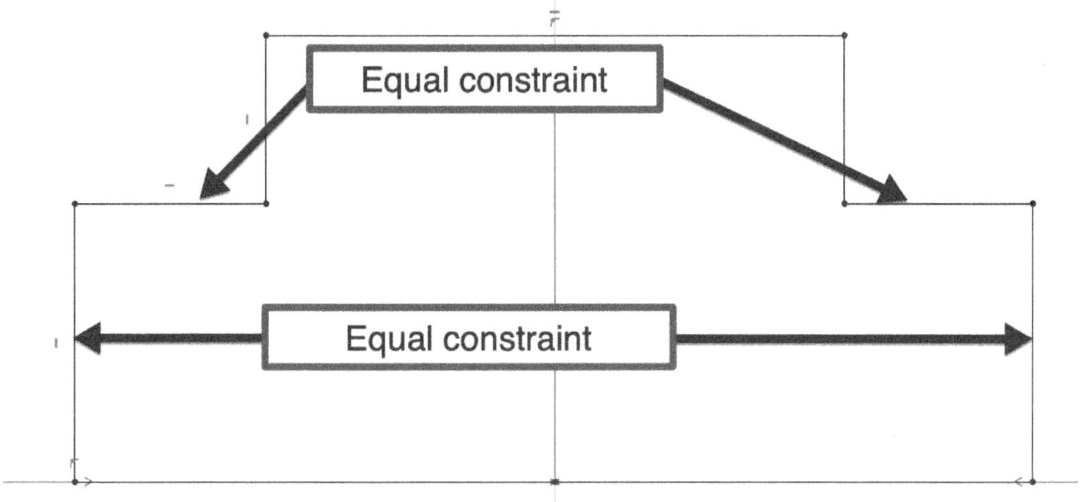

24. Create horizontal distance and vertical distance constraints, as shown.

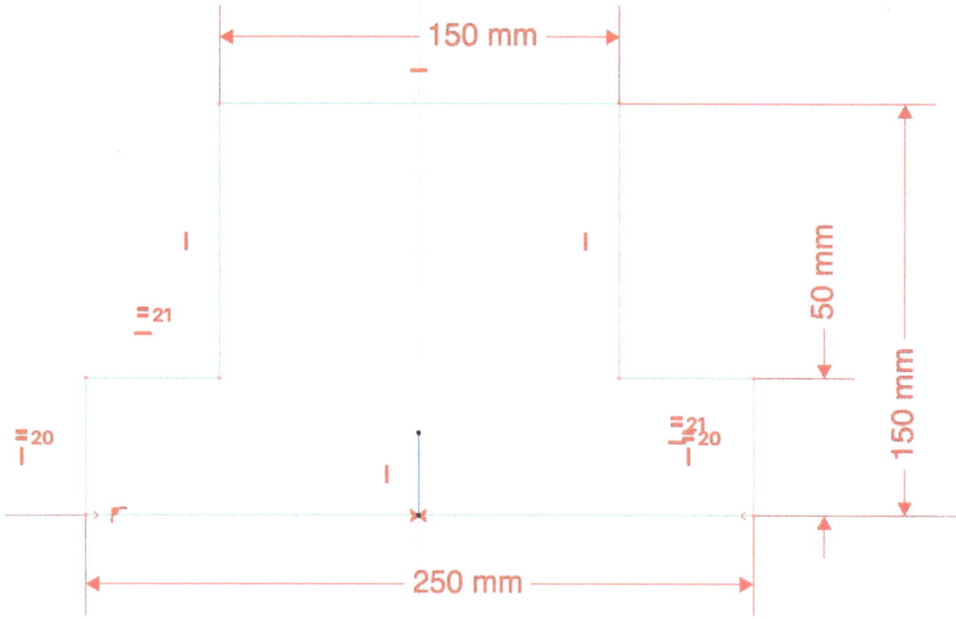

25. Click the **Rectangle** drop-down > **Rounded Rectangle**  on the **Sketcher geometries** toolbar.
26. Click on the left side to define the first corner of the rectangle. Next, move the cursor diagonally and click to define the second corner of the rectangle.

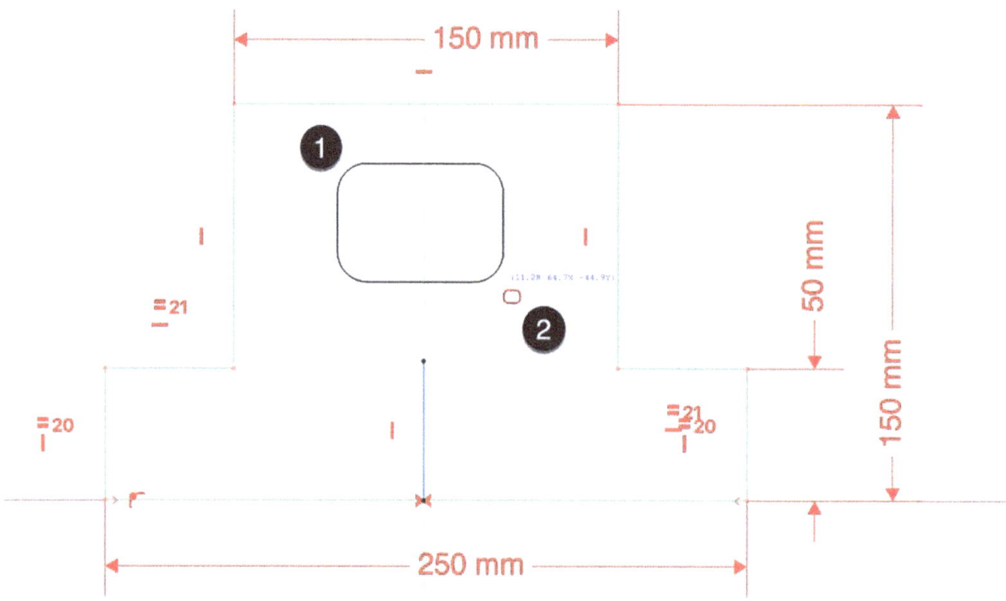

27. Move the pointer inward and click to specify the corner radii of the rectangle.

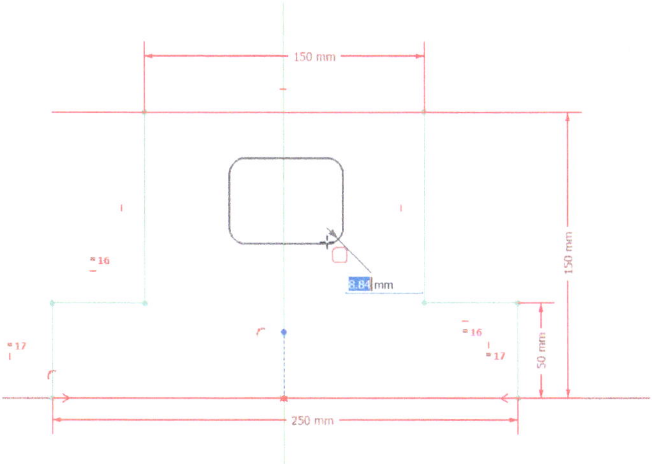

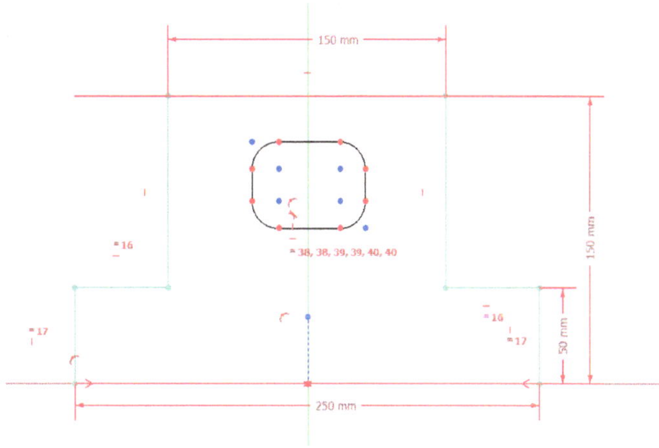

28. Click the **Dimension** drop-down > **Constrain radius** icon on the **Sketcher constraints** toolbar.
29. Select any one of the fillets. Type **6** in the **Radius** box and click **OK**.
30. On the menu bar, click **Sketch > Sketcher constraints > Constrain horizontal distance**.
31. Select the centerpoints of the two lower fillets. Next, type 18 in the **Length** box and click **OK**.

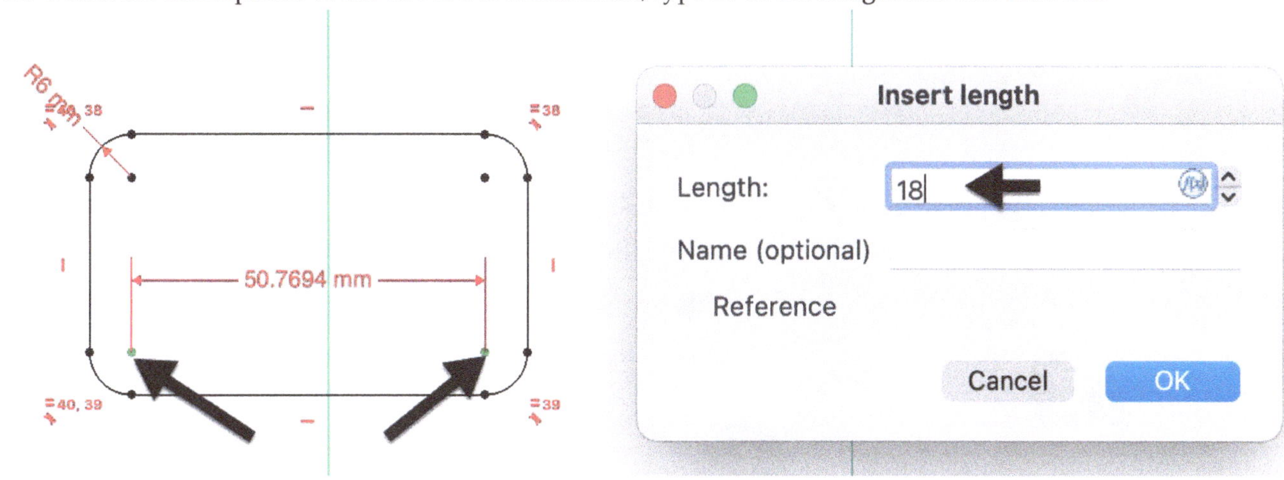

32. On the menu bar, click **Sketch > Sketcher constraints > Constrain vertical distance**.
33. Select the centerpoints of the two right fillets. Next, type **38** in the **Length** box and click **OK**.

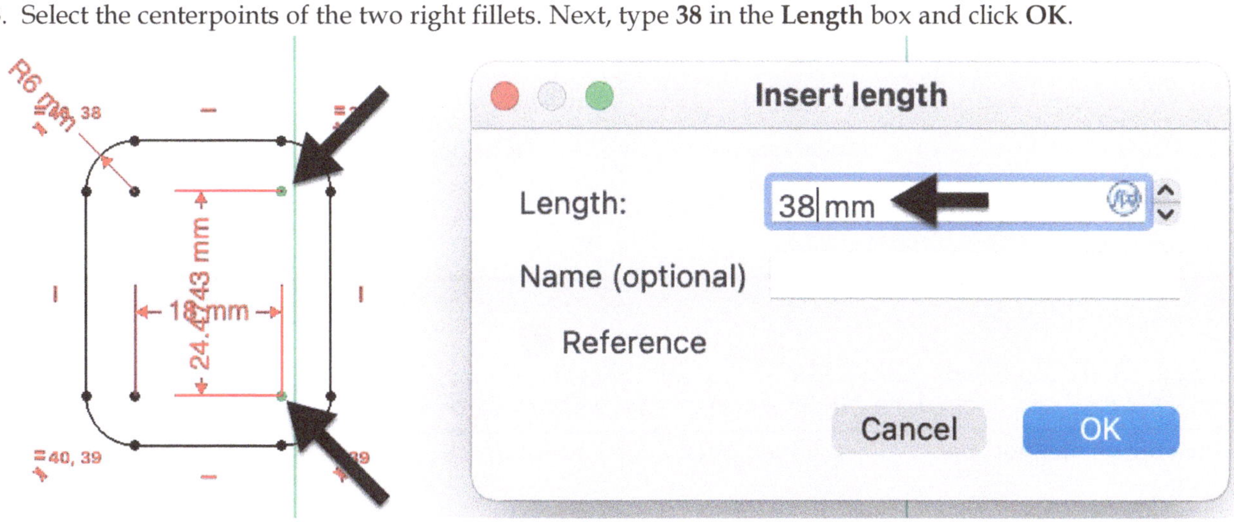

34. Click the **Dimension** drop-down > **Constrain horizontal distance** icon on the **Sketcher constraints** toolbar.
35. Select the origin point of the sketch and the center point of the bottom-left fillet of the rectangle.
36. Type **9** in the **Length** box and click **OK**.

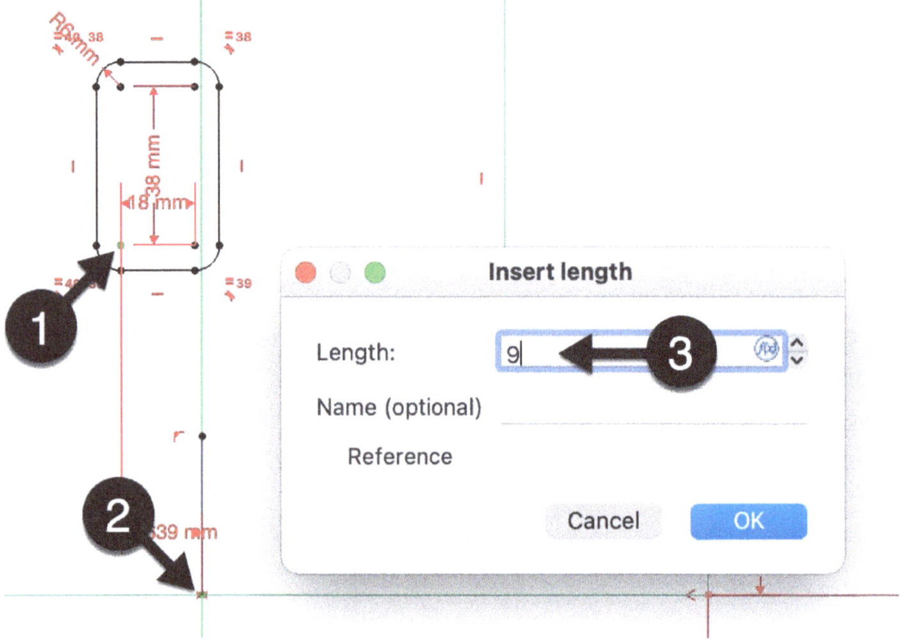

37. Click the **Constrain vertical distance** icon on the **Sketcher constraints** toolbar.
38. Select the top-left corner of the outer loop. Next, select the top left corner of the rectangle.
39. Type 25 in the **Length** box and click **OK**.

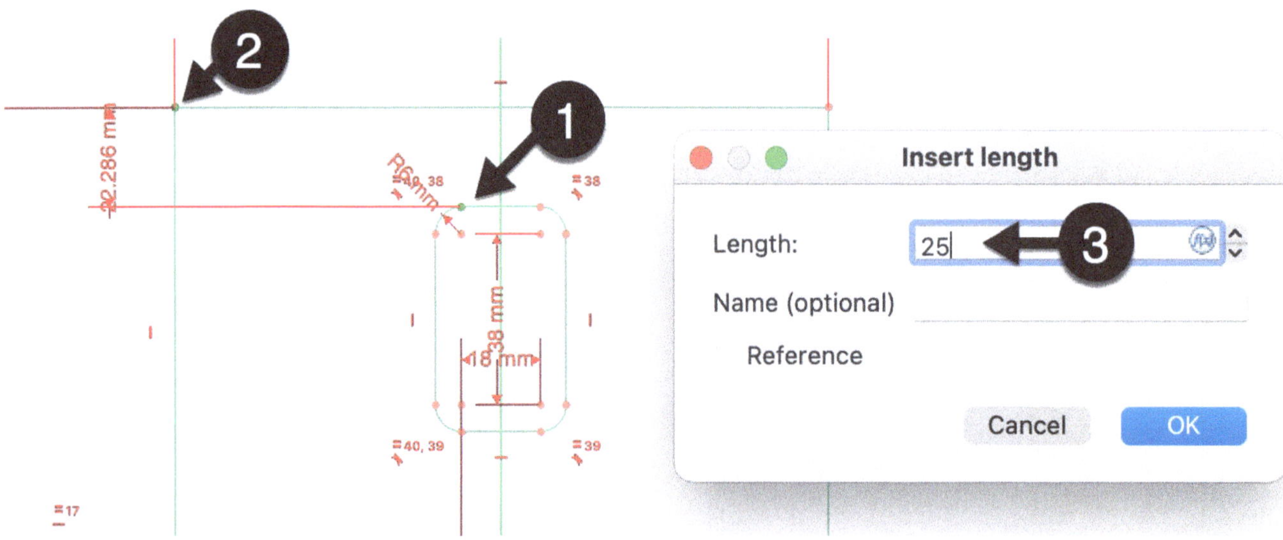

40. Click the **Slot** drop-down **> Create slot** on the **Sketcher geometries** toolbar.
41. Specify the center point of the slot end on the left side of the sketch.
42. Move the pointer horizontally toward the right and click to specify the other end of the slot.

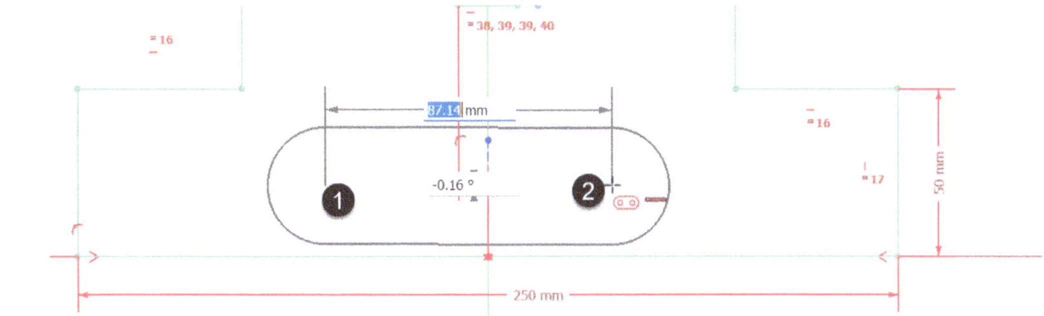

43. Move the pointer outward or inward and click to specify the slot width

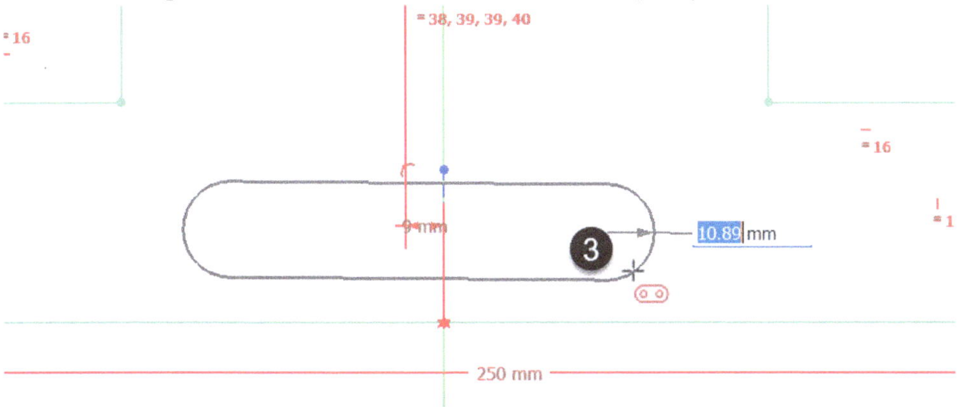

44. Click the **Constrain symmetrical** icon on the **Sketcher constraints** toolbar.
45. Select the left endpoint of the slot, right endpoint of the slot, and the top endpoint of the vertical construction line. The two endpoints are made symmetric about the top endpoint of the vertical construction line.

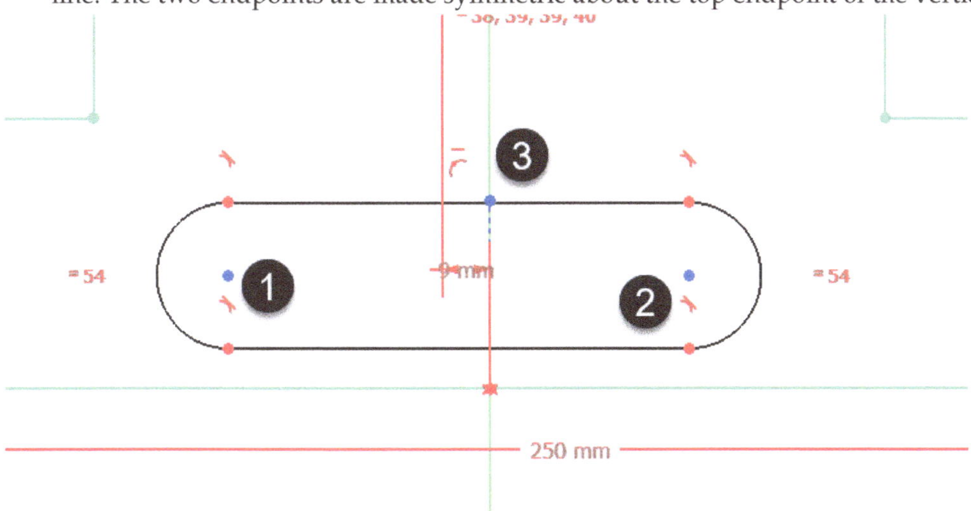

46. Add constraints to the slot and the vertical construction line, as shown.

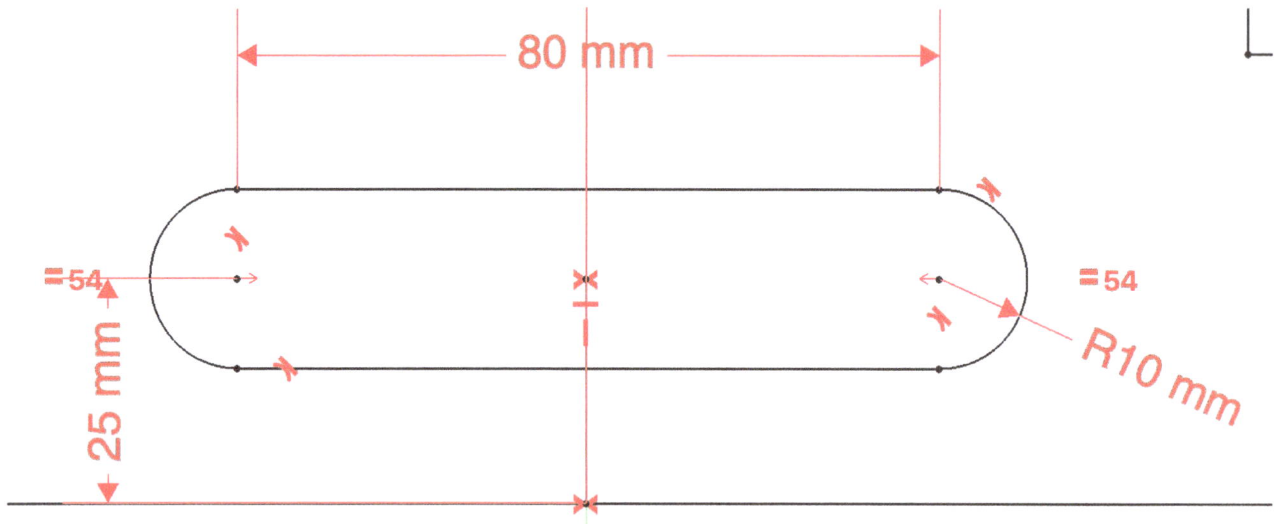

47. Click the **Close** button on the **Tasks** panel.
48. Click **File > Save** on the Menu bar. Next, browse to the required location on your computer and type **C2_example3** in the **File name** box. Click **Save**.
49. Close the file tab on the bottom left corner of the window.

Questions

1. What is the procedure to create sketches in FreeCAD?
2. List any two sketch *Constraints* in FreeCAD.
3. List any two distance constraints.
4. Describe two methods to create circles.
5. How to define the shape and size of a sketch?
6. How to create a tangent arc?
7. Which command is used to create multiple lines?
8. List the commands to create arcs?
9. What is the command to create slots?
10. What are inferred constraints?

Exercises

Exercise 1

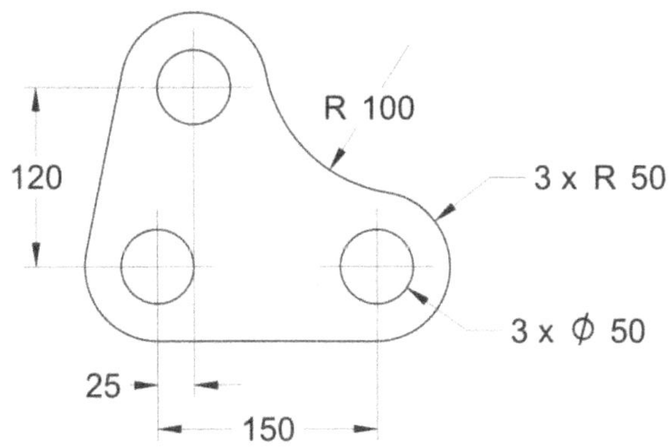

Exercise 2

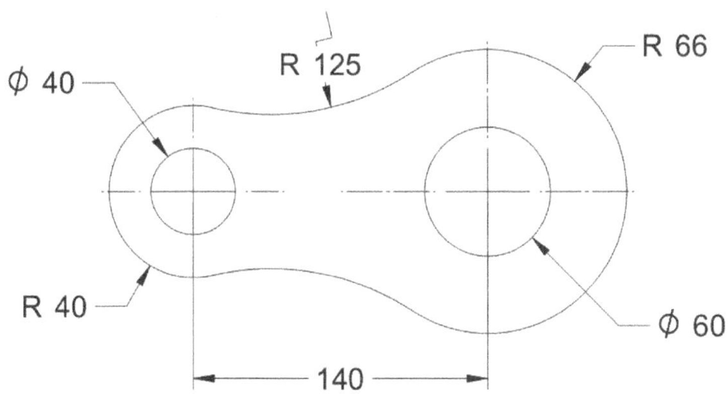

Exercise 3

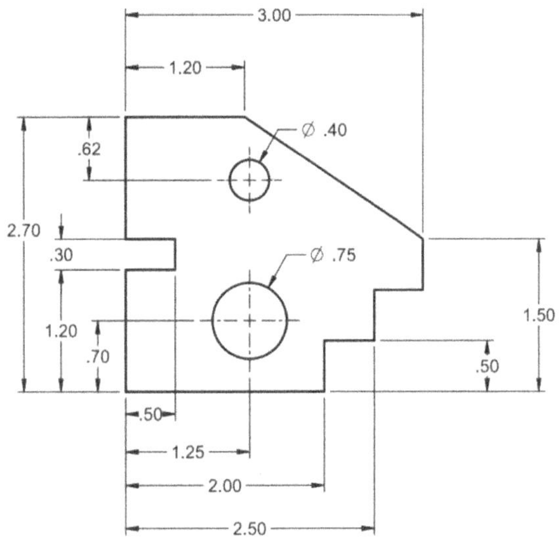

Chapter 3: Pad and Revolve Features

Pad and revolve features are used to create basic and simple parts. Most of the time, they form the base for complex parts, as well. These features are easy to create and require a single sketch. Now, you will learn the commands to create these features.

In this chapter, you will learn to:

- Create the *Pad* and *Revolve* features
- Create Construction Planes
- Work with additional options in the *Pad* and *Revolve* commands

Pad Features

Padding is the process of taking a two-dimensional profile and converting it into a 3D model by giving it some thickness. A simple example of this would be taking a circle and converting it into a cylinder. Once you have created a sketch profile or profiles you want to *Pad*, click the **Pad** icon on the **Part Design Modeling** toolbar; the sketch is selected automatically. Type-in a value in the **Length** box to specify the Pad length.

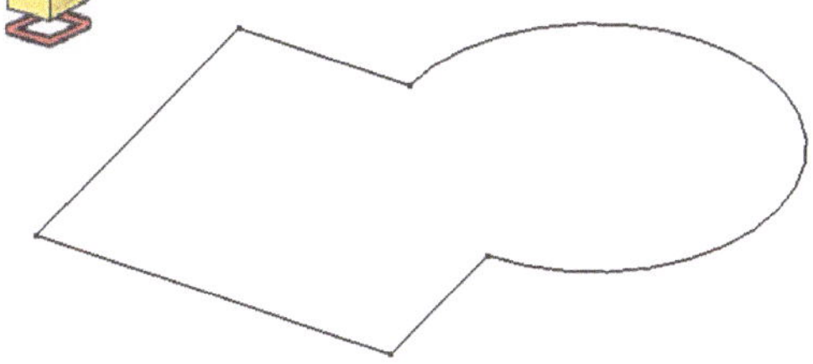

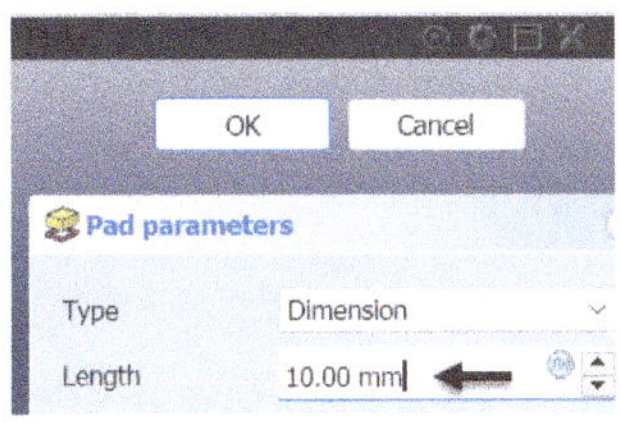

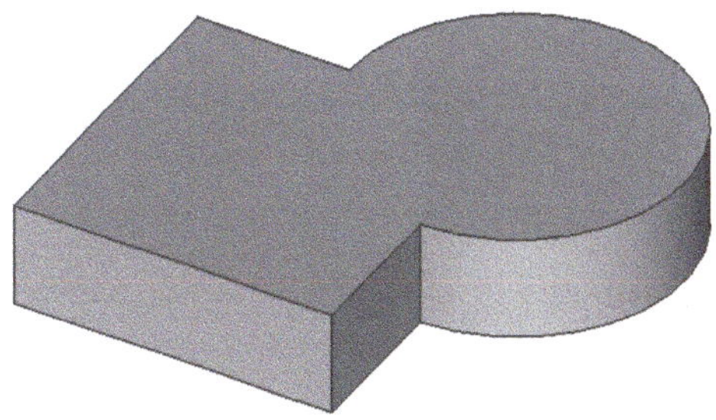

You can select **Symmetric to plane** option on the **Combo View** panel to Pad the sketch symmetrically about the sketch plane.

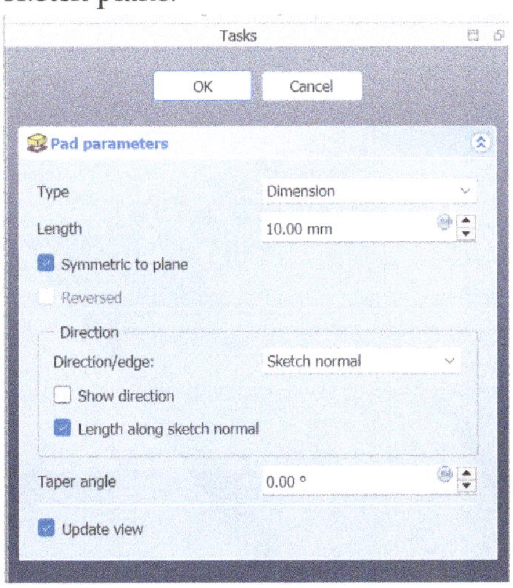

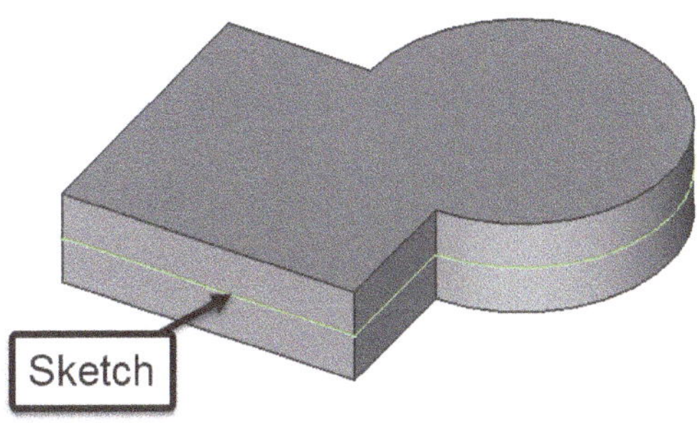

Click **OK** on the **Tasks** panel to complete the *Pad* feature.

Extruding the Sketch in the Custom Direction

By default, the sketch is extruded in the direction normal to the sketch plane. However, you can define the extrude direction selecting the **Select reference** option from the **Direction/edge** drop-down. Next, type-in the length and click **OK**.

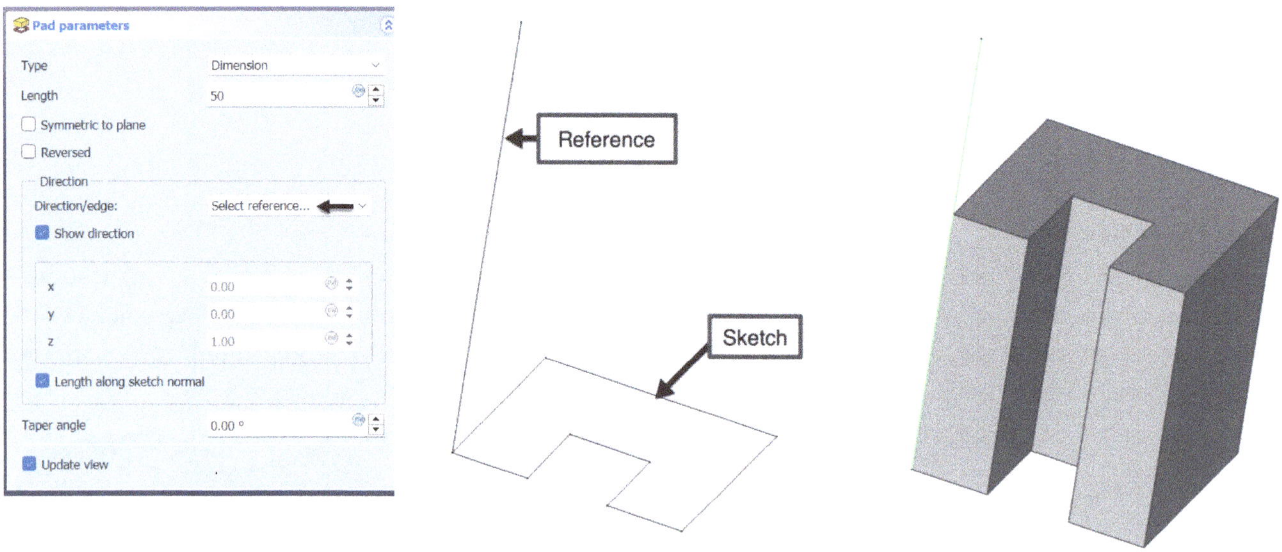

You can also select the **Custom Direction** option from the **Direction/edge** drop-down to specify the custom direction. After selecting this option, check the **Show Direction** option and enter values in the **x**, **y**, and **z** boxes. The extrusion will be skewed along the X, Y, and Z directions.

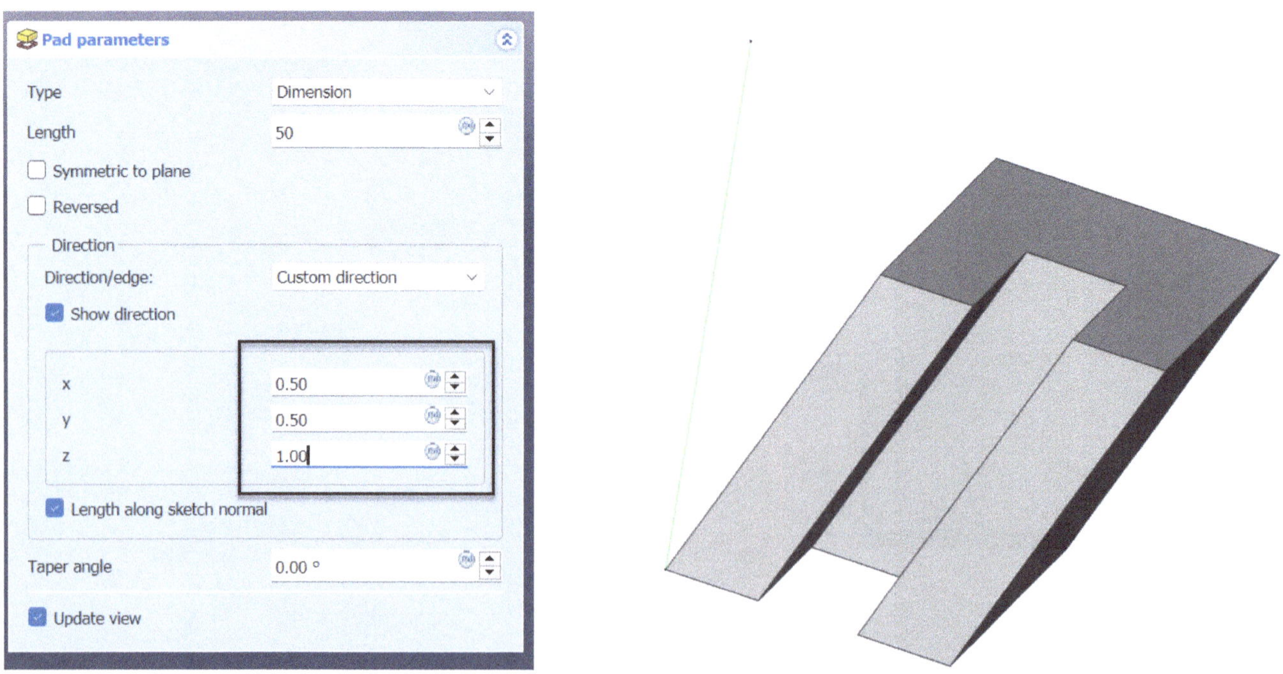

Revolved Features

Revolving is the process of taking a two-dimensional profile and revolving it about a centerline to create a 3D geometry (shapes that are axially symmetric). This command is useful when you're working on designs like screws, bolts, wheels, or any cylindrical or symmetrical components. While creating a sketch for the *Revolved* feature, it is vital to think about the cross-sectional shape that will define the 3D geometry once it is revolved around an axis. For instance, the following geometry has a hole in the center. This could be created with a separate *Pocket* or *Hole* feature. But in order to make that hole part of the *Revolved* feature, you need to create the profile at a distance from the axis of revolution. The distance value should be the radius of the hole to be created at the center. You can define the axis of revolution using the vertical or horizontal axis, or by creating a construction line in the sketch.

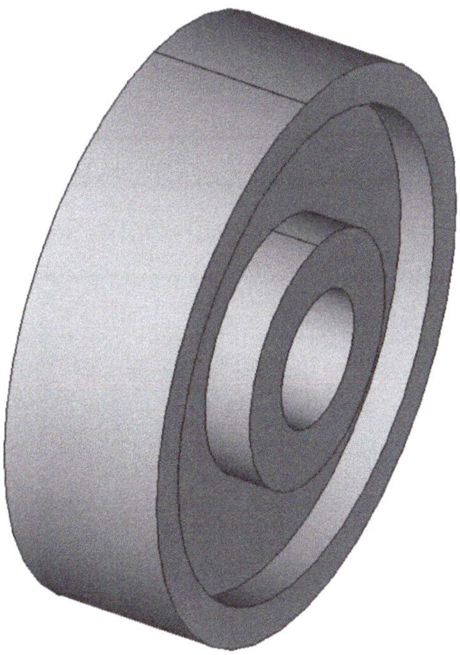

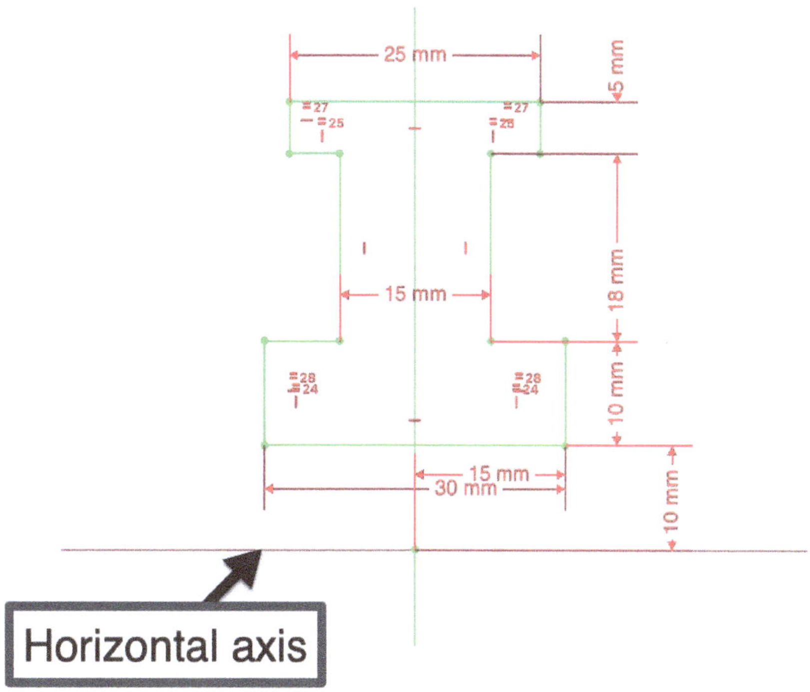

After completing the sketch, click the **Revolution**  icon on the **Part Design** toolbar (or) click **Part Design > Create an additive feature > Revolution**; the sketch profile is selected automatically. Next, you have to select the axis of revolution from the **Axis** drop-down available on the **Tasks** tab of the **Combo View** panel. You can select the Vertical sketch axis, Horizontal sketch axis, Construction line, or Base X, Y, or Z axes. You can also select a part edge or other reference element using the **Select reference** option available in the **Axis** drop-down.

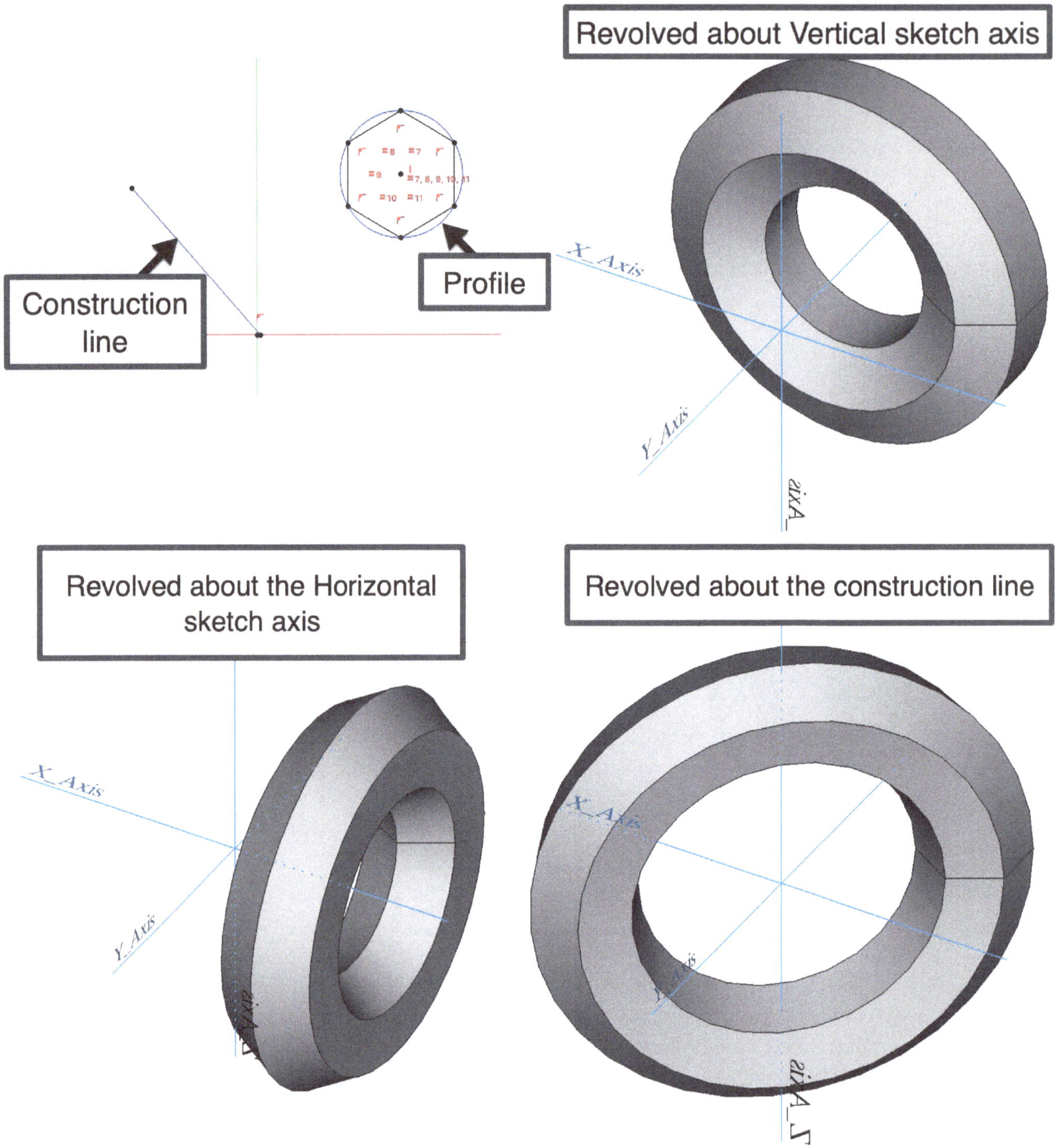
Revolved about Vertical sketch axis
Construction line
Profile
X_Axis
Y_Axis
Revolved about the Horizontal sketch axis
Revolved about the construction line
X_Axis
Y_Axis
X_Axis

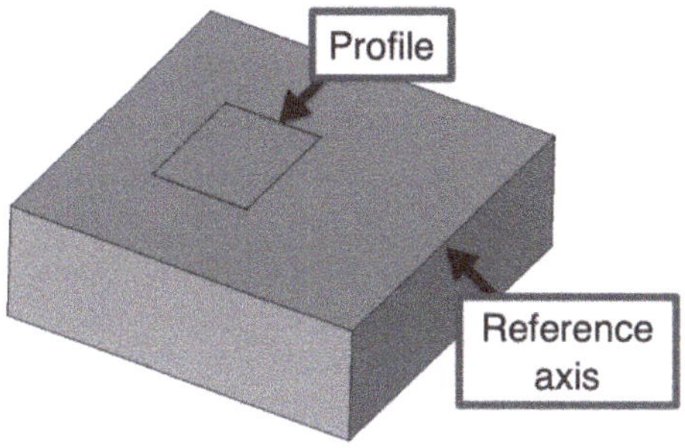

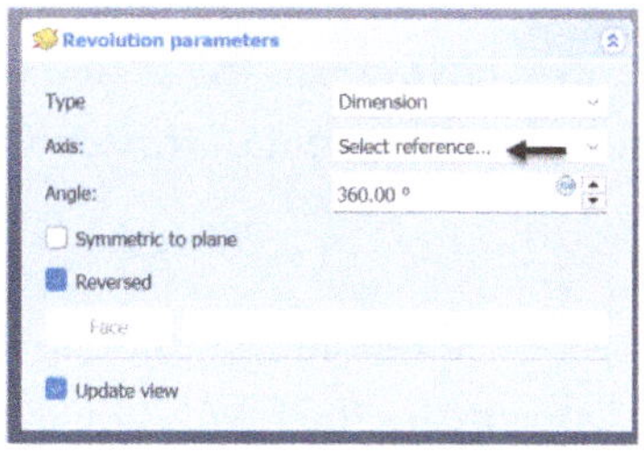

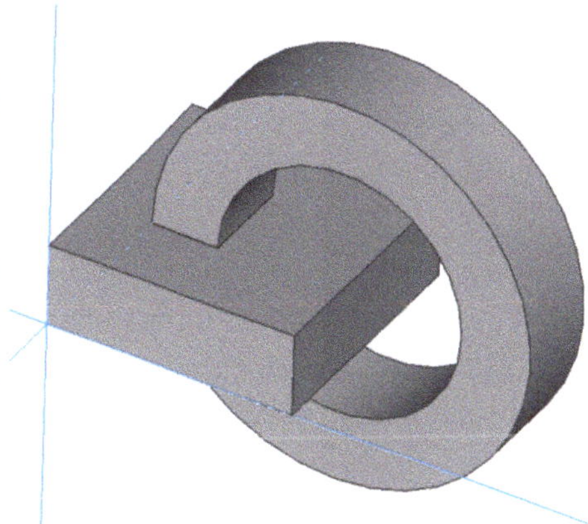

Next, you need to type-in a value in the **Angle** box. Check the **Reversed** option, if you want to reverse the direction of revolution.

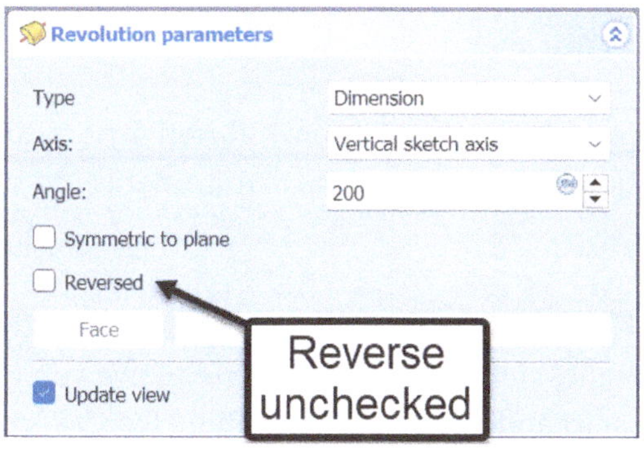

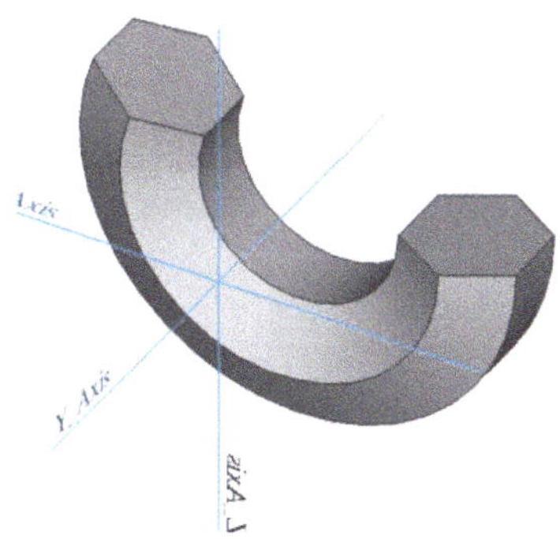

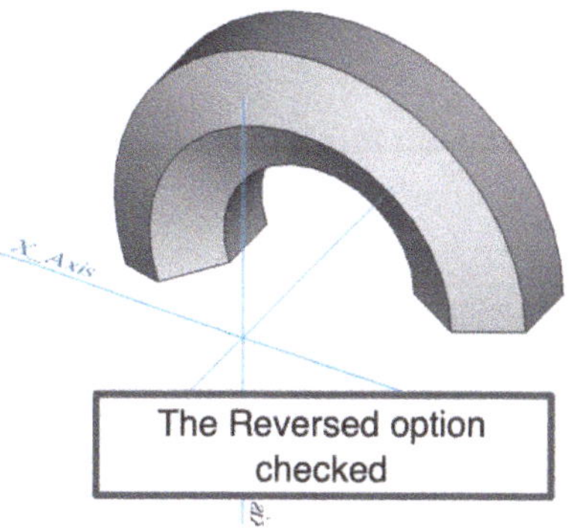

In addition to that, you can check the **Symmetric to plane** option to revolve the sketch symmetrically on both sides of the sketch plane.

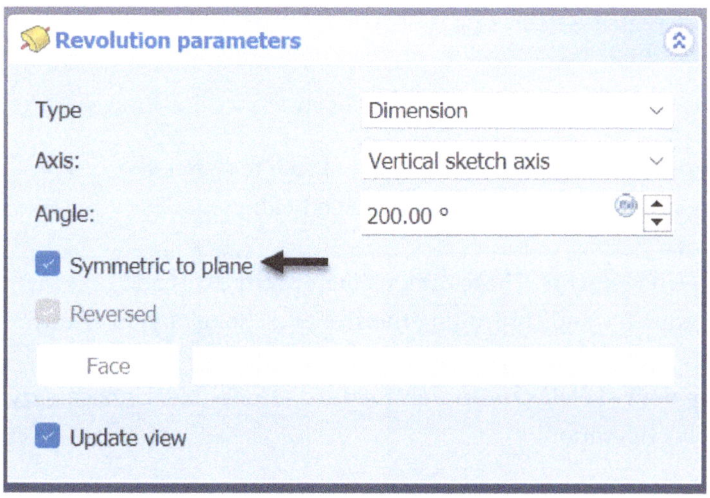

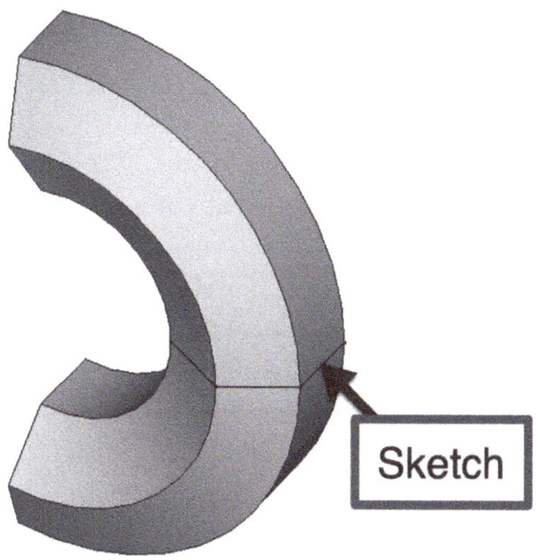

The Type drop-down on the **Revolution parameters** section has four options: **Dimension**, **To Last**, **To first**, **Up to face**, and **Two dimensions**.

Dimension:
The **Dimension** option lets you set a specific angle for the revolution. You can manually input the desired angle, such as 90°, 180°, or 360°, to control how far the 2D sketch revolves around the chosen axis. This option is ideal when you need precise control over the extent of the revolution.

To Last:
The **To Last** option automatically extends the revolution until it reaches the last possible face or surface in the design. It calculates the required angle to ensure the revolution extends to the furthest boundary of the model, making it useful for creating features that span the entire length of the geometry.

To First:
The **To First** option stops the revolution when it encounters the first face or surface in the design. It adjusts the angle automatically to ensure the revolution ends at the first intersecting geometry, providing a quick way to limit the revolution to a specific boundary.

Up to Face:
The **Up to Face** option allows you to select a specific face or surface where the revolution will stop. By choosing a target face, you can precisely control where the revolution ends, ensuring the feature aligns perfectly with your design requirements.

Two Dimensions:
The **Two Dimensions** option enables you to define two separate angles for the revolution. This allows you to create more complex shapes by specifying different angles for the start and end of the revolution. It's particularly useful for creating asymmetric or partially revolved features with greater flexibility.

Click **OK** on the **Tasks** panel to complete the *Revolved* feature.

Best Practices:

Start with a Proper Sketch: Kick off your design by creating a 2D sketch on the plane where you intend to form your revolved feature. Make sure this sketch is well-defined and accurately represents the intended cross-section of your revolving feature.

Use Construction Geometry: Employ construction lines or centerlines within your sketch to define the axis of rotation. This step ensures that your revolved feature turns out symmetric and correctly aligned.

Add Dimensions: Never skip dimensioning your sketch elements. These dimensions specify sizes and relationships, playing a pivotal role in defining the geometry and controlling the size and shape of your feature.

Keep Sketch Simple: Simplicity is key. Strive to keep your sketches as straightforward as possible. Unnecessary lines and points might lead to errors during the revolve operation.

Check for Overlaps: Be diligent in inspecting your sketch for potential overlaps. Overlapping elements can cause issues during the revolve operation.

Cautions:

Overly Complex Sketches: While revolving sketches are potent, overly complex sketches can lead to performance hiccups and a higher likelihood of errors. If your sketch becomes too intricate, consider simplifying it or breaking it into smaller, more manageable features.

Tangency and Continuity: It's vital to maintain tangency and continuity along the axis of rotation. Any gaps or overlaps in your sketch could lead to less-than-ideal results.

Avoid Self-Intersecting Geometries: Self-intersecting sketch elements should be a no-go. These can spell trouble during the revolve operation, so ensure your sketch is free from any self-intersecting entities.

Tips:

Leverage Symmetry: Whenever possible, leverage the symmetry of your sketch to your advantage. Doing so simplifies your model, reducing the workload and making future modifications a breeze.

Experiment with Angle: FreeCAD grants you the freedom to specify the angle of revolution. Experiment with different angles to understand how they influence your model, especially when crafting parts with partial rotations.

Preview the Revolve: Before committing to the final revolved feature, check how your feature will appear. This helps you to catch any issues before the operation is set in stone.

Groove: FreeCAD offers more than just creating solid features with revolving sketches. You can also employ the "Groove" feature to hollow out or create holes within your components.

External Geometry

This command projects the edges of a 3D geometry onto a sketch plane. To do this, select a plane or model face and click the **Create sketch** icon on the **Part Design Helper** toolbar. Next, click the **Create external Geometry** icon on the **Sketcher tools** toolbar. Click on the edges of the model geometry. Click **OK** on the **Project** dialog to project the edge on to the sketch plane.

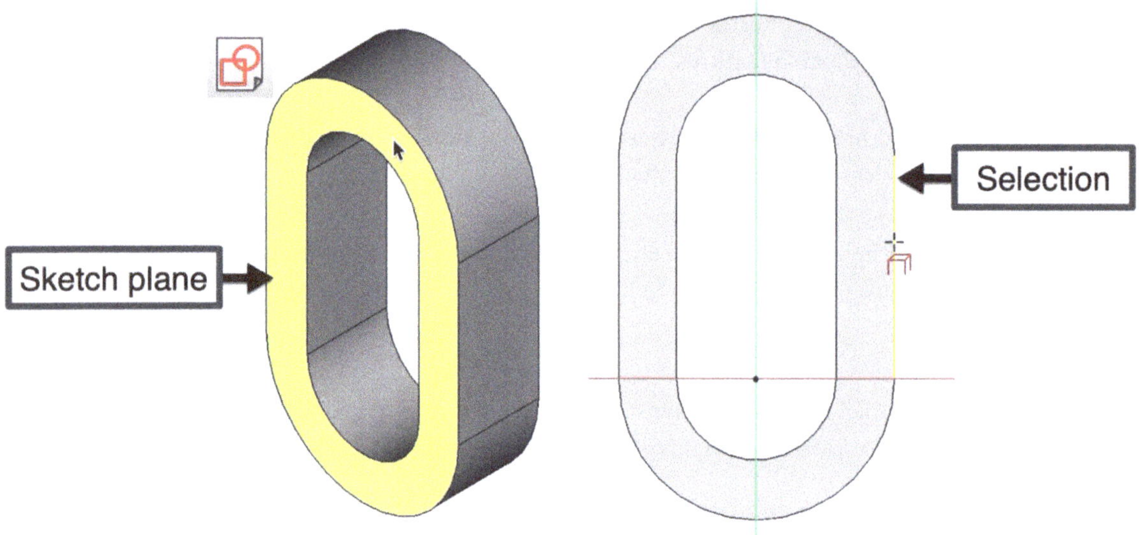

The projected element will be red in color and can be used to connect the sketch with the existing geometry. For example, create a rectangle and apply the **Coincident** constraint between the vertex of the rectangle and the endpoint of the projected element.

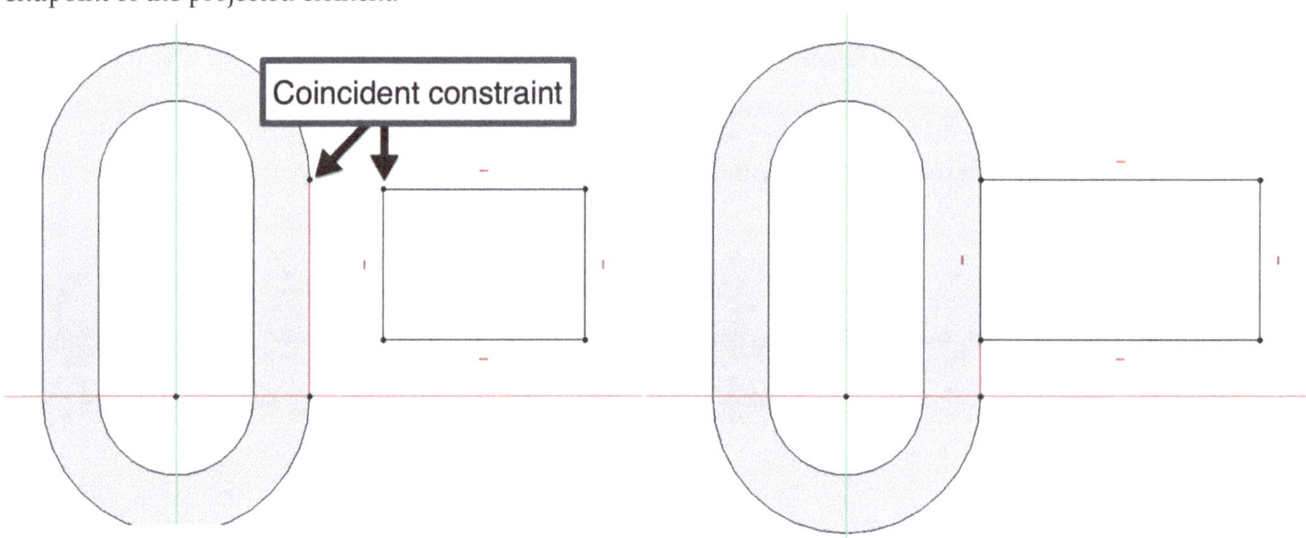

Pocket

This command removes material from the geometry by extruding a sketch. It functions on the same lines as the **Pad** command. Draw a sketch on a plane or a model face. Next, click the **Pocket**  icon on the **Part Design Modeling** toolbar (or) click **Part Design > Create a subtractive feature > Pocket** on the Menu bar; the sketch is selected automatically. On the **Pocket parameters** section, type in a value in the **Length** box; the pocket's preview appears in the direction normal to the sketch. Click **OK** to create the pocket feature.

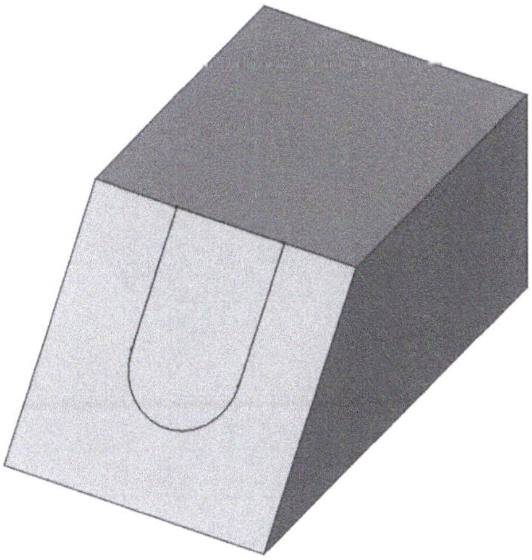

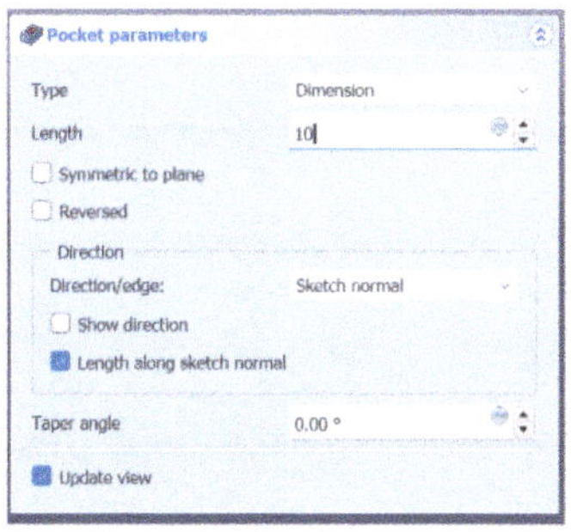

You can change the direction of the pocket feature. To do this, select **Direction/edge > Select reference** from the combo view panel. Next, select an edge or sketched element from the graphics window. Next, check the Reversed option, if the pocket feature is not displayed. Click **OK** to create the pocket feature.

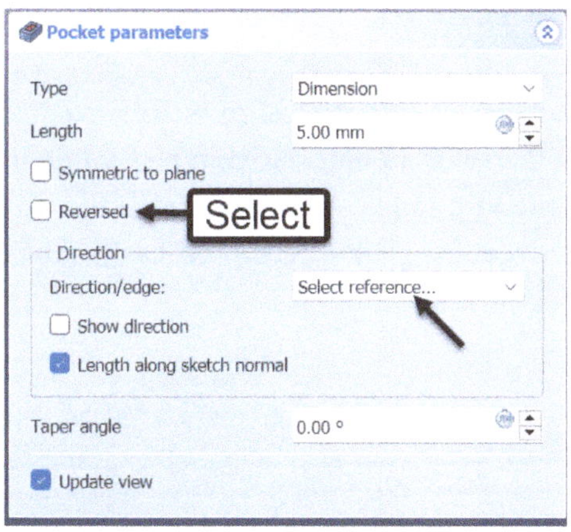

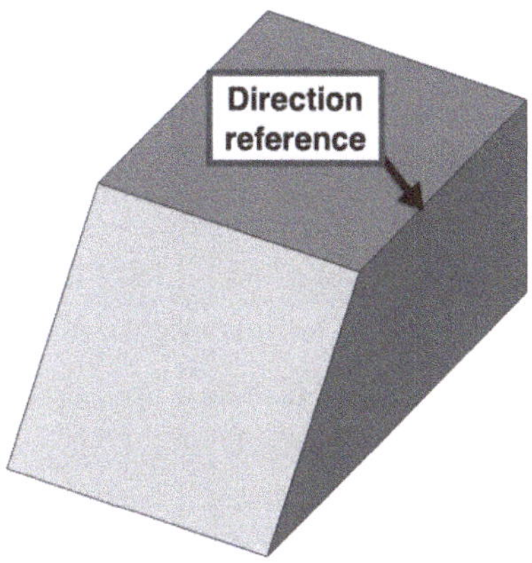

The Groove command

This command removes material from the geometry by revolving a sketch about an axis. It functions in a way similar to the **Revolution** command. Draw a sketch on a plane or a model face. Next, create an axis using the **Datum line** command. Click the **Groove** icon on the **Part Design Modeling** toolbar (or) click **Part Design > Create a subtractive feature > Revolution** on the Menu bar; the sketch is selected automatically. Select the **Construction Line 1** from the **Axis** drop-down. Next, specify the revolution angle and click **OK** to complete the groove feature.

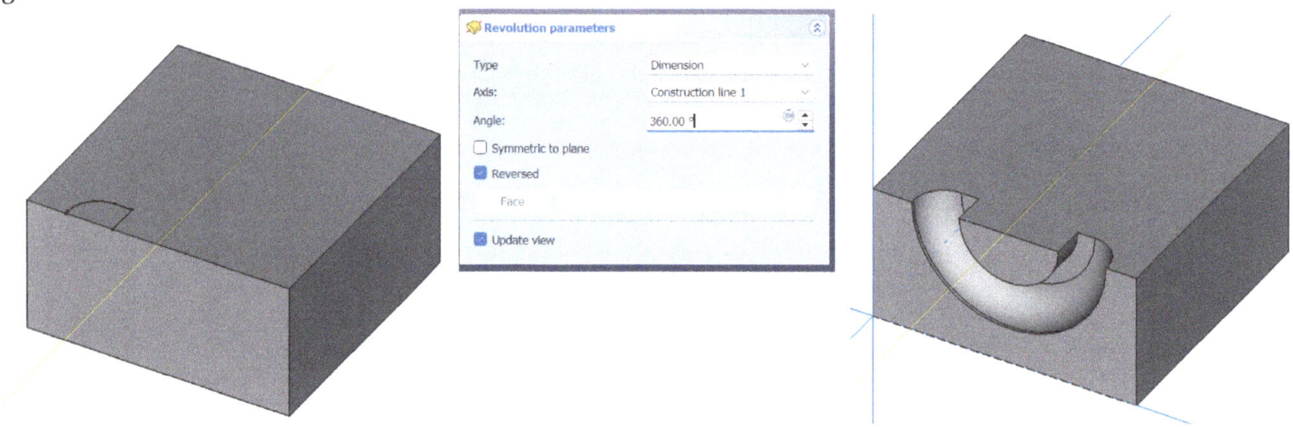

Planes

Planes are a specific type of element in FreeCAD 1.0, known as datum features. These features act as supports to your 3D geometry. Each time you start a new part file, FreeCAD 1.0 automatically creates default planes (XY, YZ, and XZ planes). Until now, you have learned to create sketches on any of the default planes. If you want to create sketches and geometry at locations other than default planes, you can create new planes manually. You can do this by using the **Create datum plane** command.

Creating a Parallel plane

Click the **Create datum plane** icon on the **Part Design Helper** toolbar (or) click **Part Design > Create a datum > Create a datum plane** on the menu bar. Click on a flat face of goemetry or a plane. Next, type a value in the **In z-direction** box on the **Tasks** tab of the **Combo View** panel. Check the **Flip sides** option located at the bottom of the **Combo View** panel to change the side on which the plane is created. Click **OK** on the **Tasks** tab of the **Combo View** panel to create a plane parallel to the selected face or another plane.

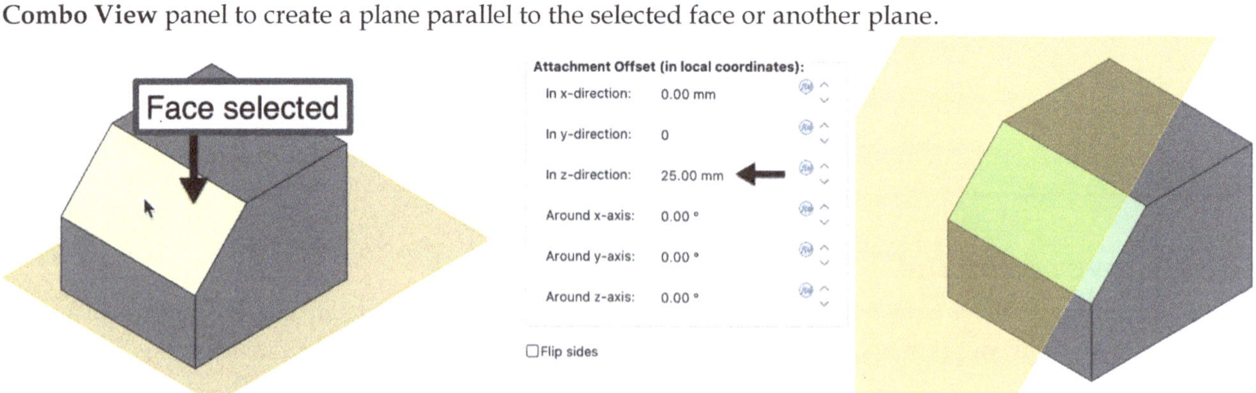

Inertia 2-3

Click the **Create datum plane** icon on the **Part Design Helper** toolbar (or) click **Part Design > Create a datum > Create a datum plane** on the menu bar. Select an edge from the model geometry and select the **Inertia 2-3** option from the **Attachment mode** section; the plane is created perpendicular to the selected edge and positioned at the midpoint.

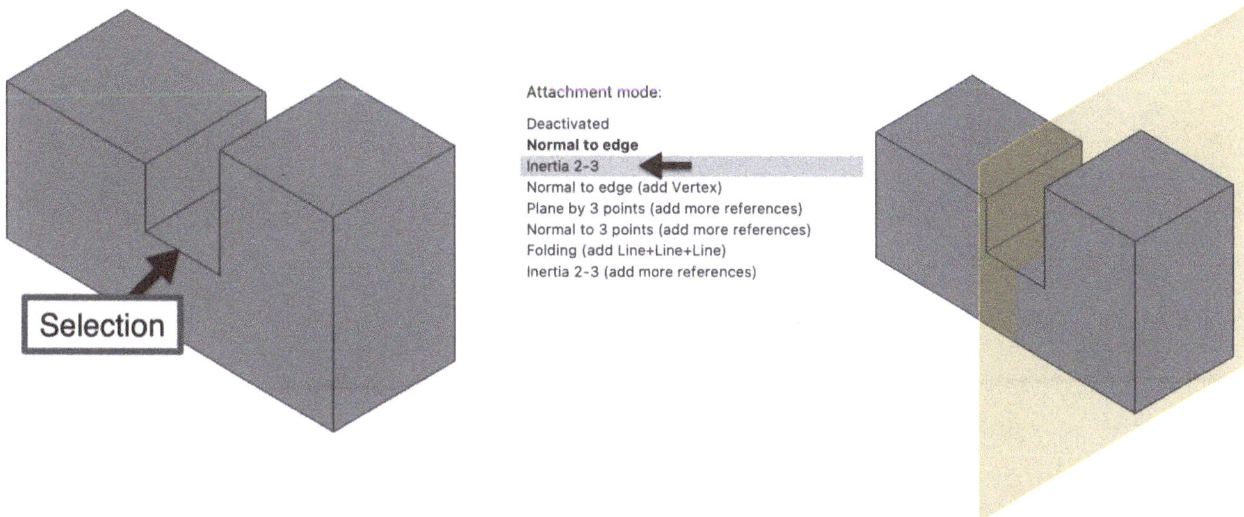

Plane at Angle

Click the **Create datum plane** icon on the **Part Design Helper** toolbar. Click on a face of the part geometry. Next, type in a value in the **Around x-axis** box; the plane is rotated at the specified angle around the x-axis of the selected face. You can also rotate the plane around the Y-axis of the selected face by entering a value in the **Around y-axis** box.

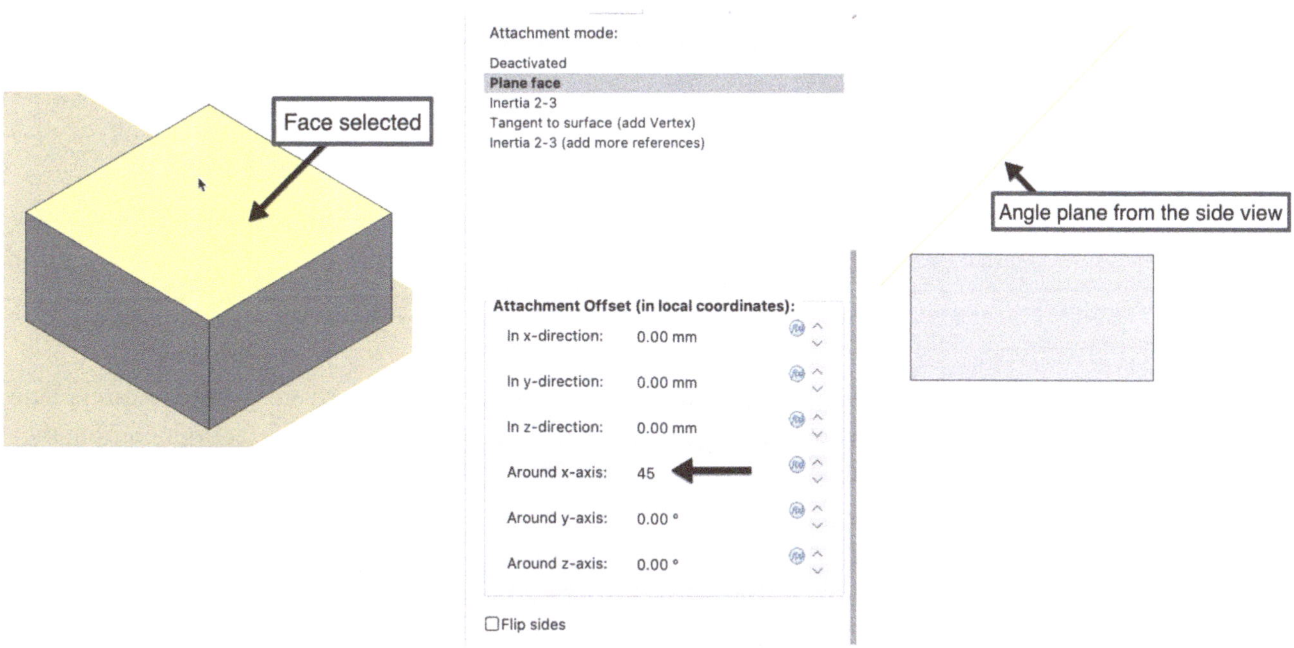

Plane by 3 Points

This option creates a plane passing through three points. Activate the **Create a datum plane** command and select three points from the model geometry. Next, select the **Plane by 3 Points** option from the **Attachment mode** section and click **OK**. The plane will be created, passing through the selected points.

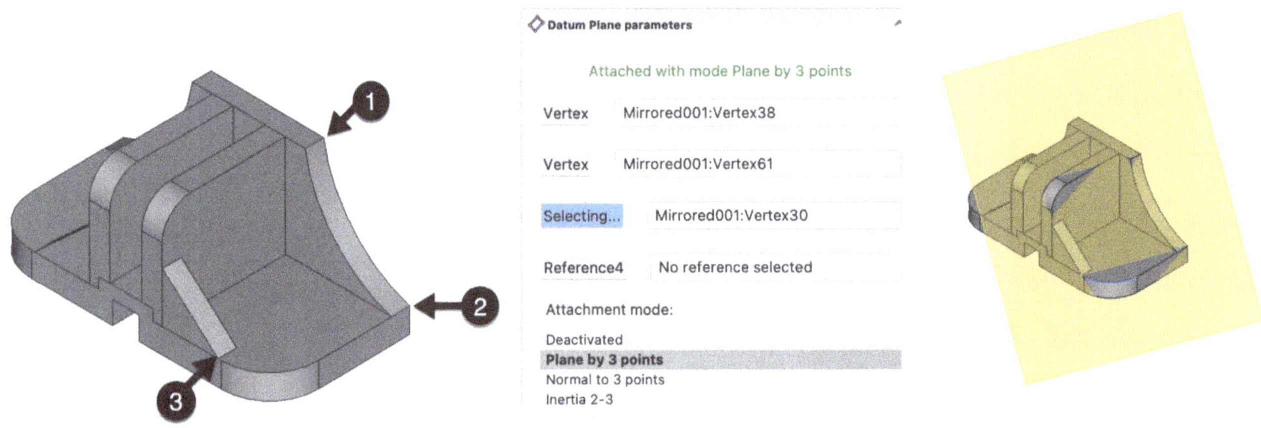

Normal to 3 Points

This option creates a plane normal three points. Activate the **Create a datum plane** command and select three points from the model geometry. Next, select the **Normal to 3 Points** option from the **Attachment mode** section and click **OK**. The plane will be created, normal to the selected points.

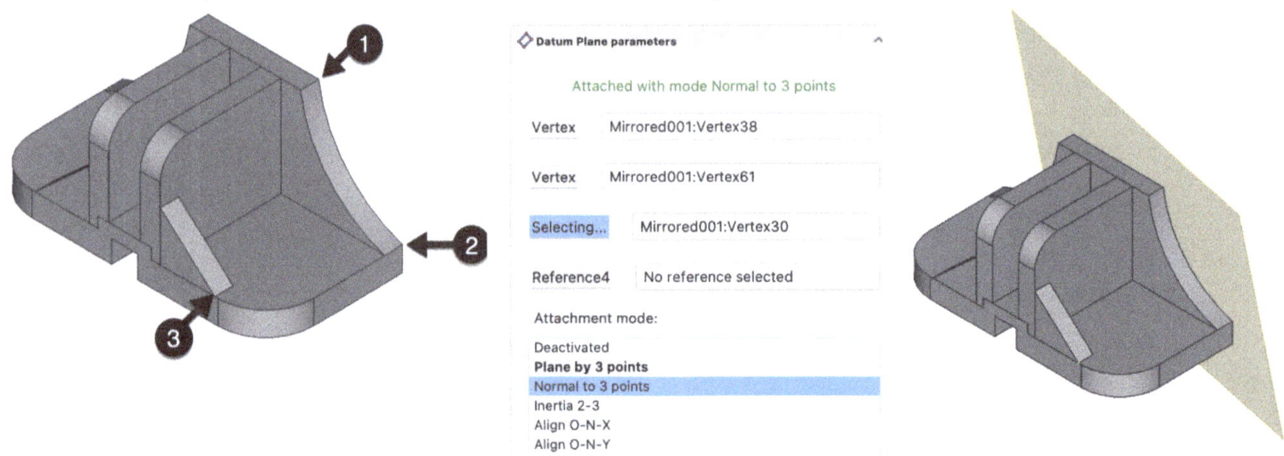

Tangent to Surface

This option creates a plane passing through a point and tangent to a curved face. Activate **Create a datum plane** command and select a curved face. Next, select a point or vertex. Select the **Tangent to Surface** option from the **Attachment mode** section and click **OK**. A plane tangent to the curved face passing through a point will be created.

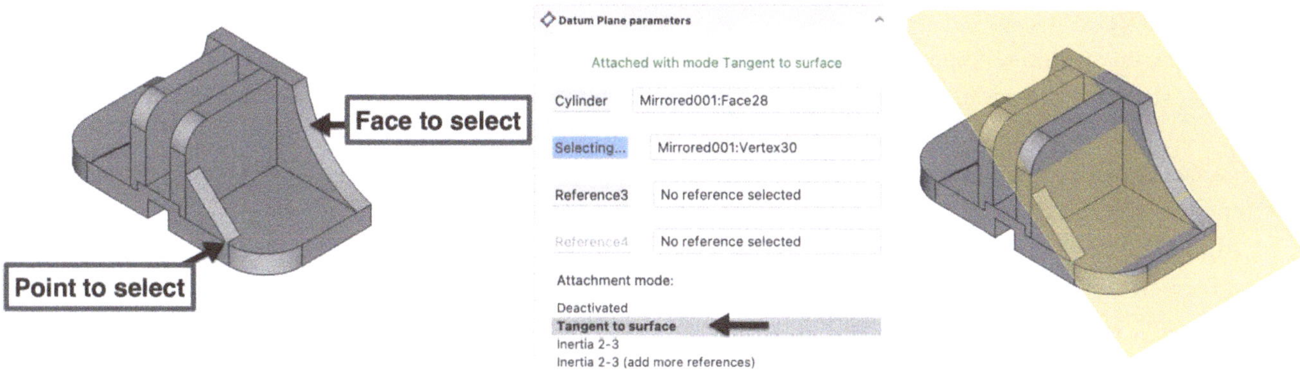

Normal to edge

This option creates a plane, which will be normal to a line, curve, or edge. Activate the **Create a datum plane** command and select an edge, line, curve, arc, or circle. Next, you need to specify the location of the plane on the selected path. To do this, select a point from the graphics window. Next, select the **Normal to edge** option from the **Attachment mode** section and click **OK**. A plane normal to the edge will be created.

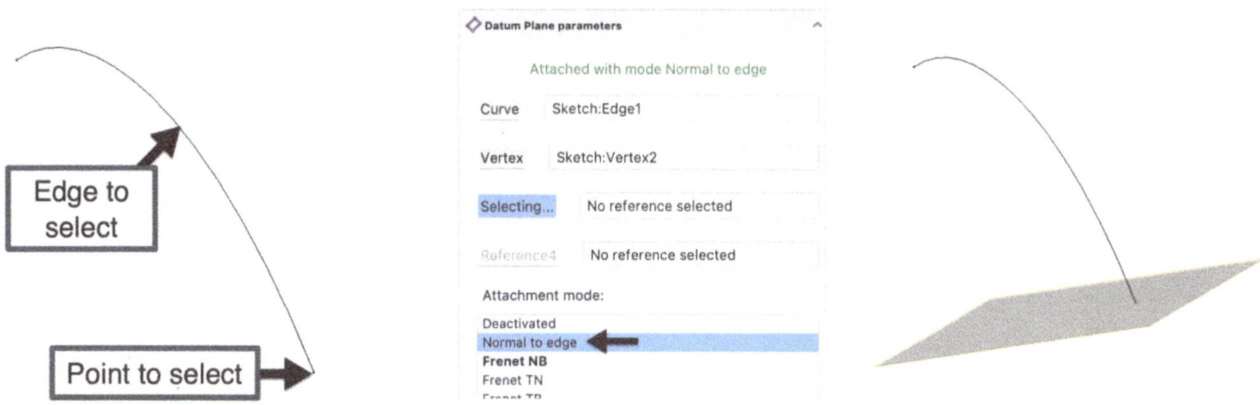

Revolution section

This option creates a plane, which will be perpendicular to a circular edge. Activate the **Create a datum plane** command and select circular edge. Next, you need to specify the location of the plane by selecting a point from the graphics window. Select the **Revolution section** option from the **Attachment mode** section and click **OK**. A plane normal to the edge will be created.

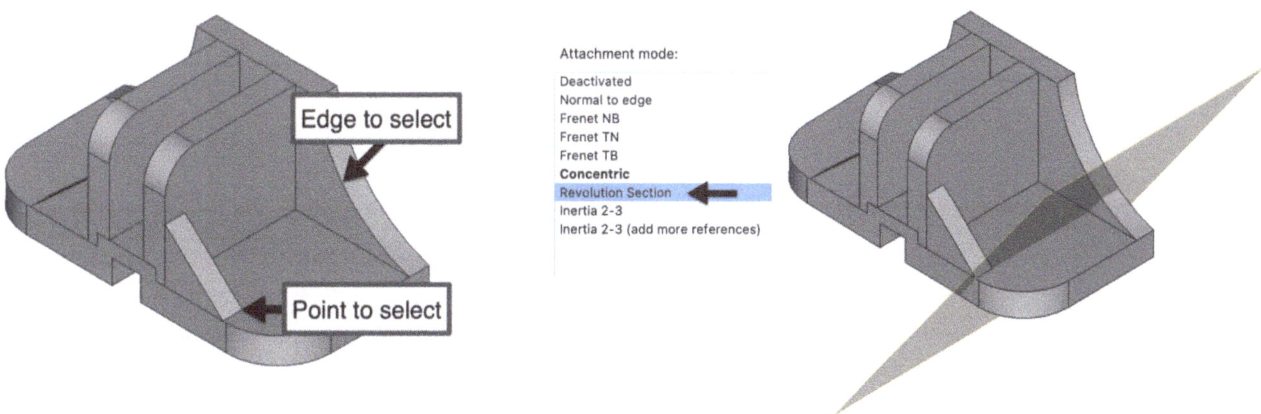

Best Practices:

1. **Naming Conventions:** When working with datum planes, it's a smart practice to assign clear and descriptive names. This makes it easier to identify and manipulate them, especially as your models become more complex. Meaningful names like "TopView" or "SideSymmetry" can go a long way in keeping your work organized. You can rename a datum plane by simply right-clicking on it in the **Model** tree and selecting the **Rename** option.
2. **Utilize Default Planes:** FreeCAD offers standard datum planes, such as the XY, XZ, and YZ planes. These act as excellent starting points for your design. Incorporating them when applicable ensures consistency in your models and saves you time on recreating basic reference planes.
3. **Symmetry:** In cases where your components or features exhibit symmetry, consider creating datum planes to simplify your model. Symmetrical datum planes assist in maintaining balance and precision, resulting in more efficient designs.

Cautions:

1. **Avoid Overuse:** While datum planes are valuable, it's important to strike a balance. Creating an excessive number of datum planes can clutter your model, making it harder to manage. Only generate datum planes that are essential for your design.
2. **Consistent Naming:** Ensure that your datum plane names are not only clear but also follow a consistent pattern. Inconsistent naming can lead to confusion, especially when collaborating with others. A shared naming convention ensures everyone is on the same page.
3. **Dependency Awareness:** Changes to datum planes can ripple through your model and affect dependent sketches and features. Whenever you modify datum planes, be sure to review your model and update any elements that rely on them.

Tip:

Visibility Control: Datum planes can be toggled on and off, which aids in decluttering your workspace. This is particularly helpful when working on specific parts of your model, allowing you to focus on one aspect at a time. To turn ON or OFF the visibility of a datum plane. To do this, select it from the **Model** tab of the **Combo View** panel and click the **View** tab located at the bottom. On the **View** tab, select **Visibility > false** to turn OFF its visibility.

Datum Line

A datum line is another type of construction element that helps you in building a 3D model. For example, you can use a datum line to create a revolved feature. You can create various types of axes in FreeCAD 1.0. They are discussed next.

1st principal axis

This option creates an axis through a cylinder or cone or torus. Click the **Create a datum line**  icon on the **Part Design Helper** toolbar (or) click **Part Design > Create a datum > Create a datum line** on the menu bar. Next, select a round face, cone, or torus. Select the **1st principal axis** option from the **Attachment mode** section. You can also create a datum line perpendicular to flat face.

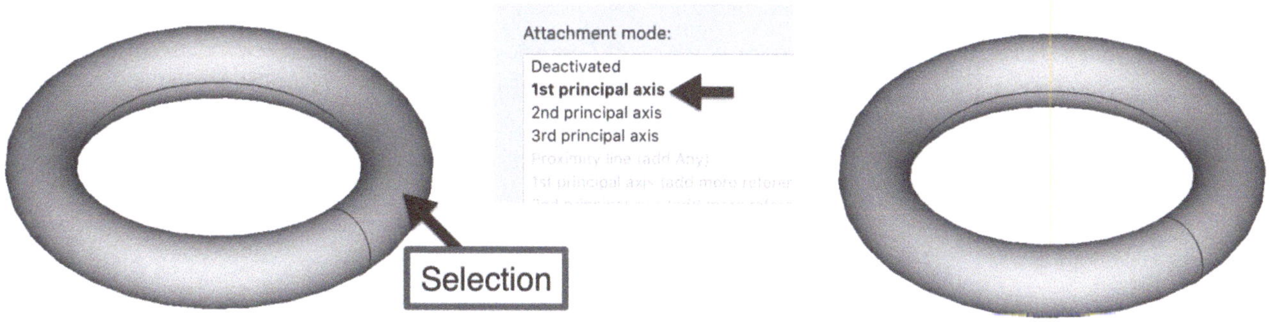

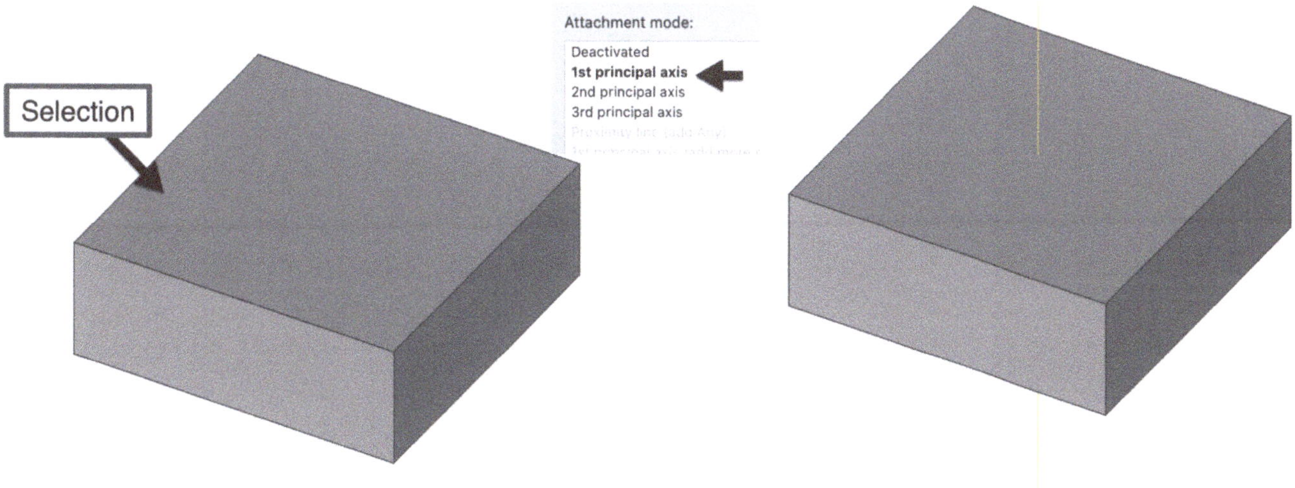

Through Two Points

This option creates a datum line passing through two selected points. Activate **Create a new datum line** command and select two points. Select two points or vertices, and then select the **Through two points** option from the **Attachment mode** section.

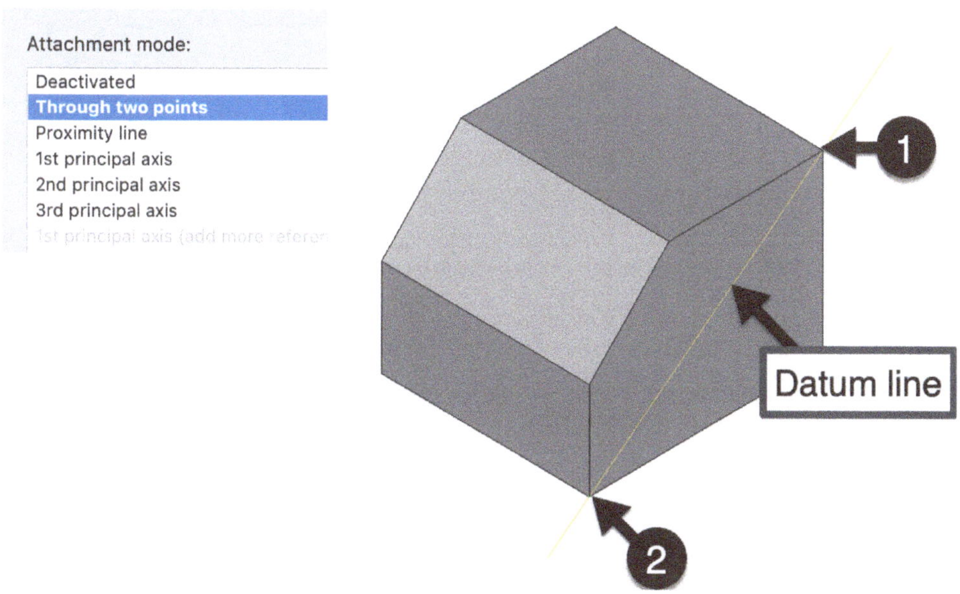

Normal to surface

This option creates an axis, which will be perpendicular to a face and point. Activate **Create a new datum line** command and select a face. Next, click on a point to define the location of the axis. Select the **Normal to surface** option from the **Attachment mode** section.

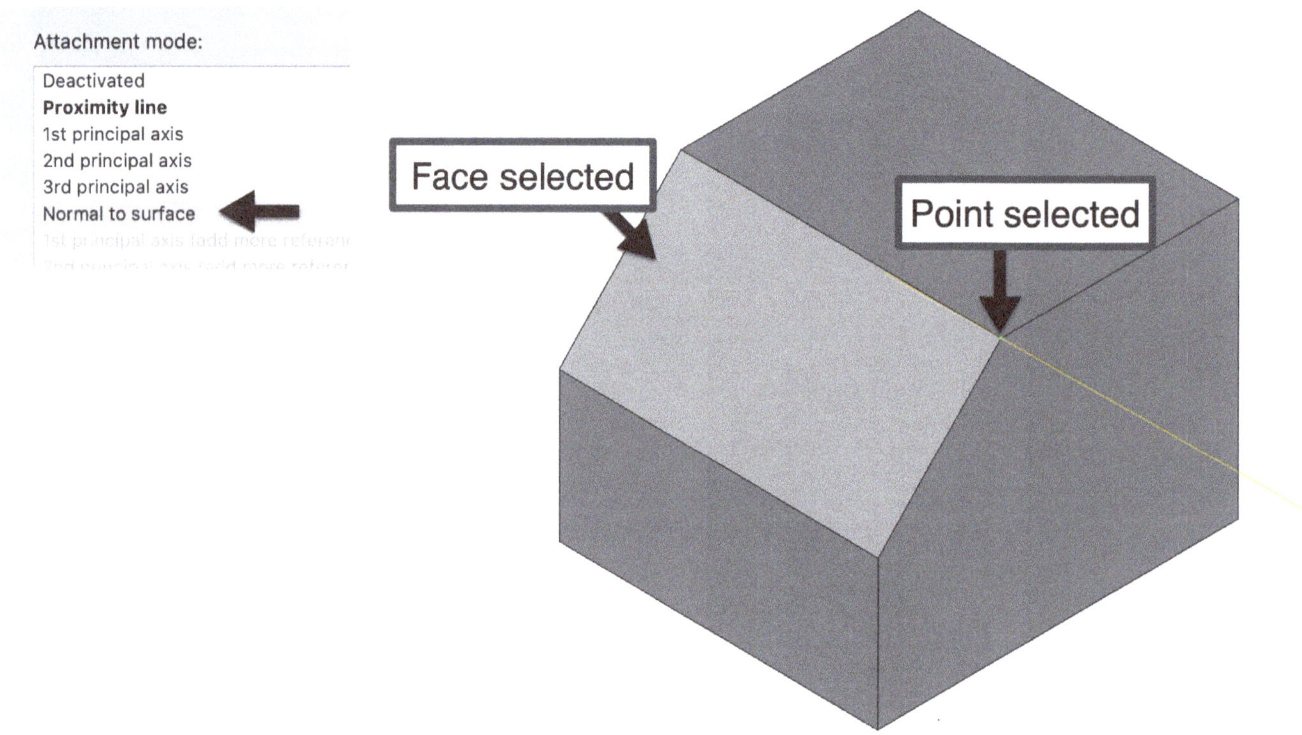

Datum Point

Points are another type of construction element in addition to planes and axes. The options to create construction points are explained next.

Center of mass

This option creates a datum point at the center of mass of a body. Click the **Create a new datum point** icon on the **Part Design Helper** toolbar (or) click **Part Design > Create a datum > Create a datum point** on the menu bar. Next, select a solid body and select the **Center of mass** option from the **Attachment mode** section.

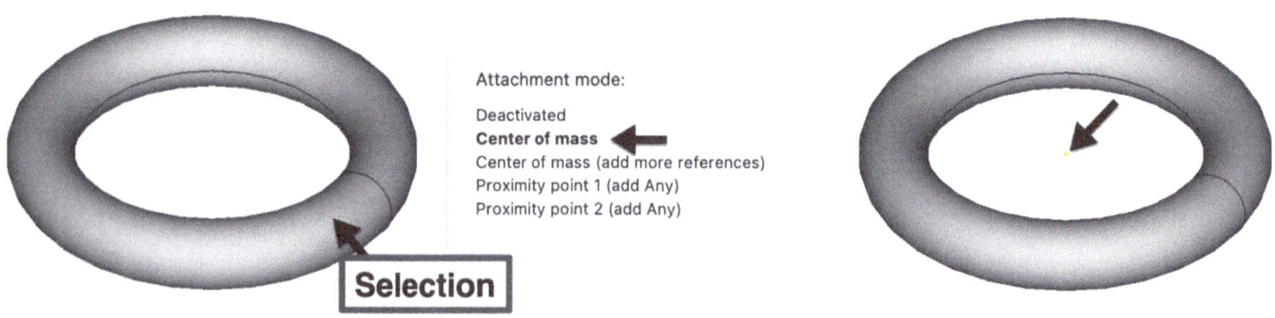

Vertex

This option creates a datum point at a selected point or vertex. Click the **Create a new datum point** icon on the **Part Design Helper** toolbar and select a point or vertex of the model. Next, select the **Vertex** option from the **Attachment mode** section.

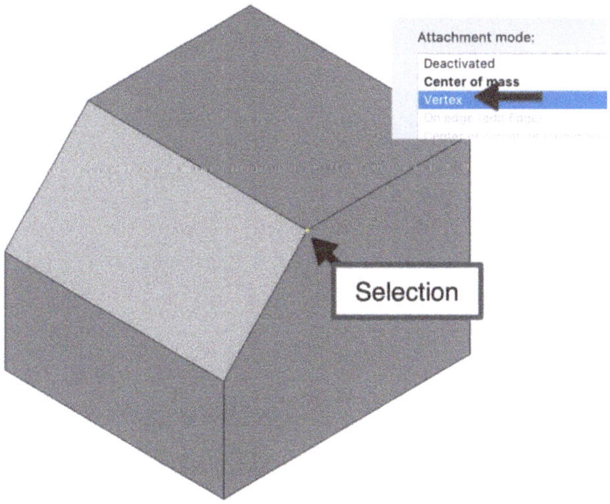

Additional options of the Pad and Pocket commands

The **Pad** and **Pocket** commands have some additional options to create complex features of a 3D geometry.

Extent Type

The **Type** drop-down has five options to define the end limit of the *Pad* feature. These options are **Dimension, To Last, To first, Up to face,** and **Two Dimensions**.

The **Dimension** option pads the sketch up to the specified distance. On the **Tasks** panel, select **Dimension** from the **Type** drop-down. Next, specify the distance in the **Length** box.

The **Two dimensions** option pads the sketch in both the directions normal to the sketch plane. Select this option from the **Type** drop-down. Next, enter values in the **Length** and **2nd length** boxes.

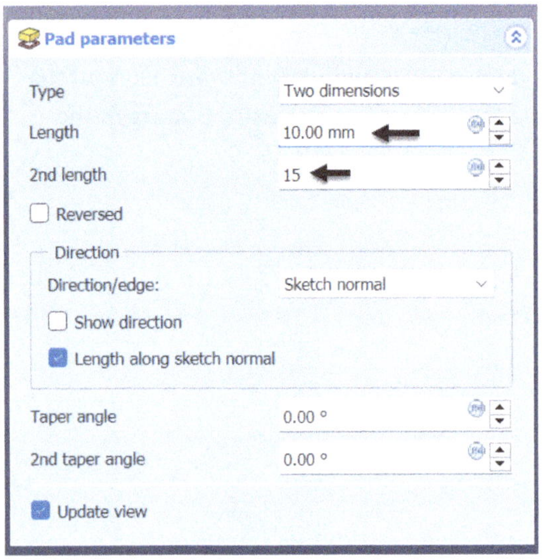

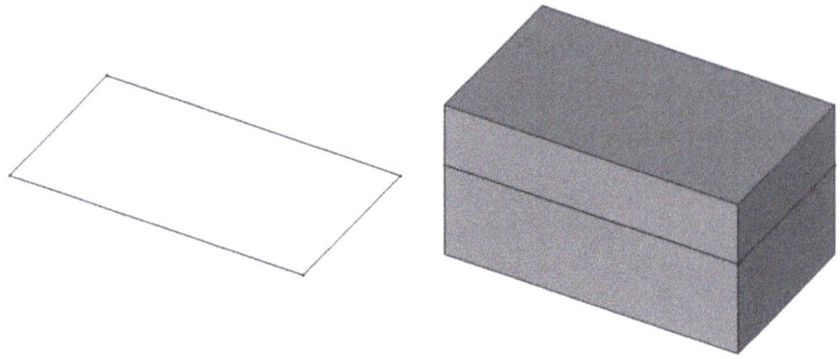

The **Up to face** option extrudes the sketch up to a selected face. On the **Tasks** tab of the **Combo View** panel, select **Up to face** from the **Type** drop-down (check the **Reversed** option if nothing is displayed in the graphics window). Next, select the face or plane; the sketch will be extruded up to the selected face or plane.

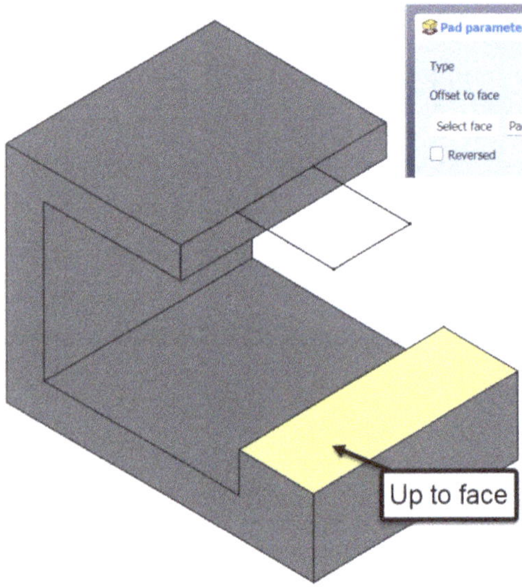

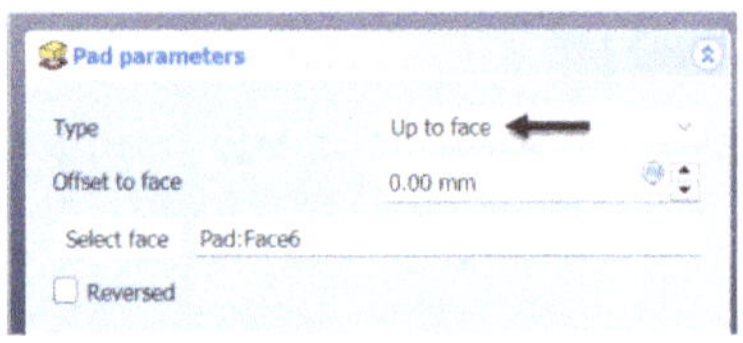

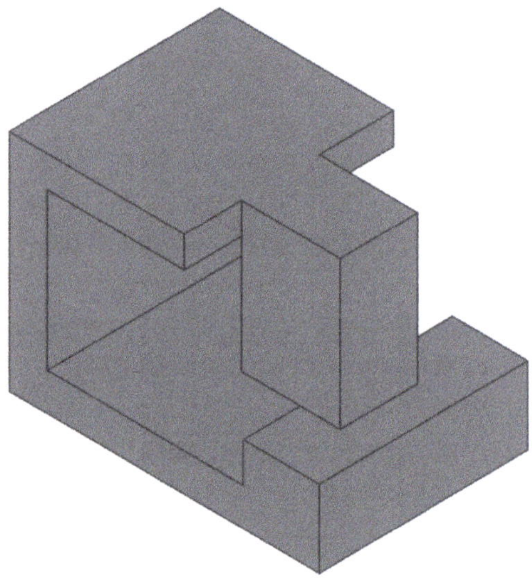

You can enter a value in the **Offset to face** box to offset the extrusion from the selected face.

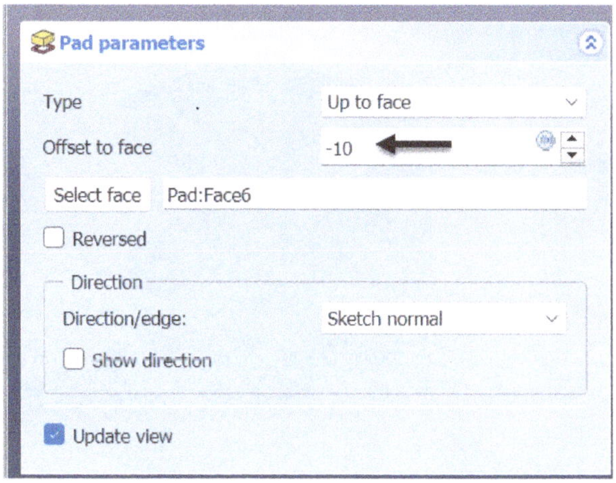

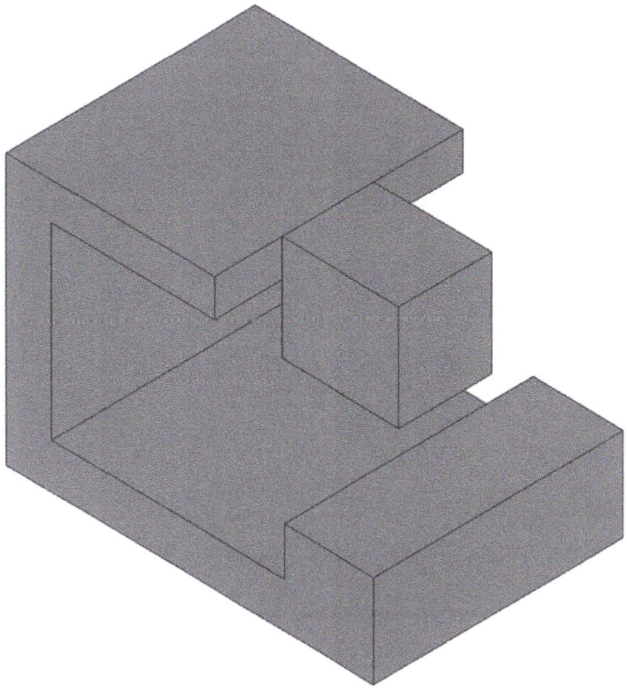

The **To first** option extrudes the sketch up to the next surface. Select **To first** from the **Type** drop-down. Check the **Reversed** option to reverse the direction.

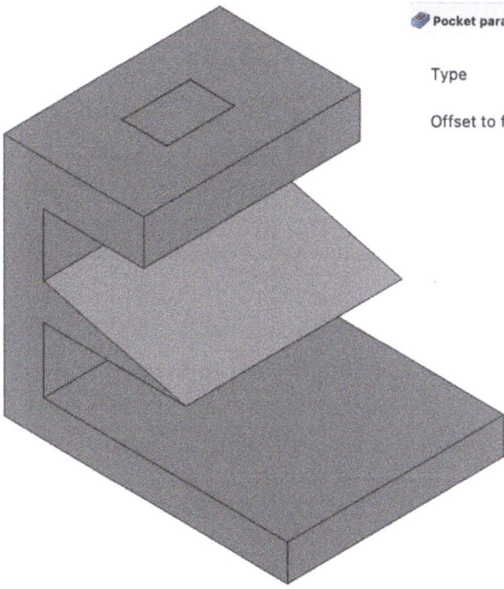

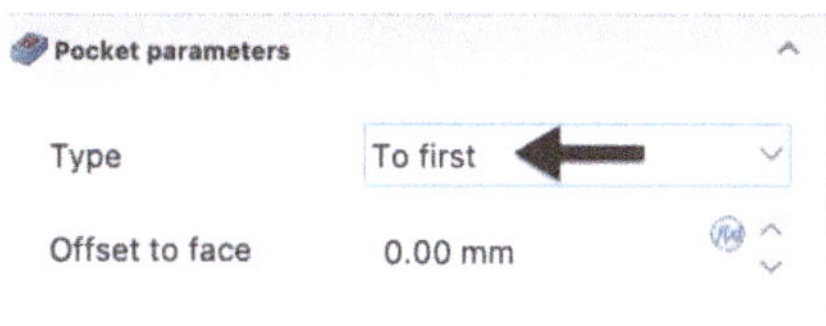

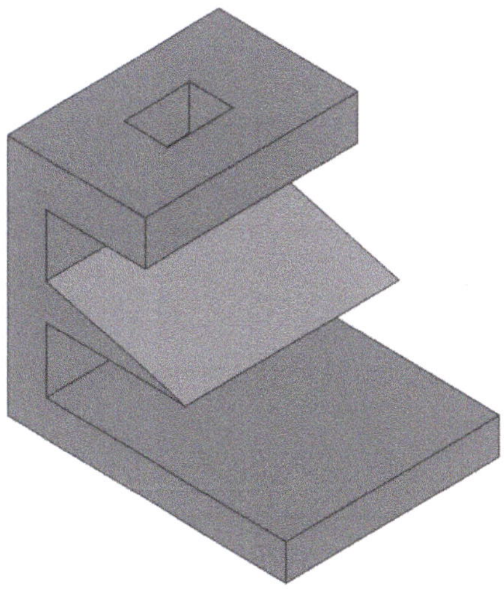

The **Through All** option (the **To Last** option for the **Pad** feature) extrudes the sketch throughout the 3D geometry. Select **Through all** from the **Type** drop-down.

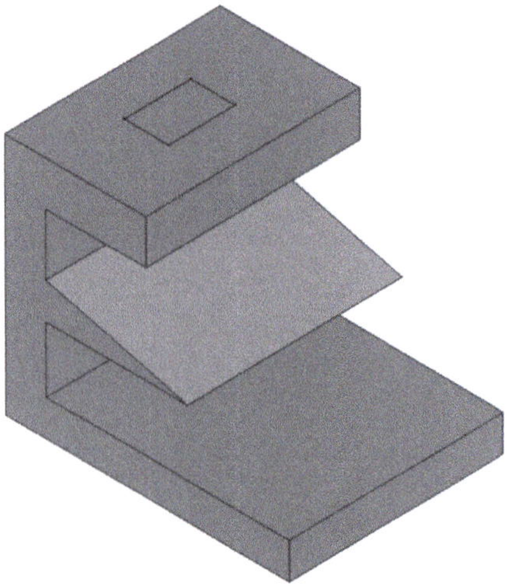

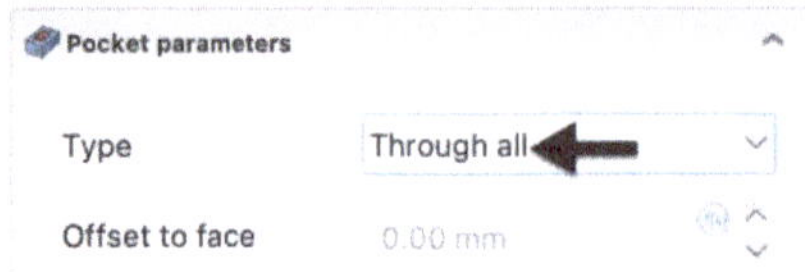

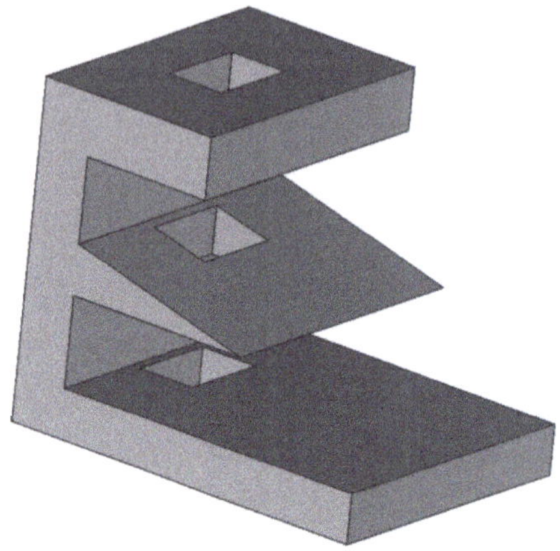

Adding Taper to the Pad Feature

The **Taper angle** box will help you to apply taper to the extrusion. On the **Combo View** panel, type-in the angle value in the **Taper angle** box. After specifying the taper angle, click the **Type** drop-down and select anyone of the direction icons.

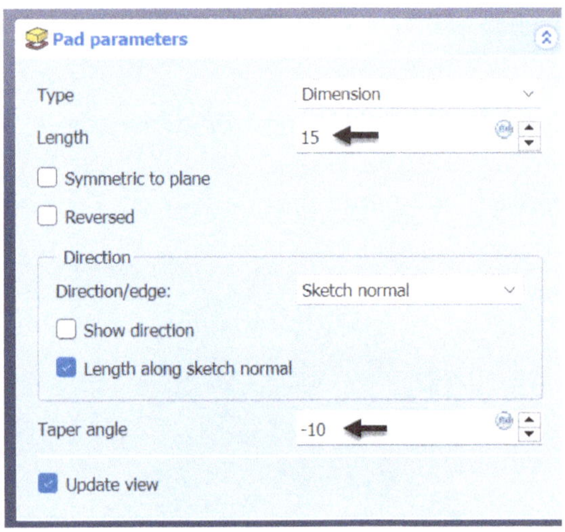

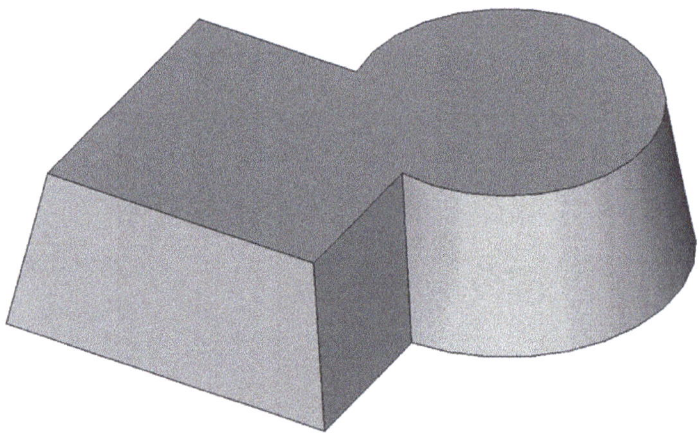

Select **Type > Two Dimensions** from the **Combo View** panel and specify the **2nd length** and **2nd taper angle** values.

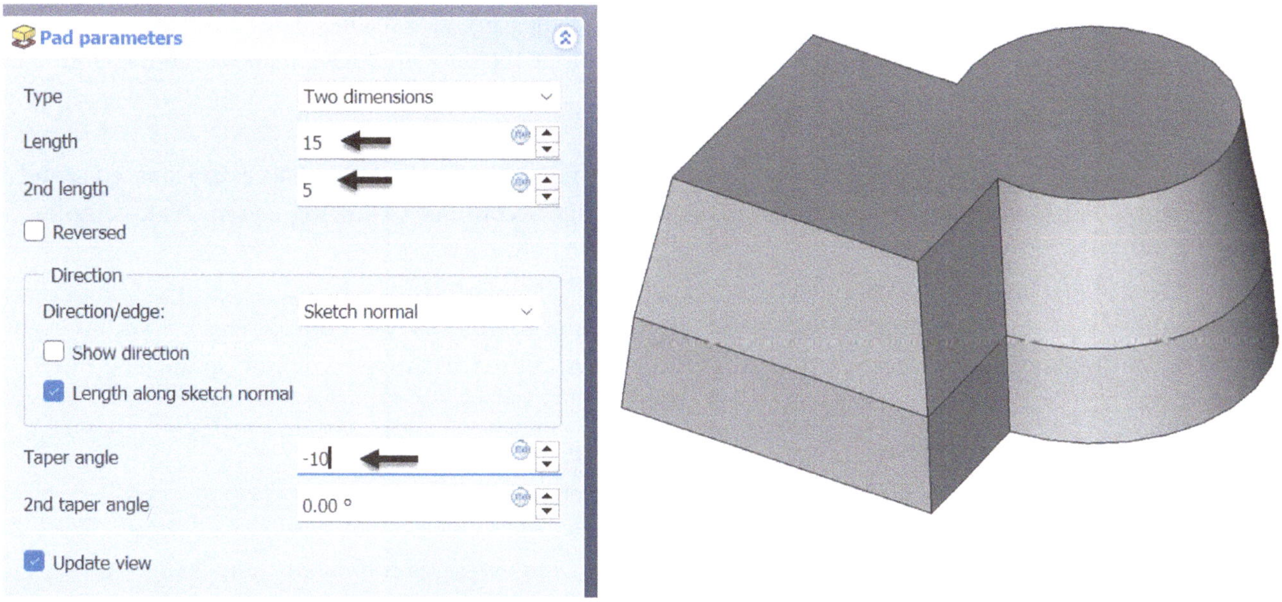

Select **Type > Dimension** and check the **Symmetric to plane** option. Next, type a value in the **Taper angle** box; the taper is applied to the extrusion on both sides of the sketch plane.

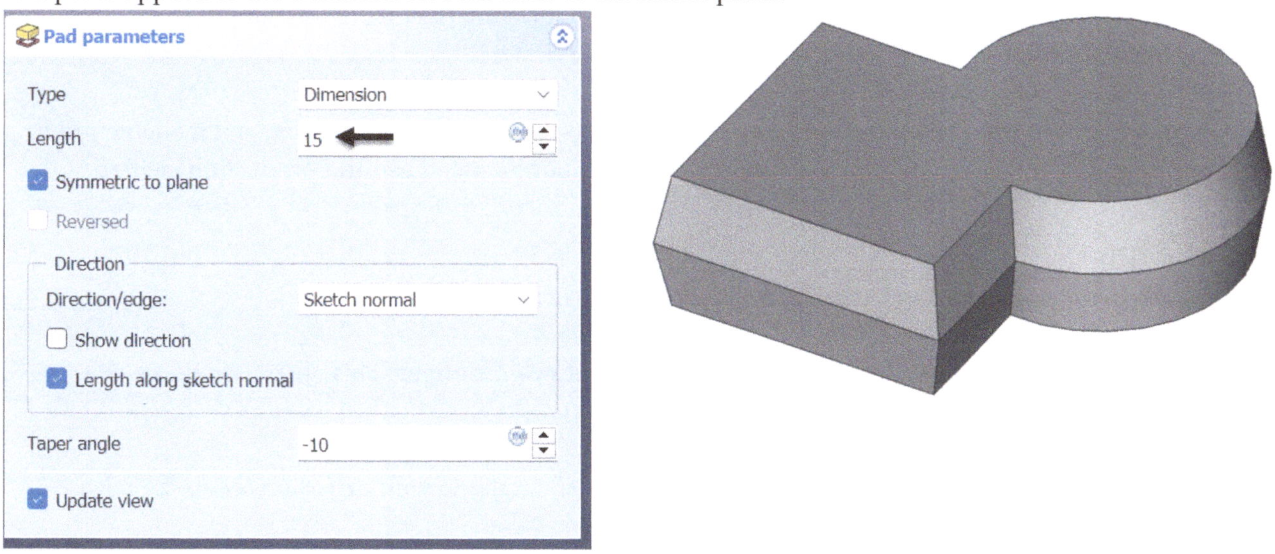

Click **OK** to complete the Pad feature.

Best Practices while Extruding Sketches

To ensure a smooth workflow in FreeCAD, follow these best practices:

1. Start with a Clear Sketch: Before diving into extrusions, make sure your initial 2D sketch is well-defined and accurately represents the shape you intend to create. Utilize dimensions and constraints to lock down essential aspects.

2. Sketch on Appropriate Planes: Select the suitable working plane for your sketches. The choice of the plane affects the orientation of your extrusion. It's often a good practice to begin with the XY plane and build from there.

3. Combine Features: Leverage FreeCAD's capability to combine various features, such as extrusions, cuts, and fillets. Consider how these features interact and plan your design accordingly, allowing you to create complex shapes.

4. Reevaluate as You Go: As your model gains more features and complexity, periodically reassess your design to ensure it continues to meet your requirements. This proactive approach can save you time in the long run.

Cautions to Keep in Mind

While exploring FreeCAD's capabilities, remember these cautionary points:

1. Avoid Over-Complexity: FreeCAD permits intricate designs, but excessive complexity may lead to performance issues and make your model challenging to work with. Strive for simplicity without compromising functionality.

2. Check for Intersecting Geometry: When extruding, be vigilant for intersecting or overlapping geometry. These issues can create problems in your model, especially in intricate designs.

3. Watch for Thin Features: Thin extrusions may pose problems, especially in 3D printing and manufacturing. Ensure your parts maintain a minimum thickness suitable for your intended use and production method.

Useful Tips

Consider these handy tips for an enhanced FreeCAD experience:

1. Use Symmetry: Whenever feasible, incorporate symmetry into your designs. This not only reduces your workload but also ensures balance in your design.

2. Utilize Draft Angles: If your part will be molded, adding draft angles to your extrusions eases the release of the part from the mold.

3. Experiment with Type Options: FreeCAD provides diverse extrusion options like "Up to face" or "To first." Experiment with these choices to achieve your desired results.

4. Use Reference Geometry: Employ reference geometry, such as planes, axes, and points, to accurately position and orient your sketches and extrusions. It simplifies the modeling process.

By following these practices, staying vigilant, and experimenting with the software's features, you'll be on your way to mastering FreeCAD with confidence and efficiency.

View Modification commands

The model displayed in the graphics window can be changed using various view modification commands. These commands can be accessed from the **View toolbar** (or) the **View** menu. The following are some of the main view modification commands:

	**Fit all**	The model will be fitted in the current size of the graphics window so that it will be visible completely. You can also fit the model in the graphics window by clicking the cube next to the Viewcube and selecting the **Zoom to fit** option.
	**Fit to Selection**	The **Fit to Selection** option automatically adjusts the view to make selected edge, face, or point fit perfectly within the screen.
	**Align to Selection**	This option adjusts the view to make the selected face or object parallel to the screen.
	**Pan**	Press and hold the middle mouse button, and then drag the pointer to move the model view on the plane parallel to screen.
	**Free Orbit**	Press and hold the middle and right mouse button. Next, drag the pointer to rotate the model view.
	**Rotate Left**	On the menu bar, click **View** > **Standard Views** > **Rotate Left**; the model rotates to left.
	**Rotate right**	On the menu bar, click **View** > **Standard Views** > **Rotate right**; the model rotates to right.
	**Zoom In**	On the menu bar, click **View** > **Zoom** > **Zoom In** to zoom into the model.
	**Zoom Out**	On the menu bar, click **View** > **Zoom** > **Zoom Out** to zoom out of the model.
	**Box Zoom**	On the menu bar, click **View** > **Zoom** > **Box Zoom** and drag a rectangle. The contents inside the rectangle will be zoomed.

Draw Style	**Flat Lines**	This represents the model with shades along with visible edges.	
	Shaded	This represents the model with shades without visible edges.	
	Hidden line	This represents the model faces with triangular meshes.	
	Wireframe	This represents the model in wireframe along with the hidden edges	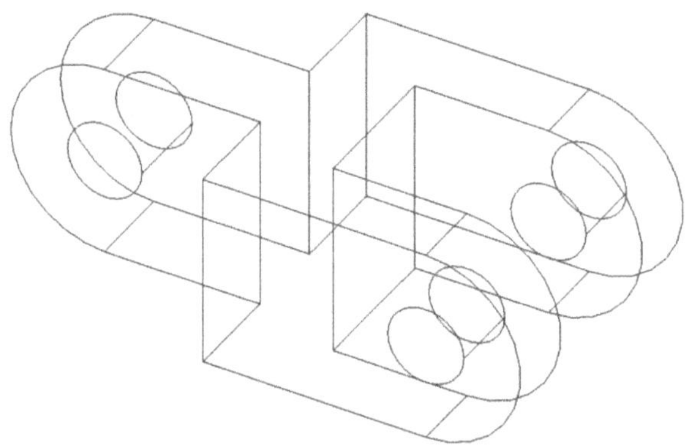

	Points	Only the vertices of the model are displayed	
	No Shading	This represents the model without any shading. The model edges, vertices and faces are displayed in solid color.	
Selection filters	**Vertex selection**	Limits selection to individual vertices of the model.	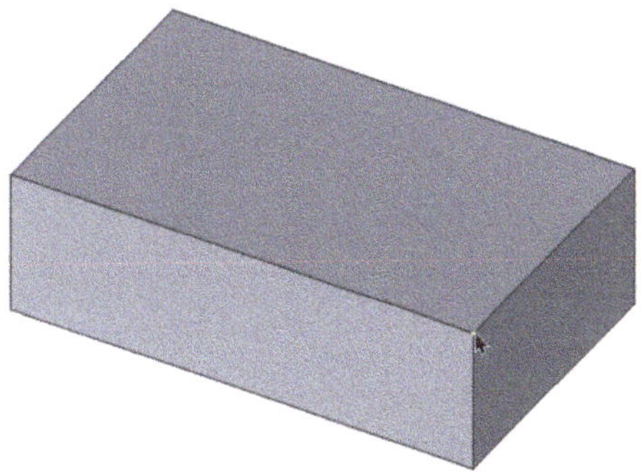
	**Edge selection**	Restricts selection to edges of the model.	
	**Face selection**	Filters selection to faces, allowing you to work on entire surfaces or apply materials to specific areas.	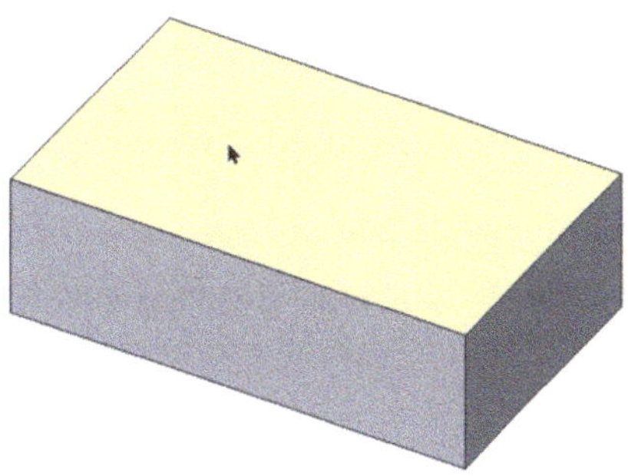

	All selection filters cleared	Removes any active selection filters, enabling unrestricted selection of vertices, edges, faces, or other elements.	

Tutorial 1 (Millimeters)

In this example, you create the part shown below.

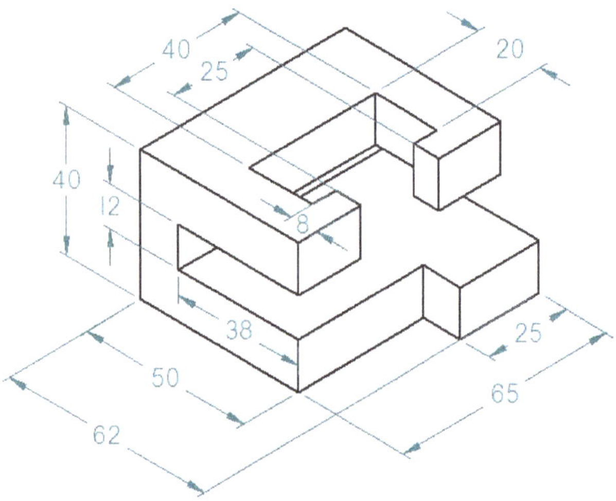

Creating a New Document

1. Click **FreeCAD 1.0** on the desktop to start.
2. On the menu bar, click **File > New**; it creates a new document.
3. On the **Workbench** toolbar, select **Workbench** drop-down **> Part Design**.
4. Click **Edit > Preferences** on the **Menu** bar (or) click **FreeCAD 1.0. > Preferences** on the title bar if you are working in MacOS; the **Preferences** dialog appears on the screen.
5. Click **General** tab and select **Default Unit system > Standard (mm/kg/s/degree)**.
6. Select **Number of decimals > 2** and click **OK** on the **Preferences** dialog.

Creating a Sketch

1. Click the **Create sketch** icon on the **Part Design Helper** toolbar, and then select the XZ-Plane.
2. On the **Sketcher geometries** toolbar, click the **Create rectangle** icon.
3. Click the origin point to define the first corner of the rectangle.
4. Move the pointer toward the top right. Type-in **50** in the width dimension box and press the TAB key
5. Type-in **40** in the height dimension box and press ENTER to create the rectangle.

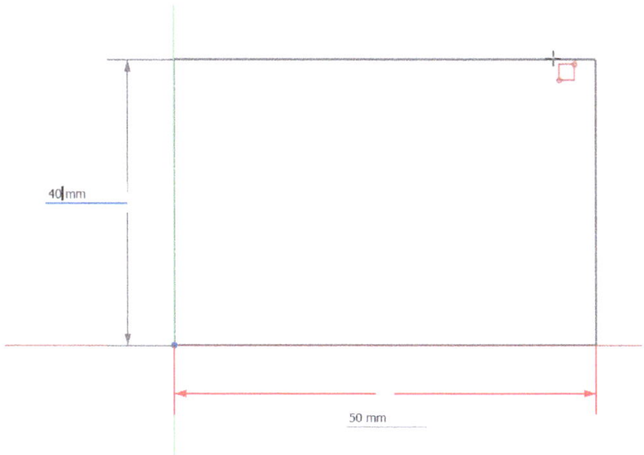

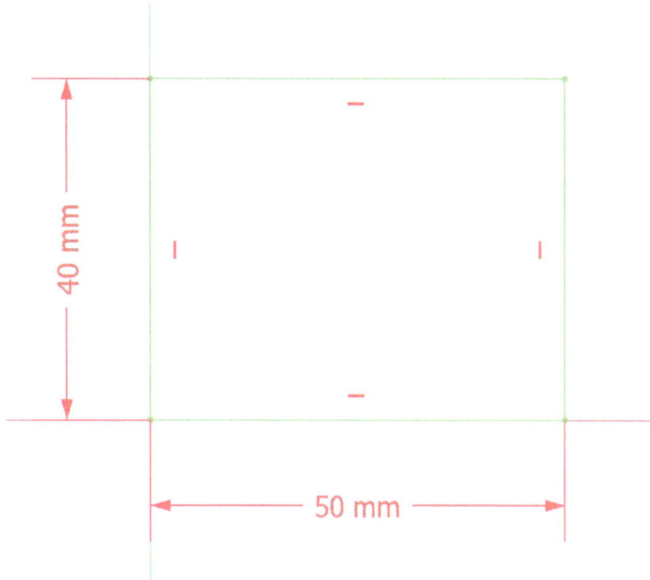

6. Click **Leave Sketch** on the **Sketcher edit mode** toolbar.

Creating a Pad Feature

1. Click the **Pad** icon on the **Part Design Modeling** toolbar.
2. Check the **Symmetric to plane** option on the **Pad parameters** panel.
3. Set the **Length** to **65** and click **OK** to create the pad feature.
4. Click the **Isometric** icon on the **View** toolbar.

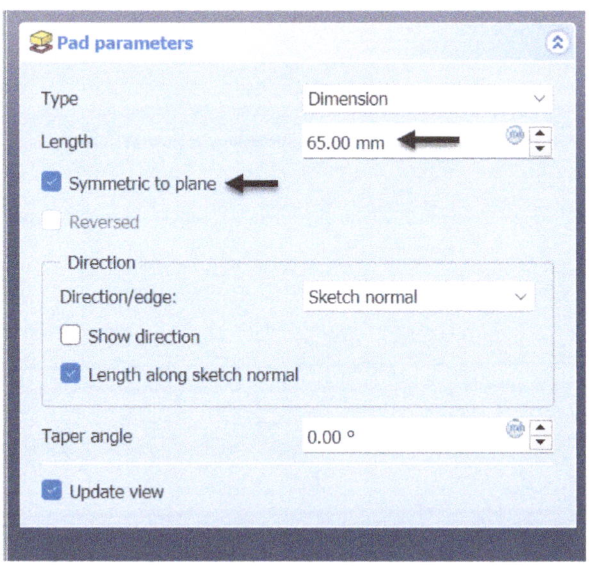

Creating a Pocket Feature

1. Click on the front face of the part geometry. Next, click the **Create Sketch** icon on the **Part Design Helper** toolbar.
2. Click the **Create external geometry** icon on the **Sketcher tools** toolbar. Click on the right edge of the model.
3. On the **Sketcher geometries** toolbar, click the **Create rectangle** icon.
4. Click on the right edge of the model, move the pointer toward left.
5. Type-in **38** in the width box and press TAB. Next, type-in **12** in the height box and press ENTER.

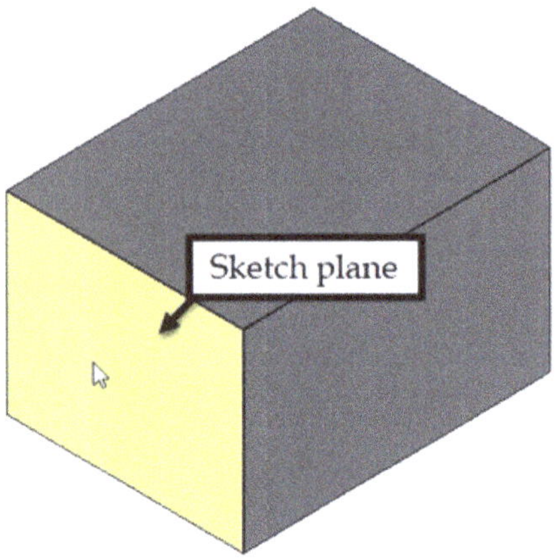

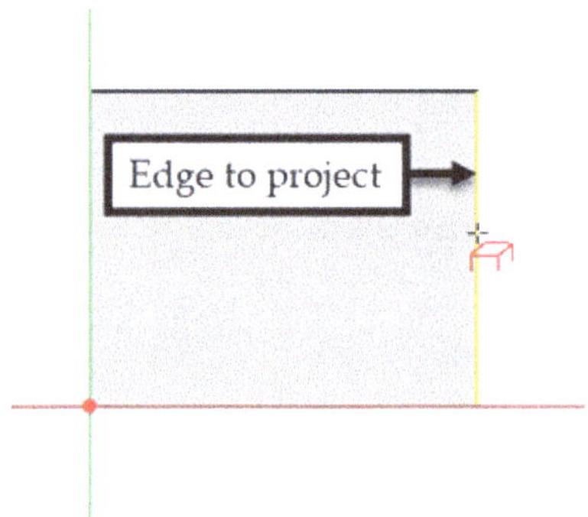

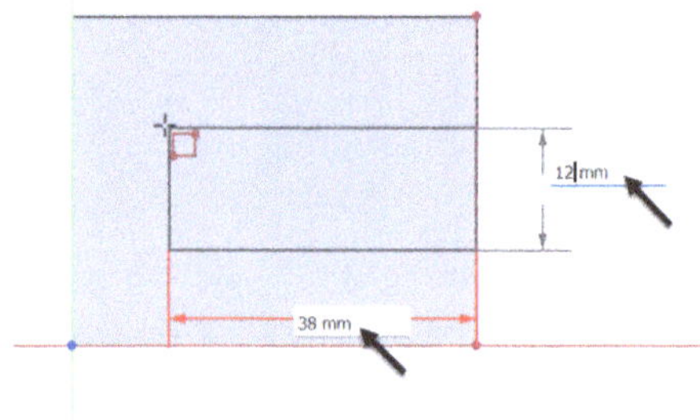

6. Click the **Constraint vertical distance** command.
7. Select the bottom right corner of the rectangle and the bottom endpoint of the projected edge, as shown.
8. Type-in **14** in the **Length** box and click **OK**.
9. Click **Leave Sketch** on the **Sketcher edit mode** toolbar.

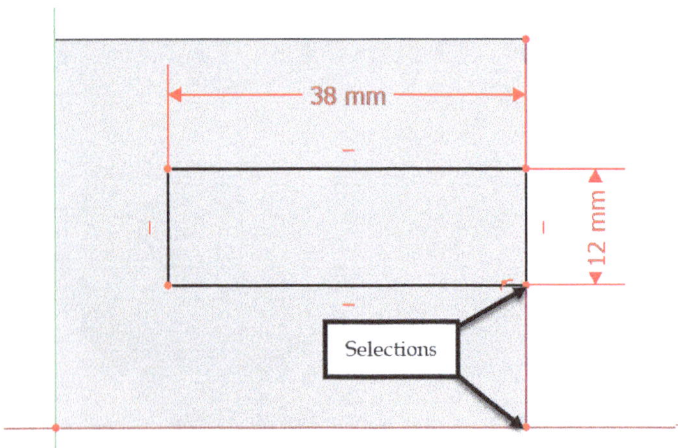

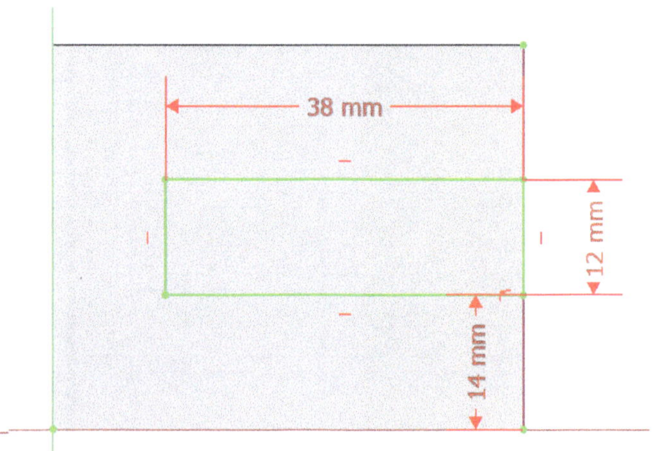

10. Click the **Pocket** icon on the **Part Design Modeling** toolbar.
11. On the **Tasks** panel, under the **Pocket Parameters** section, select **Type > Through All**.
12. Click **OK** on the **Tasks** panel to create the cut throughout the part design.

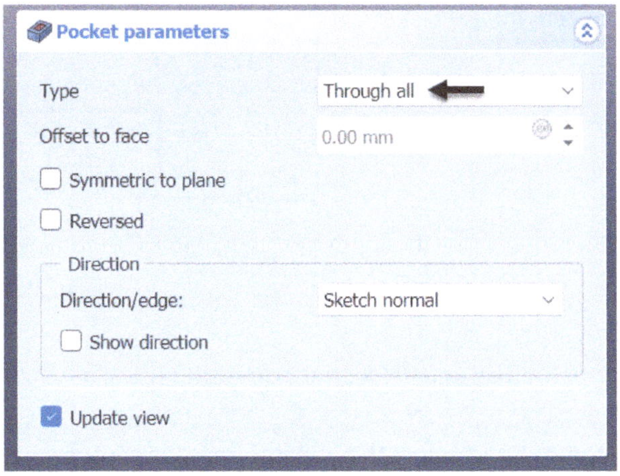

Extruding a sketch up to the Face next to the sketch plane

1. Click on the top face of the part design. Click the **Create Sketch** command on the **Part Design Helper** toolbar.
2. Click the **Orientation** drop-down **> Top** icon on the **View** toolbar.
3. Click the **Create external Geometry** icon on the **Sketcher tools** toolbar. Next, select the right vertical edge of the model; the selected edge is projected.
4. Activate the **Polyline** command (click the **Polyline** icon on the **Sketcher geometries** toolbar).
5. Click the drop-down available on the **Constraints** section on the **Combo View** panel and check the **Auto remove redundants** option
6. Create the sketch, as shown.
7. Select the inclined and click the **Constrain vertical** icon on the **Sketcher constraints** toolbar, as shown.

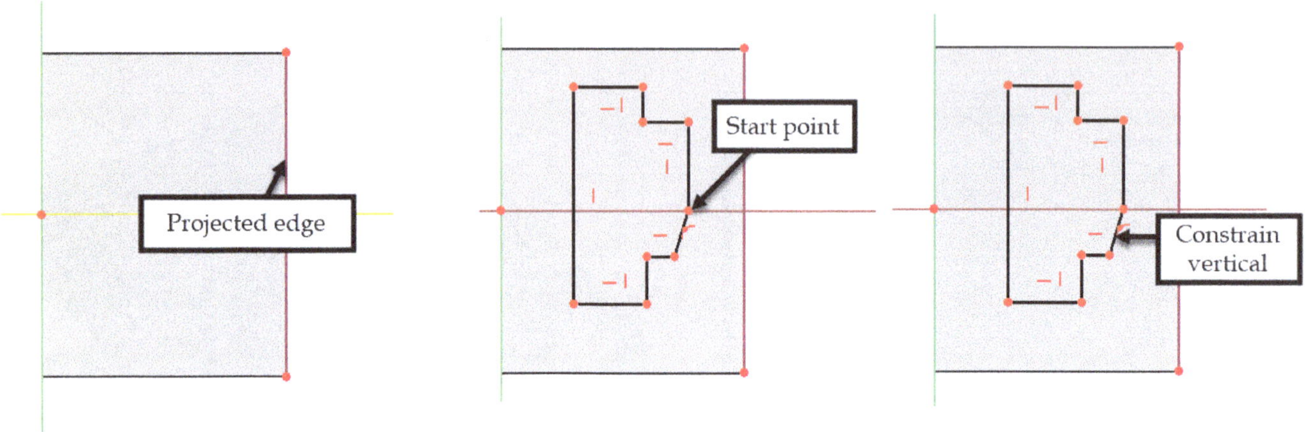

8. Click the **Constrain equal** icon on the **Sketcher constraints** toolbar and select the horizontal lines, as shown. Next, select the vertical lines, as shown.
9. Click the **Constrain equal** icon on the **Sketcher constraints** toolbar and select the vertical lines, as shown.

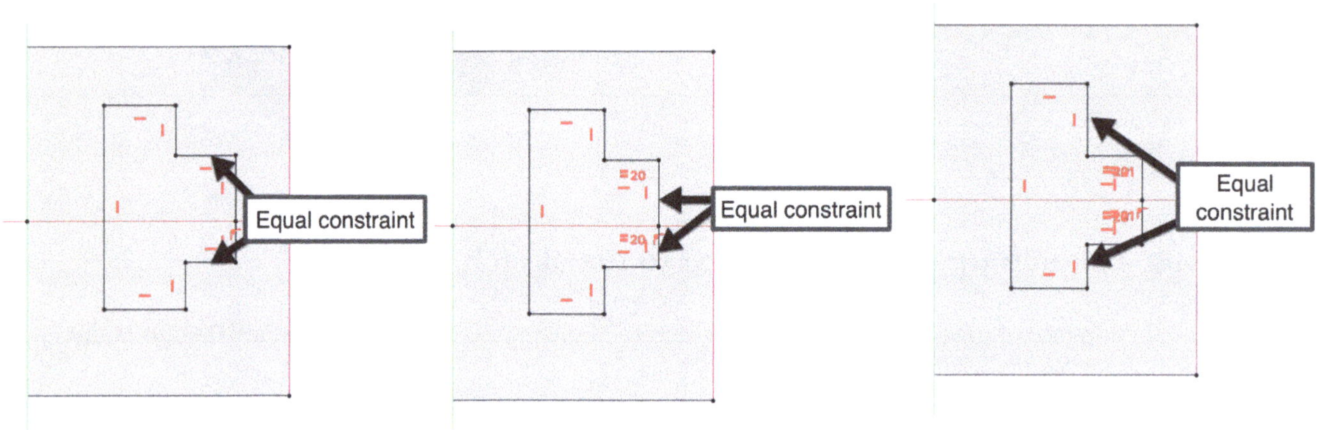

10. Click the **Constrain point onto an object** icon on the **Sketcher constraints** toolbar and select the projected edge and the start point of the sketch. The selected point is made coincident to the projected edge.

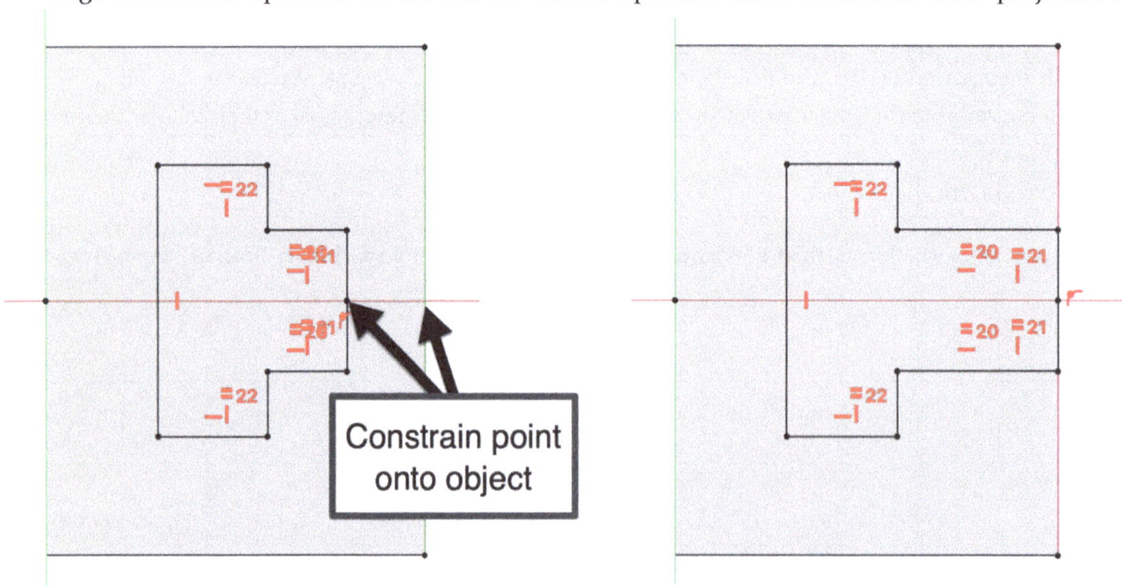

11. Click the **Constrain vertical distance** icon on the **Sketcher constraints** toolbar. Next, select the left vertical line. Type **40** in the **Length** box and click **OK**.
12. Select the endpoints of the right vertical line. Next, type **25** in the **Length** box, and then click **OK**.
13. Click the **Constrain horizontal distance** icon on the **Sketcher constraints** toolbar, and then select the left horizontal line. Next, type **20** in the **Length** box and click **OK**.
14. Select the right horizontal line and type **8** in the **Length** box, and then click **OK**.

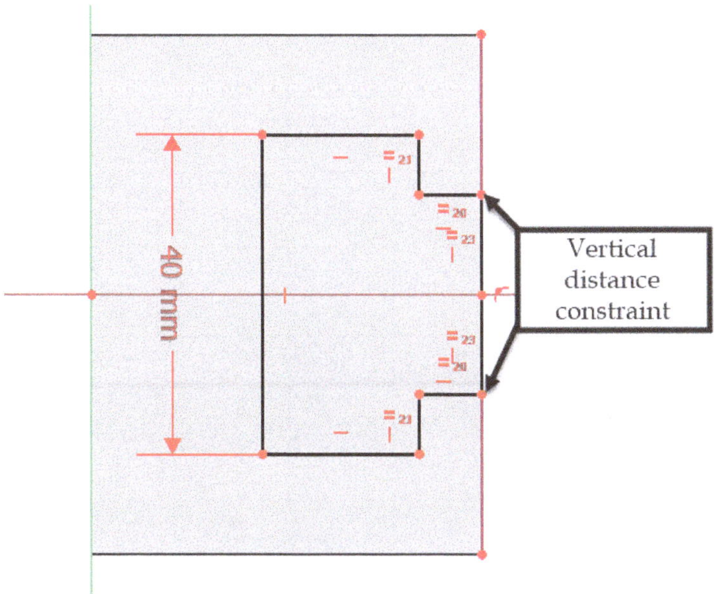

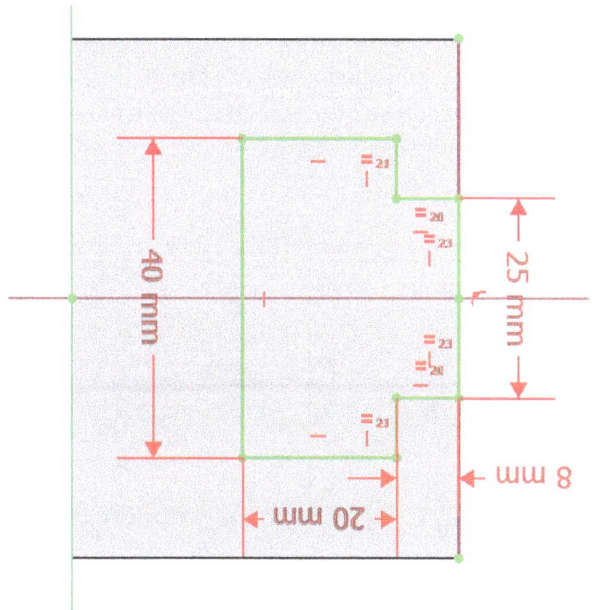

15. Click the **Close** button on the **Tasks** panel to close the sketch.
16. Activate the **Pocket** command (on the **Part Design Modeling** toolbar, click the **Pocket** icon)
17. On the **Pocket parameters** section, select **Type > To first**.
18. Click **OK** to remove the material up to the surface next to the sketch plane.

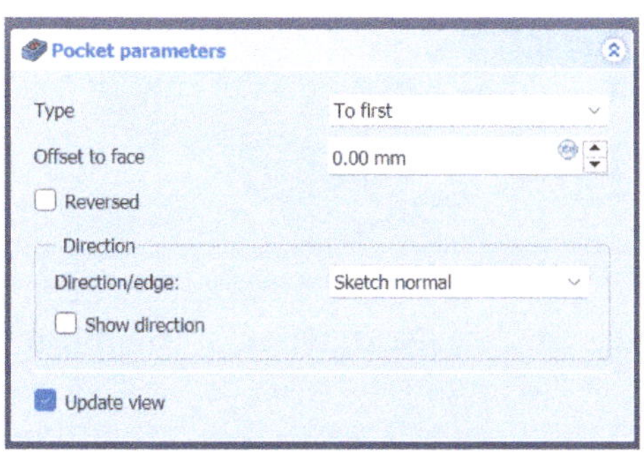

Extruding a sketch up to a selected face

1. Activate the **Create Sketch** command and select the XY plane.
2. Click the **Create external Geometry**  icon on the **Sketcher tools** toolbar. Next, select the right vertical edge of the model; the selected edge is projected.
3. Draw a rectangle and apply constraints to it, as shown.
4. On the **Sketcher constraints** toolbar, click **Constrain Coincident** . Next, select the corner point of the rectangle and the model, as shown.
5. Click the **Close** button on the **Tasks** panel to close the sketch.

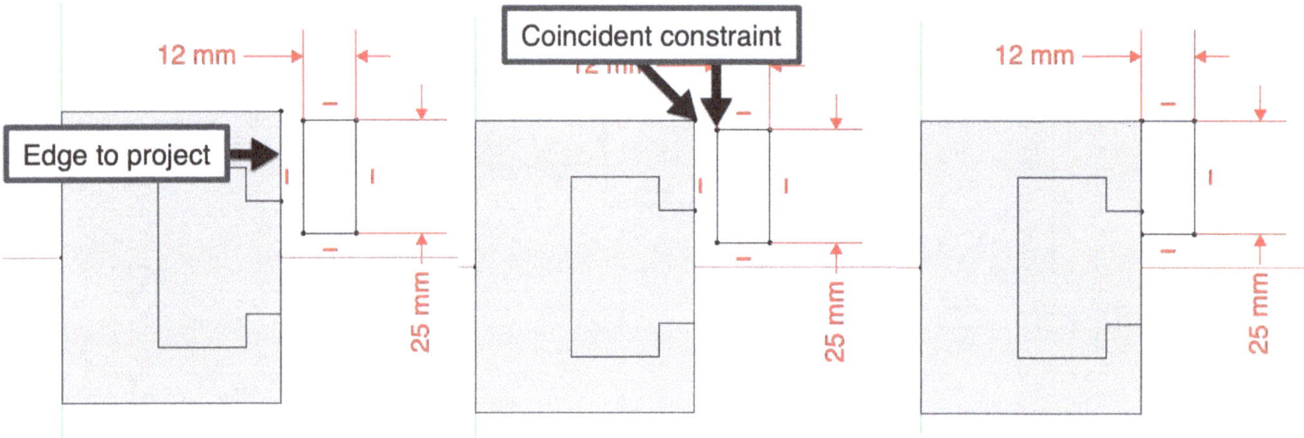

6. Activate the **Pad** command (on the **Part Design Modeling** toolbar, click the **Pad**  icon)
7. Select **Type > Up to face** from the **Pad Parameters** section on the **Tasks** panel. Next, select the horizontal face of the part geometry, as shown.
8. Click **OK** on the **Pad parameters** section to complete the part.

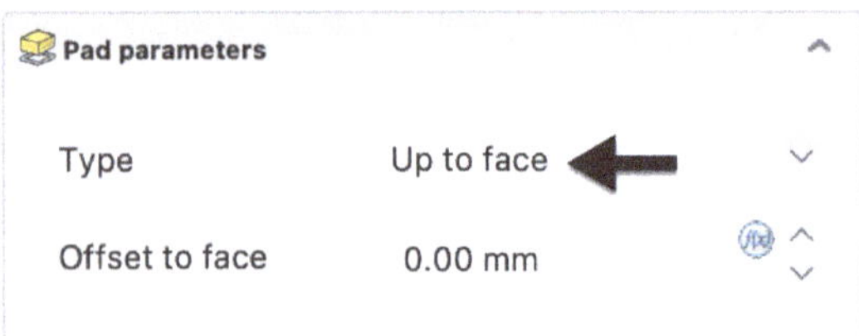

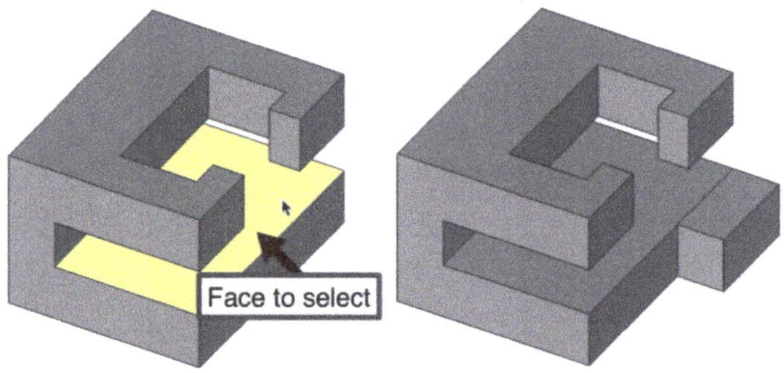

9. Click the **Save** icon on the **File** toolbar located at the top-left corner of the window. Next, type C3_exampl1 in the **File name** box, and then click **Save**.
10. Click **File > Close** on the menu bar to close the document.

Tutorial 2 (Inches)

In this example, you create the part shown below.

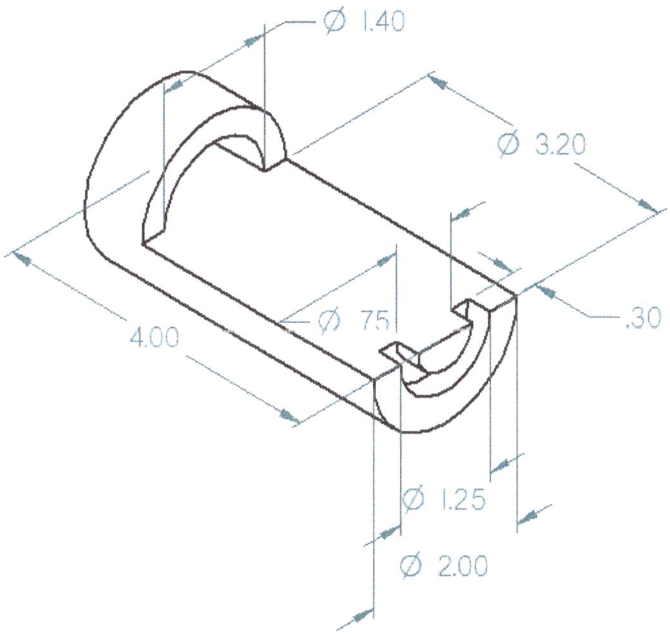

Creating a New document

1. Open a new **FreeCAD 1.0** file.
2. Click **Edit > Preferences** on the **Menu** bar (or) click **FreeCAD 1.0 > Preferences** on the title bar if you are working on MacOS; the **Preferences** dialog appears on the screen.
3. Click the **General** tab on the **Preferences** dialog.
4. Select **Default unit System > Imperial decimal (in, lb)** and type-in **3** in the **Number of decimals** box.
5. Click **OK** on the **Preferences** dialog.
6. Select the **Part Design** from the **Workbenches** drop-down.

Creating a Revolved Feature

1. Click the **Create sketch**  icon on the **Part Design Helper** toolbar, and then select the XY_Plane.
2. On the **Sketcher geometries** toolbar, click the **Create rectangle** 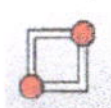 icon.
3. Click on the origin point to define the first corner of the rectangle.
4. Move the pointer toward the top right corner and type-in **4** in the **width** box. Next, press the TAB key and type-in **1** in the height box and press ENTER.

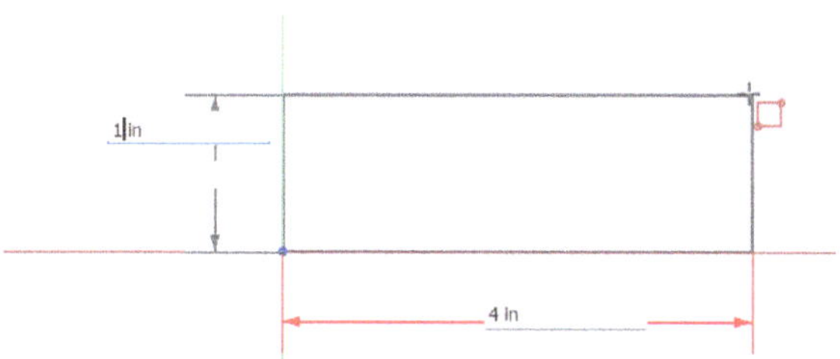

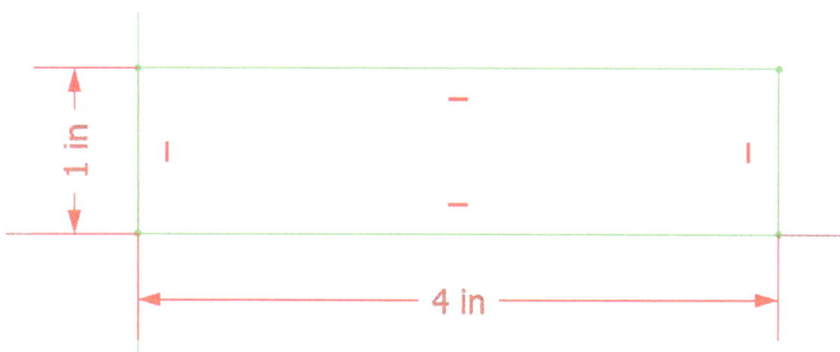

5. Click **Leave Sketch**  on the **Sketcher edit mode** toolbar. Next, click the **Isometric**  icon on the **View** toolbar.
6. Click the **Revolution**  icon on the **Part Design Modeling** toolbar.
7. Select **Axis > Horizontal Sketch Axis** from the **Revolution parameters** section on the **Tasks** panel.
8. Type-in **180** in the **Angle** box and check the **Reversed** option. Next, click **OK** on the **Tasks** panel to create the *Revolution* feature.

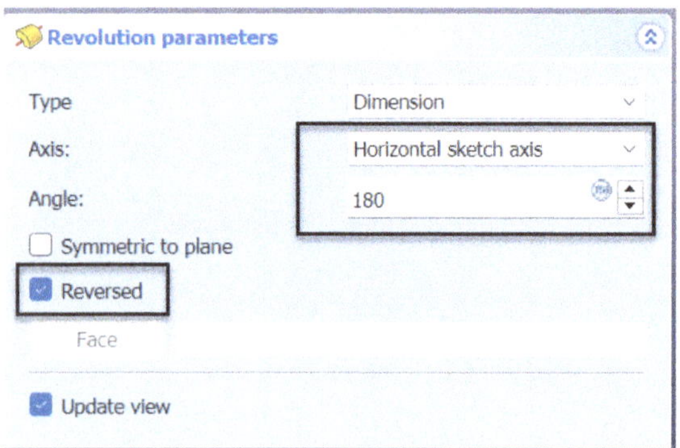

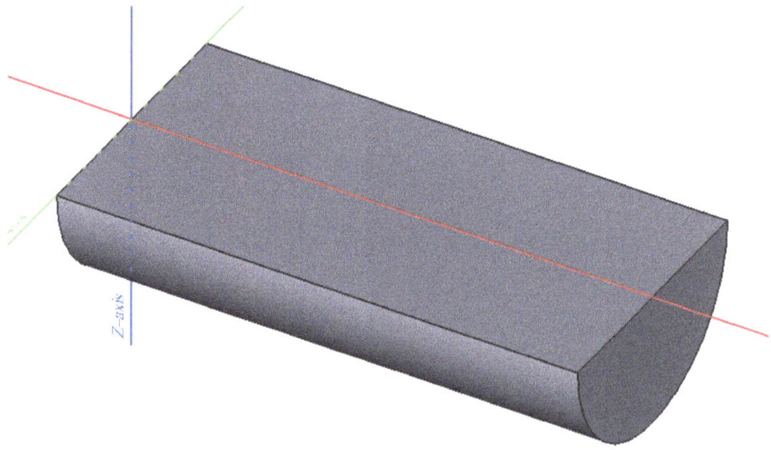

Creating a Groove feature

1. Select the top face of the part geometry and click the **Create Sketch**  tool on the **Part Design Helper** toolbar.
2. Draw a rectangle and apply the dimensional constraints to it, as shown.
3. Click the **Create external geometry**  icon on the **Sketcher tools** toolbar and select the right vertical edge.
4. Click the **Dimension** drop-down > **Constrain vertical distance** icon on the **Sketcher constraints** toolbar.
5. Select the top right corner of the rectangle and the top endpoint of the projected edge. Type **0.375** in the **Length** box and click **OK**.
6. Click the **Constrain Coincident**  icon on the **Sketcher constraints** toolbar and select the top right corner of the rectangle. Next, select the projected edge. Click the **Close** button on the **Combo View** panel.

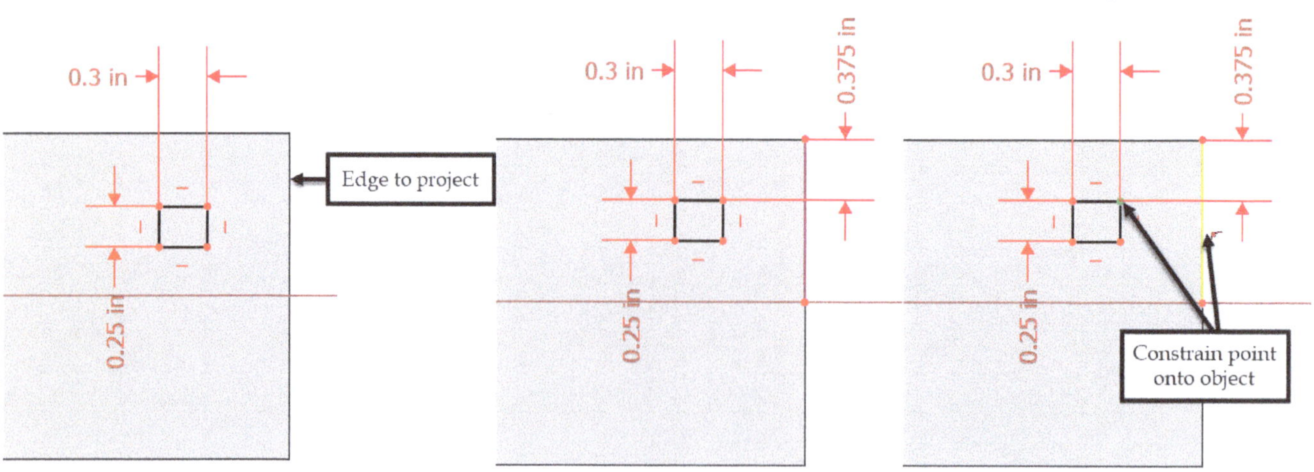

7. On the **Part Design Modeling** toolbar, click the **Groove** icon.
8. On the **Groove parameters** section, select **Axis > Horizontal sketch axis**. Next, type **180** in the **Angle** box and click **OK** to create the groove feature.

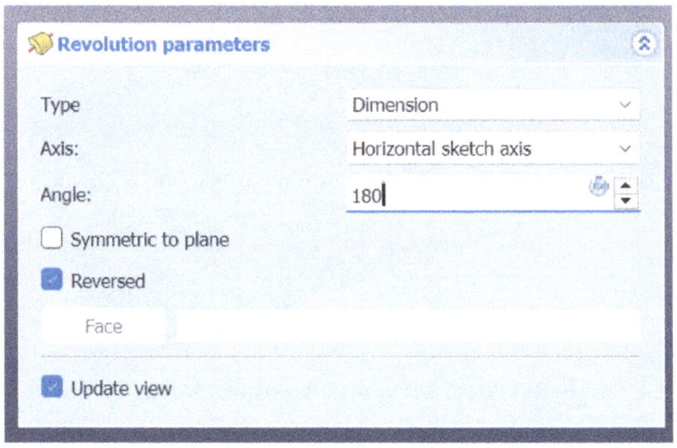

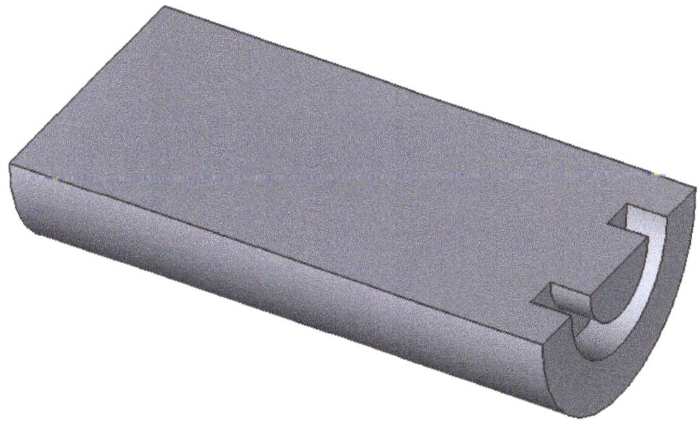

Adding a Revolution Feature to the Model

1. Select the top face of the part geometry and click the **Create Sketch** tool on the **Part Design Helper** toolbar.
2. Draw a rectangle and add dimensional constraints to it, as shown.
3. Click the **Create external geometry** icon on the **Sketcher tools** toolbar and select the bottom horizontal edge.
4. Click the **Constrain coincident** icon on the **Sketcher constraints** toolbar. Next, select the bottom left corner point of the rectangle and the left endpoint of the projected edge.
5. Click the **Close** button on the **Tasks** panel.

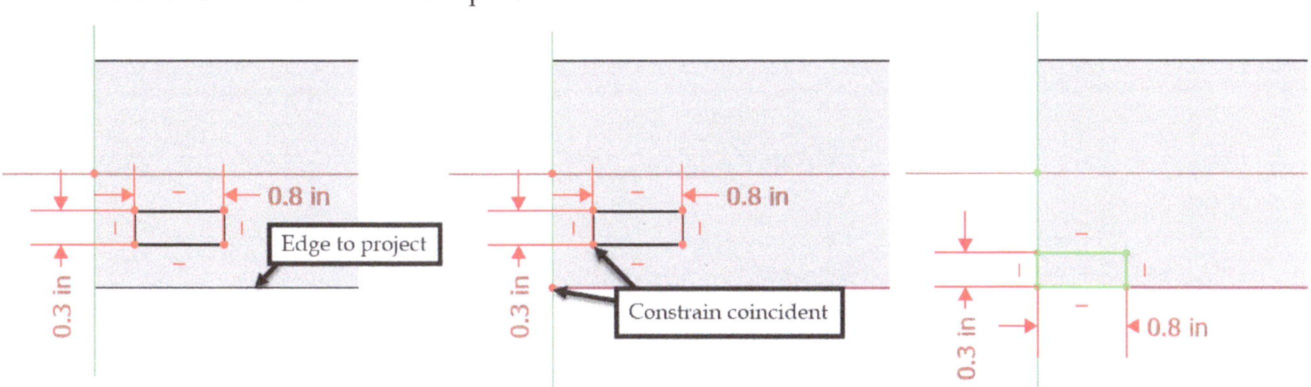

6. Click the **Revolution** icon on the **Part Design Modeling** toolbar.
7. On the **Revolution parameters** section, select **Axis > Horizontal sketch axis**.
8. Type 180 in the **Angle** box and click **OK**.

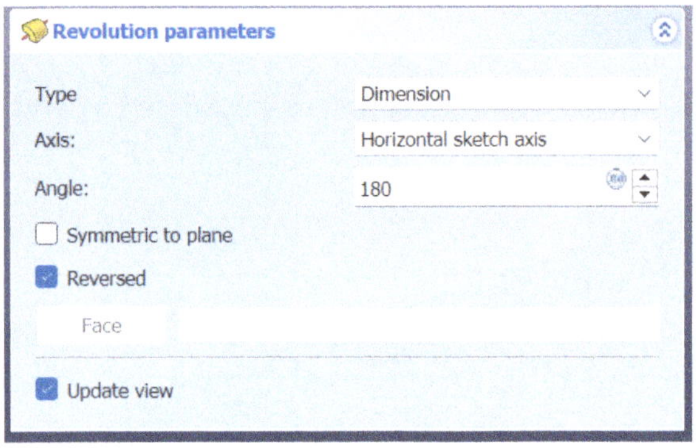

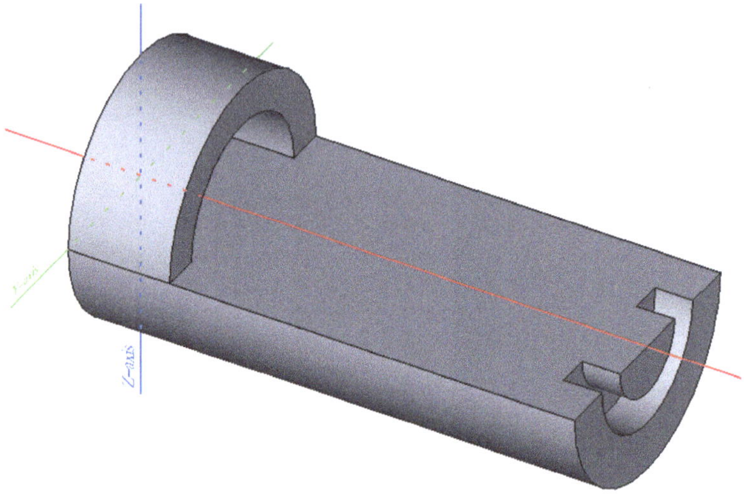

9. Click **File > Save** on the menu bar. Next, type **C3_example2** in the **File name** box, and then click **Save**.
10. Click **Close Tab** on the bottom left corner of the window.

Questions

1. How to create parallel planes in FreeCAD?
2. What are the **Type** options available on the **Pad Parameters** section?
3. How to create angled planes in FreeCAD?

Exercises

Exercise 1

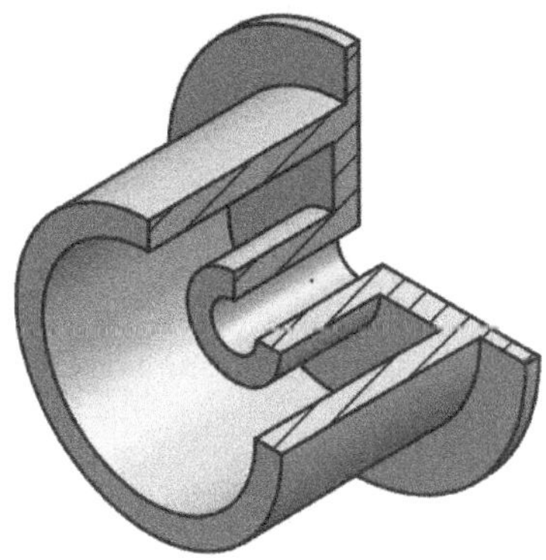

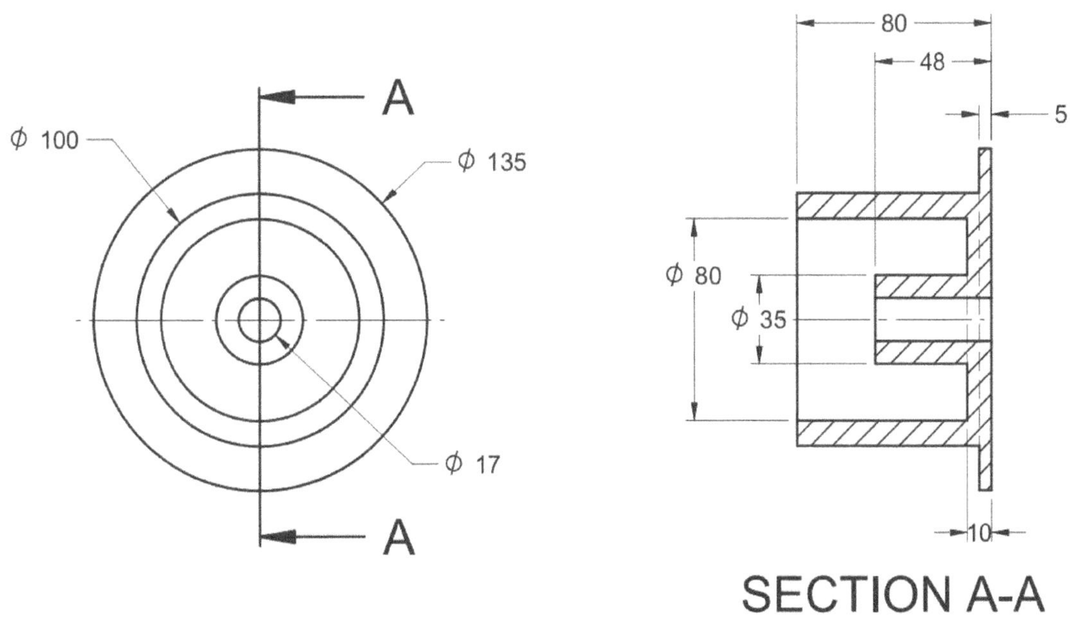

Exercise 2

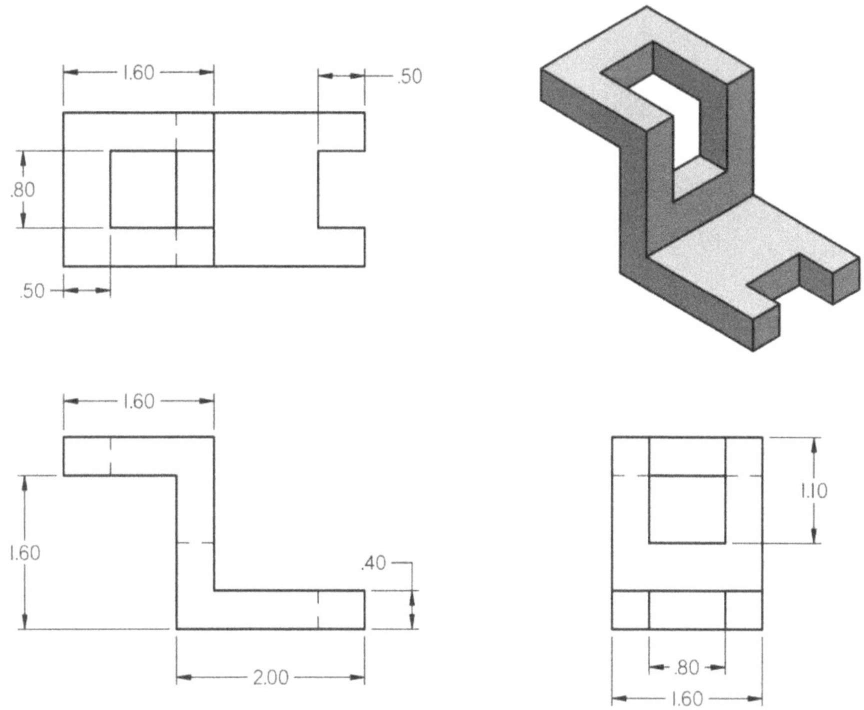

Exercise 3

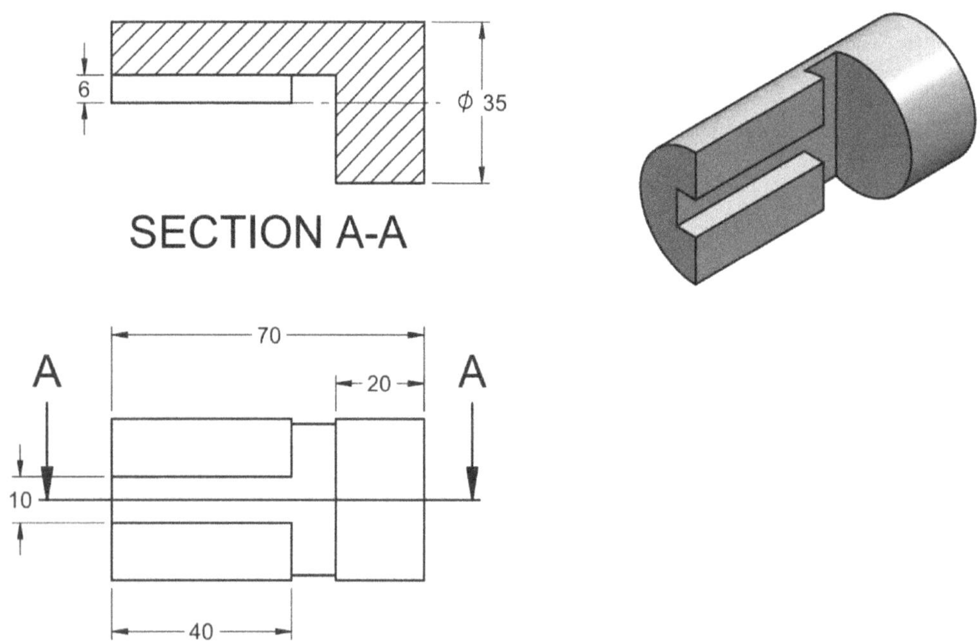

Chapter 4: Dress-up Features

So far, all of the features that were covered in the previous chapter were based on two-dimensional sketches. However, there are certain features in FreeCAD 1.0 that do not require a sketch at all. Features that do not require a sketch are called dress-up features. You can simply place them on your models. However, to do so, you must have some existing geometry. Unlike a sketch-based feature, you cannot use a dress-up feature for the first feature of a model. For example, to create a *Fillet* feature, you must have an already existing edge. In this chapter, you will learn how to add dress-up features to your design.

The topics covered in this chapter are:

- *Holes*
- *Threads*
- *Fillets*
- *Chamfers*
- *Drafts*
- *Shells*

Hole

As you know, it is possible to use the *Extrude* command to create cuts and remove material. But, if you want to drill holes that are of standard sizes, the **Hole**  command is a better way to do this. The reason for this is it has many hole types already predefined for you. All you have to do is choose the correct hole type and size. The other benefit is when you are going to create a 2D drawing, FreeCAD can place the correct hole annotation automatically. To create a hole first, click on the placement face and then click **Create Sketch**  on the **Part Design Helper** toolbar. Next, create one or more circles, and then add dimensions and constraints to them.

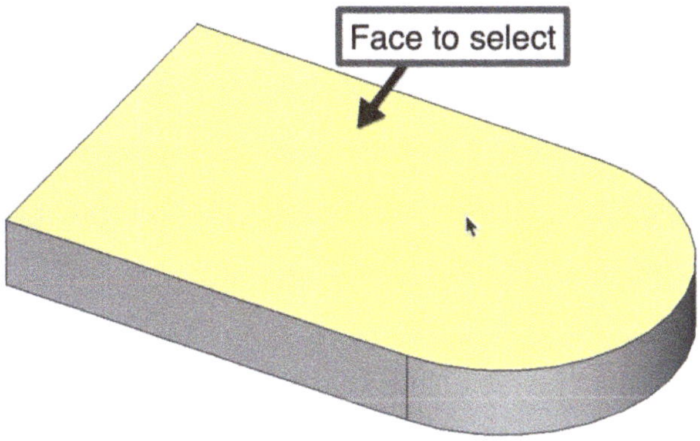

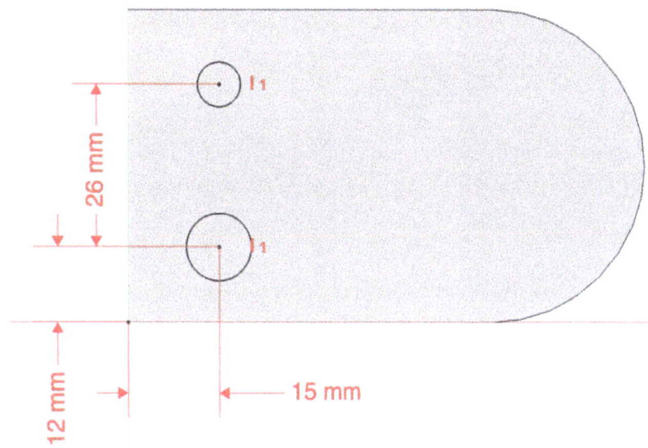

If you want to create a hole concentric to a circular edge, then click the **Create external geometry** icon on the **Sketcher tools** toolbar. Next, click on the circular edge. Activate the **Create circle** command and select the centerpoint of the external geometry. Move the pointer outward and click to create the circle. Click **Leave Sketch** on the **Sketcher** toolbar.

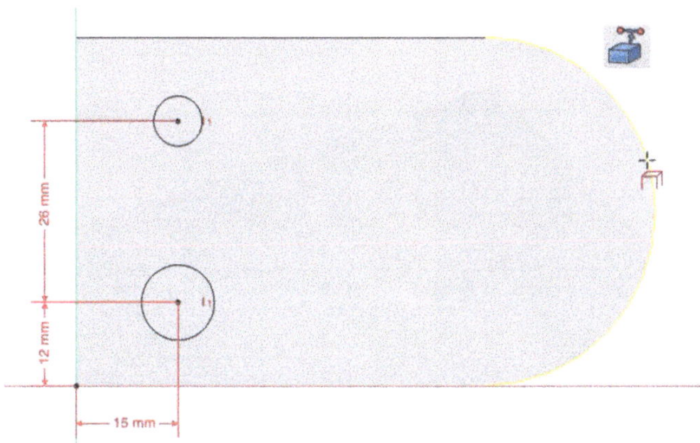

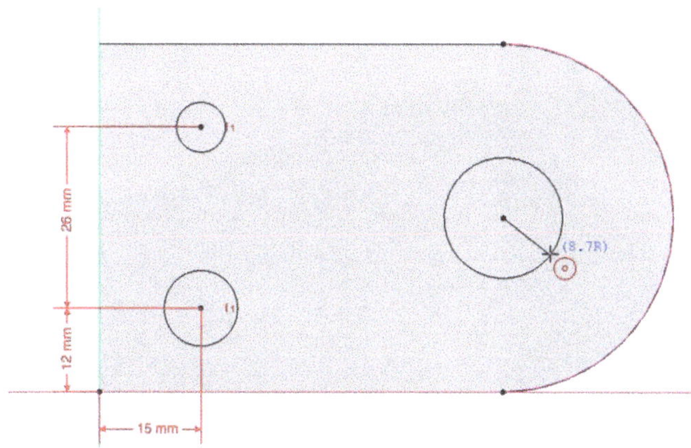

Activate **Hole** command (Click the **Hole** icon on the **Part Design Modeling** toolbar (or) click **Part Design > Create a subtractive feature > Hole** on the menu bar); you will notice that the **Hole Parameters** panel appears on the left-side. There are options on this panel that make it easy to create different types of holes.

Simple Hole

To create a simple hole feature, select **Hole cut type > None** on the **Hole Parameters** panel. Next, select the **Depth** type. If you want a through-hole, select **Depth > Through all**. If you want the hole only up to some depth, then select **Depth > Dimension**, and then type-in a value in the **Depth** box.

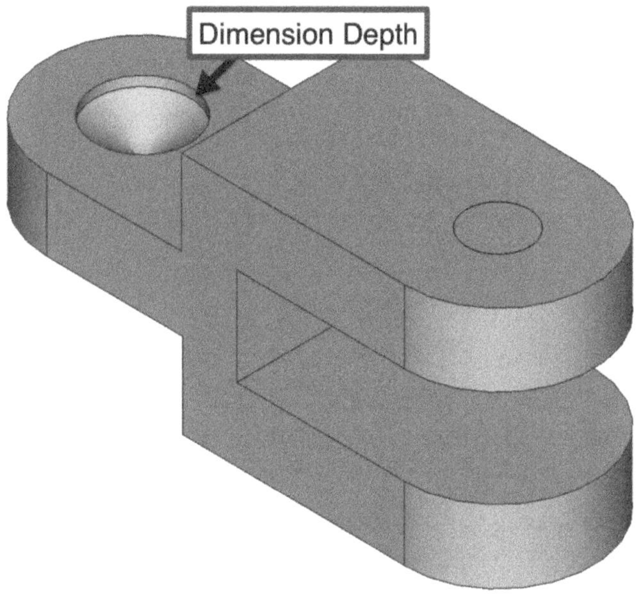

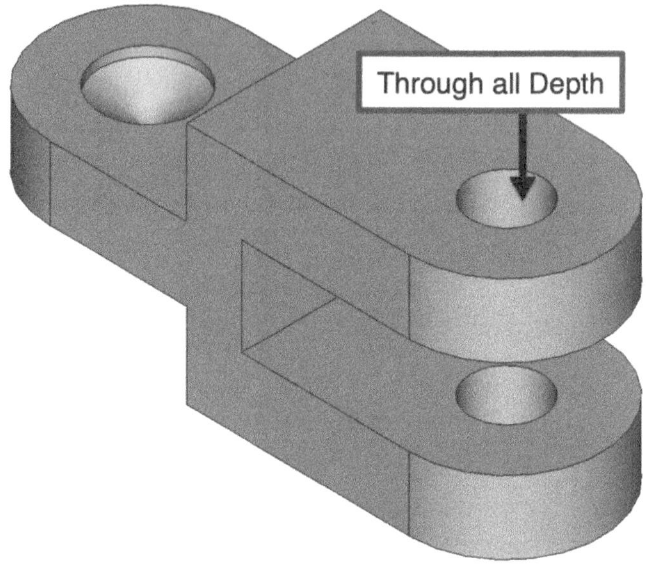

The **Drill Point** section has two options to define the depth of the hole: **Flat** and **Angled**. The **Flat** option creates a hole with a flat bottom. The **Angle** option creates a hole with an angled bottom. The **Angled** box defines the angle of the cone tip at the bottom.

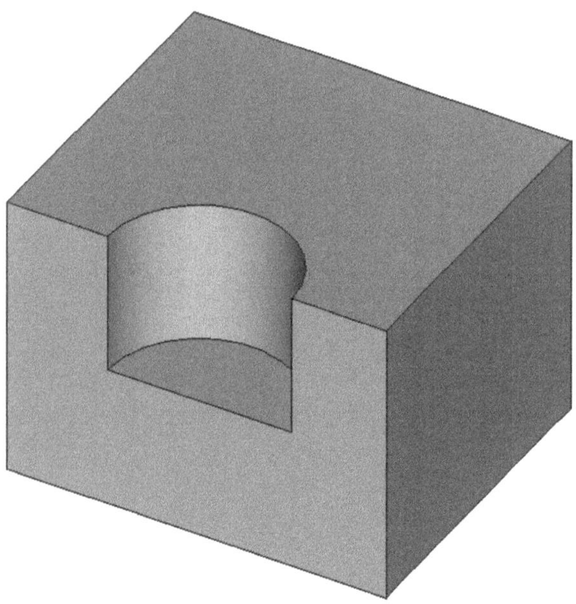

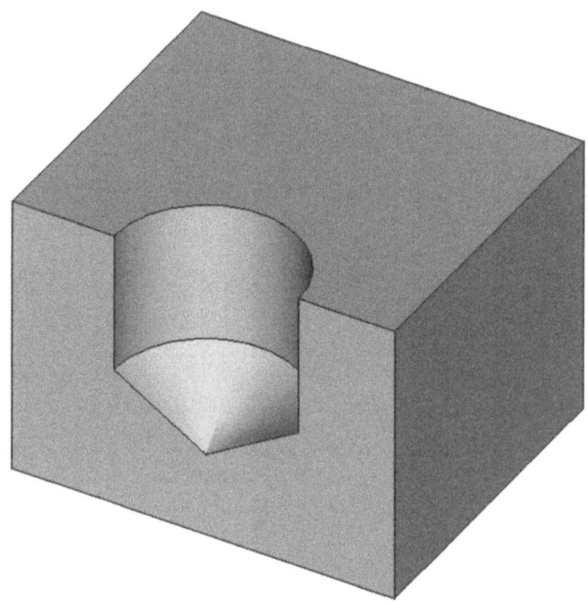

The **Take into account for depth** checkbox includes the tip of the angled bottom in the hole depth. If you uncheck this option, the angled bottom is excluded from the hole depth.

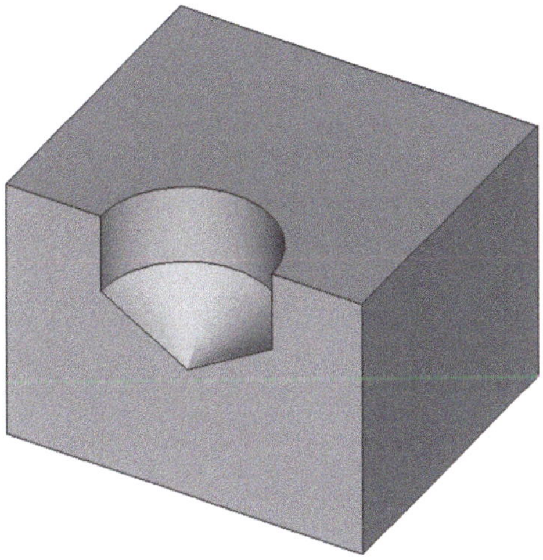

Take into account for depth checked

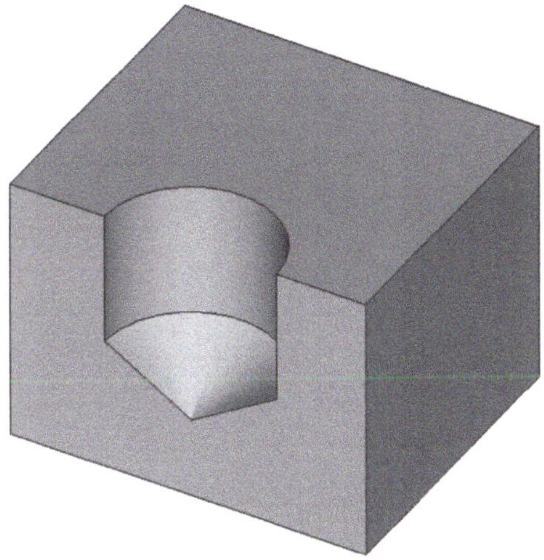

Take into account for depth unchecked

Next, specify the **Diameter** of the hole and click **OK** to complete the hole feature.

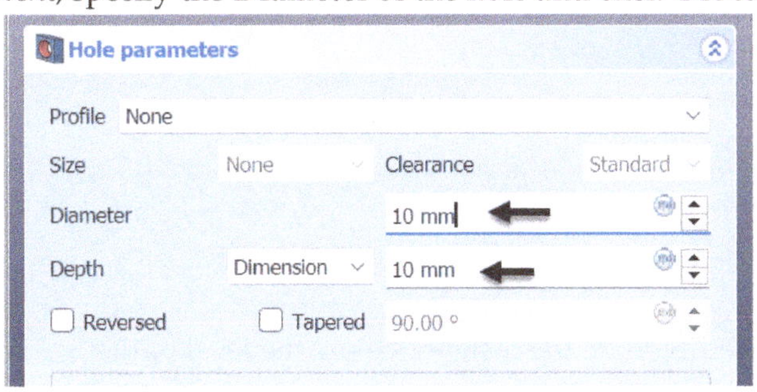

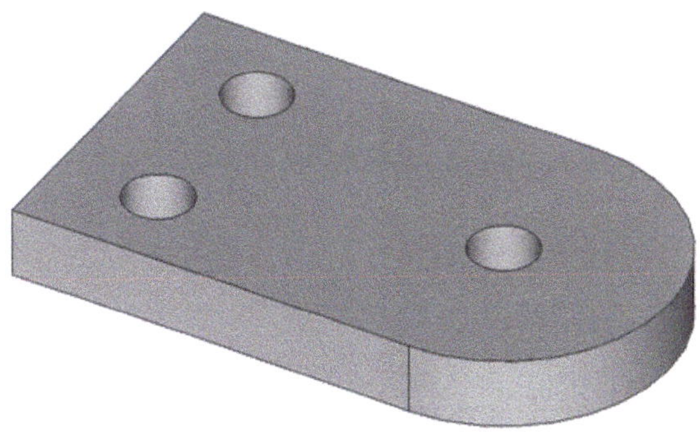

Counterbored Hole

A counterbore hole is a large diameter hole added at the opening of another hole. It is used to accommodate a fastener below the level of the workpiece surface. To create a counterbore hole, select **Hole Cut Type > Counterbore from**. Next, specify the Hole Diameter, Hole Depth, Counterbore Diameter, and Counterbore Depth. Next, specify the desired **Drill Point** type (**Flat** or **Angled**). If you click the **Angled** option, then specify the **Tip Angle** value.

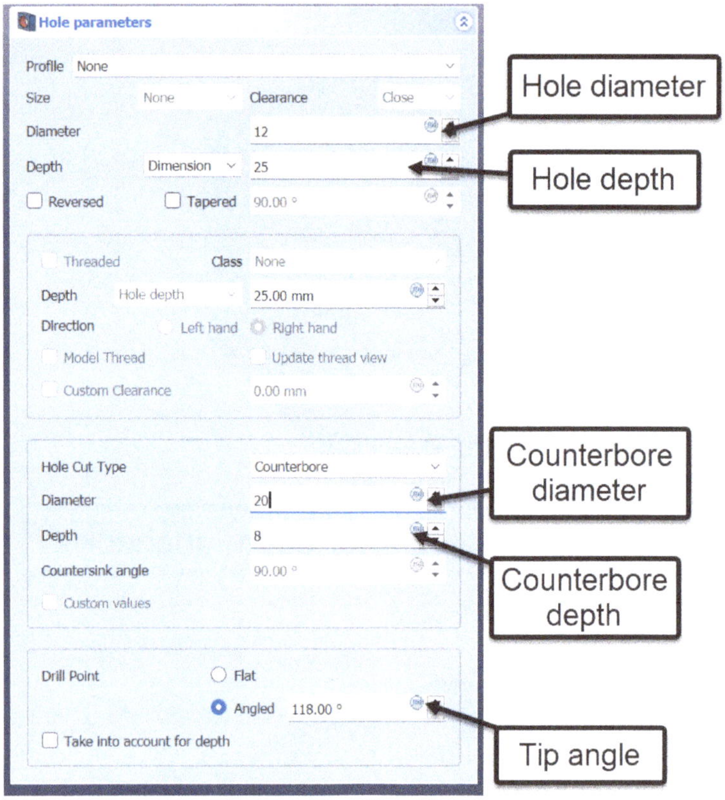

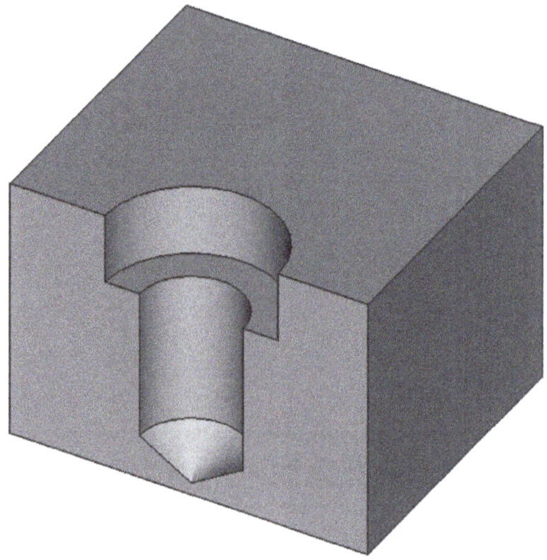

Countersink Hole

A countersunk hole has an enlarged V-shaped opening to accommodate the fastener below the level of the workpiece surface. To create a countersink hole, select **Type > Countersink** from the **Hole cut** section. Next, specify the Hole Diameter, Countersink Diameter, and Countersink angle. Set the hole diameter and drill point.

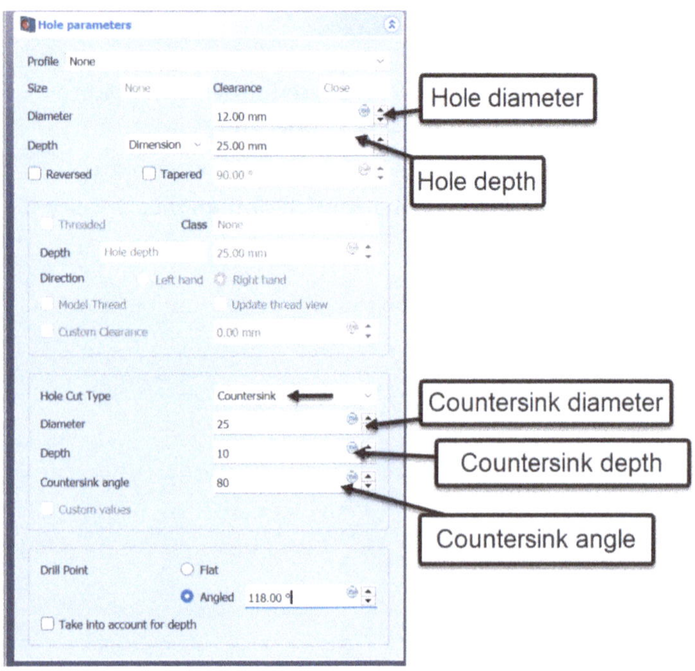

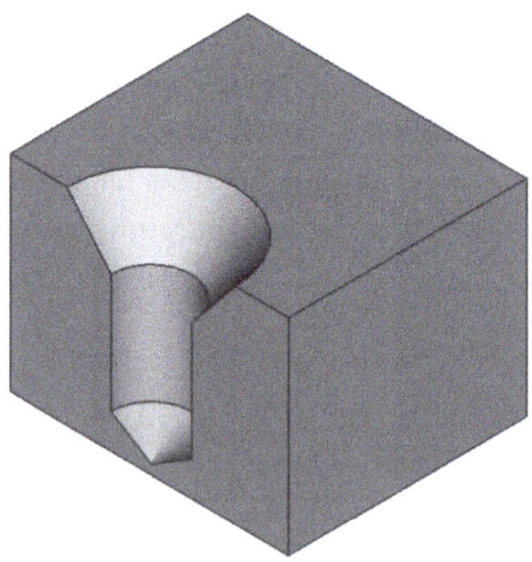

Counterdrill Hole

If you select the **Counterdrill** option from the **Type** drop-down, a counterbore hole will be added on top of the countersink hole. After selecting option from the **Type** drop-down, you need to specify the Hole Diameter, Countersink Diameter, Counterbore Depth, and Countersink angle.

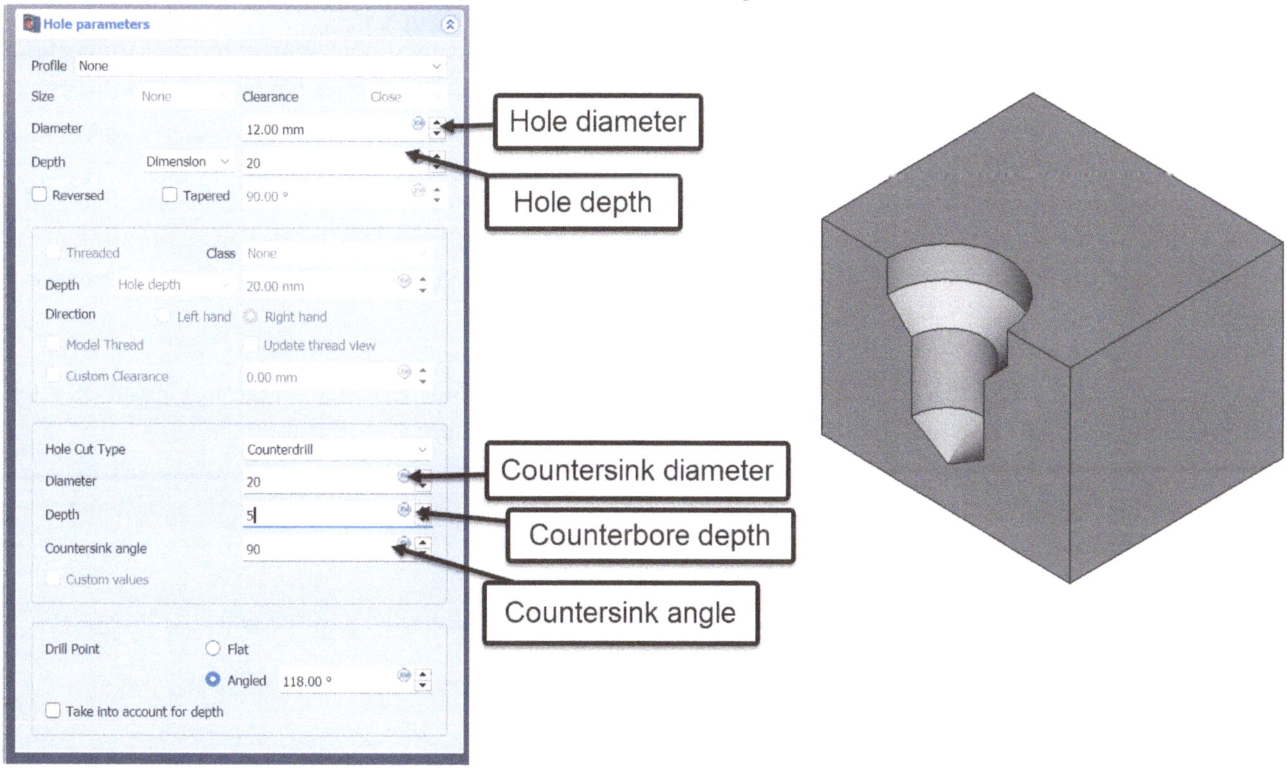

Threaded Hole

To create a threaded hole feature, first start by choosing the appropriate thread profile from the options available in the **Profile** drop-down menu. This profile defines the characteristics of the threads you want to incorporate into the hole. Next, enable the **Threaded** option; this step is pivotal because it signals the software that you intend to create a threaded hole. Next, specify the **Direction**, **Size**, and **Class**.

Direction

You can define the direction of a threaded hole by choosing between the **Right Hand** or **Left Hand** option. Right-hand threads are the most common and are used in standard applications like screws, bolts, and nuts. When you turn a fastener clockwise, it moves into the hole, making right-hand threads ideal for typical fasteners that tighten by turning to the right. On the other hand, left-hand threads are less common but serve specific purposes, such as preventing unintentional loosening due to vibrations or rotation. These threads tighten when turned counter-clockwise and are often used in specialized cases, like the left side of a bicycle pedal. If your threaded hole needs to accommodate a fastener that tightens counter-clockwise, you should select the **Left Hand** option for the thread direction.

Size

The **Size** drop-down menu simplifies the creation of threaded holes by offering predefined settings based on global standards like ISO and UTS, ensuring compatibility with international norms. For ISO profiles, common thread types such as M6x1.0 are provided, where "M6" denotes the diameter and "1.0" the pitch. Similarly, UTS, used primarily in the United States, includes options like 1/4-20, where "1/4" represents the diameter and "20" indicates threads per inch.

Class

Choose a thread class to specify the degree of fit and tolerance for your threaded hole, matching your application and engineering standards. In the context of creating threaded holes, the **Class** drop-down menu offers options tailored to the selected profile, such as ISO or UTS.

The **Class** setting is crucial for defining the fit and tolerance for both the threaded hole and the fastener that will be used with it. For ISO thread profiles, you'll typically find classes like "4h" and "6g" in the **Class** drop-down. "4h" indicates a tight fit with minimal tolerance, suitable for precision and vibration resistance. "6g" represents a looser fit with more tolerance, common in general-purpose applications.

For UTS thread profiles, the **Class** drop-down includes options like "2A" and "3B." "2A" suggests a looser fit, often used for rapid assembly, while "3B" implies a tighter fit with higher precision.

Choosing the right class is critical as it ensures proper alignment between the threaded hole and the fastener, tailored to the specific needs of your project.

Specify the remaining hole options that are similar to the simple hole feature. Click **OK** to create the threaded hole.

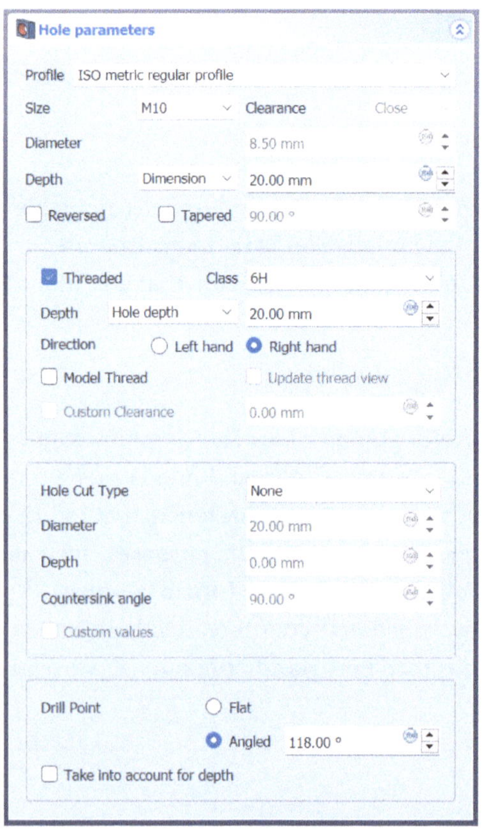

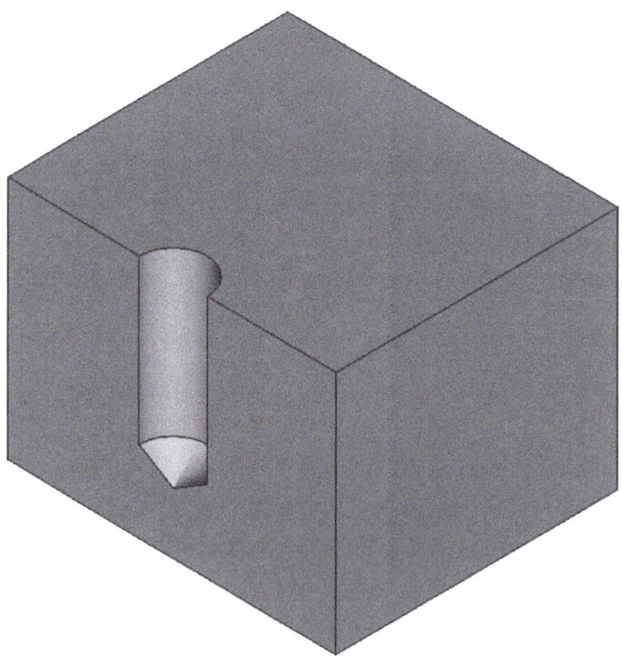

Creating a Hole with a Modelled Thread

You have the option to include the threaded feature directly in the 3D file when creating the hole. Begin by choosing the **Model Thread** option. This tells the software to incorporate threads directly into the hole, giving it both form and function. After opting for **Model Thread**, check the **Update thread view** setting. This ensures that any changes you make to the thread are instantly reflected in the hole's appearance. If your design requires extra clearance around the threaded feature, use the **Custom Clearance** option. This allows you to define specific clearances, ensuring a precise fit for your design needs.

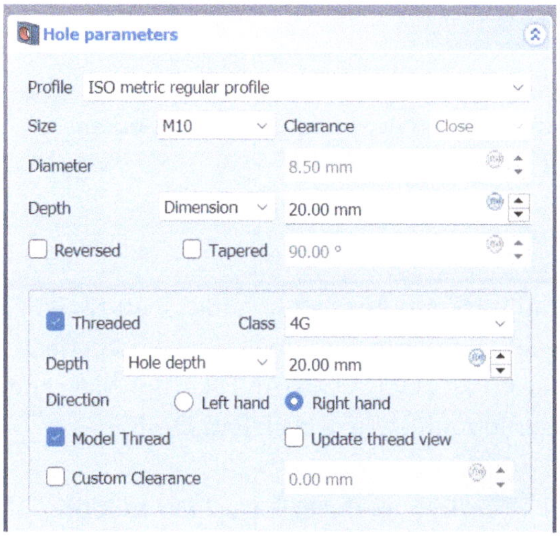

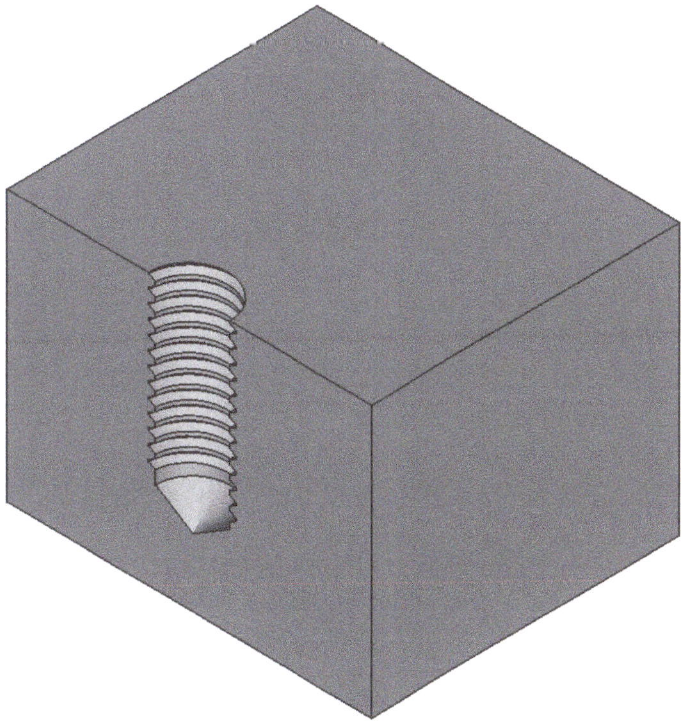

Best Practices

To ensure a smooth design process, it's essential to follow these best practices when creating holes in FreeCAD:

Plan Your Design: Before diving into hole creation, take the time to plan your design thoroughly. Identify the hole size, location, and quantity based on the specific requirements of your project.

Start with a Sketch: Begin by sketching the hole's geometry on the surface where you intend to create it. This initial sketch is crucial for accurately defining the hole's position.

Dimension the Sketch: Properly dimension the sketch for the hole. Ensure that the dimensions are clear and align with your design specifications.

Choose the Right Hole Type: FreeCAD provides various hole types, such as simple holes, counterbored holes, and countersunk holes. Select the type that best matches your design needs.

Prevent Overlapping Holes: When creating multiple holes on the same face, exercise caution, as overlapping holes can weaken the material and compromise the integrity of your design.

Cautions

Consider Material Thickness: Make sure that the material thickness is sufficient to accommodate the hole size and type. Drilling a hole too close to an edge or the material's limit can result in structural issues.

Be Mindful of Updates: Keep in mind that modifications to your model's geometry may require corresponding updates to hole positions and sizes.

Tips

Leverage Thread Features: When creating threaded holes, take advantage of FreeCAD's thread features to specify thread size and type, especially when working with fasteners.

Check for Interferences: After creating holes, carefully examine for any interferences with other components in the assembly. FreeCAD offers tools for detecting and resolving interferences

Fillet

The **Fillet** tool simplifies sharp edges on a 3D model by smoothly blending them. Also, adding fillet features is crucial to improve the aesthetics, functionality, and manufacturability of your parts. You don't need a predefined sketch for this. To start, ensure you can see the model's edges. Hold the CTRL key (COMMAND key for Mac) and click on the edges you want to fillet. This helps you choose which edges to round. Next, click **Part Design** >

Apply a dress-up feature > **Fillet** on the menu bar (or) click the **Fillet**  icon on the **Part Design Modeling** toolbar. Next, click the Preview button on the Fillet parameters panel to preview the fillet.

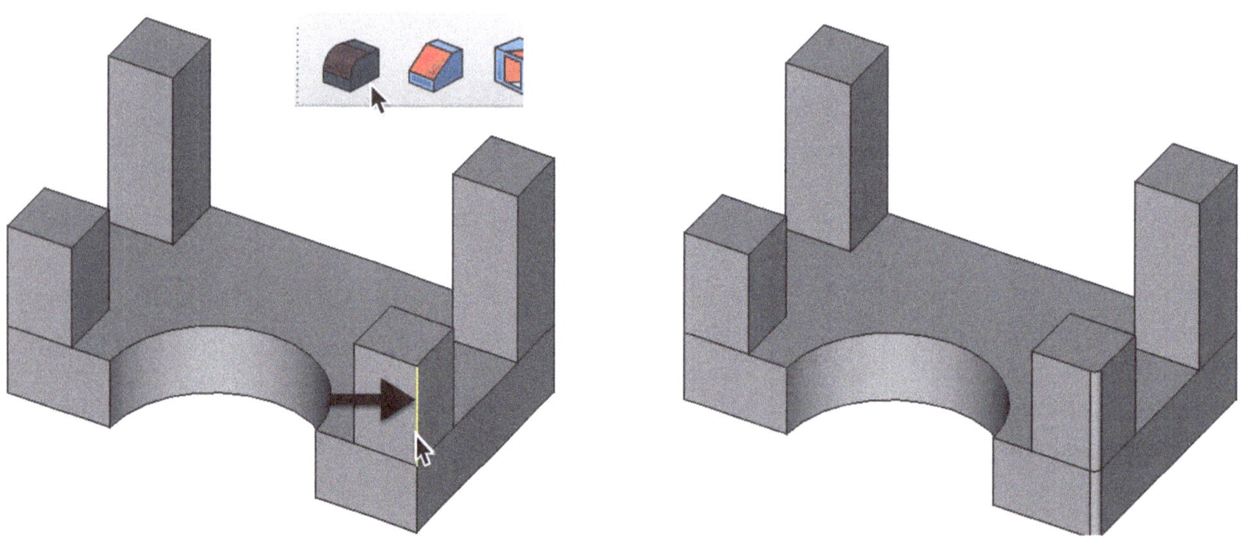

If you want to select more edges to be filleted, then click the **Select** button on the **Fillet parameters** panel and select the edges to be filleted. By mistake, if you have selected the wrong edge, you can deselect it. To do this, click the **Remove** button on the **Fillet parameters** panel and select the edge(s) to be removed. You can change the radius by typing a value in the **Radius** box available on the **Fillet parameters** panel. As you change the radius, all the selected edges will be updated. This is because they are all part of one instance. If you want the edges to have different radii, you must create fillets in separate instances.

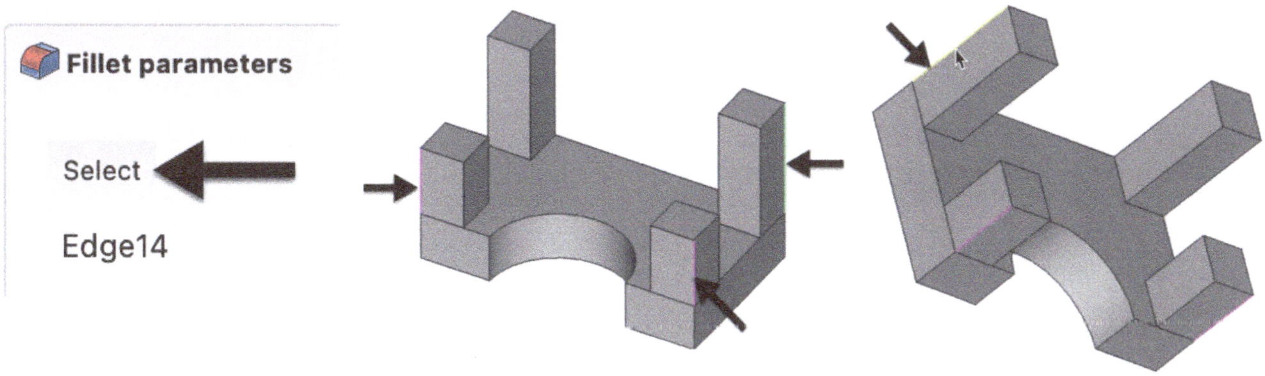

Select the required number of edges and click **OK** to complete the fillet feature. The *Fillet* feature will be listed in the **Model** tab of the **Combo View** panel.

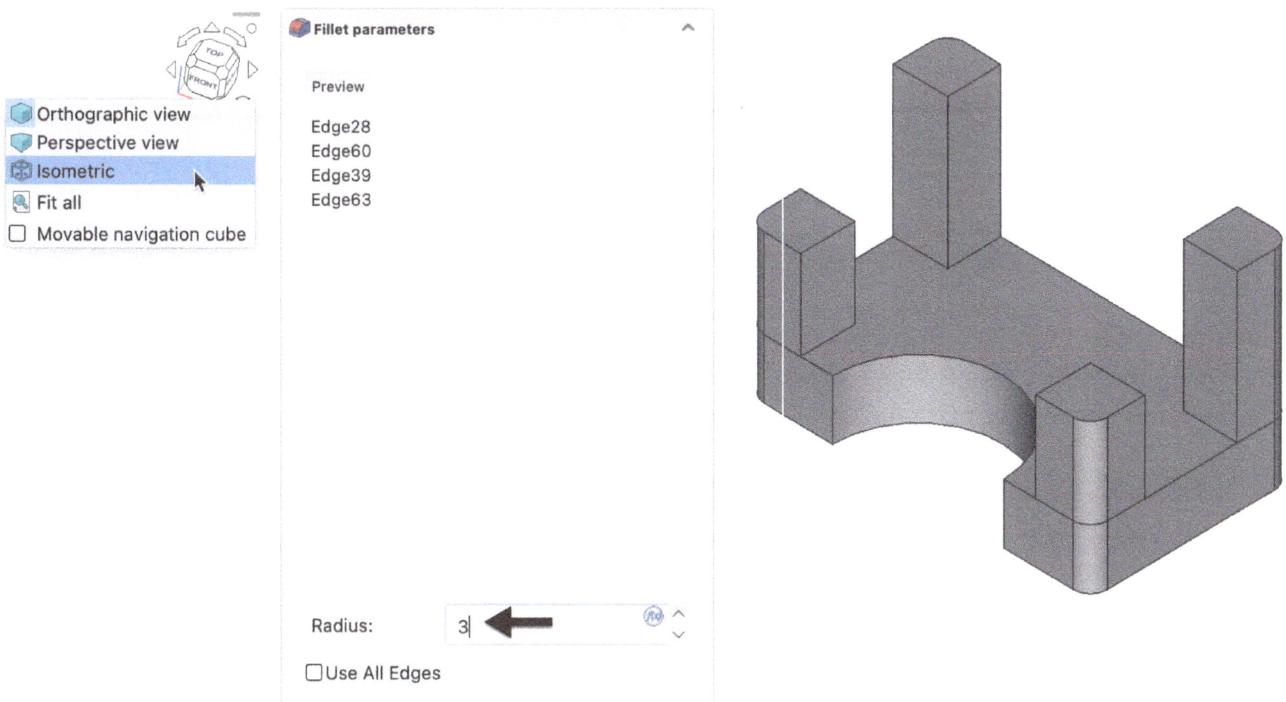

Selection Modes

The **Fillet** command allows you to select the edges to be filleted using two selection modes: **Edges** and **Faces**.

You can select individual edges just by clicking on them.

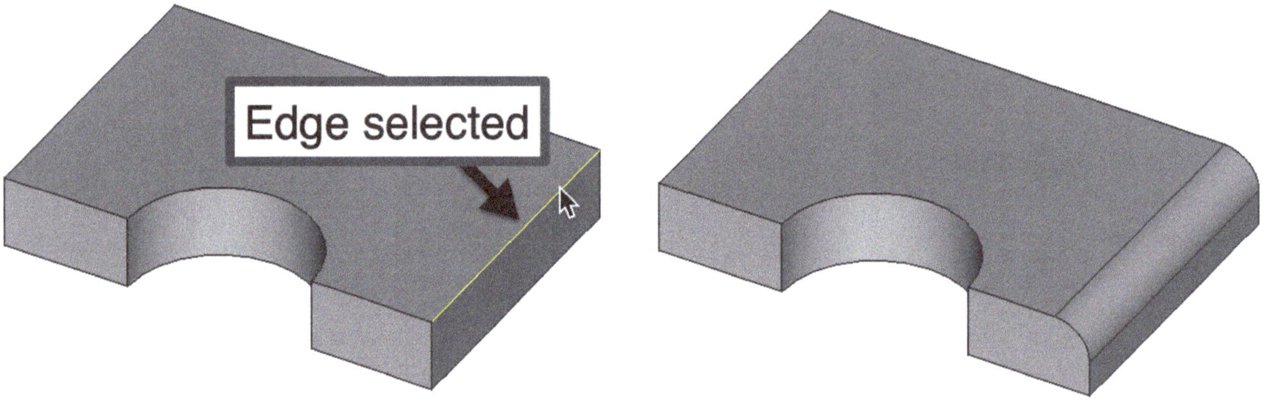

You can select all the edges of a face by merely clicking on it. If you want to select all the edges of the model, then check the **Use All Edges** option.

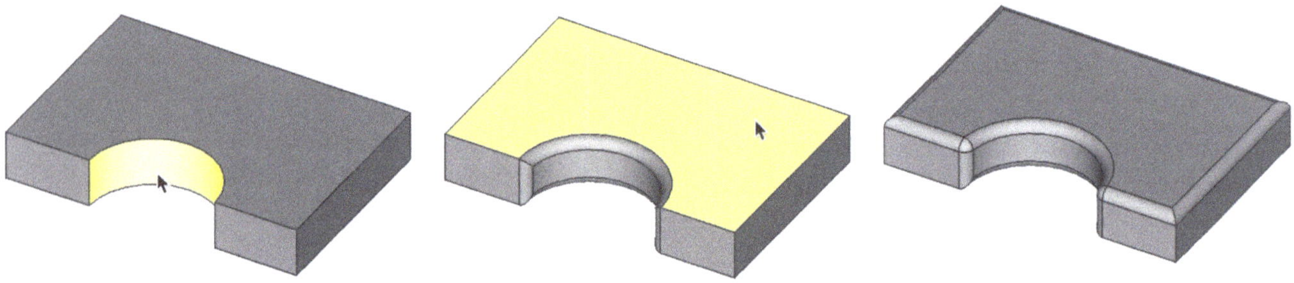

Best Practices

Understanding Design Intent: Before adding fillets, have a clear understanding of your design's purpose and how fillets will enhance the part's functionality and look.

Design Guidelines: Establish specific design guidelines for fillets, such as minimum and maximum fillet radii. This ensures consistency in your models.

Base Feature First: Begin by adding fillets to the base feature, then proceed to subsequent features. This helps maintain predictability in your modeling process.

Segmented Edges: For complex geometries, consider dividing edges into smaller segments and apply fillets to these segments separately. This method results in smoother transitions.

Balanced Filleting: Avoid excessive filleting, which can lead to model inaccuracies and larger file sizes. Use fillets thoughtfully and with purpose.

Consider Feature Order: Pay attention to the order in which fillets are applied. Sometimes, changing the order can make filleting easier and reduce errors.

Cautions:

Watch File Size: Extensive or overly complex filleting can increase file sizes and impact system performance, especially in larger projects.

Sharp Edges: Be cautious when applying fillets to very sharp edges, as it might result in small or unnecessary fillet radii.

Avoid Overlapping Fillets: Do not create fillets that overlap or intersect each other, as this can lead to modeling errors.

Timing of Filleting: Avoid adding fillets too early in the design process, especially when expecting significant design changes. Fillets can be challenging to modify once applied.

Chamfer

The **Chamfer** and **Fillet** commands are commonly used to break sharp edges. The difference is that the **Chamfer** command adds a beveled face to the model. In machined parts, the choice between chamfers and fillets depends on the specific requirements of the design and ease of machining. Chamfers can be more accessible for certain toolpaths.

In forged parts, chamfers can be used strategically to control material flow during the forging process. Chamfers can make it easier to shape the material into the desired form. Chamfers serve multiple purposes, such as improving the part's aesthetics, reducing stress concentration, and facilitating assembly

A chamfer is also a dress-up feature. There are three different chamfer types: *Equal Distance, Two Distances* and *Distance and Angle*. The default Chamfer **Type** is Equal distance.

Equal Distance chamfer

This option is used to create a chamfer with equal distance on both sides of the edge. Press and hold the CTRL key (COMMAND key of Mac users) and select the edges to fillet. Next, click **Part Design > Apply a dress-up feature > Chamfer** on the menu bar (or) click the **Chamfer** icon on the **Part Design Modeling** toolbar. On the **Chamfer parameters** panel, select **Type > Equal Distance**. Next, type-in a value in the **Size** box. Click **OK** to complete the chamfer.

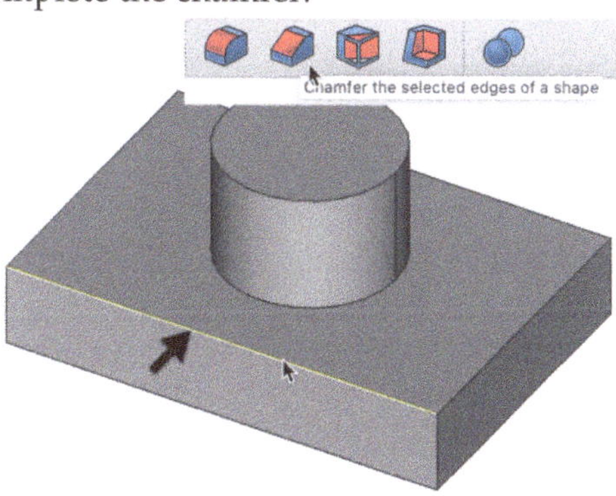

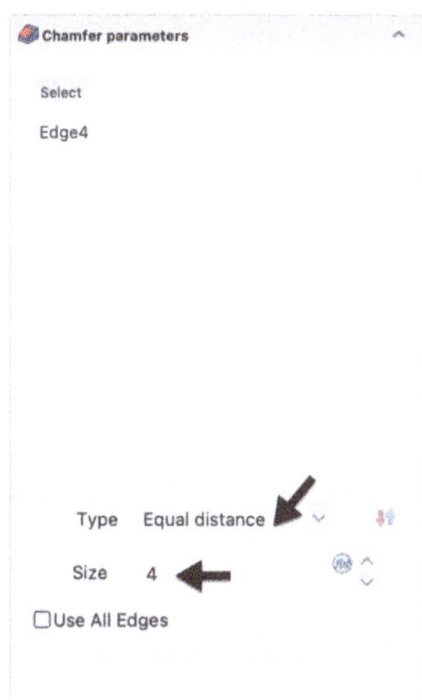

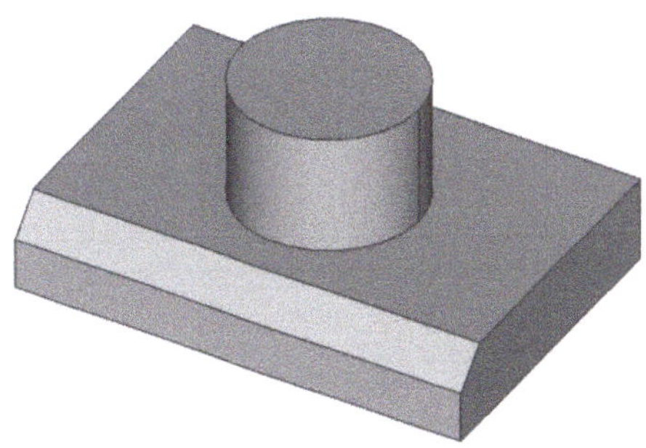

Distance and Angle chamfer

This option lets you create a chamfer by defining its distance and angle values. Select the edge to chamfer and click the **Chamfer** icon on the **Part Design Modeling** toolbar. On the **Chamfer parameters** panel, select **Type > Distance and angle.** Type-in values in the **Size** and **Angle** boxes; the distance and angle values are measured from the vertical and horizontal faces, respectively. Click **OK** to complete the feature.

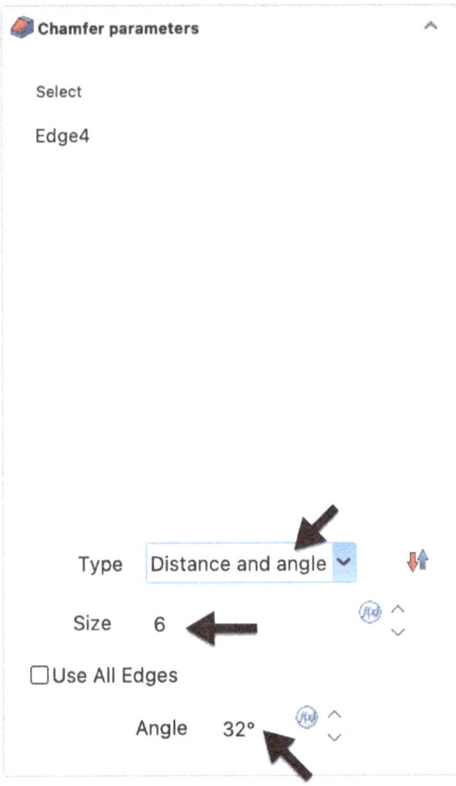

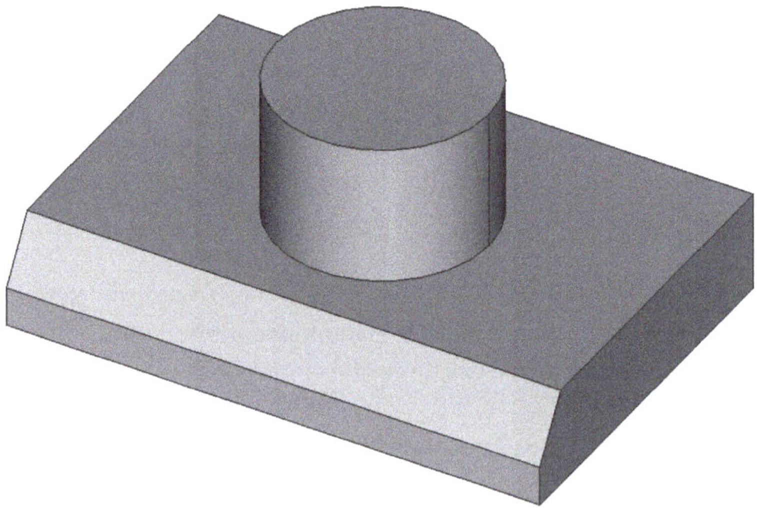

Two Distances chamfer

If you want a chamfer to have different setbacks on both sides of the edge, then select **Type > Two distances** option on the **Chamfer parameters** panel. Type-in values in the first **Distance** and the second **Distance** boxes on the **Chamfer parameters** panel. Click the **Flip Direction** icon to reverse the sides. Click **OK** to complete the feature.

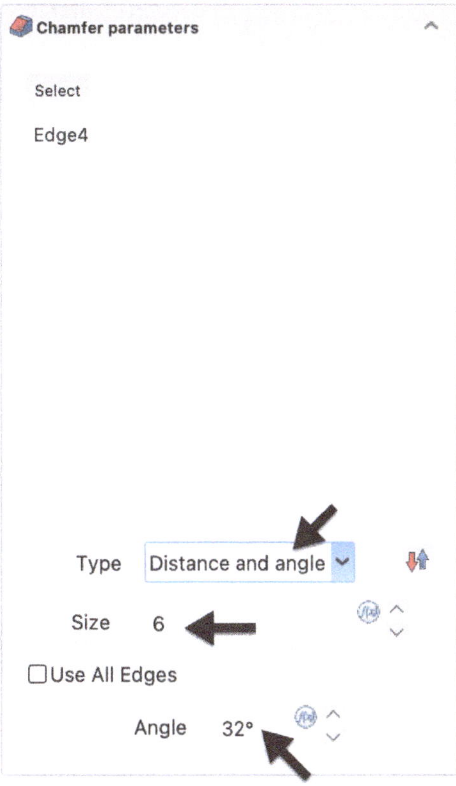

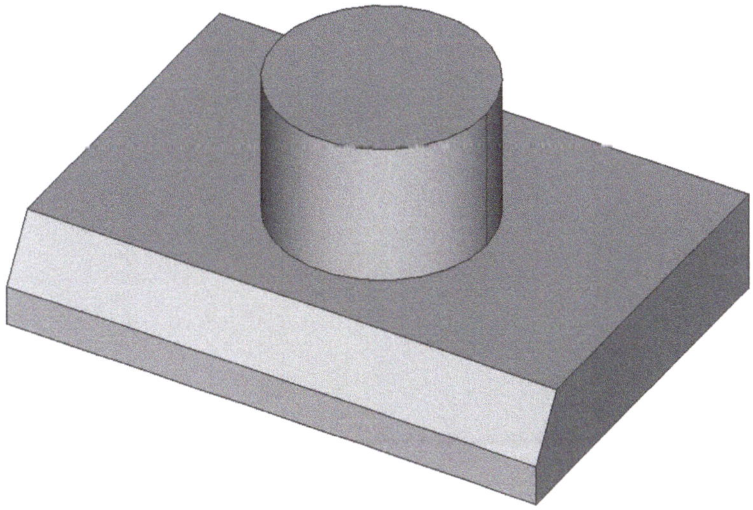

The Draft command

When creating cast or plastic parts, you are often required to add a draft on them so that they can be molded easily. A draft is an angle or taper applied to the faces of components so that they can be removed from the mold easily. The following illustration shows a molded part with and without a draft.

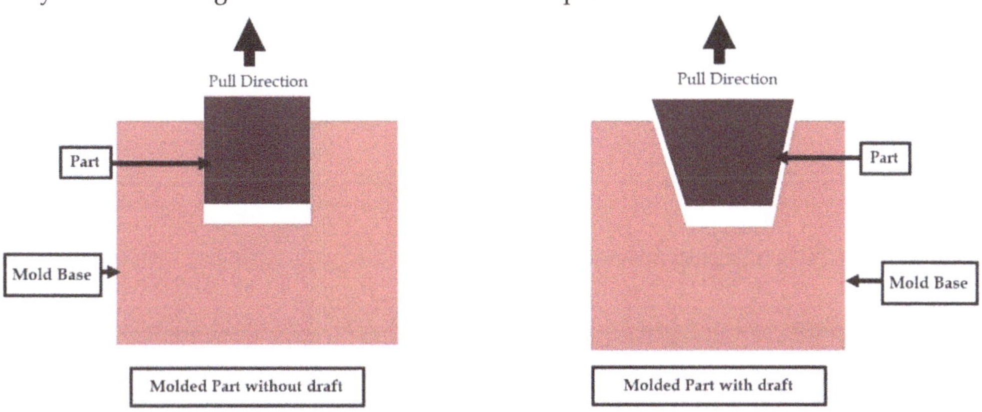

The **Draft** command will help you to apply a draft to the model geometry. To do this, first select the face to be drafted. Next, click **Part Design > Apply a dress-up feature > Draft** on the menu bar (or) click the **Draft** icon on the **Part Design Modeling** toolbar. On the **Draft parameters** panel, click the **Neutral plane** button and select the plane or face to define the neutral plane. Next, click the **Pull direction** button and select an edge to define the pull direction. Type-in a value in the **Draft angle** box to specify the angle.

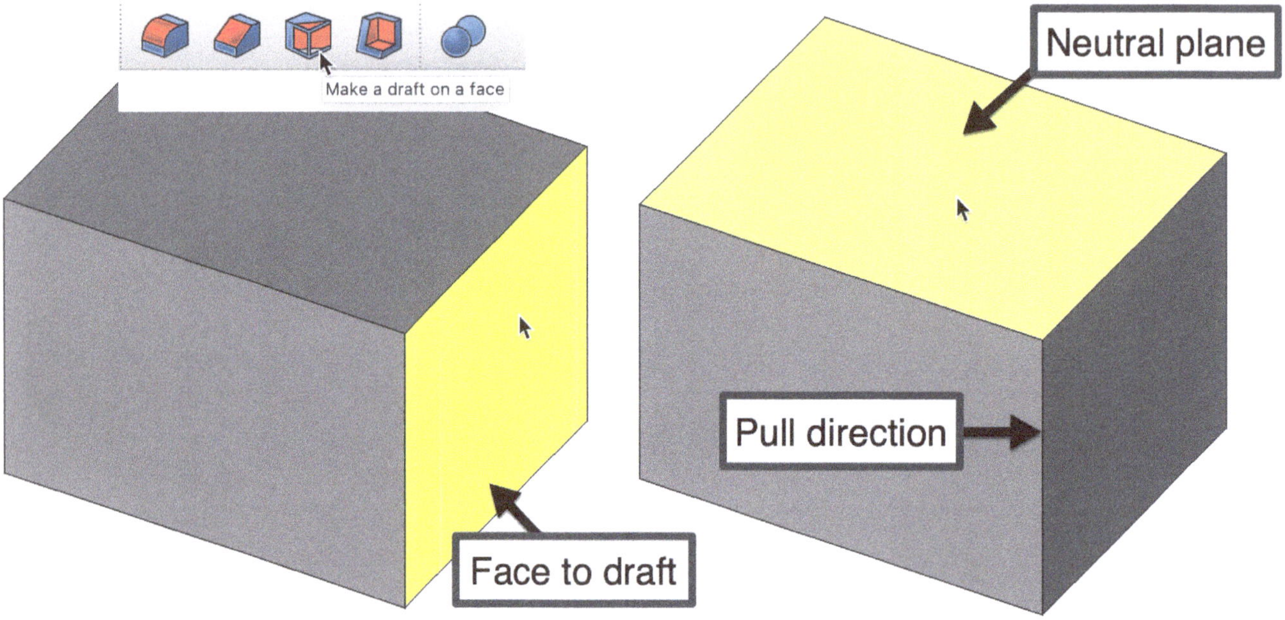

Check the **Reverse pull direction** option to reverse the direction of the draft. Click **OK** to create the draft feature.

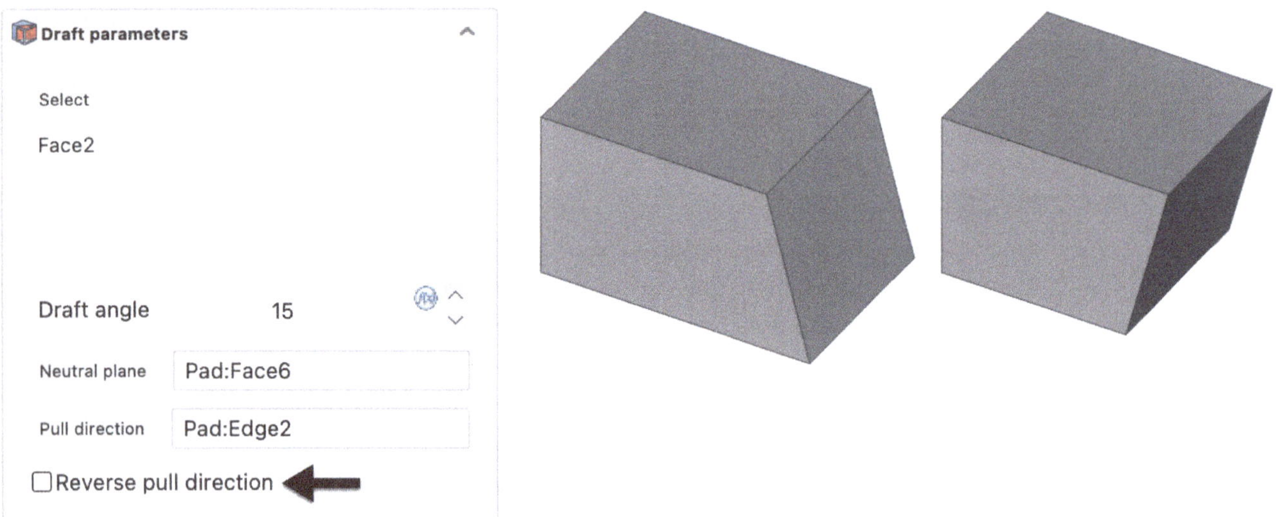

You can select tangentially connected faces by clicking anyone of them.

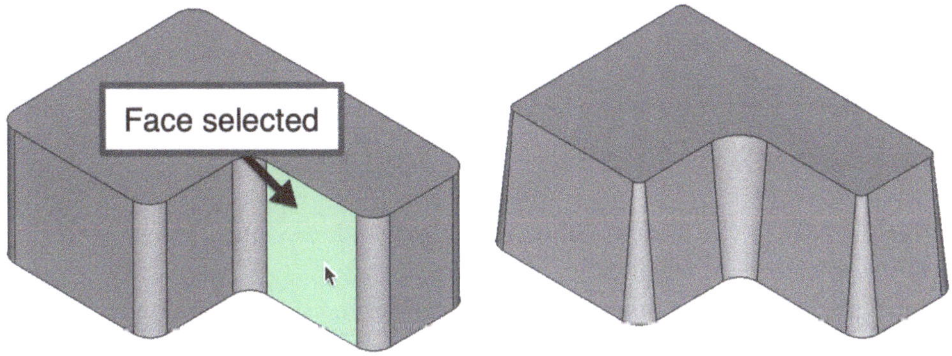

Note that it is a best practice to apply fillets at the end of the model. You may get some undesired geometry if you apply fillets before the draft feature.

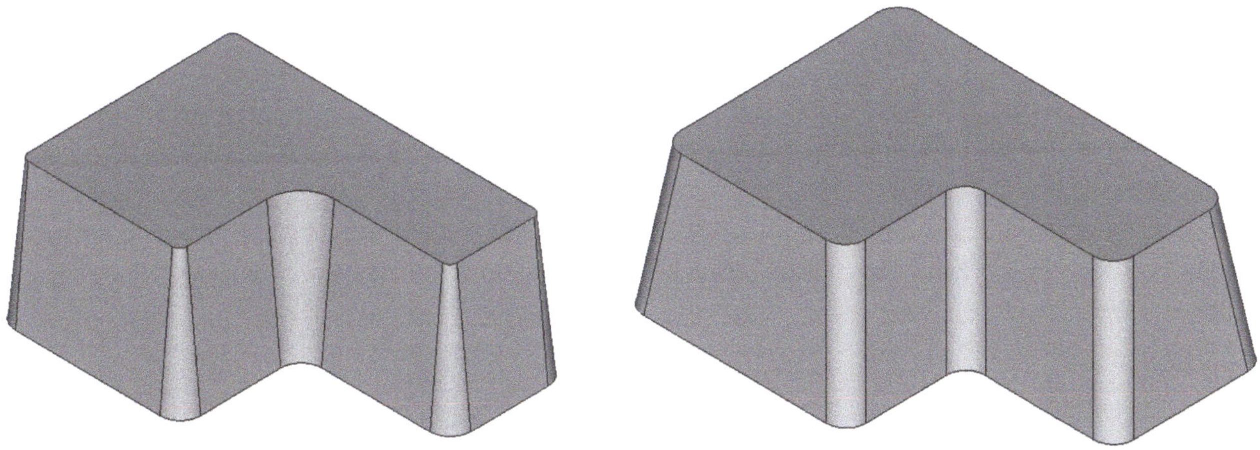

Fillets created before the draft

Fillets created after the draft

General Guidelines

1. **Early Planning:** Start thinking about draft angles early in your design process. It's easier to incorporate them from the beginning rather than making changes later.
2. **Material Consideration:** Different materials have different requirements for draft angles. Always consult material guidelines to determine the right draft for your chosen material.
3. **Minimum Draft:** Apply the minimum amount of draft required to facilitate proper ejection without overdoing it. Excessive draft can increase part size and material usage.
4. **Protect Functional Surfaces:** Avoid adding draft to surfaces that need to mate precisely or create seals. These surfaces should be as close to vertical as possible.

Drafting Tips for Different Part Types

Plastic Parts:

1. **Uniform Draft:** Aim for a consistent draft angle on all vertical surfaces when designing plastic parts. This helps with ejection and minimizes warping during cooling.
2. **Core/Cavity Feature:** FreeCAD provides tools to apply draft specifically to the mold features while preserving your original part's geometry. This maintains the original part's shape.

3. **Ribs and Bosses:** When designing features like ribs and bosses on plastic parts, apply draft to the walls of these features while keeping the critical dimensions unaffected.

Casted Parts:

1. **Parting Lines:** Consider where the parting lines in the mold will be for casted parts. Apply draft to the surfaces facing away from these lines.
2. **Maintain Wall Thickness:** Avoid excessive draft that might thin the part's walls too much. Proper wall thickness is essential for casted parts' structural integrity.
3. **Smooth Transitions:** Ensure that draft angles have smooth transitions on curved surfaces to prevent sharp changes in wall thickness.

Forged Parts:

1. **Varied Draft Angles:** For forgings, draft angles may vary based on the specific shape of the part. Curved or complex surfaces may need different draft angles compared to flat or simpler areas.
2. **Thick Sections:** Be cautious when adding draft to heavily loaded sections, as they might need additional material for strength. Consider using fillets or other design features to maintain strength.

Machined Parts:

1. **Limited Draft:** For machined parts, draft angles are typically not required. These parts are produced by removing material, not molding or casting. However, minimal draft can ease machining and deburring processes.
2. **Preserve Design Intent:** When adding draft to machined parts, take care to maintain the design intent. Overdrafting can change the part's shape and size, so proceed with caution.

Cautions:

1. **Overdrafting:** Adding excessive draft can increase costs and alter the part's size and shape. Always aim for the minimum draft required to achieve ejection.
2. **Functionality:** Be mindful of how draft impacts the functionality of the part. Avoid adding draft to surfaces that require precise mating or sealing.
3. **Mold Complexity:** Complex molds with intricate parts may require additional considerations. Consult with mold designers or casting experts when needed to align your design with manufacturing capabilities.

Thickness

The **Thickness** command is another useful command that can be applied directly to a solid model. It allows you to take a solid geometry and make it hollow. This can be a powerful and timesaving technique when designing parts that call for thin walls such as bottles, tanks, and containers. This command is easy to use. You should have a solid part to use this command. Select a face to remove and click **Part Design** > **Apply a dress-up feature** > **Thickness** on the menu bar (or) click the **Thickness** icon on the **Part Design Modeling** toolbar. Type-in the wall thickness in the **Thickness** box. The thickness is added outside the model. Check the **Make thickness inwards** option, if you want to add thickness inside the model.

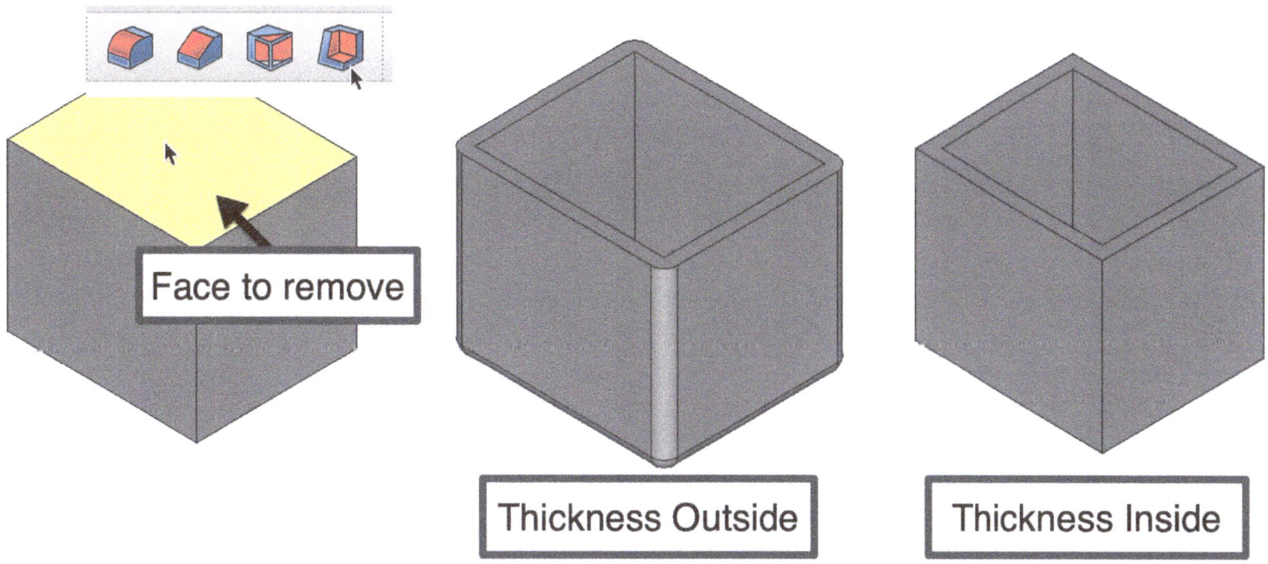

Next, specify the **Join Type**: **Arc** or **Intersection**. The **Arc** option creates an arc at the intersections of two faces. The **Intersection** option leaves sharp edges at the intersection of two faces. Click **OK** to create the *Thickness* feature.

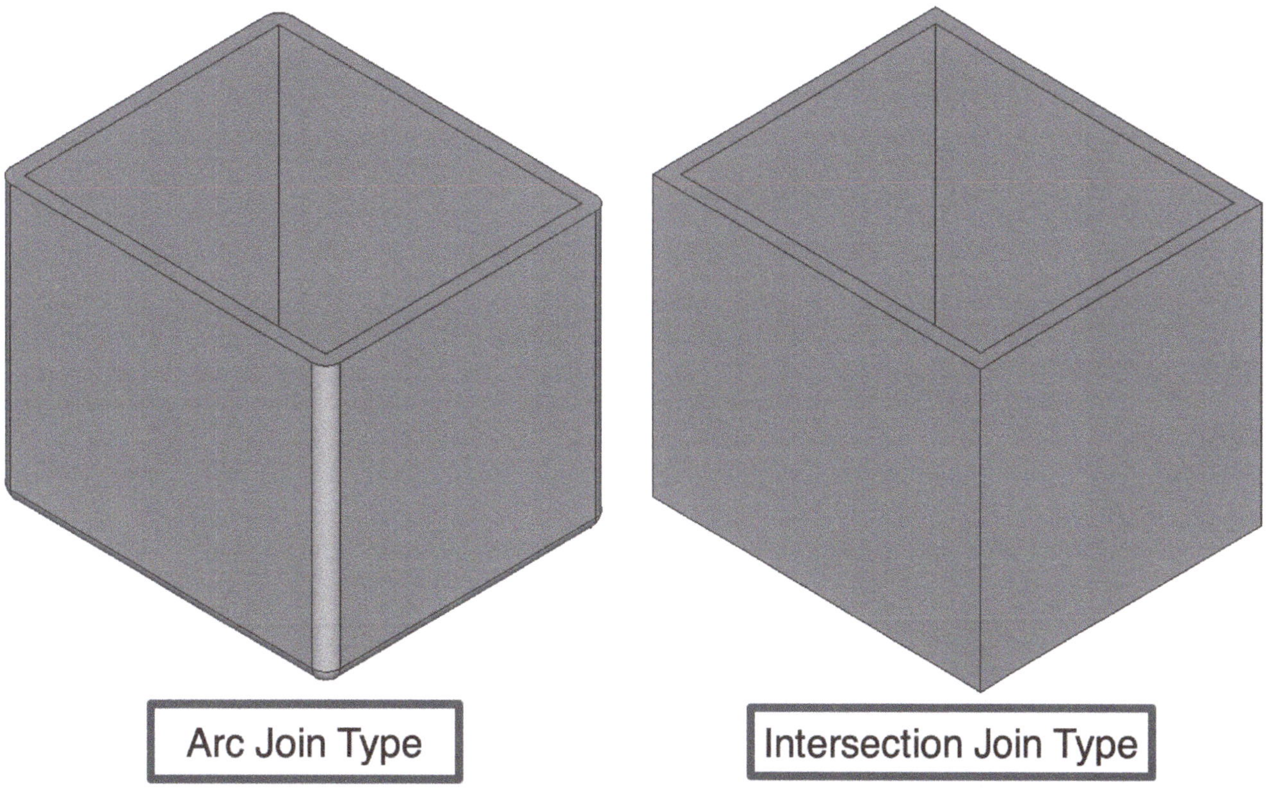

Best Practices

Proper Design Intent: Before creating a shell feature, define the purpose and functional requirements of the part. Understand why you need to create a shell and how it affects the part's behavior.

Keep Wall Thickness Uniform: Maintain a consistent wall thickness in your shell feature. Uneven wall thickness can lead to weak spots or defects in the part.

Parametric Design: Use parametric modeling techniques to ensure that changes in the part design (e.g., dimensions, angles, etc.) update the shell feature accordingly. This keeps your design flexible.

Cautions

Wall Thickness Limits: Be aware of the minimum and maximum wall thickness limitations for the manufacturing process and material you intend to use. Different processes have different requirements.

Avoid Sharp Corners: Avoid creating sharp corners or abrupt changes in wall thickness, as this can lead to stress concentration and possible failure in the part.

Material Selection: The choice of material can greatly impact the feasibility of a shell feature. Make sure the material can be molded, cast, forged, or machined effectively with the desired wall thickness.

Tips

Draft Angles (Plastic Parts):
Consider adding draft angles to the walls of the shell feature for easier mold release in plastic injection molding.

Ribbing and Gussets (Plastic Parts):
For added strength, consider adding ribs or gussets to the interior of the shell feature in plastic parts.

Material Shrinkage (Plastic Parts):
Compensate for material shrinkage during the cooling phase of plastic injection molding in your design to achieve the desired final dimensions.

Tapered Walls (Casted Parts):
Design tapered walls in the shell feature to facilitate the removal of the pattern and reduce the risk of casting defects.

Parting Lines (Casted Parts):
Keep parting lines in mind when creating the shell, as they can affect the ease of casting and part quality.

Minimize Undercuts (Casted Parts):
Minimize or eliminate undercuts in the shell feature to simplify the casting process.

Allow for Draft Angles (Forged Parts):
Include draft angles in the shell feature to aid in the forging process.

Avoid Sudden Changes (Forged Parts):
Avoid sharp corners and abrupt transitions, which can be challenging to forge.

Maintain Consistency (Forged Parts):
Ensure consistent wall thickness for even deformation during forging.

Consider Post-Machining (Machined Parts):
Plan for post-machining operations if necessary, as shell features can create internal cavities that need to be machined after initial manufacturing.

Select Suitable Tooling (Machined Parts):
Use appropriate tooling and cutting strategies to machine the thin-walled areas of the shell feature efficiently and with precision.

Tutorial 1 (Millimetres)

In this example, you create the part shown below.

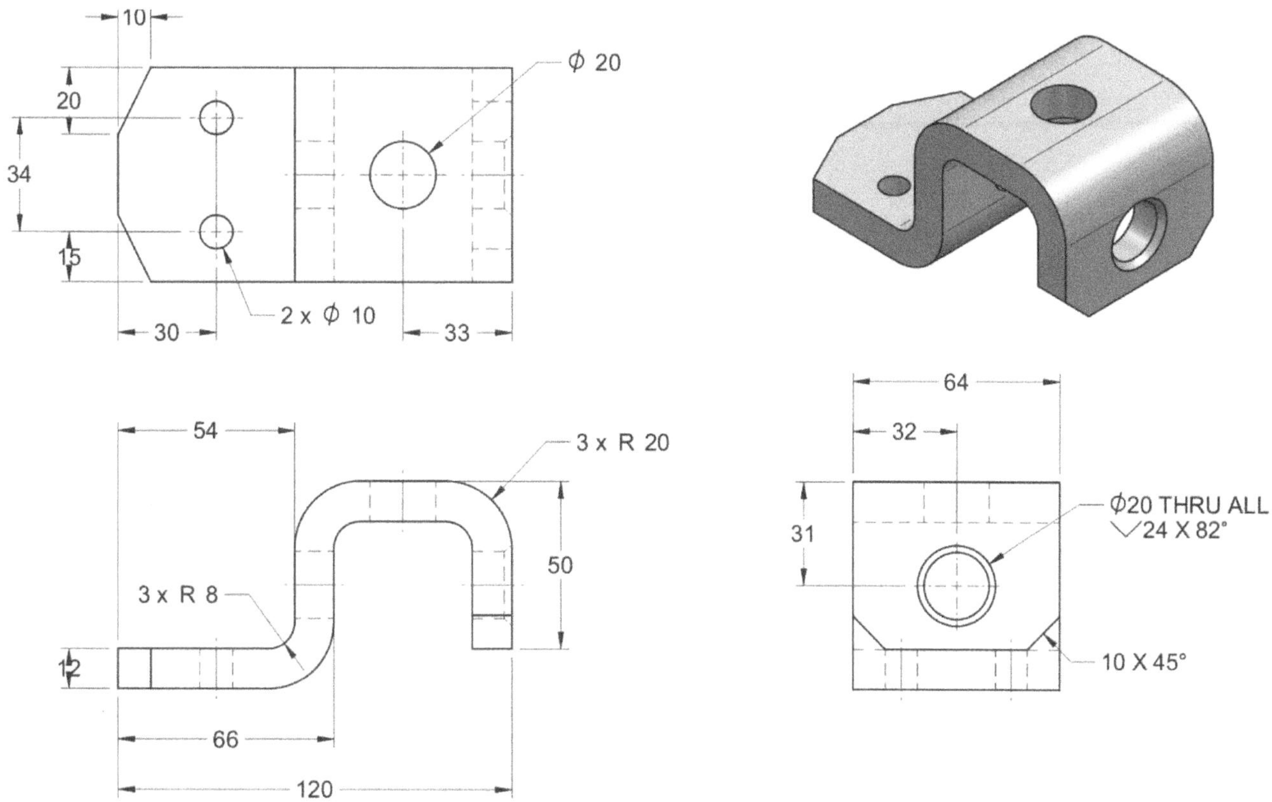

Creating a New document

1. Click **FreeCAD 1.0** on the desktop to start.
2. On the menu bar, click **File > New**; a new document opens.
3. On the **Workbench** toolbar, select **Workbench** drop-down **> Part Design**.
4. Click **Edit > Preferences** on the **Menu** bar (or) click **FreeCAD 1.0 > Preferences** on title bar, if you are working on MacOS; the **Preferences** dialog appears on the screen.
5. Click **General** tab and select **Unit system > Standard (mm/kg/s/degree)**.
6. Select **Number of decimals > 2** and click **OK** on the **Preferences** dialog.

Creating the Pad Feature

1. Click **Create Sketch** command on the **Part Design Helper** toolbar and then select the **XZ** plane.
2. On **Tasks** panel, click the down-arrow located on the **Constraints** section and check the **Auto remove redundants** option.

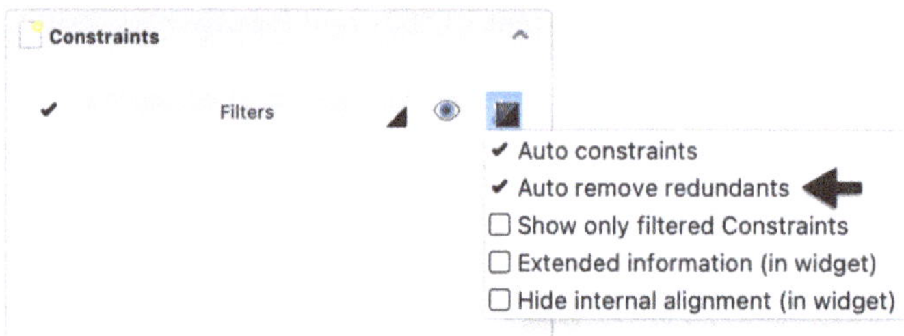

3. Click the **Create line** icon on the **Sketcher geometries** toolbar. Next, select the origin point of the sketch.
4. Move the pointer horizontally toward the right. Type 66 and press the TAB key. Next, type 0 and press and ENTER.

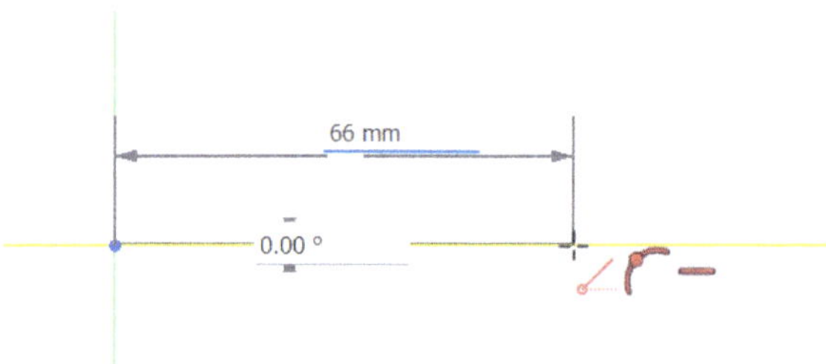

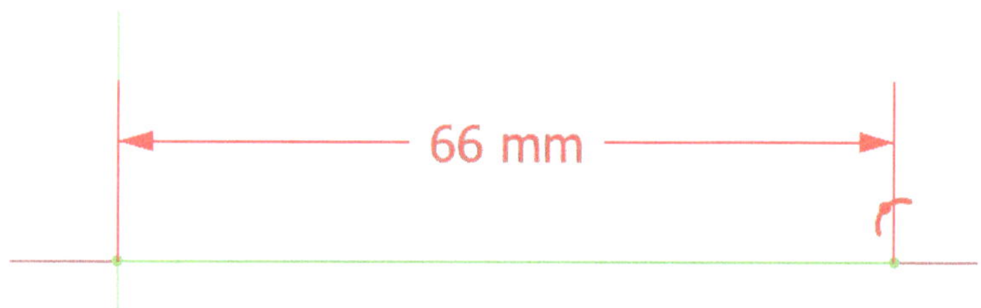

5. Click the **Create polyline** icon on the **Sketcher geometries** toolbar. Select the endpoint of the horizontal line.

6. Create a closed sketch, as shown below. Use the **Constrain Coincident** command and the endpoints, if they are not connected properly.

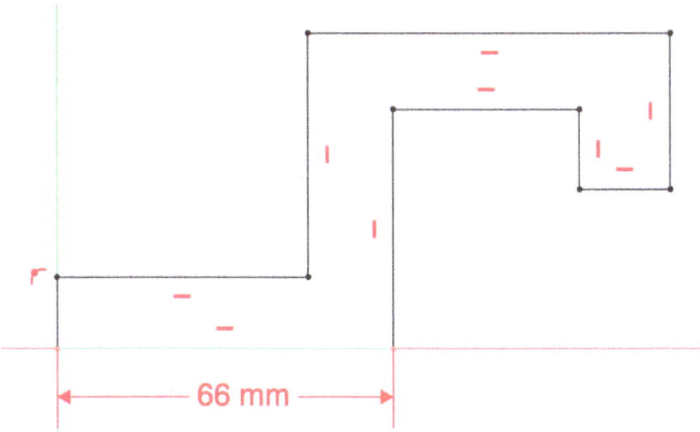

7. Click the **Constrain equal** icon on the **Sketcher constraints** toolbar. Next, select the small vertical and horizontal lines, as shown.

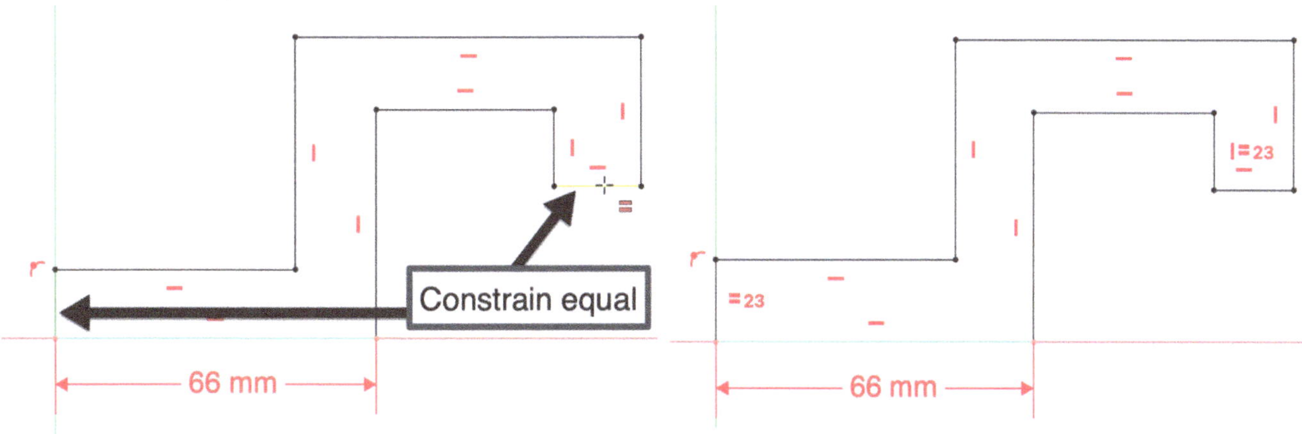

8. Click the **Dimension** drop-down > **Constrain horizontal distance** icon on the **Sketcher constraints** toolbar. Next, select the points of the vertical lines, as shown. Type **120** and click **OK**.

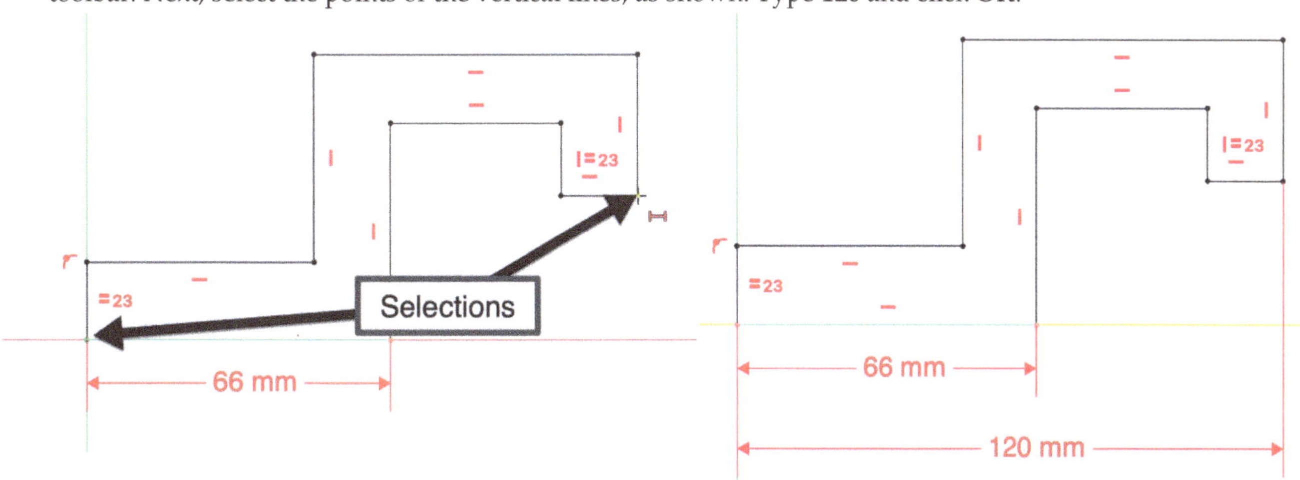

9. Click the **Constrain vertical distance** icon on the **Sketcher constraints** toolbar. Select the corner point of the sketch, as shown. Type **62** and click **OK**.

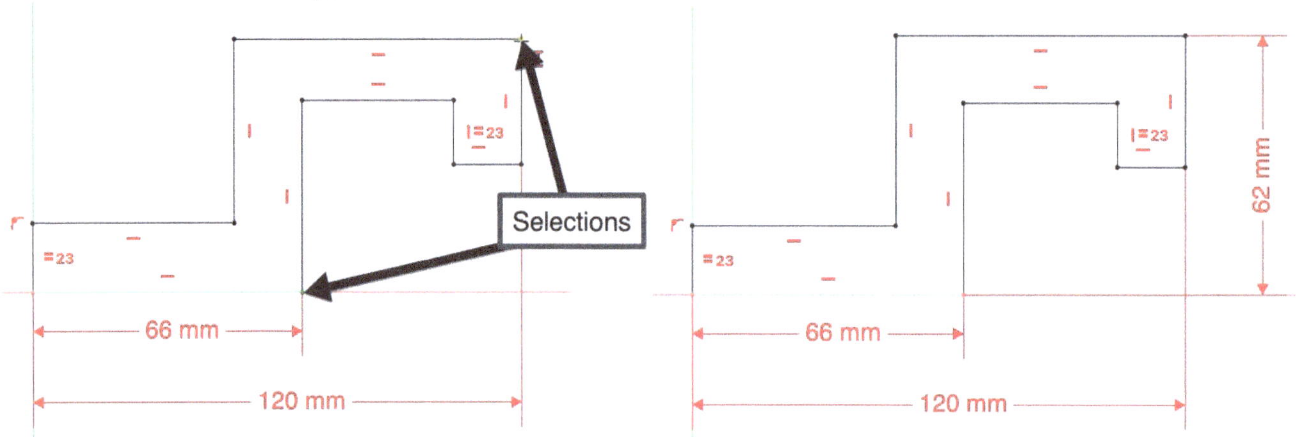

10. Add the remaining vertical and horizontal distance constraints, as shown.

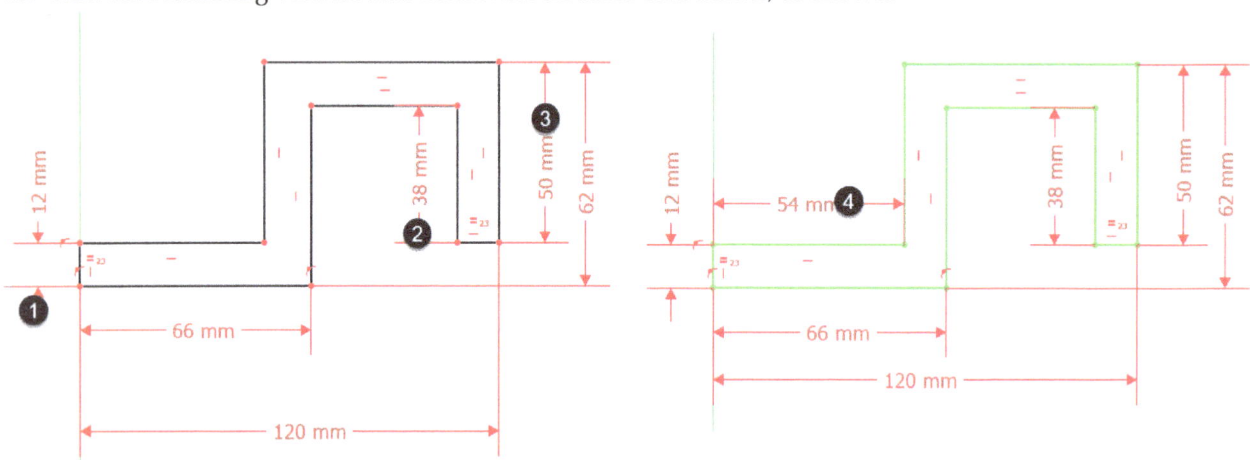

11. Click the **Leave Sketch** icon on the **Sketcher edit mode** toolbar.
12. Click the **Pad** icon on the **Part Design Modeling** toolbar.
13. Type **64** in the **Length** box under the **Pad Parameters** section of the **Combo View** panel.
14. Select the **Symmetric to plane** option and click **OK** to create the *Pad* feature.

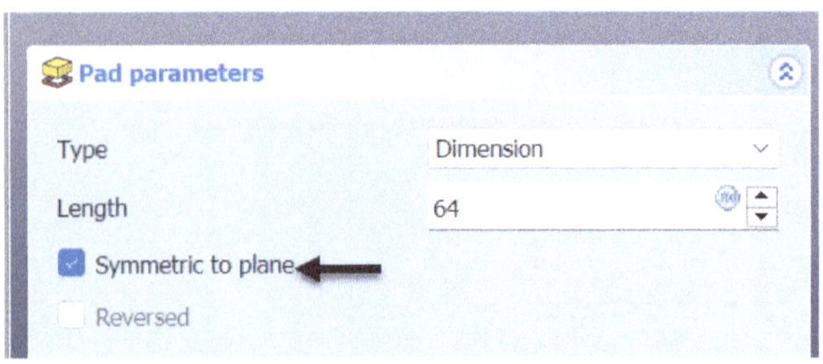

Creating the Hole Features

1. Select the right-side face of the model and click the **Create Sketch** icon on the **Part Design Helper** toolbar.

2. Click the **View Orientation** drop-down > **Right** icon on the **View** toolbar.

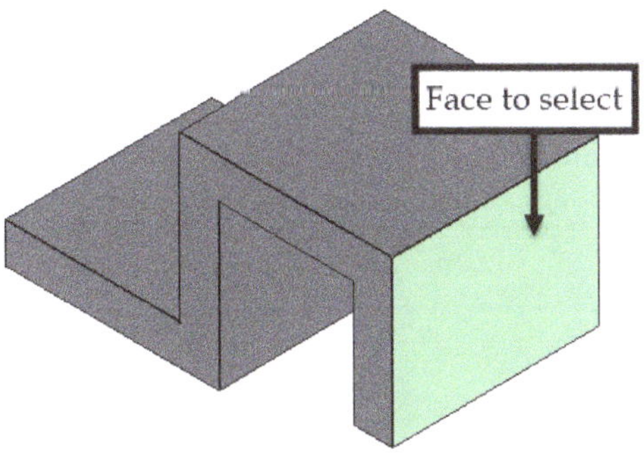

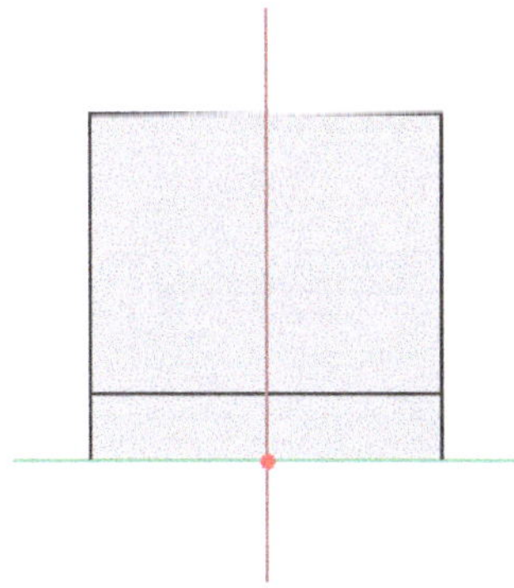

3. Click the **Create external geometry** icon on the **Sketcher tools** toolbar.
4. Select the right vertical edge and the upper horizontal edge of the model, as shown.

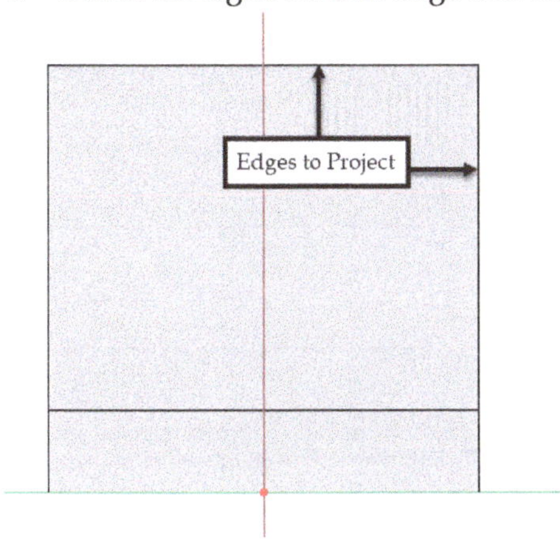

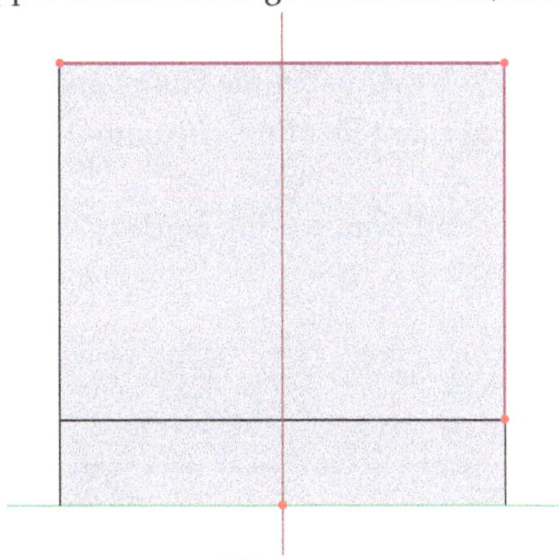

5. Click the **Circle** drop-down > **Create circle by center** icon on the **Sketcher geometries** toolbar. Next, select the vertical axis of the sketch to define the center point. Move the pointer outward and click to create a circle.

6. Click the **Dimensions** drop-down > **Constrain horizontal distance** icon on the **Sketcher constraints** toolbar. Next, select the center point of the circle and the top right corner.
7. Type-in **31** in the **Length** box on the **Insert Length** dialog. Click **OK**.

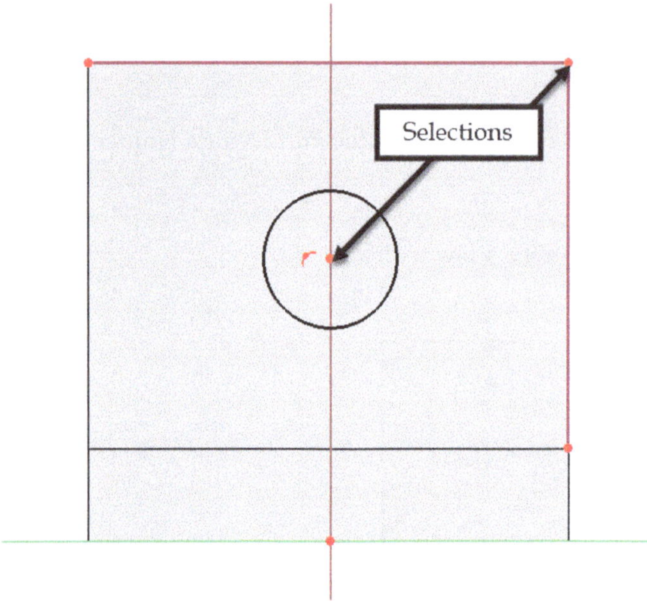

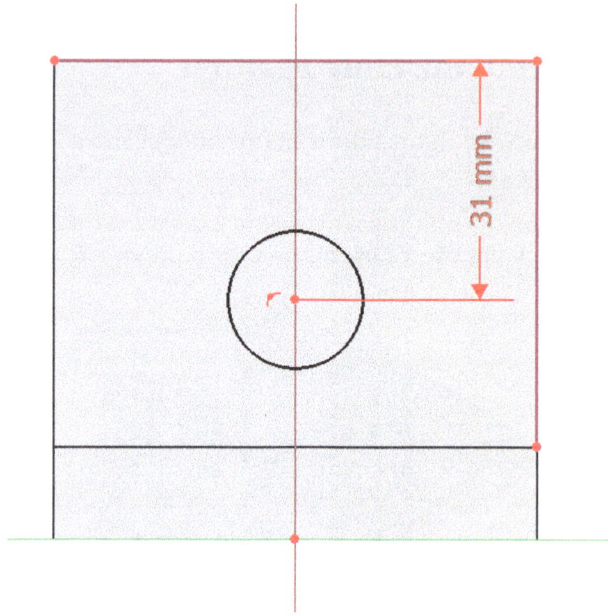

8. Click the **Leave Sketch**  icon on the **Sketcher edit mode** toolbar.
9. Click the **Hole**  icon on the **Part Design Modeling** toolbar; the **Hole parameters** section appears on the **Tasks** panel.
10. On the **Tasks** panel, select **Profile > None** under the **Hole Parameters** section.
11. Type-in **21** in the **Diameter** box and select **Depth > Through All**.
12. Select **Hole cut Type > Countersink**.
13. Type-in **24** and **82** in the **Diameter** and **Countersink angle** boxes, respectively.
14. Click **OK** to create the *Hole* feature.

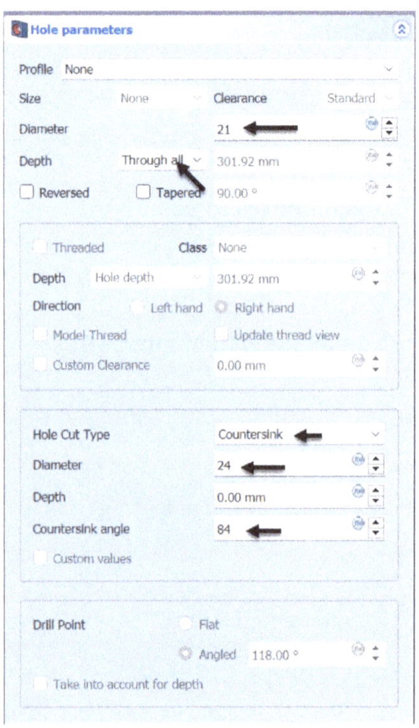

15. Select the top face and click the **Create Sketch** command on the **Part Design Helper** toolbar.
16. On the **Sketcher geometries** toolbar, click the **Create circle by center** icon and then select the horizontal axis. Move the pointer outward and click to create a circle.
17. Click the **Create external geometry** icon on the **Sketcher tools** toolbar.
18. Select the left vertical edge and the upper horizontal edge of the model, as shown.
19. Click the **Dimension** drop-down > **Constrain horizontal distance** icon on the **Sketcher constraints** toolbar. Next, select the center point of the circle and the bottom left corner.
20. Type-in **33** in the **Length** box on the **Insert Length** dialog. Click **OK**.

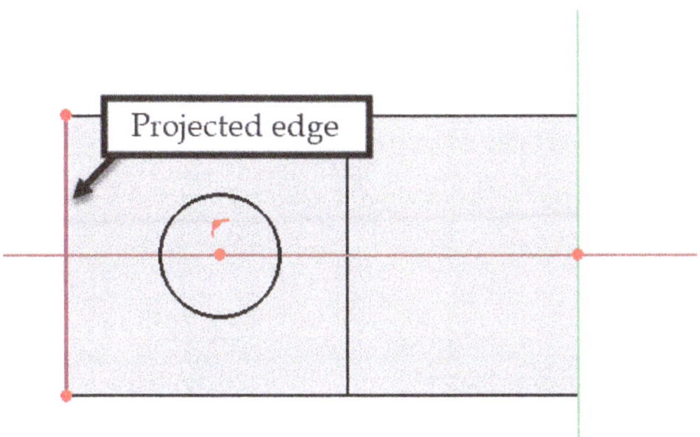

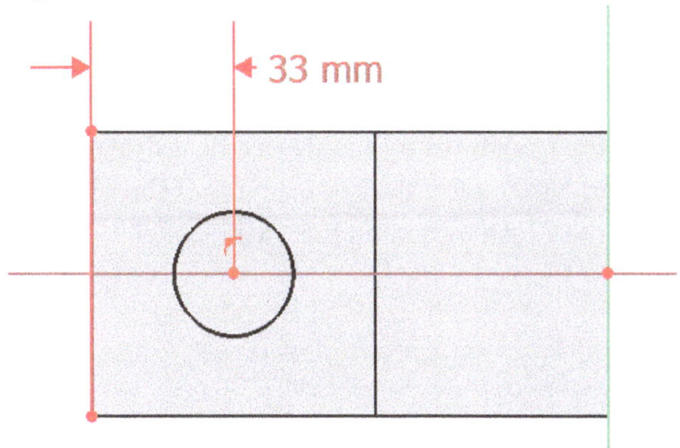

21. Click **Close** on the **Tasks** panel.
22. Click the **Hole** icon on the **Part Design Modeling** toolbar. Next, select **Profile > None** from the **Hole parameters** section.
23. Select **Depth > Through all**. Next, type-in 20 in the **Diameter** box.
24. Click **OK** to create the hole feature.

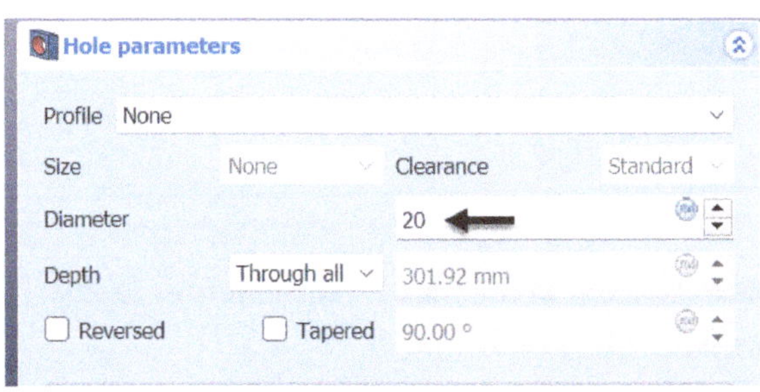

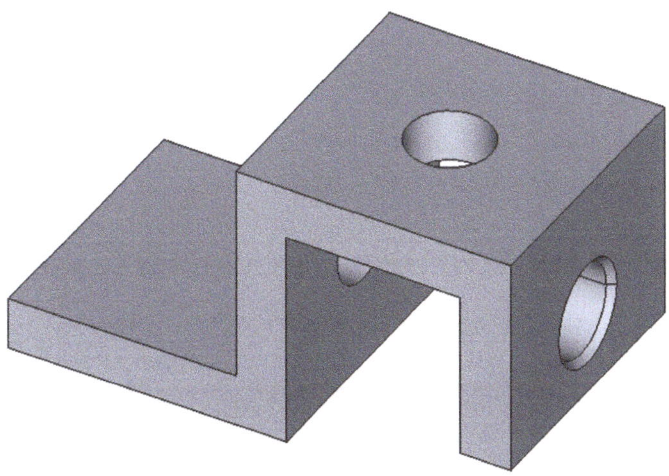

25. Select the lower top face of the model and click the **Create Sketch** icon on the **Part Design Helper** toolbar.

26. Click the **Circle** drop-down > **Create circle by center** icon on the **Sketcher geometries** toolbar and create two circles, as shown.

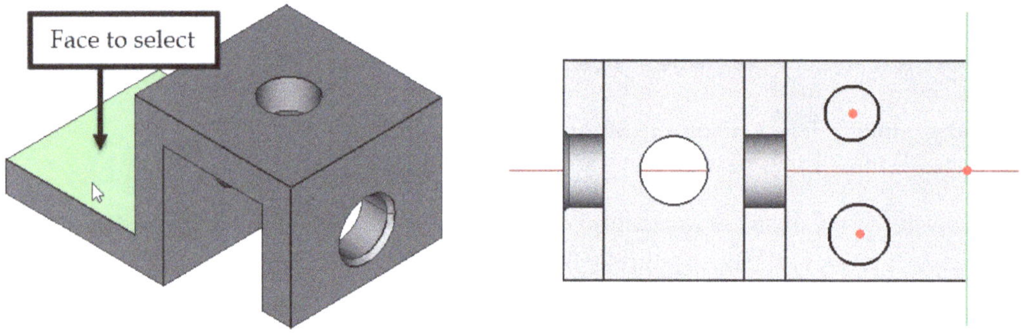

27. Create the dimensional constraints between the circles and the sketch origin.
28. Click the **Constrain horizontal/vertical** drop-down > **Constrain vertical** icon on the **Sketcher constraints** toolbar. Next, select the centerpoints of the two circles to align them vertically.
29. Click the **Close** button on the **Tasks** panel.

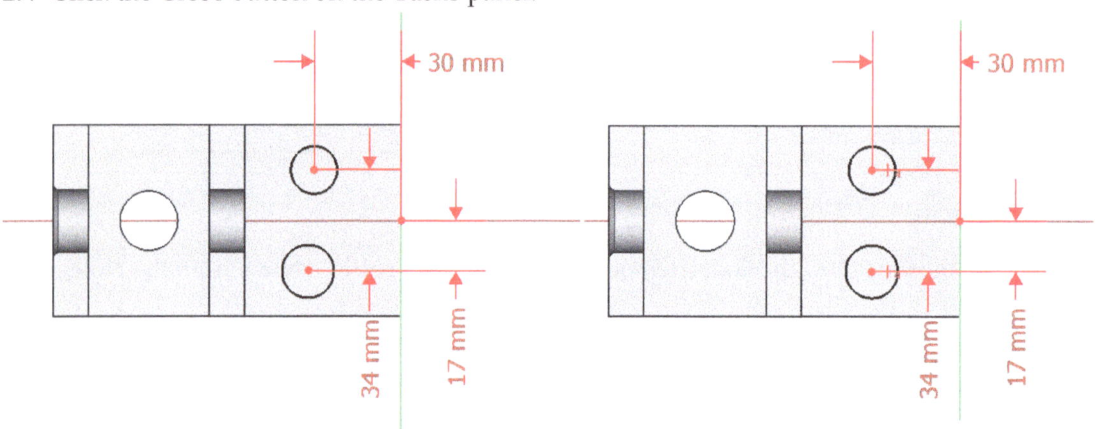

30. Click the **Hole** icon on the **Part Design Modeling** toolbar. Next, select **Profile > None** from the **Hole parameters** section.
31. Select **Depth > Through all**. Next, type-in 10 in the **Diameter** box.
32. Click **OK** to create the hole feature.

Creating the Two Distance Chamfer features

1. Select vertical edge of model, as shown. Next, click the **Chamfer** icon on the **Part Design Helper** toolbar.
2. Select **Type > Two distances** from the **Chamfer parameters** section of the **Tasks** panel.
3. Type **20** and **10** in the **Size 2** boxes, respectively.
4. Click the **Select** button on the **Chamfer parameters** section. Next, rotate the model and select the vertical edge on the back side, as shown.
5. Click **OK** to create the chamfer feature.

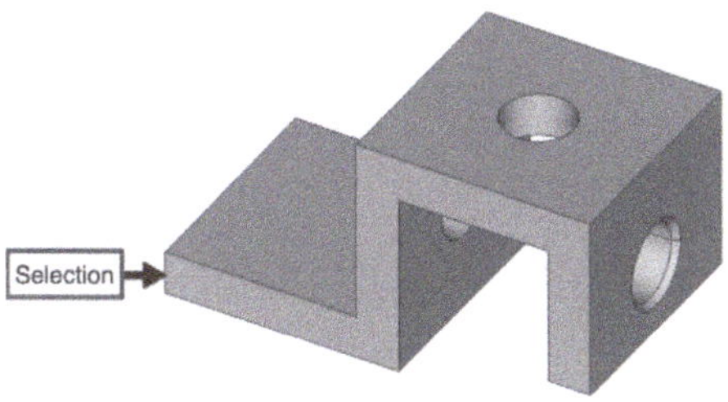

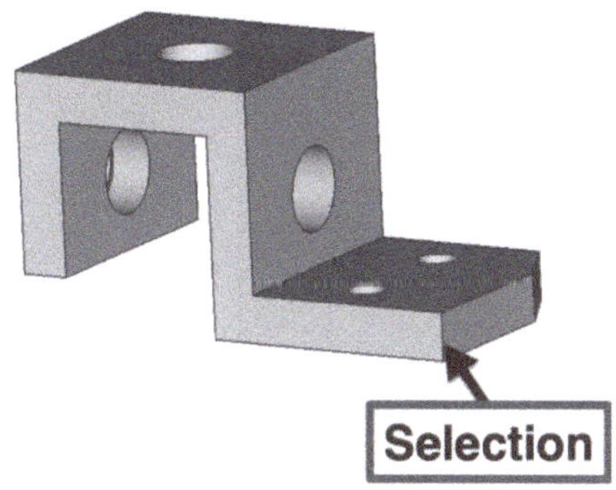

Creating Fillets and Chamfers

1. Press and hold the Ctrl key and select the edges of the model, as shown.
2. Click the **Fillet**  icon on the **Part Design Modeling** toolbar.
3. Type **20** in the **Radius** box available on the **Fillet parameters** section of the **Tasks** panel. Click **OK** to create the fillets.

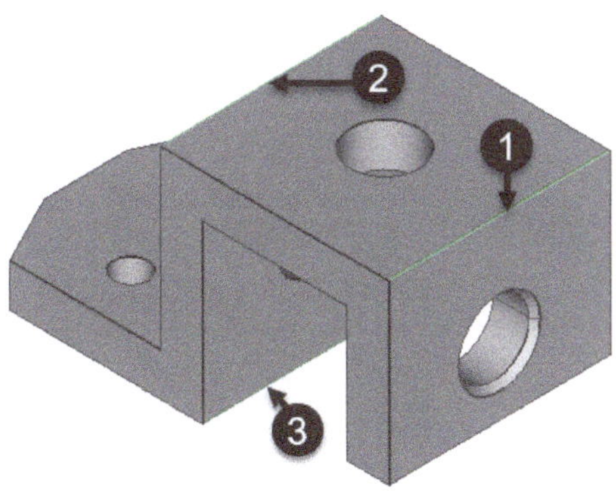

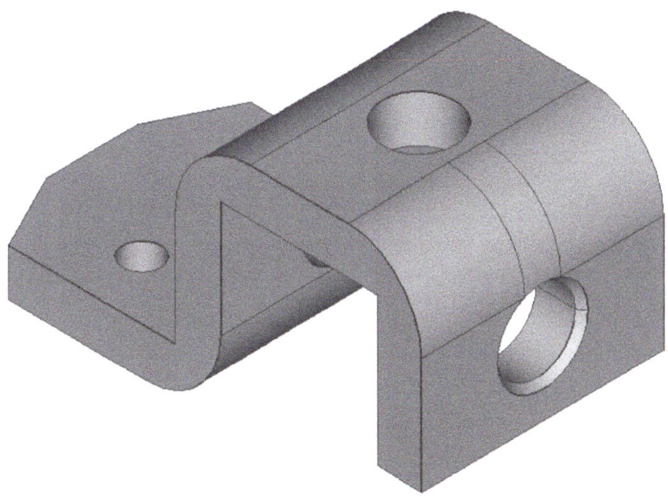

4. On the **View** toolbar, select **Draw style** drop-down > **Wireframe**.
5. Press and hold the Ctrl key and select the horizontal edges of the geometry, as shown.

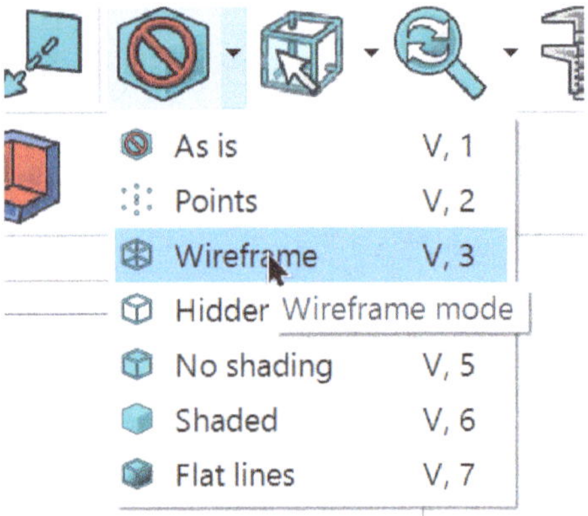

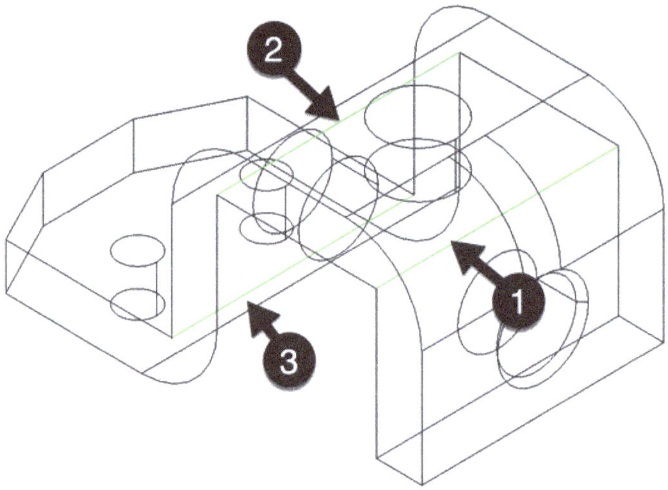

6. Click the **Fillet** icon on the **Part Design Modeling** toolbar. Type 8 in the **Radius** box of the **Fillet parameters** section, and click **OK**.
7. On the **View** toolbar, select **Draw style** drop-down > **Flat lines**.

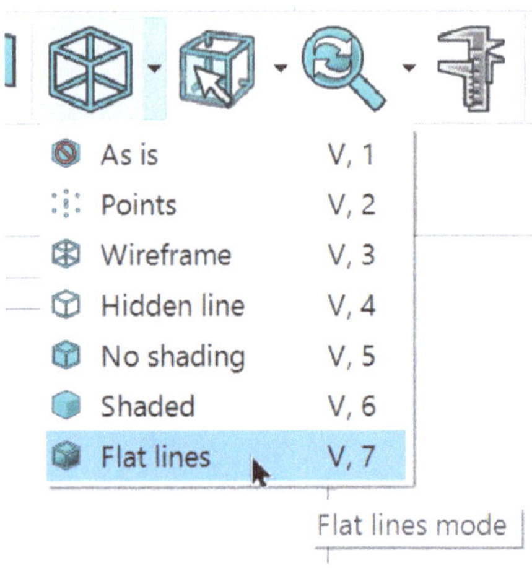

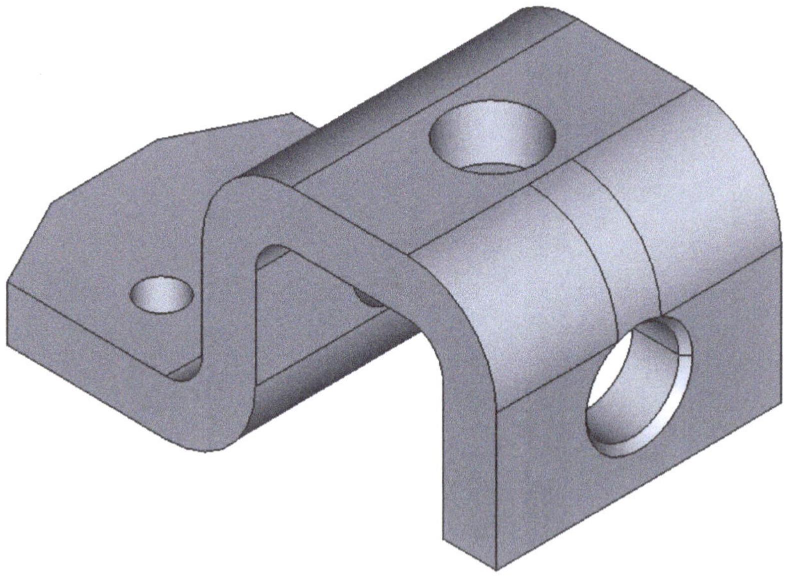

8. Press and hold the middle and right mouse button, and then drag the cursor in the forward direction.
9. Press and hold the Ctrl key and select the edges of the model, as shown.
10. Click the **Chamfer**  icon on the **Part Design Modeling** toolbar.
11. Select **Type > Equal distance** from the **Chamfer parameters** section of the **Tasks** panel
12. Type 10 in the **Size** box in the **Chamfer parameters** section. Next, click **OK** to chamfer the edges.
13. Click the **Save** icon on the **File** toolbar located at the top-left corner of the window. Next, type C4_example1 in the **File name** box, and then click **Save**.
14. Click **File > Close** on the menu bar to close the document.

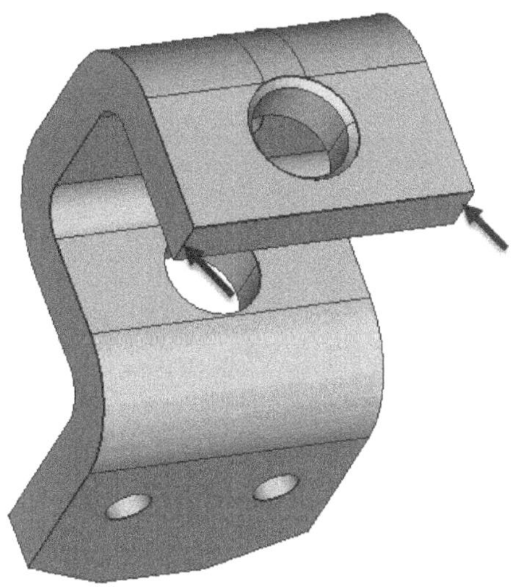

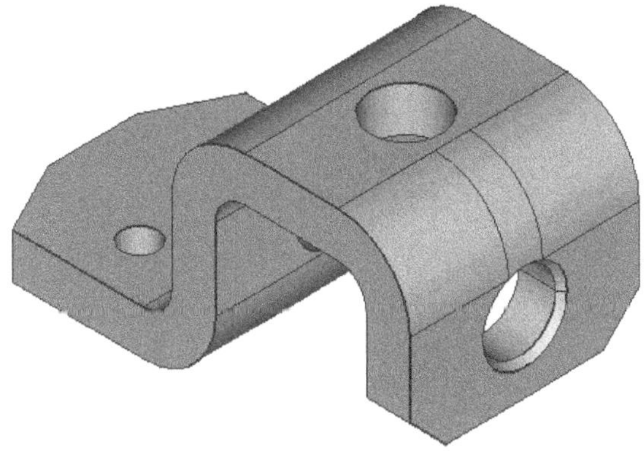

Tutorial 2 (Inches)

In this example, you create the part shown next.

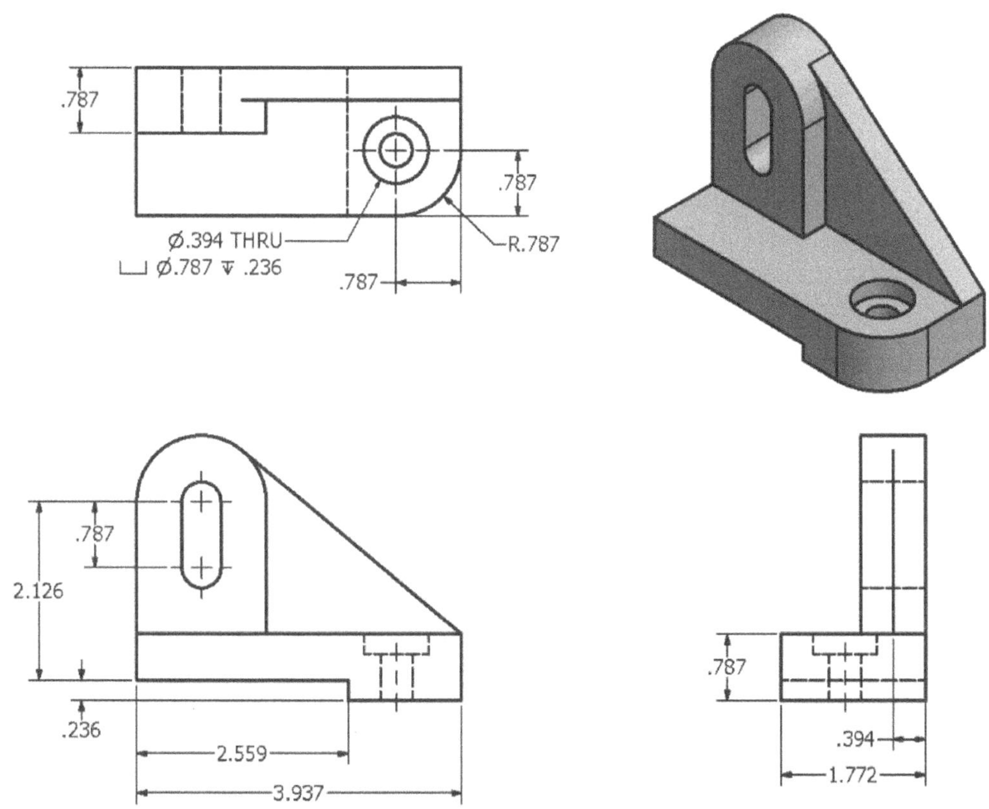

Creating a New document

1. Click **FreeCAD 1.0** on the desktop to start the application.
2. On the menu bar, click **File > New**; it creates a new document.

3. On the **Workbench** toolbar, select **Workbench** drop-down **> Part Design**.
4. Click **Edit > Preferences** on the **Menu** bar (or) click **FreeCAD 1.0 > Preferences** on title bar, if you are working on MacOS; the **Preferences** dialog appears on the screen.
5. Click the **General** tab and select **Default unit system > Imperial decimal (in/lb)**.
6. Select **Number of decimals > 3** and click **OK** on the **Preferences** dialog.

Creating the Pad features

1. Click the **Create Sketch** icon on the **Part Design Helper** Toolbar and select the XY_plane. Next, click **OK**.
2. Click the **Create rectangle** icon on the **Sketcher geometries** toolbar and select the origin point of the sketch. Next, move the pointer toward the bottom right corner and click.
3. Type-in **3.937** in the **width dimension** box and press TAB.
4. Type-in **1.772** in the **height dimension** box and press ENTER.

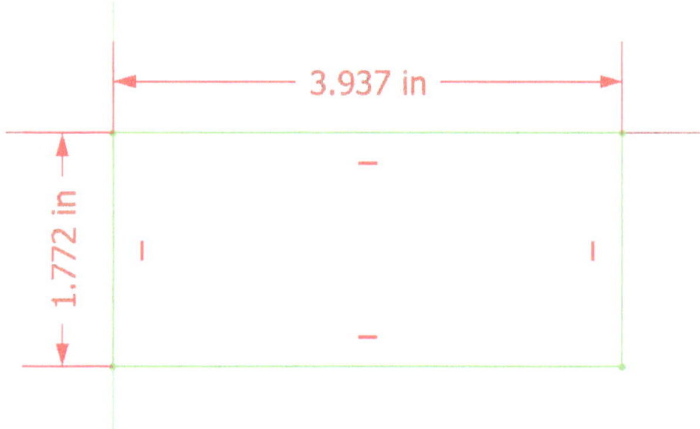

5. Click the **Close** button on the **Tasks** panel.
6. On the **Part Design Modeling** toolbar, click the **Pad asks** command.
7. On the **Pad parameters** section, select **Type > Dimension** and enter **0.787** in the **Length** box. Click **OK** to create the *Pad* feature.

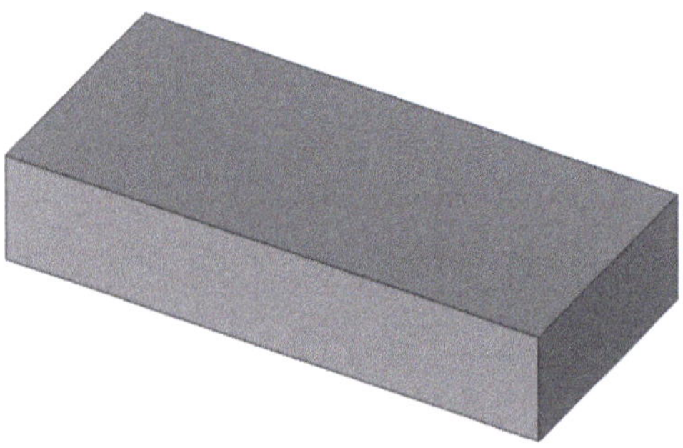

8. Activate the **Create Sketch** command and select the **XZ_plane** on the **Tasks** panel. Next, click **OK**.
9. Click the **Create slot** drop-down **> Create slot** on the **Sketcher geometries** toolbar and click in the graphics window.
10. Move the pointer upward and type-in **1.575** in the length dimension box and press TAB.
11. Type **90** in the angle dimension box and press TAB.

12. Type-in **0.787** in the radius dimension box and press ENTER to create the slot.

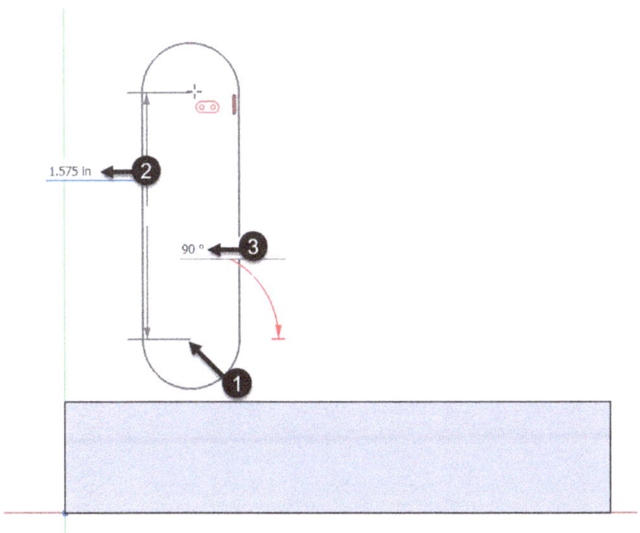

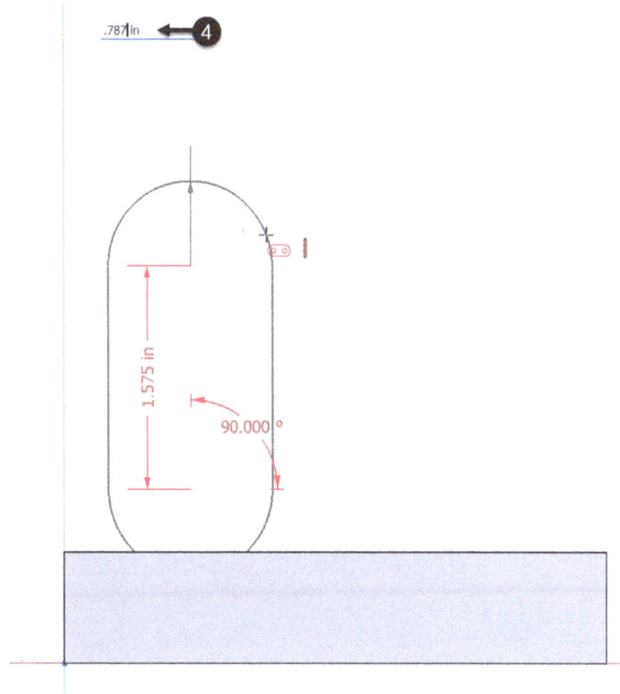

13. Select the lower arc of the slot and press DELETE on your keyboard.
14. On the **Sketcher geometries** toolbar, click **Create line** icon and select the lower endpoint of the left vertical line.
15. Move the pointer toward right and select the lower endpoint of the right vertical line.

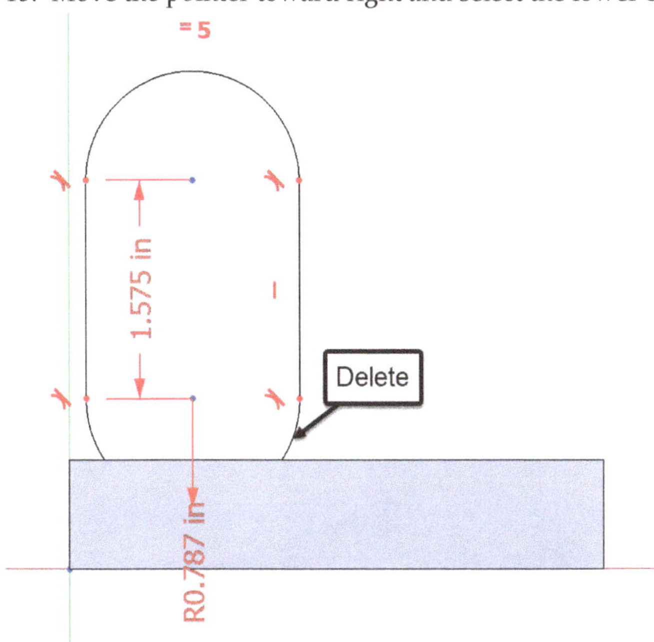

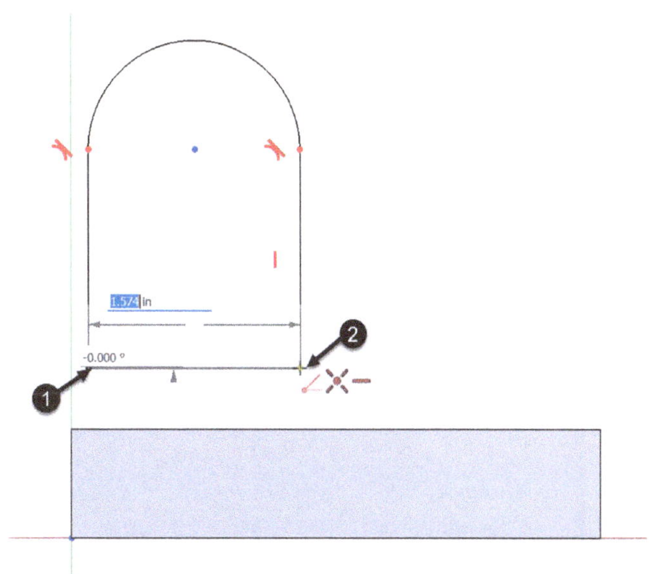

16. Click the **Create external geometry** command on the **Sketcher tools** toolbar and select the horizontal edge of the part geometry, as shown.

17. On the **Sketcher constraints** toolbar, click the **Constrain coincident** and select the lower left corner of the sketch. Next, select the endpoint of the projected edge.
18. On the Sketcher constraints toolbar, click **Constrain horizontal/vertical** drop-down > **Constrain vertical**. Next, select the left vertical line.

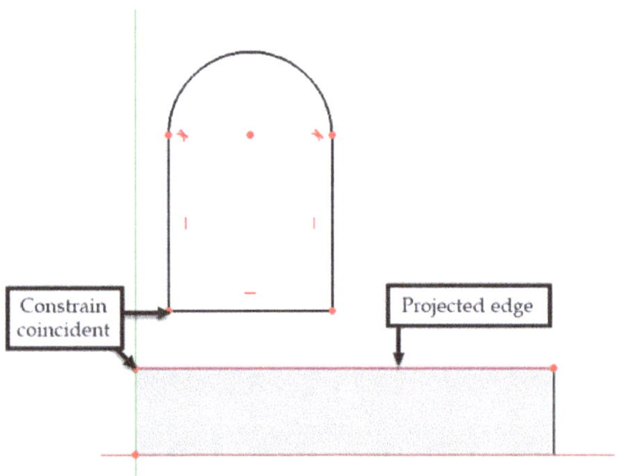

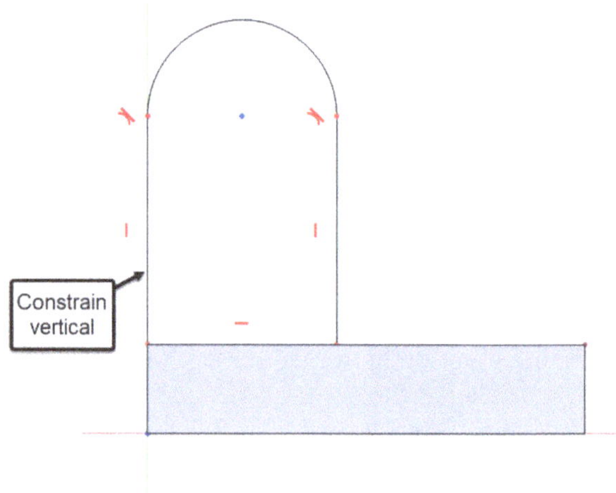

19. Click **Dimension** drop-down **> Constrain vertical distance** on the **Sketcher constraints** toolbar. Next, select the left vertical line of the sketch.
20. Type-in **1.575** in the **Length** box on the **Insert Length** dialog. Click **OK**.
21. Click the **Dimension** drop-down > **Constrain radius** icon on the **Sketcher constraints** toolbar. Next, select the arc, type **0.787** in the **Radius** box, and then click **OK**.
22. Click **Close** on the **Tasks** panel.
23. Activate the **Pad** command select **Type > Dimension**. Next, enter 0.787 in the **Length** box. Click **OK** to complete the Pad feature.

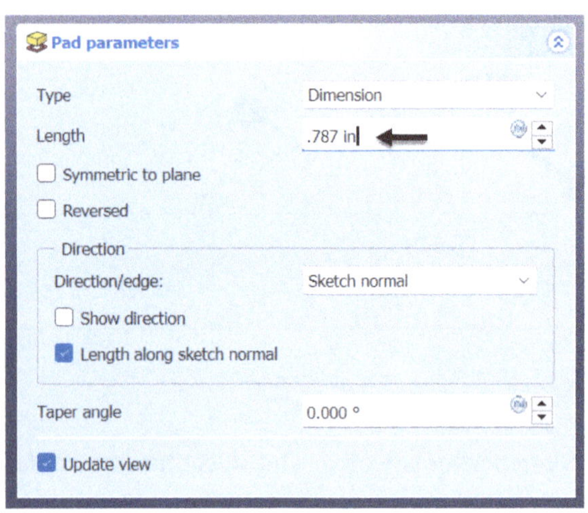

Creating the Rib

1. Activate the **Create Sketch** command and select the XZ_plane. Draw an inclined line, as shown.
2. Click **Sketch > View section** on the menu bar.
3. Click the **Create external geometry** icon on the **Sketcher tools** toolbar. Next, select the curved, vertical, and horizontal edges, as shown.

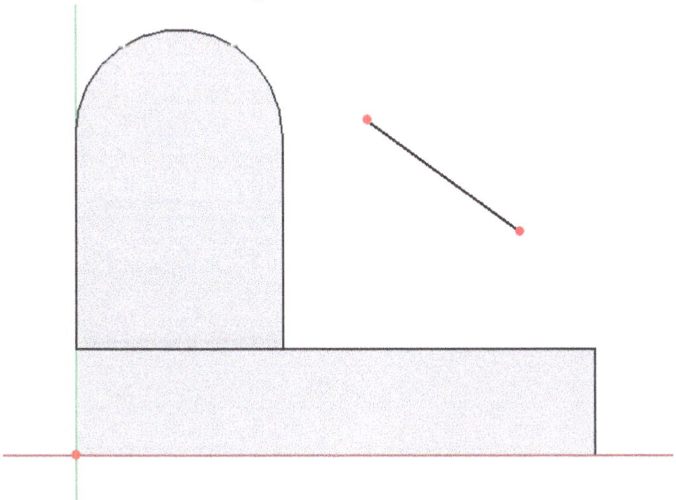

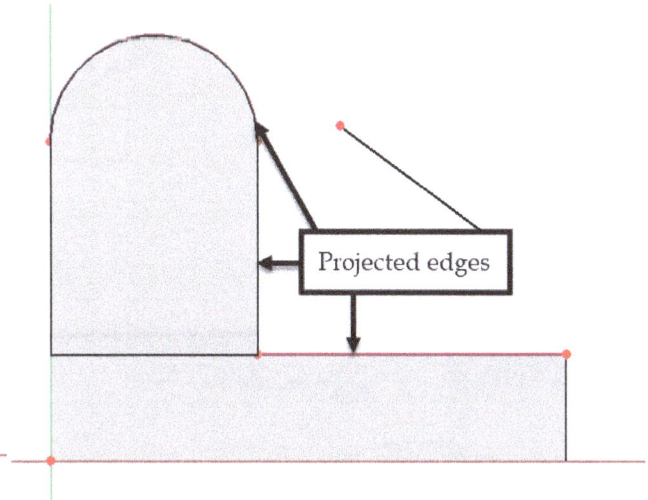

4. Create an arc and two lines, as shown.
5. On the **Sketcher constraints** toolbar, click **Constrain tangent** , and then select the vertical line and the arc; the line is made tangent to the arc. Click **OK** on the **Sketcher Constraint Substitution** dialog.

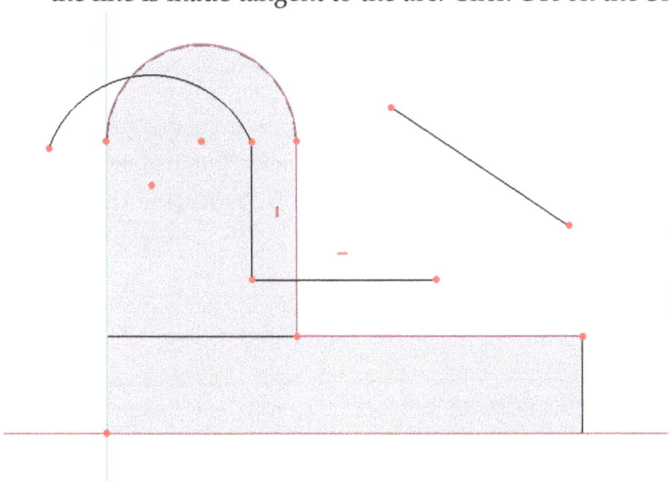

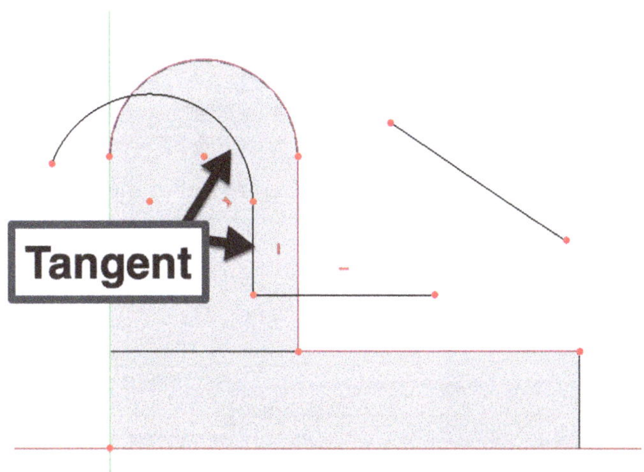

6. Click the **Constrain equal** icon on the **Sketcher constraints** toolbar. Next, select the arc and curved edge.
7. Click the **Constrain coincident** icon on the **Sketcher constraints** toolbar. Next, select the endpoint of the arc and the endpoint of the curved edge.
8. Select the endpoint of the horizontal line and the endpoint of the horizontal edge.

9. On the **Sketcher constraints** toolbar, click **Constrain tangent** , and then select the inclined line and the arc; the line is made tangent to the arc.

10. Click the **Constrain coincident** icon on the **Sketcher constraints** toolbar. Next, select the lower endpoint of the inclined line and the endpoint of the horizontal line. Right-click to deactivate the **Constrain coincident** command.

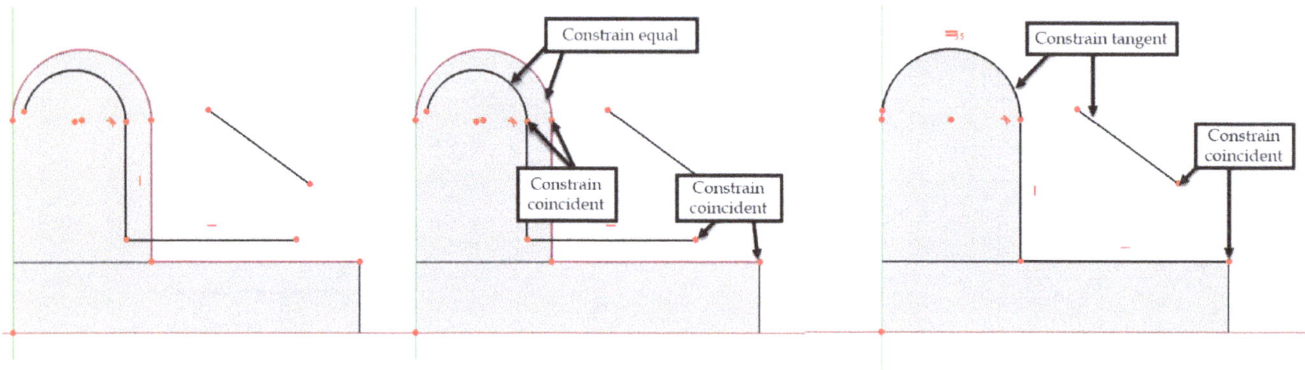

11. Click on the endpoint of the arc and drag it toward the right.

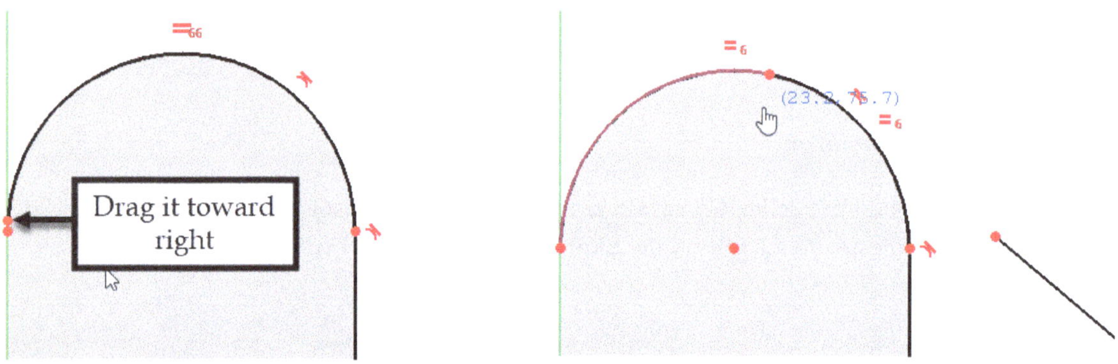

12. Click the **Constrain coincident** icon on the **Sketcher constraints** toolbar. Next, select the upper endpoint of the inclined line and the endpoint of the arc. Click **OK** on the **Sketcher Constraint Substitution** dialog.

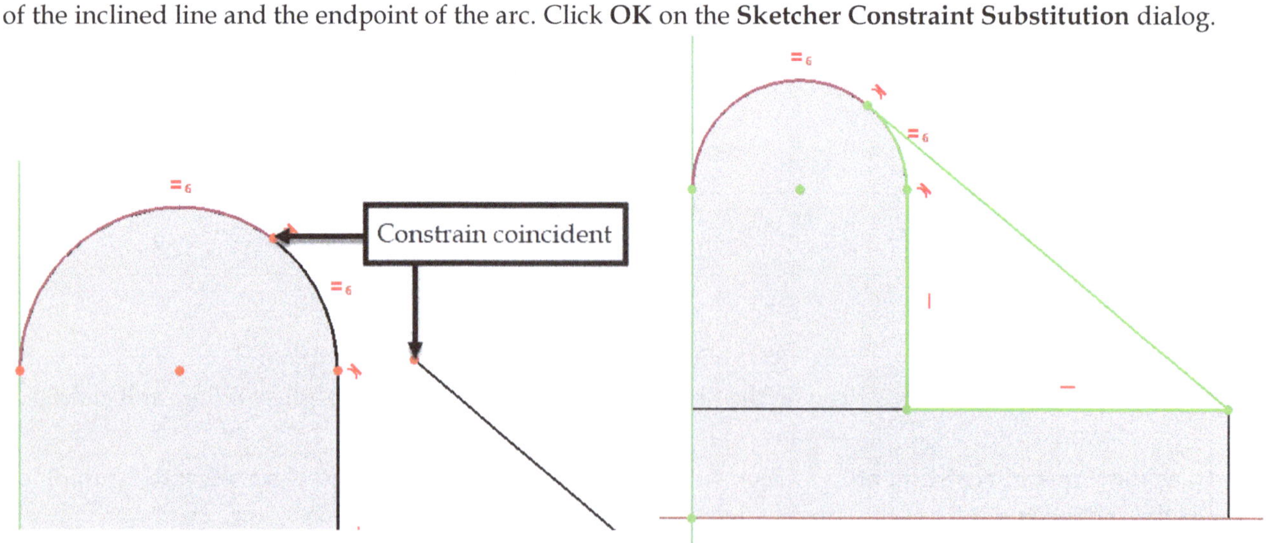

13. Click **Close** on the **Tasks** panel.

14. Click the **Pad** icon on the **Part Design Modeling** toolbar.
15. Type-in 0.394 in the **Length** box. Next, click **OK** to create the *Pad* feature.

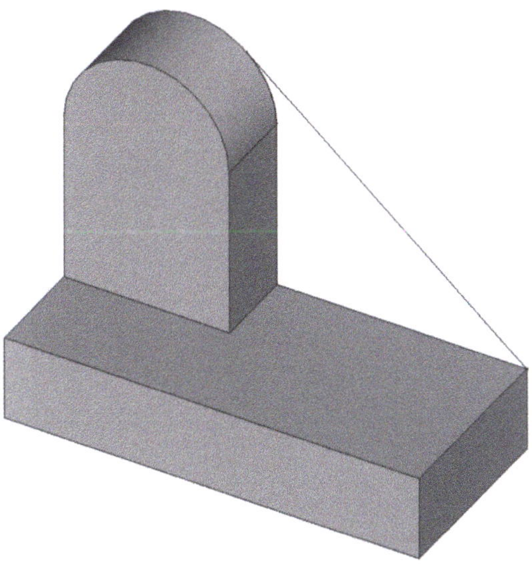

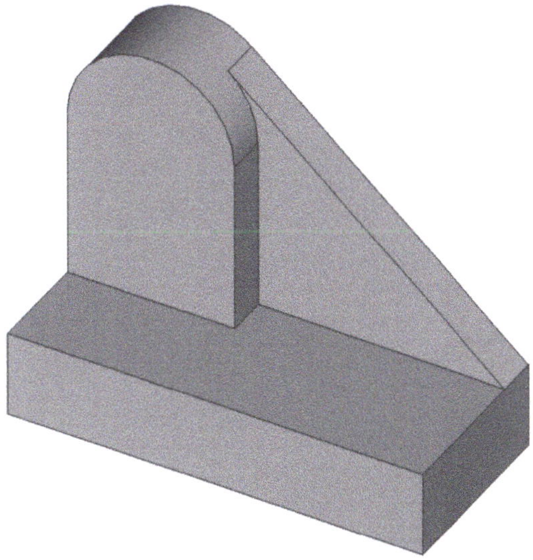

Creating the Pocket features

1. Select the front face of the second feature and click the **Create Sketch** icon on the **Part Design Helper** toolbar.
2. On the **Sketcher geometries** toolbar, click the **Slot** drop-down > **Create slot** .
3. Click on the sketch plane to specify the first end of the slot. Next, move the pointer downward and click.
4. Click the **Create external geometry** icon on the **Sketcher tools** toolbar.

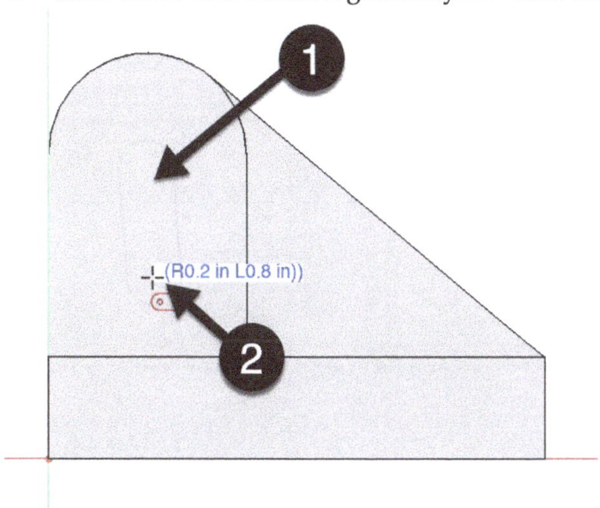

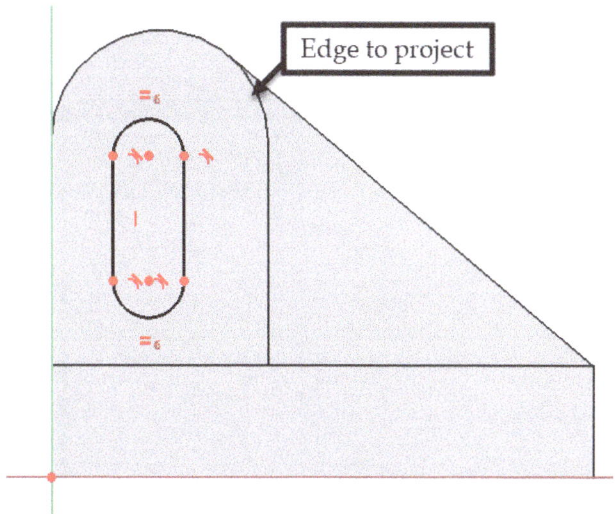

5. Click **Constrain horizontal/vertical > Constrain vertical** on the **Sketcher constraints** toolbar. Next, select anyone of the linear edges of the slot.

6. Click **Constrain coincident** on the **Sketcher constraints** toolbar. Next, select the center point of the projected curve edge and the centerpoint of the slot endcap.
7. Create the radius and vertical distance constraints, as shown.

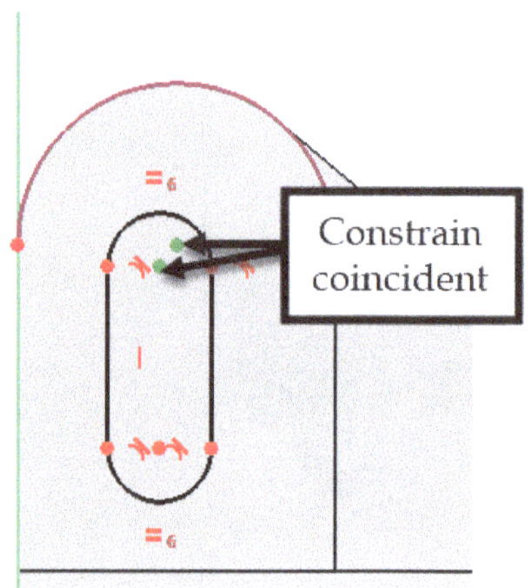

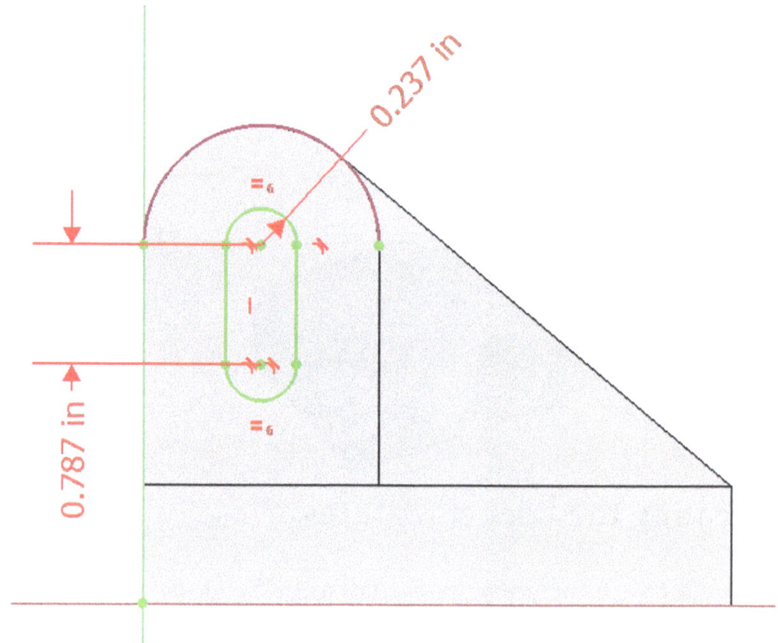

8. Click **Close** on the **Tasks** panel.
9. Click the **Pocket** icon on the **Part Design Modeling** toolbar.
10. On the **Pocket parameters** section, select **Type > Through all**. Next, click **OK**.

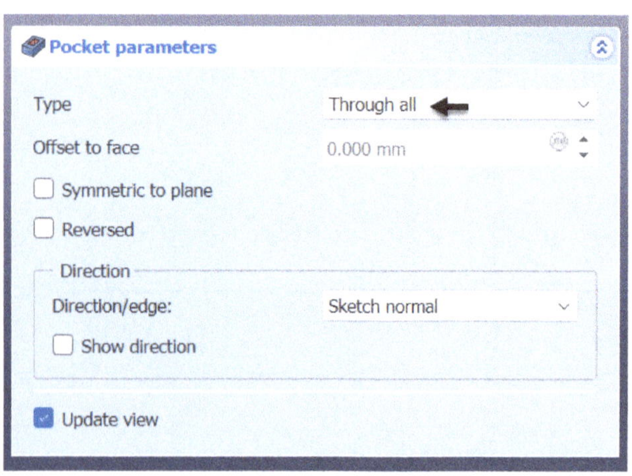

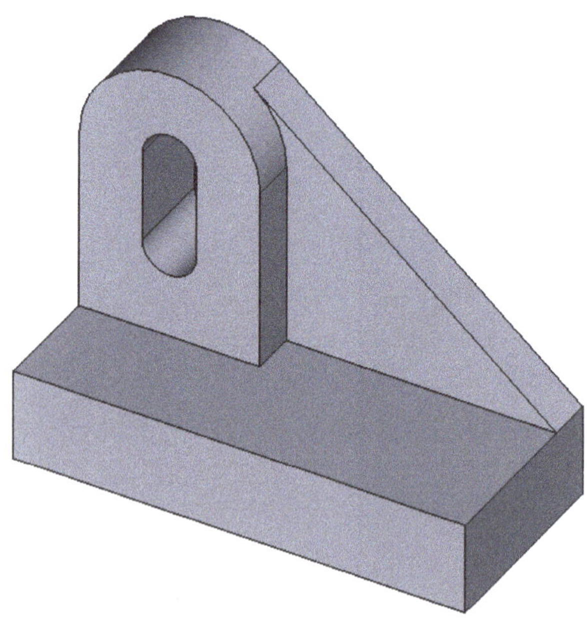

Creating the Fillet and Hole features

1. Select the right vertical edge and click **Create fillet** on the **Part Design Modeling** toolbar.
2. Type **0.787** in the **Radius** box and click **OK**.
3. Select the top face of the first feature and click the **Create Sketch** icon on the **Part Design Helper** toolbar.
4. Click **Create external geometry** on the **Sketcher tools** toolbar. Next, select the curved edge, as shown.
5. Click the **Circle** drop-down > **Create circle by center** on the **Sketcher geometries** toolbar. Next, select the center point of the projected edge. Move the pointer outward and click to create a circle.
6. Click **Close** on the **Tasks** panel.

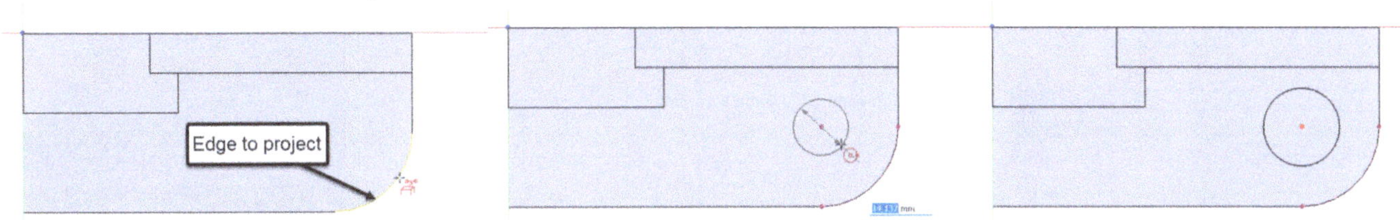

7. Click the **Hole** icon on the **Part Design Modeling** toolbar.
8. On the **Hole parameters** section, specify the settings, as shown. Next, click **OK** to create the hole.787

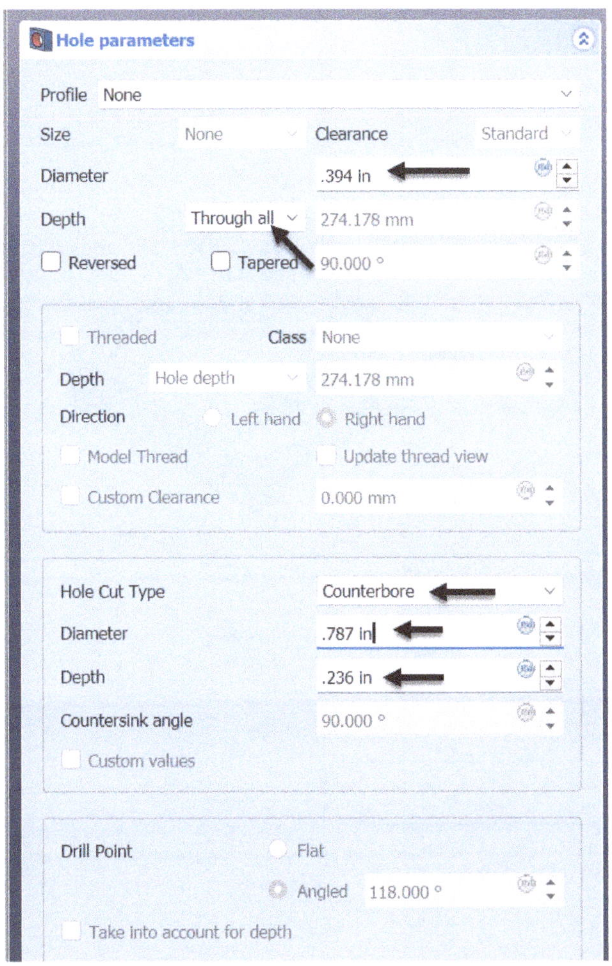

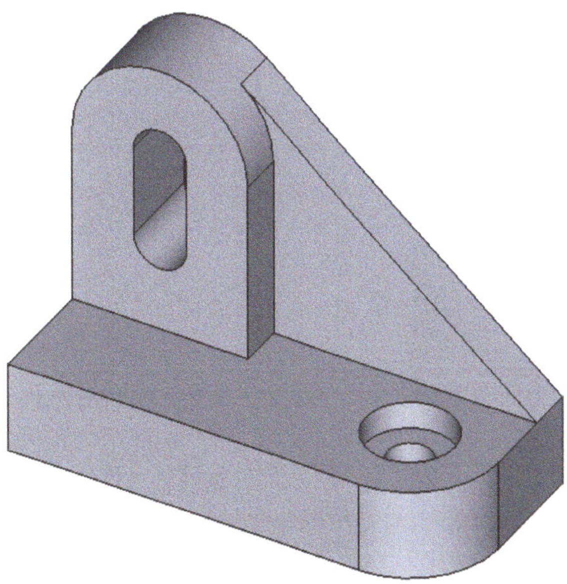

9. Select the front face of the rectangular base and click the **Create Sketch**  icon on the **Part Design Helper** toolbar.
10. Draw a sketch and add dimensions to it. Click **Close** on the **Tasks** panel.
11. Create a *Pocket* feature using the sketch.

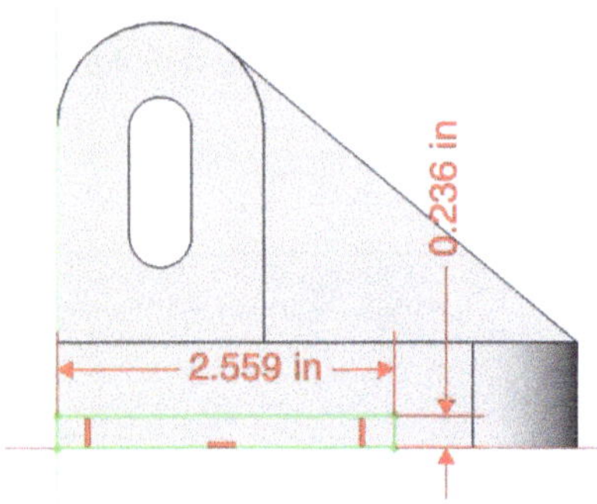

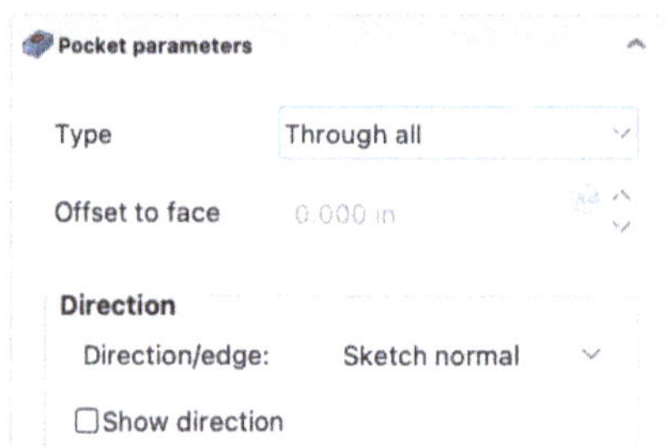

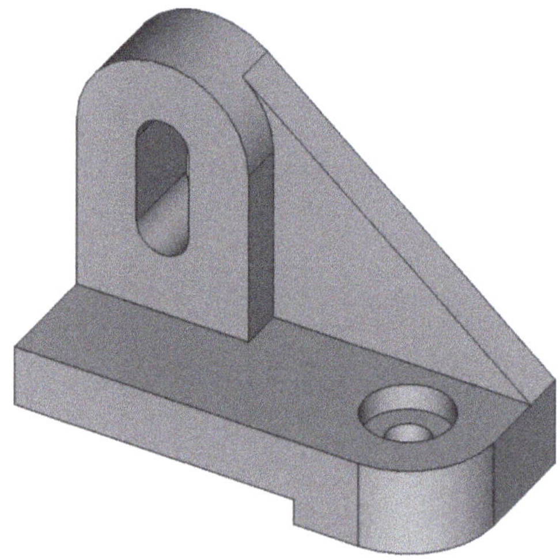

12. Save and close the part file.

Tutorial 3 (Millimeters)

In this example, you create the part shown next.

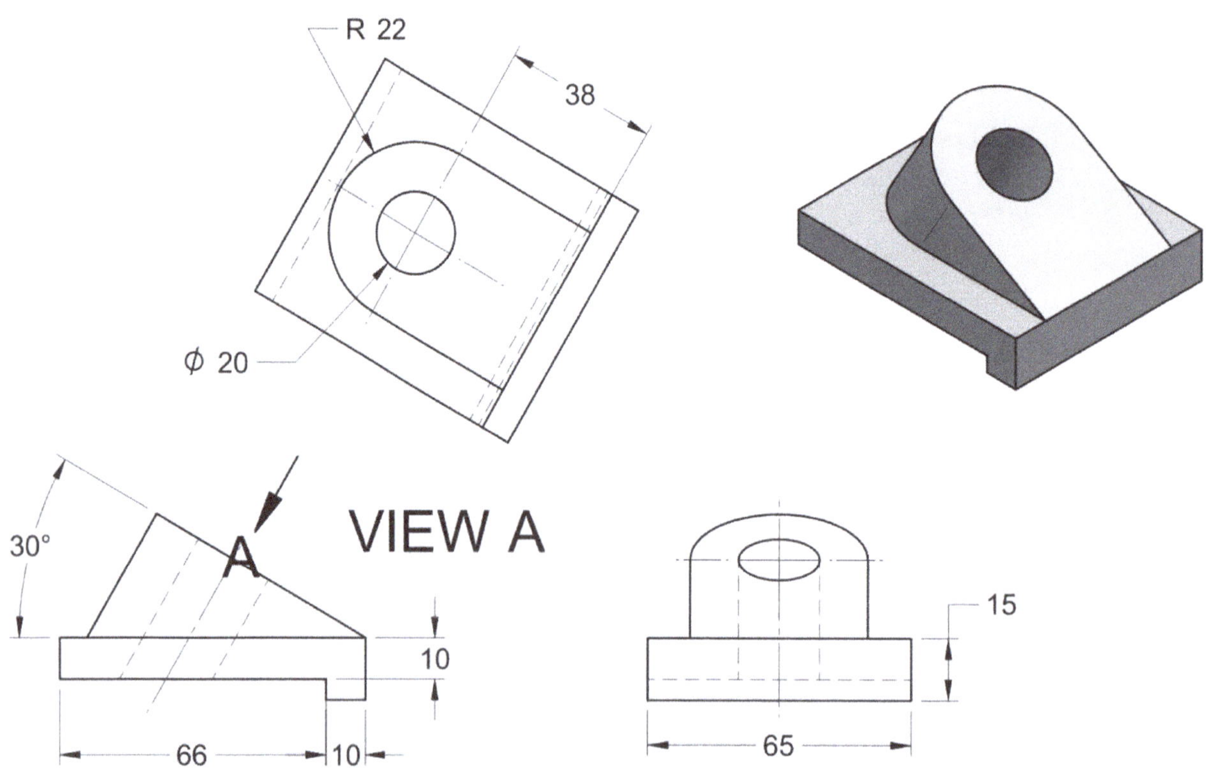

Creating a New document

1. Click **FreeCAD 1.0** on the desktop to start the application.
2. On the menu bar, click **File > New**; it creates a new document.
3. On the **Workbench** toolbar, select **Workbench** drop-down **> Part Design**.
4. Click **Edit > Preferences** on the **Menu** bar (or) click **FreeCAD 1.0.1 > Preferences** on title bar, if you are working on MacOS; the **Preferences** dialog appears on the screen.
7. Click the **General** tab and select **Default unit system > Standard (mm/kg/s/degree)**.
8. Select **Number of decimals > 2** and click **OK** on the **Preferences** dialog.

Creating the Pad features

1. Click the **Create Sketch**  icon on the **Part Design Helper** Toolbar and select the XZ_plane. Next, click **OK**.
2. Click the **Create polyline**  icon on the **Sketcher geometries** toolbar. Next, select the sketch origin.
3. Move the pointer downward and click on the vertical axis of the sketch.
4. Move the pointer toward left up to a small distance and click to create a horizontal line.
5. Move the pointer vertically upward up to a small distance and click.
6. Move the pointer toward left and click.
7. Move the pointer vertically upward and click on the horizontal axis of the sketch.
8. Move the pointer toward right and select the sketch origin.
9. Add dimensional and geometric constraints, as shown.

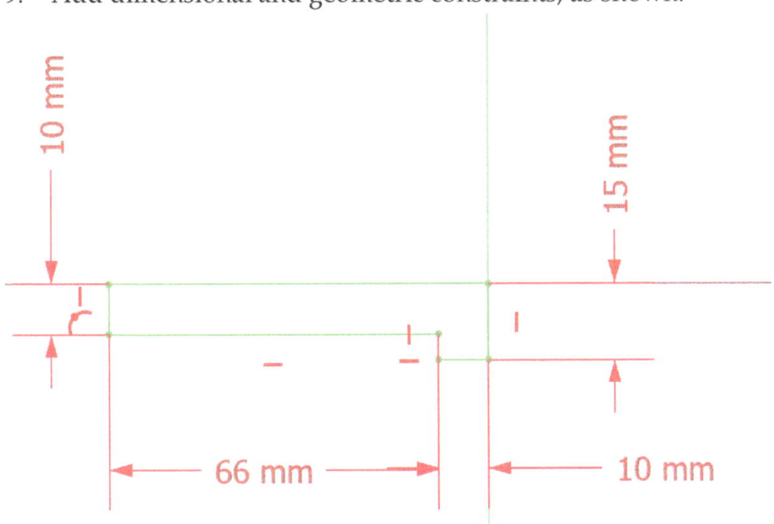

10. Click the **Close** button on the **Tasks** panel.
11. On the **Part Design Modeling** toolbar, click the **Pad**  command.
12. On the **Pad parameters** section, select **Type > Dimension** and enter **65** in the **Length** box.
13. Check the **Symmetric to plane** option and click **OK** to create the *Pad* feature.

Creating the Angled Plane

1. Click the **Create a datum plane** icon on the **Part Design Helper** toolbar and select the top face of the model.
2. Type -30 in the **Around y-axis** box. Next, click **OK**.

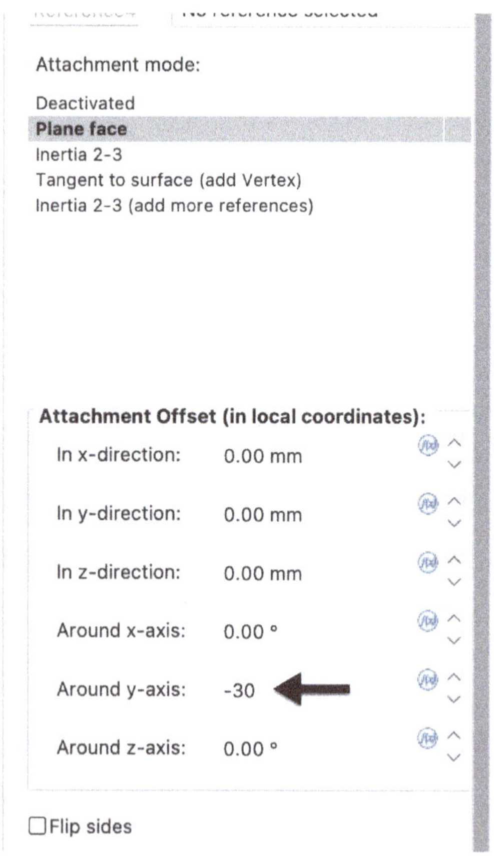

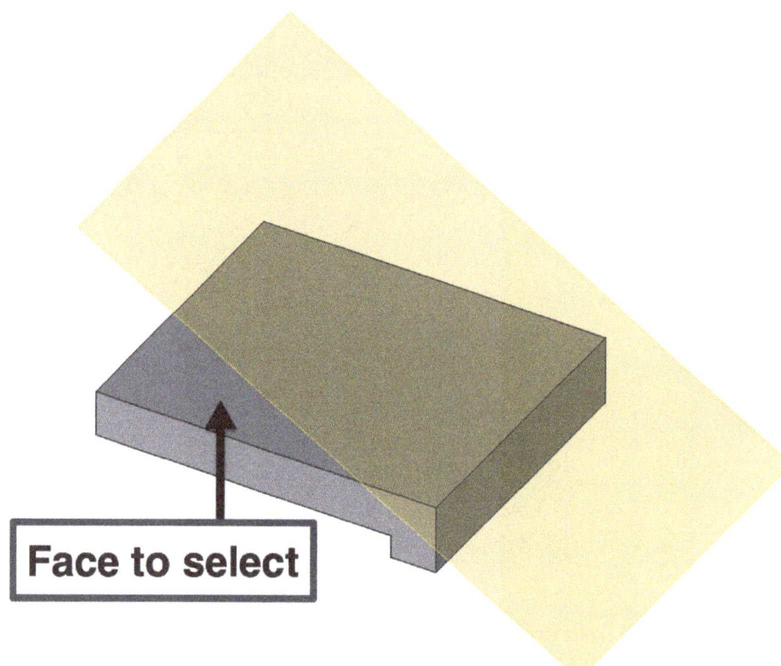

Creating the Pad feature

1. Click the **Create Sketch** icon on the **Part Design Helper** Toolbar and select the newly created datum plane. Next, click **OK**.

2. Click the **Slot** drop-down **> Create slot** icon on the **Sketcher geometries** toolbar. Next, select the sketch origin.
3. Move the pointer toward right and click on the horizontal axis of the sketch. Move the pointer outward and click.
4. Click the **Create line** icon on the **Sketcher geometries** toolbar. Next, left endpoint of the upper horizontal line.
5. Move the pointer downward and select the left endpoint of the lower horizontal line.

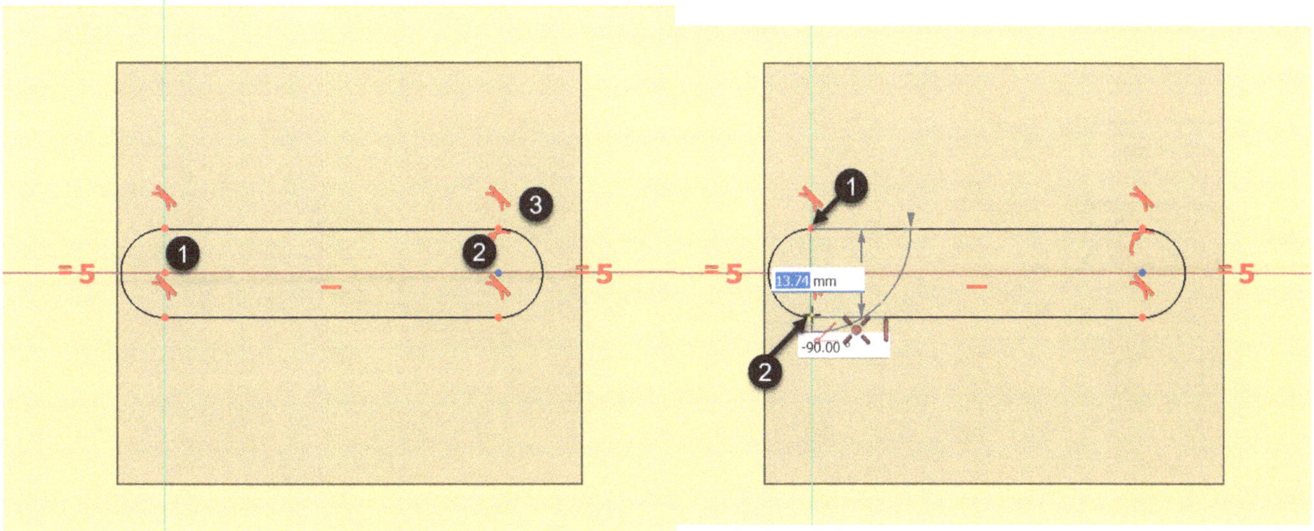

6. Click the **Trim edge** icon on the **Sketcher tools** toolbar. Next, select the left arc of the slot.

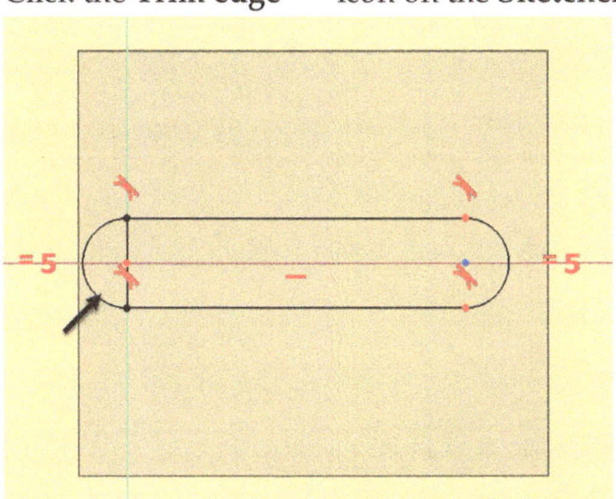

7. Add dimensional and geometric constraints, as shown.

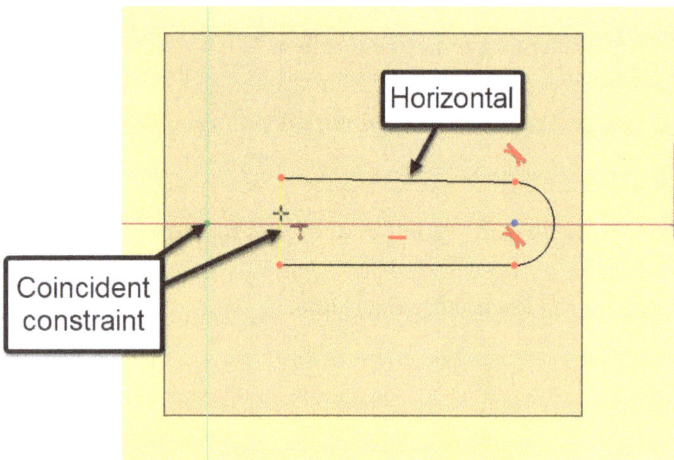

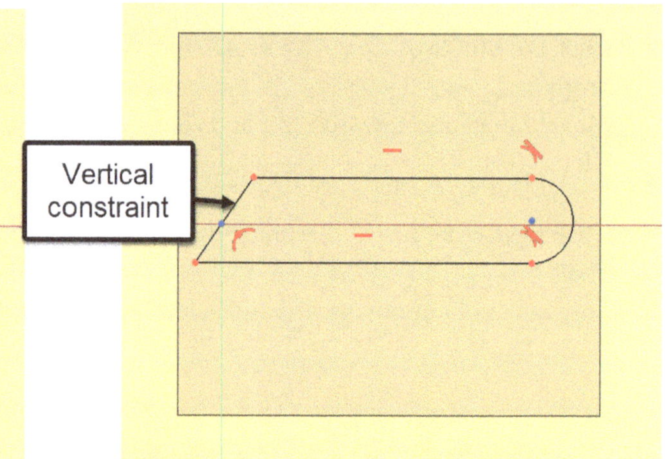

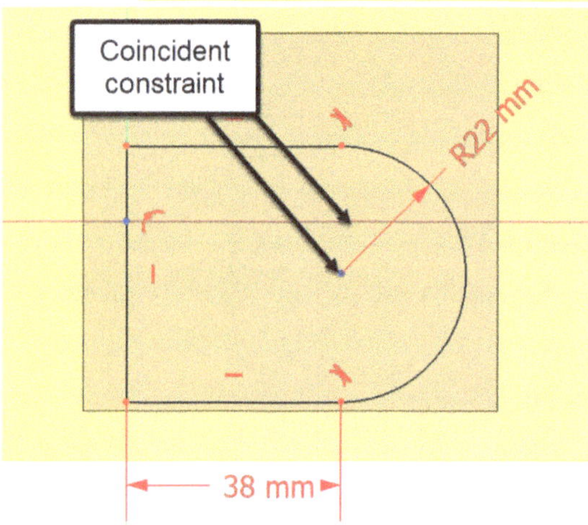

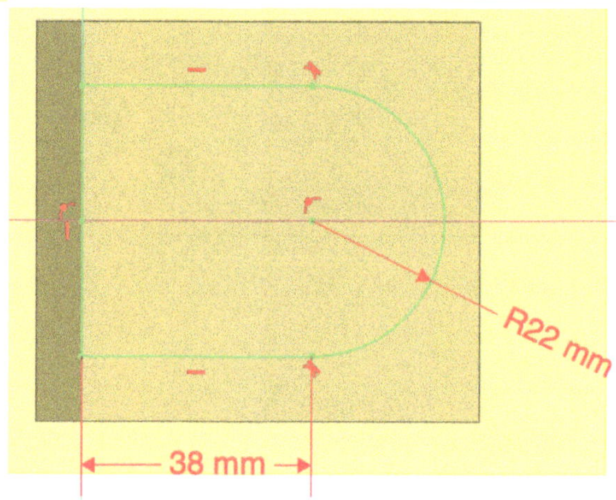

8. Click the **Close** button on the **Tasks** panel.
9. On the **Part Design Modeling** toolbar, click the **Pad**  command.
10. Check the **Reversed** option on the **Pad parameters** section of the **Tasks** panel.
11. Select **Type > To Last** from the **Pad parameters** section and click **OK**.

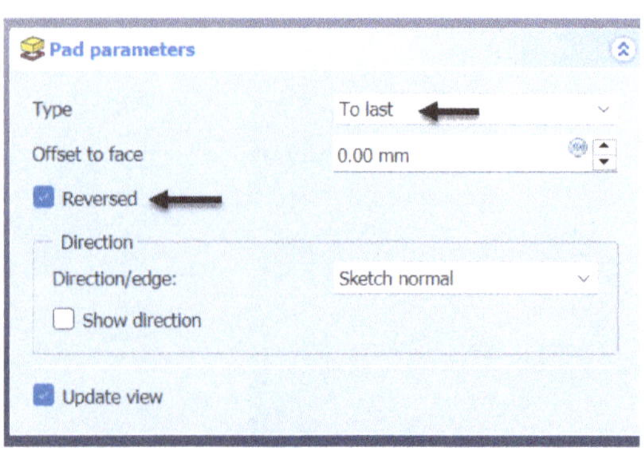

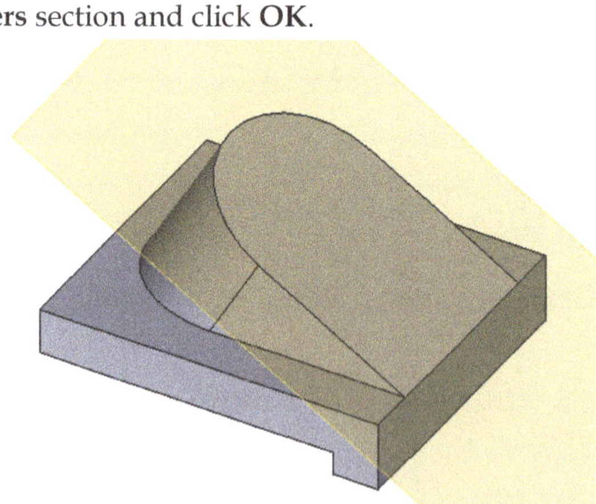

Creating the Hole feature

1. Select inclined face and click the **Create Sketch**  icon on the **Part Design Helper** toolbar.

2. Click **Create external geometry** on the **Sketcher tools** toolbar. Next, select the curved edge, as shown.
3. Click the **Create circle by center** icon on the **Sketcher geometries** toolbar. Next, select the center point of the projected edge. Move the pointer outward and click to create a circle.

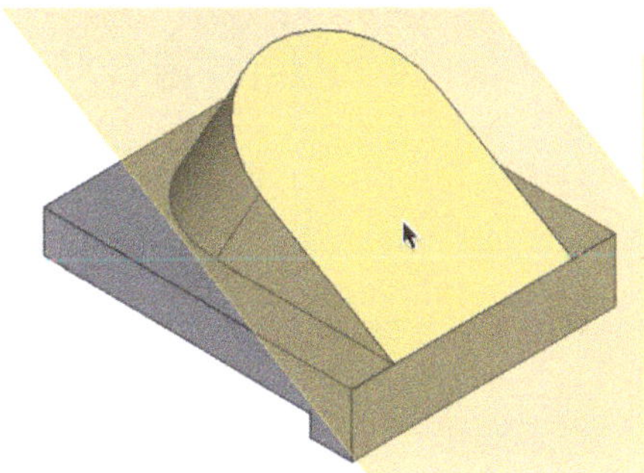

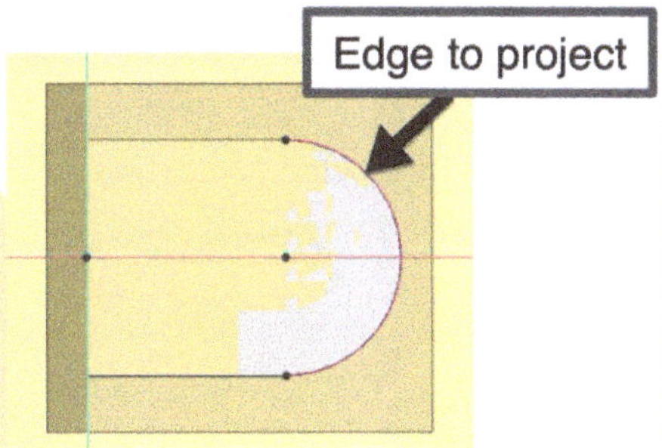

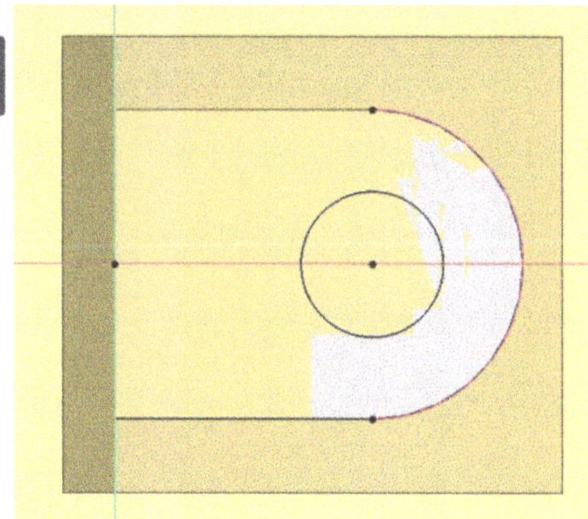

4. Click **Close** on the **Tasks** panel.
5. Click the **Hole** icon on the **Part Design Modeling** toolbar.
6. On the **Hole parameters** section, specify the settings, as shown. Next, click **OK** to create the hole.

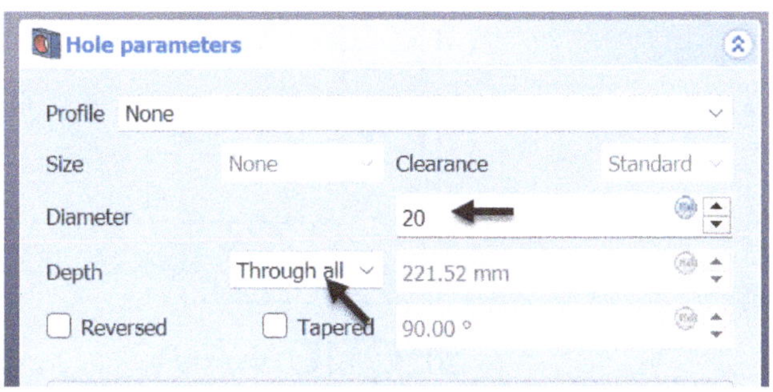

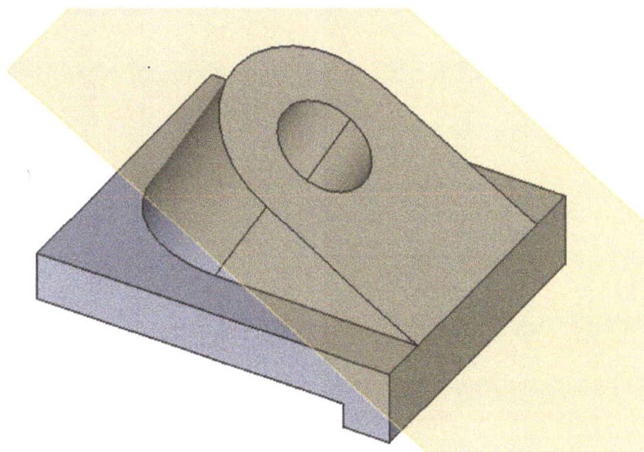

7. Save and close the file.

Questions

1. What are the dress up features?
2. How to create a counterbored hole?
3. Which option allows you to create chamfer with unequal setbacks?
4. How to create a fillet?

Exercises

Exercise 1 (Inches)

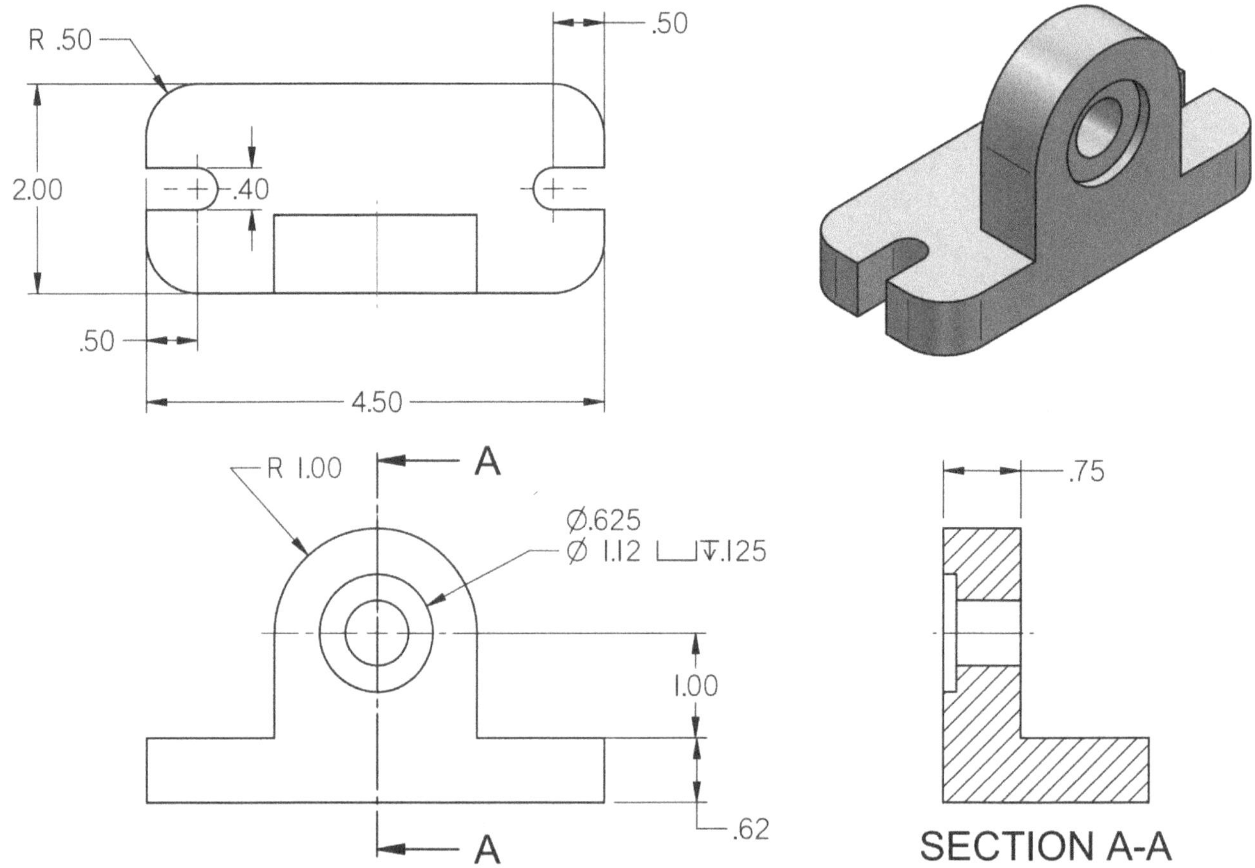

Exercise 2 (Millimeters)

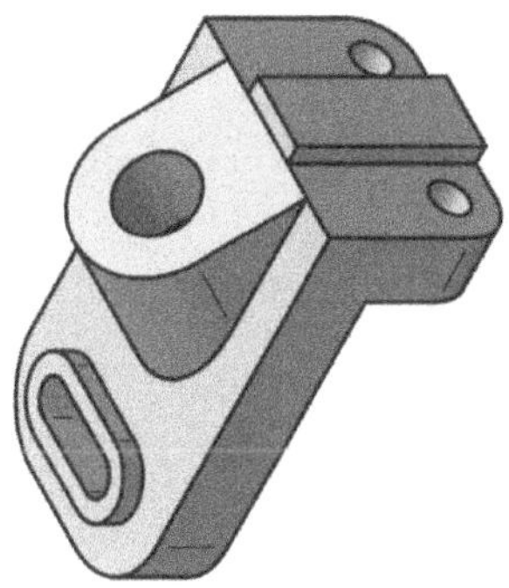

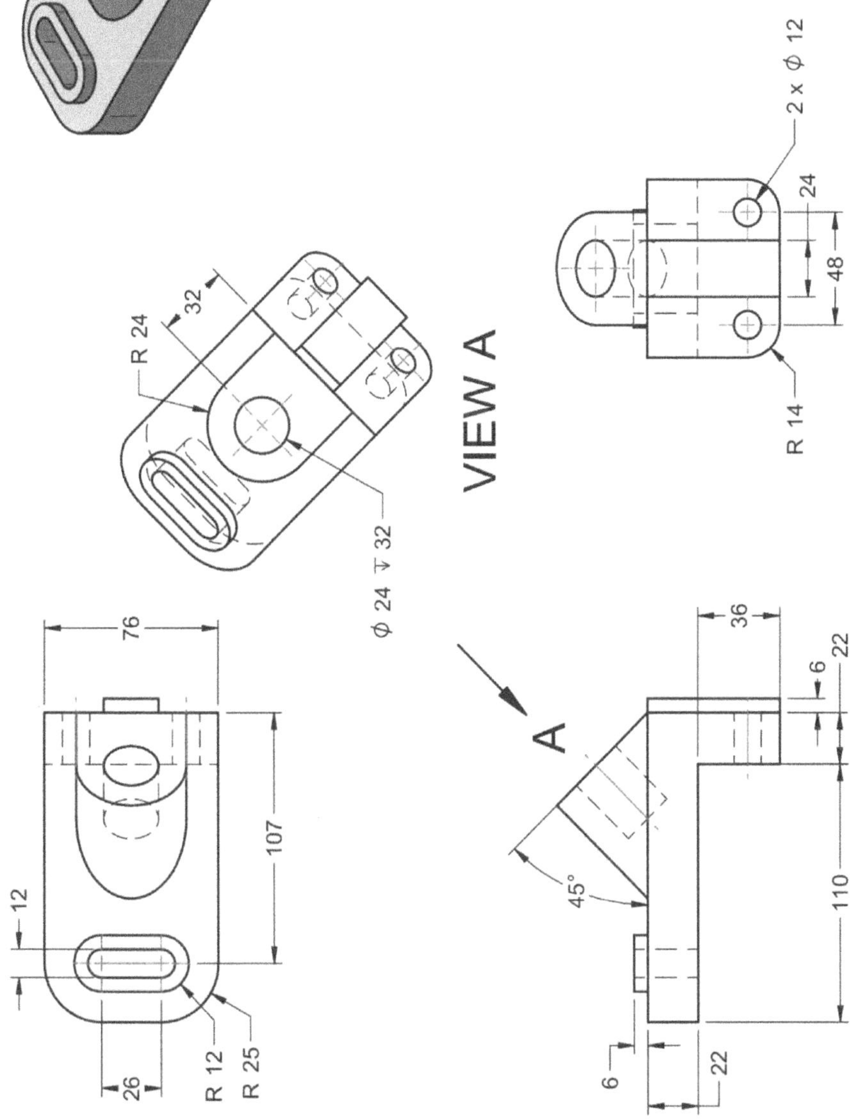

Chapter 5: Patterned Geometry

When designing a part geometry, most of the time, there are elements of symmetry in each part, or there are at least a few features that are repeated multiple times. In these situations, FreeCAD 1.0 offers some commands that save you time. For example, you can use mirror features to design symmetric parts, which makes designing the part quicker. This is because you only have to design a portion of the part and use the mirror feature to create the remaining geometry.

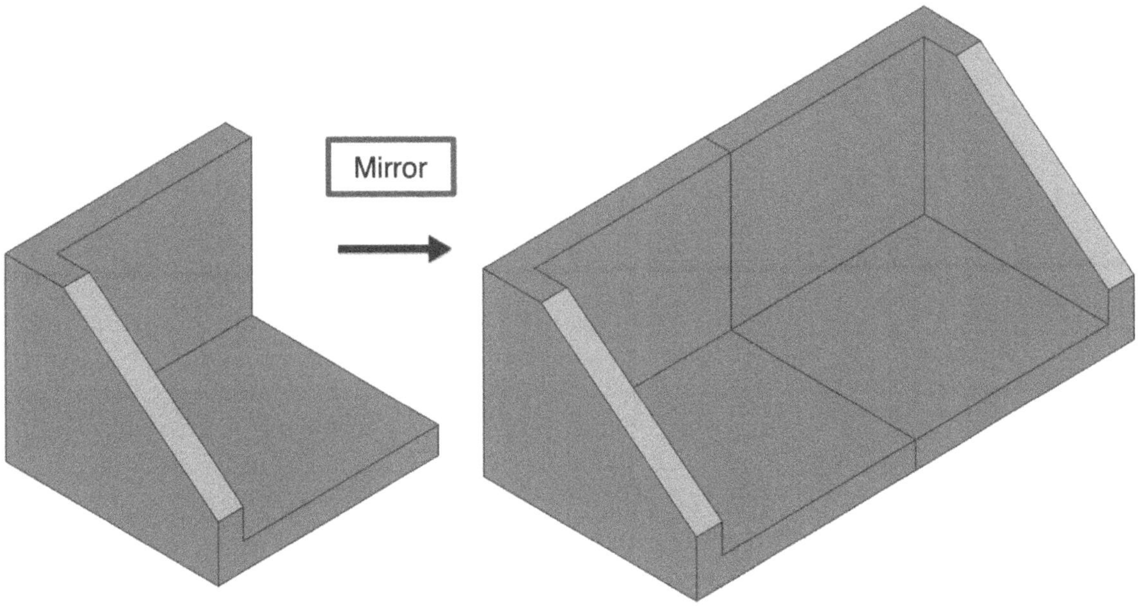

In addition, there are some pattern commands to replicate a feature throughout a part quickly. They save you time from creating additional features individually and help you modify the design easily. If the design changes, you only need to change the first feature; the rest of the pattern features will update automatically. In this chapter, you will learn to create mirrored and pattern geometries using the commands available in FreeCAD 1.0.

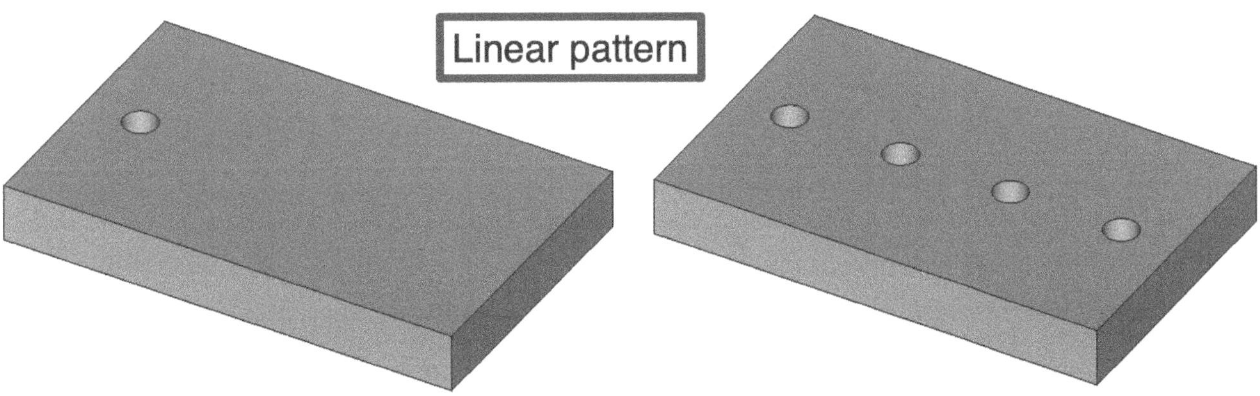

The topics covered in this chapter are:

- *Mirror* features
- *Linear Patterns*
- *Polar Pattern*

- *Multi Transforms*

Mirrored

In FreeCAD part modeling, symmetry plays a crucial role, and mirror functions emerge as a fundamental and frequently employed tool for achieving this symmetry. This essential concept of utilizing mirroring techniques transcends various industrial sectors, proving to be invaluable in the design and development of a wide array of components and products. This includes machinery parts, sheet metal assemblies, injection-molded items, as well as cast and forged elements. Proficiency in creating mirrored features is a key skill for efficiently building symmetrical and well-balanced 3D models.

Our exploration of these 3D mirroring techniques aims to enhance your FreeCAD modeling capabilities, making them a valuable addition to your skillset, irrespective of the specific type of part you're designing.

When working on a symmetric part, you can significantly save time and effort by utilizing the '**Mirrored**' command. This command allows you to duplicate individual features of the entire body, ensuring the symmetry you desire. To mirror features, which include 3D geometry, you'll need a face or plane to use as a reference. This reference can be a model face, a default plane, or, if necessary, you can create a new plane to fulfill the mirroring requirements.

Press and hold the Shift key and select the features to mirror from the **Model** panel. On the Menu bar, click **Part Design > Create a pattern > Mirrored** (or) click the **Mirrored** icon on the **Part Design Modeling** toolbar. On the **Mirrored parameters** section, notice that the **Transform tool shapes** option is active and the selected features are listed. Next, select a mirroring plane from the **Plane** drop-down. You can select a sketch axis or a base plane from the **Plane** drop-down. Alternately, you can select a user-defined Datum plane from the graphics window to define the mirroring plane. To do this, select the **Select reference** option from the **Plane** drop-down and select the datum plane about which the features are to be mirrored. Click **OK** to mirror the selected features.

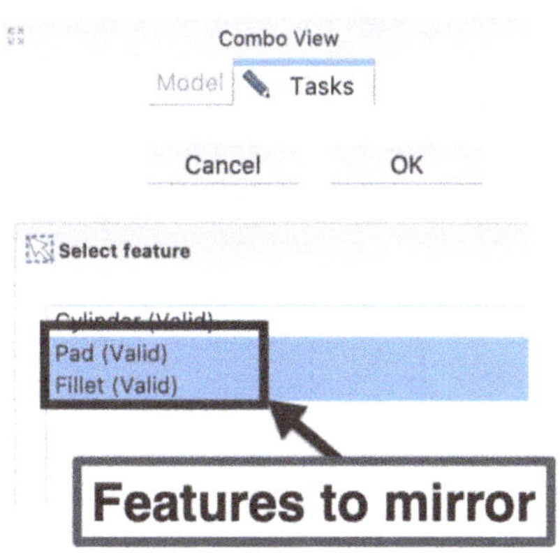

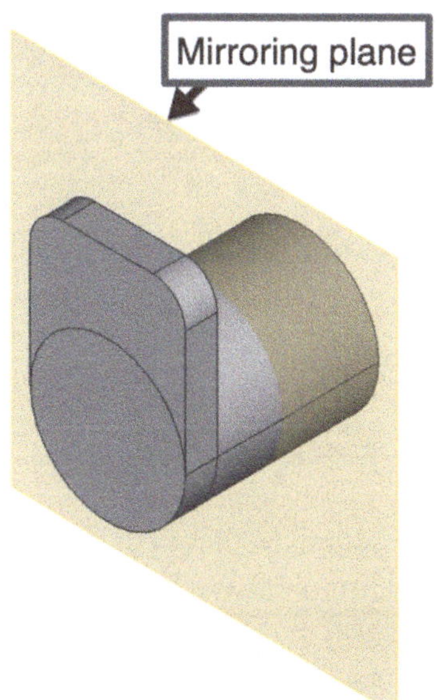

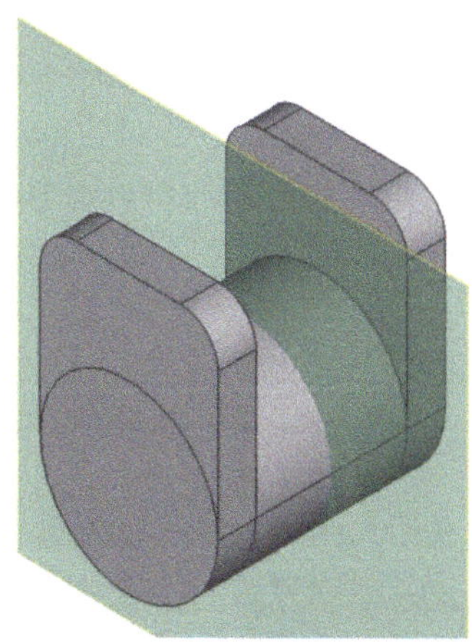

In FreeCAD, when you're working on mirroring multiple features, it's often a good idea to streamline your process. Instead of creating separate mirror features for each of them, consider using a single mirror feature that encompasses all the features you want to mirror.

To achieve this, you may need to create the mirrored feature after creating all the features to be mirrored. Try to make sure to position the mirror feature lower down the **Model** tree. This helps keep your project well-organized and easy to follow. While this approach can be useful, it's important not to overcomplicate your design or take convoluted steps just to make it work. The key is to strike a balance between simplicity and efficiency in your modeling process. Choose when to create mirrors based on your project's needs without making things unnecessarily intricate.

Mirror Bodies

If the part you are creating is entirely symmetric, you can save more time by creating half of it and mirroring the entire geometry rather than individual features. Activate the **Mirrored** command (On the menu bar, click **Part Design > Apply a pattern > Mirrored**) and select the **Transform body** option. Next, select **Plane > Select reference** from the **Mirrored parameters** section. Select the face or plane about which the geometry is to be mirrored. Click **OK** to complete the mirror geometry.

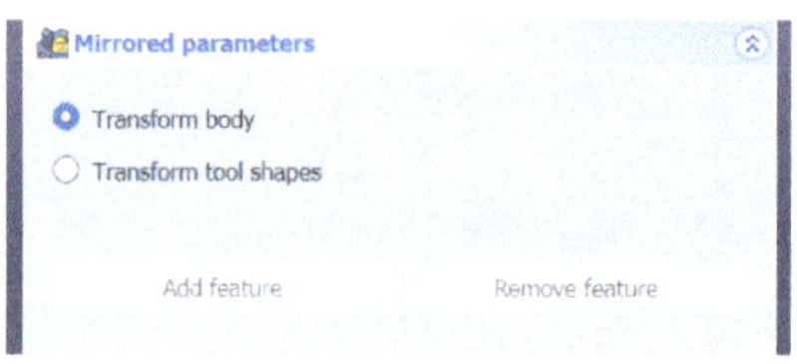

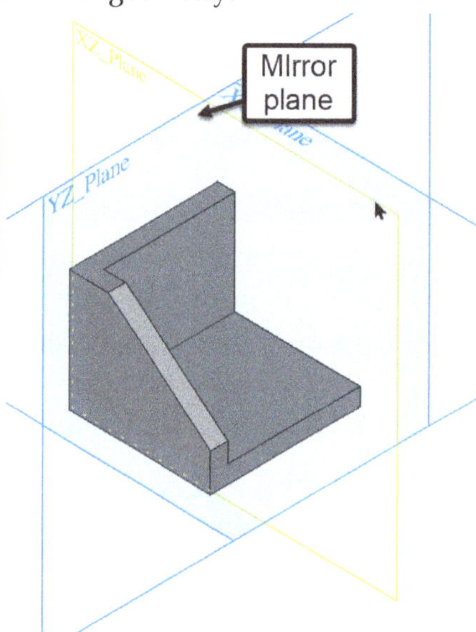

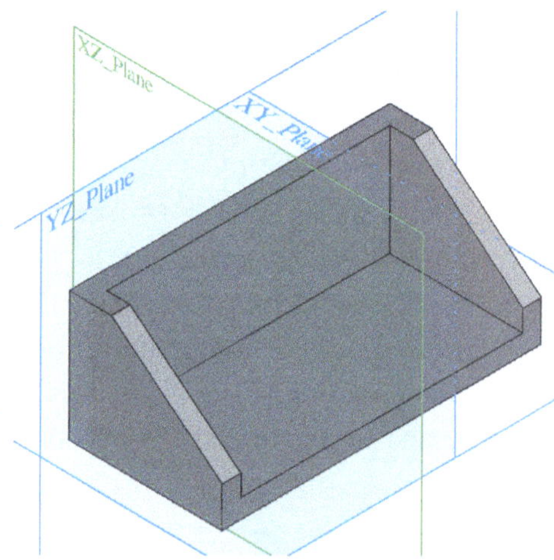

Best Practices

- **Symmetry**: Ensure your part exhibits clear symmetry. Place the features you want to mirror in an appropriate position relative to the axis or plane you intend to use as a mirror reference.

- **Part Modeling Order**: Construct the initial features of your part in the right sequence. It's generally best to create the primary features before applying the mirror feature.

- **Reference Planes or Axes**: Establish reference planes or axes that define the symmetry and mirror plane. This facilitates consistency and simplifies future design modifications.

- **Fully Defined Sketches**: Ensure your sketches are fully defined to prevent unintentional changes during the mirroring process.

- **Check for Interferences**: After mirroring, check for interferences, particularly in complex designs. Sometimes mirrored features may overlap or interfere with other design elements.

- **Keep Fillets and Rounds for After Mirroring**: If possible, add fillets and rounds after mirroring to simplify future modifications without needing to adjust multiple mirrored features.

Cautions

- **Asymmetrical Features**: Be cautious when mirroring features that lack perfect symmetry. This can lead to unexpected results and design issues.

- **Bodies with Internal Features**: In multi-body parts, be careful when dealing with internal features. Hide or exclude any internal bodies or features that shouldn't be mirrored.

- **Revisions and Revisions**: When you need to modify one side of the mirrored part, remember to adjust the mirrored features accordingly.

Tips for Specific Part Types

Plastic Parts: Account for draft angles and undercuts, especially when mirroring complex shapes. Utilize the draft feature and check for draft analysis to identify issues.

Casted Parts: Be mindful of parting lines and draft angles in casted parts. Note that mirrored features can complicate the design process and affect mold creation.

Forged Parts: Forging often involves extensive machining after the initial forging. Consider this when mirroring, and allow for machining allowances in your design.

Machined Parts: Machined parts are more flexible for mirroring. However, ensure mirrored features don't result in excessive material that requires machining.

Create Patterns

FreeCAD 1.0 allows you to replicate a feature using the pattern commands: **Linear Pattern**, **Polar Pattern**, and **MultiTransform**. The following sections explain the different patterns that can be created using the three pattern commands.

Linear Pattern

To create a pattern in a linear fashion, you must first select the feature(s) to pattern from the graphics window or Model panel. Next, click the **Linear Pattern** icon on the **Part Design Modeling** toolbar (or) click **Part Design > Apply a pattern > Linear Pattern** on the menu bar. Next, select an axis from the **Direction** drop-down. You can select a sketch axis or a base X, Y, or Z axis from the **Direction** drop-down. Alternately, you can select an edge or face from the graphics window to define the pattern direction. To do this, select the **Select reference** option from the **Direction** drop-down and select an edge along which the features are to be patterned.

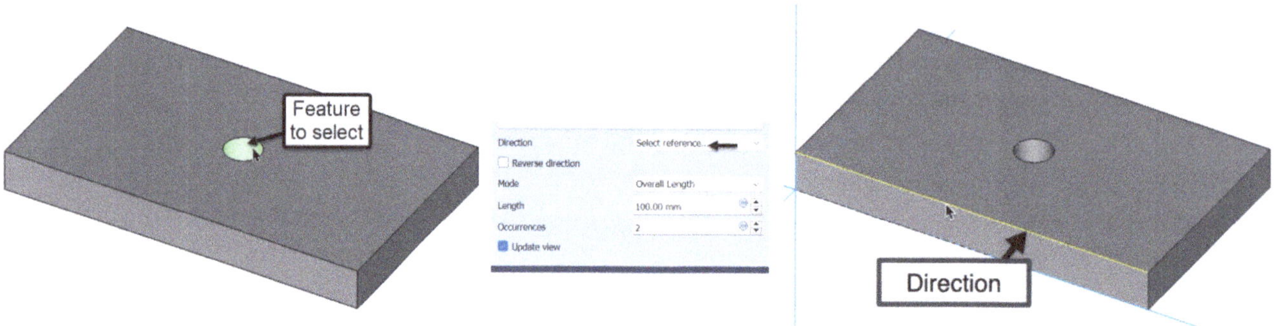

Next, select an option from the **Mode** drop-down (**Overall Length** or **Offset**). If you select the **Overall Length** option, you need to type-in values in the **Length** and **Occurrences** boxes; the value entered in the **Length** box defines the total length of the pattern. Check the **Reverse direction** option, if you want to reverse the pattern direction.

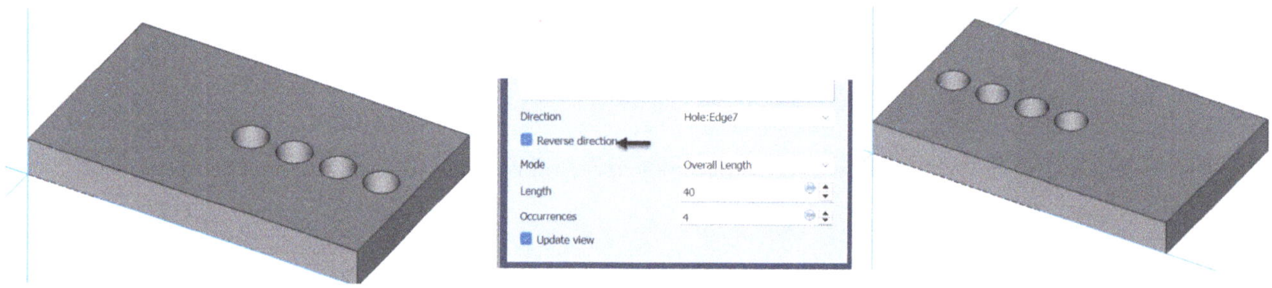

If you select the **Offset** option from the **Mode** drop-down, you need to type-in values in the **Offset** and **Occurrences** boxes. The value entered in the **Offset** box define the distance between the individual occurrences of the pattern.

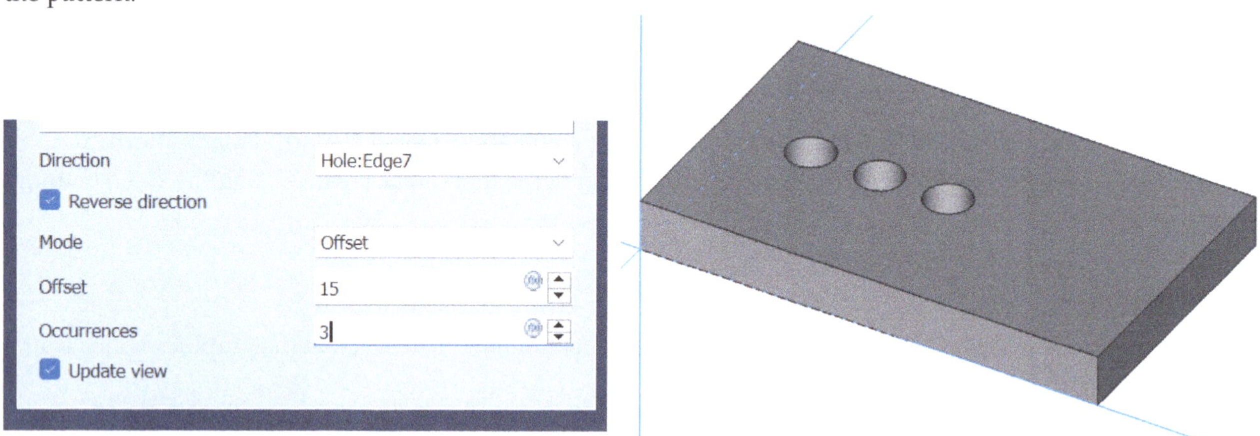

Next, click **OK** to complete the pattern.

Polar Pattern

The polar pattern is used to pattern the selected features in a circular fashion. To create a pattern in a polar fashion, you must first select the select the feature(s) to pattern from the graphics window or **Model** panel.

click the **Polar Pattern**  icon on the **Part Design Modeling** toolbar (or) click **Part Design > Apply a pattern >**

Polar Pattern on the menu bar. Next, select an axis from the **Axis** drop-down. You can select a sketch axis or a Base X, Base Y, or Base Z axis from the **Axis** drop-down. Alternately, you can select the axis from the graphics window. To do this, select the **Select reference** option from the **Axis** drop-down and select axis of the rotation.

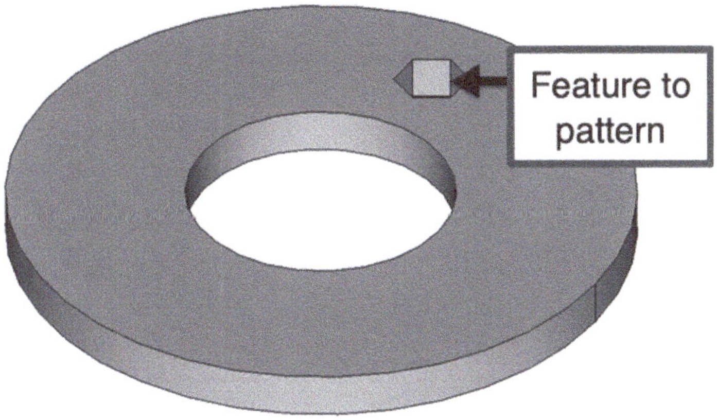

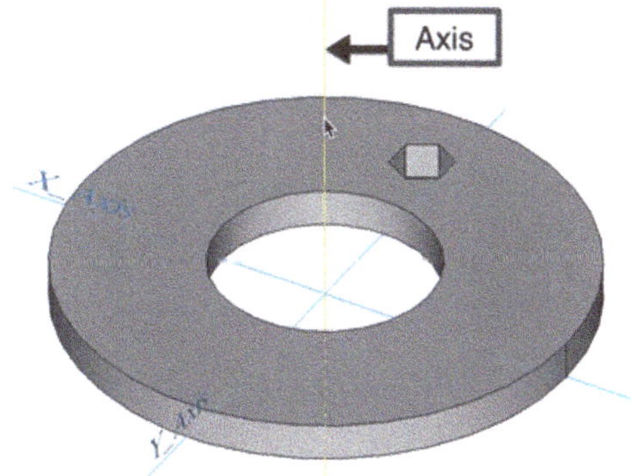

Next, select an option from the **Mode** drop-down (**Overall Angle** or **Offset Angle**). If you select the **Overall Angle** option, specify the angle and number of occurrences values in the **Angle** and **Occurrences** boxes, respectively. The value entered in the **Angle** box defines the total angle of the pattern.

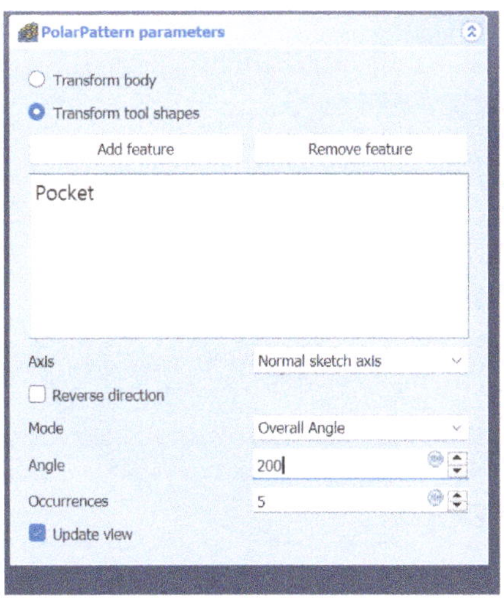

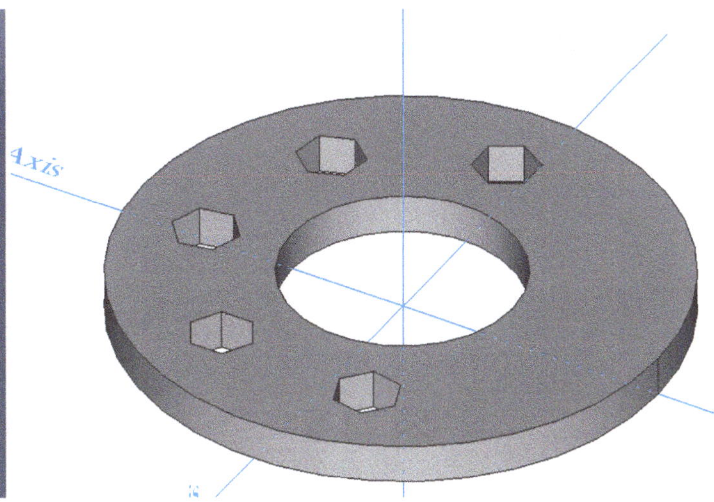

If you select the **Offset Angle** option from the **Mode** drop-down, you need to type-in values in the **Offset** and **Occurrences** boxes. The value entered in the **Offset** box defines the angle between the individual occurrences of the pattern.

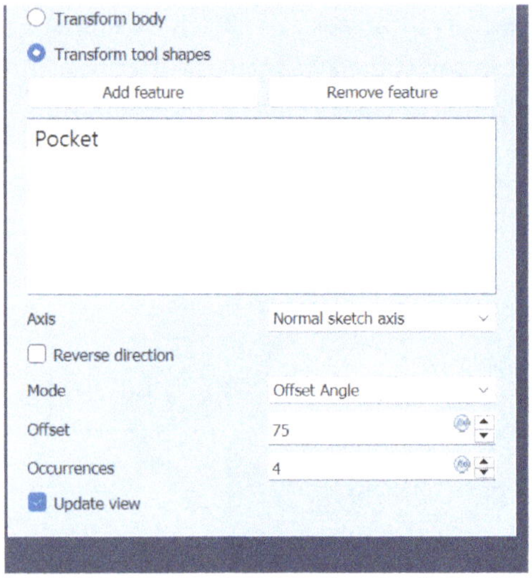

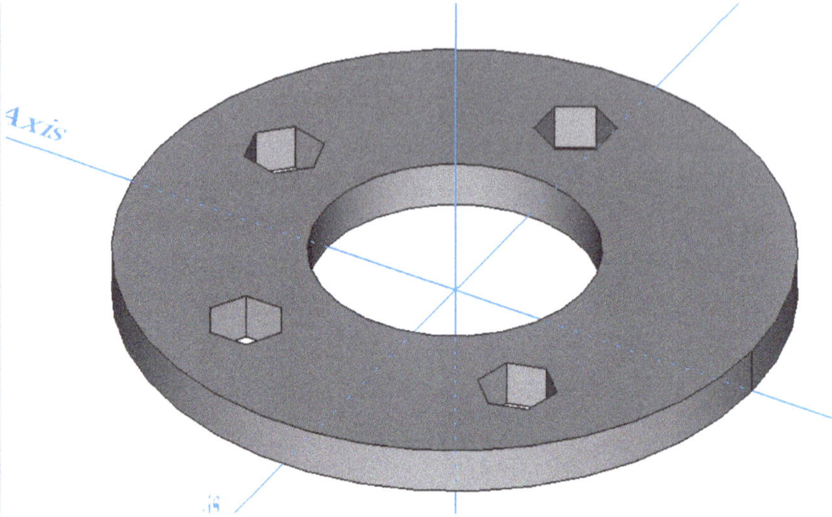

Click **OK** to create a polar pattern.

Multi Transform

The **MultiTransform** command is used to create patterns of multiple patterns. For example, you can pattern the pocket feature shown in the following image using three types of patterns (Linear Pattern, Scaled Pattern, and Polar Pattern) at a time.

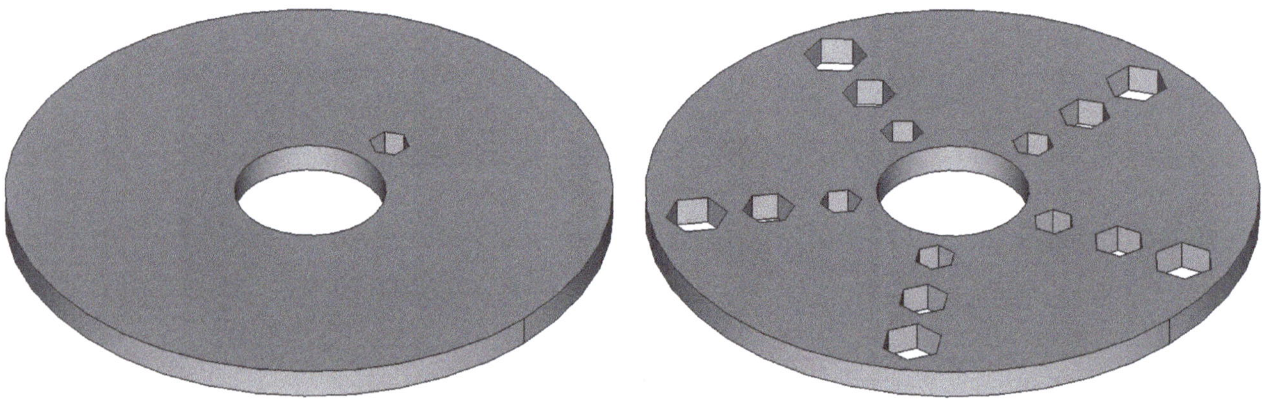

Click the **MultiTransform**  icon on the **Part Design Modeling** toolbar (or) click **Part Design > Apply a pattern > Create MultiTransform** on the menu bar. Next, select the feature to pattern from the **Combo View** panel, and then click **OK**. Next, right-click in the **Transformations** section and select **Add linear pattern**. Specify the **Direction**, **Length**, and **Occurences**.

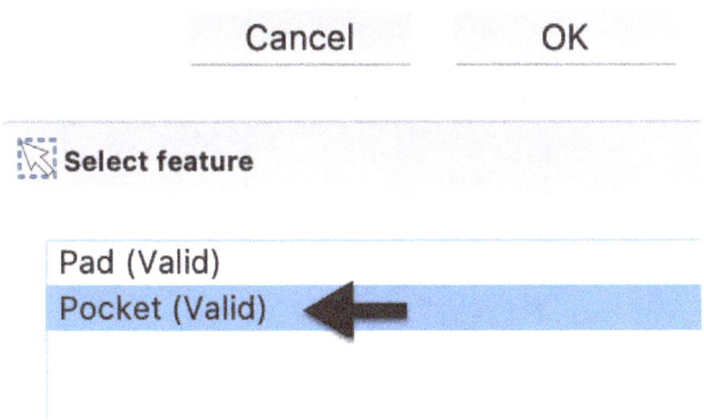

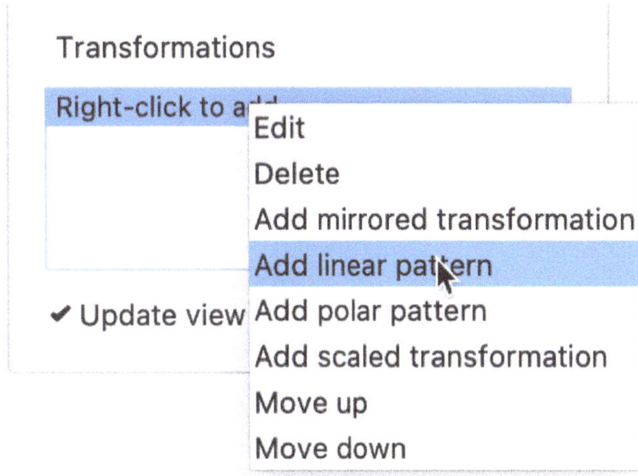

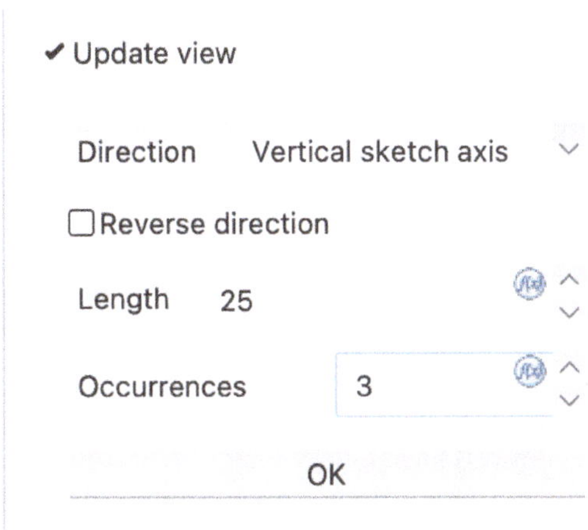

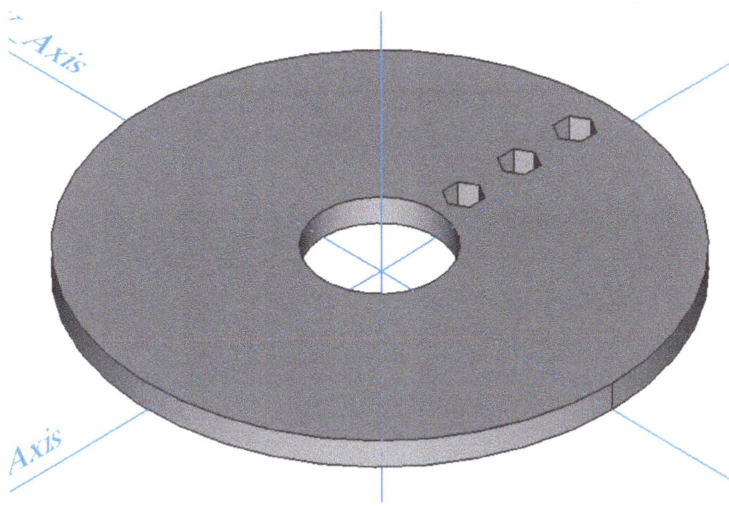

Right-click in the **Transformations** section and select **Add scaled transformation**. Specify the scale factor and occurrences to be scaled in the **Factor** and **Occurrences** boxes, respectively.

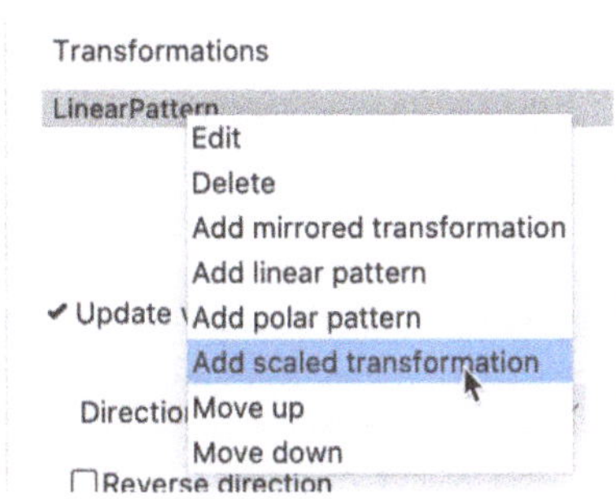

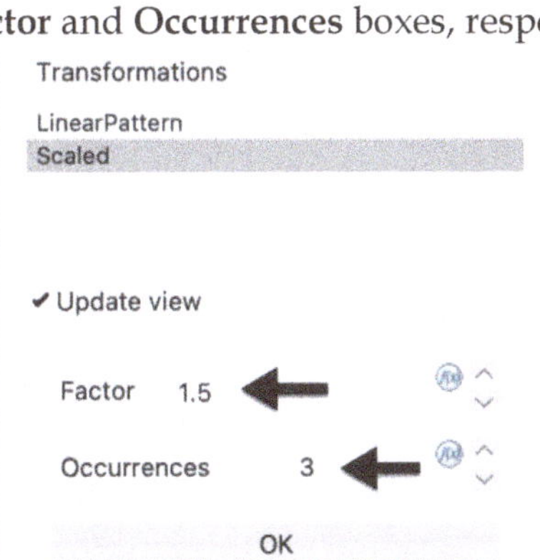

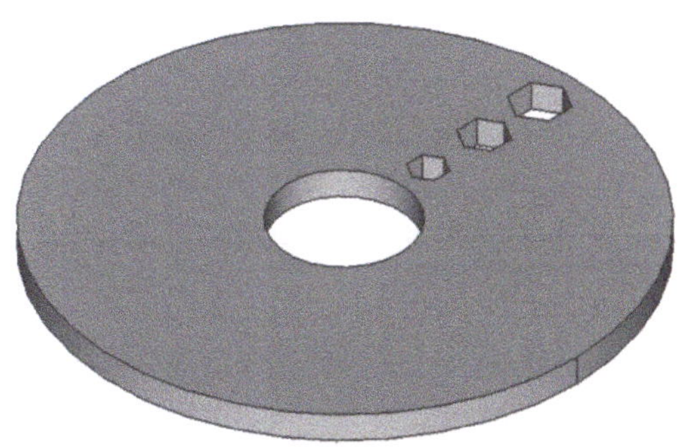

Right-click in the **Transformations** section and select **Add polar pattern**. Specify the rotation **Axis, Angle**, and **Occurrences**. Next, click **OK** twice.

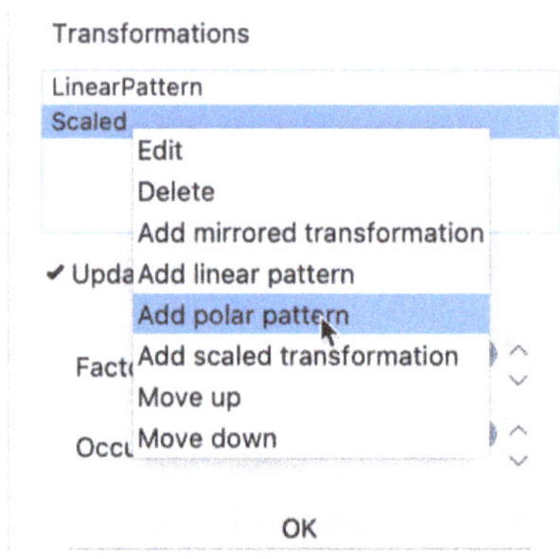

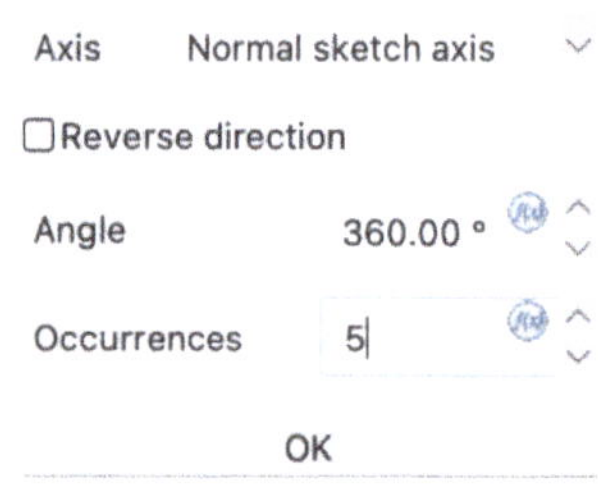

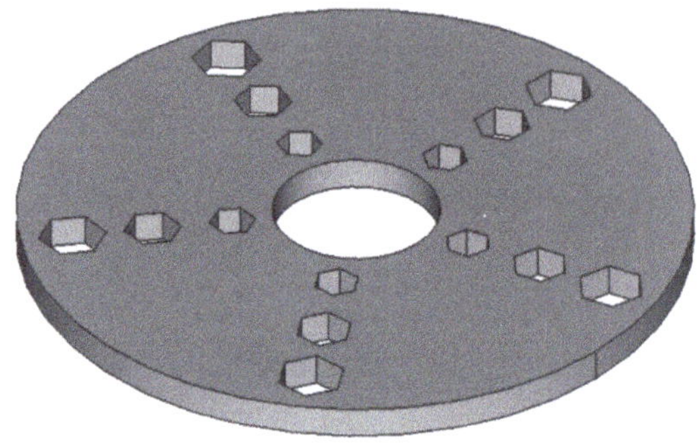

Best Practices for Using Patterns in Design

Design Intent

Start by understanding your design intent. Determine where patterns are necessary to save time and ensure that changes to the original feature are automatically reflected in the pattern.

For polar patterns, ensure the original feature is accurately positioned and designed, as errors will propagate through the pattern.

Efficient Geometry

Use well-constructed geometry for patterning. Avoid overly complex or detailed features, as patterns can increase file size and slow down system performance.

Maintain consistent wall thickness, especially in plastic parts, to avoid structural issues.

Standard Units

Always work in standard units and set them correctly in the document properties to ensure accuracy and consistency in patterns.

Use Patterns Sparingly

Patterns are powerful but can make models overly complex. Use them only when necessary to avoid performance issues and maintain model manageability.

Cautions When Using Patterns

Overdefinition

Avoid over-defining sketches or features with excessive dimensions or relations, as this can cause issues when creating patterns.

Complex Patterns

Be cautious with complex patterns, especially in large assemblies. Overuse can lead to performance issues and make the model harder to modify.

Interference

In assemblies, check for potential interference between patterned components to ensure they do not intersect or interfere with each other.

Maintain Modifiers

Update any modifiers or dependent features when patterns are updated to avoid unintended consequences in the design.

Tips for Different Types of Parts

Plastic Parts

Pay attention to draft angles and material flow to avoid undercuts or molding issues.

Ensure patterned features maintain consistent wall thickness and structural integrity.

Use polar patterns for symmetric rib and boss features to save time and ensure uniformity.

Casted Parts

Use patterns to replicate features like ribs, bosses, gating, and runner systems for structural integrity and balanced layouts.

Consider draft angles and parting lines to ensure ease of removal from molds.

Forged Parts

Use patterns for symmetrical impressions or shapes in forging dies.

Account for heat treatment requirements, as they may alter material properties and dimensions.

Machined Parts

Use patterns for replicating holes, pockets, or fasteners in machined parts.

Consider toolpath planning to ensure patterned features are accessible and can be efficiently machined.

Additional Considerations

Symmetry

Polar patterns are ideal for symmetric parts, such as regularly spaced bolts or screws.

Feature Order

Ensure the central feature is created before applying a polar pattern. Changing the order can impact the pattern's outcome.

Performance

Overusing patterns can slow down performance, particularly in complex assemblies. Suppress patterns if necessary to improve system efficiency.

Flexibility

Strike a balance between patterned features and individually designed components to maintain design flexibility.

Tutorial 1

In this example, you create the part shown next.

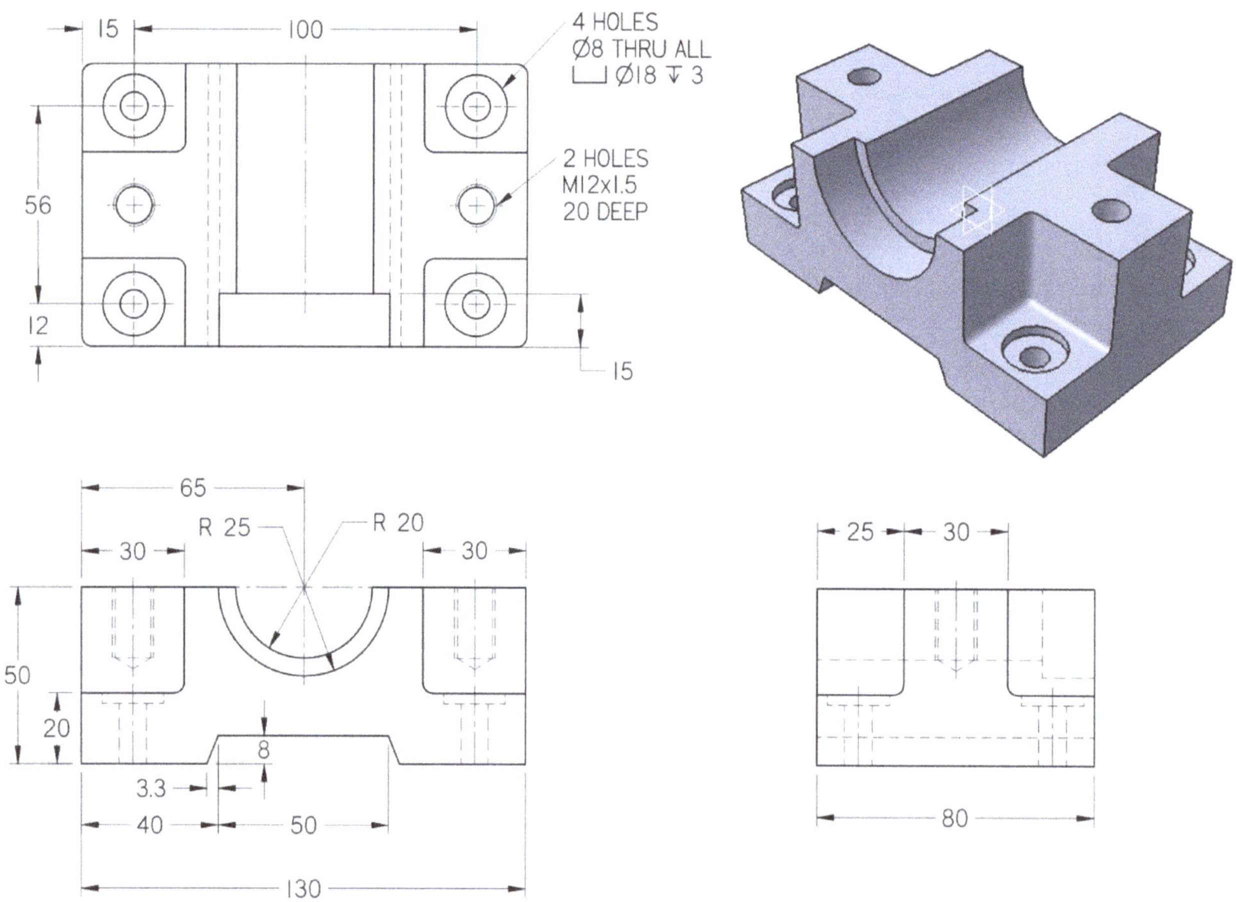

Creating a New document

1. Click **FreeCAD 1.0** on the desktop to start.
2. On the menu bar, click **File> New**; it creates a new document.
3. On the **Workbench** toolbar, select **Workbench** drop-down **> Part Design**.
4. Click **Edit > Preferences** on the **Menu** bar (or) click **FreeCAD 1.0 > Preferences** on title bar, if you are working on MacOS; the **Preferences** dialog appears on the screen.

5. Click the **General** tab and select **Default unit system > Standard (mm/kg/s/degree)**.
6. Select **Number of decimals > 2** and click **OK** on the **Preferences** dialog.

Creating the Pad features

1. To start a sketch, click **Create Sketch** on the **Part Design Helper** toolbar.
2. Click on the XZ_Plane and click **OK** on the **Tasks** panel; the selected plane orients normal to the screen.
3. On the **Sketcher geometries** toolbar, click **Rectangle**. Next, specify the two corners of the rectangle.

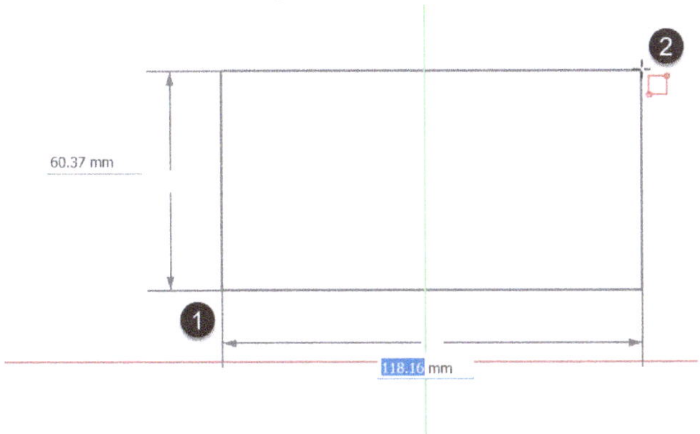

4. Click the **Constrain symmetric** icon on the **Sketcher constraints** toolbar. Next, select the lower right corner point of the rectangle.
5. Select the lower-left corner of the rectangle and the sketch origin point; the two corners of the rectangle are made symmetric about the sketch origin.
6. Add vertical and horizontal distance constraints to the rectangle.

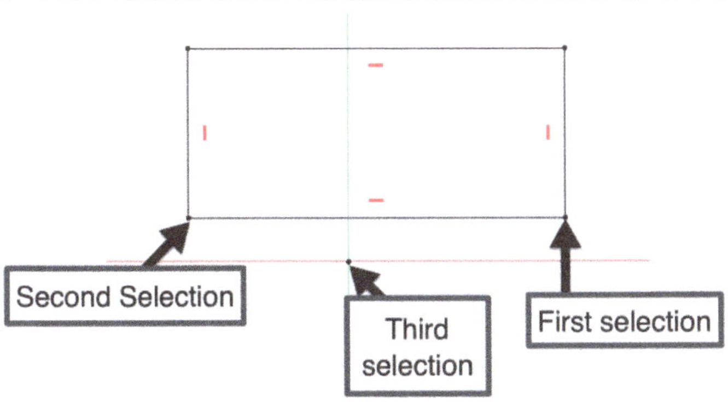

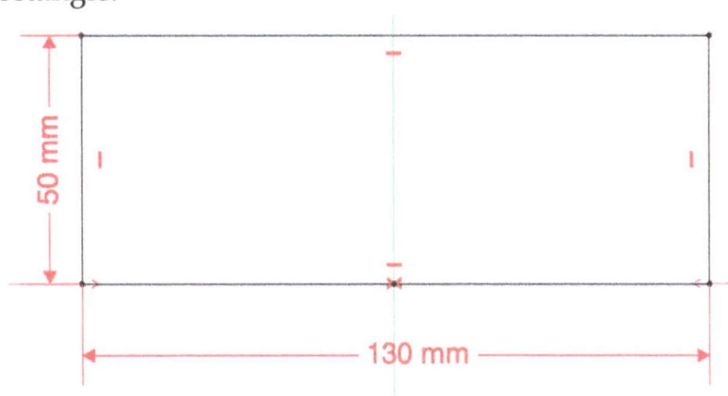

7. Click the **Close** button on the **Tasks** panel.
8. Activate the **Pad** tool on the **Part Design Modeling** toolbar.
9. On the **Pad parameters** section, check the **Symmetry to plane** option. Type **80** in the **Length** box and click **OK** to create the *Pad* feature.

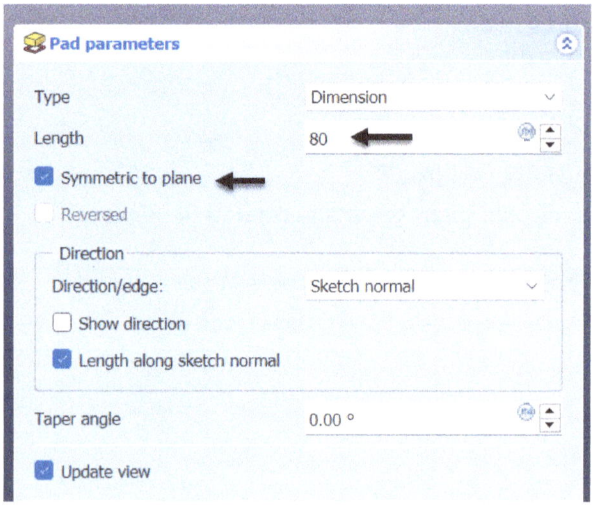

10. Select the top face of the model and click the **Create Sketch** icon on the **Part Design Helper** toolbar.
11. Click the **Create external geometry** icon on the **Sketcher tools** toolbar.
12. Select the right vertical edge of the top face of the *Pad* feature, as shown. Next, create a rectangle.
13. Click the **Constrain coincident** icon on the **Sketcher constraints** toolbar.
14. Select the bottom-right corner point of the rectangle. Next, select the bottom endpoint of the projected edge; the two selected points are constrained coincidentally.

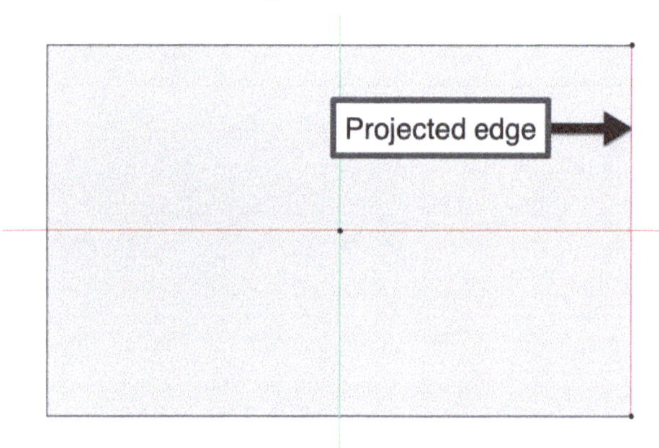

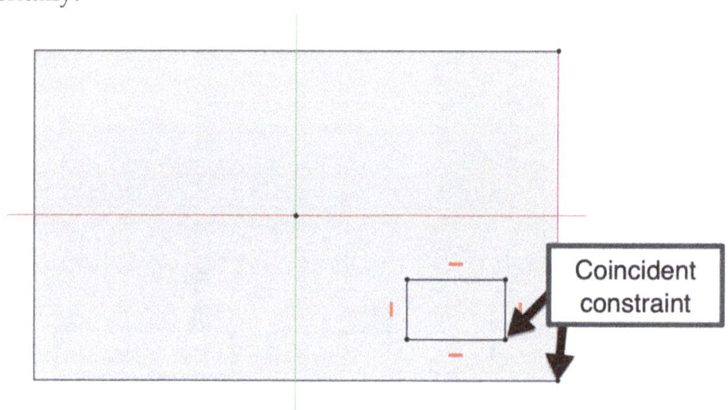

15. On the **Sketcher constraints** toolbar, click the **Dimension** icon.
16. Select the horizontal line and move the pointer downward and click. Next, type-in **30** in the **Length** box on the **Insert Length** dialog, and then click **OK**.
17. Select the vertical line and type-in **25** in the **Length** box on the **Insert Length** dialog, and click **OK**.
18. Click the **Close** button on the **Tasks** panel.
19. Click the **Pocket** icon on the **Part Design Modeling** toolbar; the **Pocket parameters** section appears on the **Tasks** panel.
20. Type-in **30** in the **Length** box on the **Tasks** panel and click **OK** to create the *Pocket* feature.

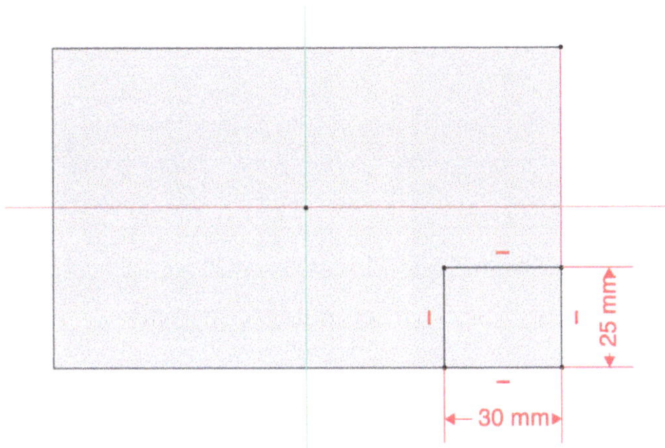

Creating the Hole features

1. Select the horizontal face of the *Pocket* feature and click the **Create Sketch** on the **Part Design Helper** toolbar.

2. On the **Sketcher tools** toolbar, click the **Create external geometry** icon to project the edges.
3. Select the horizontal and vertical edges of the *Pocket* feature, as shown.

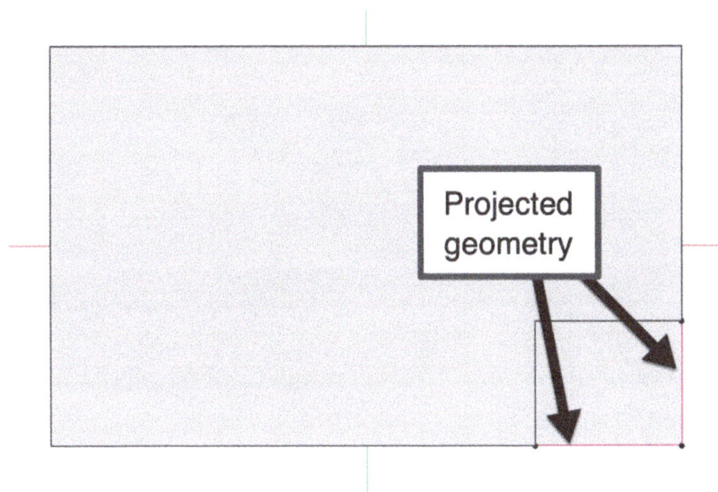

4. Click the **Circle** drop-down > **Center and rim point** on the **Sketcher geometries** toolbar.
5. Create a circle and horizontal and vertical distance constraints, as shown.

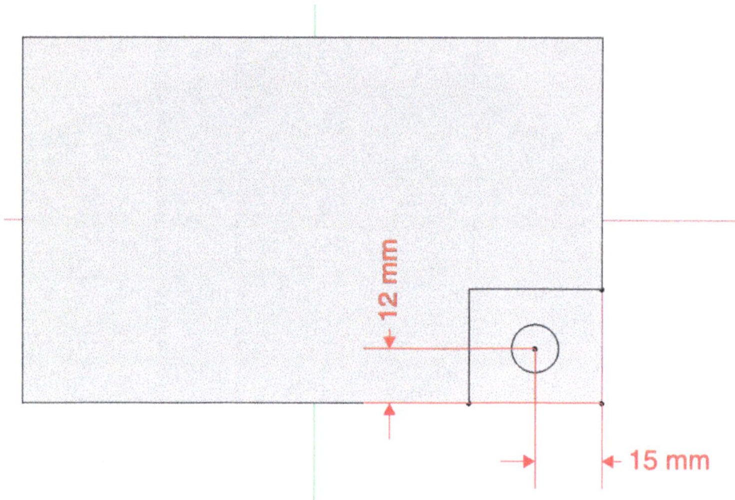

6. Click the **Close** button on the **Tasks** panel.
7. Click the **Hole**  tool on the **Part Design Modeling** toolbar; the sketch is selected automatically.
8. Type-in **8** in the **Diameter** box and select **Depth > Through All**.
9. On the **Hole Parameters** section, select **Hole Cut Type > Counterbore**.
10. Type-in **18** and **3** in the **Diameter** and **Depth** boxes, respectively.
11. Click **OK** on the **Tasks** panel; the counterbore hole is created.

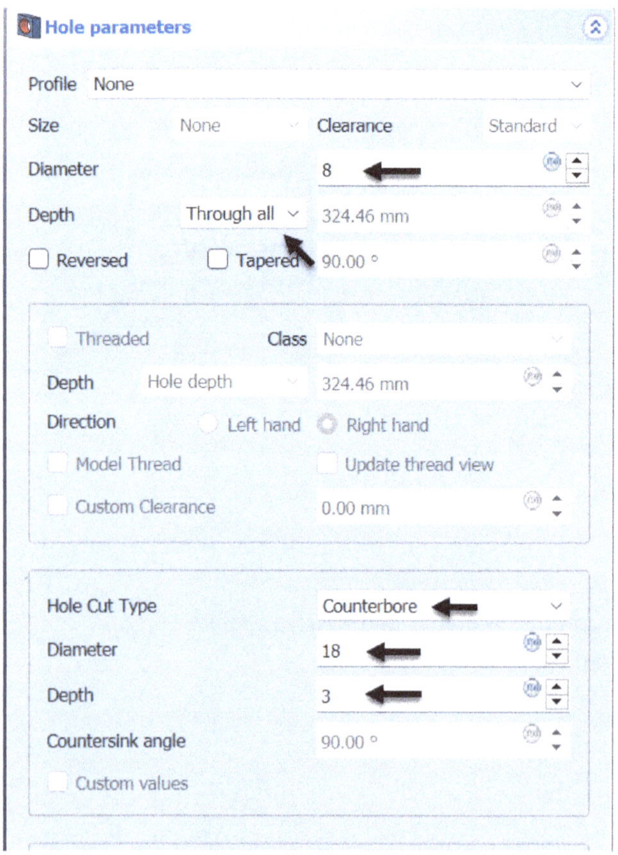

Creating the Multi transform feature

1. Click the **Create MultiTransform** icon on the **Part Design Modeling** toolbar.
2. On the **MultiTrasnform parameters** section of the **Tasks** panel, select the **Transform tool shapes** option
3. Click the **Add feature** button, and then click the **Model** panel. Next, select the **Pocket** feature.
4. Click the **Tasks** panel and click the **Add feature** button on the **MultiTransform parameters** section and select the cylindrical face of the counterbore hole.

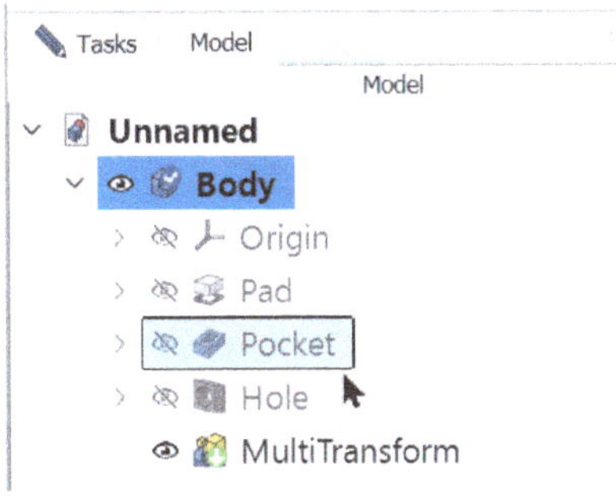

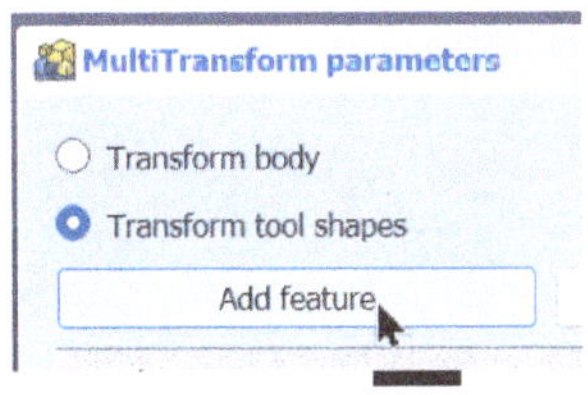

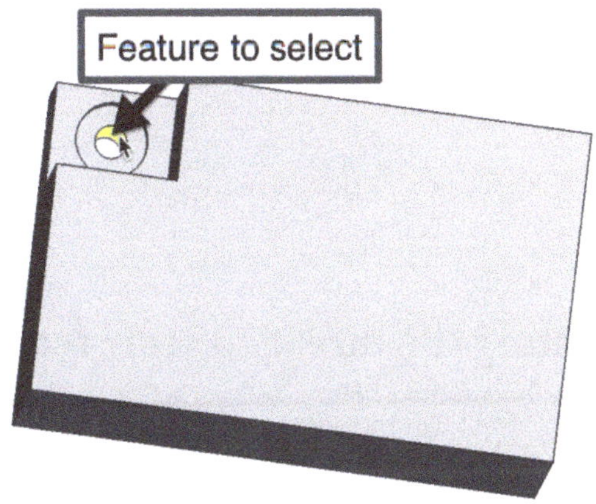

5. Right-click in the **Transformations** section and select **Add linear pattern**.
6. On the **MultiTransform parameters** section, select **Direction > Base X axis**.
7. Type **100** and **2** in the **Length** and **Occurrences** boxes, respectively.

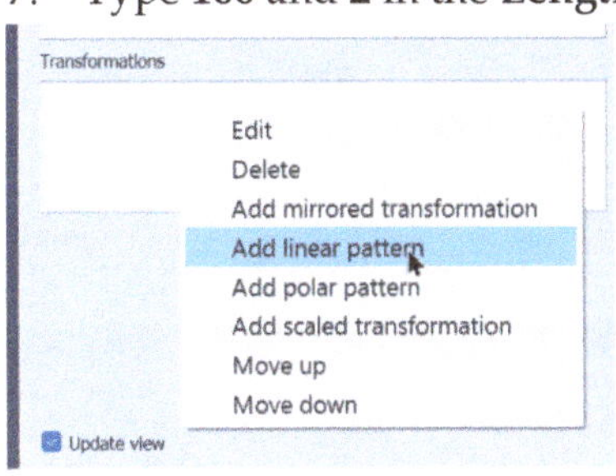

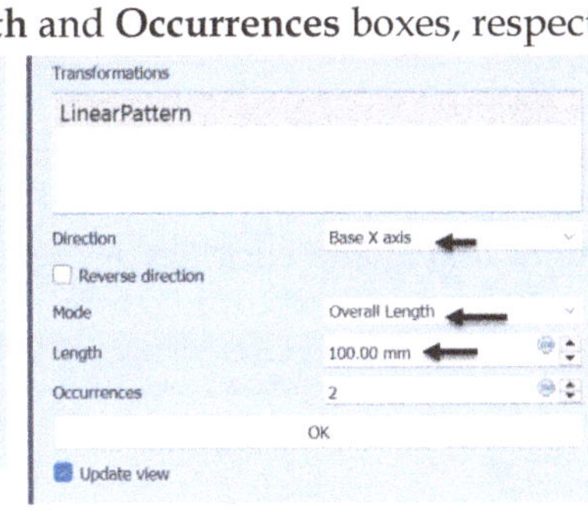

8. Right-click in the **Transformations** section and select **Add mirrored transformation**.
9. Select **Plane > Base XZ plane**. Next, click **OK** to create the linear pattern.

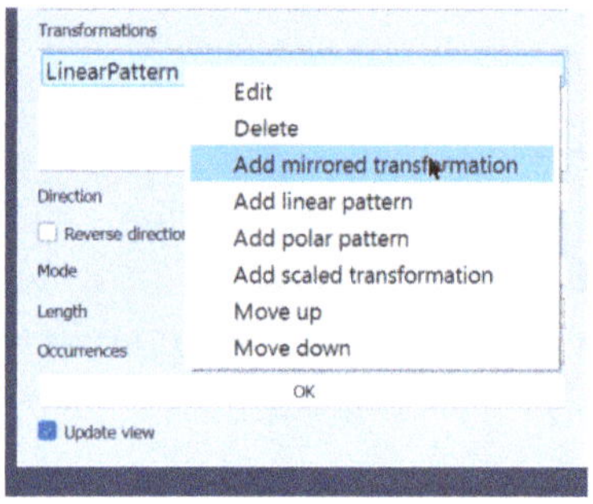

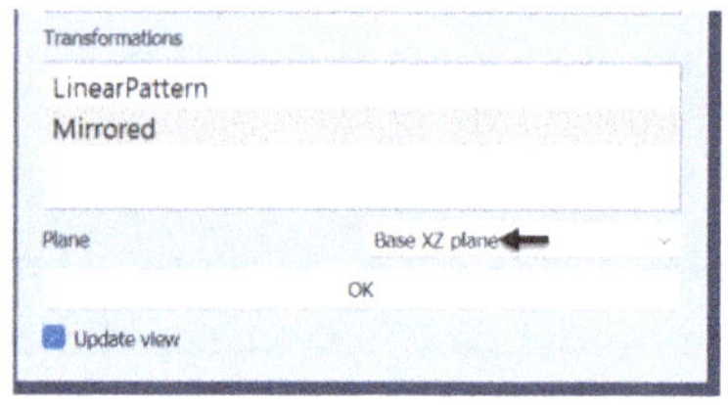

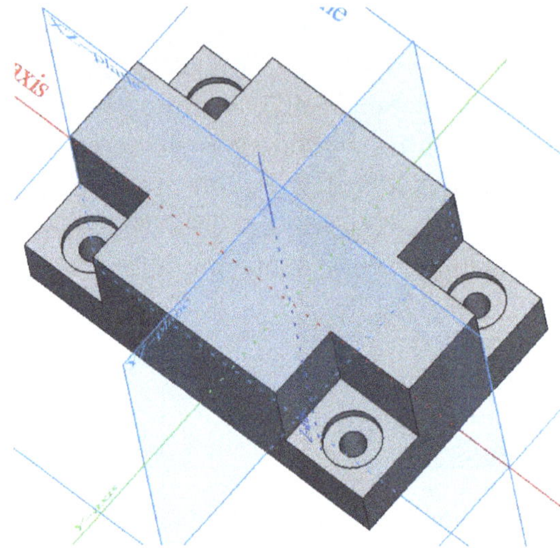

Creating the threaded Hole feature

1. Select the top face of the model and click the **Create Sketch** on the **Part Design Helper** toolbar.
2. Click the **Create external geometry** icon on the **Sketcher tools** toolbar.
3. Select the left vertical edge of the part, as shown. Press **Esc** to deactivate the tool.
4. Click the **Create circle** icon on the **Sketcher geometries** toolbar.
5. Click on the horizontal sketch axis to define the center of the circle. Next, move the pointer outward and click to create a circle, as shown.
6. On the **Sketcher constraints** toolbar, click the **Dimension > Constrain horizontal distance** tool.
7. Select the center point of the circle and the endpoint of the projected vertical edge, as shown.
8. Type-in **15** in the **Length** box of the **Insert Length** dialog and click **OK.**

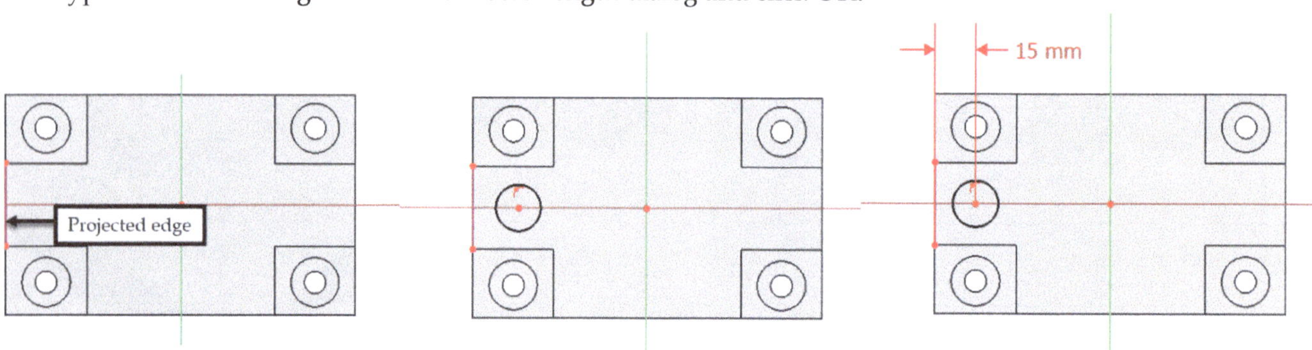

9. Click **Close** on the **Tasks** panel.
10. Click the **Hole** icon on the **Part Design Modeling** toolbar; the **Hole parameters** section appears on the screen.
11. Select **Profile > ISO metric regular profile.**
12. Check the **Threaded** option, and then select **Direction > Right hand**.
13. Check the **Model Thread** option and check the **Update thread view** option.
14. Select **Size > M12** and **Class > 4G**.
15. Select **Depth > Dimension** and type-in **20** in the dimension box.

16. Select **Depth > Hole depth**.
17. Select **Drill point > Angled** option. Next, type **118** in the angle box.
18. Click **OK** on the **Combo View** panel.

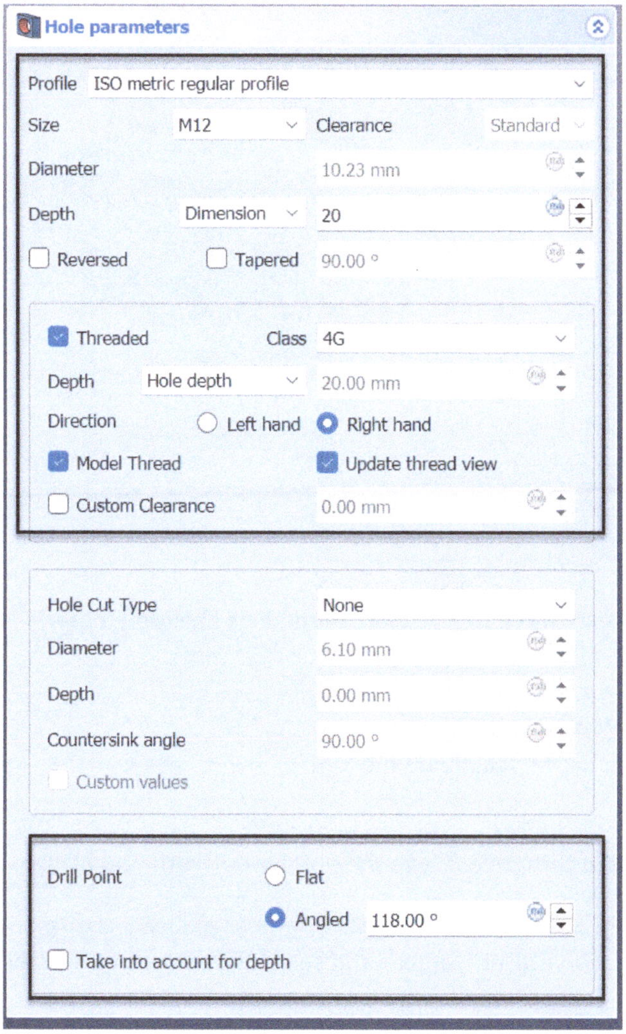

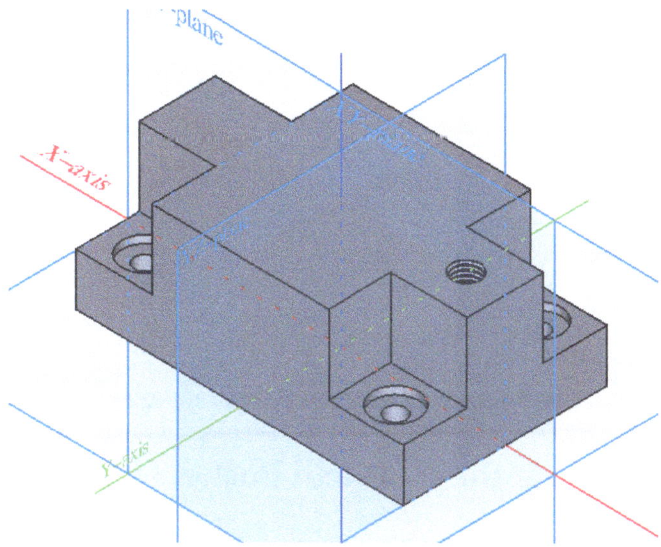

Mirroring the Features

1. On the **Part Design Modeling** toolbar, click the **Mirrored**  icon.
2. On the **MultiTrasnform parameters** section of the **Tasks** panel, select the **Transform tool shapes** option
3. Click the **Add feature** button, and then click the **Model** panel. Next, select the **Hole001** feature.
4. Click the **Tasks** panel, select **Plane> Base YZ plane** option under the **Mirrored parameters** section.
5. Click **OK** to mirror the *Hole* feature.

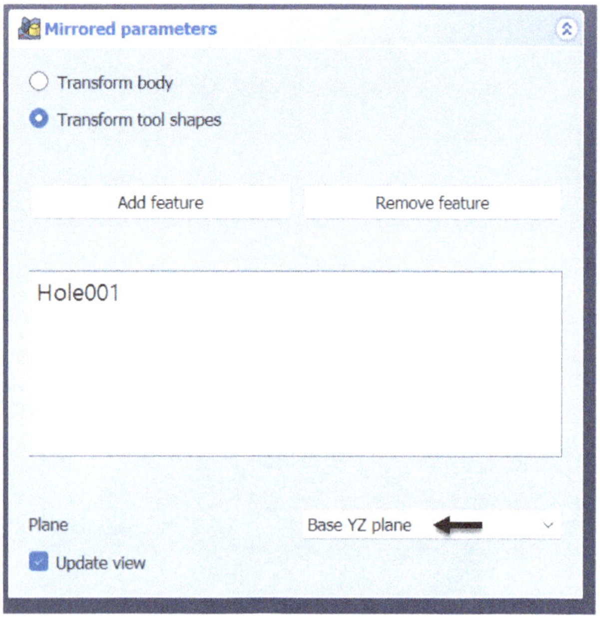

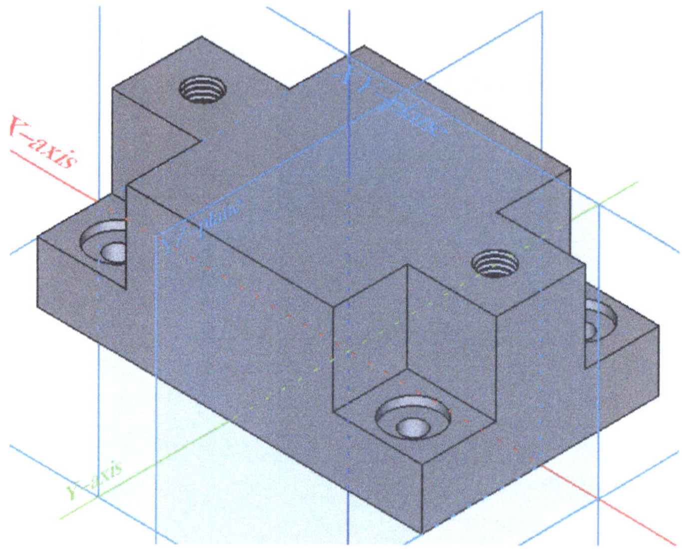

Creating the Hole and Pocket features

1. Select the front face of the part geometry and click the **Create Sketch** icon on the **Part Design Helper** toolbar.
2. Click the **Create external geometry** icon on the **Sketcher tools** toolbar.
3. Select the top horizontal edge of the part, as shown. Press **Esc** to deactivate the tool.
4. Click the **Create circle** icon on the **Sketcher geometries** toolbar.
5. Click on the vertical sketch axis to define the center point of the circle. Move the pointer outward and click to create a circle.
6. Click the **Constrain Coincident** icon on the **Sketcher constraints** toolbar and select the center point of the circle. Next, select the projected edge.
7. Click **Close** on the **Tasks** panel.

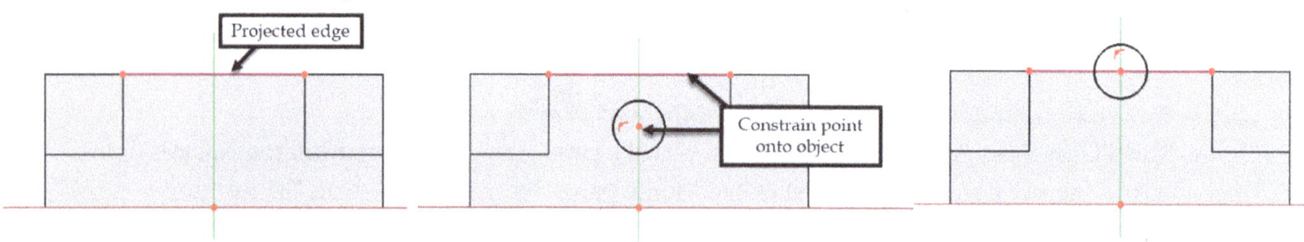

8. Click the **Hole** icon on the **Part Design Modeling** toolbar.
9. On the **Hole parameters** section, select **Profile > None**.
10. Type 40 in the **Diameter** box. Next, select the **Depth > Through all**.
11. In the section, select **Hole Cut Type > Counterbore**.
12. Type-in **50** and **15** in the **Diameter** and **Depth** boxes, respectively.
13. Click **OK** to create the counterbore hole.

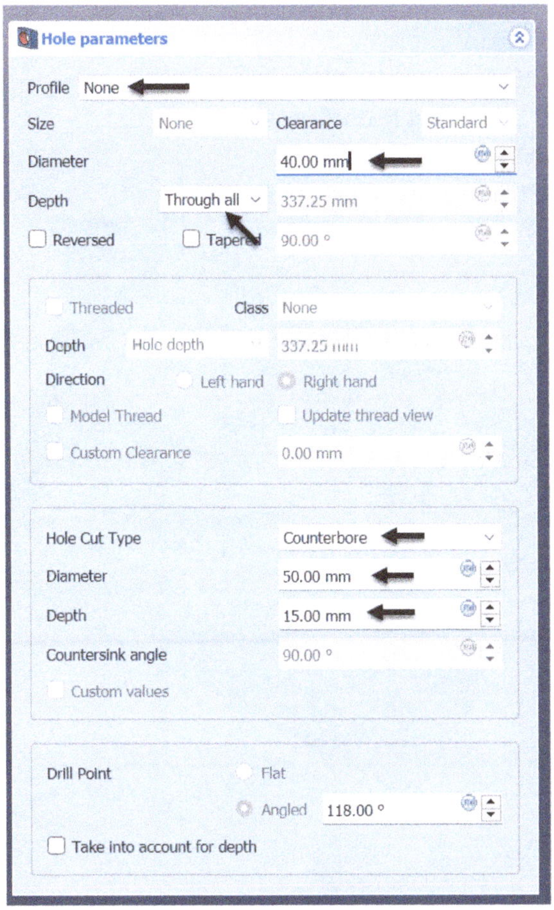

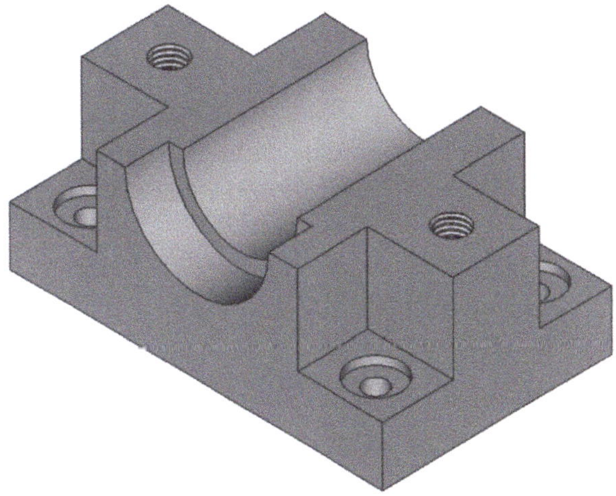

14. Select the front face of the part geometry and click the **Create Sketch** icon on the **Part Design Helper** toolbar.
15. Create a closed sketch using the **Create Polyline** command. Next, add vertical and horizontal distance constraints to it.
16. Click the **Constrain symmetrical** icon on the **Sketcher constraints** toolbar and select an endpoint of the lower horizontal line. Next, select the other endpoint of the lower horizontal line.
17. Select the sketch origin; the two endpoints of the lower horizontal line are made symmetric about the sketch origin.
18. Click the **Constrain equal** icon on the **Sketcher constraints** toolbar. Next, select the two inclined lines, as shown.

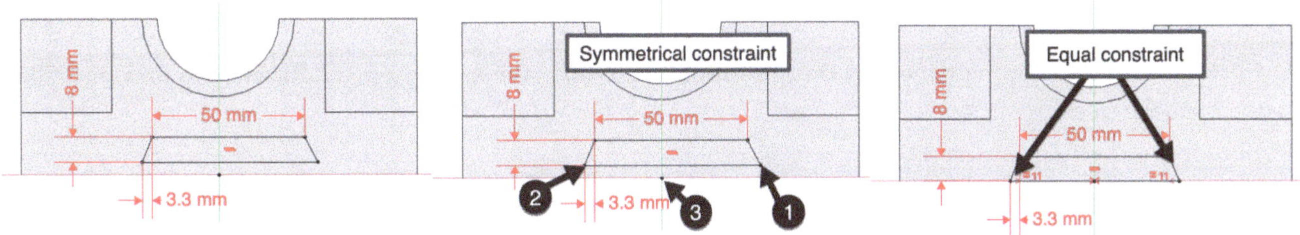

19. Click **Close** on the **Tasks** panel.

20. Click the **Pocket** icon on the **Part Design Modeling** toolbar.
21. Select **Type > Through all** from the **Pocket parameters** section. Next, click **OK**.
22. Press and hold the Ctrl key and select the internal edges of the pocket feature, as shown.
23. Press and hold the middle and right mouse buttons, and then drag the cursor.
24. Press and hold the Ctrl key and select the internal edges of the remaining pocket features.

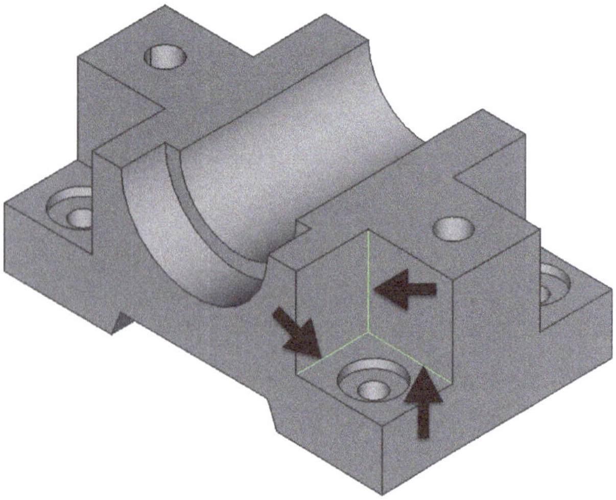

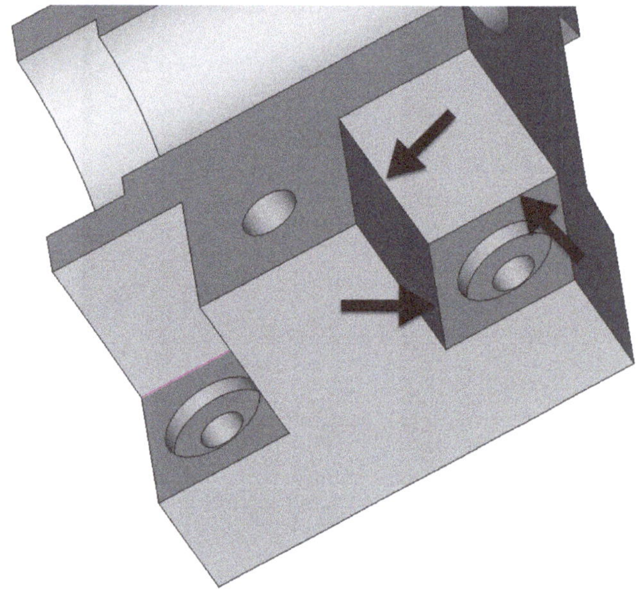

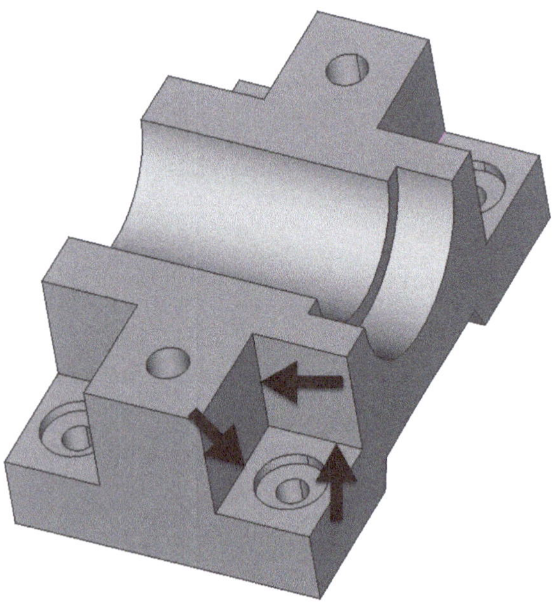

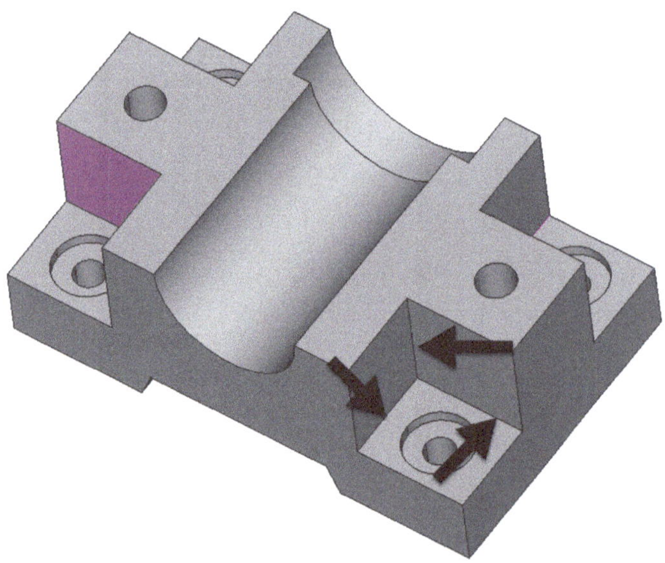

25. Click the **Fillet** icon on the **Part Design Modeling** toolbar. Next, type 2 in the **Radius** box and click **OK** to create the fillets.

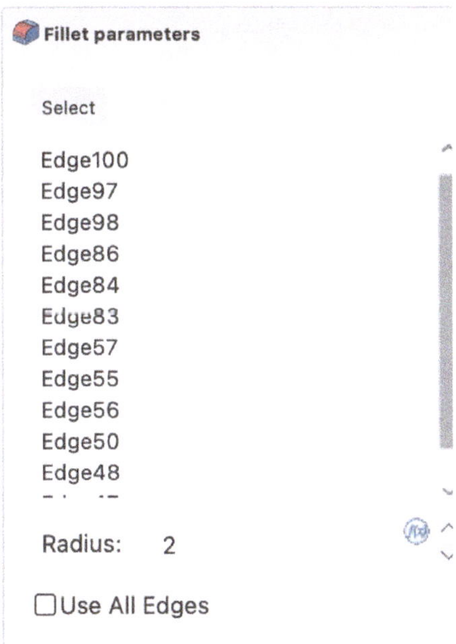

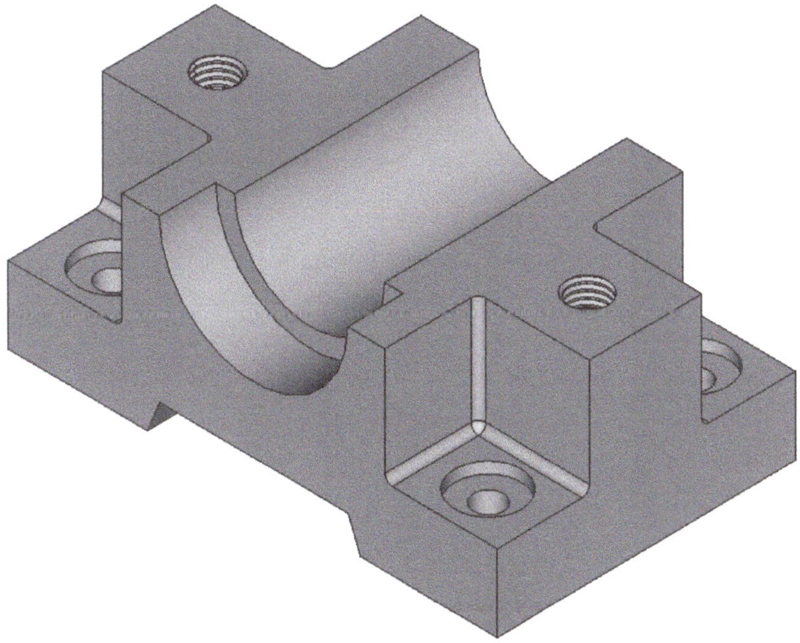

26. Click the **Save** icon on the **File** toolbar located at the top-left corner of the window. Next, type C5_exampl1 in the **File name** box, and then click **Save**.
27. Click **File > Close** on the menu bar to close the document.

Tutorial 2 (Millimetres)

In this example, you create the part shown next.

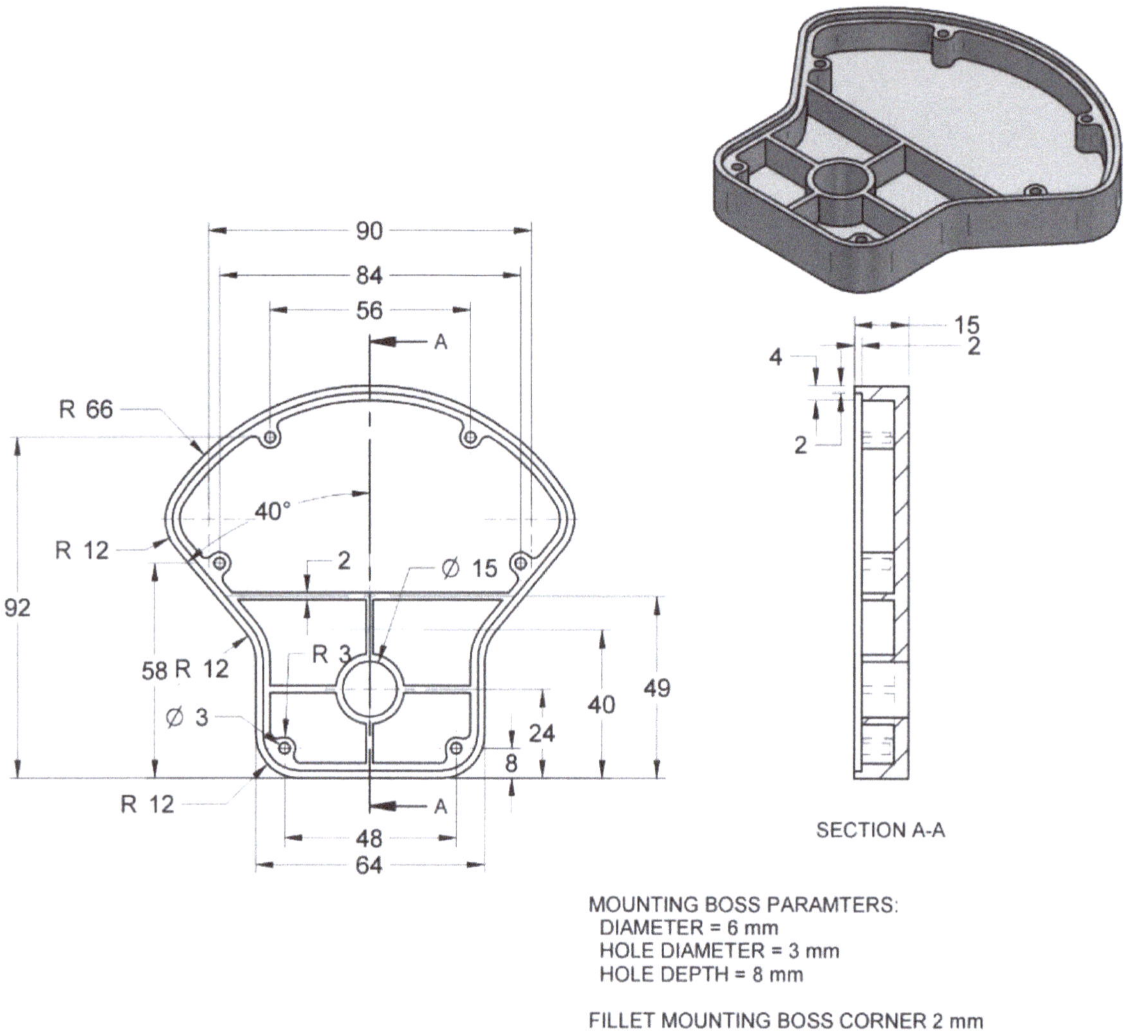

Creating a New document

1. Click **FreeCAD 1.0** on the desktop to start.
2. On the Menu bar, click **File > New**; it creates a new document.
3. On the **Workbench** toolbar, select **Workbench** drop-down **> Part Design**.
4. Click **Edit > Preferences** on the **Menu** bar (or) click **FreeCAD 1.0 > Preferences** on title bar, if you are working on MacOS; the **Preferences** dialog appears on the screen.
5. Click the **General** tab and select **Default unit system > Standard (mm/kg/s/degree)**.
6. Select **Number of decimals > 2** and click **OK** on the **Preferences** dialog.

Creating the Pad Feature

1. Click the **Create Sketch** command on the **Part Design Helper** toolbar and start a new sketch on the **XY** plane.
2. On the **Sketcher geometries** toolbar, click the **Create polyline** command and draw the sketch, as shown

in the figure below.

3. On the **Sketcher geometries** toolbar, click the **Arc** drop-down > **Create arc by three points** command, and then create an arc by specifying the points in the sequence, as shown.

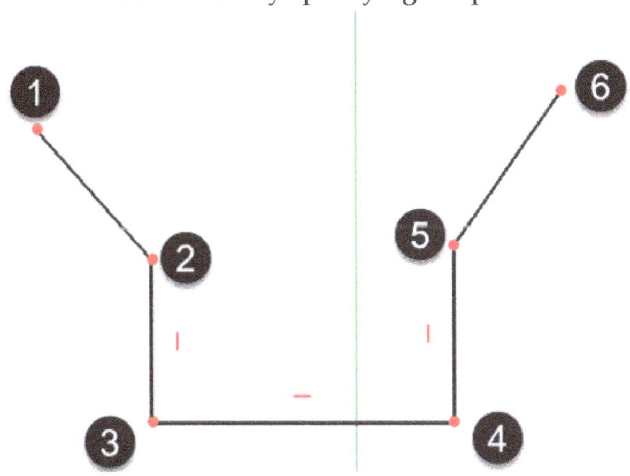

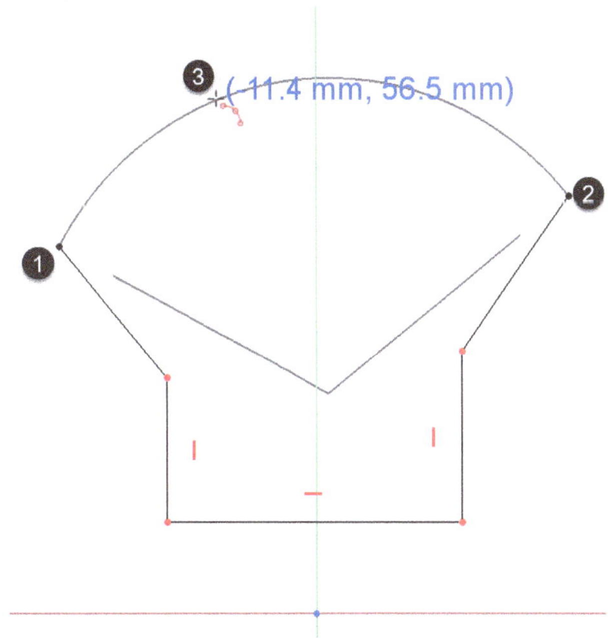

4. Click the **Sketch Fillet** command on the **Sketcher tools** Toolbar, and then select the sharp corners to fillet.
5. Select the arc and the inclined line connected to it; the fillet is created at the corner.
6. Likewise, select the arc and the inclined line connected to it at the other end.

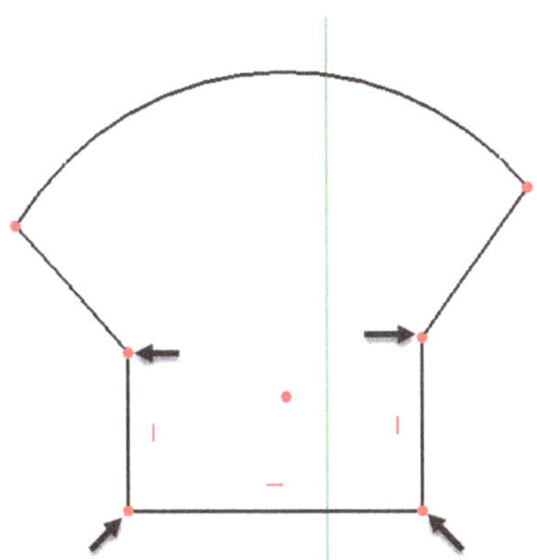

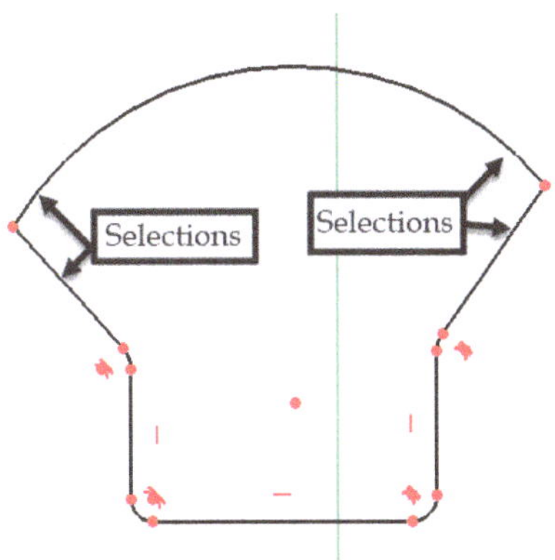

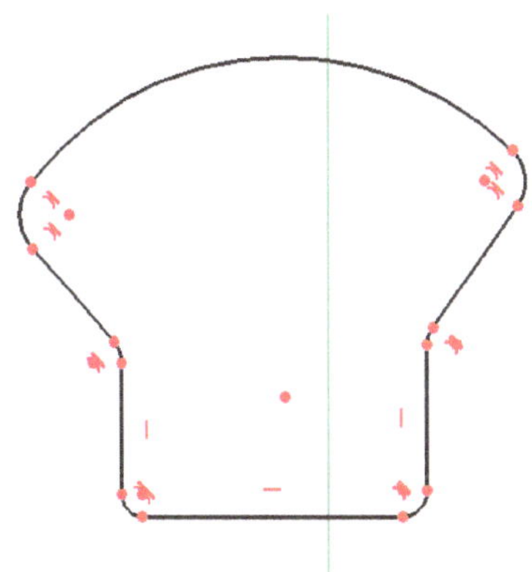

7. Click the **Constrain equal** icon on the **Sketcher constraints** toolbar. Next, apply the **Equal** constraint between the fillets, as shown.
8. Apply the **Equal** constraint between the fillets, as shown.

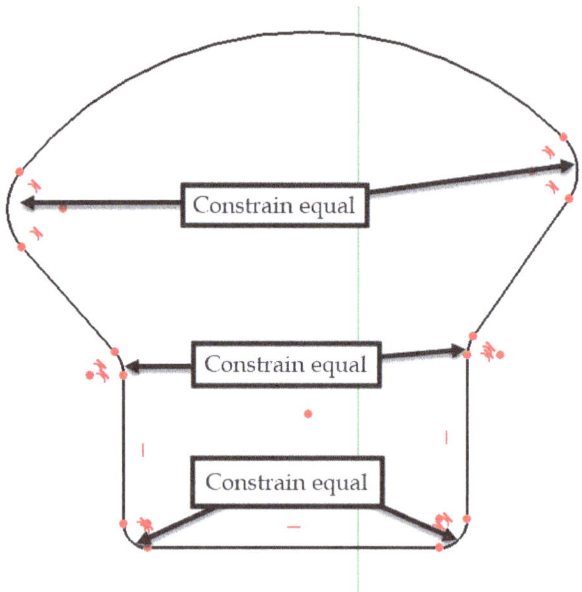

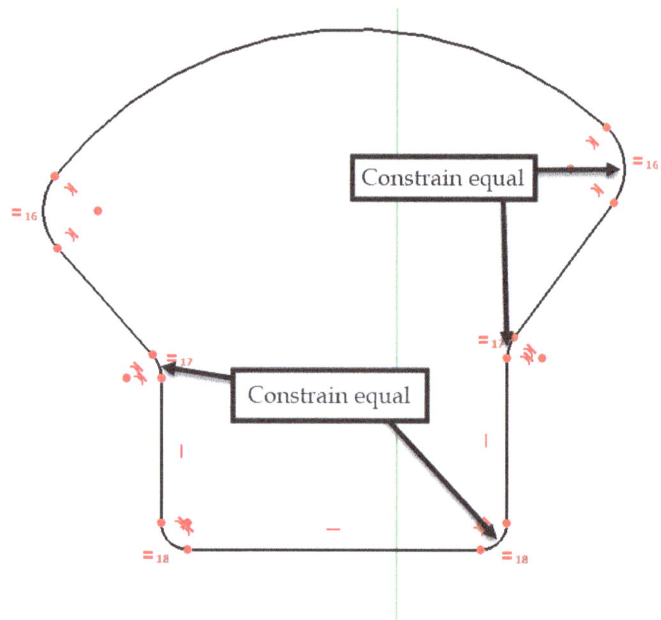

9. Apply the **Equal** constraint between the two vertical lines.
10. Apply the **Equal** constraint between the two inclined lines. Next, right click in the graphics window.
11. Select the centerpoints of the two fillets, as shown. Next, click the Constrain horizontal/vertical drop-down > **Constrain horizontal** icon on the **Sketcher constraints** toolbar.

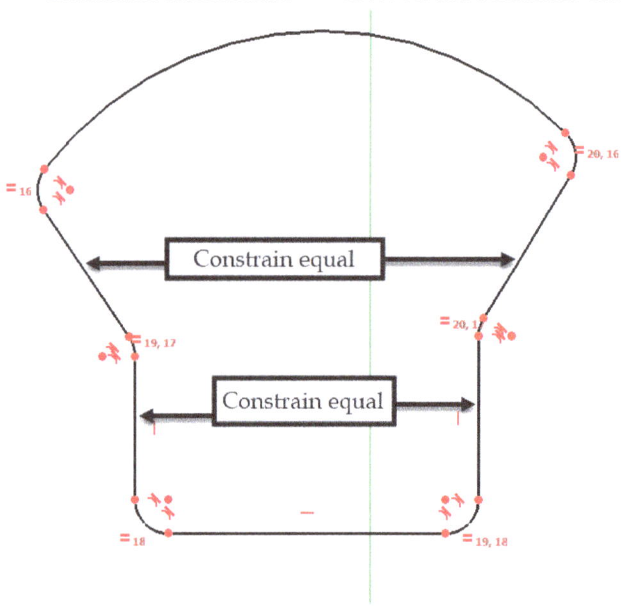

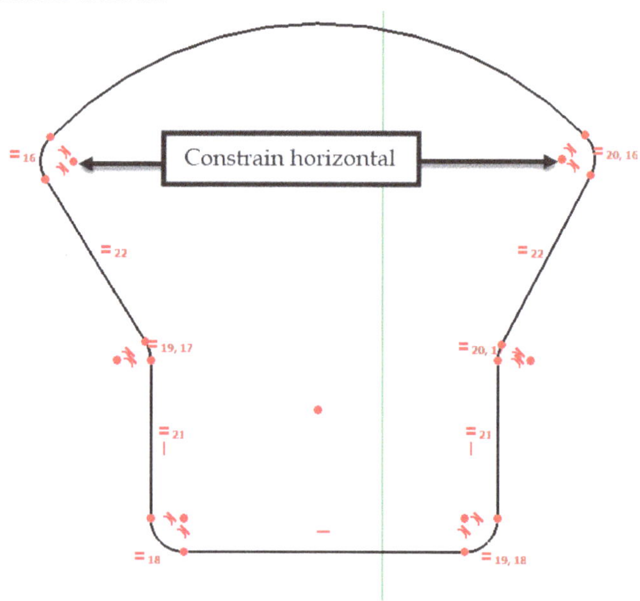

12. Click the **Constrain symmetrical** icon on the **Sketcher constraints** toolbar and select the points in the sequence, as shown.

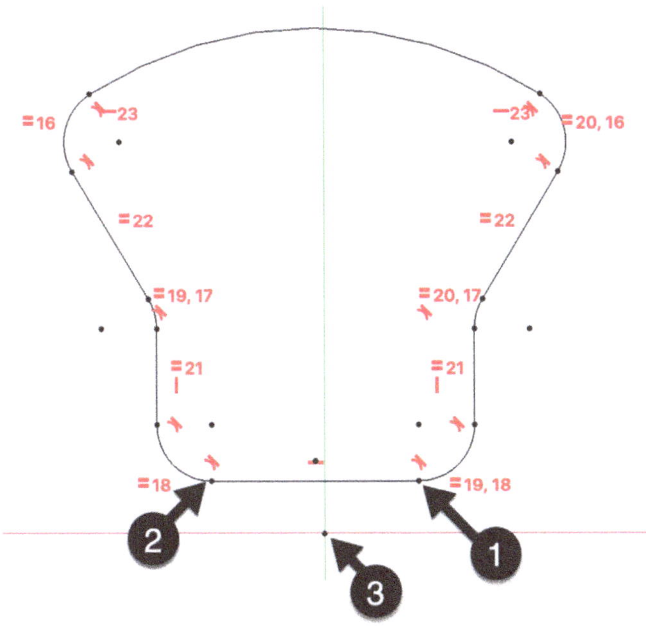

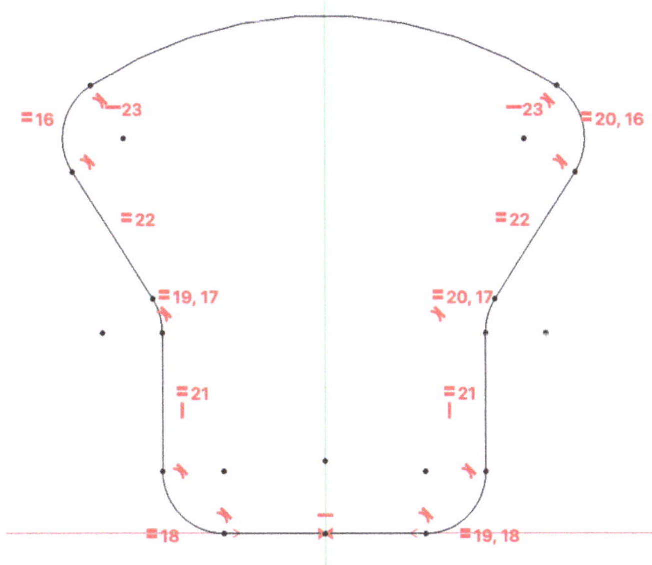

13. Click the **Dimension drop-down > Constrain angle** icon on the **Sketcher constraints** toolbar. Next, select the left inclined and vertical lines, as shown. Type **140** in the **Angle** box and click **OK**.
14. Apply the dimensional constraints to the sketch in the sequence, as shown.

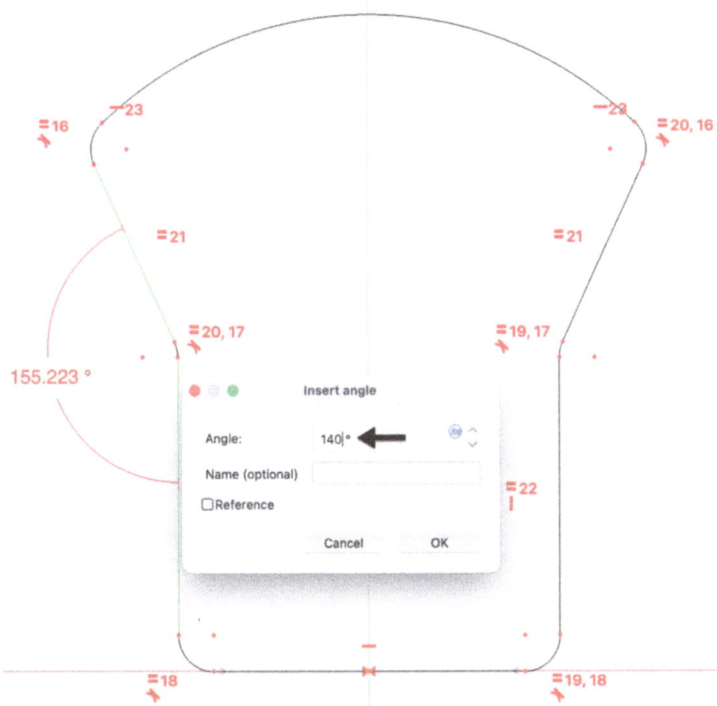

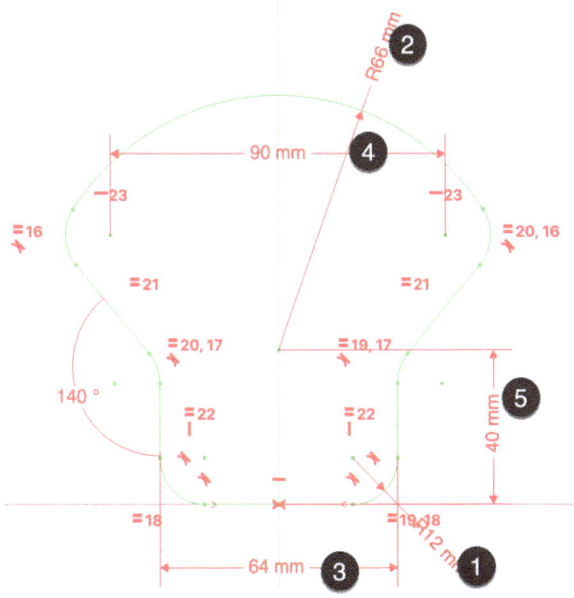

15. Click the **Close** button on the **Tasks** panel.
16. Activate the **Pad** command. Next, type-in **14** in the **Length** box under the **Pad parameters** section of the **Tasks** panel.
17. Click **OK** to create the *Pad* feature.

18. Select the top face of the pad feature and click the **Thickness** icon on the **Part Design Modeling** toolbar.
19. Type-in **4** in the **Thickness** box on the **Thickness parameters** section.
20. Check the **Make thickness inwards** option and click **OK**.

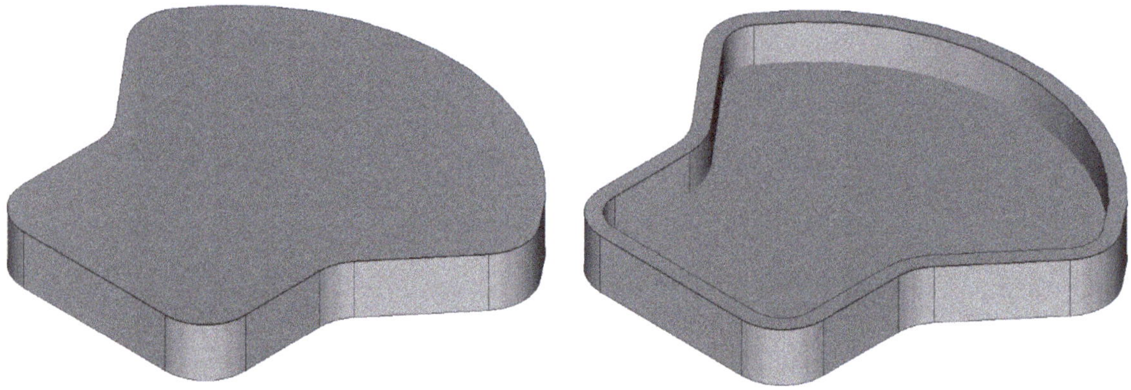

Adding a Lip to the model

1. In the **Tasks** panel, expand the **Origin** node and
2. Click the **Create Sketch** icon on the **Part Design Helper** toolbar. Select the YZ Plane.
3. Click the **View Section** icon on the **Sketcher edit mode** toolbar.
4. Click **Create external geometry** on the **Sketcher tools** toolbar, and then select the internal vertical edge.
5. Click the **Create rectangle** icon on the **Sketcher geometries** toolbar.
6. Select the top endpoint of the projected edge. Next, move the pointer toward the bottom left corner.
7. Type 2 in the width box and press the TAB key. Type-in 2 in the height box and press ENTER.

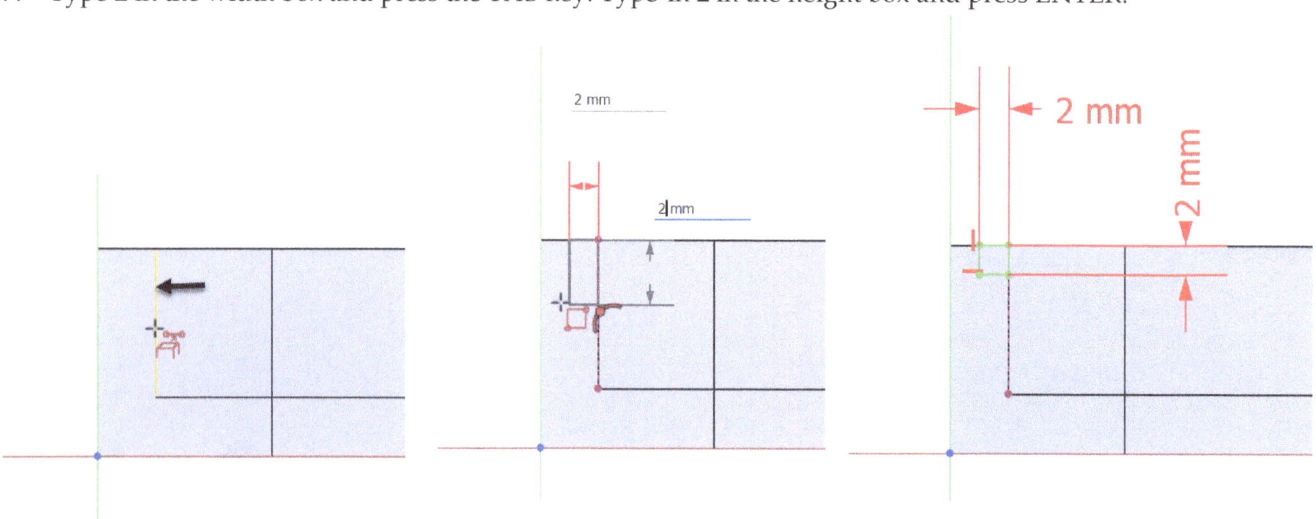

8. Click **Close** on the **Tasks** panel.
9. In the **Model** panel, expand the **Pad** feature and select the **Sketch**.
10. Right-click and select **Toggle Visibility**.
11. In the **Properties** panel, scroll down and click the drop-down next to the **Visibility** property. Next, select **true** from the drop-down; the sketch used for the Pad feature is visible in the graphics window.

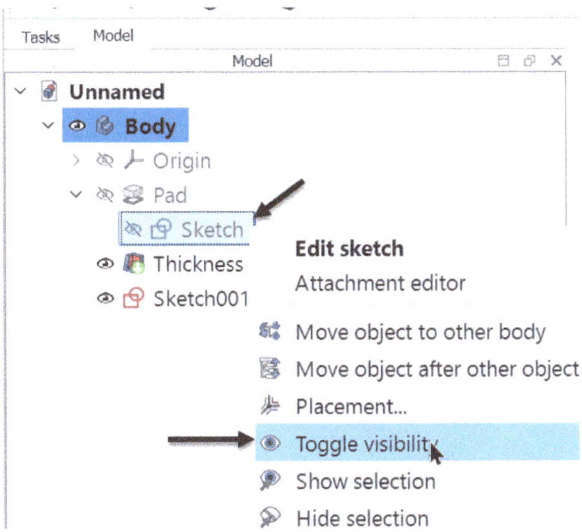

12. Click in the graphics area to deselect the sketch of the Pad feature.
13. Click the **Subtractive Pipe** icon on the **Part Design Modeling** toolbar; the sketch created on the YZ plane is selected as the profile.
14. Press and hold middle and right mouse buttons. Next, drag the cursor such that the bottom face of the model is displayed.
15. On the **Pipe parameters** section, click the **Object** button under **Pipe to sweep along** section.
16. Select the sketch used for the *Pad* feature. Next, click **OK** to create the subtractive pipe feature.
17. Click the **Set to isometric view** icon on the **View** toolbar to change the view to isometric.

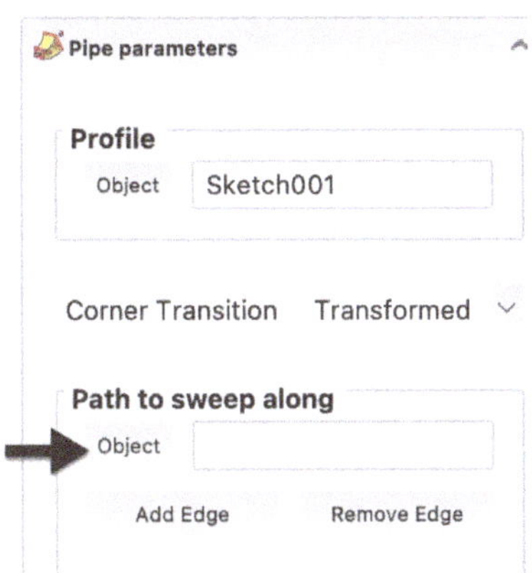

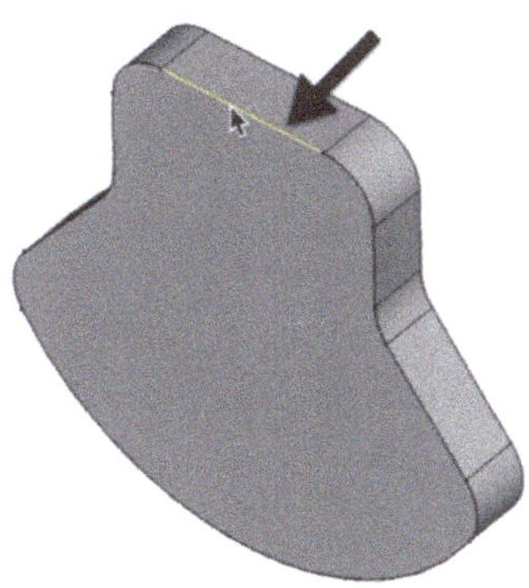

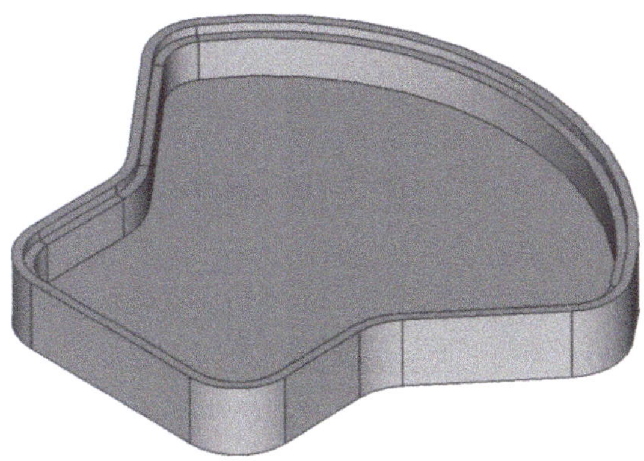

Creating Bosses

1. Click on the horizontal face create by the subtractive pipe feature. Next, click the **Create sketch** icon on the **Part Design Helper** toolbar.
2. Draw the three circles on the sketch plane. Next, click **Constrain equal** on the **Sketcher constraints** toolbar.
3. Select the first two circles to make them equal in diameter. Next, select the second and third circles to make them equal.

4. Add dimensional constraints to them, as shown.

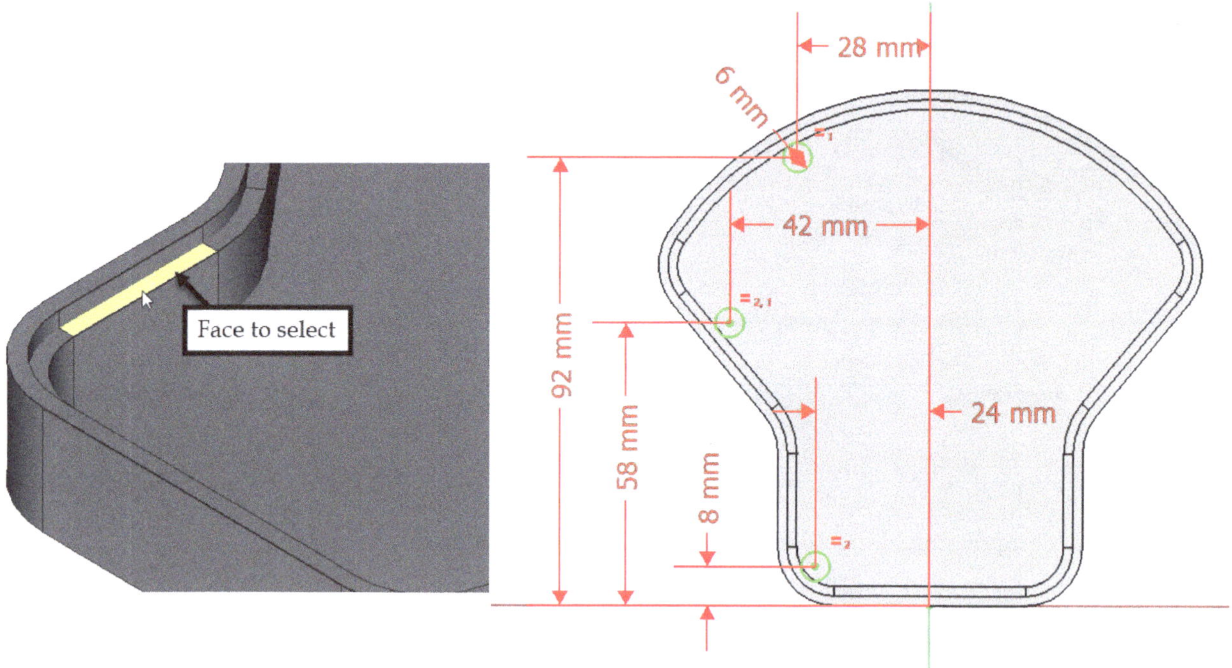

5. Click the **Create circle** icon on the **Sketcher geometries** toolbar. Next, select any one of the centerpoints of the circles. Move the pointer outward and click to create a circle.
6. Likewise, create two more circles concentric to the other two circles.

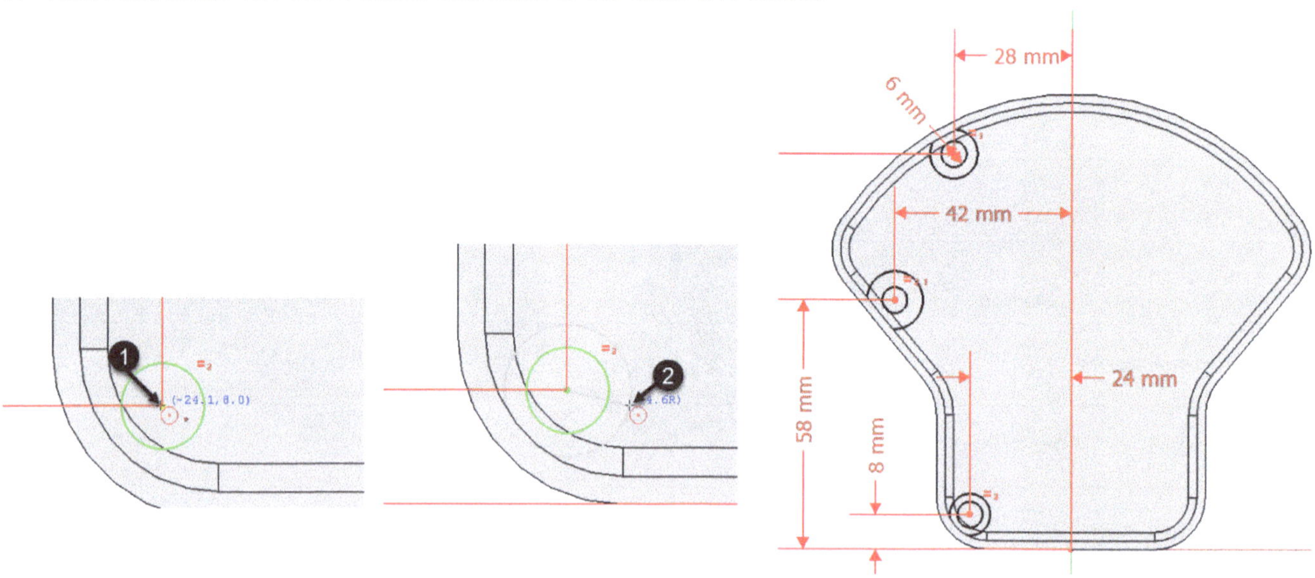

7. Click the **Constrain equal** icon on the **Sketcher constraints** toolbar and select two new circles; the two circles are made equal in diameter.
8. Likewise, make the third new circle equal to the second new circle.
9. Click the **Dimension** drop-down **> Constrain diameter** icon on the **Sketcher constraints** toolbar and select any one of the new circles.
10. Type 3 in the **Diameter** box and click **OK**.

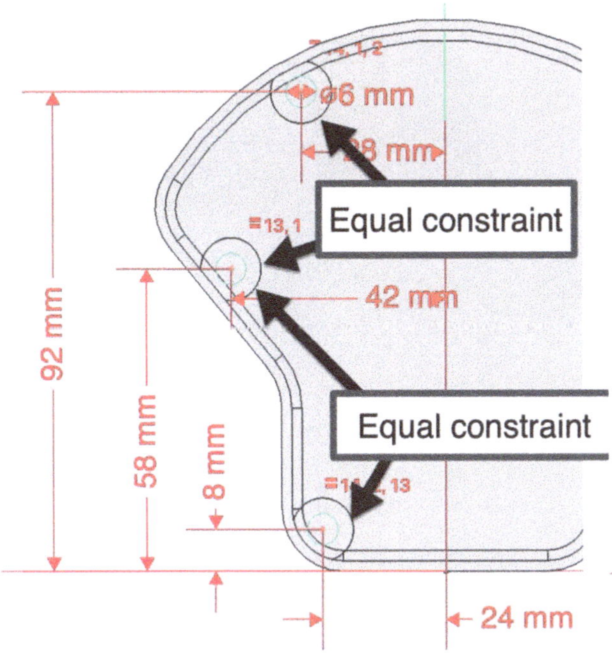

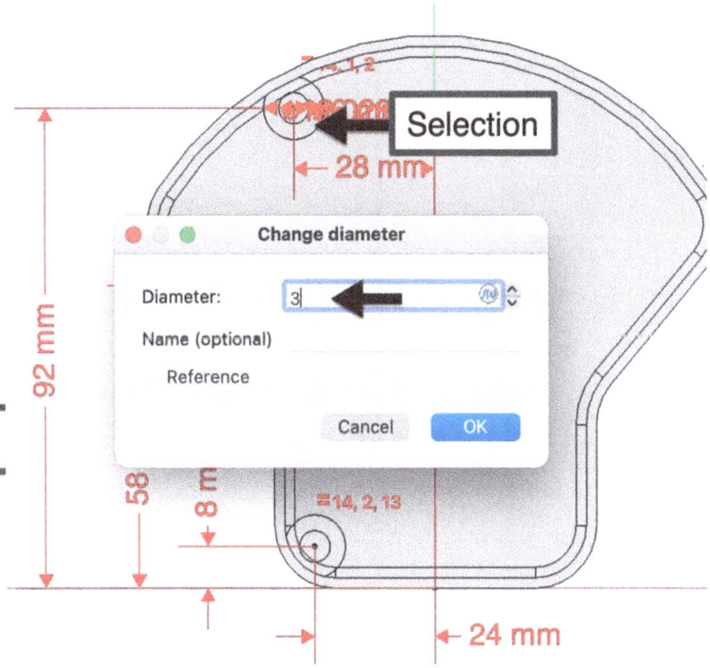

11. Click the **Close** button on the **Tasks** panel.

12. On the **Part Design Modeling** toolbar, click the **Pad**  icon.
13. On the **Pad parameters** section, enter **8** in the **Length** box. Next, check the **Reversed** option and click **OK**.

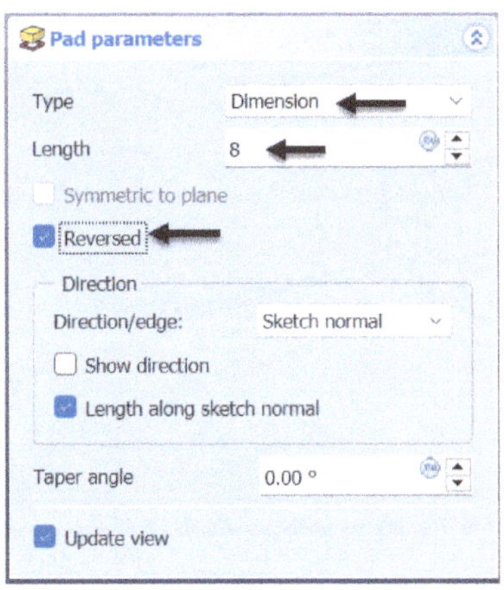

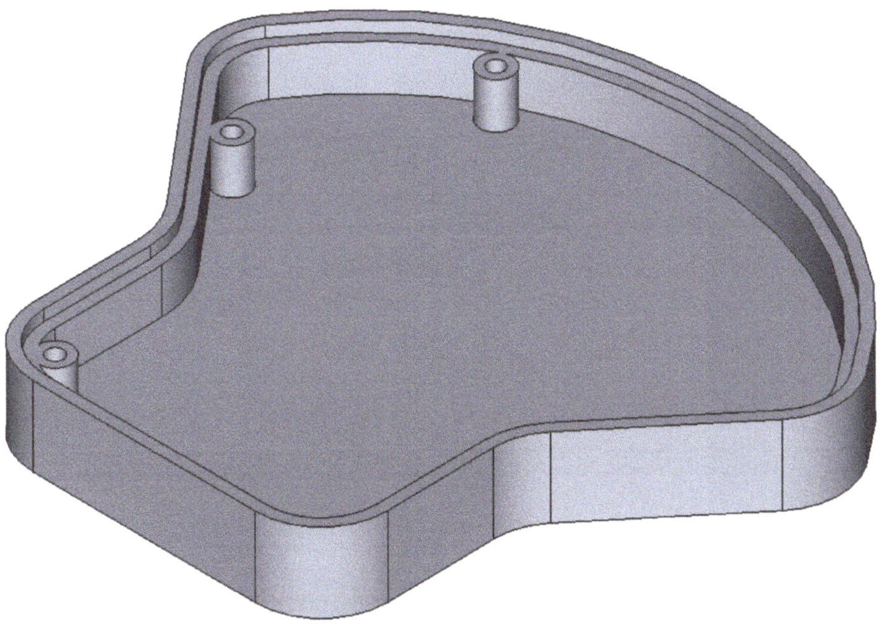

14. Click the **Model** panel and click the Pad001 feature.

15. On the toolbar, click the **Mirror**  command.
16. Select **Base YZ plane** from the **Plane** drop-down, and click **OK**.

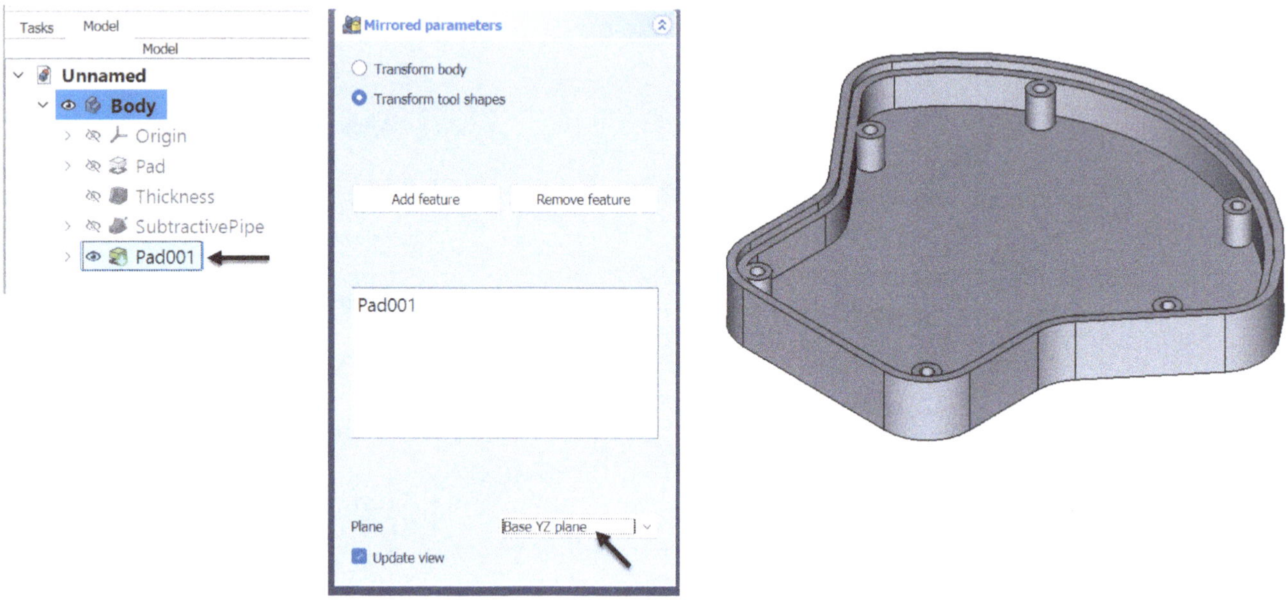

17. Click **View > Draw Style > Wireframe** on the Menu bar.
18. Zoom-in to anyone of the pad features. Next, press and hold the Ctrl key and select the edges where the pad feature meets the wall of the geometry.
19. Click the **Create fillet** icon on the **Part Design Modeling** toolbar. Next, type 1 in the **Radius** box and click **OK**.

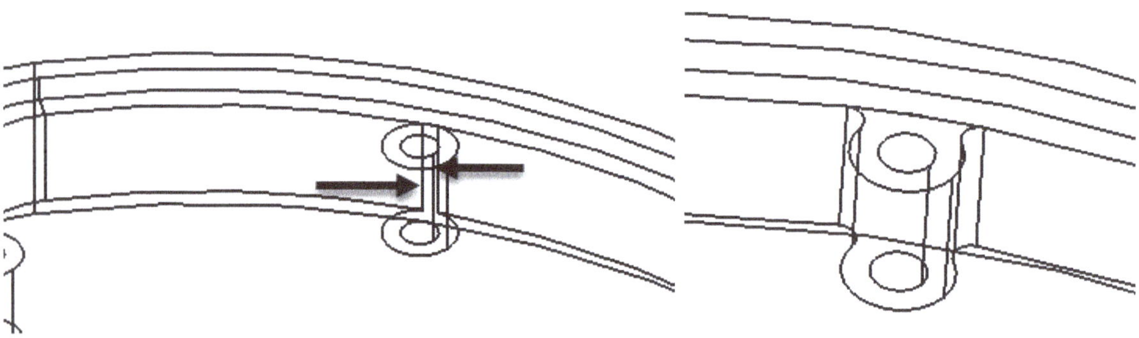

20. Likewise, create fillets for the remaining pad features.
21. Click **View > Draw style > Flat lines** on the menu bar.

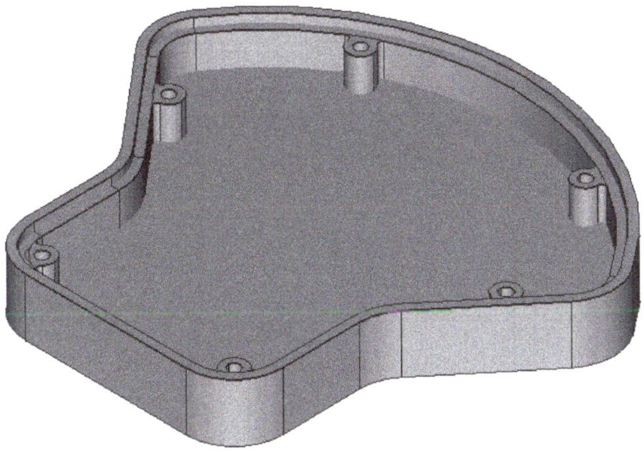

Creating Ribs

1. Select the bottom face of the shell feature and click **Create sketch** on the **Part Design Helper** toolbar.
2. Click the **Create external geometry** icon on the **Sketcher tools** toolbar. Next, select the edges of the model, as shown,
3. Click the **Create circle by center** command on the **Sketcher geometries** toolbar and create two circles, as shown.

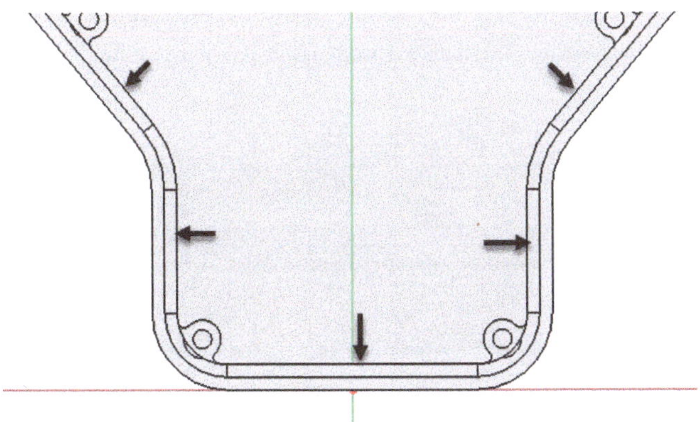

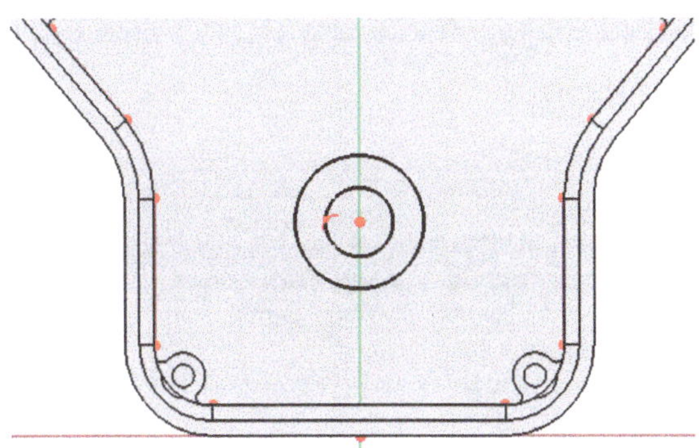

4. Add dimensional constraints to the sketch, as shown.

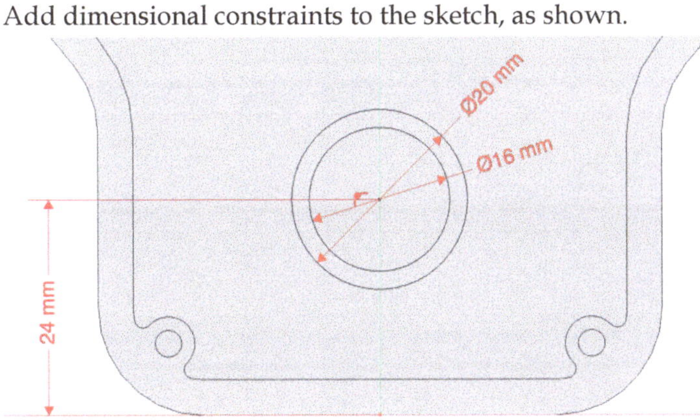

5. Click the **Create rectangle** command on the **Sketcher geometries** toolbar and create two rectangles, as shown.

6. On the **Sketcher constraints** toolbar, click **Constrain point onto object**. Next, constrain the corners of the rectangles onto the projected edges, as shown.

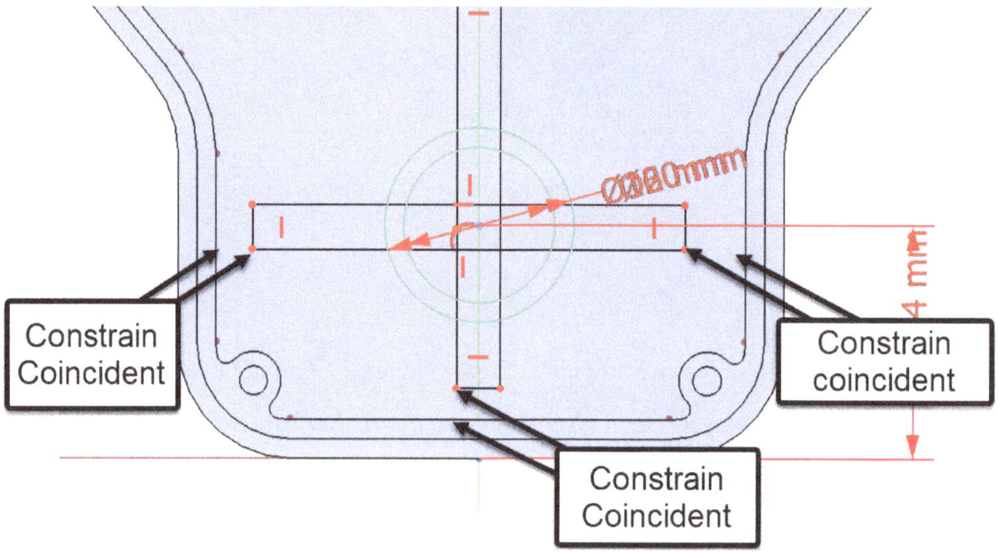

7. Click the **Trim edge** command on the **Sketcher geometries** toolbar and trim the portions of the sketch, as shown.

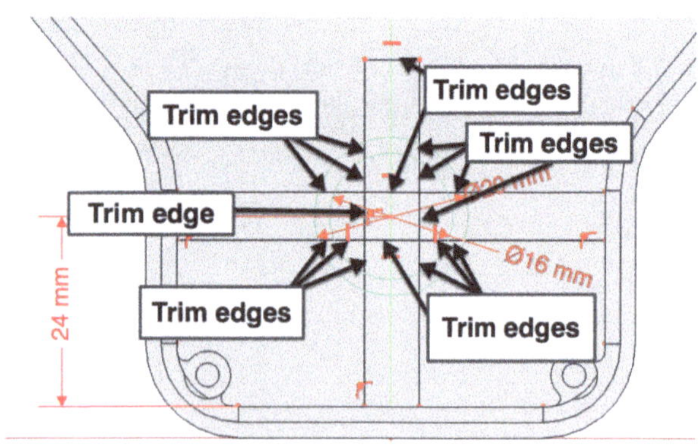

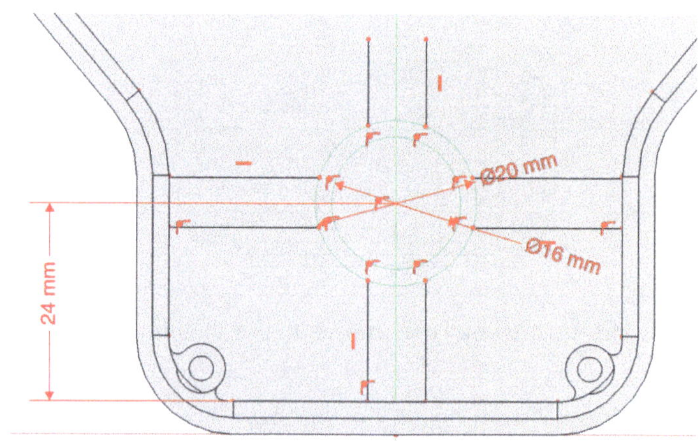

8. Use the **Trim edge** command and trim the portions of the circles, as shown.

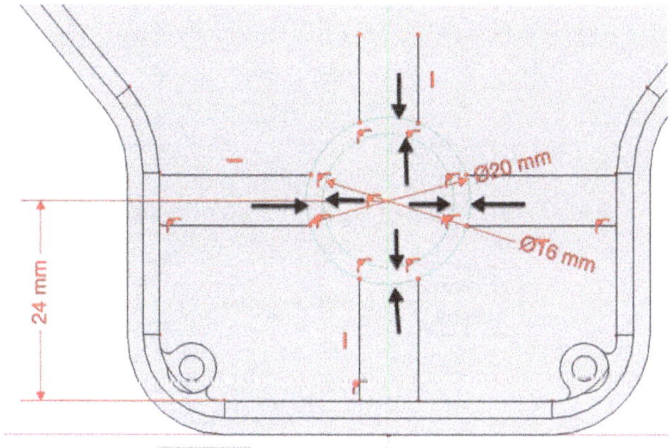

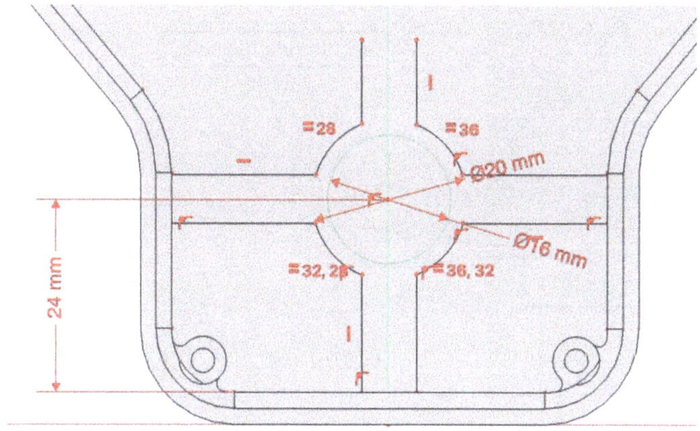

9. Click the **Create polyline** command on the **Sketcher geometries** toolbar and create the lines, as shown.

10. On the **Sketcher constraints** toolbar, click **Constrain Coincident** . Next, constrain the endpoints of the line onto the projected edges, as shown.

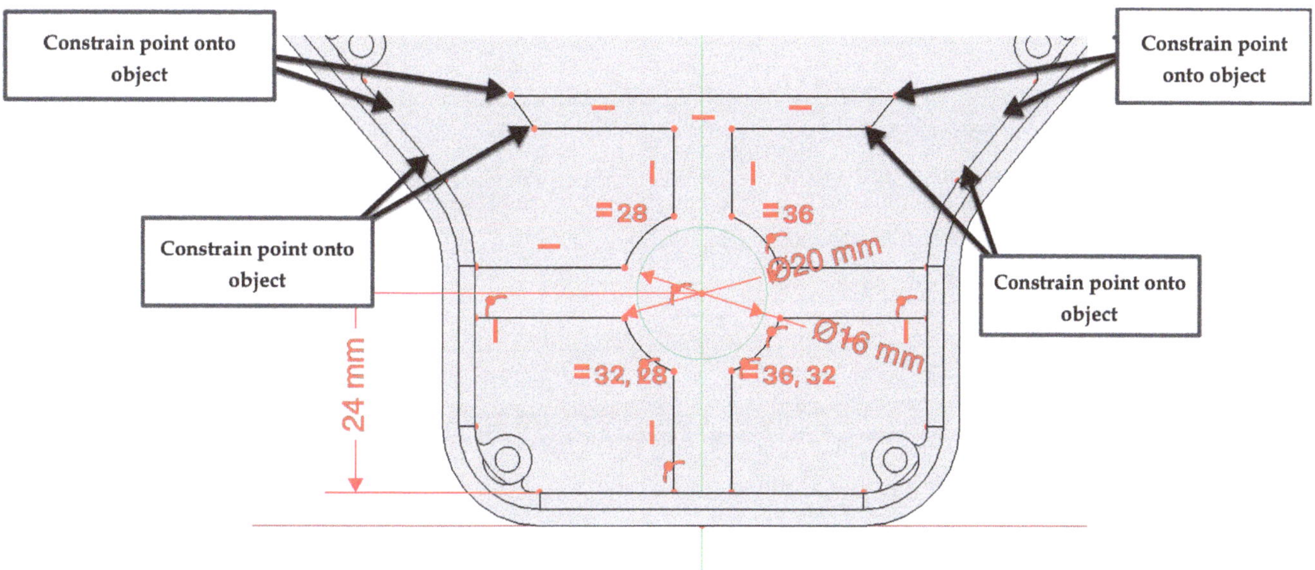

11. Apply the horizontal and vertical constraints between the endpoints of the lines, as shown.

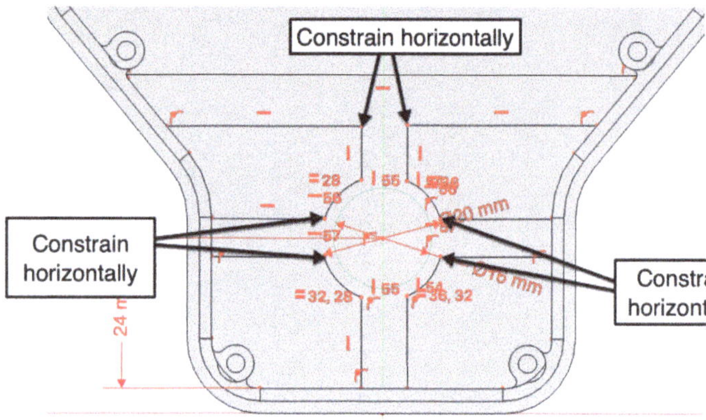

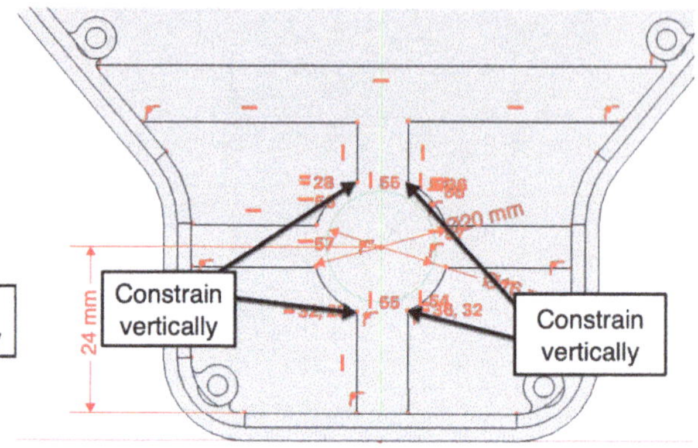

12. Create vertical distance and horizontal distance constraints, as shown.

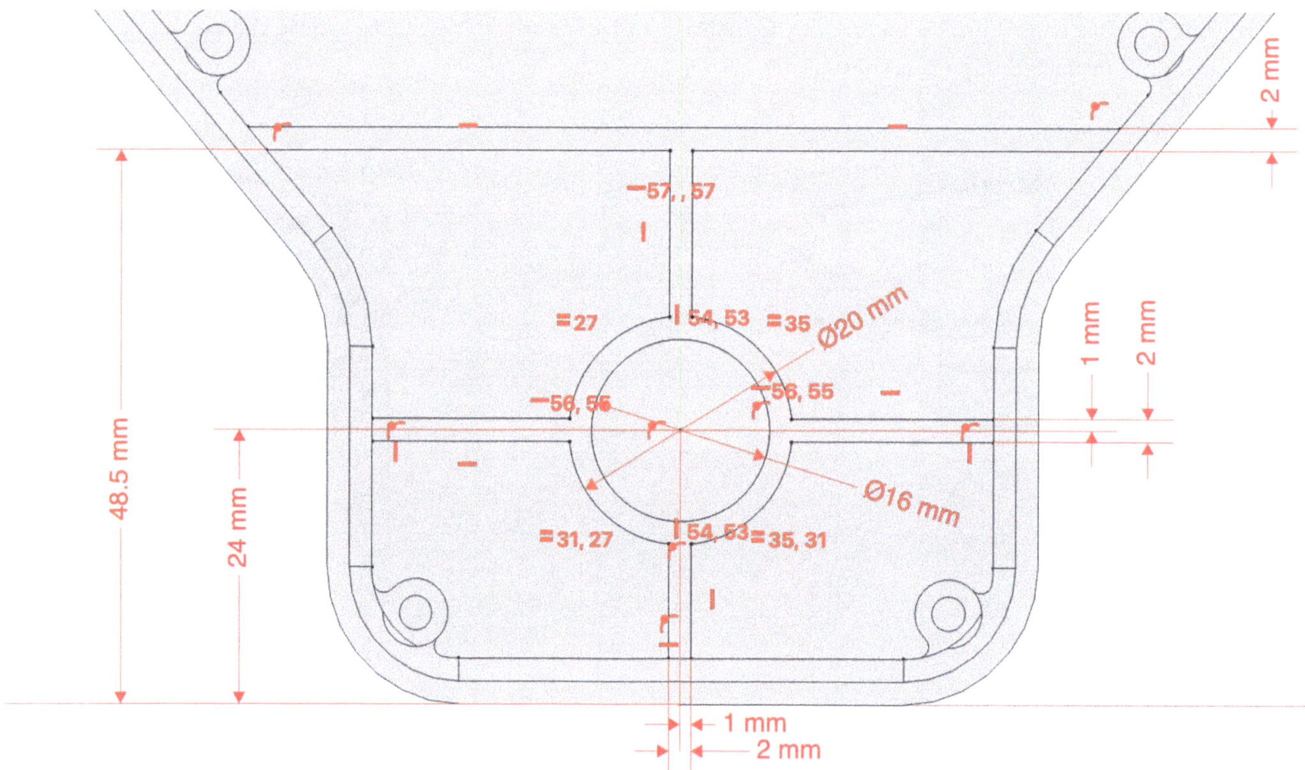

13. Click the **Close** button on the **Tasks** panel.
14. Click the **Pad**  icon on the **Part Design Modeling** toolbar. Next, select **Type > Up to face** from the **Pad parameters** section.
15. Select the horizontal face of the Subtractive pipe feature. Next, click **OK**.

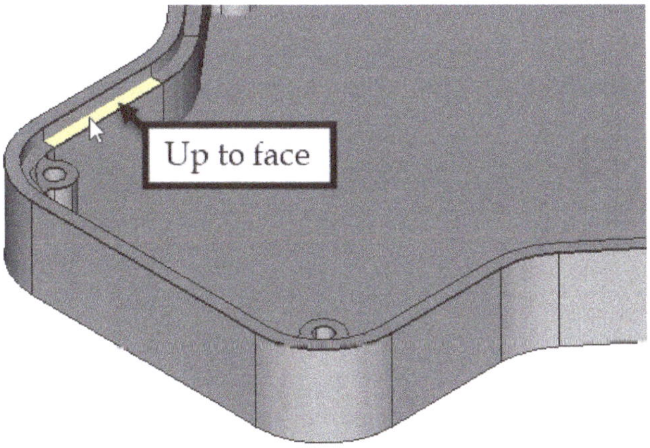

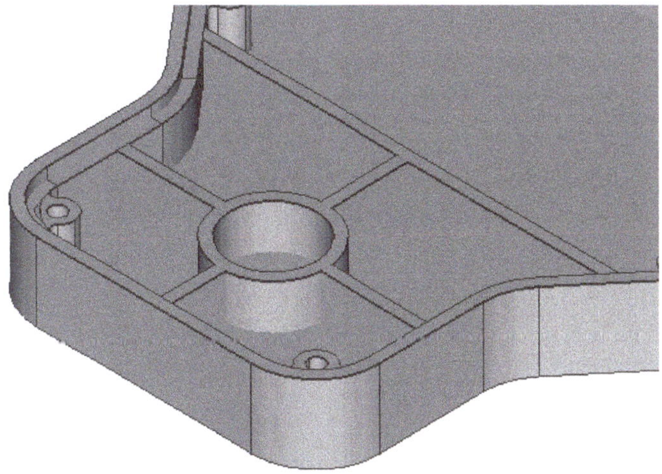

16. Click **File > Save** on the menu bar. Next, type **C5_example2** in the **File name** box, and click **Save**.
17. Click **File > Close** on the menu bar.

Tutorial 3 (Millimeters)

In this example, you create the part shown next.

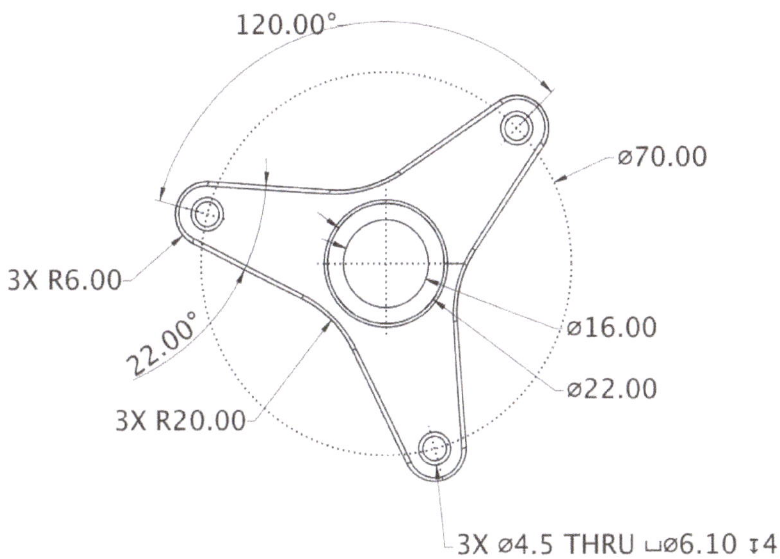

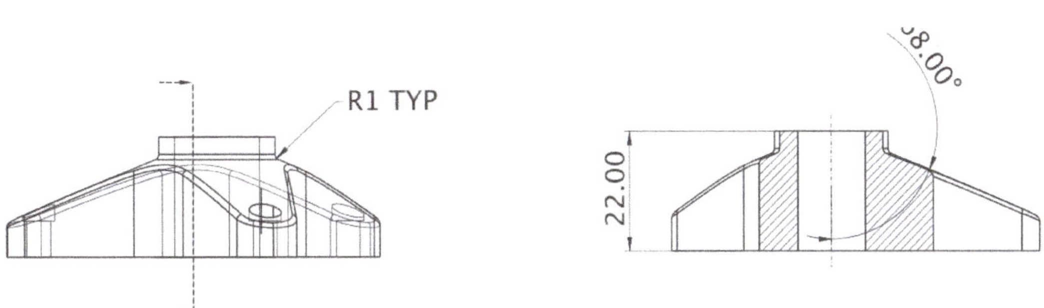

Creating a New document

1. Click **FreeCAD 1.0** on the desktop to start the application.

2. On the menu bar, click **File > New**; it creates a new document.
3. On the **Workbench** toolbar, select **Workbench** drop-down **> Part Design**.
4. Click **Edit > Preferences** on the **Menu** bar (or) click **FreeCAD 1.0 > Preferences** on title bar, if you are working on MacOS; the **Preferences** dialog appears on the screen.
9. Click the **General** tab and select **Default unit system > Standard (mm/kg/s/degree)**.
10. Select **Number of decimals > 2** and click **OK** on the **Preferences** dialog.

Creating the Pad feature

1. Click the **Create Sketch**  icon on the **Part Design Helper** Toolbar and select the XY_plane. Next, click **OK**.
2. On the **Tasks** panel, click the down-arrow on the **Constraints** section and check the **Auto remove redundants** option.
3. On the **Sketcher geometries** toolbar, click the **Create polyline**  icon. Next, specify the start point of the line.
4. Move the pointer horizontally toward right and click. Move the pointer downward and click.

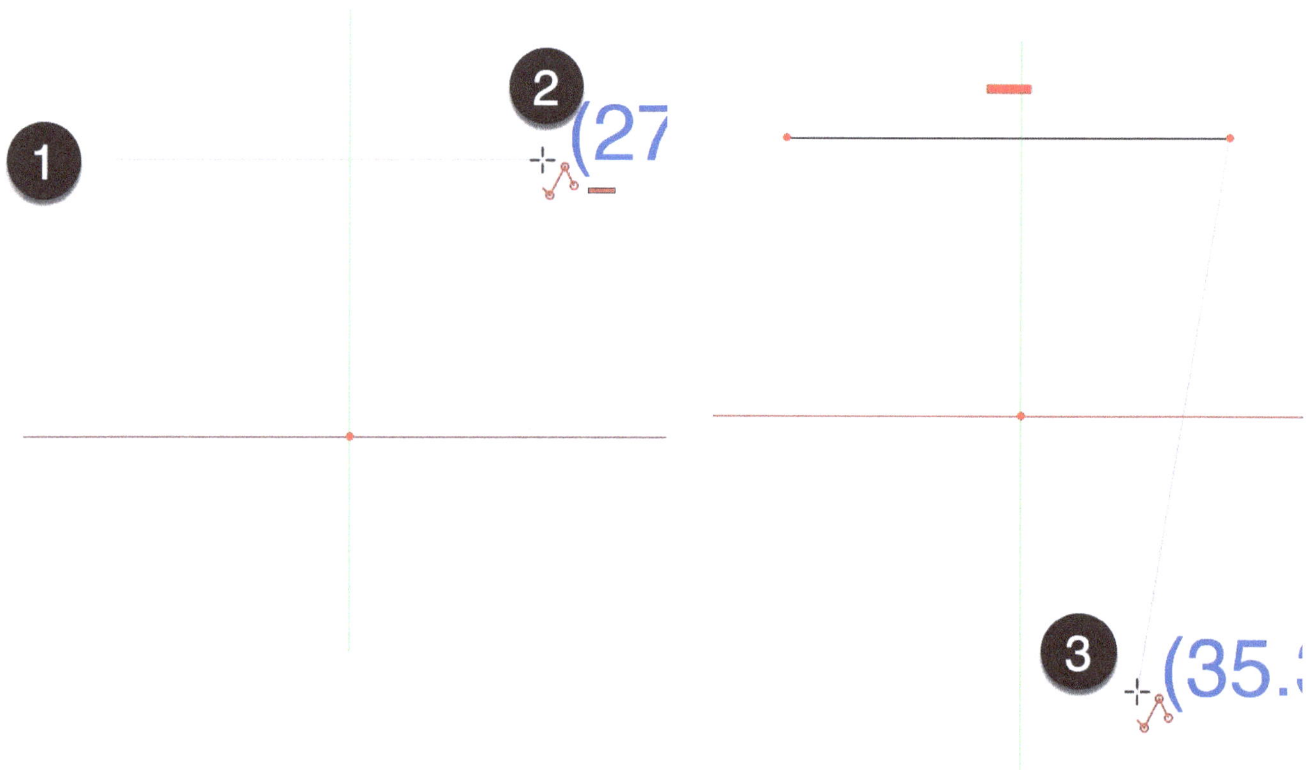

5. Press the **M** key thrice to change to the Arc mode. Next, move the pointer toward left and click to create an arc tangent to the previous line.
6. Press the **M** key twice to change to the Line mode. Move the pointer upward and select the start point of the first line.

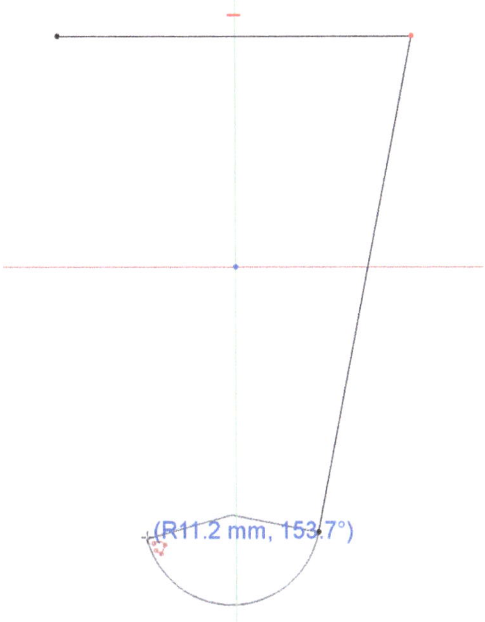

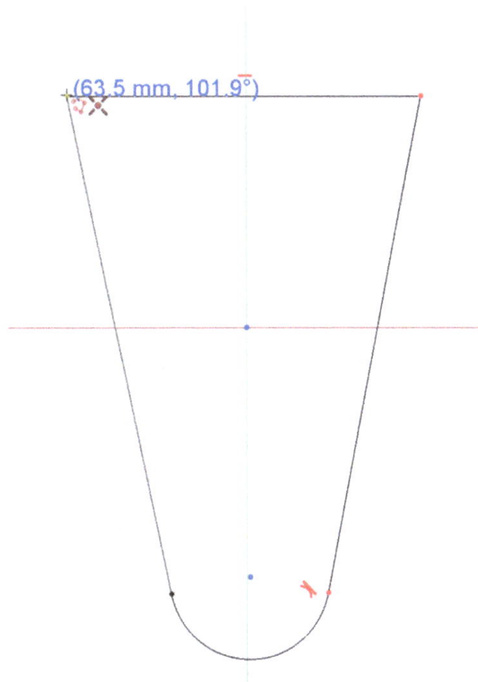

7. Click the **Constrain Symmetrically** icon on the **Sketcher Constraints** toolbar and select the horizontal line.
8. Select the sketch origin to make the endpoints of the horizontal line symmetrical about the sketch origin.
9. Click the **Constrain Tangent** icon on the **Sketcher Constraints** toolbar and select the arc and left inclined line.

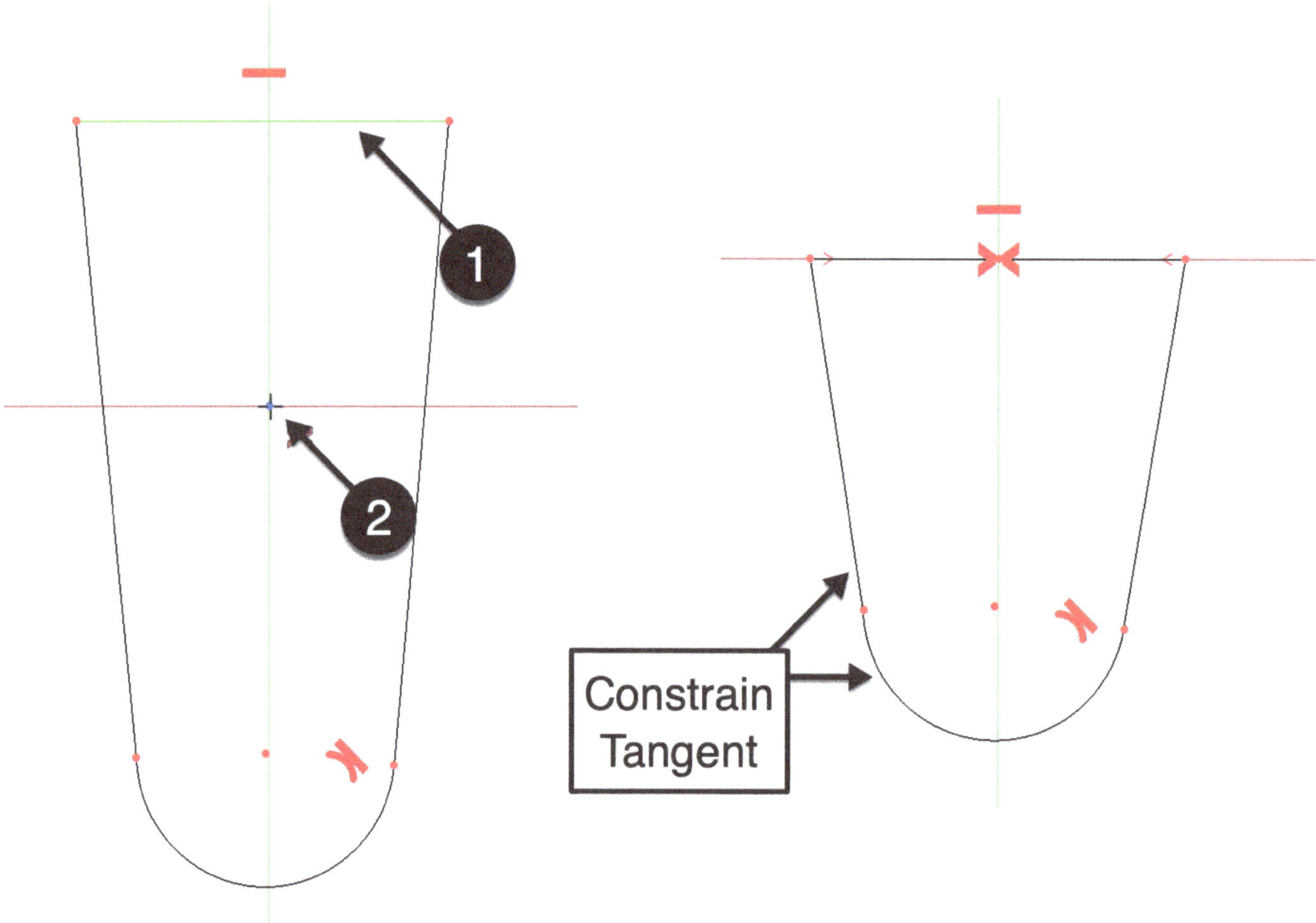

10. Click the **Dimension** drop-down > **Constrain arc or circle** icon on the **Sketcher Constraints** toolbar and select the arc.
11. Type **6** in the **Radius** box and click **OK.**
12. Click the **Constrain Angle** icon on the **Sketcher Constraints** toolbar and select the inclined lines of the sketch.
13. Type **22** in the **Angle** box and click **OK**.
14. Click the **Dimension** drop-down **> Constrain vertical distance** icon on the **Sketcher Constraints** toolbar. Next, select the sketch origin and the center point of the arc.
15. Type 35 in the **Length** box and click **OK**.
16. Click the **Constrain coincident** icon on the **Sketcher Constraints** toolbar and select the center point of the arc and the vertical sketch axis.

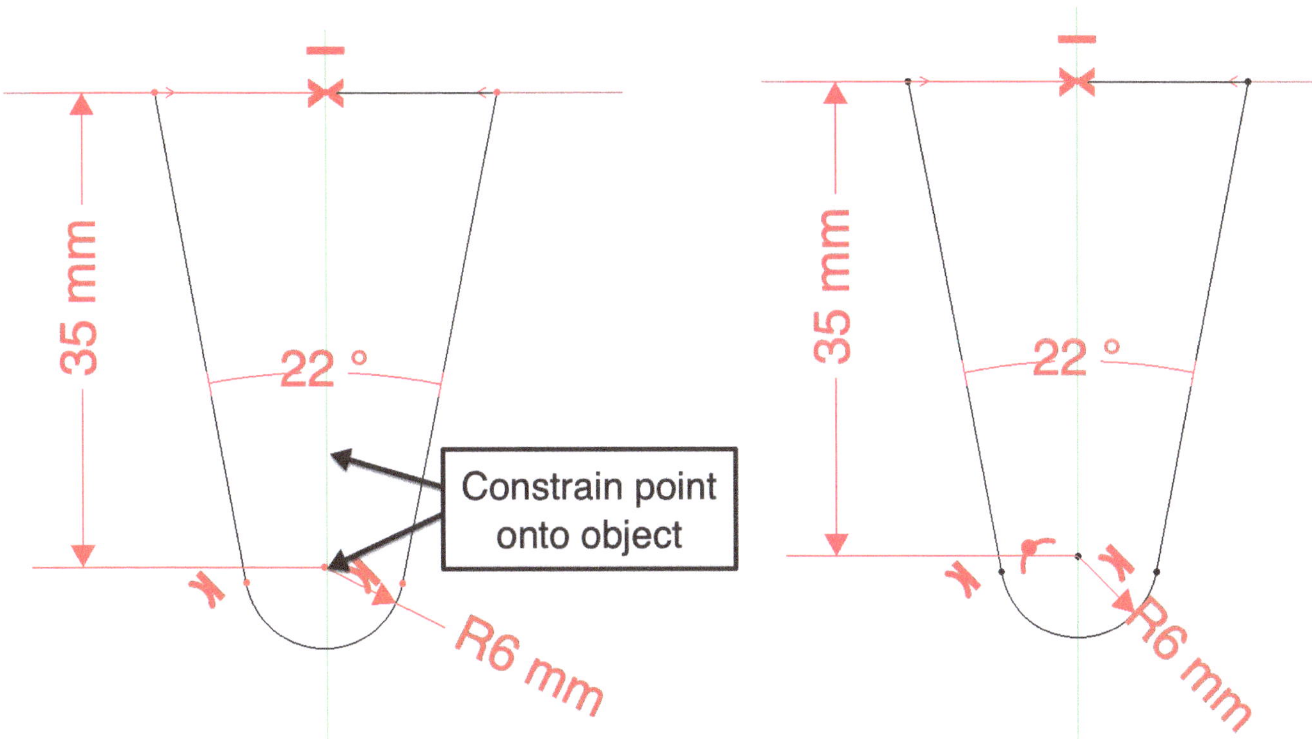

17. Click the **Close** button on the **Tasks** panel.
18. On the **Part Design Modeling** toolbar, click the **Pad** command.
19. On the **Pad parameters** section, select **Type > Dimension** and enter **22** in the **Length** box. Next, click **OK** to create the *Pad* feature.

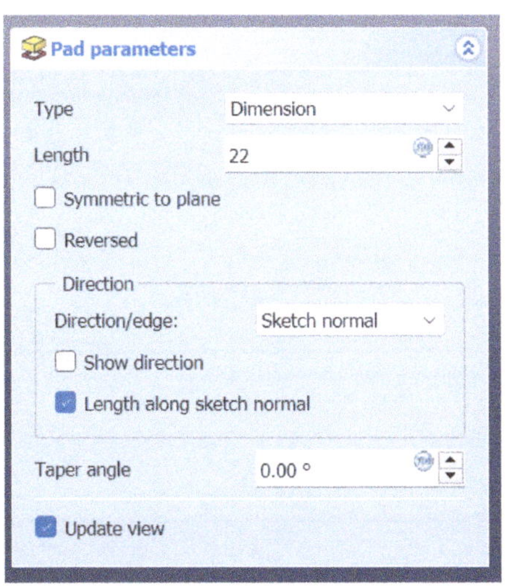

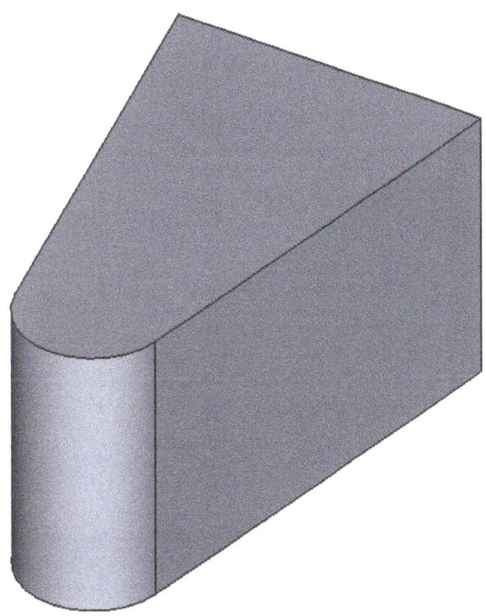

Creating the Counterbore Hole

1. Select the horizontal face of the *Pad* feature and click the **Hole**  tool on the **Part Design Modeling** toolbar.
2. Select **Profile > ISO metric regular profile**. Next, select **Size > M4**.
3. Select **Depth > Through All**.
4. On the **Hole Parameters** section, select **Hole Cut Type > Counterbore**.
5. Type-in **6.10** and **17** in the **Diameter** and **Depth** boxes, respectively.
6. Click **OK** on the **Combo View** panel; the counterbore hole is created.

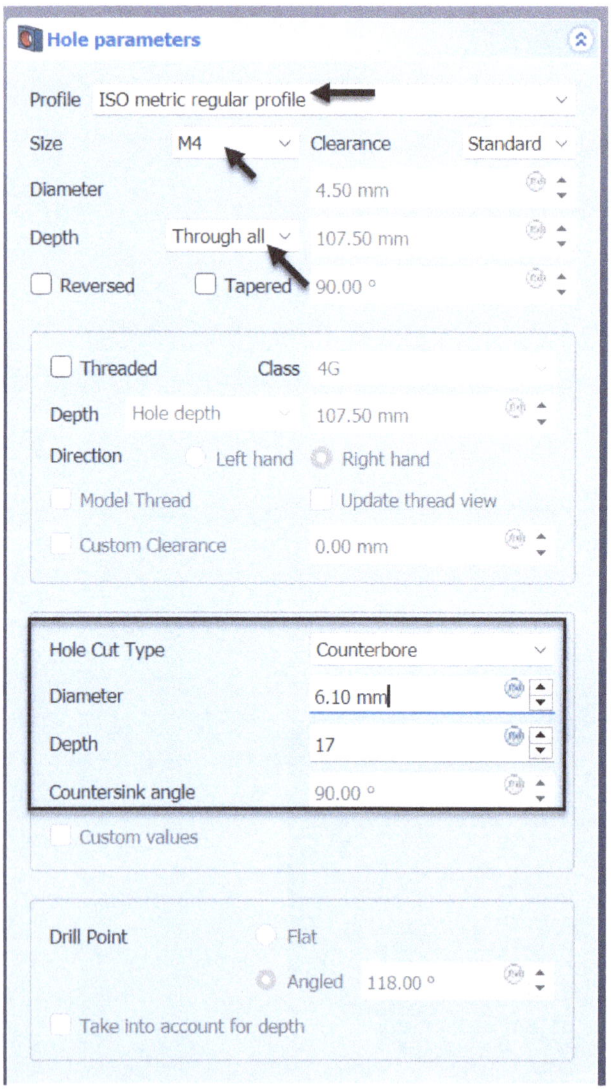

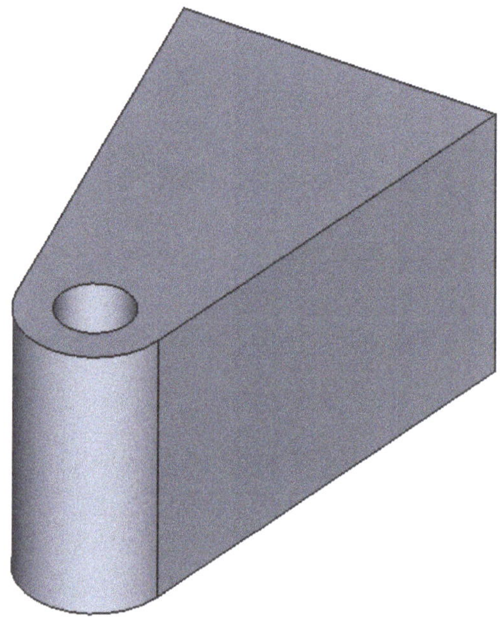

Creating the Polar Pattern

1. Click the **Create a polar pattern feature**  command on the **Part Design Modeling** toolbar.
2. Under the **PolarPattern parameters** section, select the **Transform body** option
3. Under the **PolarPattern parameters** section and select **Axis > Base Z axis**.
4. Type-in **360** and **3** in the **Angle** and **Occurrences** boxes, respectively.
5. Click **OK** to create the pattern.

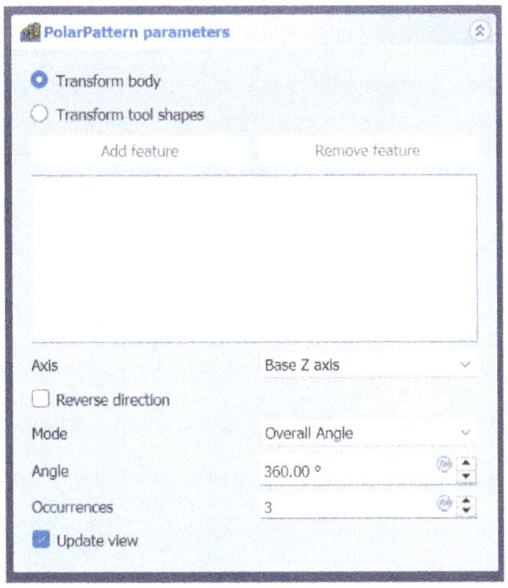

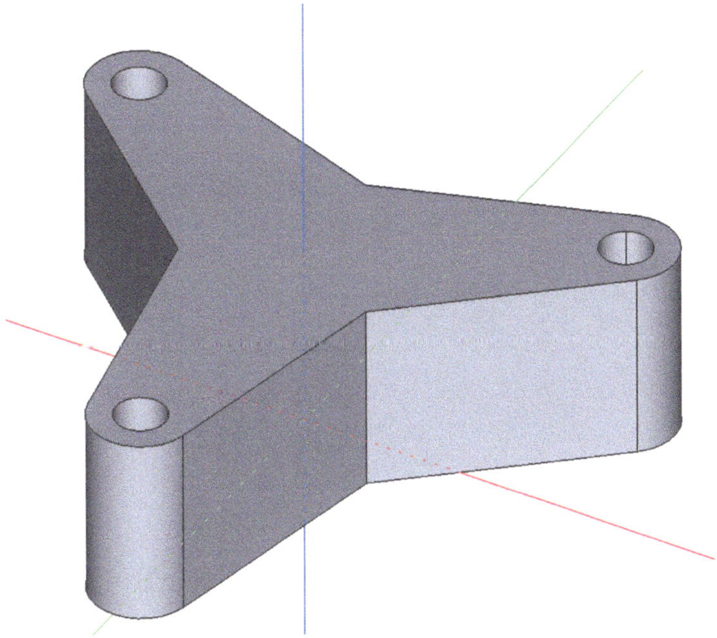

Creating a New Body

1. Click the **Create Body** command on the **Part Design Helper** toolbar; a new body is created.
2. Click the **Create Sketch** icon on the **Part Design Helper** Toolbar and select the XZ_plane.
3. Click the **View Section** icon on the **Sketcher edit mode** toolbar.
4. On the **Sketcher geometries** toolbar, click the **Create Polyline** icon. Next, select the origin point of the sketch, move the pointer upward and click on the vertical axis of the sketch.
5. Next, specify the other points of the sketch, as shown. Next, apply constraints and dimensions to the sketch and click **Close**.

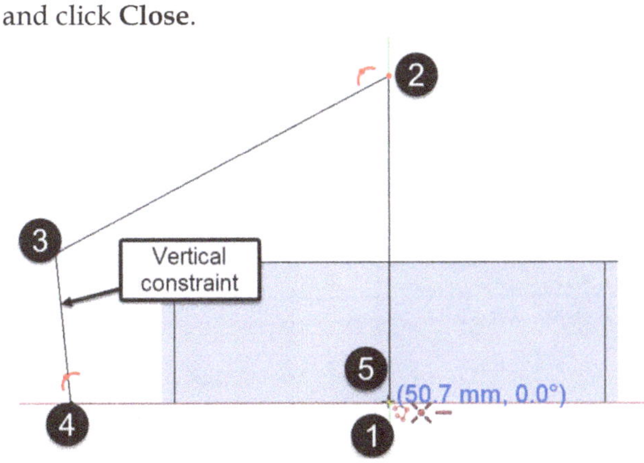

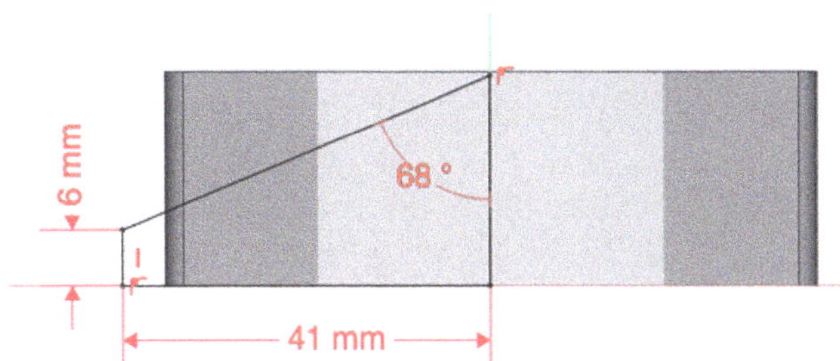

6. Click the **Revolution** icon on the **Part Design** toolbar (or) click **Part Design > Create an additive feature > Revolution**; the sketch profile is selected automatically.
7. Select **Axis > Vertical sketch axis** and type **360** in the **Angle** box. Next, click **OK**.

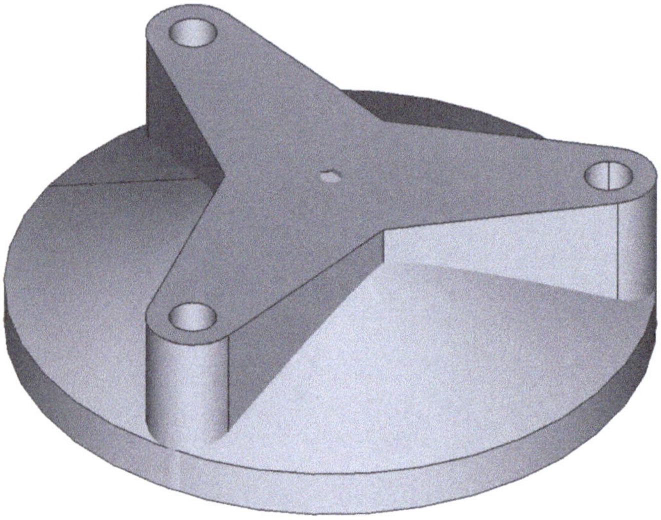

Creating a Common Body Between the Two Bodies

1. Click the **Boolean** command on the **Part Design Modeling** toolbar; the second body is selected automatically.
2. Click the **Add Body** button on the **Combo View** panel and select the first body.
3. Select the **Common** option from the drop-down available on the **Tasks** panel and click **OK**; a common body is created between the two selected bodies.

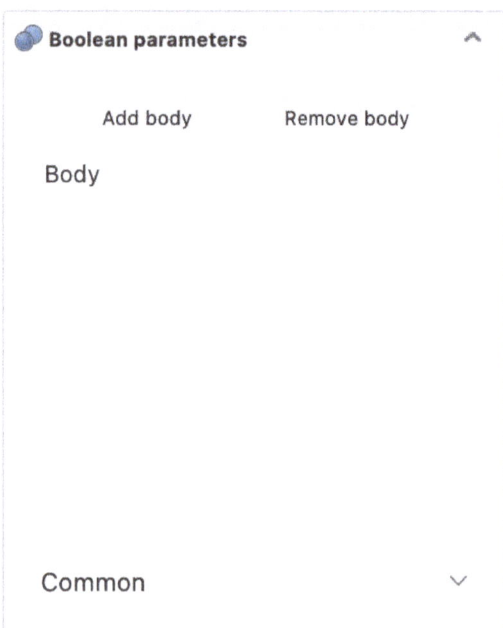

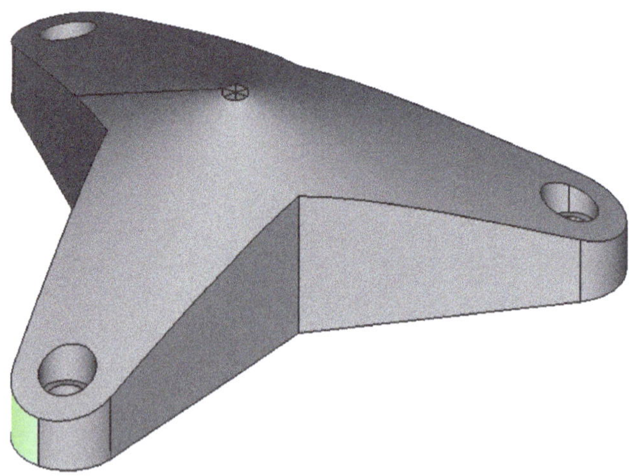

Creating Cylindrical Feature and Hole at the center

1. Click the **Create Sketch** icon on the **Part Design Helper** Toolbar and select the XY_plane. Next, click **OK**.
2. Click the **View Section** icon on the **Sketch edit mode** toolbar.

3. On the **Sketcher geometries** toolbar, click the **Create circle by center** icon. Next, select the origin point of the sketch, move the pointer outward and click.
4. Click the **Dimension** drop-down > **Constrain arc or circle** icon on the **Sketcher Constraints** toolbar and select the arc.
5. Type **22** in the **Diameter** box and click **OK.** Next, click **Close** on the **Tasks** panel.
6. Activate the **Pad** tool on the **Part Design Modeling** toolbar.
7. On the **Pad parameters** section, type **22** in the **Length** box and click **OK** to create the *Pad* feature.

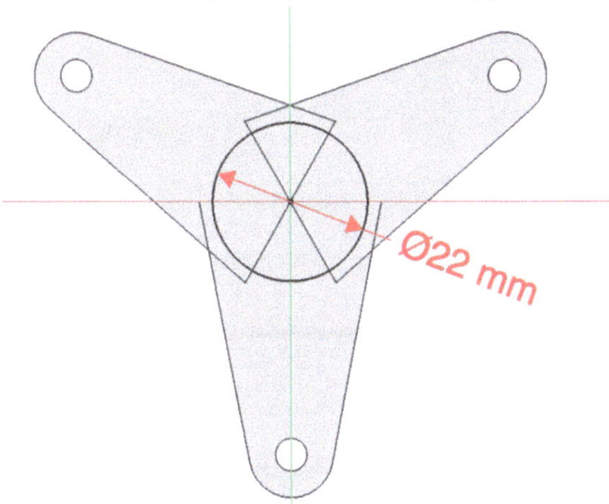

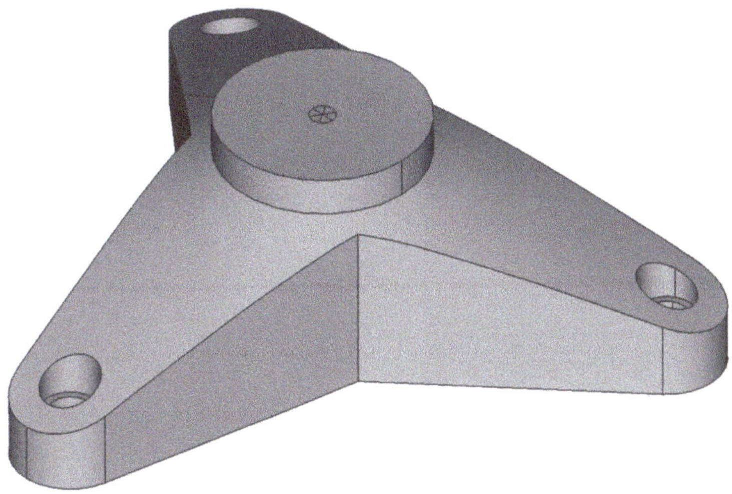

8. Click on the top face of the cylindrical feature and click the **Create Sketch** icon on the **Part Design Helper** Toolbar.
9. Create a circle by selecting the sketch origin as it center. Next, click **Close** on the **Tasks** panel.
10. Select the horizontal face of the *Pad* feature and click the **Hole** tool on the **Part Design Modeling** toolbar.
11. Select **Profile > None**. Next, type **16** in the **Diameter** box.
12. Select **Depth > Through All**. Next, click **OK** on the **Combo View** panel; the hole is created.

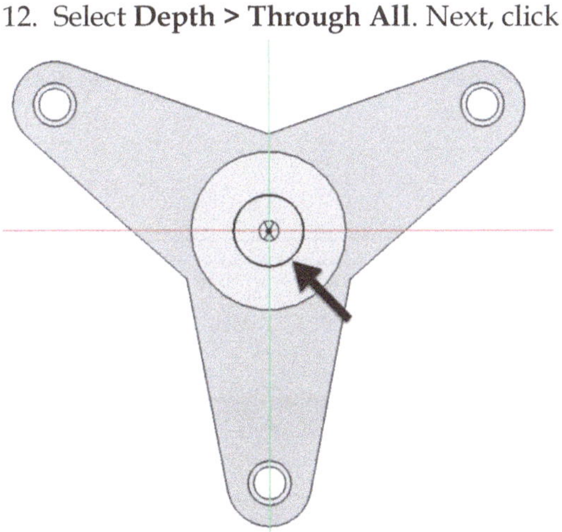

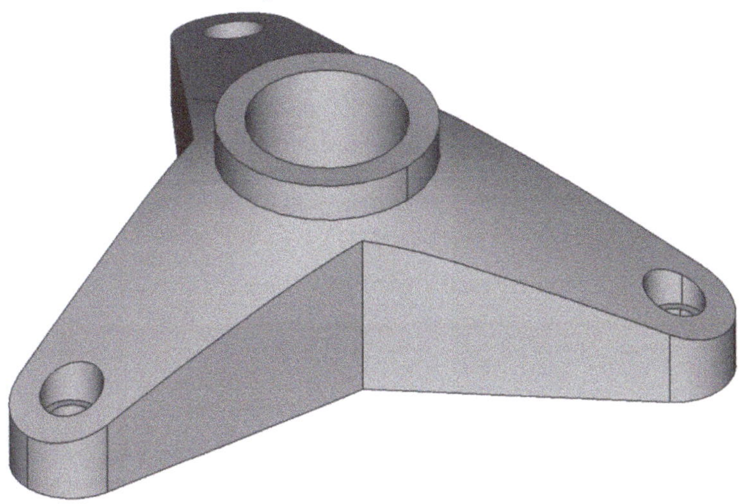

Creating Fillets

1. Click **View > Draw Style > Wireframe** on the Menu bar.
2. Press and hold the Ctrl key and select the edges, as shown.
3. Click the **Create fillet** icon on the **Part Design Modeling** toolbar. Next, type 20 in the **Radius** box and click **OK**.
4. On the **View** toolbar, click **Draw Style > Normal Mode**.

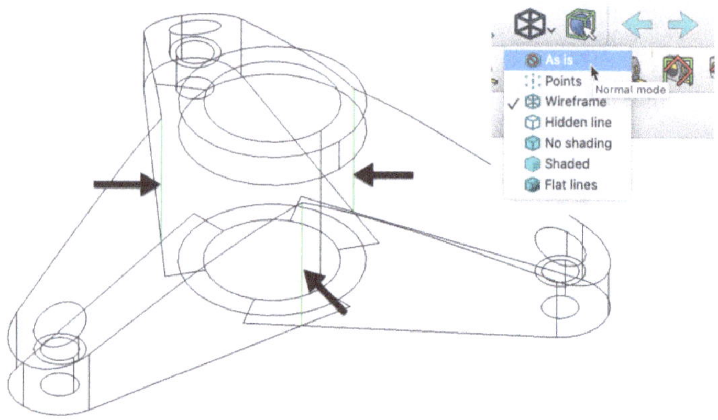

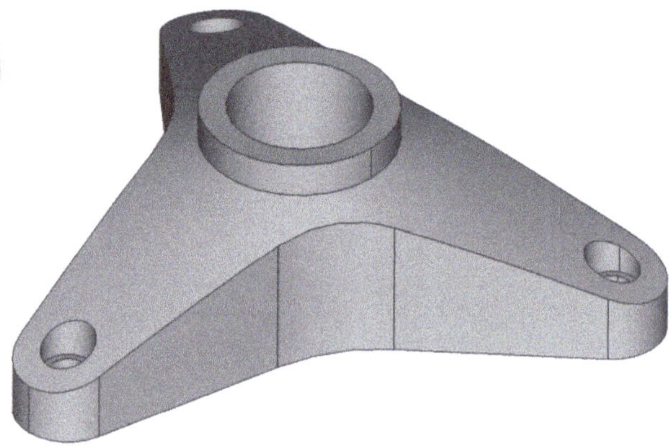

5. Press and hold the CTRL key and select the edges of the model, as shown.
6. Click the **Create fillet** icon on the **Part Design Modeling** toolbar. Next, type 1 in the **Radius** box and click **OK**.

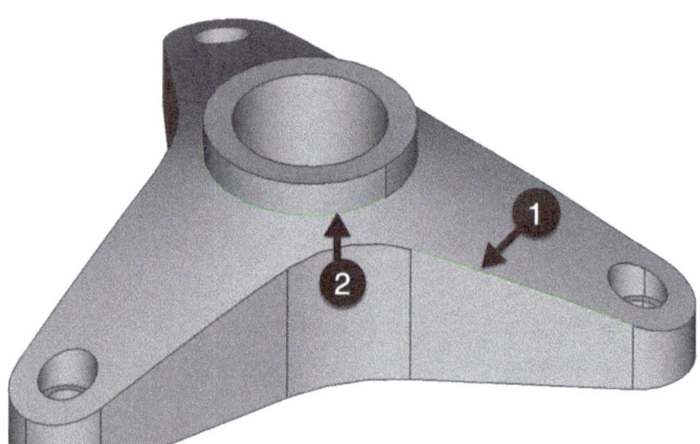

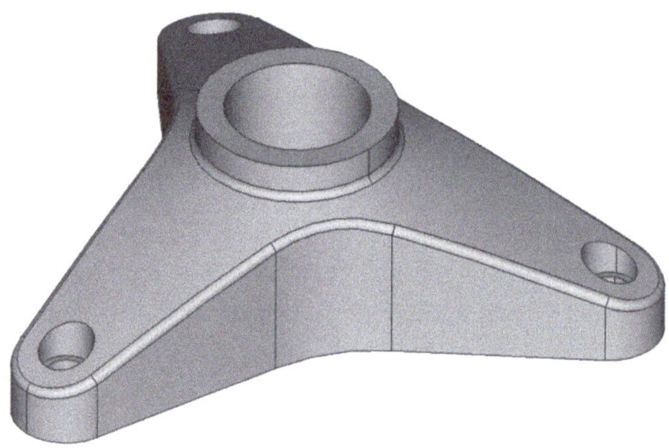

7. Save and close the design file.

Tutorial 4 (Millimeters)

In this example, you create the part shown next.

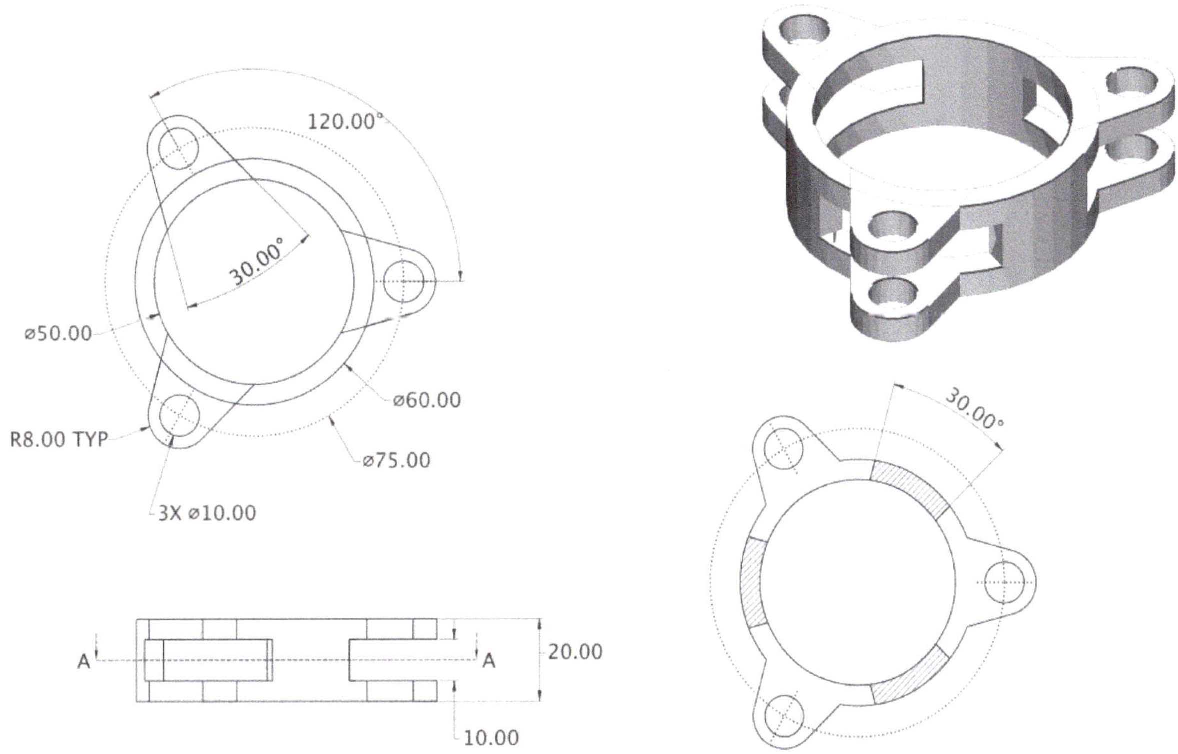

Creating a New document

1. Click **FreeCAD 1.0** on the desktop to start the application.
2. On the menu bar, click **File > New**; it creates a new document.
3. On the **Workbench** toolbar, select **Workbench** drop-down **> Part Design**.
4. Click **Edit > Preferences** on the **Menu** bar (or) click **FreeCAD 1.0 > Preferences** on title bar, if you are working on MacOS; the **Preferences** dialog appears on the screen.
5. Click the **General** tab and select **Default unit system > Standard (mm/kg/s/degree)**.
6. Select **Number of decimals > 2** and click **OK** on the **Preferences** dialog.

Creating the Pad feature

1. Click the **Create Sketch** icon on the **Part Design Helper** Toolbar and select the XY-plane.
2. Create a circle of **60** mm diameter.
3. Click the **Close** button on the **Tasks** panel.
4. On the **Part Design Modeling** toolbar, click the **Pad** command.
5. On the **Pad parameters** section, select **Type > Dimension** and enter **20** in the **Length** box. Next, check the **Symmetric to plane** option and click **OK** to create the *Pad* feature.

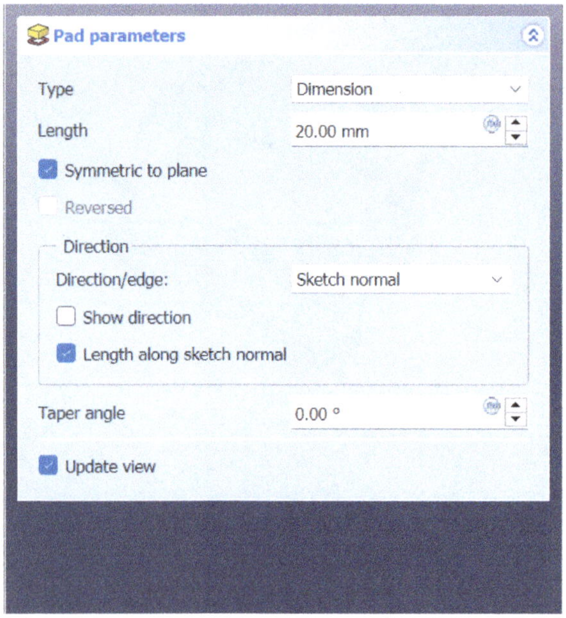

Adding the Pad feature

1. Click the **Create Sketch** icon on the **Part Design Helper** Toolbar and select the XY_plane.
2. Click **Sketch > View section** on the menu bar.
3. On the **Sketcher geometries** toolbar, click the **Polygon** drop-down > **Triangle**. Next, click on the horizontal axis of the sketch, move the pointer toward left. Again, click on the horizontal axis of the sketch to create a triangle.
4. Delete the construction circle touching the vertices of the triangle.
5. Click the **Fillets** icon on the **Sketcher geometries** toolbar and select the two inclined lines of the triangle.

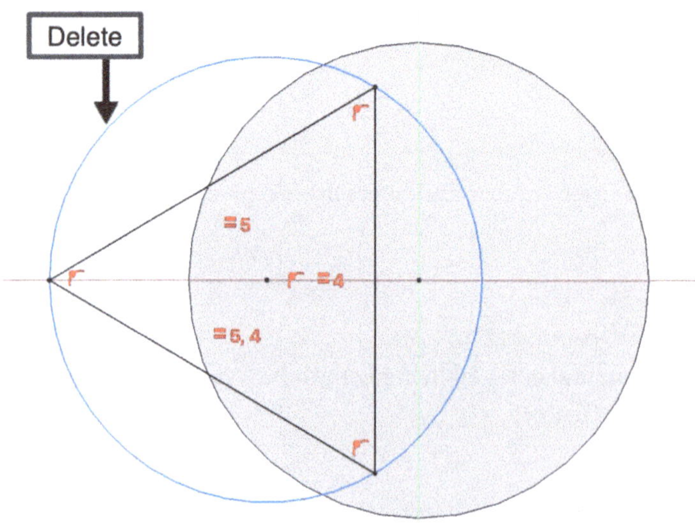

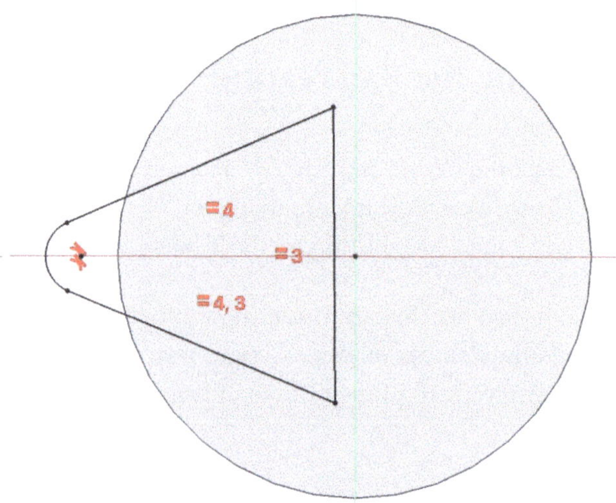

6. Apply the **Constrain Radius** to the fillet. Next, apply the **Constrain Angle** between the two inclined lines, as shown.
7. Apply the **Constrain Coincdinent** constraint between the center point of the fillet and the horizontal axis.
8. Apply the **Constrain Angle** between the horizontal axis and anyone of the inclined lines of the triangle.

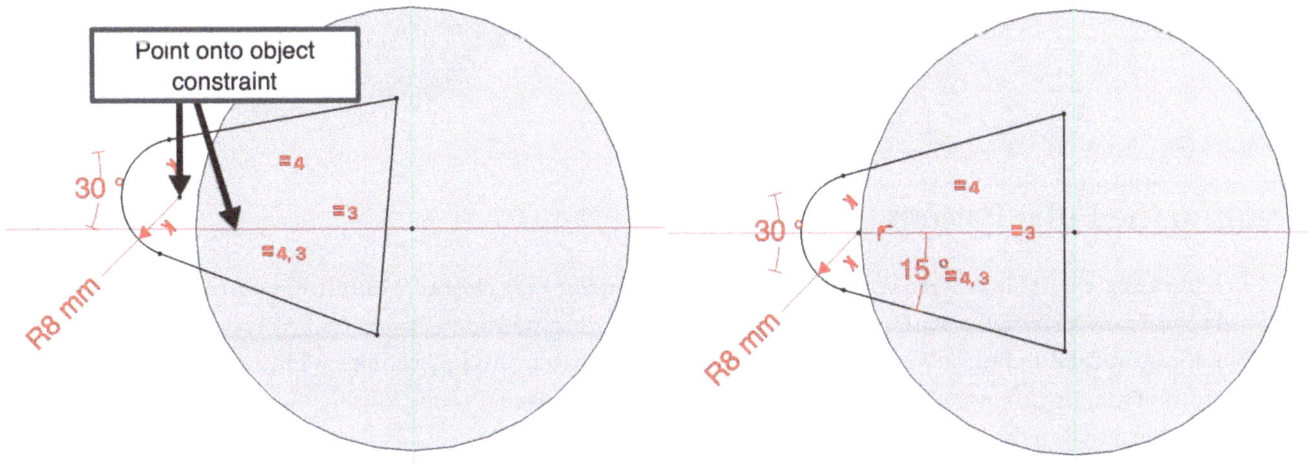

9. Add the **Horizontal distance** constraint between the center point of the arc and the sketch origin, as shown.
10. Create a circle concentric to the center point of the arc. Next, add the **Constrain diameter** to it.

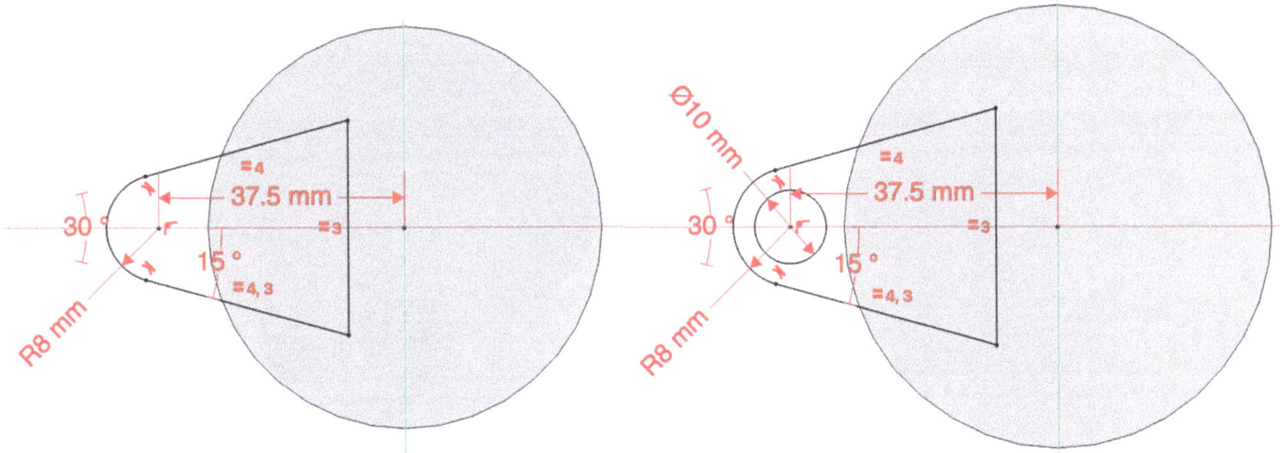

11. Apply the **Vertical constraint** to the right vertical line.
12. Click the **Close** button on the **Tasks** panel.
13. On the **Part Design Modeling** toolbar, click the **Pad** command.
14. On the **Pad parameters** section, select **Type > Dimension** and enter **20** in the **Length** box. Next, check the **Symmetric to plane** option and click **OK** to create the *Pad* feature.

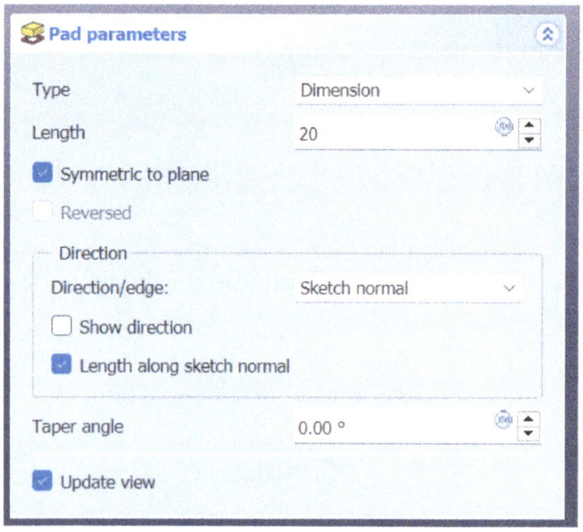

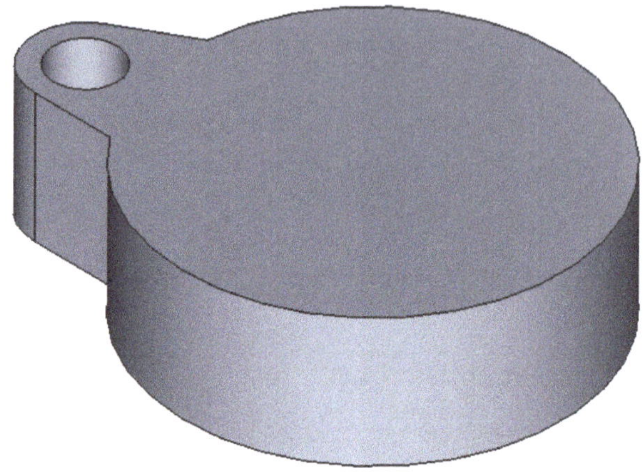

Creating the Polar Pattern

1. Click the **Create a polar pattern feature** command on the **Part Design Modeling** toolbar.
2. Select the **Transform tool shapes** option from the **PolarPattern parameters** section.
3. Click the **Add feature** button and select the second Pad feature from the graphics window.
4. Under the **PolarPattern parameters** section and select **Base Z axis**.
5. Type-in **360** and **3** in the **Angle** and **Occurrences** boxes, respectively.
6. Click **OK** to create the pattern.

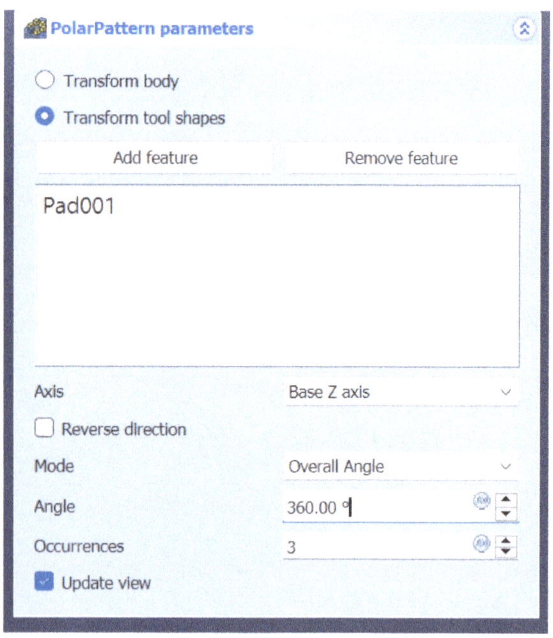

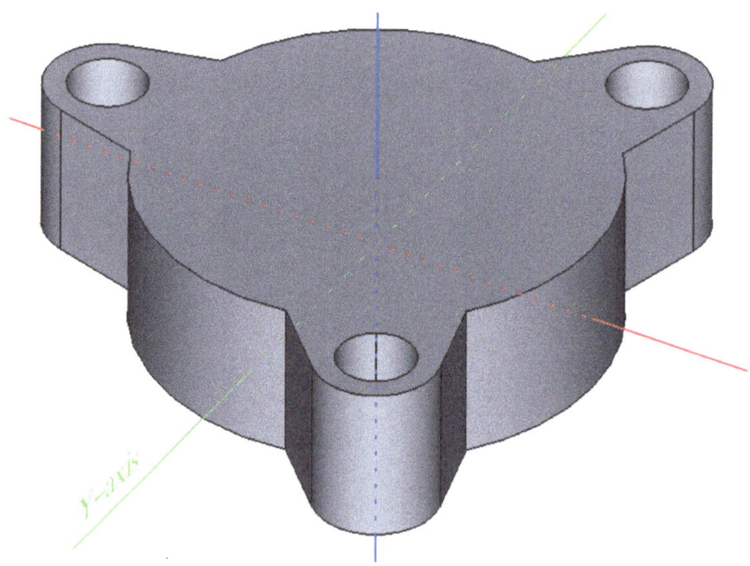

Creating the Pocket Features

1. Click on the top face of the model and click the **Create Sketch** command on the **Part Design Helper** toolbar.

2. On the **Sketcher geometries** toolbar, click the **Create circle by center** icon. Next, select the origin point of

the sketch, move the pointer outward and click.

3. Apply the **Constrain diameter** to the circle and click **Close** on the **Tasks** panel.
4. Click the **Pocket** icon on the **Part Design** toolbar; the sketch profile is selected automatically.
5. Select **Type > Through all** and click **OK**.

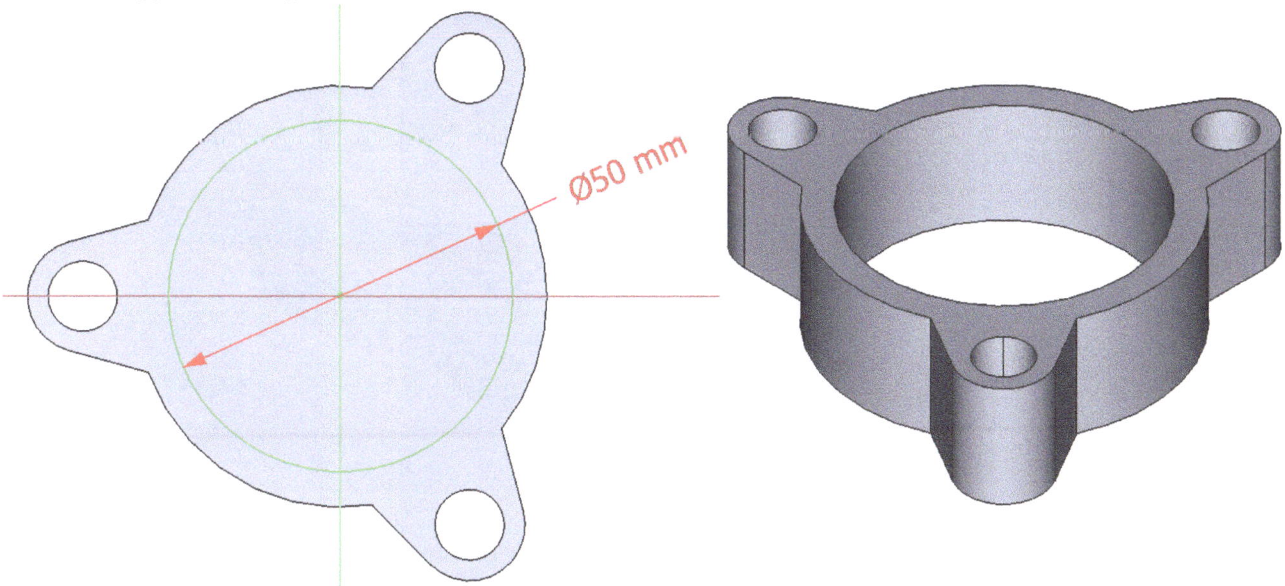

6. Click the **Create Sketch** command on the **Part Design Helper** toolbar. Next, select the XY-Plane from the graphics window.
7. On the **Sketcher geometries** toolbar, click the **Create Polyline** icon. Next, click on the horizontal axis of the sketch, move the pointer to top-left corner and click.
8. Move the pointer vertically downward and click to create a vertical line.
9. Move the pointer and select the start point of the sketch.
10. Apply the **Constrain Equal** between the two inclined lines. Next, apply the **Constrain angle** between the two inclined lines.
11. Apply the **Horizontal distance** constraint between the endpoint of the vertical line and the sketch origin.
12. Apply the **Horizontal distance** constraint between the start point of the sketch and the sketch origin.
13. Click **Close** on the **Tasks** panel.
14. Click the **Pocket** icon on the **Part Design** toolbar; the sketch profile is selected automatically.
15. On the **Pocket parameters** section, select **Type > Dimension** and enter **10** in the **Length** box. Next, check the **Symmetric to plane** option and click **OK** to create the *Pocket* feature.

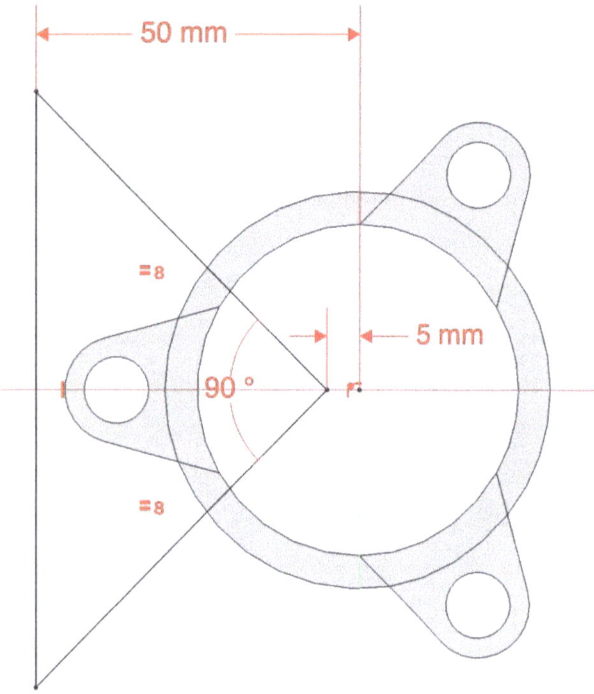

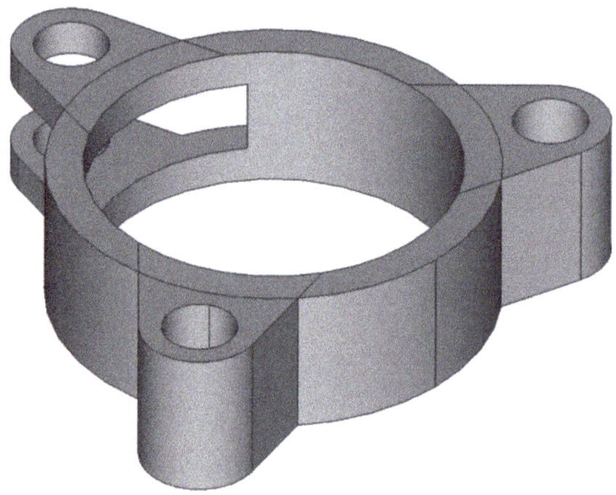

Creating a Polar Pattern

1. Click the **Create Polar Pattern**  icon on the **Part Design Modeling** toolbar.
2. Select the **Transform tool shapes** option from the **PolarPattern parameters** section.
3. Click the **Add feature** button and select the pocket feature from the graphics window.
4. Under the PolarPattern parameters section, select **Axis > Base Z axis**.
5. Type **360** and **3** in the **Angle** and **Occurrences** boxes, respectively.

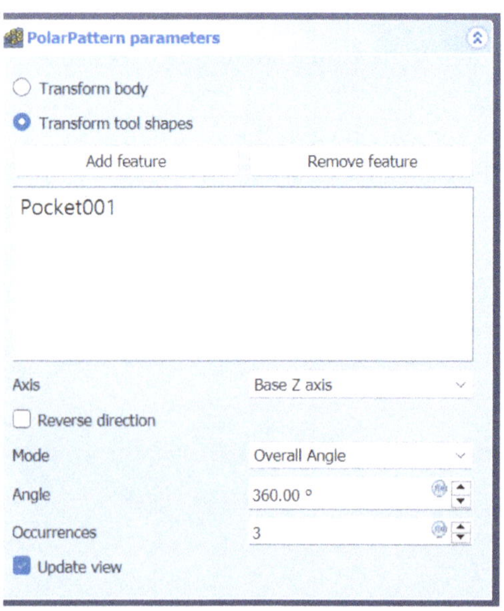

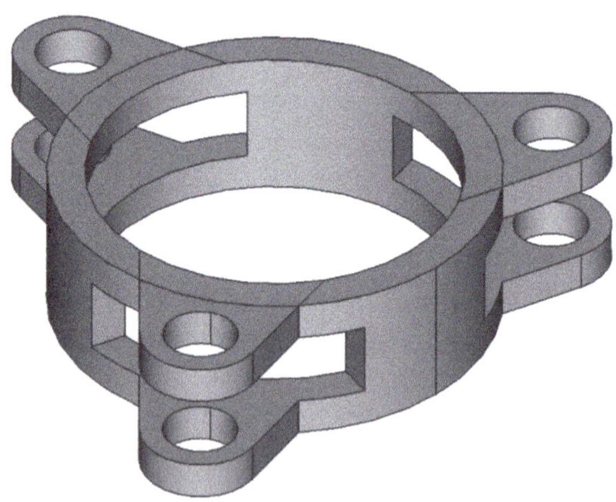

6. Click **OK**.

7. Save and close the design file.

Questions

1. Describe the procedure to create a mirror feature.
2. List any two pattern types.
3. Describe the procedure to create a multi transform feature.
4. How to define spacing in a linear pattern.

Exercises

Exercise 1

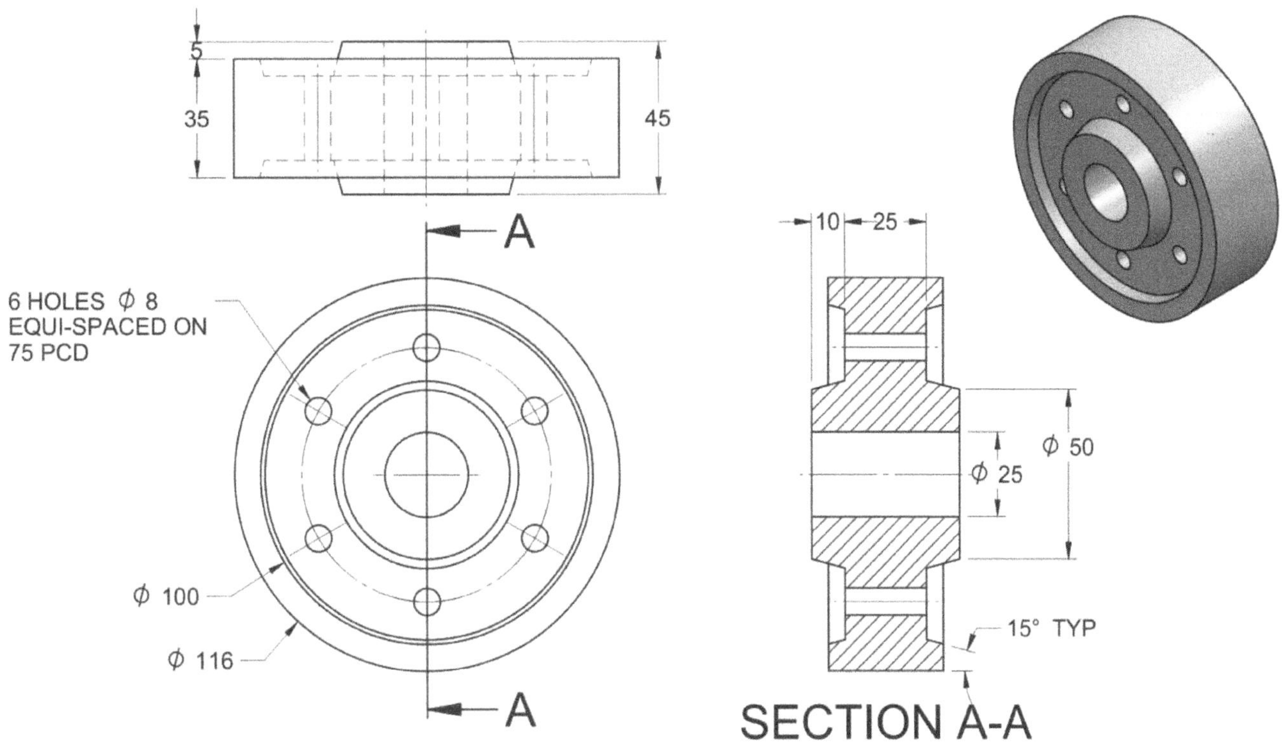

Chapter 6: Pipe Features

The **Additive Pipe** command is one of the basic commands available in FreeCAD 1.0 that allow you to generate solid geometry. It can be used to create simple geometry as well as complex shapes. An additive pipe is composed of two items: a profile and a path. The profile controls the shape of the pipe while the path controls its direction. For example, take a look at the angled cylinder shown in the figure. This is created using a simple pipe with the circle as the profile and an angled line as the path.

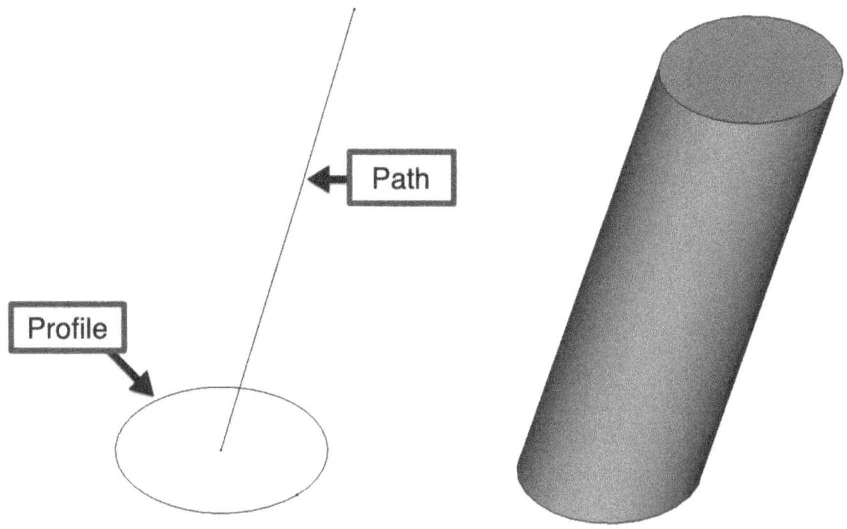

By making the path a bit more complex, you can see that a pipe allows you to create shapes you would not be able to create using commands such as **Pad** or **Revolution**.

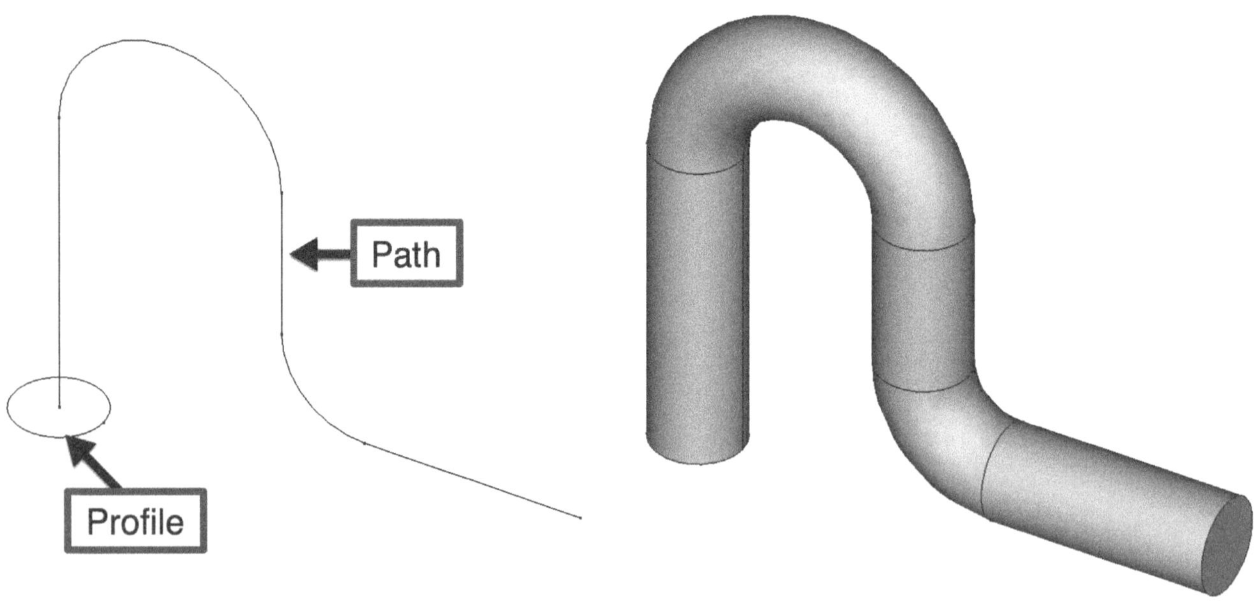

To take the pipe feature to the next level of complexity, you can add another profile and section orientation curve. By doing so, the shape of the geometry is controlled by section orientation curve. For example, the circular profile in the figure varies in size along the path because a section orientation curve controls it.

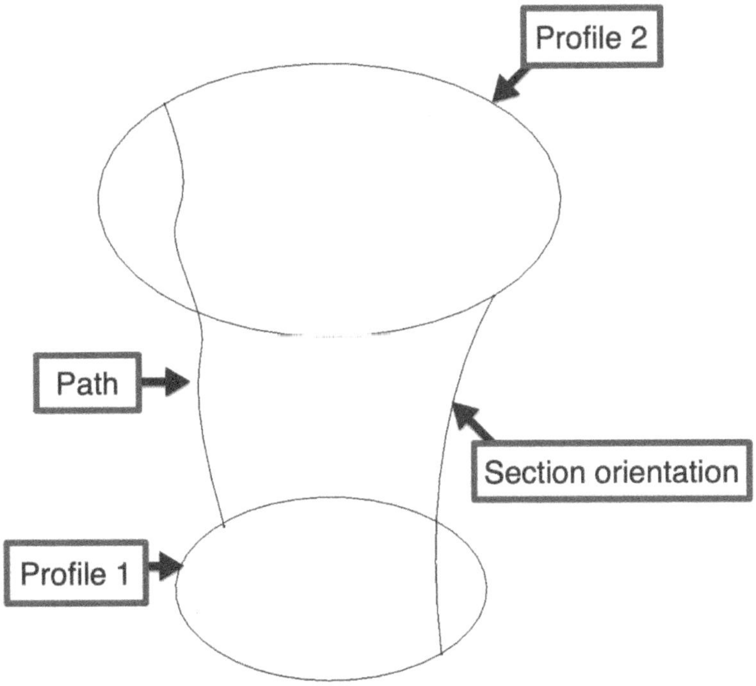

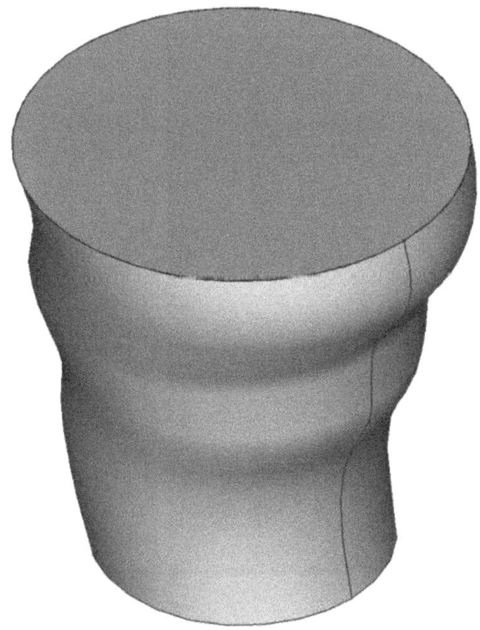

The topics covered in this chapter are:

- *Additive Pipe*
- *Subtractive Pipe*
- *Helix*

Additive Pipe

This feature requires two elements: a path and profile. The profile defines the shape of the sweep along the path. A path is used to control the direction of the profile. A path can be a sketch or an edge. To create a pipe, you must first create a path and a profile. Create a path by drawing a sketch. It can be an open or closed sketch. Next, click the **Datum plane** icon on the **Part Design Helper** toolbar, and then click on an element of the path. Next, select the **Normal to edge** option from the **Attachment mode** section of the **Datum Plane parameters** panel. Click **OK** to create a plane normal to the path. Sketch the profile on the plane normal to the path.

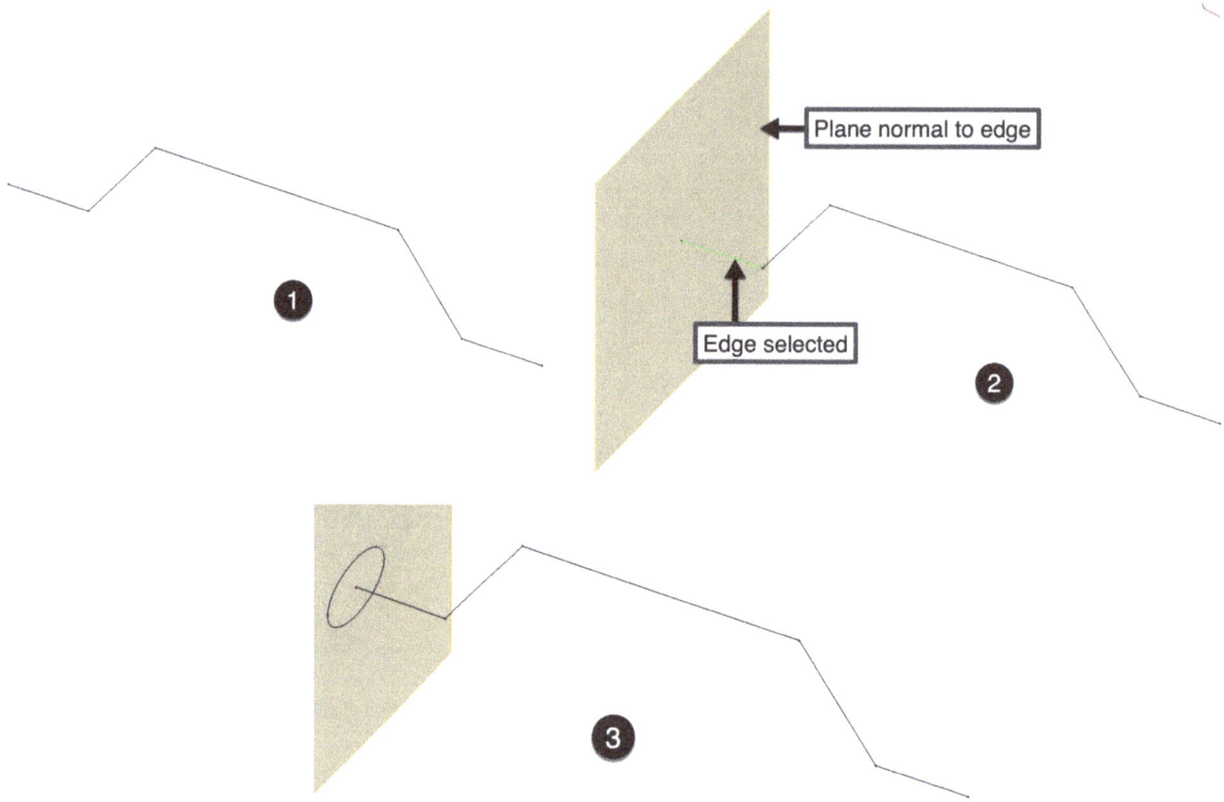

Click the **Additive Pipe**  on the **Part Design Modeling** toolbar (or) click **Part Design > Create an additive feature > Additive Pipe**. Select the profile from the graphics window and click **OK**. Next, click the **Object** button in the **Path to sweep along** section and select the path. You can add edges to the path one-by-one by using the **Add Edge** button. Alternatively, you can select the entire sketch by clicking the **Model** tab on the **Combo View** panel and selecting the path sketch from the **Model** tree.

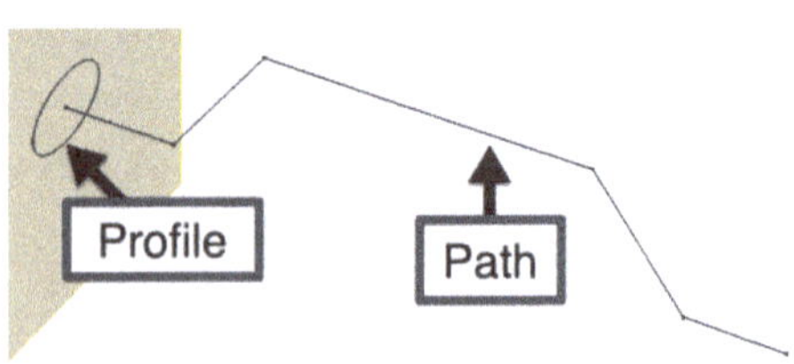

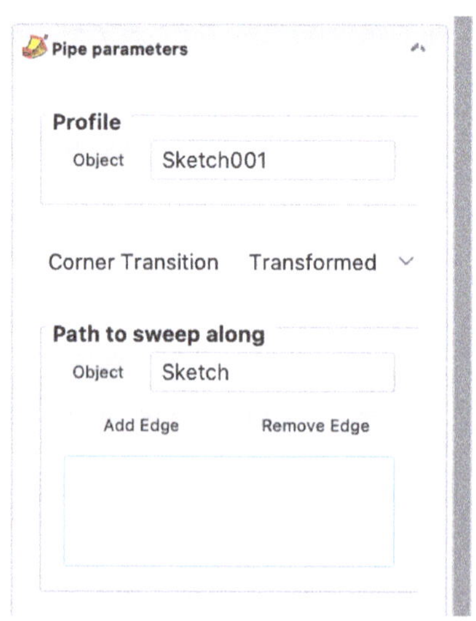

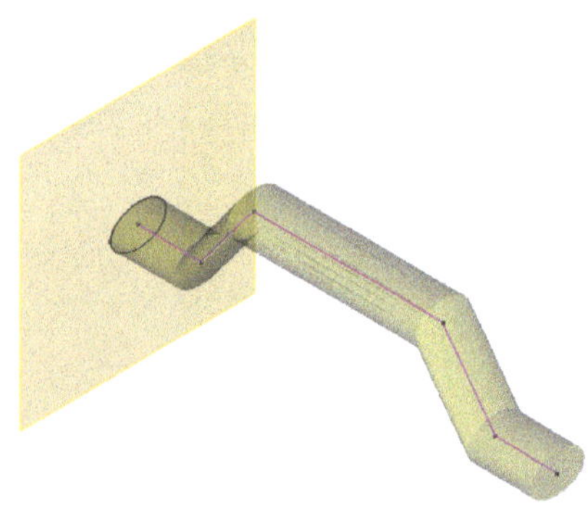

After selecting the path, specify the **Corner Transition** option. There are three **Corner Transition** options: **Transformed**, **Right Corner**, and **Round Corner**. The **Transformed** option creates corners that are parallel to the sketch plane of the profile. The **Right Corner** option creates the corners that are perpendicular to the path. The **Round Corner** option creates the rounded corners.

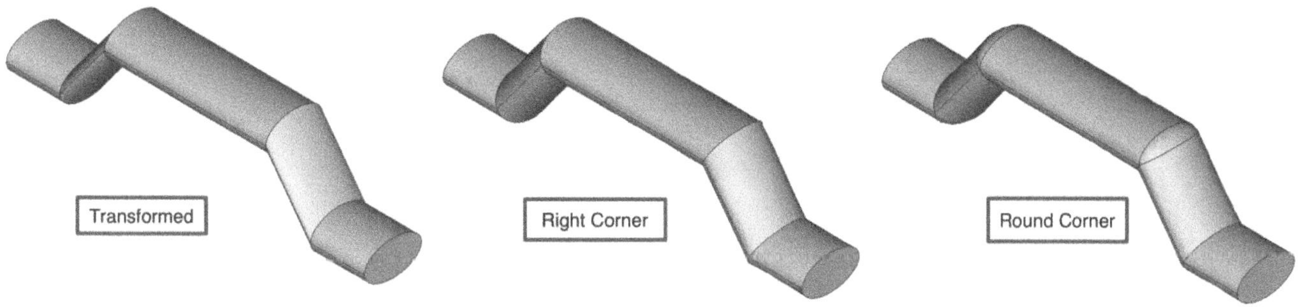

A sweeping profile must be created as a sketch. However, a path can be a sketch or an edge. The following illustrations show various types of paths and resultant pipe features.

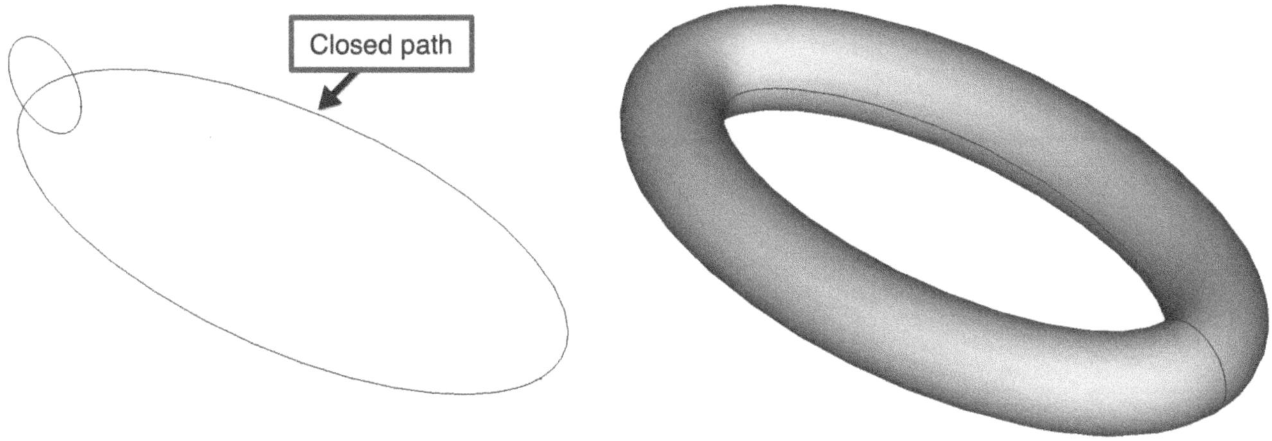

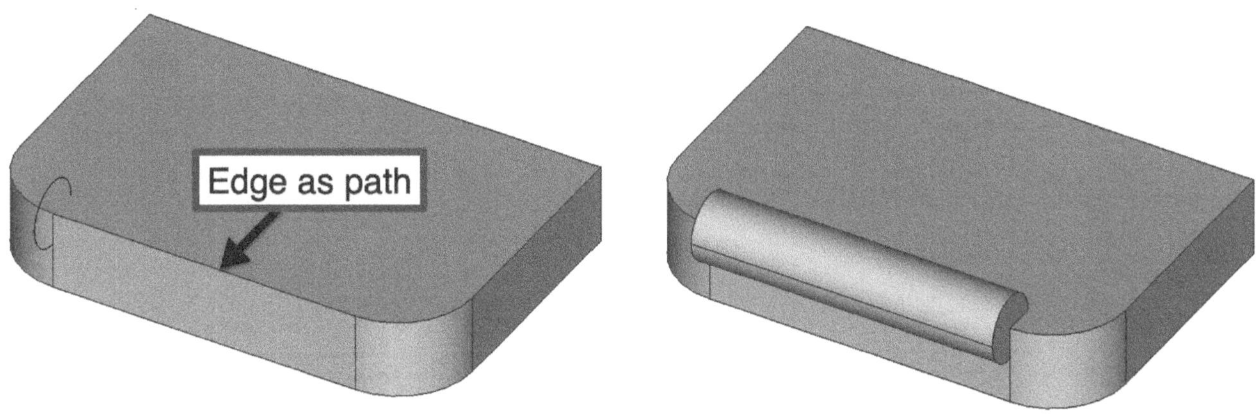

Section Orientation

The **Section Orientation** options define the orientation of the resulting geometry. The **Standard** option pipes the cross-section in the direction perpendicular to the path. The **Fixed** option pipes the cross-section in the direction parallel to itself.

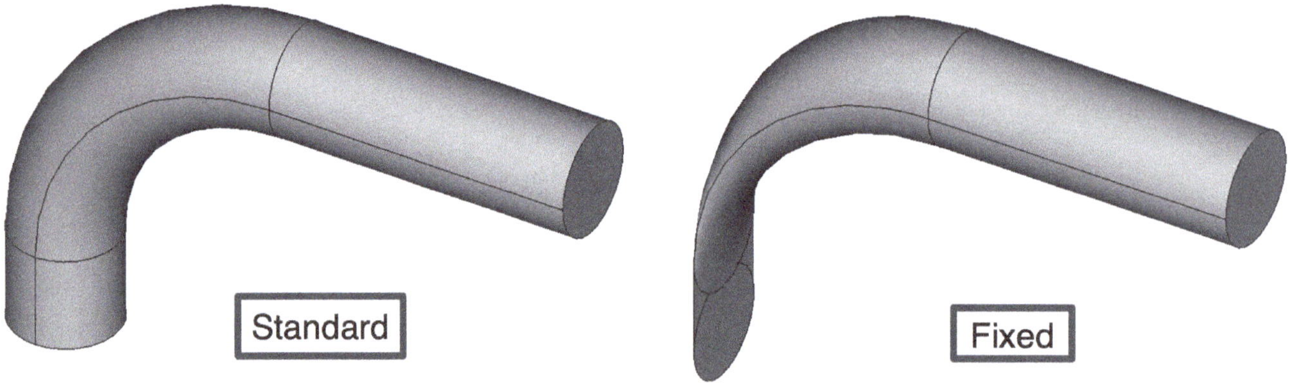

The **Auxiliary** option orients the cross-section perpendicular to a selected auxiliary element. Select this option from the **Orientation mode** drop-down and click the **Object** button under the **Profile** section. Next, select the auxiliary element.

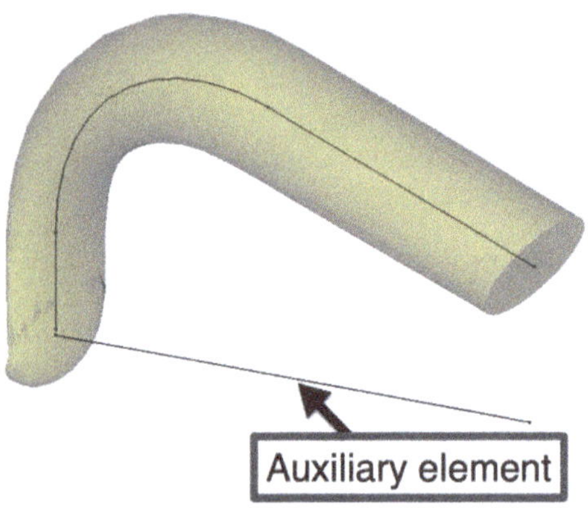

Creating an Additive Pipe between two Cross-sections

Create two cross-sections, as shown. Next, create a path connecting the two cross-sections. For example, start a sketch on the plane intersecting with the cross-sections, and then create a spline.

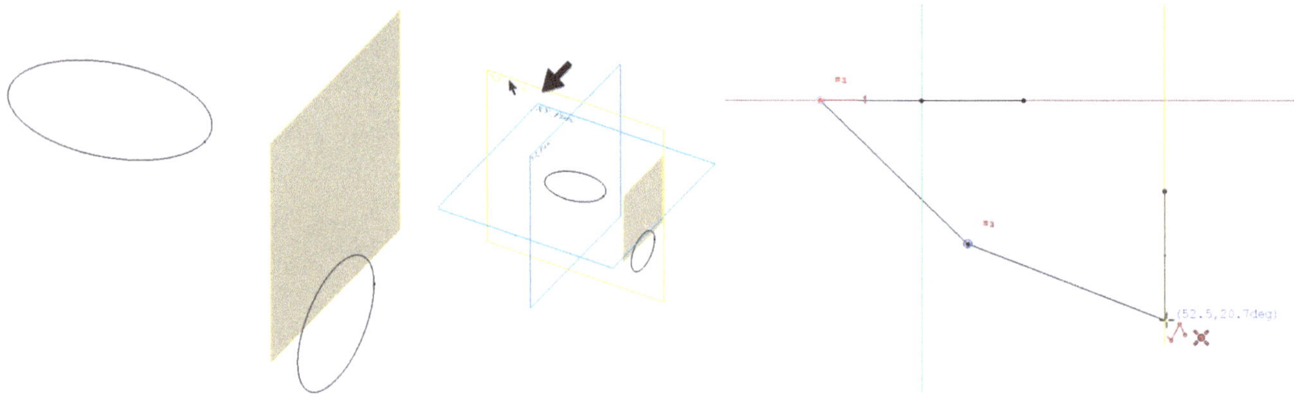

Next, you need to connect the endpoints of the spline with the profiles. Click the **Create External geometry** icon on the **Sketcher tools** toolbar. Next, select the two existing cross-section. Next, make the endpoints of the spline coincident with the external geometry using the **Constrain coincident** command. Click **Close** on the **Tasks** tab of the **Combo View** panel.

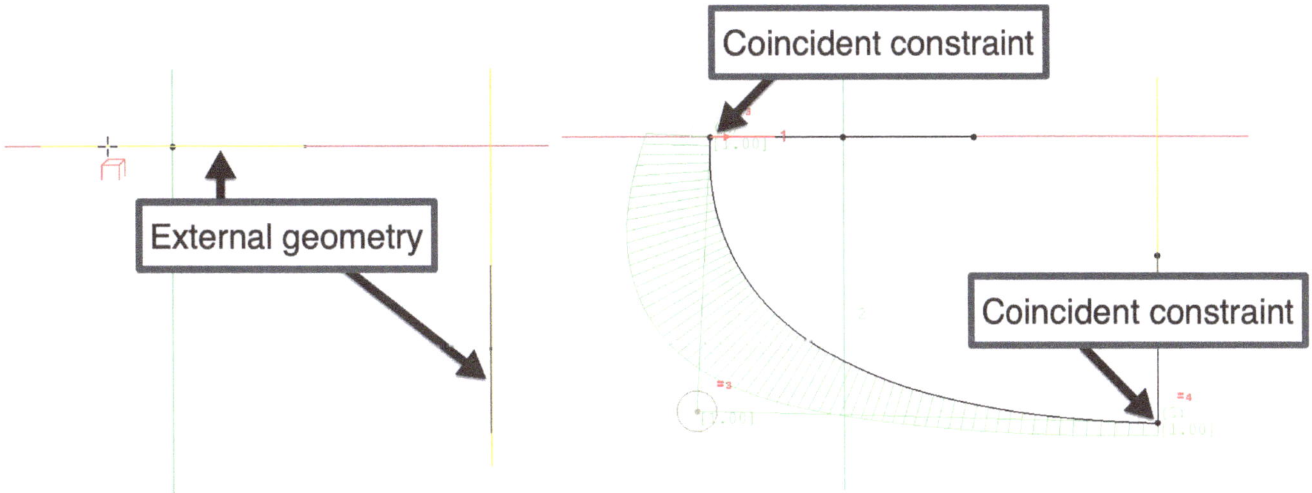

Activate the **Additive Pipe** command and select the first cross-section, and then click **OK**. Click the **Object button** in the **Path to sweep along** section. Next, select the path. You can add more paths by clicking the **Add edge** button in the **Path to sweep along** section and selecting the path; the preview updates. Next, select **Transform mode > Multisection** from the **Section Transformation** section. Click the **Add section** button and select the second cross-section. Notice that the edges with rails are affected. Select **Orientation mode > Fixed** and click **OK**.

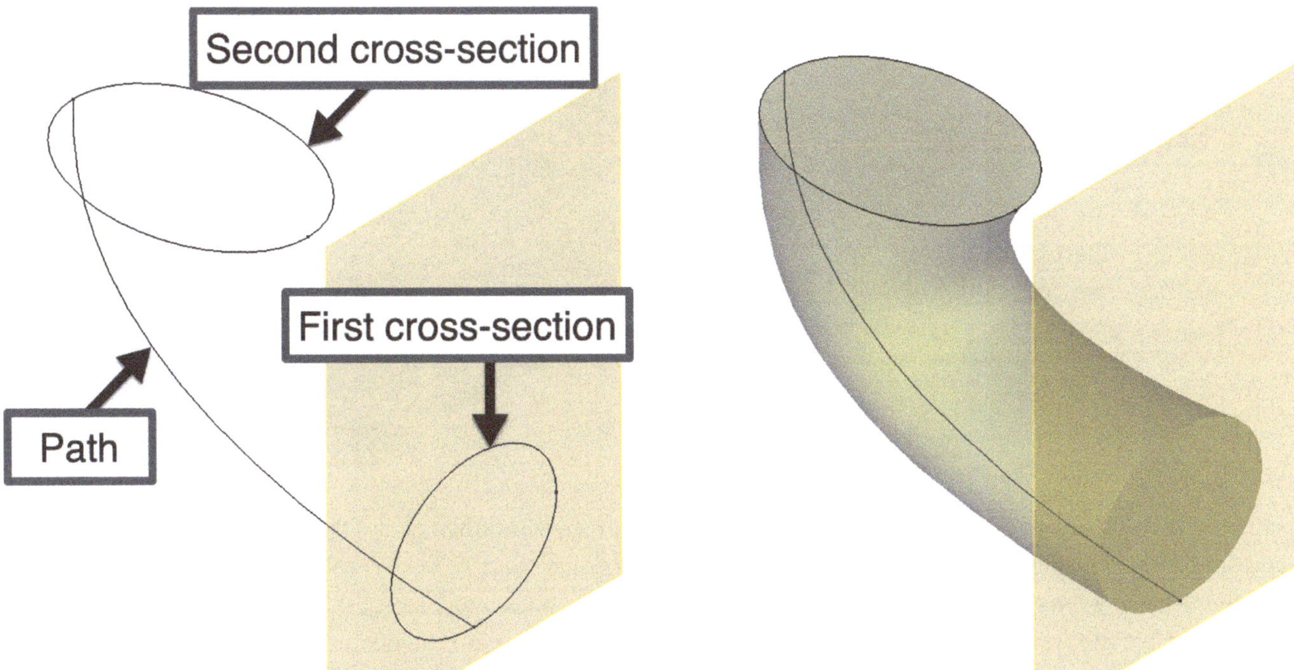

Subtractive pipe

In addition to adding pipe features, FreeCAD 1.0 allows you to remove geometry using the **Subtractive Pipe**  command. Click the **Subtractive pipe** icon on the **Part Design Modeling** toolbar (or) click **Part Design > Create a subtractive feature > Subtractive pipe.** Next, select the profile and click **OK**. Next, click the **Add edge** button and select the path. Click **OK** to create the subtractive pipe.

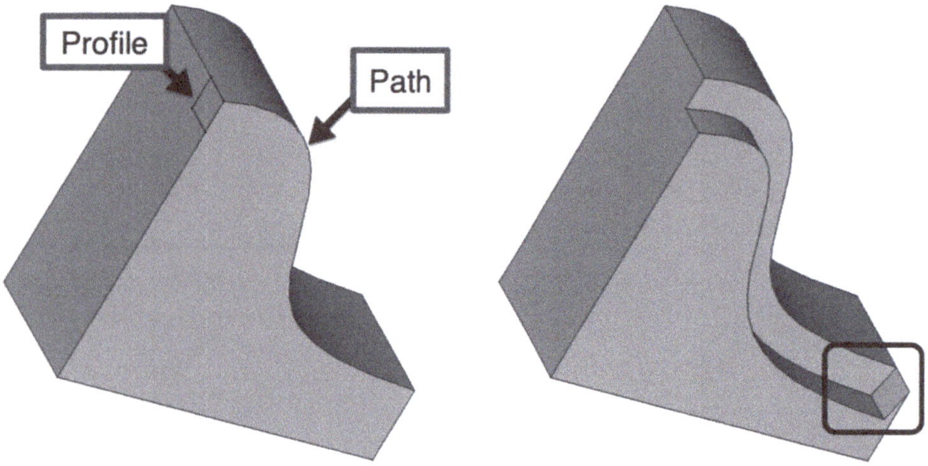

You will notice that the swept cutout is not created throughout the geometry. This is because the profile is swept only up to the endpoints of the path. You can solve this problem by adding another profile at the end face of the model. To do this, right-click on the **Subtractivepipe** feature and select **Delete**. Next, create a sketch on the end face similar in size and shape of the first profile.

Activate the **Subtractive pipe** command and select the first profile, and then click **OK**. Click the **Add Edge** button under the **Path to sweep along** section and select the curved edge. Next, select **Transform mode > Multisection** from the **Section Transformation** section. Click the **Add Section** button and select the newly created sketch. Click **OK** to complete the feature. The resultant swept cutout will be throughout the geometry.

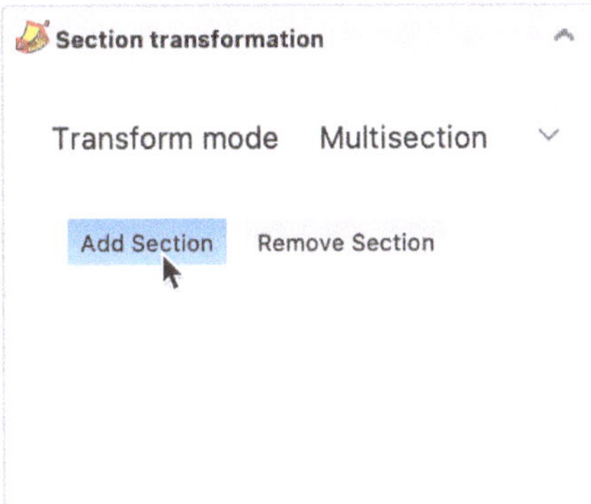

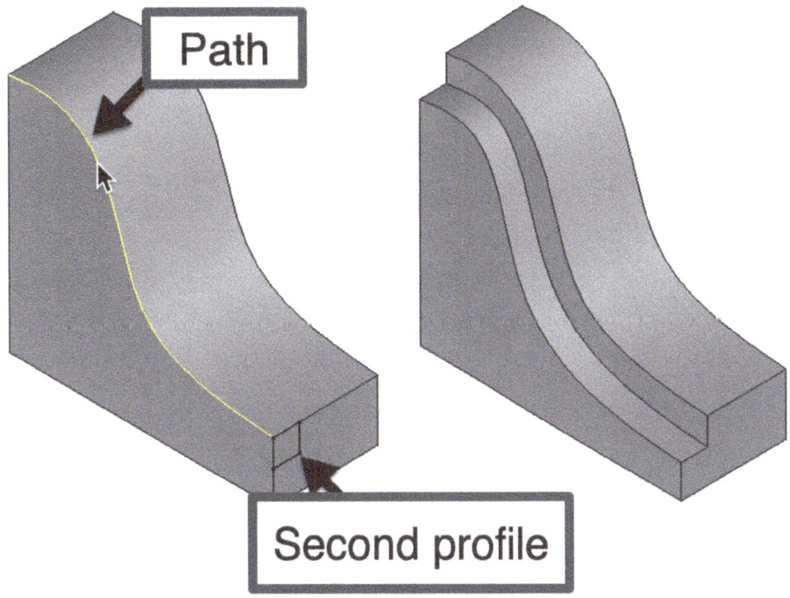

Best Practices for Pipe features

General Swept Features:

Before creating a swept feature in FreeCAD, start by planning your design carefully. Understand the path and profile you'll be working with. Keep in mind that complex paths or profiles may slow down your system or lead to errors. It's advisable to start with simple sweeps and gradually increase complexity as you become more comfortable with the tool.

Plastic Parts:

When designing for plastic parts, ensure the path and profile are suitable for the plastic manufacturing process. Consider draft angles and wall thickness. Avoid overly intricate or tight sweeps, as they may be difficult to mold or may lead to defects. When designing for 3D printing, remember that support structures may be necessary, especially for overhanging or intricate geometries.

Casted Parts:

For casted parts, pay attention to draft angles and avoid undercuts in your swept features. This will make the part easier to remove from the mold. Sharp internal corners can be problematic in casted parts, as they may lead to defects or difficulty in the casting process. Add fillets and use more gradual transitions in your swept features to facilitate the casting process.

Forged Parts:

When designing for forged parts, make sure your swept features have smooth transitions to avoid stress concentrations and material discontinuities. Be cautious with intricate shapes, as they may be difficult or costly to forge. Using a lofted feature in conjunction with sweeps can help create complex, smooth transitions that are easier to forge.

Machined Parts:

Design your swept features for machined parts with smooth transitions to avoid internal stresses or challenging geometries for machining. Ensure that the geometry doesn't create deep pockets or sharp angles that could be difficult to access with cutting tools. Design parts with proper clearances, and consider the toolpath to ensure that the swept features can be machined efficiently.

3D Printed Parts for Makers:

When creating swept features for 3D printed parts, remember to design with the layering process in mind. Pay attention to overhangs and consider adding support structures if needed. Utilize features like fillets and chamfers to reduce sharp angles, as these can be challenging to 3D print. Keep an eye on wall thickness to ensure structural integrity in the printed part.

Additive helix

This command creates a spring or spiral-shaped feature. To create this type of feature, you must have a cross-section. First create a closed sketch and click the **Additive helix**  icon on the **Part Design Modeling** toolbar (or) click **Part Design > Create an additive feature > Additive helix**; the cross-section is selected automatically. Also, the default axis is selected from the **Axis** drop-down and the preview of the geometry is displayed. You can select the required axis from the **Axis** drop-down.

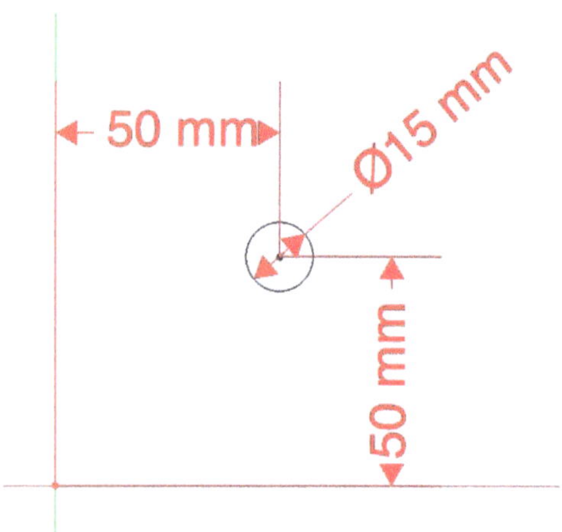

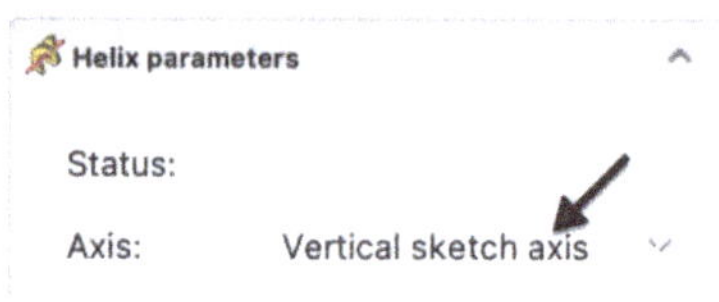

Next, select the method to define the size of the helix from the **Mode** drop-down available on the **Helix parameters** panel. It has three options: **Pitch-Height-Angle**, **Pitch-Turns-Angle**, **Height-Turns-Angle**, and **Height-Turns-Growth**.

The **Height-Turns-Angle** option allows you to create a helix by entering its height and number of turns in the **Height** and **Turns** boxes, respectively. The **Height** parameter refers to the vertical distance or elevation over which the helix will extend. Essentially, it defines how tall or long the helix will be along its central axis. The **Number of Turns** parameter is a numeric value you input to determine how many complete spirals or coils the helix will make from the bottom to the top. Each turn represents a full rotation of the helix around its central axis. It defines how tightly or loosely the spirals are wound around the central axis.

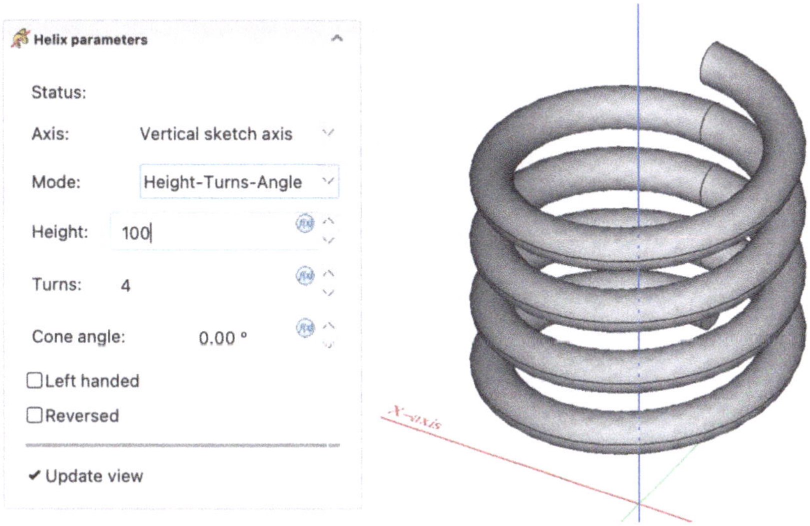

The **Pitch-Turns-Angle** option allows you to create a helix by entering the number of turns and the distance between the turns in the **Turns** and **Pitch** boxes, respectively. The pitch, in this context, refers to the vertical distance or height between each coil or turn of the helix. It's essentially the amount the helix rises or descends as it winds around a central axis. The pitch is a crucial parameter when creating helical structures, as it determines the separation between each revolution. The term **Turns** pertains to the number of complete revolutions or cycles that the helix makes along its path. This parameter allows you to specify how many times the helix wraps around the central axis. The number of turns is typically an integer, representing the whole number of cycles the helix completes.

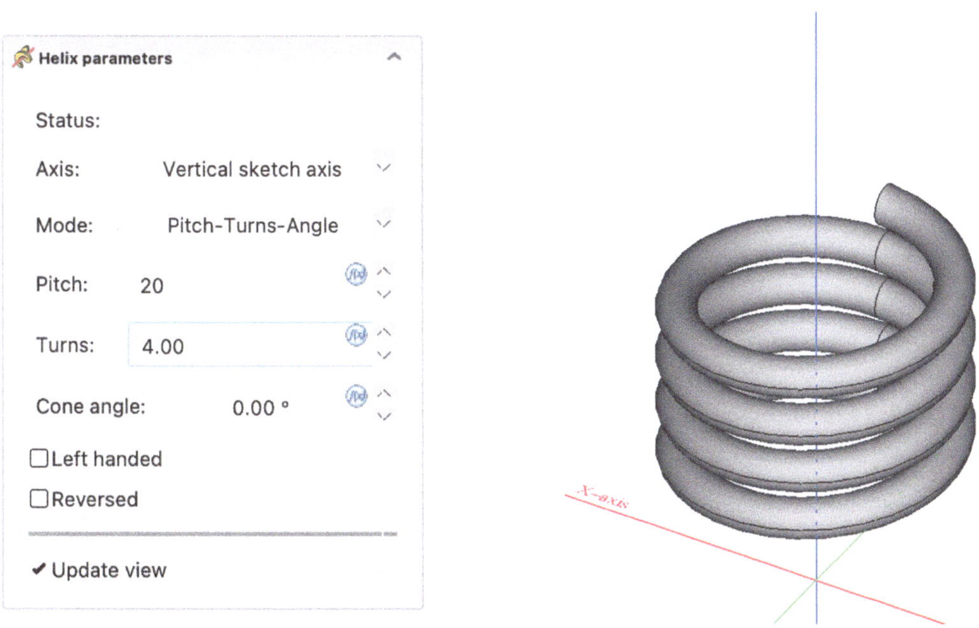

The **Pitch-Height-Angle** option allows you to create a helix by entering its height and the distance between the turns in the **Height** and **Pitch** boxes, respectively.

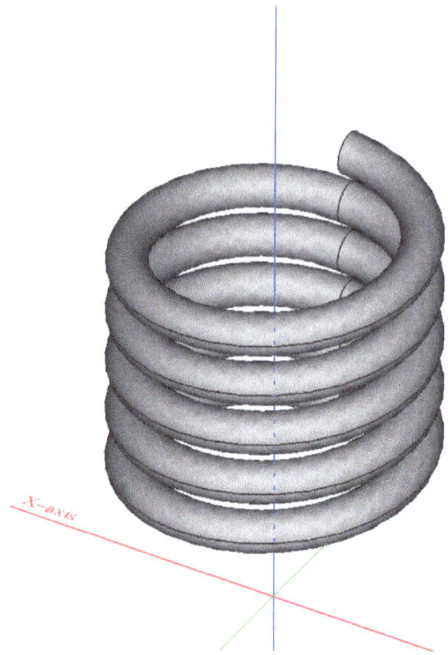

The default rotation direction of the helix is clockwise (i.e., Right-hand side). Check the **Left handed** option to change the rotation direction. Check the **Reversed** option, if you want to create the helix in the opposite direction.

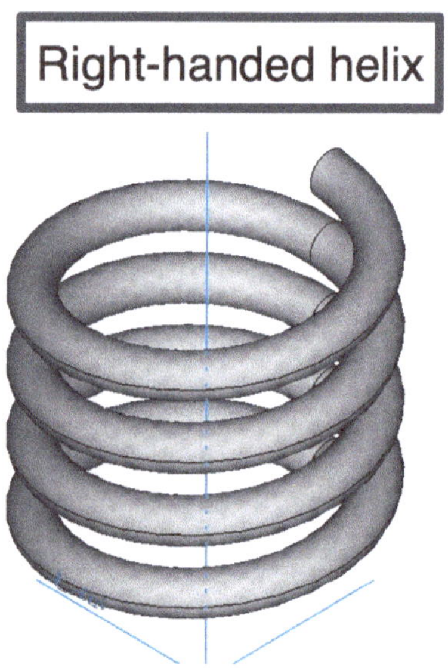

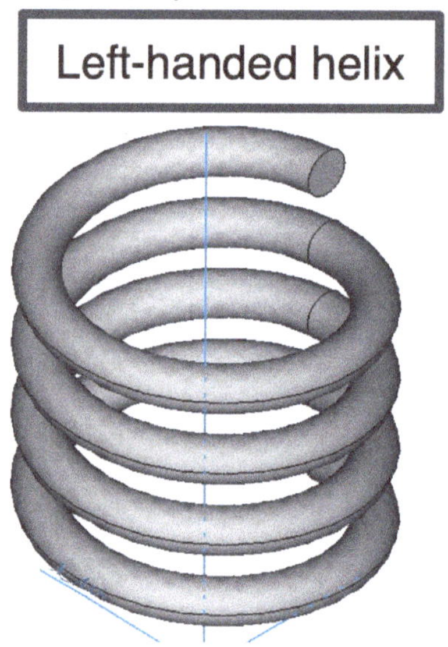

The **Cone angle** box helps you to apply taper to the helix. You can apply taper to the coil by entering a value in the **Cone angle** box. The negative angle reverses the taper direction.

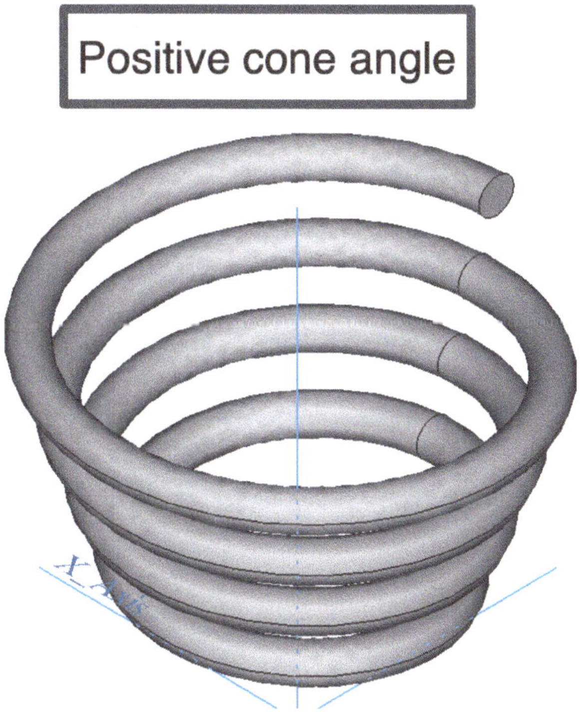

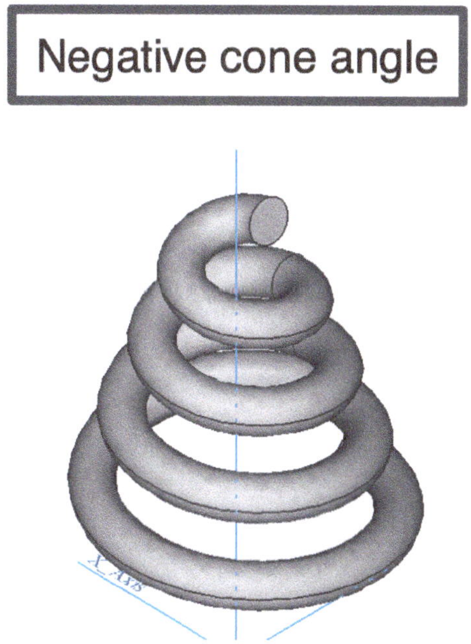

The **Height-Turns-Growth** option allows you to create a helix by entering its height and number of turns in the **Height** and **Turns** boxes, respectively. In addition to that, you can taper the helix by entering a value in the **Radial growth** box. The diameter of the helix is increased per each turn by the value that you enter in the **Radial growth** box. For example, if you enter 10 mm in the **Radial growth** box, the diameter of the helix is increase by 10 mm for each turn of the helix.

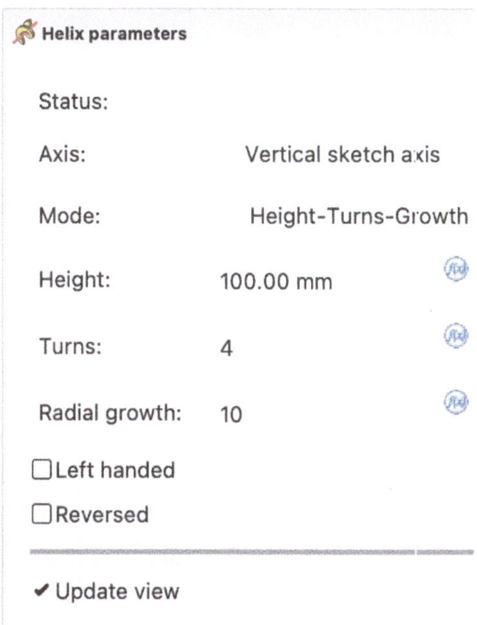

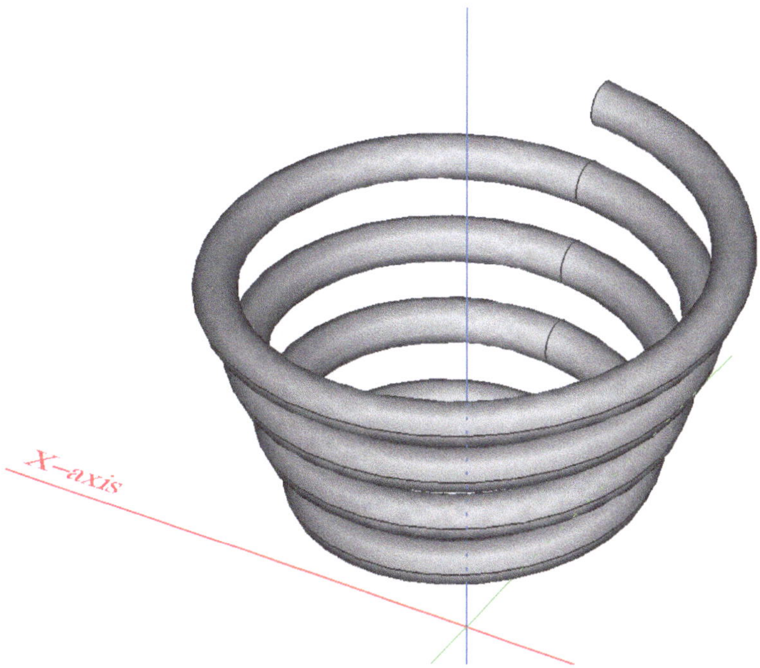

Click **OK** after specifying all the required options.

Subtractive helix

The **Subtractive helix** command can be used to remove material from the part geometry by creating a helical feature. The **Subtractive Helix** command is commonly employed in various design and manufacturing scenarios. For instance, it can be used to create threaded holes, spiraled grooves, or any feature that requires a helical shape. It's particularly useful when working on designs that involve screws, bolts, springs, or any other component with a spiral or helical structure. To create this feature, first, you must have an existing geometry and sketch of the cross-section. Click the **Subtractive helix** icon on the **Part Design Modeling** toolbar (or) click **Part Design > Create a subtractive feature > Subtractive helix**; the cross-section is selected automatically. Define the number of turns and pitch using anyone of the **Modes** described in the previous topic. Next, click **OK** to create the subtractive helix.

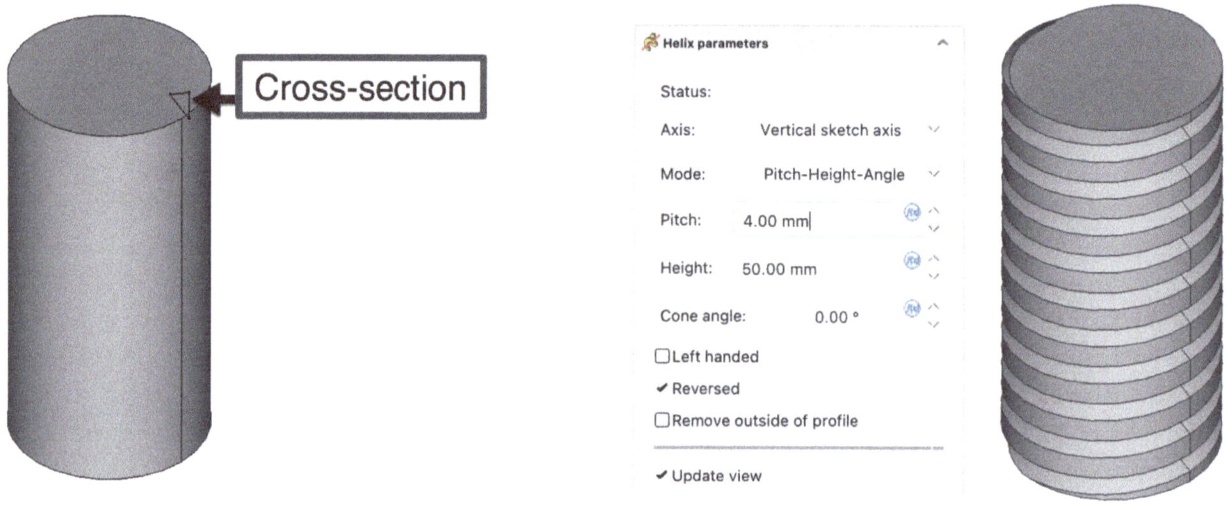

Best Practices

Define the Purpose:

Clearly understand the function and purpose of the helical feature. Is it for threading, guiding, or aesthetic reasons? This will help you determine the appropriate dimensions and pitch.

Understand Material Properties:

Different materials have different properties. Know the material you're working with to design the feature accordingly. For instance, threads in plastic parts may have different tolerances than those in metal parts.

Cautions

- Be mindful of your modeling intent. Ensure that the helical feature is properly constrained and aligned with other components in your design.
- Avoid overly complex helical shapes, as these may lead to issues with solid modeling or manufacturing.

Tips for Different Types of Parts

Plastic Parts:

- Consider draft angles in your design to facilitate mold ejection for threaded plastic parts.
- Self-tapping screws can be a good alternative for plastic parts if they need to be fastened to other components.

Casted Parts:

- Ensure that the pattern allows for easy removal of the part from the mold.
- Consider using inserts or threaded components instead of casted threads for better durability.

Forged Parts:

- Be aware that forging involves material deformation, so your design should consider the change in material properties and how it affects helical features.
- Forged threads may require post-forging machining to achieve the desired precision.

Machined Parts:

- Ensure that the helical feature is accurately dimensioned and positioned for machining.
- Consider the choice of cutting tools and the type of machining operation (e.g., turning or milling).

3D Printed Parts:

- Design the helical feature with additive manufacturing in mind. Be aware of overhangs, support structures, and printing orientation.
- Consider tolerances, as 3D printing may not achieve the same precision as traditional manufacturing methods.

Always collaborate closely with your manufacturing or production team to ensure that your design can be effectively translated into a physical part. Testing and prototyping can also be beneficial to verify the functionality of helical features in real-world applications.

Tutorial 1

In this example, you create the part shown below.

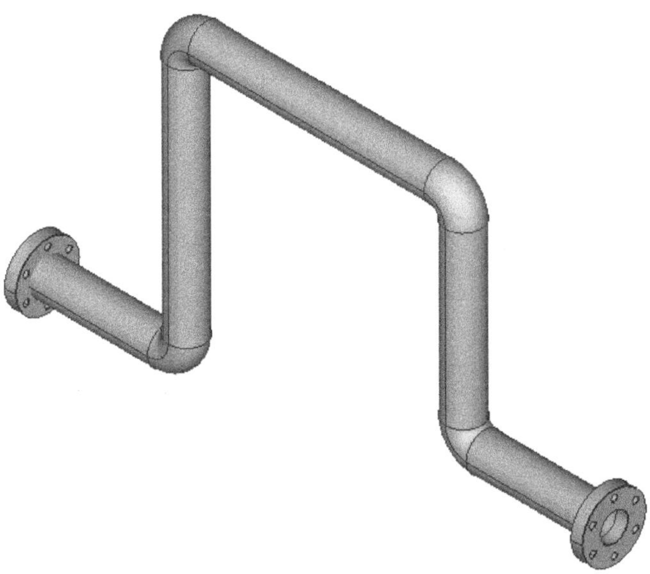

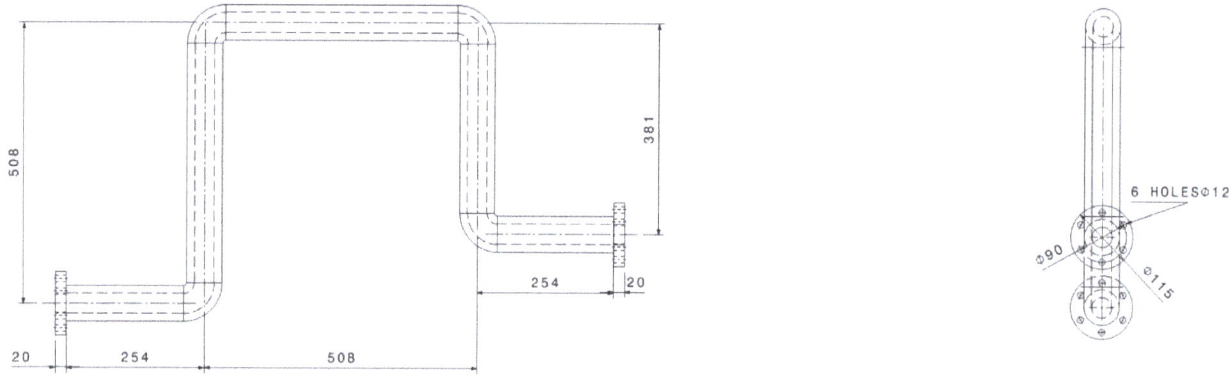

PIPE I.D. 51

PIPE O.D. 65

Creating a New document

1. Click **FreeCAD** on the desktop to start.
2. On the **Home** page, click **Documents > Create New**; it creates a new document.
3. On the **Workbench** toolbar, select **Workbench** drop-down **> Part Design**.
4. Click **Edit > Preferences** on the **Menu** bar (or) click **FreeCAD 1.0 > Preferences** on title bar, if you are working on MacOS; the **Preferences** dialog appears on the screen.
5. Click the **General** tab and select **Default unit System > Standard (mm/kg/s/degree)**.
6. Select **Number of decimals > 2** and click **OK** on the **Preferences** dialog.

Creating the Pipe Feature

1. Click **Create Sketch** command on the **Part Design Helper** toolbar and then select **XZ-plane**.
2. Click **OK** on the **Combo View** plane.
3. Click the **Create polyline** icon on the **Sketcher geometries** toolbar. Next, create the lines, as shown.

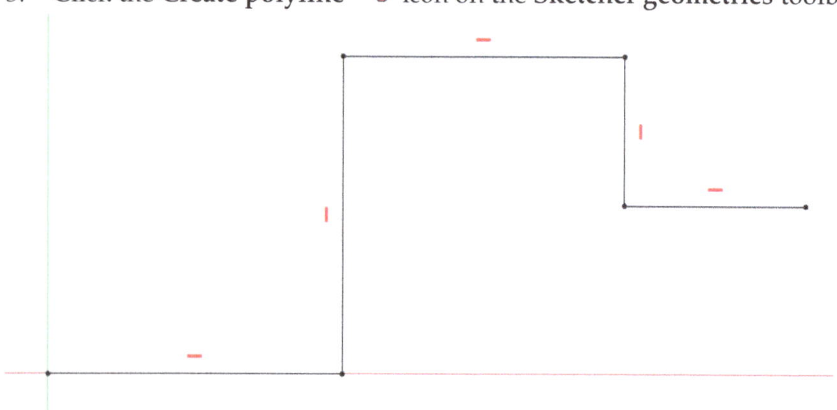

4. On the **Sketcher geometries** toolbar, click the **Create fillet**. Select the corner points of the sketch.

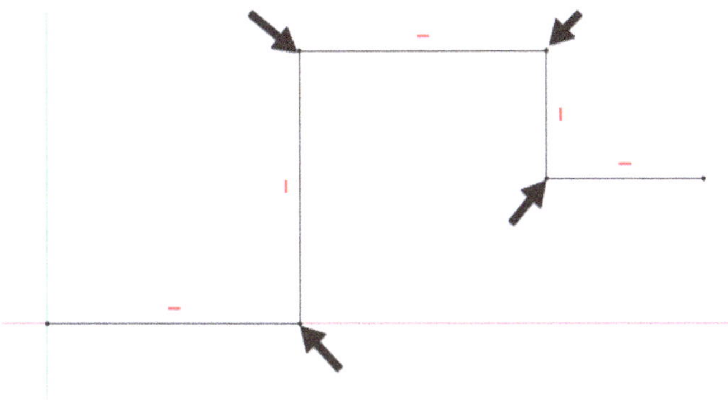

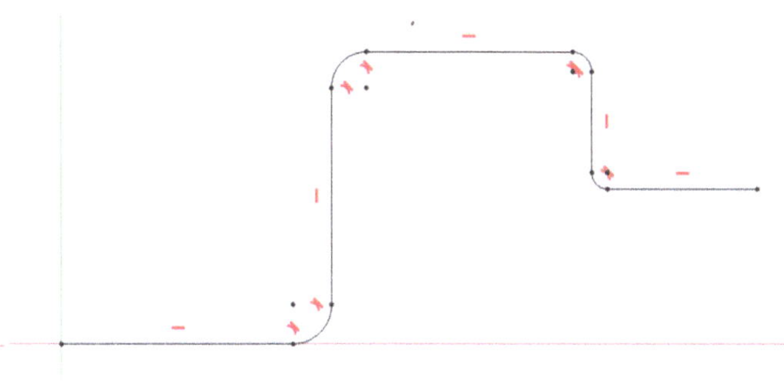

5. Click the **Constrain horizontal distance** icon on the **Sketcher constraints** toolbar.
6. Select the lower horizontal line of the sketch. Click **OK** on the **Insert Length** dialog.
7. Likewise, create the horizontal distance constraints, as shown.

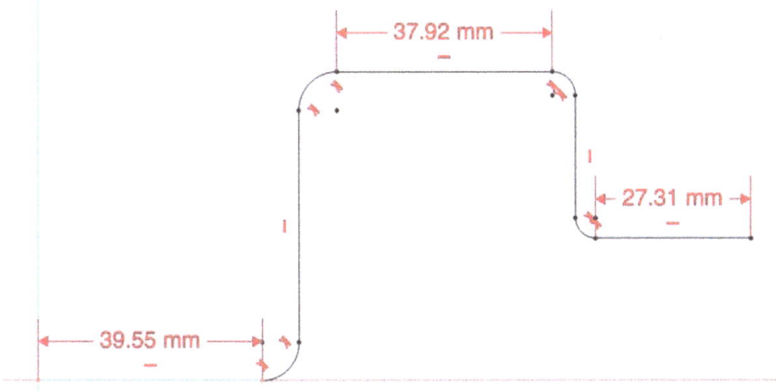

8. Click the **Constrain vertical distance** icon on the **Sketcher constraints** toolbar.
9. Select the left vertical line and click **OK** on the **Insert Length** dialog.
10. Likewise, select the right vertical line and **OK** on the **Insert Length** dialog.

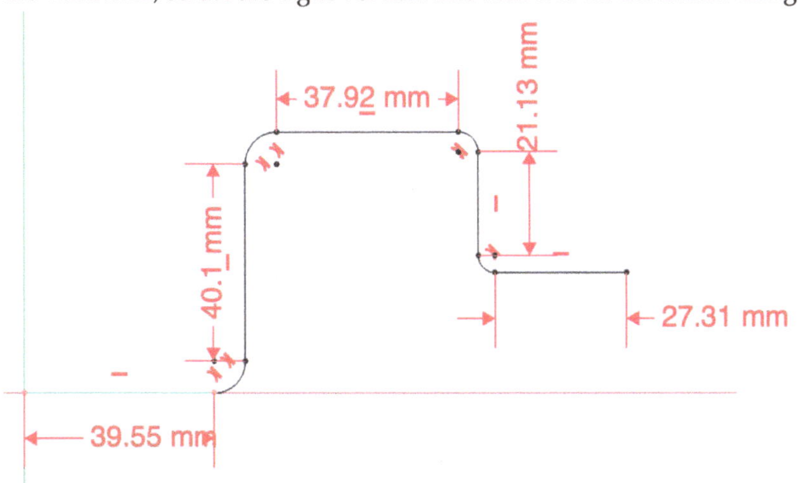

11. Click the **Constrain equal** icon on the **Sketcher constraints** toolbar. Select all the fillets.
12. Again, select the first and last fillets.

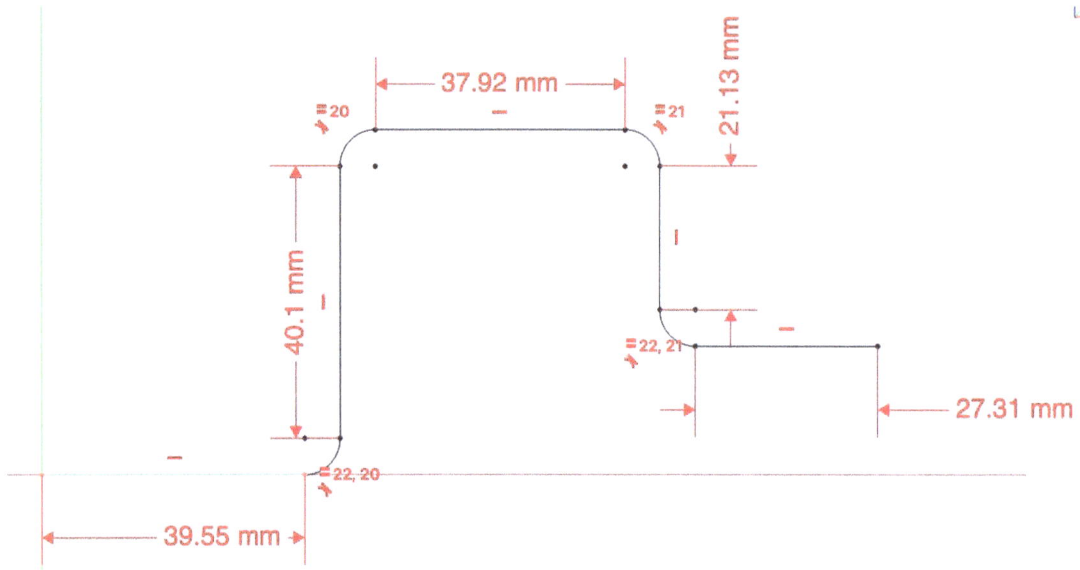

13. Ensure that all the lines are either vertical or horizontal. To achieve this, utilize the **Constrain vertical** or **Constrain horizontal** commands. If any lines are not aligned as desired, use these commands to constrain them to the vertical or horizontal orientation, ensuring uniformity in the sketch.
14. Click the **Constraint radius** on the **Sketcher constraints** toolbar.
15. Select any one fillet and click **OK** on the **Insert Length** dialog.

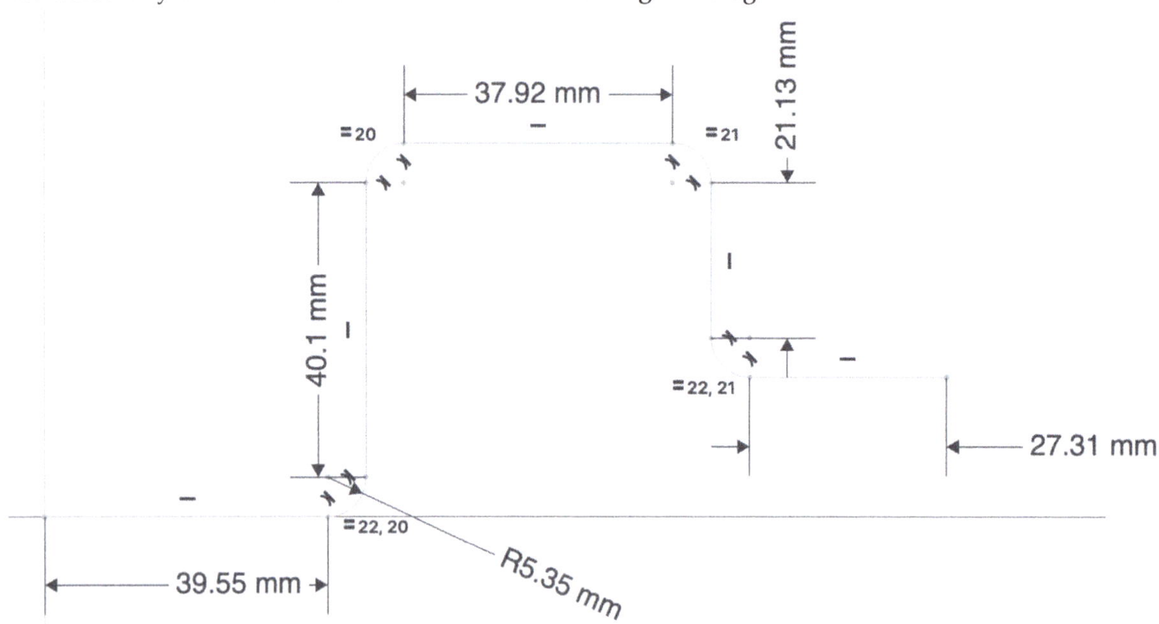

16. Double-click on the left vertical dimension and type-in **432** in the **Length** box on the **Insert Length** dialog.
17. Click **OK** to edit the dimension.
18. Likewise, edit all the values of the dimensions, as shown in the figure.

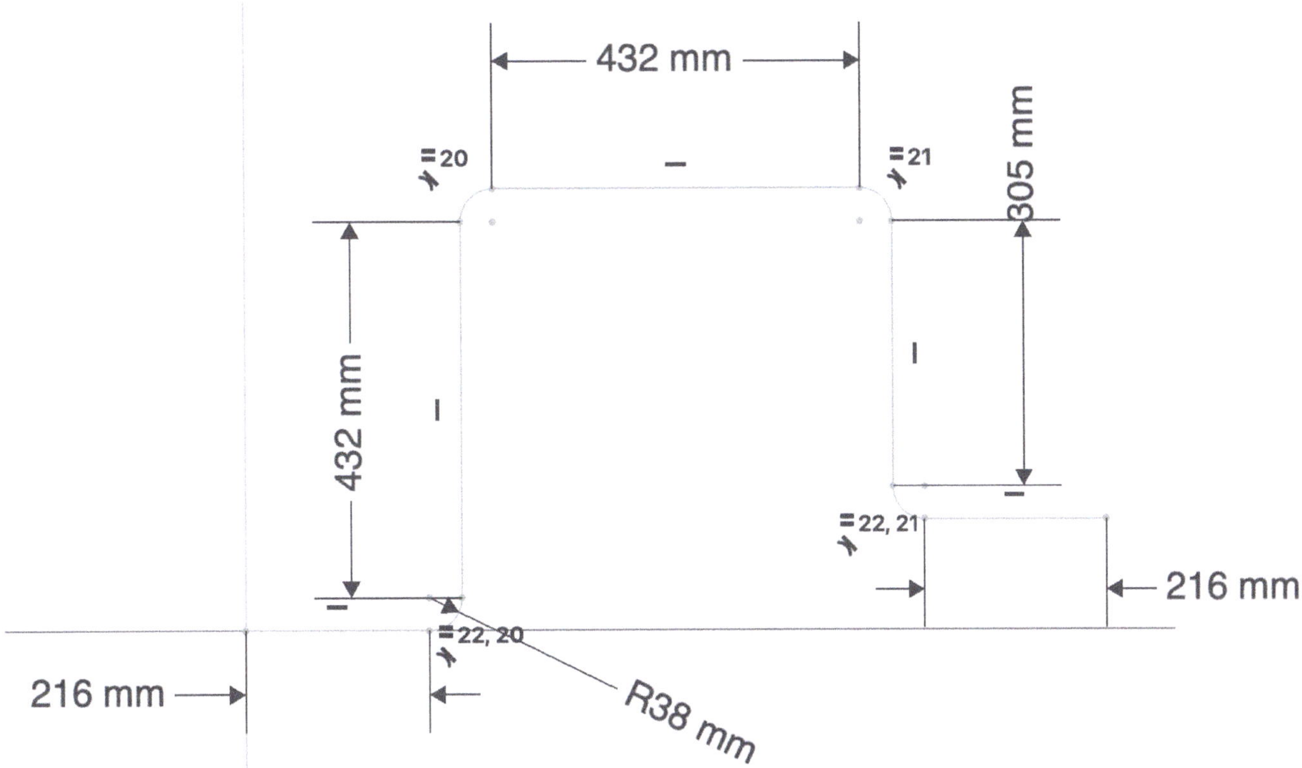

19. Click the **Close** button on the **Tasks** panel. Next, click in the graphics window to deselect the newly created sketch.

20. On the **Part Design Helper** toolbar, click the **Create a datum plane**  icon.
21. Select the right horizontal line of the sketch to define the first reference.
22. Select the endpoint of the horizontal line to define the second reference.
23. Select **Normal to edge** from the **Attachment mode** section and click **OK**.

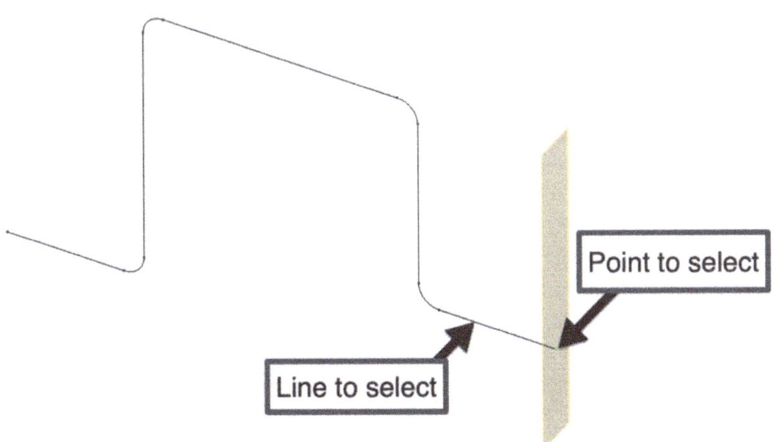

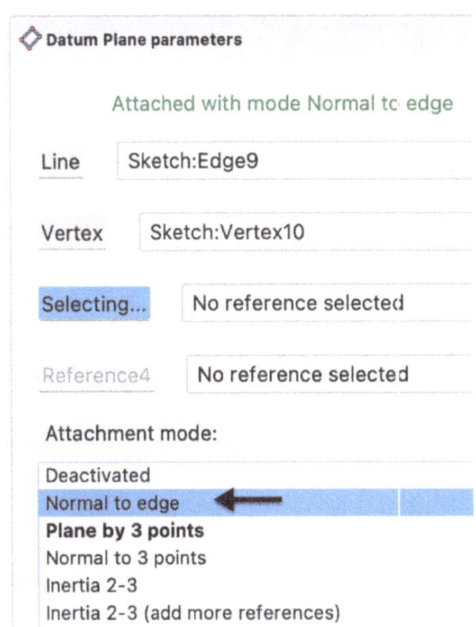

24. Click the **Create Sketch**  icon on the **Part Design Helper** toolbar. Next, select the newly created datum plane and click **OK**.
25. Click the **Create circle by center**  tool on the **Sketcher geometries** toolbar.
26. Change the view orientation to the Isometric view. (on the graphics area, click the **Camera and render options > Isometric** from the right-side).
27. Click on the sketch origin to define the center point of the circle.
28. Move the pointer outward and click to create a circle.
29. Again, click on the sketch origin to define the center point of the circle.
30. Move the pointer and click to create another circle. Make sure that the center points of the circles coincident with each other.

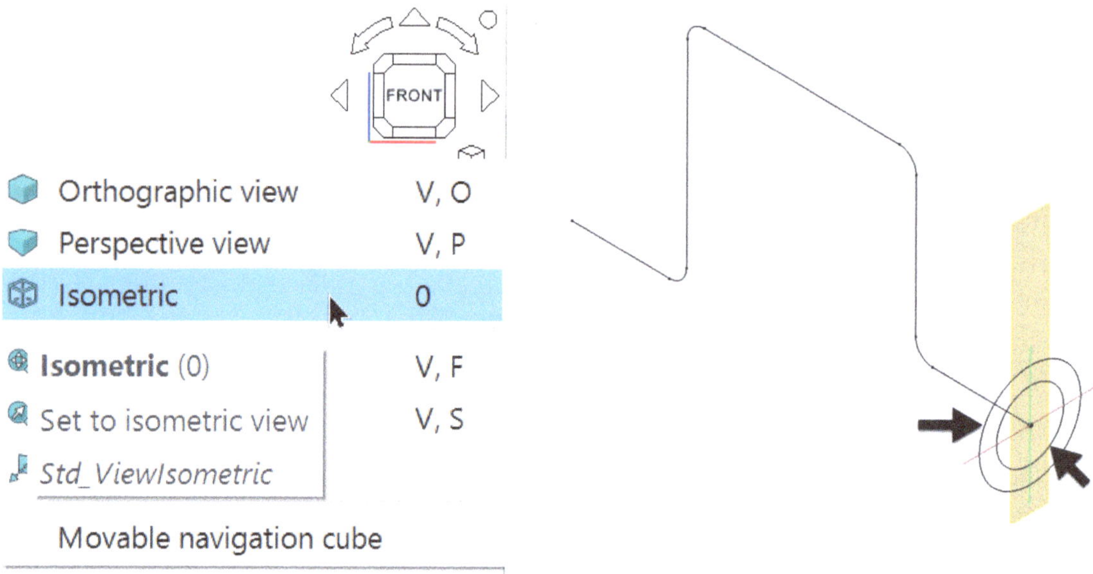

31. On the **Sketcher constraints** toolbar, click the **Constrain an arc or circle** drop-down and select **Constrain diameter**.
32. Select the inner circle. Next, type-in **51** in the **Length** box and click **OK** on the **Insert Length** dialog.
33. Select the outer circle. Next, type-in **65** in the **Length** box and click **OK** on the **Insert Length** dialog.

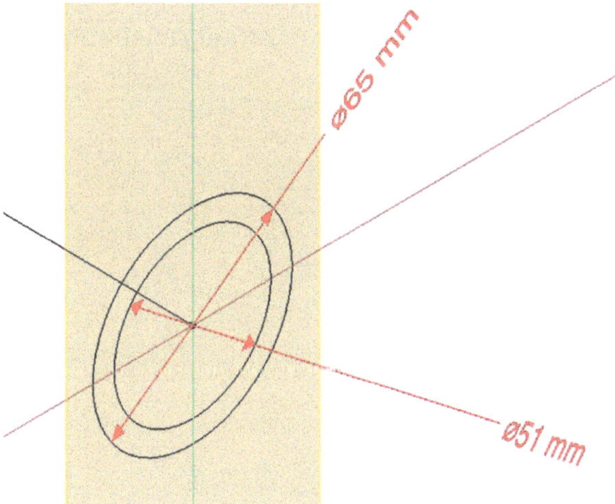

34. Click the **Close** button on the **Tasks** panel.
35. On the **Part Design Modeling** toolbar, click the **Additive pipe** icon. Next, select the **Sketch001** from the **Select feature** section on the **Tasks** panel.
36. Click **OK** on the **Tasks** panel.
37. Under the **Pipe parameters** section on the **Tasks** panel, click the **Object** button under the **Path to sweep along** section.
38. Select the first sketch from the graphics area and click **OK** to create the *Pipe* feature.

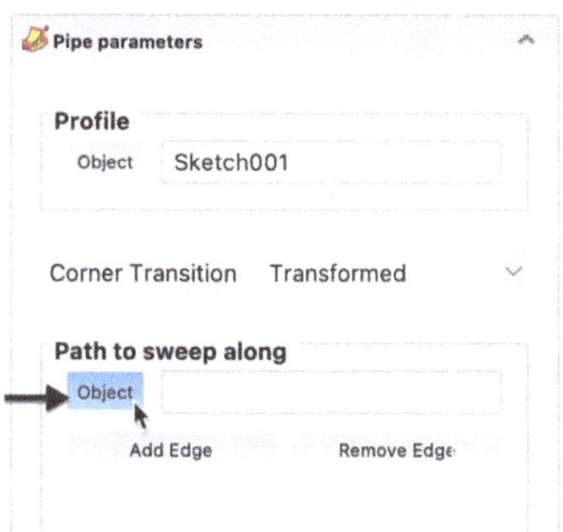

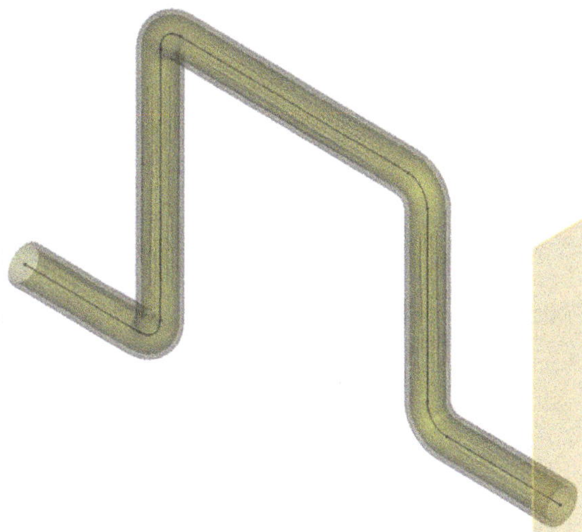

Adding the Pad Feature

1. Click the **Create Sketch** command on the **Sketcher geometries** toolbar.
2. Click on the datum plane displayed on the front-end face of the *Pipe* feature.
3. Change the view orientation to the Isometric view. (on the graphics area, click the **Camera and render options > Isometric** from the right-side).
4. Create two circles that are concentric with each other.
5. Click the **Constrain coincident** icon on the **Sketcher constraints** toolbar. Next, select the centerpoint of the circles and the sketch origin.

6. Click the **Dimension** drop-down and select the **Constrain diameter** icon on the **Sketcher constraints** toolbar.

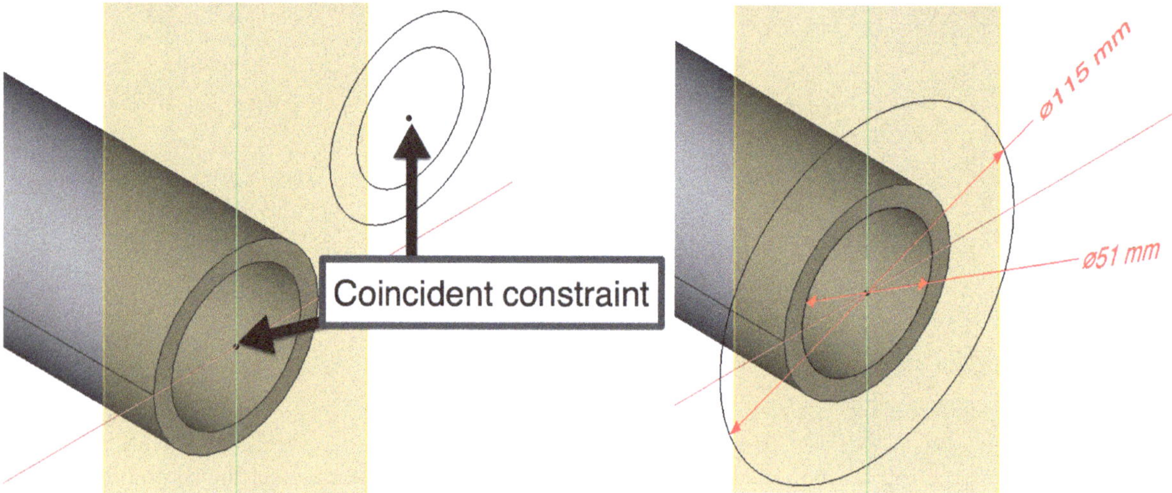

7. Click the **Close** button on the **Tasks** panel to confirm the sketch.
8. Activate the **Pad** command; the sketch is selected automatically.
9. Type-in **20** in the **Length** box under the **Pad parameters** section on the **Tasks** panel. Next, check the **Reversed** option.

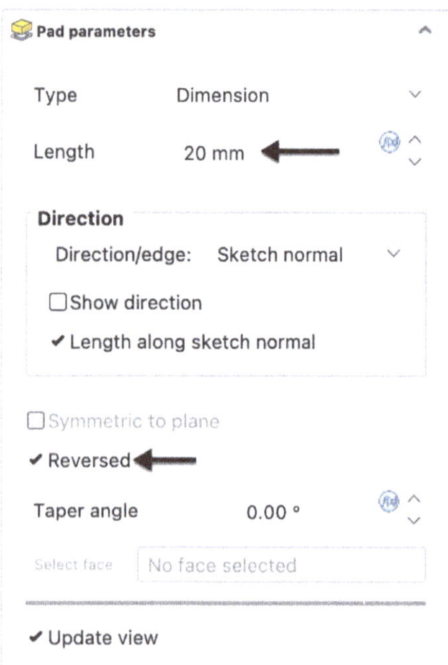

10. Click **OK** on the **Tasks** panel to complete the *Pad* feature.

Creating the Polar pattern

1. Select the face of the pad feature and activate the **Create Sketch** command.

2. Click the **Create circle by center** icon on the **Sketcher geometries** toolbar. Next, click the vertical sketch axis and move the pointer outward. Again, click to create a circle.

3. On the **Sketcher constraints** toolbar, click **Constrain radius** drop-down > **Constrain diameter**.
4. Select the circle and enter 12 in the **Diameter** box. Next, click **OK** to add a diameter constraint.

5. Click the **Constrain vertical** icon on the **Sketcher constraints** toolbar. Next, select the sketch origin and the centerpoint of the circle.
6. Type **45** in the **Length** box and click **OK**.

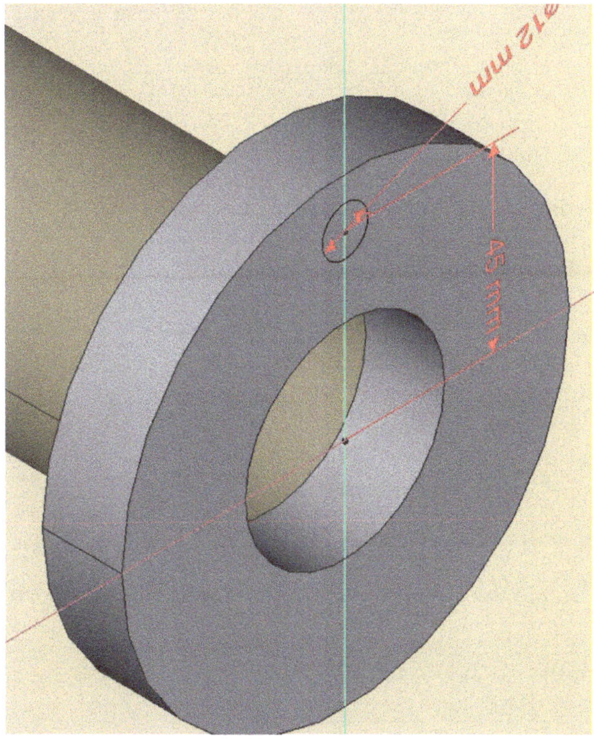

7. Click the **Close** button on the **Tasks** panel.
8. Click the **Pocket** icon on the **Part Design Modeling** toolbar.
9. Select **Type > To first** on the **Pocket parameters** section of the **Tasks** panel. Next, click **OK**.
10. Click the **Create a polar pattern feature** command on the **Part Design Modeling** toolbar.
11. Select the **Pocket** from the **Select feature** panel. Next, click **OK**.
12. Under the **PolarPattern parameters** section and select **Axis > Normal sketch axis**.
13. Type-in **360** and **6** in the **Angle** and **Occurrences** boxes, respectively.
14. Click **OK** to create the pattern.

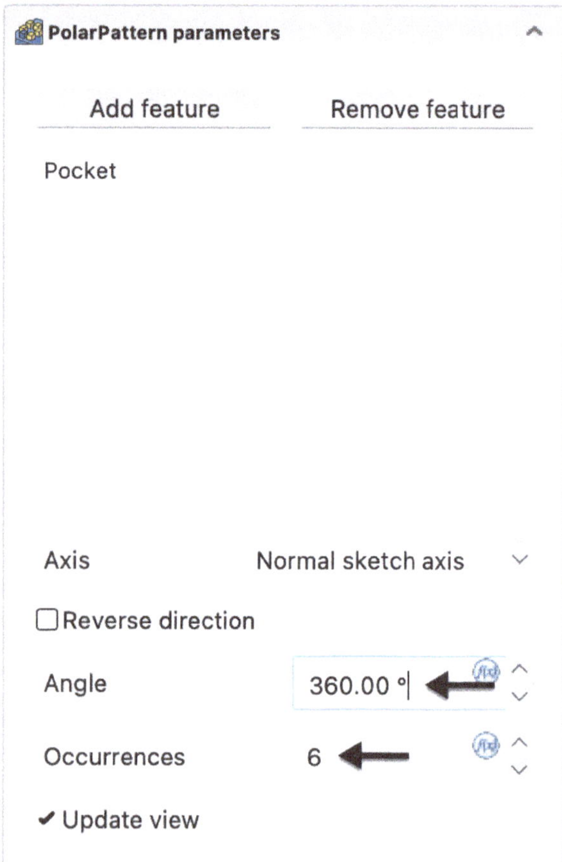

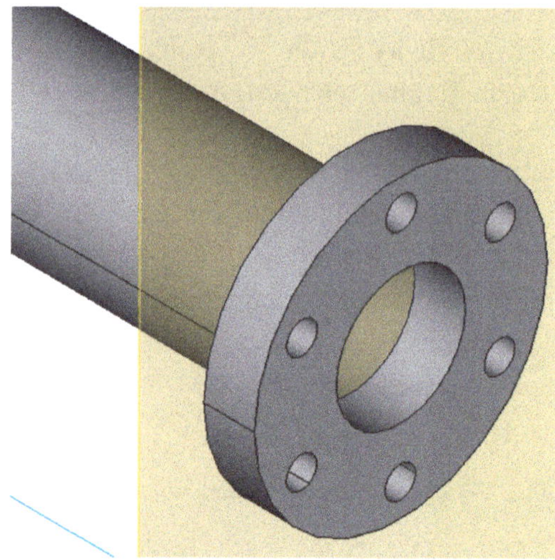

15. Create the *Pad*, *Pocket*, and *Polar pattern* features on the other end of the model.

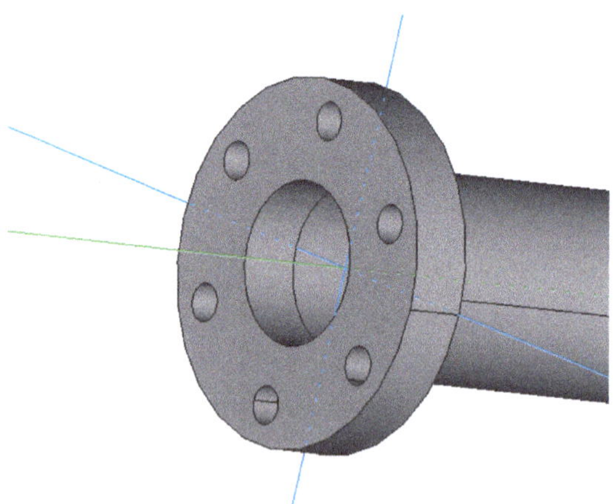

16. Click **File > Save** on the menu bar. Next, type C6_example1 in the **File name** box and click the **Save** button.

17. Click **File > Close** to close the document.

Questions

1. What are the section orientation options?
2. How to create a *Pipe* feature between two cross-sections?
3. List any two options to define the size of the helix features.

Exercises

Exercise1

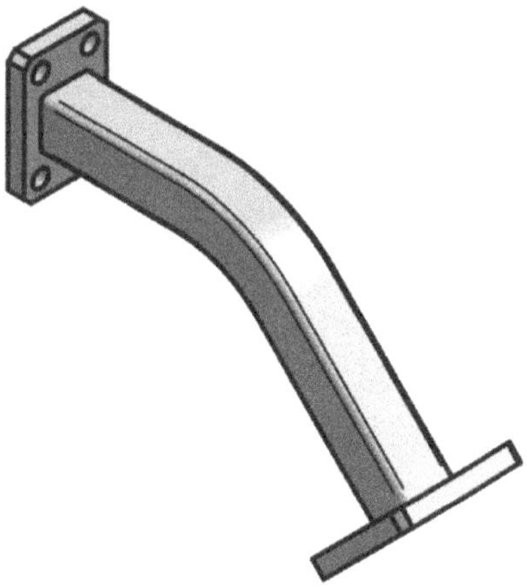

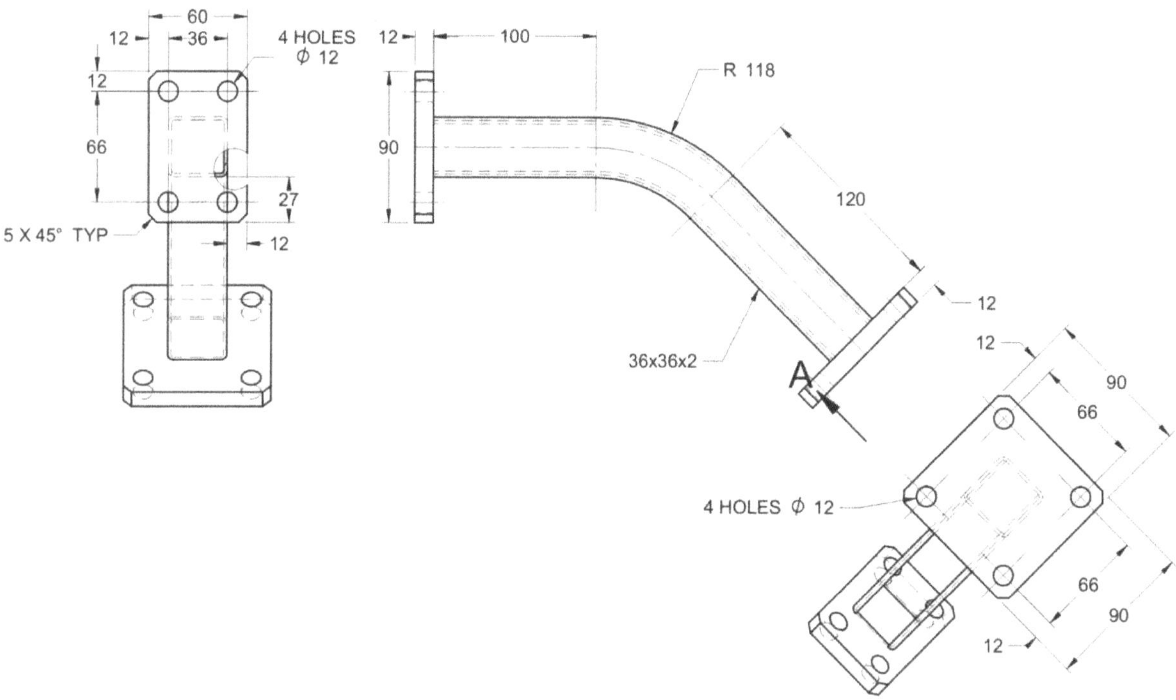

Chapter 7: Loft Features

The **Additive Loft** command is one of the advanced commands available in FreeCAD 1.0 that allows you to create simple as well as complex shapes. A loft in 3D modeling is like connecting two shapes, sort of like linking point A to point B. It's the software's job to fill in all the in-between parts, making it smooth and seamless.

Now, remember when I mentioned using just two profiles for a loft? It's a bit like drawing a straight line with a ruler. But things get more fascinating when you have more than two profiles. The software blends from one to the next, like your hand-drawn line turning into a graceful curve.

Choosing between using a loft or a sweep in 3D modeling can pose a challenge, especially for those starting out. While these features share some similarities, your decision-making becomes more straightforward with experience.

Here's a basic rule of thumb to assist you:

1. **Sweep:** If you can control the cross-sectional shape of your feature by tweaking a single sketch's dimensions, opt for a sweep. Sweeps work well when you can maintain consistent control over the feature's cross-section using a single sketch.

2. **Loft:** Conversely, if your feature's cross-section undergoes significant changes or takes on varying shapes along its length, a loft is generally the better choice. Lofts provide greater flexibility as they enable you to precisely define the cross-section at various points along the feature.

3. **Loft for Complex Shapes:** If you require a specific shape at both ends and potentially in the middle of your feature, a loft provides the precision to craft your feature exactly as needed at any location.

4. **Sweep for Outlines:** When the outer shape of your feature is of paramount importance compared to the cross-section, a sweep is often the preferred option. Sweeps also come in handy when the path or trajectory that your feature follows holds significant importance.

The topics covered in this chapter are:

- *Additive Loft*
- *Subtractive Loft*

Additive Loft

The **Additive Loft** command enables the creation of a loft feature between different profiles. To initiate the lofting process, you should begin by creating two or more profiles on separate planes. These planes can either run parallel or be positioned perpendicular to each other.

Once your profiles are ready, proceed as follows:

1. Access the **Additive Loft**  icon, which can be found on the **Part Design Modeling** toolbar. Alternatively, you can navigate to **Part Design** on menu bar, then select **Create an additive feature**, and finally choose **Additive Loft**.
2. After selecting the **Additive Loft** command, a dialog box will appear. Start by choosing the first cross-section you want to use for the loft. Once selected, click **OK**.
3. Click the Add Section button and continue by selecting the second cross-section for the loft. You can also pick the profiles directly from the graphics window to define the loft. After making your selections, click **OK** to confirm and complete the loft creation.

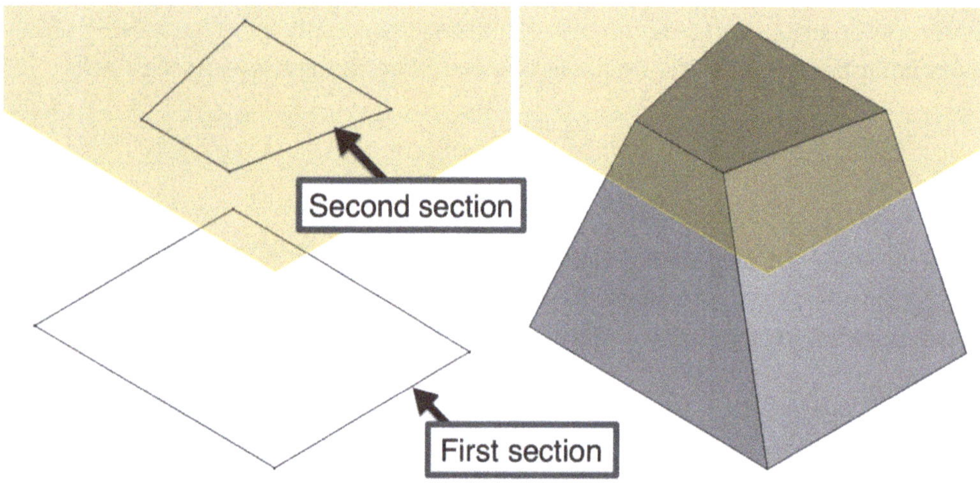

Ruled Surface

When you opt for the **Ruled Surface** option in FreeCAD, it connects the corresponding points on your chosen cross-sections using straight lines. This process results in a direct, linear transition from one cross-section to the next. The resulting shape is commonly referred to as a "ruled surface."

Ruled surfaces are characterized by their simplicity and efficiency because they are composed of straight lines or linear segments. These surfaces are particularly valuable when you need to create geometric features like prisms, cylinders, or other linear shapes.

However, it's important to note that the **Ruled Surface** option may not be the best choice when you're aiming to generate features with highly organic or curvilinear forms.

Additionally, keep in mind that for this option to take effect, you must select more than two cross-sections. This selection of multiple cross-sections is necessary to fully appreciate the impact of the Ruled Surface feature.

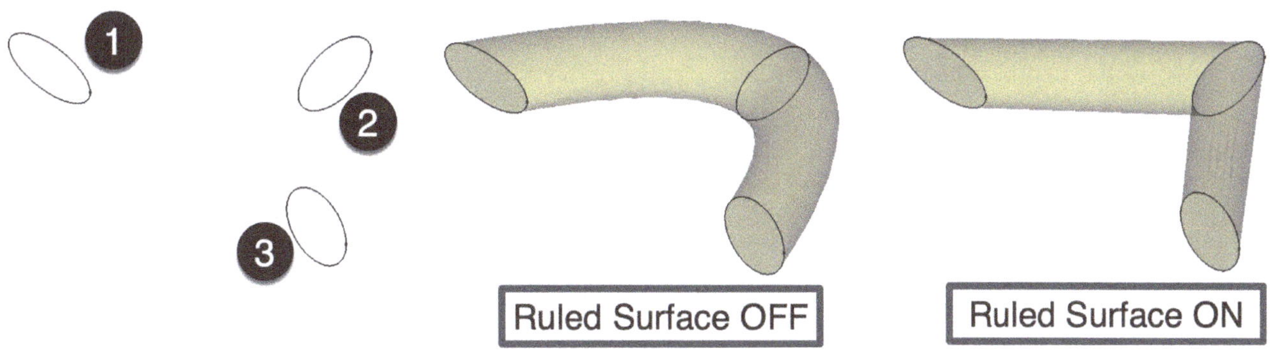

Closed

In FreeCAD, you can create a closed loft to seamlessly connect multiple shapes. Here's how:

1. **Select Sketches**: Start by selecting the initial sketch. Then, use the **Add Section** button to choose each subsequent sketch that defines the shapes you wish to connect. Ensure you select at least three sketches as your base.
2. **Enable the Closed Option**: In the **Loft Parameters** panel, activate the **Closed** option. This directs FreeCAD to generate a loft that seamlessly connects back to itself, creating a fully enclosed, watertight shape from the selected sketches.
3. **Confirm**: Click **OK** to finalize and execute the lofting process. This will produce a complete, closed lofted shape.

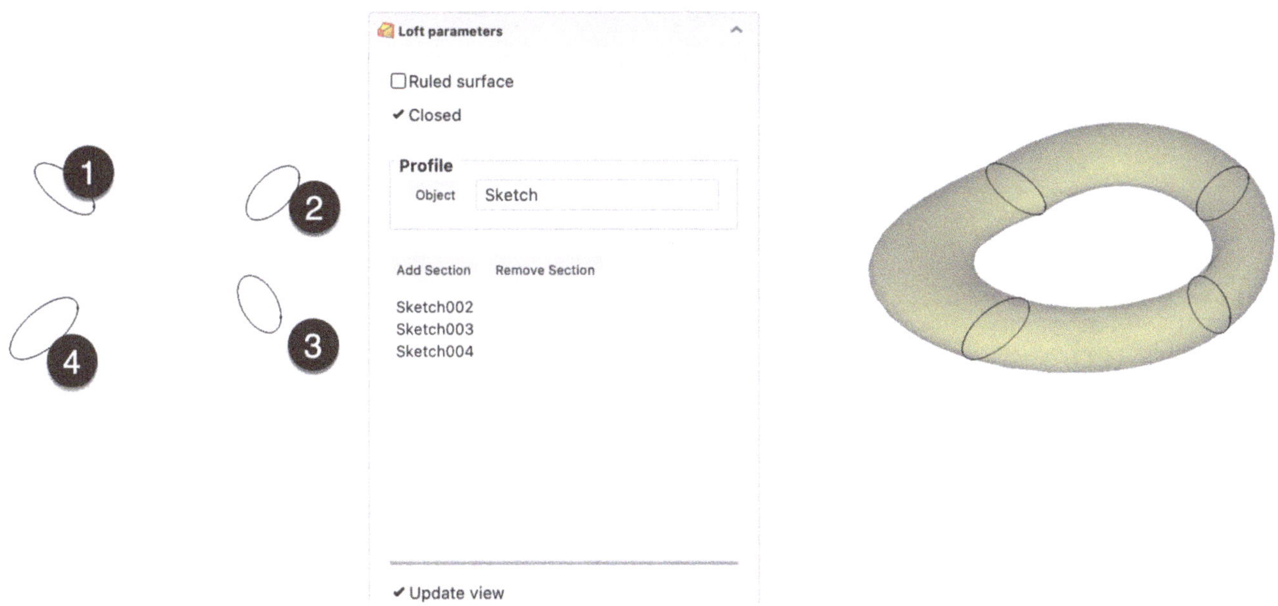

Subtractive Loft

In a manner similar to other standard features like extrude, revolve, and pipe, the loft feature in FreeCAD serves the purpose of adding or removing material. For material removal, you can effectively employ the **Subtractive Loft** command. Here's how you can do it:

1. Start by navigating to the **Part Design Modeling** toolbar, where you'll find the **Subtractive Loft** icon. Alternatively, you can access it through the menu bar by selecting "**Part Design**," then "**Create a subtractive feature**," and finally, "**Subtractive Loft**."
2. Once you've selected the **Subtractive Loft** command, the next step is to choose the initial cross-section. After making your selection, click "**OK**."
3. Now, you can proceed to add further sections to define the shape of the lofted cutout. To do this, click the "**Add section**" button and select the second cross-section.
4. Continue using the "**Add section**" button to pick the remaining cross-sections that collectively define the loft cutout.
5. Finally, once you've selected all the necessary cross-sections, click "**OK**." This action will execute the loft cutout operation, precisely creating the desired subtractive feature in your design.

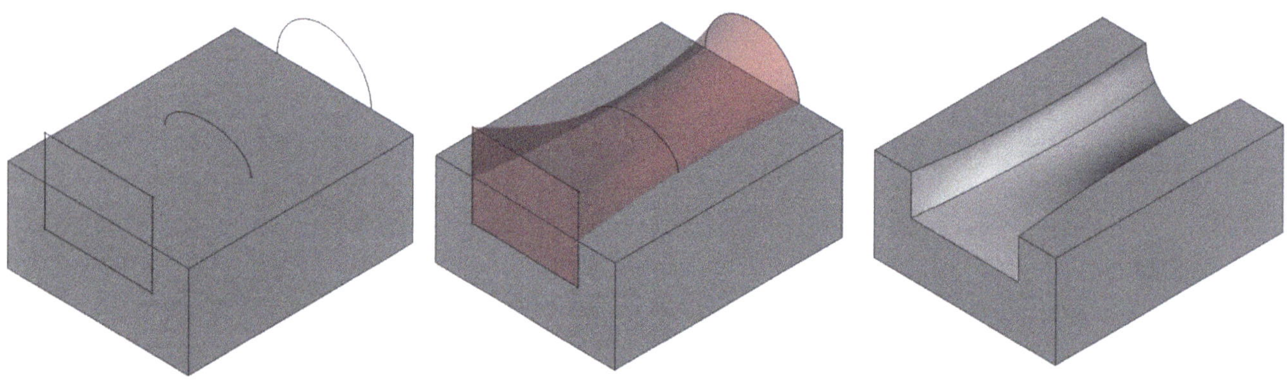

Best Practices

Plan Your Design: Before you begin, make sure you have a clear design plan in mind. Sketch the profiles that you intend to loft between to save time and avoid design errors.

Profile Sketching: Be sure that the profile sketches have the same number of vertices and are consistently oriented to prevent twisting in the loft.

Maintain Tangency: To achieve smooth transitions, ensure that there is tangency or curvature continuity between the profiles and guide curves. This minimizes abrupt changes in the shape.

Simplify Sketches: Keep your sketches as simple as possible. Complex geometric elements in your profiles can make the lofting process more intricate and prone to issues.

Cautions:

Profile Compatibility: Exercise caution when lofting between profiles with significantly different shapes or dimensions. It can result in sudden jumps or intersections, which may affect the quality of your design.

Tips for Specific Types of Parts:

Plastic Parts:

- Consider incorporating draft angles in your design to aid in the ejection of parts from molds.

Casted Parts:

- Account for the shrinkage that occurs during the casting process when designing lofted features.
- Make sure the geometry is conducive to the casting process without creating areas where molten material might get trapped.

Forged Parts:

- Plan for the deformation that takes place during the forging process, as it can affect the shape of lofted features.

Machined Parts:

- Lofted features are ideal for parts with complex contours, such as aircraft components.
- Remember that machining intricate designs can be time-consuming.

3D Printed Parts:

- Be mindful of the limitations of your 3D printer, such as minimum feature sizes and support requirements.
- Lofted features can create unique shapes suitable for 3D printing, but ensure they are feasible for your specific printing setup.

For all cases, consider testing your design by creating prototypes or conducting simulations to identify potential issues like stress concentrations, material flow, and manufacturability. FreeCAD offers simulation tools to help analyze the behavior of your designs under different conditions. Save your work frequently to avoid data loss in case of software crashes or other unexpected incidents. Building proficiency with lofted features in FreeCAD comes with practice and experience.

Tutorial 1

In this example, you create the part shown below.

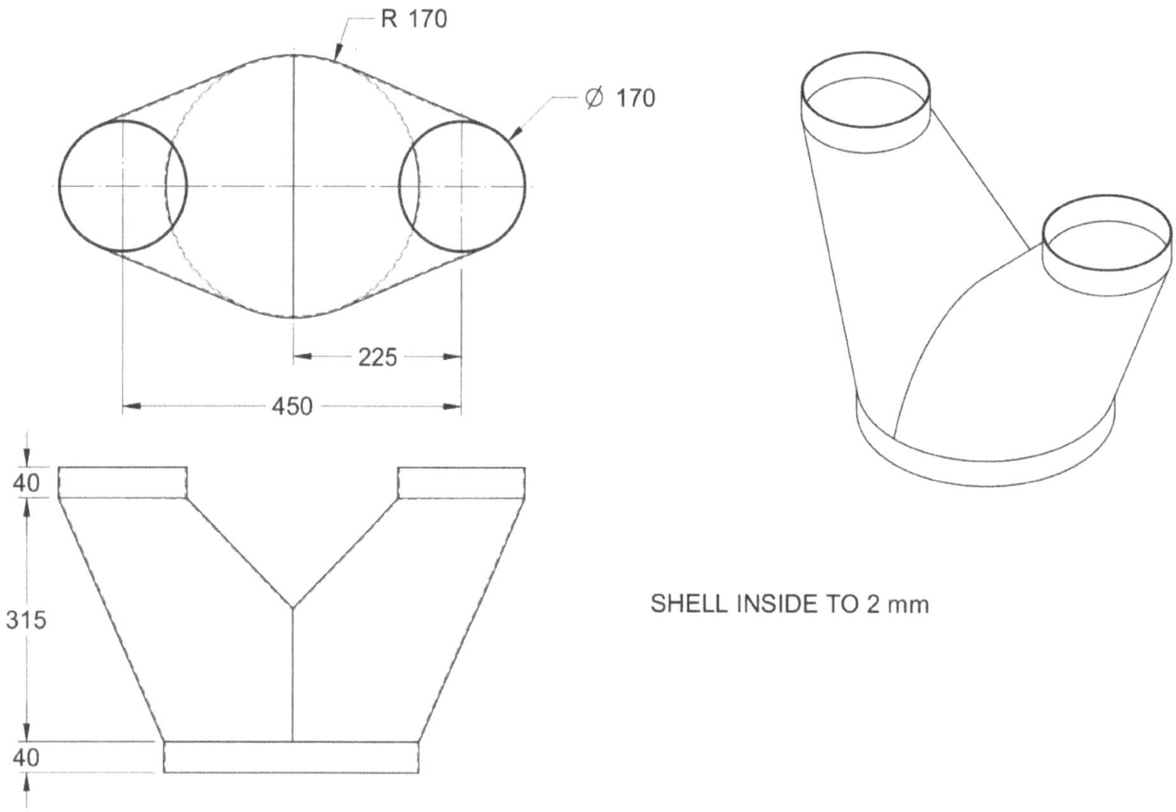

Creating a New document

1. Click **FreeCAD** on the desktop to start.
2. On the menu bar, click **File > New**; it creates a new document.
3. On the **Workbench** toolbar, select **Workbench** drop-down > **Part Design**.
4. Click **Edit > Preferences** on the **Menu** bar (or) click **FreeCAD 1.0 > Preferences** on title bar, if you are working on MacOS; the **Preferences** dialog appears on the screen.
5. Click the General tab and select **Default unit system > Standard (mm/kg/s/degree)**.
6. Select **Number of decimals > 2** and click **OK** on the **Preferences** dialog.

Creating a Loft Feature

1. On the **Part Design Helper** toolbar, click the **Create Sketch** icon. Select the XY_Plane and click **OK**.
2. Draw two circles of **338** and **340** mm diameters. Next, click the **Close** button on the **Tasks** panel.

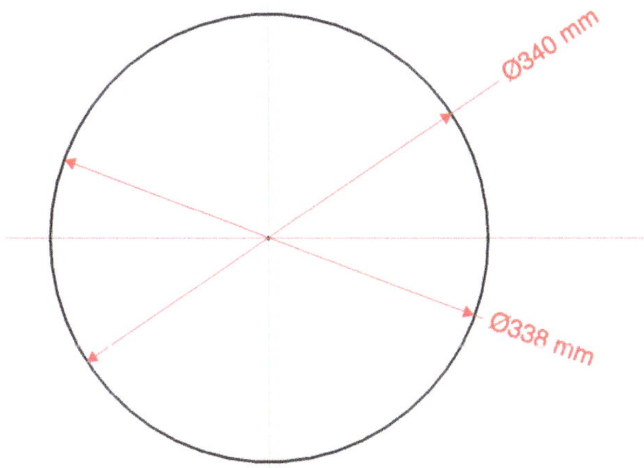

3. Click the **Model** panel. Next, expand the **Origin** node and select the **XY-Plane**.
4. On the **Part Design Helper** tool, click the **Create a new datum plane**  tool.
5. Type **315** in the **Z** box of the **Attachment Offset** section. Next, click **OK**.

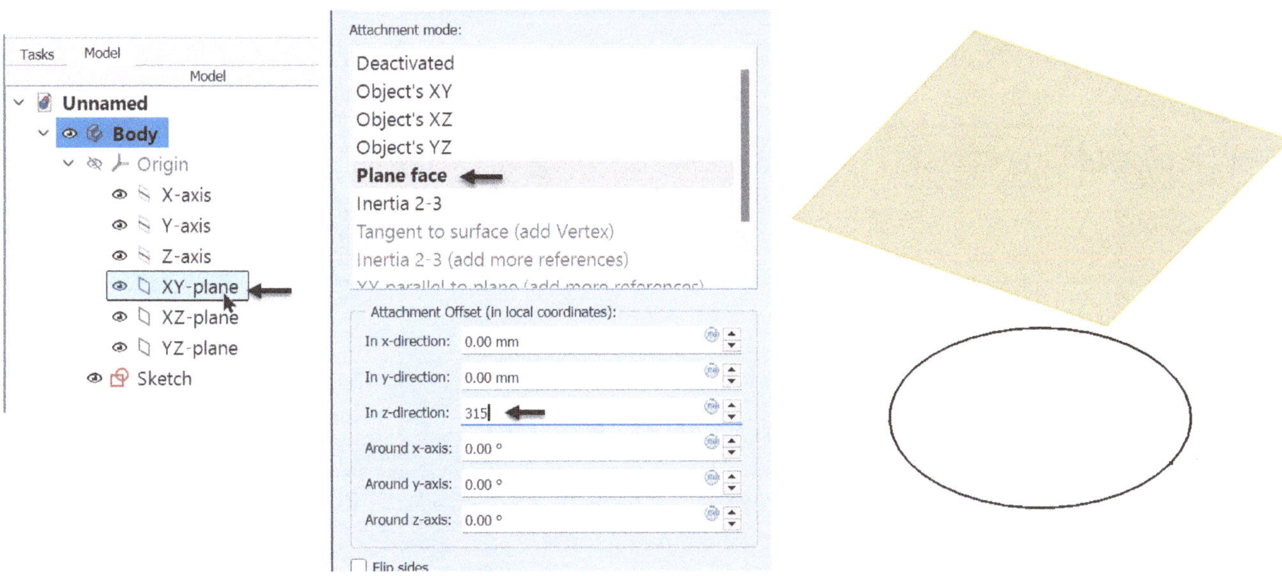

6. Click the **OK** button on the **Tasks** panel.
7. Select the newly created datum plane and click the **Create Sketch** icon on the **Part Design Helper** toolbar.
8. Draw two circles of **168** and **170** mm diameters and add constraints to them, as shown.
9. Click the **Close** button on the **Tasks** panel. Click in the graphics window to deselect the circle.

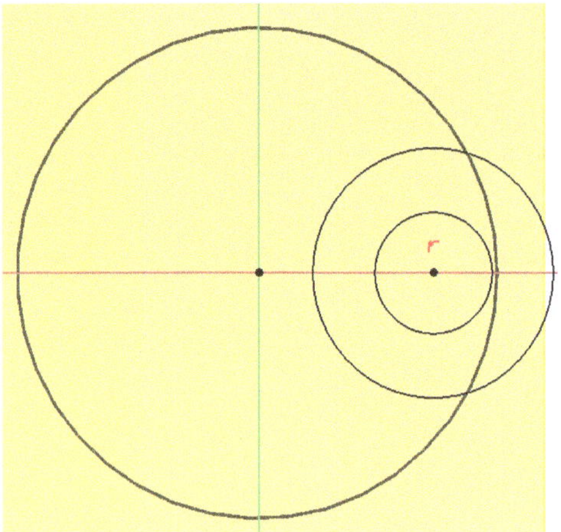

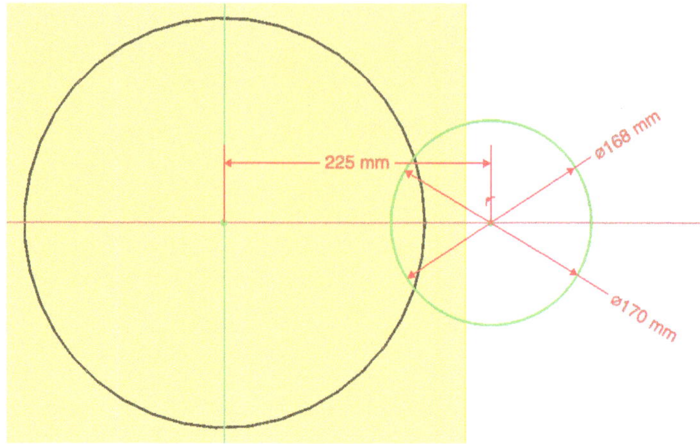

10. On the **Part Design Modeling** toolbar, click the **Loft** icon. Select **Sketch** from the **Select feature** section of the **Tasks** panel. Next, click **OK**.
11. Click the **Add section** button on the **Loft parameters** section and select the circle from the graphics window.
12. Click **OK**.

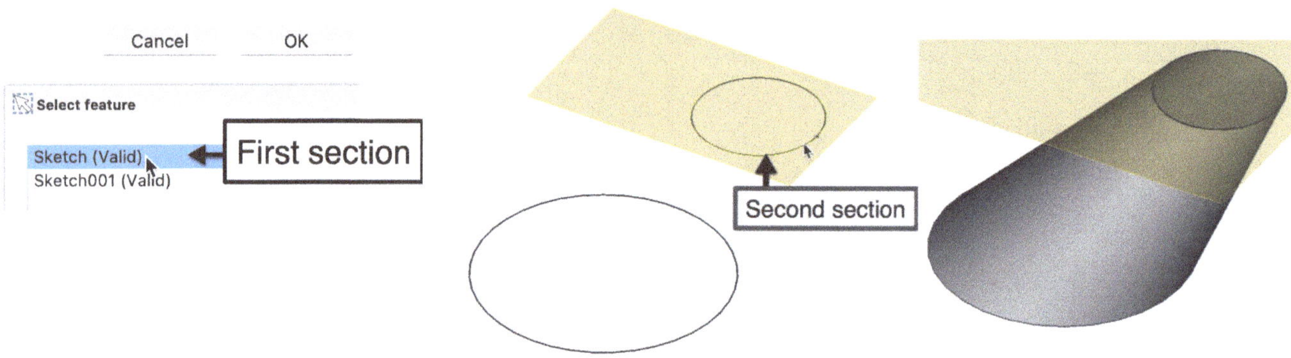

13. In the **Tasks** panel, expand the **AdditiveLoft** feature and select the first sketch.
14. Click the **Pad** icon on the **Part Design Modeling** toolbar. Next, check the **Reversed** option.
15. Enter **40** in the **Length** box and click **OK** to create a pad feature.

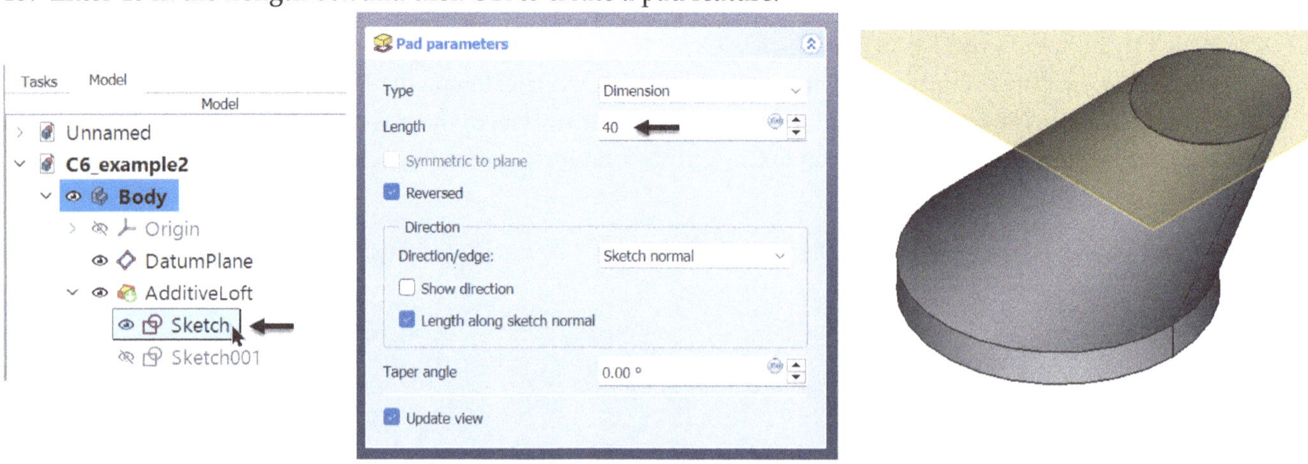

16. In the **Tasks** panel, expand the **AdditiveLoft** feature and select the second sketch.

17. Click the **Pad**  icon on the **Part Design Modeling** toolbar. Next, enter **40** in the **Length** box and click **OK**.

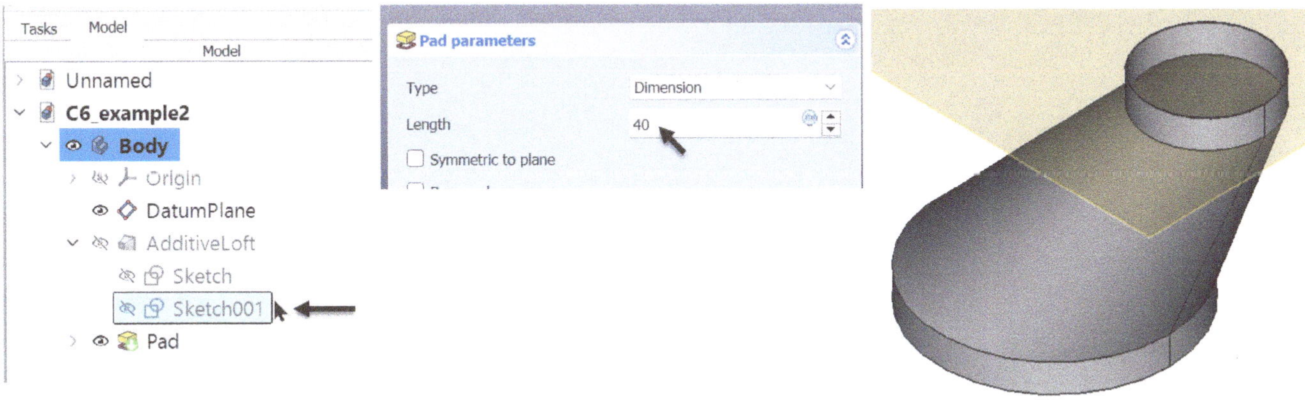

Mirroring the Loft and Pad features

1. Select the **AdditiveLoft** feature from Model panel or from graphics window.
2. On the **Part Design Modeling** toolbar, click the **Mirrored**  icon.
3. Click the **Add feature** button on the **Mirrored parameters** section. Next, select the *Pad* feature from the graphics window.
4. Select the **Base YZ plane** option from the **Plane** drop-down
5. Click **OK** to mirror the *Loft* and *Pad* features.

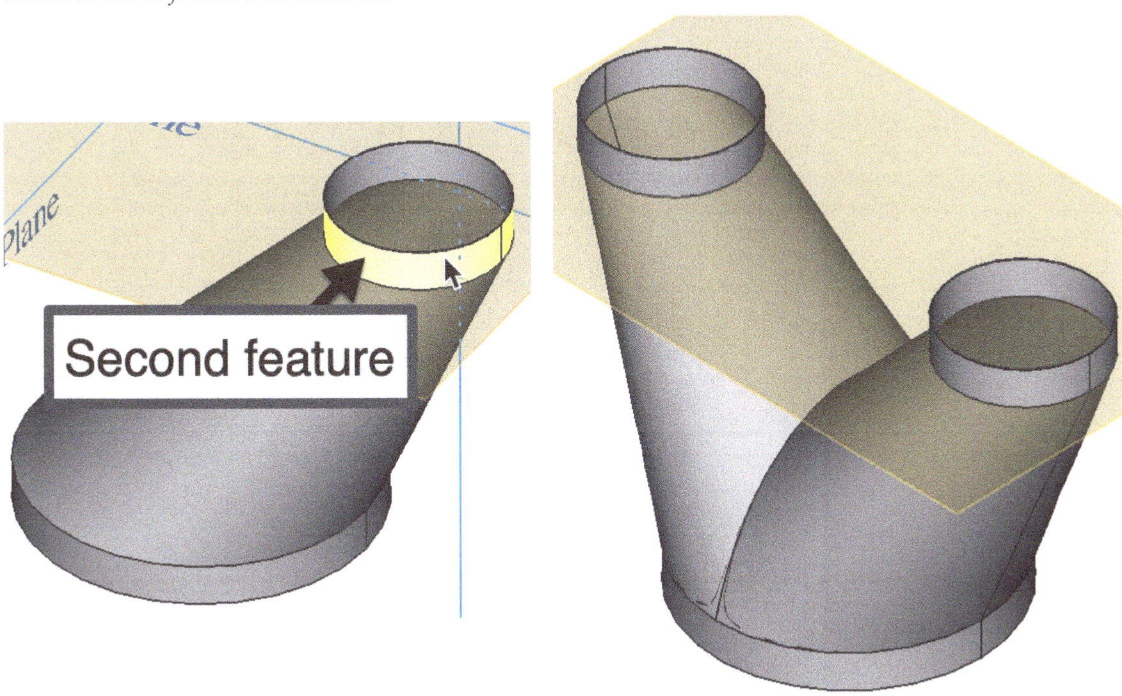

6. Click **File > Save** on the Menu bar. Next, enter C6_example2 in the **File name** box. Click **Save** to save the document
7. Click **File > Close** to close the document.

Questions

1. Describe the procedure to create a *Loft* feature.
2. What is the use of the **Ruled Surface** option?

Exercises

Exercise 1

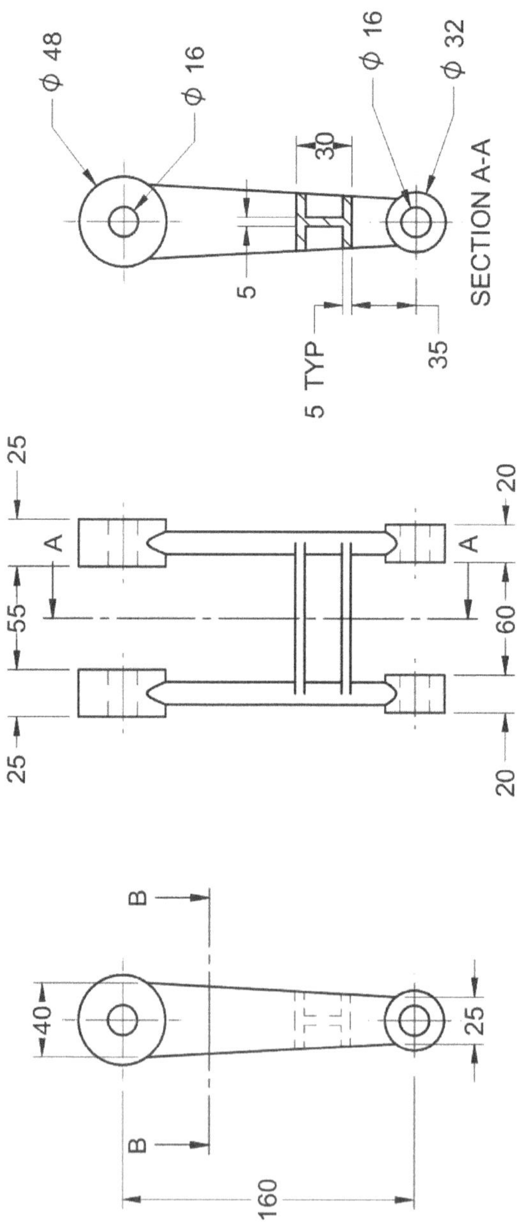

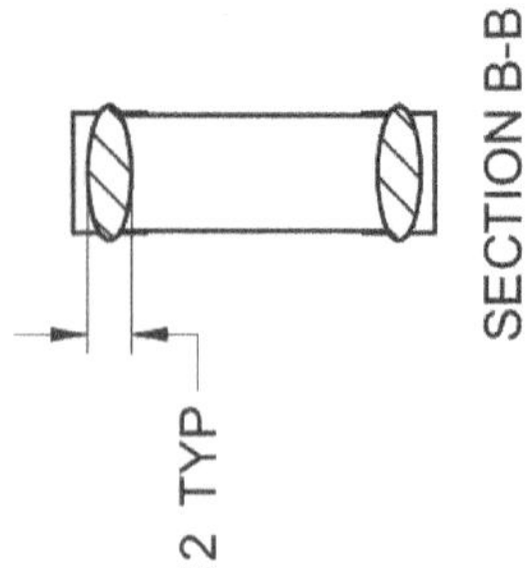

Chapter 8: Modifying Parts

In the design journey, it's important to understand that achieving the final model doesn't typically happen on the first try. Instead, it's common to refine and tweak existing parts to reach the desired part geometry. This iterative process is a fundamental aspect of successful design.

In this chapter, we'll explore a range of commands and techniques that will empower you to make these necessary changes to a part. By the end, you'll be well-equipped with the skills to modify and enhance your designs, allowing you to fine-tune your work until it perfectly matches your vision.

The topics covered in this chapter are:

- *Edit Sketches*
- *Edit Features*
- *Deleting Sketches*
- *Attachment Editor*

Edit Sketches

Sketches serve as the foundational blueprints for creating 3D geometry. They are crucial in controlling the size and shape of your 3D objects. When you need to make changes to your 3D geometry, it often starts with editing these sketches.

Making Changes through Sketch Editing: To modify your 3D geometry, the process usually involves tweaking the underlying sketches. Here's how you can do it:

1. **Open the Model Panel**: Go to the **Model** panel, where all the features of your 3D object are listed.
2. **Find the Feature**: Look for the feature linked to the part of the geometry you want to modify. Expand it to see its details.
3. **Edit the Sketch**: Inside the feature, locate the sketch you want to change. Right-click on it and select "**Edit Sketch**" to open it for editing.
4. **Adjust the Sketch**: Modify the sketch as needed—change dimensions, add or remove elements, or tweak relationships between components.
5. **Save Changes**: Once done, click "**Close**" in the **Tasks** panel to save your edits.

Immediate Geometry Update: As you close the sketch edit, watch closely. You'll notice that the changes you've made to the sketch translate instantly into your 3D part geometry. This immediate update ensures that your 3D object accurately reflects the modifications you've applied to the sketch. It's a real-time connection between your 2D sketches and the 3D world, making the design process smooth and dynamic.

So, whether you're fine-tuning the contours of a car's body or designing intricate architectural details, the ability to edit sketches and see the immediate impact on your 3D geometry empowers you to create, iterate, and perfect your designs efficiently.

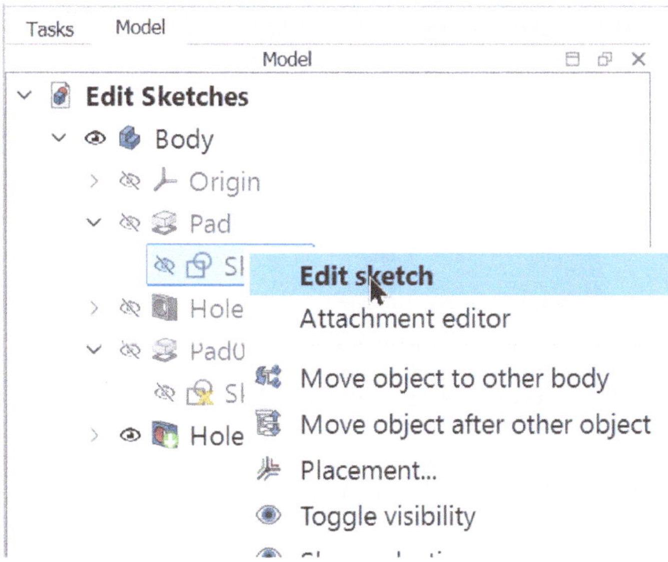

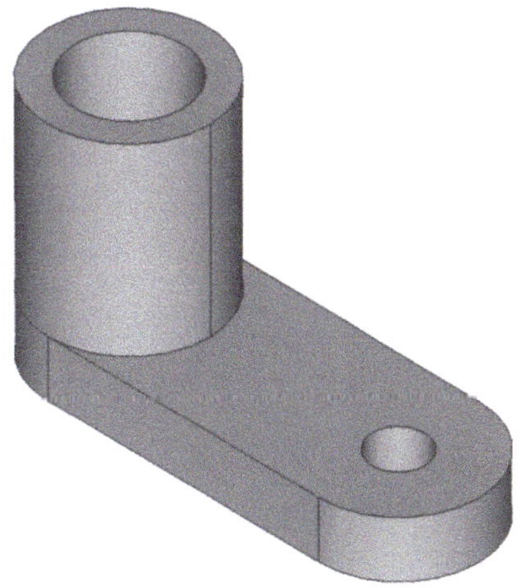

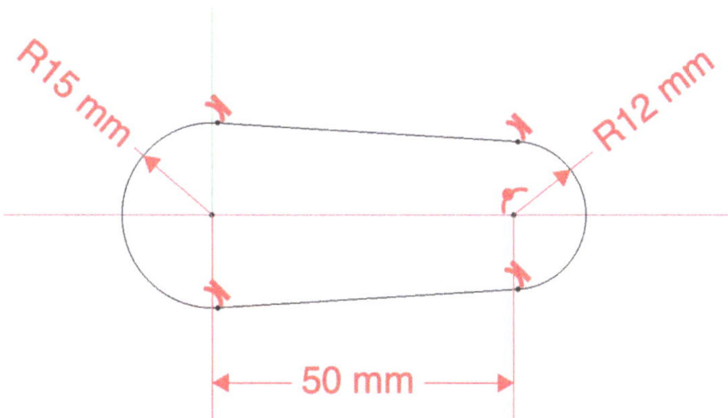

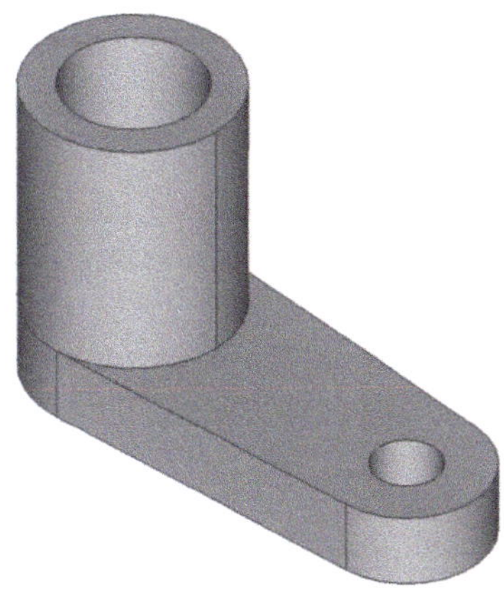

Edit Feature

Features serve as the fundamental components that shape the geometry of your model. When you want to make changes to a specific feature, follow these steps for a seamless process:

1. Right-click on the feature you wish to modify.
2. From the context menu that appears, select **Edit (Feature name)**. This action triggers the parameters panel associated with the chosen feature to open. This panel is where you'll adjust the various settings that define the feature.
3. Now, take your time to make the necessary adjustments to the feature's parameters based on your design requirements. You can tweak dimensions, angles, or any other relevant characteristics that need modification.
4. Once you've fine-tuned the parameters to your satisfaction, simply click the "**OK**" button. Your changes will take effect immediately.

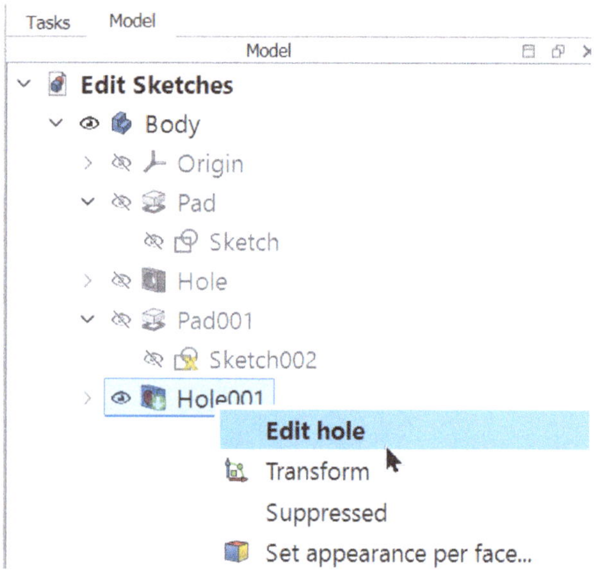

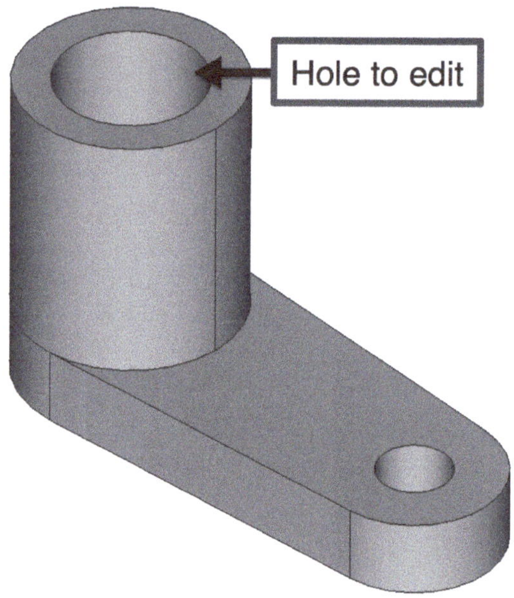

Deleting Sketches

In 3D modeling, particularly in FreeCAD, the "**Delete**" command should be used carefully, especially when dealing with sketches. Deleting sketches can cause problems in your model and its references. Here's why:

1. **Loss of References**: FreeCAD often loses references easily. If you delete a sketch that other sketches depend on, those dependent sketches may become overdefined or unsolvable, leading to errors in your model.
2. **Editing Challenges**: Deleting a sketch can make future edits harder. It's usually better to keep the original sketch and modify it as needed, rather than deleting it and starting over. This keeps your model more flexible and easier to manage.
3. **Unintended Effects**: Deleting a sketch can have ripple effects. For example, removing a line from a parent sketch and replacing it with a new one can cause issues for dependent features. They might still reference the original line, leading to rebuild errors.

In summary, whether you're using FreeCAD or other 3D modeling software, **sketch management is crucial**. Use the "**Delete**" command sparingly. Focus on preserving sketches and their constraints to maintain a stable modeling process. This will save time and prevent unnecessary complications. If you must delete a sketch, follow the steps provided next.

1. **Locate the Sketch**: Go to the **Model panel**, where all the features of your 3D object are listed.
2. **Expand the Feature**: Find the feature linked to the geometry you want to edit. Expand it to see the associated sketches.
3. **Delete the Sketch**: Select the sketch you want to remove, then either choose **Edit > Delete** from the menu bar or right-click and select **Delete**. Confirm by clicking **Yes**.

Attachment Editor

The **Attachment Editor** option is a useful feature that allows you to modify the attachment plane of your sketch in a smooth and efficient manner. This comes in handy when you want to change the plane on which your sketch is originally created. For instance, if your sketch was initially made on the XY-plane but you now prefer it on the YZ-plane, here's how you can easily achieve that:

1. Begin by navigating to the **Model** panel. Once there, expand the feature that contains the sketch you wish to modify.
2. With your feature selected, right-click on the corresponding sketch, and a context menu will appear. In this menu, locate and select the **Attachment Editor** option.
3. On the **Tasks** panel, Within the '**Attachment**' section, you'll notice a '**Plane**' button. Click on it to initiate the plane selection process.

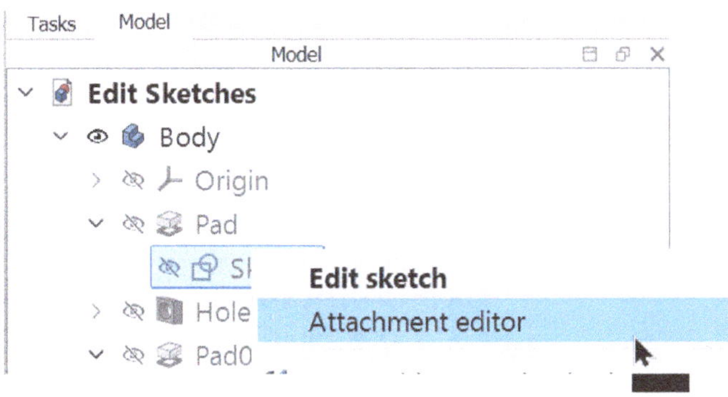

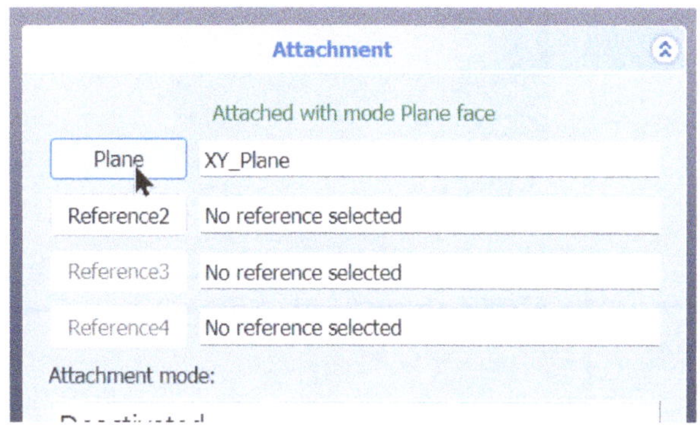

4. Now, switch back to the **Model** panel, and expand the '**Origin**' node. This is where you'll find various plane options that you can choose from.
5. Select the '**YZ-plane**' from the tree structure. This tells the system that you want your sketch to be attached to the YZ-plane.
6. To complete the process, head over to the '**Tasks**' tab and simply click '**OK**'.

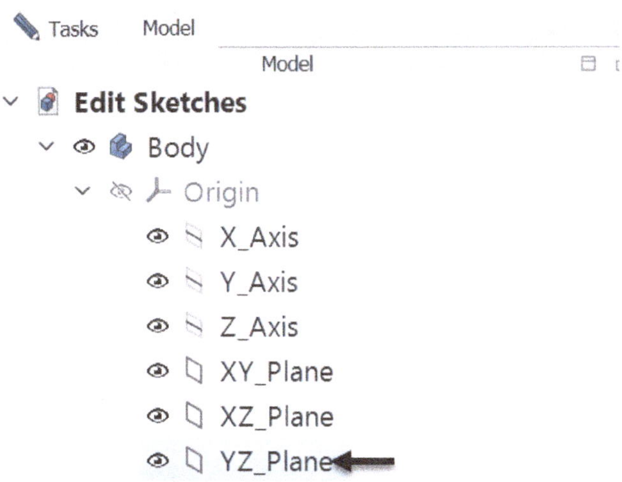

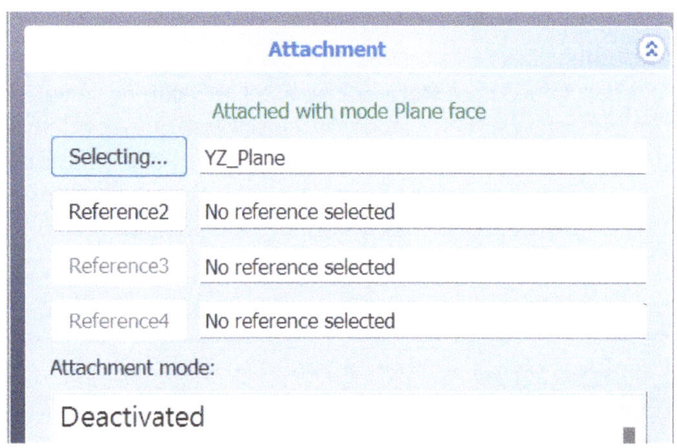

7. Once you've made this adjustment, you can ensure that your model reflects these changes by clicking the '**Refresh**' button found on the **Edit** toolbar. This update will be immediately visible in the graphics window.

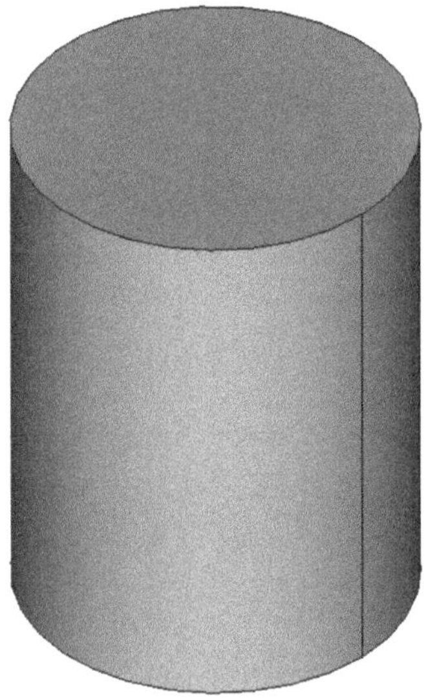

Sketch attached to XY-Plane

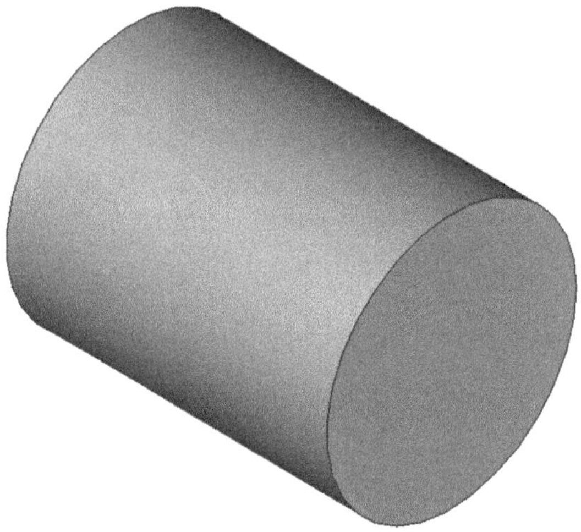

Sketch attached to YZ-Plane

Editing sketch planes is a fundamental task in FreeCAD, but it requires careful attention to ensure efficiency and avoid issues. Here are some best practices, cautions, and tips to guide you:

Best Practices

1. **Choose the Right Plane**: When creating a new sketch, select a plane that aligns logically with your design. This ensures proper orientation and simplifies the assembly process.
2. **Use Standard Planes**: Whenever possible, sketch on standard planes (e.g., XY, XZ, YZ). These serve as consistent reference points, making it easier to adjust or reposition sketches later as your design evolves.

Cautions

1. **Avoid Lost References**: FreeCAD can be sensitive to changes in sketch planes, especially if they are referenced by other sketches. Modifying or deleting a sketch plane may cause over-defined or unsolved sketches, leading to errors. Proceed with caution.
2. **Plan for Future Edits**: While editing a sketch plane might solve an immediate issue, it can complicate future modifications. Retain the original sketch plane and make adjustments as needed, rather than deleting and starting over.

Additional Tip

Keep clear documentation of your changes. This helps you track your design decisions and makes it easier to revisit and modify your model later.

Tutorial 1 (Inches)

In this example, you create the part shown below and then modify it.

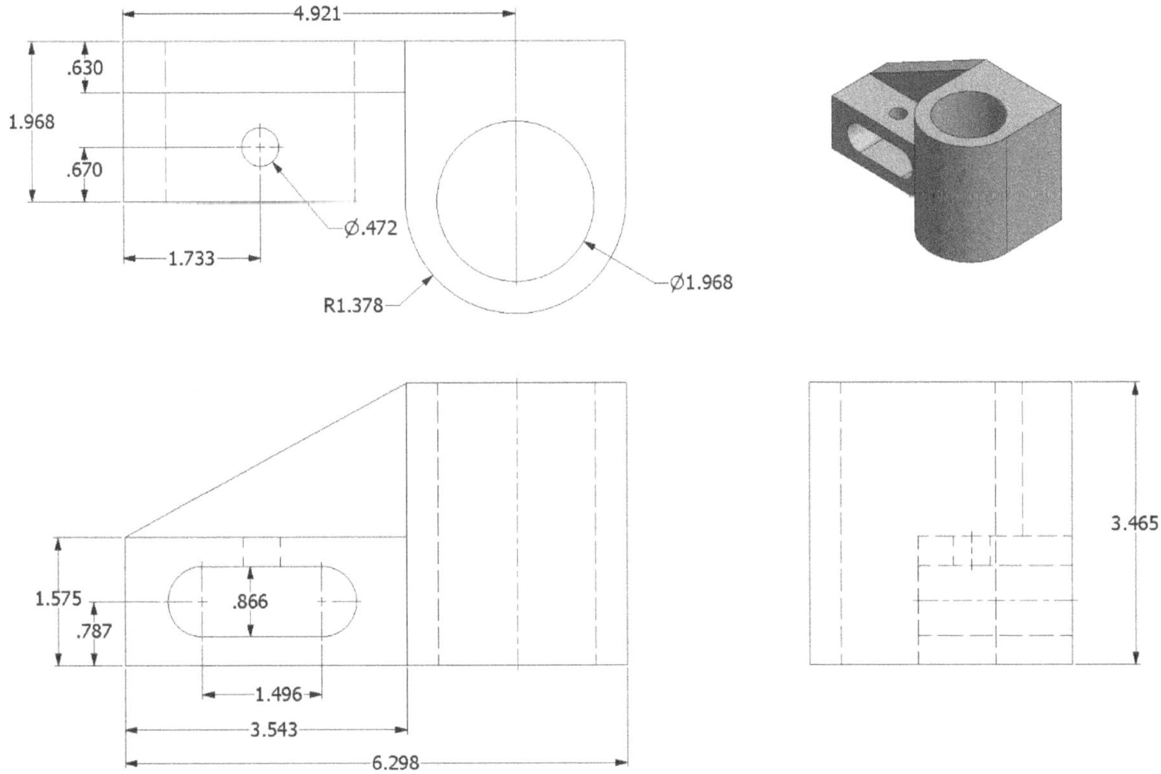

Creating a New document

1. Click **FreeCAD 1.0** on the desktop to start.
2. On the menu bar, click **File > New**; it creates a new document.
3. On the **Workbench** toolbar, select **Workbench** drop-down **> Part Design**.
4. Click **Edit > Preferences** on the Menu bar (or) click **FreeCAD 1.0 > Preferences** on title bar, if you are working on MacOS; the **Preferences** dialog appears on the screen.
5. Click the General tab and select **Default unit system > Imperial decimal**.
6. Select **Number of decimals > 3** and click **OK** on the **Preferences** dialog.
7. Create the part using the tools and commands available in FreeCAD, as shown in the figure. You can also download this file from the companion website.

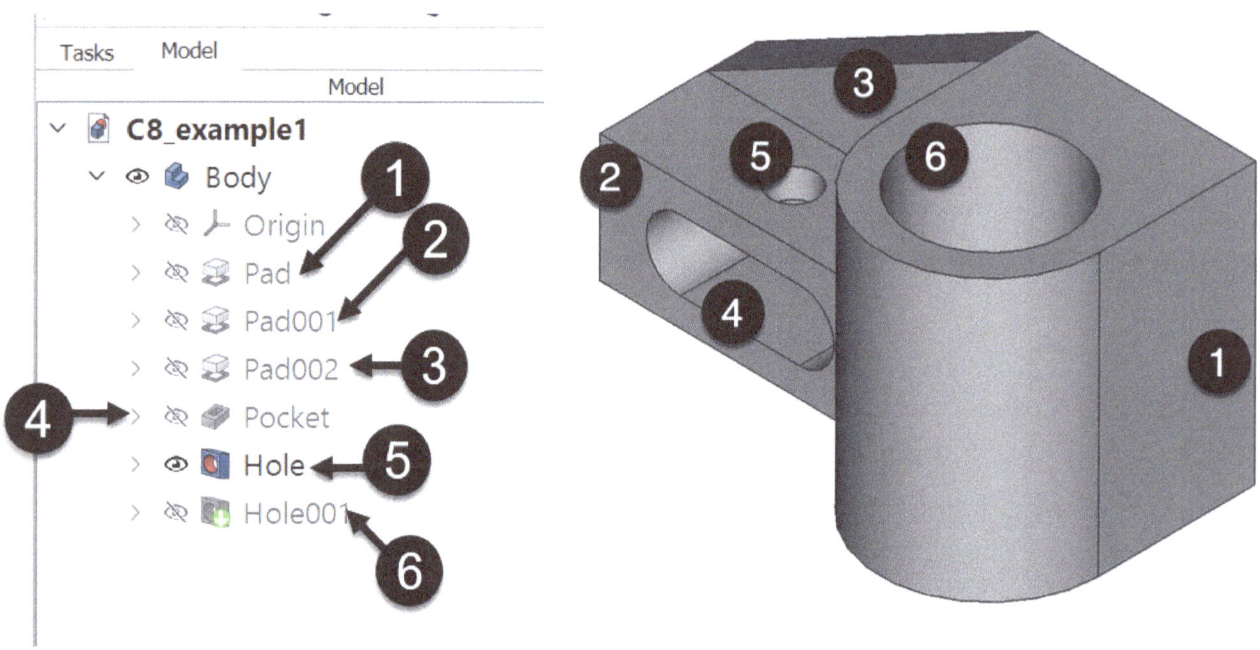

Editing a Feature

1. Click the right mouse button on the **Hole001** in the **Model** panel. Next, select **Edit hole** from the menu.
2. On the **Hole parameters** section, enter **1.378** in the **Diameter** box.
3. Select **Hole Cut Type > Counterbore**. Next, enter **1.968** and **0.787** in the **Diameter** and **Depth** boxes available under the **Hole cut** section, respectively.
4. Click **OK**.

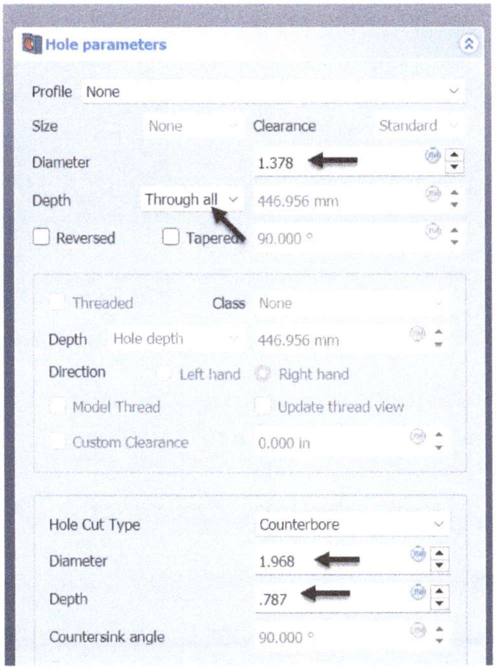

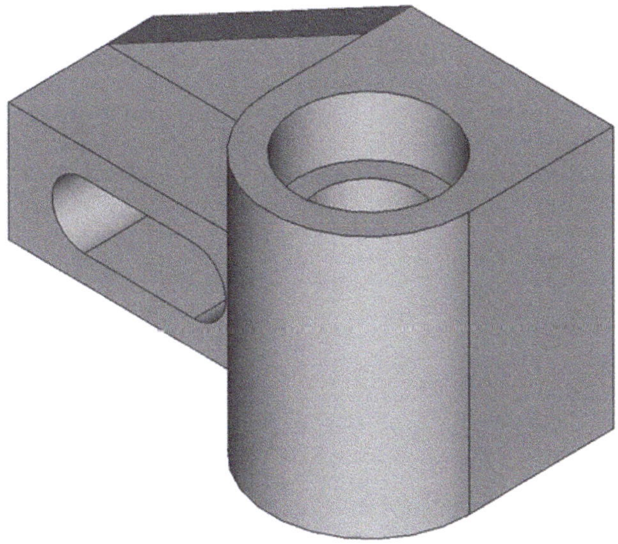

Editing Sketches

1. Expand the **Pad001** feature in the **Model** tab of the **Combo View** panel. Next, right-click on the *Sketch001* in and select **Edit sketch**. Modify the horizontal dimension of the sketch, as shown. Click **Close** on the **Combo View** panel.

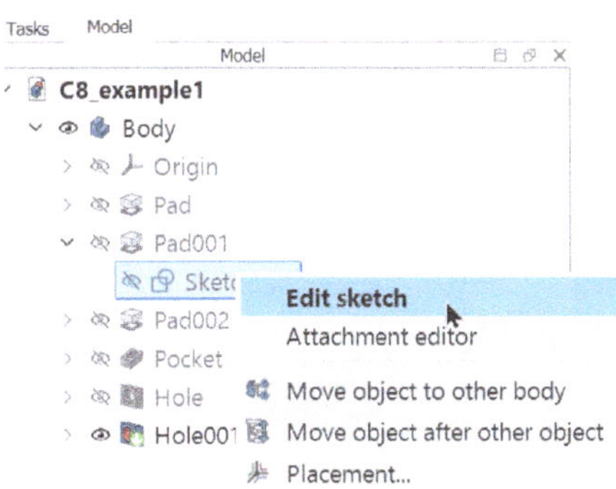

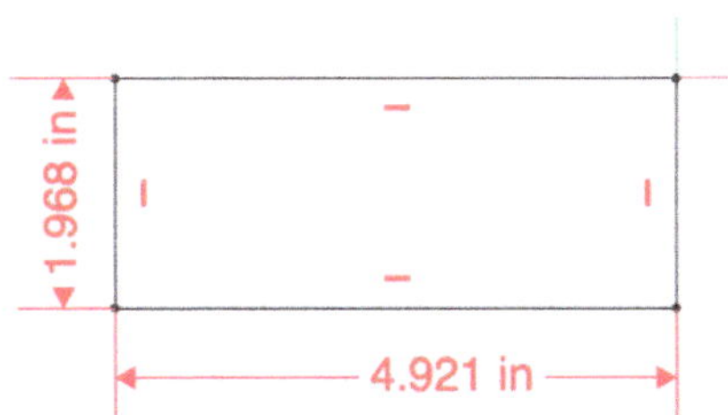

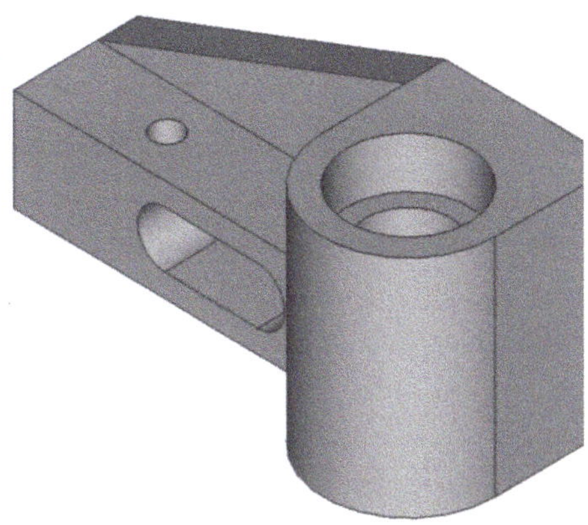

2. Expand the **Pocket** feature and right the mouse button on *Sketch003*. Next, select **Edit sketch**.

3. Click the **Create external geometry**  icon on the **Sketcher tools** toolbar. Next, select the left vertical edge.
4. Delete the horizontal distance constraint of the slot, as shown. Next, add a horizontal distance constraint between the center point of the left arc.

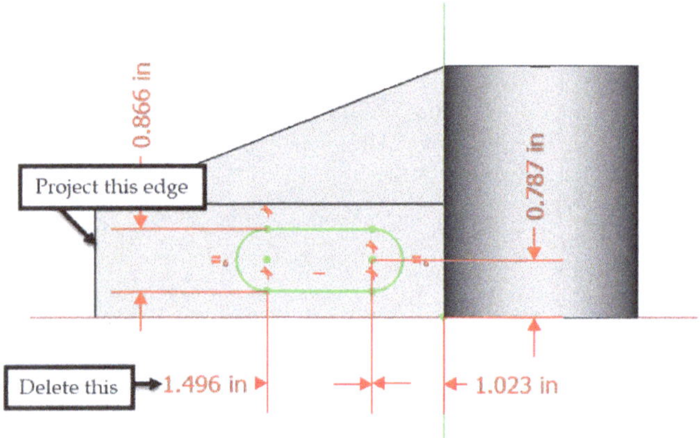

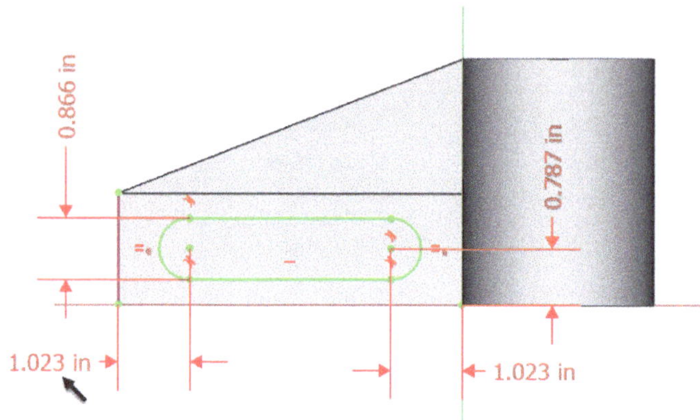

5. Delete the vertical distance constraint between the centerpoint of the right arc and the origin point.
6. Click the **Create polyline** icon on the **Sketcher geometries** toolbar. Next, select the top left corner point.
7. Select the centerpoint of the left arc. Next, select the bottom left corner point.
8. Click the **Constrain equal** icon on the **Sketcher constraints** toolbar. Next, select the two newly created lines. Right-click in the graphics window to deactivate the **Constrain equal** command.

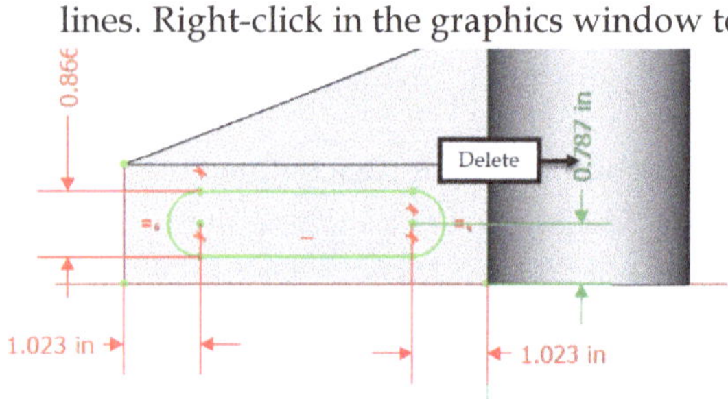

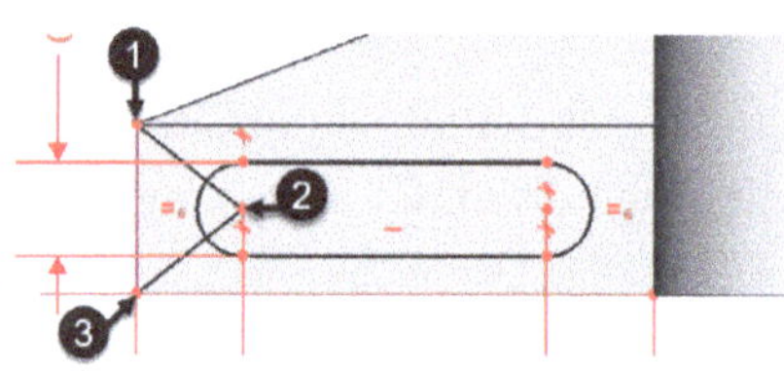

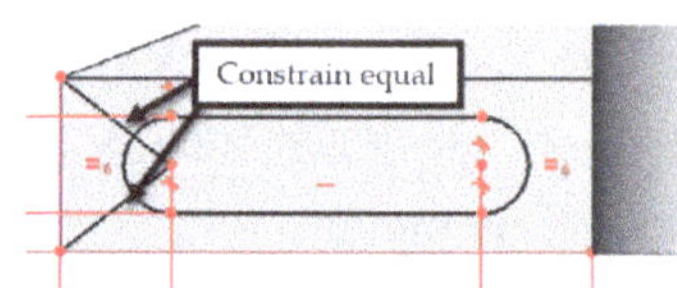

9. Select the two new lines, and click the **Toggle Construction geometry** icon on the **Sketcher geometries** toolbar.
10. Click **Close** on the **Model** panel.

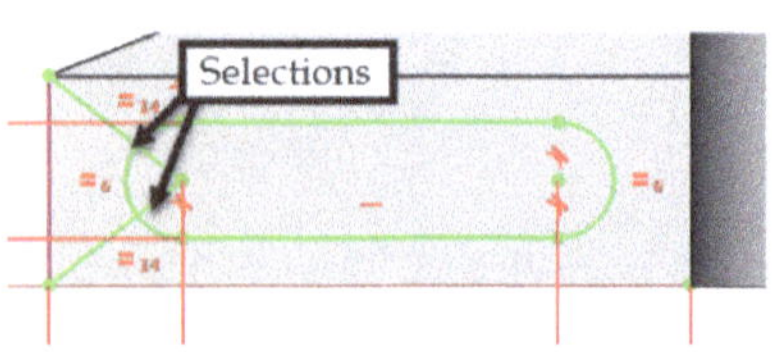

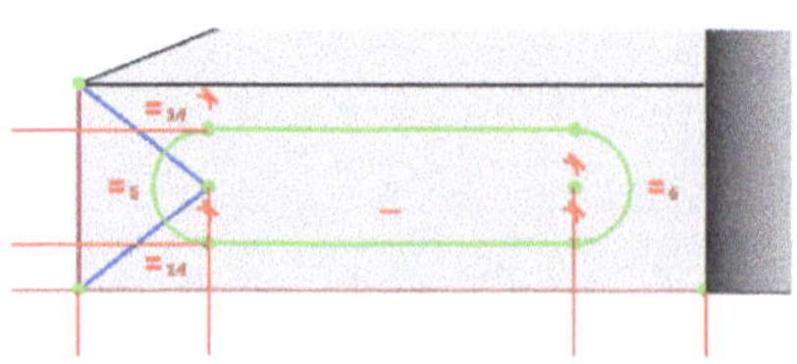

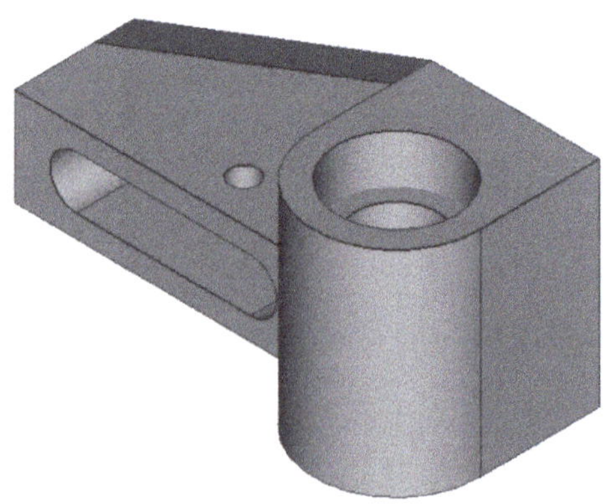

11. In the **Model** panel, expand the first **Hole** and click the right mouse button on the Sketch. Next, select **Edit sketch** from the menu.
12. Delete the vertical and horizontal distance constraints.
13. Create three lines connecting the centerpoint of the circle and the corner points, as shown.

14. Click the **Constrain equal** icon on the **Sketcher constraints** toolbar. Next, select two lines to make them equal in length. Select the third and second lines to make them equal. Right-click in the graphics window to deactivate the **Constrain equal** command.

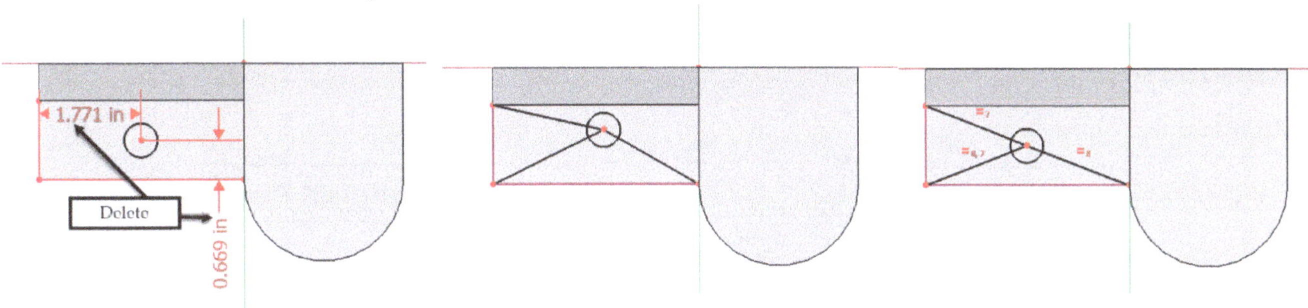

15. Select all the three lines and click the **Toggle construction geometry** icon on the **Sketcher geometries** toolbar.
16. Click **Close** on the **Model** panel.

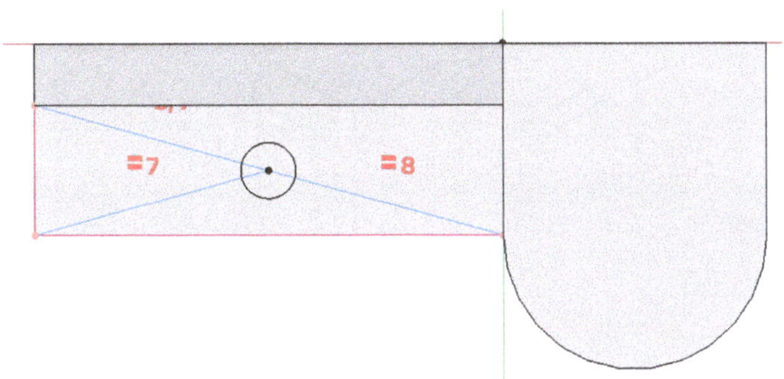

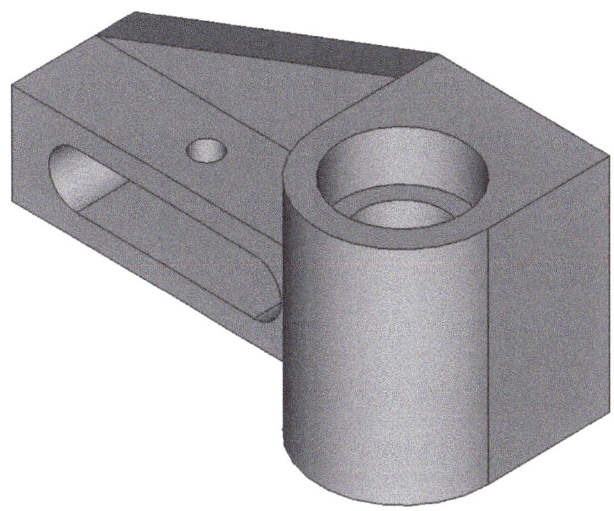

17. Now, change the size of the rectangular pad feature. Notice that the slot and hole are adjusted automatically.

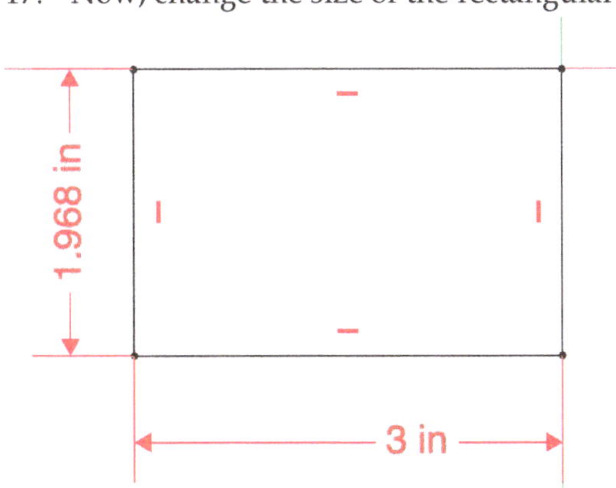

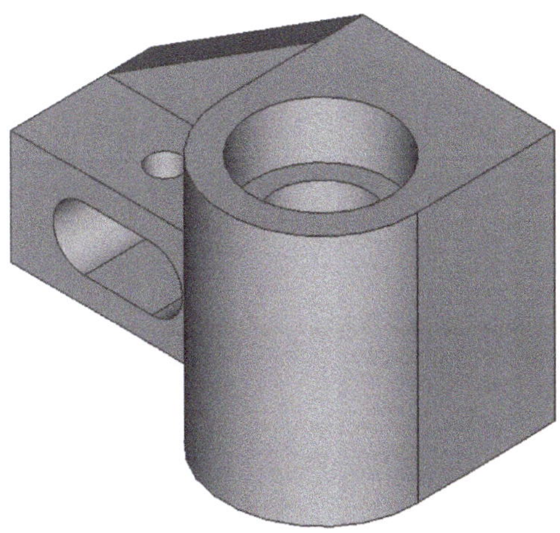

18. Save and close the file.

Questions

1. How to modify the sketch of a feature?
2. How to modify a feature directly?

Exercises

Exercise 1

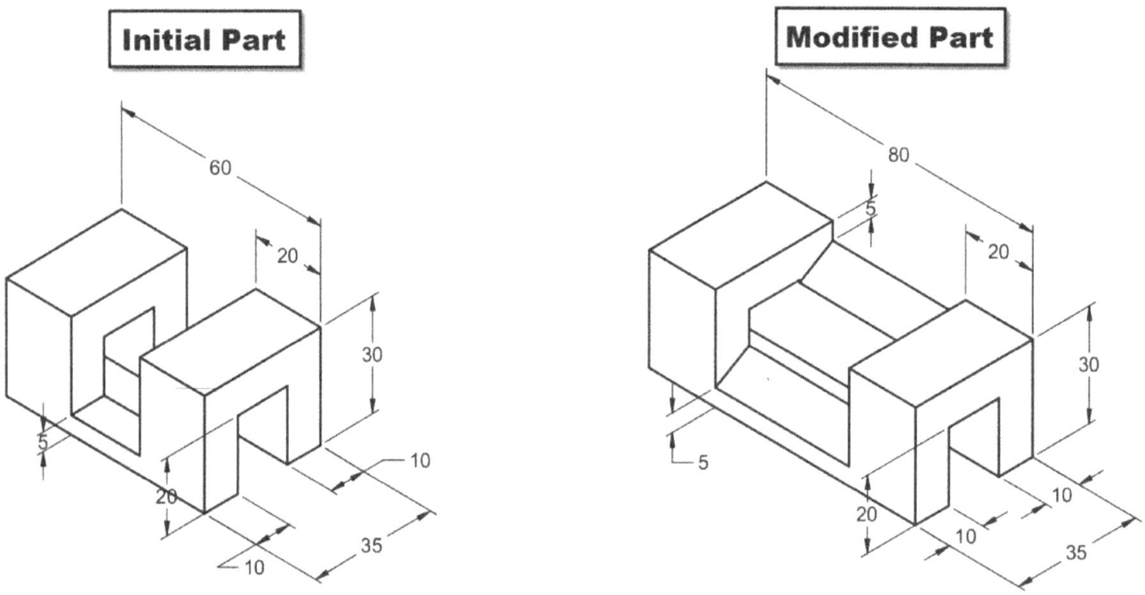

Exercise 2

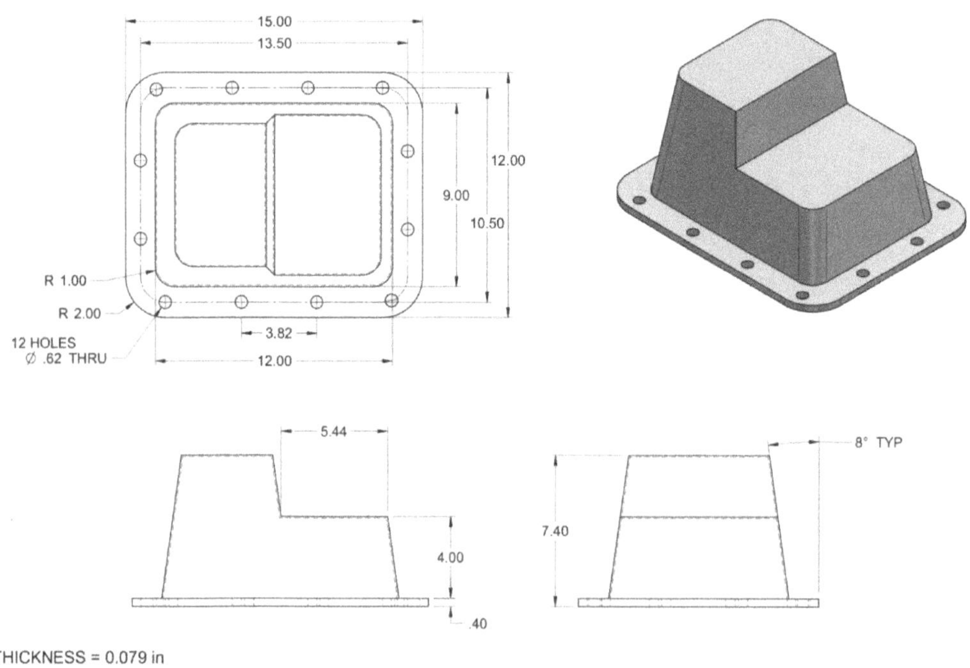

Chapter 9: Assemblies

Once you've created individual components, the next step is assembling them into an overall structure, called an assembly. This step is essential because it helps identify design problems that might not be apparent at the component level.

In this chapter, you'll learn how to put these components together and establish how they interact in real-life scenarios. Assembling components not only ensures they fit correctly but also allows you to simulate their movements and functions.

This process reveals how the parts work together, helping you spot issues, make necessary adjustments, and refine the design. It's a pivotal phase where your design transitions from separate components to a functional and coherent system.

The topics covered in this chapter are:

- *Starting an assembly*
- *Inserting Components*
- *Moving and Rotating Components*
- *Applying Constraints*
- *Editing a Component*
- *Sub-assemblies*

Starting an Assembly

In FreeCAD 1.0, while the software includes a native Assembly Workbench, this book focuses on the A2plus Workbench for creating assemblies due to the current instability of the built-in tool. To utilize A2plus, you must first install it via FreeCAD's Addon Manager. Begin by navigating to **Tools > Addon Manager** in the menu bar. Once the Addon Manager opens, locate the A2plus Workbench in the list of available workbenches, select it, and click the **Install/Update Selected** button to initiate the installation. After the process completes, close the Addon Manager.

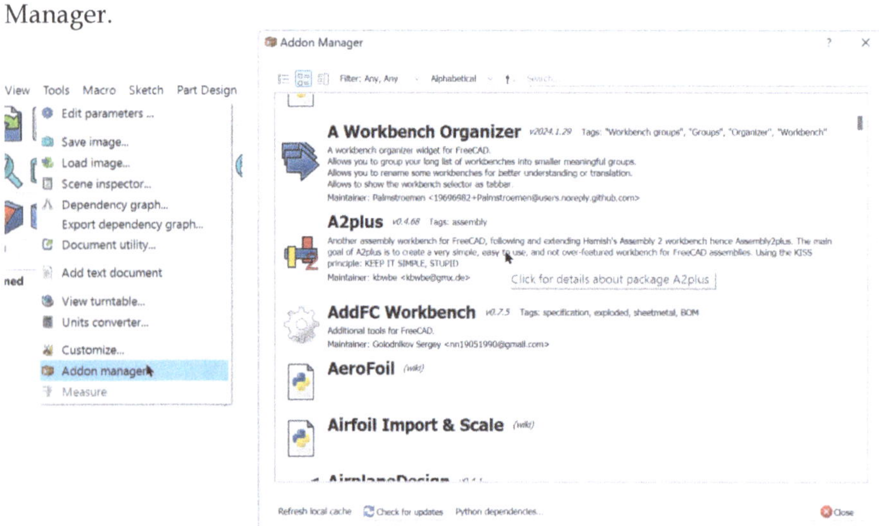

Click **OK** to restart the FreeCAD application. Next, select the A2plus workbench from the **Workbenches** drop-down. Click the **New** icon to open a new document.

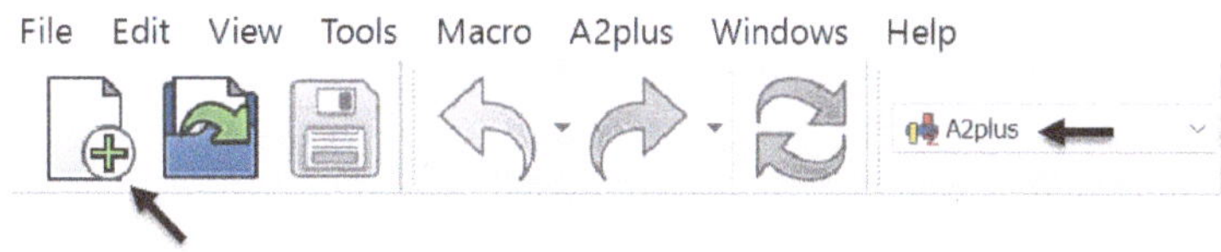

Inserting Components

To insert components into a design file, first, you need to save it. Next, Click the **Add a part from an external file** icon on the **A2p_Part** toolbar (or) click **A2plus > Add a part from an external file** on the menu bar. Go to the location of the parts and select the component. Next, click **Open** or double-click on the part to insert.

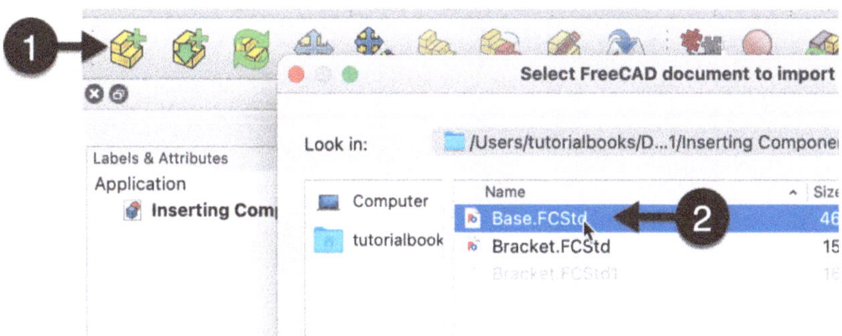

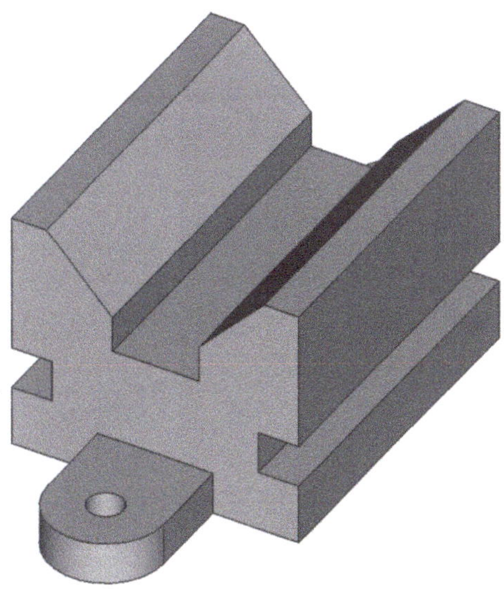

Likewise, insert the second component into the design.

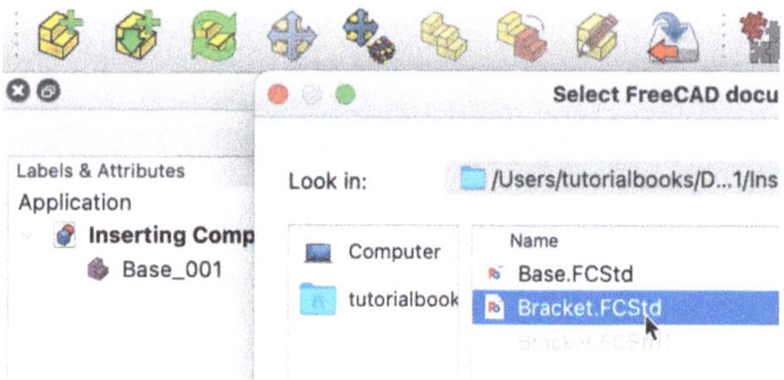

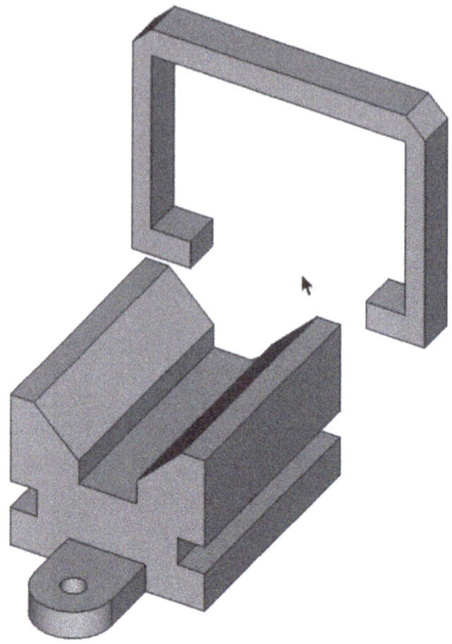

Moving and Rotating Parts

To move the component, select it and click the **Move the selected part**  icon on the **A2p_Part** toolbar (or) click **A2plus > Move the selected part** on the menu bar. Now, use the manipulator to move the part. For example, to move the part in the X-direction, select the X-axis handle and move the part (press and hold the left mouse button and drag the pointer).

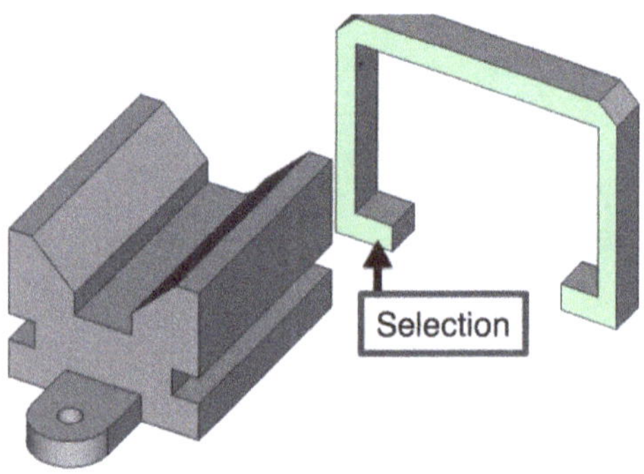

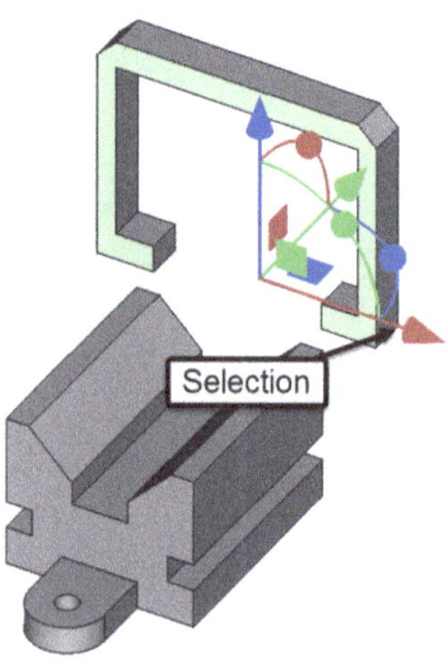

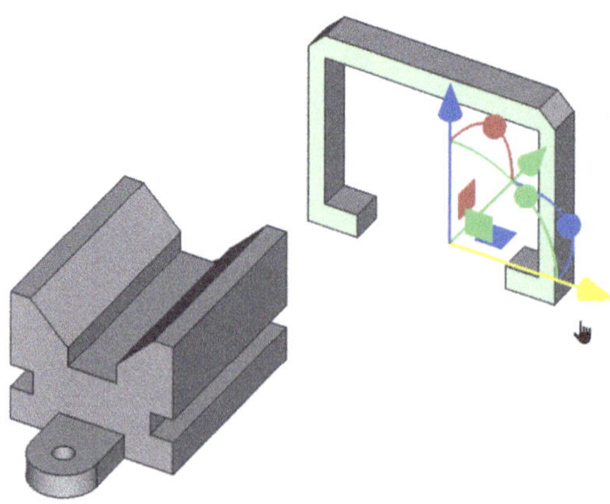

Use the rotate handles on the manipulator to rotate the part about an axis. For example, to rotate the part about the X-axis, select the sphere handle displayed between the Y and Z axes and rotate the part (press and hold the left mouse button and drag the pointer).

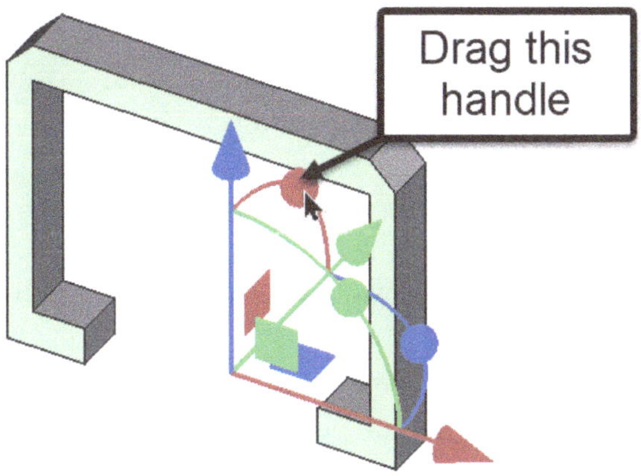

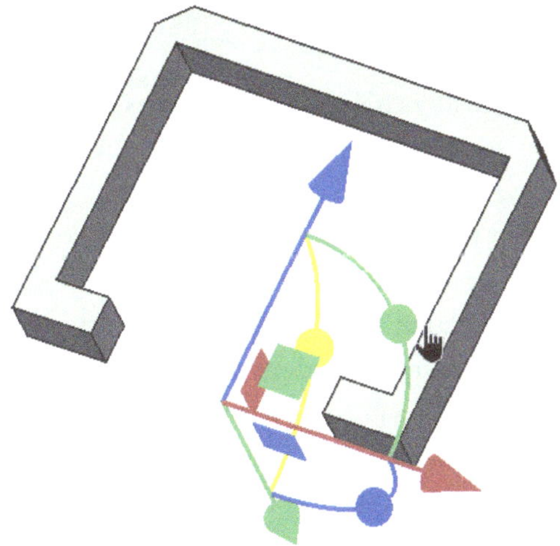

Click **OK** on the **Tasks** panel to complete the move operation.

Applying Constraints

After you've placed parts into an assembly, the next step is to apply constraints between them. Constraints serve to align parts precisely, ensuring they fit together as they should. For instance, you can make parts flush against each other or align two round faces to be concentric.

When you add constraints between parts, you effectively restrict their freedom of movement. Each part typically has six degrees of freedom by default (three for linear movement and three for rotational). By applying constraints, you remove these degrees of freedom, essentially locking the parts into a realistic interaction with each other.

In the following section, you'll learn how to establish these constraints between parts, allowing you to create assemblies that mimic real-world interactions with accuracy and precision.

Coincident Plane Constraint

The **Coincident Plane**  constraint serves the purpose of aligning two faces precisely with each other. The manner in which these two faces align is contingent upon the selection of the **Direction** type: either **Opposed** or **Aligned**. The **Opposed** and **Aligned** Direction types dictate the orientation and alignment of the mated faces, influencing how they come together in the assembly. This constraint is an essential element of ensuring the accurate positioning and alignment of components in the design or assembly process.

The Opposed direction

The "**Opposed**" direction serves as a valuable tool when aligning faces within a design. This not only brings the selected faces into coincidence but also ensures that they are oriented in opposing directions. This can be particularly useful when working with components that need to be closely fitted while maintaining a specific orientation relationship.

To apply the "Opposed direction" constraint effectively, follow these steps:

1. Initiate the process by clicking the "**Define Constraints**" icon found on the **A2p_Constraint** toolbar. Alternatively, you can access it through the menu bar by clicking "**A2plus**" > "**Constraint**" > "**Define Constraints.**"
2. While executing this operation, hold the CTRL key (Command key for Mac users) to select the faces of the two parts you intend to mate. Ensure that the selected faces are compatible for this constraint.
3. Within the "**Constraint Tools**" dialog, locate and click the "**Coincident Plane Constraint**" icon. This choice is pivotal for establishing coincidence between the selected faces.
4. In the subsequent "**Constraint Properties**" dialog, select "**Direction**" > "**Opposed**". This selection ensures that the orientation of the selected faces is opposing, a key feature of this constraint.
5. With these settings in place, the two selected faces will be mated, achieving both coincidence and an opposing orientation.

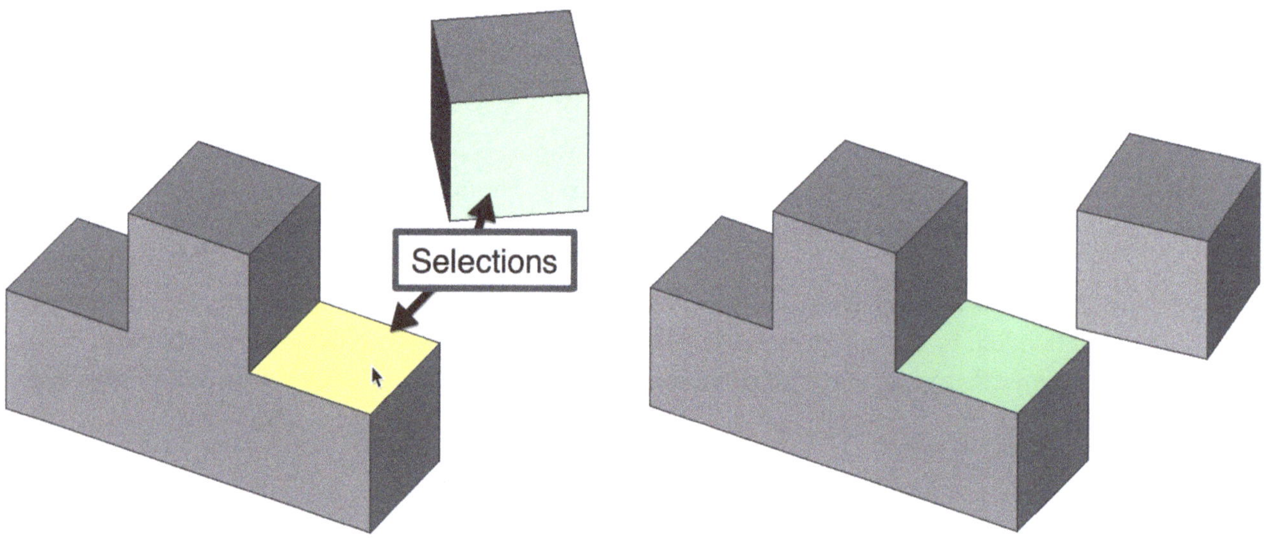

The Aligned Direction

Selecting the "**aligned**" option from the **Direction** drop-down in the **Constraint Properties** dialog serves to align the chosen faces with precision. This alignment results in the selected faces coinciding with one another, while also ensuring they share the same orientation.

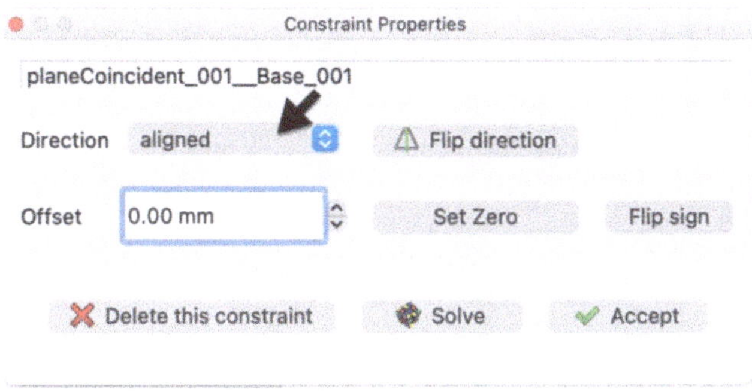

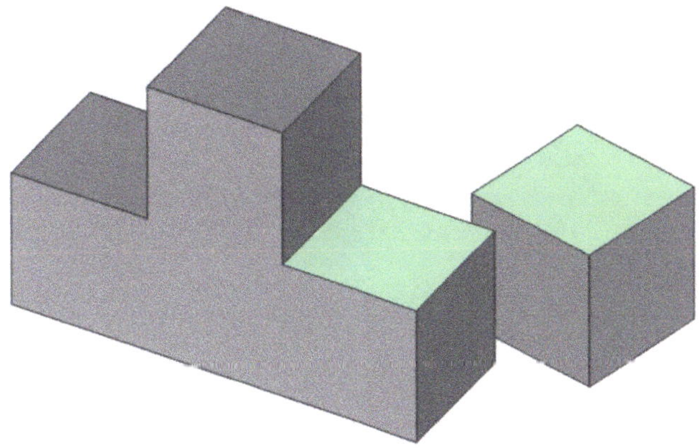

You have the option to specify an offset value within the **Offset** box located on the **Constraint properties** dialog. This offset value determines the distance between the constrained components, effectively creating a gap or overlap as needed.

After defining the desired offset, proceed by clicking the "**Accept**" button. This action finalizes the setup, establishing the Coincident Plane Constraint between the two selected faces. This constraint ensures that the specified faces align perfectly in your design, adhering to your precise engineering requirements.

Axis Coincident Constraint

The **Axis Coincident Constraint** is a valuable tool for aligning the axes of two cylindrical faces to merge them into a common axis. To apply this constraint, follow these precise steps:

1. **Press and Hold CTRL (Command for Mac) Key:** Begin by pressing and holding the CTRL key on your keyboard (Command key for Mac users). This key press prepares the software to accept your input for applying the Axis Coincident Constraint.
2. **Select Round Faces:** While holding the CTRL (Command) key, click on the round faces of both the placement and target parts. These faces are the areas where you want the cylindrical axes to coincide.

3. **Access the Constraint Icon:** Look for the "**Add axis coincident constraint**"  icon, which is located on the **A2p_Constraint** toolbar. You can find this toolbar within the software interface.

OR

   Use the Menu Bar: If the toolbar is not visible, you can access the same function through the menu bar by going to "**A2plus > Constraint > Add axis Coincident constraint**."
4. **Define Axis Coincidence:** After clicking on the "**Add axis coincident constraint**" icon or using the menu option, the software will present you with the options for this constraint. You will observe two choices in the "**Direction**" drop-down: "**Opposed**" and "**Aligned**." Select the one that suits your design requirements.

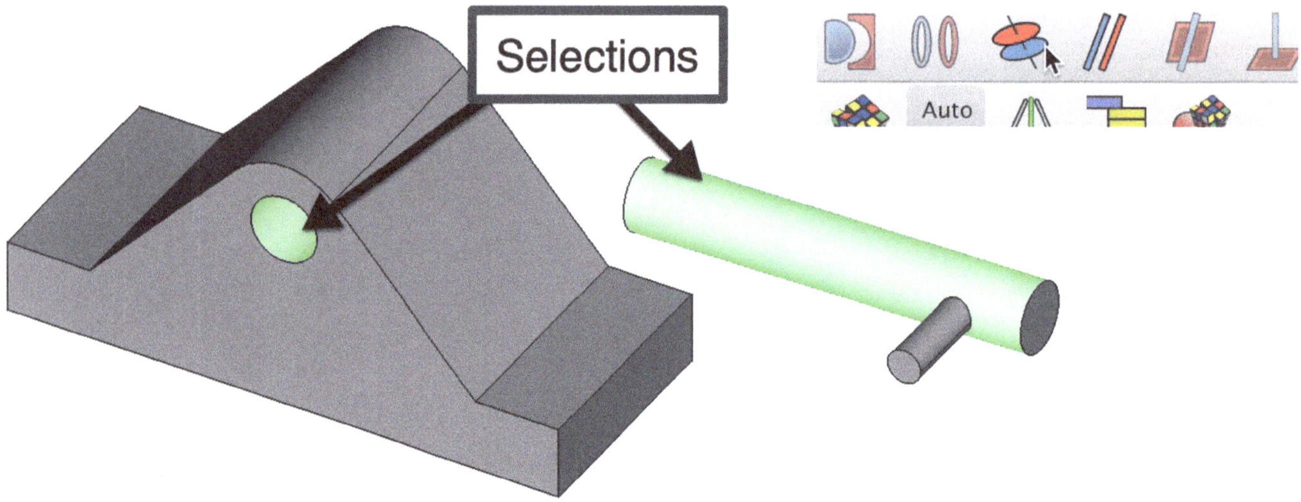

The "**opposed**" option, when selected, aligns the two chosen axes or edges in a manner where they are oriented in opposite directions, moving away from each other.

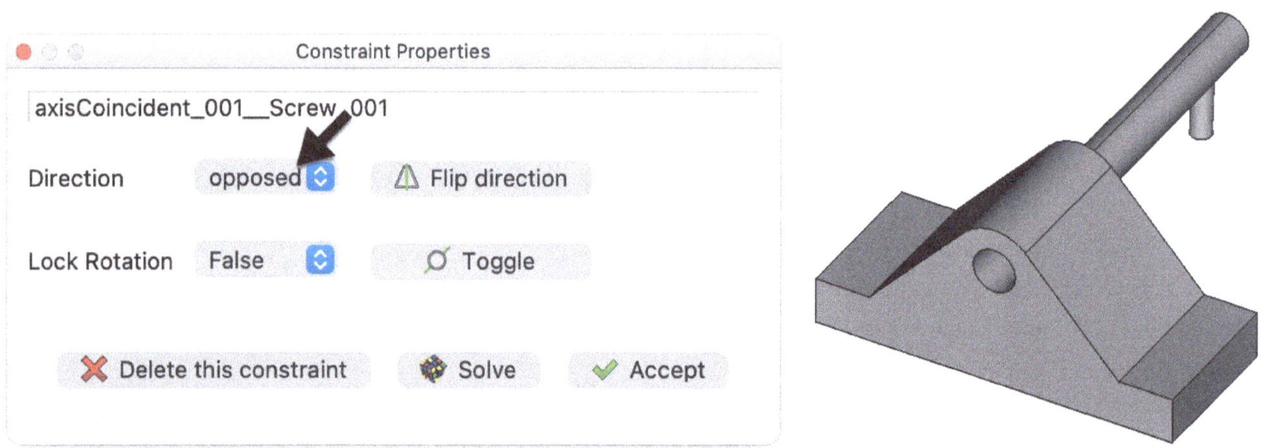

Selecting the "**Aligned**" option ensures that the axes of the parts are oriented in the same direction. This choice effectively aligns the axes, creating a consistent orientation for the parts involved

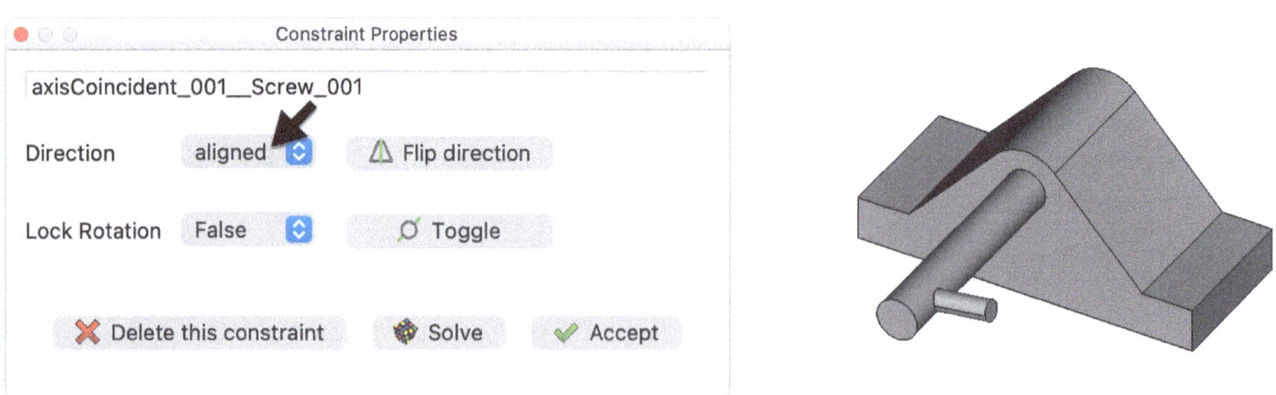

Select **Lock Rotation** > **True**, if you want to lock the rotation of the placement part. Click **Accept** to create the constraint.

Circular Edge Constraint

The **Circular Edge** constraint serves the purpose of ensuring concentricity between the circular edges of two components. To apply this constraint, follow these steps:

1. Hold down the CTRL key (or Command key for Mac users).
2. Click on the circular edges of the two components that you want to make concentric.
3. Locate and click the **Circular Edge** constraint icon on the **A2p_constraint** toolbar or navigate to **A2plus > Constraint > Add circularEdge constraint** on the menu bar.
4. Within the **Direction** drop-down menu, choose the "**Opposed**" option to align the faces of the circular edges in an opposing manner, or select "**Aligned**" to have them facing the same direction.
5. If you wish to lock the rotation of the placement part, set "**Lock Rotation**" to "**True**."
6. Confirm the constraint by clicking "**Accept**."

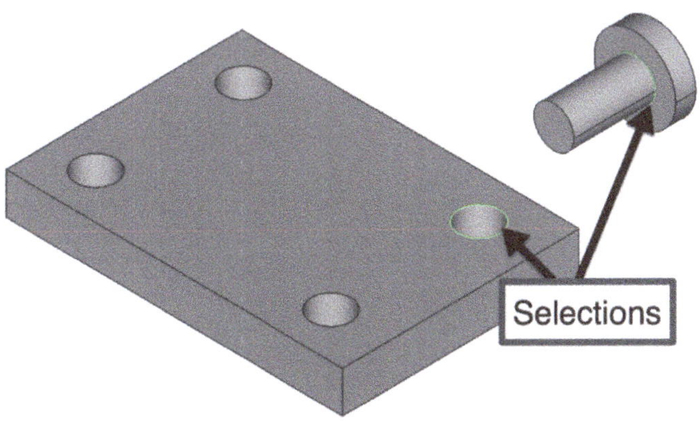

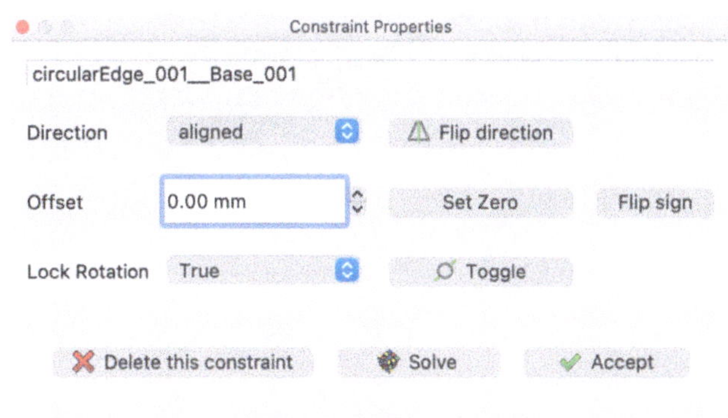

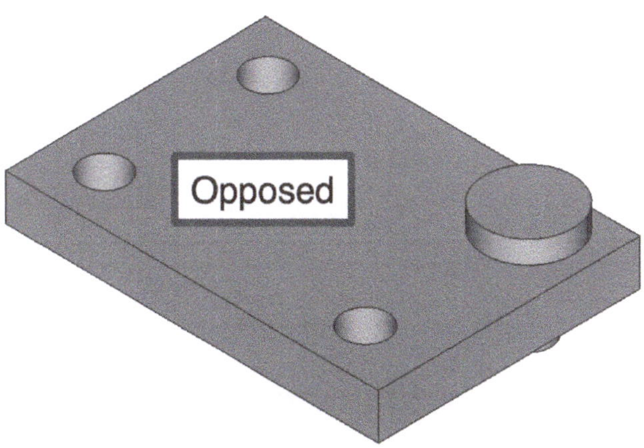

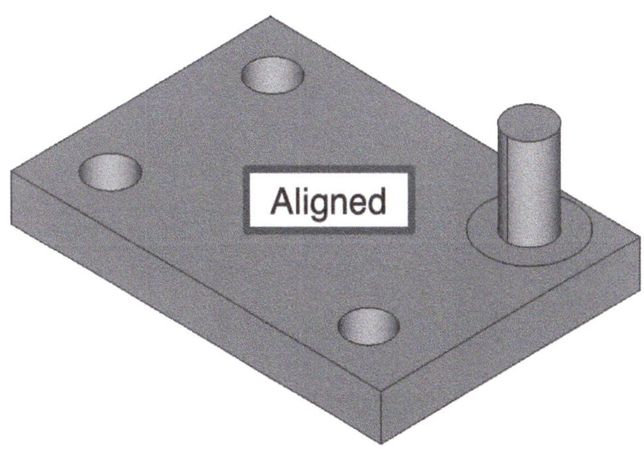

Angled Planes Constraint

The **Angled Planes** constraint serves to precisely orient faces at a specified angle within your design. To apply this constraint, follow these steps:

1. Press and hold the CTRL key (Command key for Mac users).
2. Click on the planar faces of both the first and second parts that you wish to position at a specific angle.
3. Access the **Angled Planes**  constraint by clicking the corresponding icon on the **A2p_constraint** toolbar or navigating to **A2plus > Constraint > Add angledPlanes constraint** on the menu bar.
4. In the dialog that appears, enter the desired angle value into the "**Angle**" text box. This action adjusts the orientation of the first part to match the specified angle.
5. If you need to ensure a 90-degree offset, click the "**Perpendicular**" button.
6. To finalize and implement the constraint, click the "**Accept**" button.

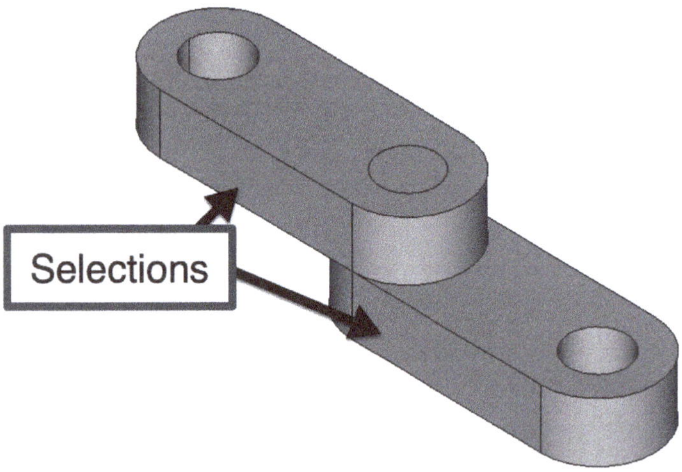

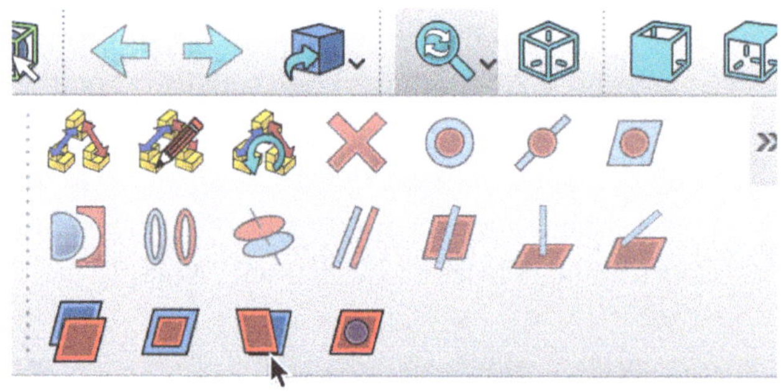

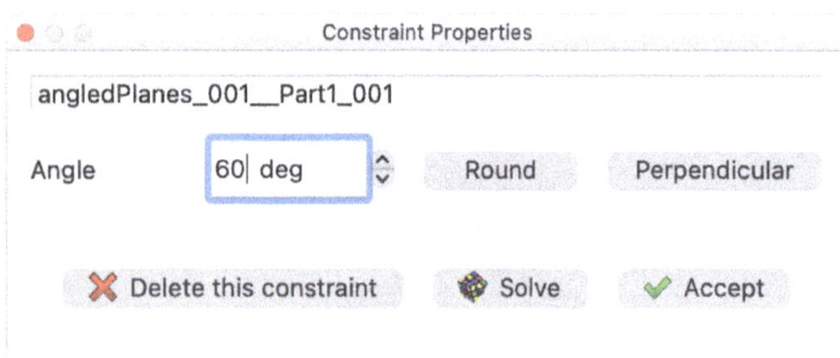

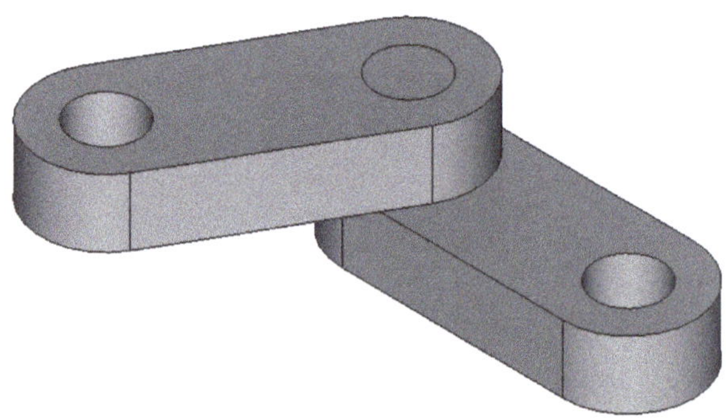

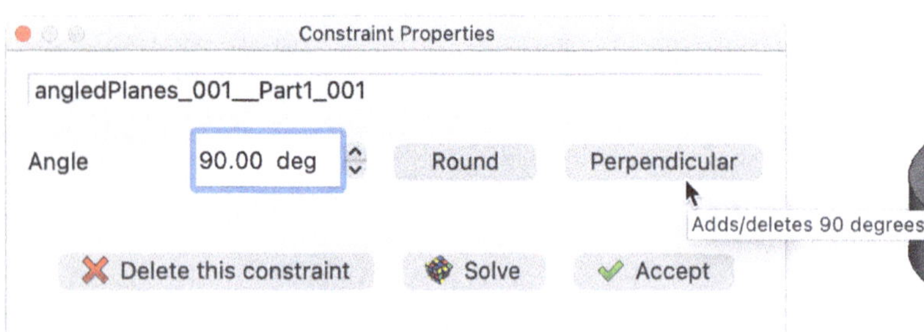

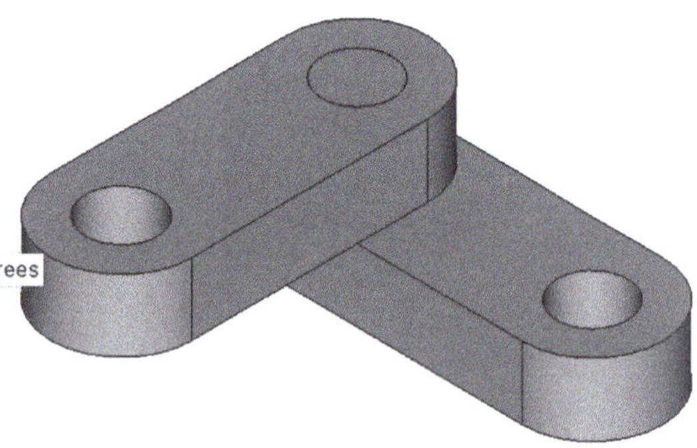

Planes Parallelism Constraint

The **Planes Parallelism constraint** serves the purpose of establishing a parallel relationship between two selected faces. To implement this constraint, start by pressing and holding the CTRL key (or Command key for Mac users) and then clicking on the planar faces of both the first and second parts.

Following this, navigate to the **A2p_constraint** toolbar, and specifically, the **Planes Parallelism** constraint icon. Alternatively, access this feature through the **A2plus** menu by choosing **Constraint** and then **Add planesParallel constraint**.

To further refine this constraint, use the **Direction** drop-down menu. If you select "**Opposed**," the constraint will align the selected faces in an opposing manner, positioning them directly across from each other. Alternatively, choosing "**Aligned**" from the **Direction** drop-down will orient the selected faces in the same direction.

Finally, once you've configured the constraint to your specifications, confirm the settings by clicking the "**Accept**" button. This action will apply the Planes Parallelism constraint according to your selected options.

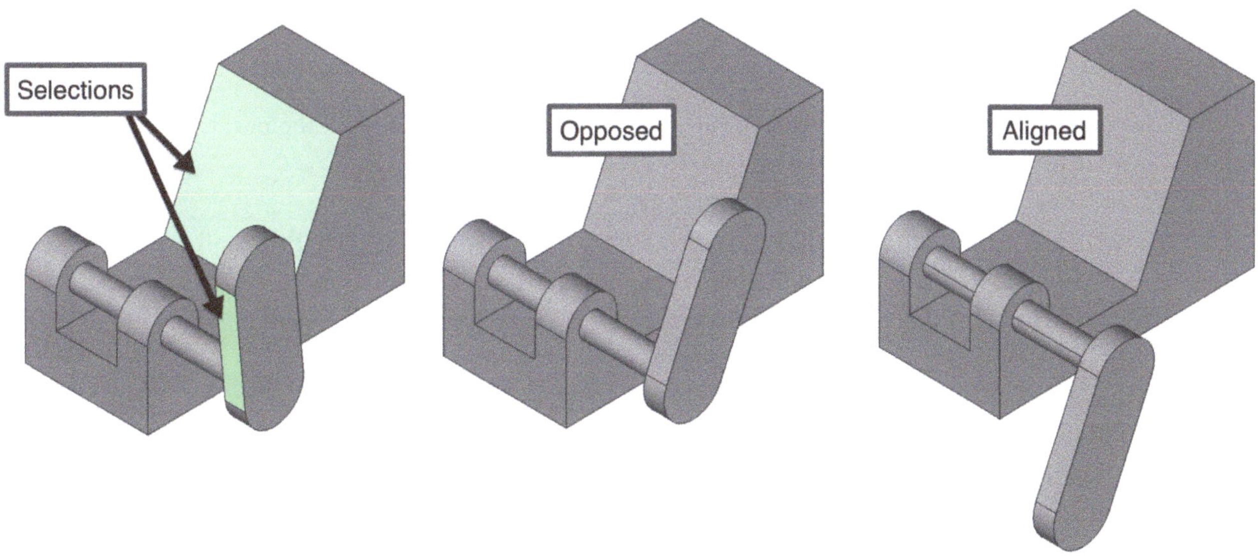

Sphere to Sphere constraint

The "**Sphere to sphere**" constraint is a mechanism used to establish a connection between two spherical faces in your design. To apply this constraint effectively, follow these precise steps:

1. Begin by pressing and holding the CTRL key (or Command key for Mac users) on your keyboard.
2. While holding the CTRL key (or Command key), click on the spherical faces of both the first and second parts that you wish to connect.
3. Proceed to the **A2p_constraint** toolbar and locate the "**Sphere-to-sphere constraint**" icon.
4. Alternatively, access this constraint through the menu bar by navigating to **A2plus > Constraint > Add sphereCenterIdent constraint**.

5. Upon selecting the appropriate constraint, click the "**Accept**" button to confirm and create the constraint.

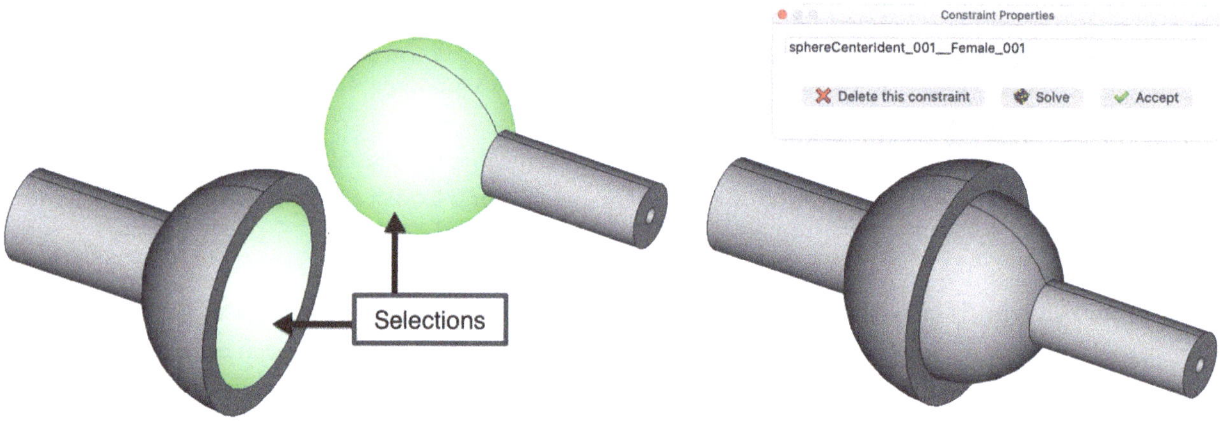

Editing an Imported Part

In the iterative design process, perfection is rarely attained on the initial attempt. Modifications and adjustments are often necessary to refine the design. Fortunately, FreeCAD facilitates this process with efficiency and ease.

To modify a part within an assembly, follow these steps:

1. Within the assembly, identify the part that requires modification. Make sure that the part to be edited is opened in another file tab.
2. Select the part, and then locate the "**Edit an imported part**"  icon on the **A2p_Part** toolbar.
3. Click on this icon, and the part model will open, ready for editing.
4. Proceed to make the necessary changes to the part as per your design requirements.
5. After making the modifications, save the part file, and then close it.
6. Return to the assembly file and locate the "**Update parts**" icon on the **A2p_Part** toolbar.
7. Click on this icon, and watch as the modified part is seamlessly updated within the assembly.

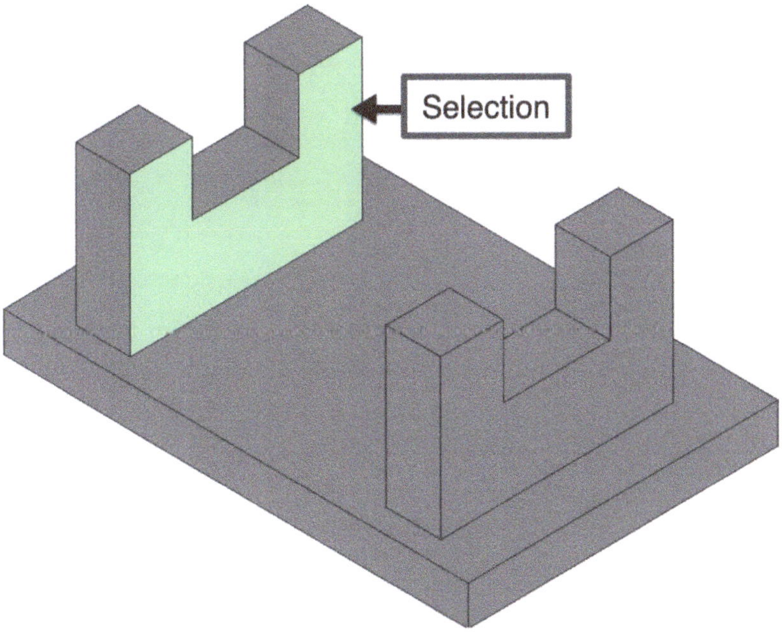
Selection

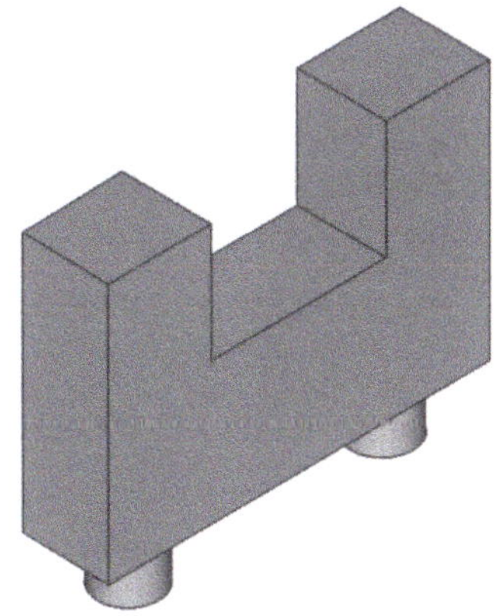

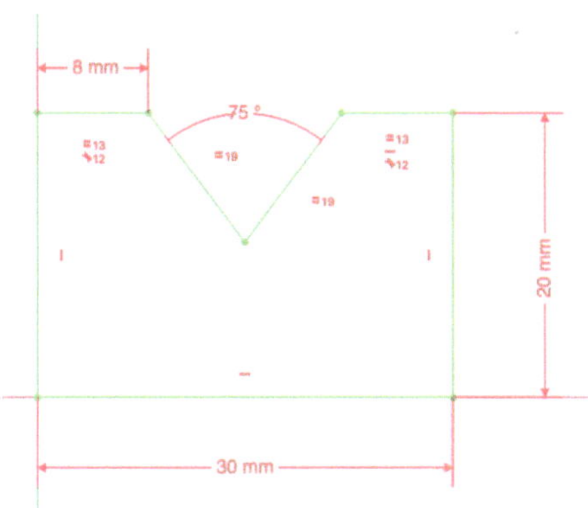
8 mm
20 mm
30 mm

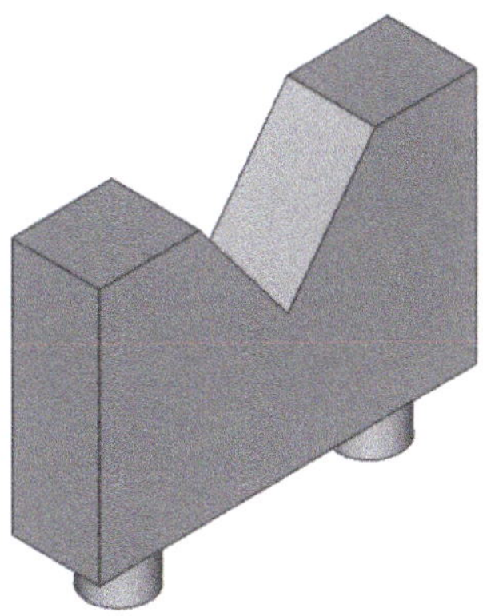

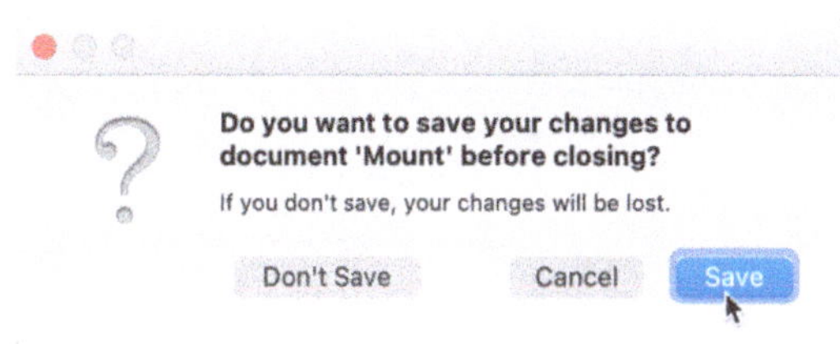
Do you want to save your changes to document 'Mount' before closing?
If you don't save, your changes will be lost.
Don't Save
Cancel
Save

Assembly : 1*
Mount : 1*

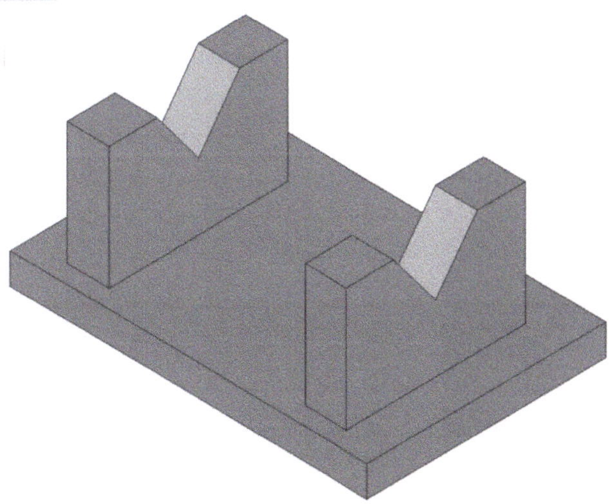

Edit selected constraint

Editing constraints within an assembly is a pivotal aspect of the design process. To make such edits, follow these steps:

1. Begin by expanding the part model you're interested in. You can find this option in the **Model** panel.
2. Identify the specific constraint you wish to modify.
3. Once you've located the constraint, select it.
4. Now, there are two methods to initiate the editing process:
    - You can click the "**Edit selected constraint**"  icon found on the **A2p_constraint** toolbar.
    - Alternatively, navigate to the menu bar, click on "**A2plus**," then select "**Constraint**," and finally, opt for "**Edit selected constraint**."
5. This will open the **Constraint Properties** dialog, where you can make the desired adjustments to the constraint settings.
6. After you've fine-tuned the constraint according to your requirements, confirm the changes by clicking the "**Accept**" button.

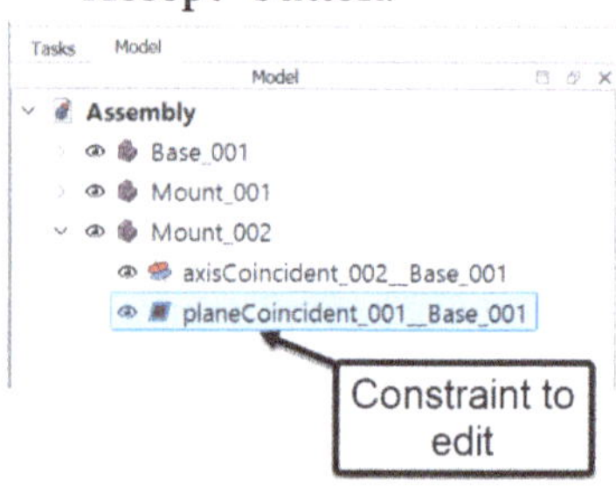

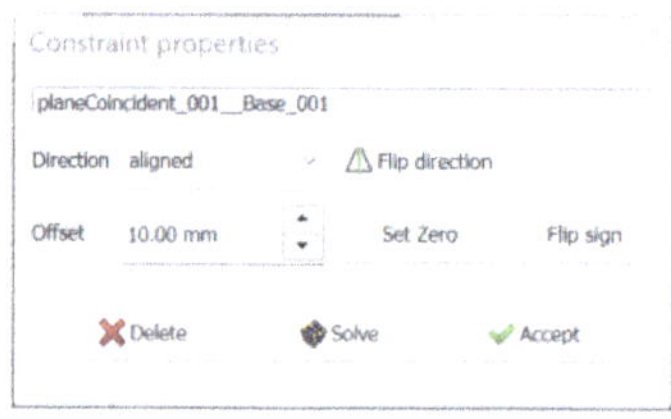

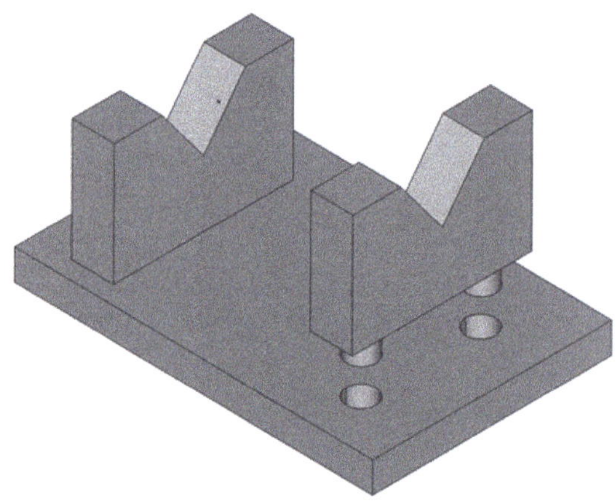

Sub-assemblies

The use of sub-assemblies has many advantages in FreeCAD 1.0. Sub-assemblies make large assemblies easier to manage. They make it easy for multiple users to collaborate on a single large assembly design. They can also affect the way you document a large assembly design in 2D drawings. For these reasons, it is important for you to create sub-assemblies in a variety of ways. The easiest way to create a sub-assembly is to insert an existing assembly into another assembly. You need to simply use the **Add a part from an existing file** command to insert the subassembly into an existing assembly. Next, apply constraints to constraint the assembly. The process of applying constraints is straightforward. You are required to apply constraints between only one part of a sub-assembly and a part of the main assembly. In addition to that, you can easily hide or suppress a group of parts with the help of sub-assemblies.

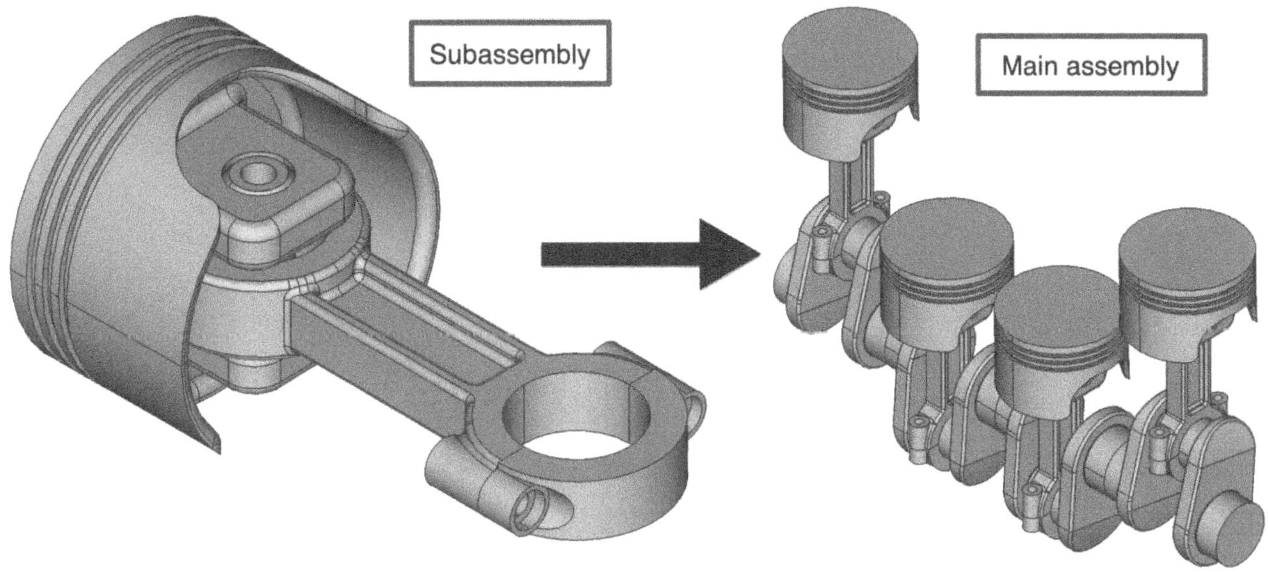

Best Practices

- **Planning Your Design:** Before starting to apply constraints, it's crucial to have a clear plan for your assembly. Understand how the components will interact, and consider factors such as clearance, motion, and alignment.
- **Naming Conventions:** Assign meaningful names to your parts and subassemblies. This keeps the assembly tree organized and easier to navigate.
- **Component Origin:** Establish a consistent origin point for your components. This helps with alignment and predictability during assembly.

General Cautions

- **Overconstraint:** Avoid overconstraint, as it can lead to errors or unexpected behavior. Apply constraints judiciously.
- **Design Changes:** Be prepared to update your assembly constraints if a part's design changes to accommodate those changes.
- **Documentation and Labeling:** Properly document your assembly constraints and use labels as needed for clarity and easier troubleshooting.

Tutorial 1 (Bottom-Up Assembly)

In this example, you create the assembly shown below.

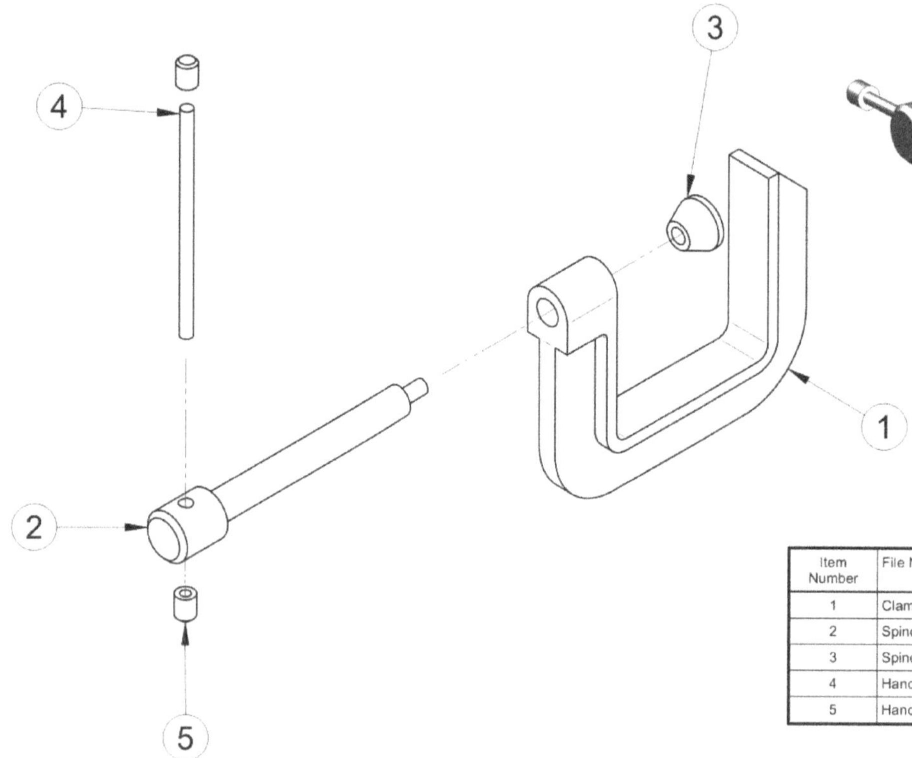

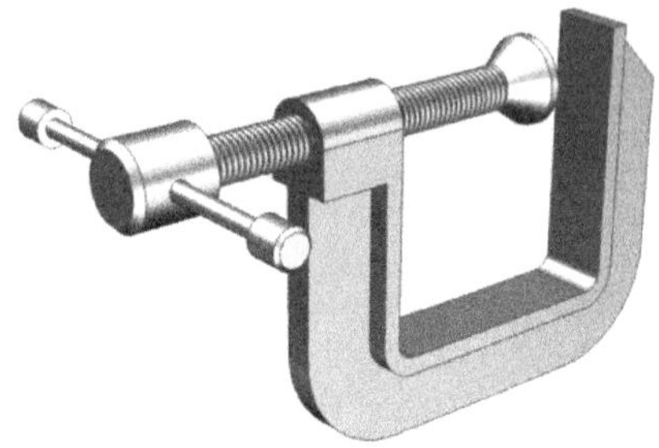

Item Number	File Name (no extension)	Quantity
1	Clamp Jaw	1
2	Spindle	1
3	Spindle Cap	1
4	Handle	1
5	Handle Cap	2

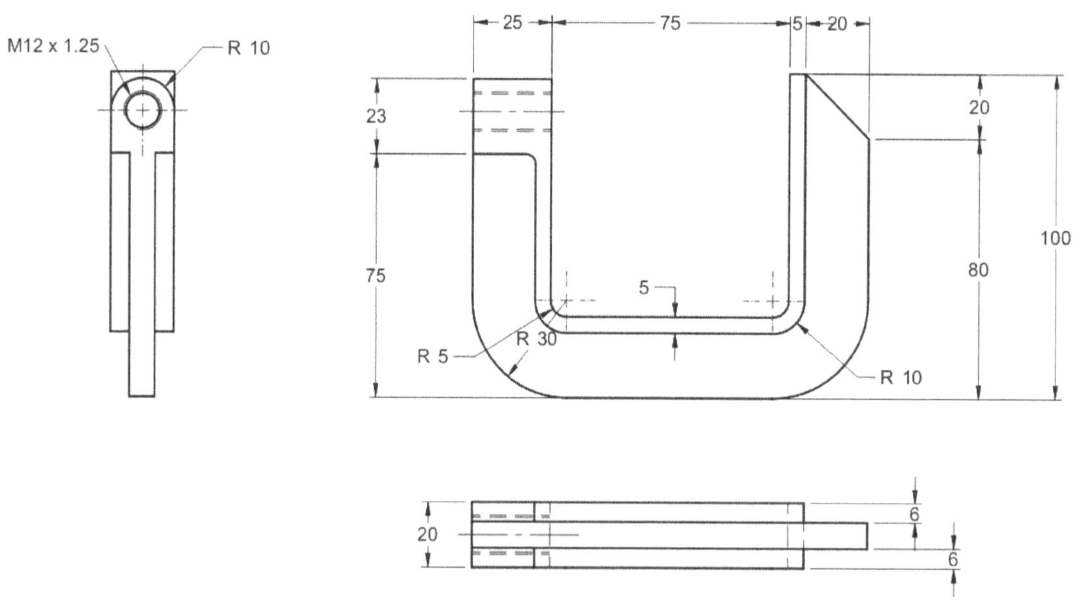

CLAMP JAW

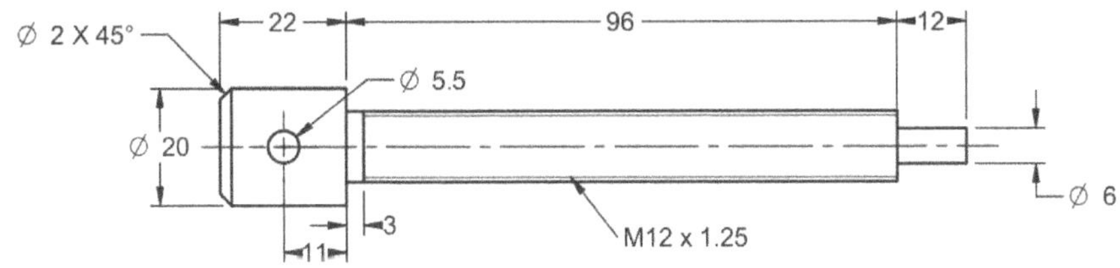

SPINDLE

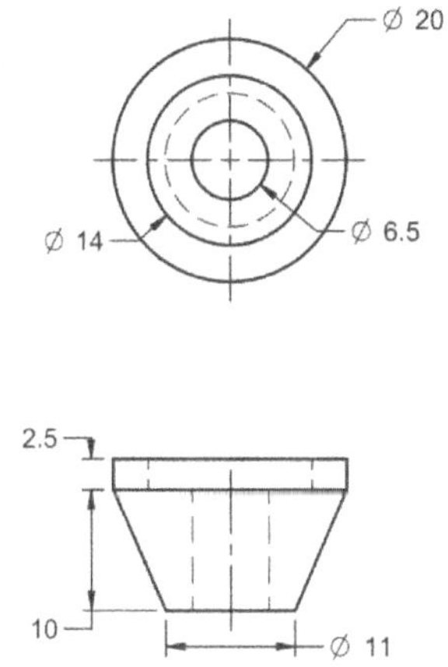

SPINDLE CAP

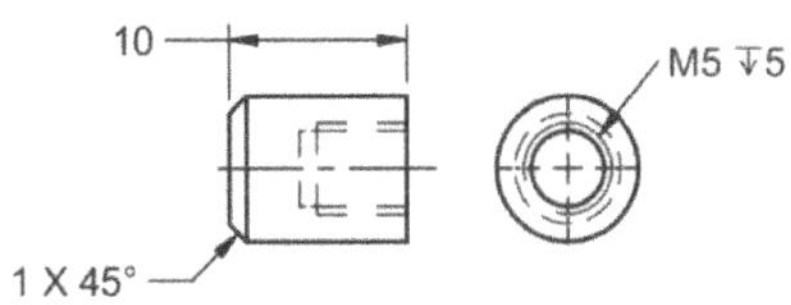

HANDLE CAP

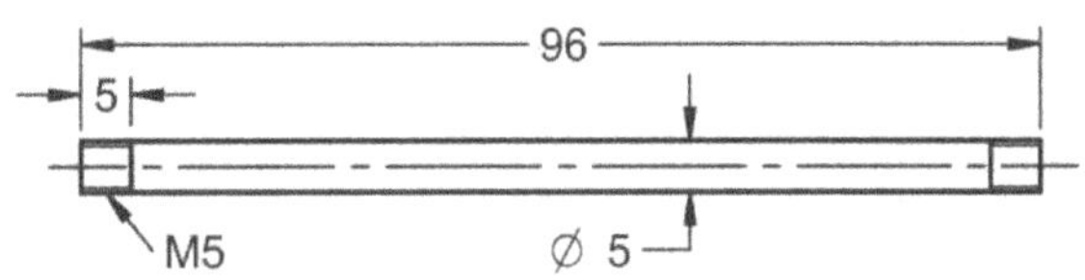

HANDLE

Creating the Assembly file

1. Create the parts of the assembly. You can also get the part files by sending us an email to *freecadtuts@gmail.com*
2. Save all the part files in a single folder.
3. Click the **FreeCAD 1.0** icon on your Desktop to start FreeCAD.
4. On the menu bar, click **File > New**; it creates a new document.
5. On the Menu bar, click **Tools > Addon manager**; the **FreeCAD** message box appears showing that the addons are not part of FreeCAD. Click **OK** to display the **Addon Manager** dialog.
6. Select the **A2plus** addon. Next, click **Install**.
7. Click **Close** twice; the **You must restart FreeCAD for changes to take effect** message appears. Click **Restart now**.
8. Close the **FreeCAD** application window. Next, click the **FreeCAD 1.0** icon on the Desktop.
9. On the **Workbench** toolbar, select **Workbench** drop-down > **A2plus**.
10. Click **Edit > Preferences** on the **Menu** bar (or) click **FreeCAD 1.0 > Preferences** on title bar, if you are working on MacOS; the **Preferences** dialog appears on the screen.
11. Click the **General** tab and select **Default unit system > Standard(mm/kg/s/degree)**.
12. Select **Number of decimals > 2** and click **OK** on the **Preferences** dialog.
13. Click **File > Save** on the Menu bar. Next, go to the location of the folder in which all the part files of the assembly are located. Enter **Tutorial 1** in the **File name** box and click **Save**.

Inserting part files in the Assemblies

1. Click the **Add a part from an external file** icon on the **A2p_Part** toolbar (or) click **A2plus > Add a part from an external file** on the menu bar; the **Select FreeCAD document to import part from** dialog appears.
2. On the **Select FreeCAD document to import part from** dialog, go to the folder in which all the part files of the assembly are located.
3. Select the **Clamp Jaw.FCStd** part file from the list, and then click **Open**; the clamp jaw is placed in the graphics window.
4. Click the **Add a part from an external file** icon on the **A2p_Part** toolbar (or) click **A2plus > Add a part from an external file** on the menu bar.
5. On the **Select FreeCAD document to import part from** dialog, click **Spindle.FCStd**, and then click **Open**. Click in the graphics window to place the component.

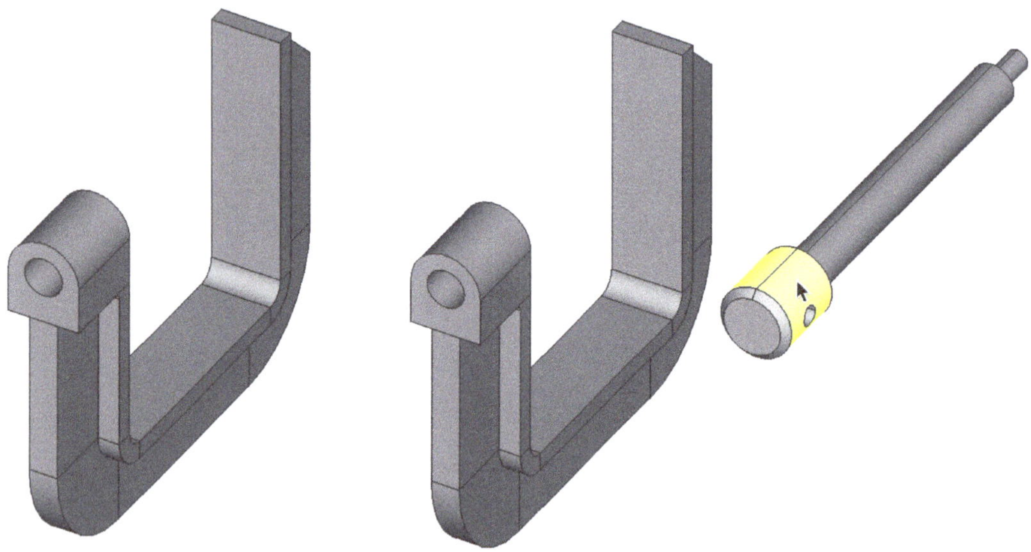

6. Likewise, insert the *Spindle Cap*, *Handle*, and two instances of *Handle Caps*. Next, click the green check on the **Insert parts and assemblies** dialog.

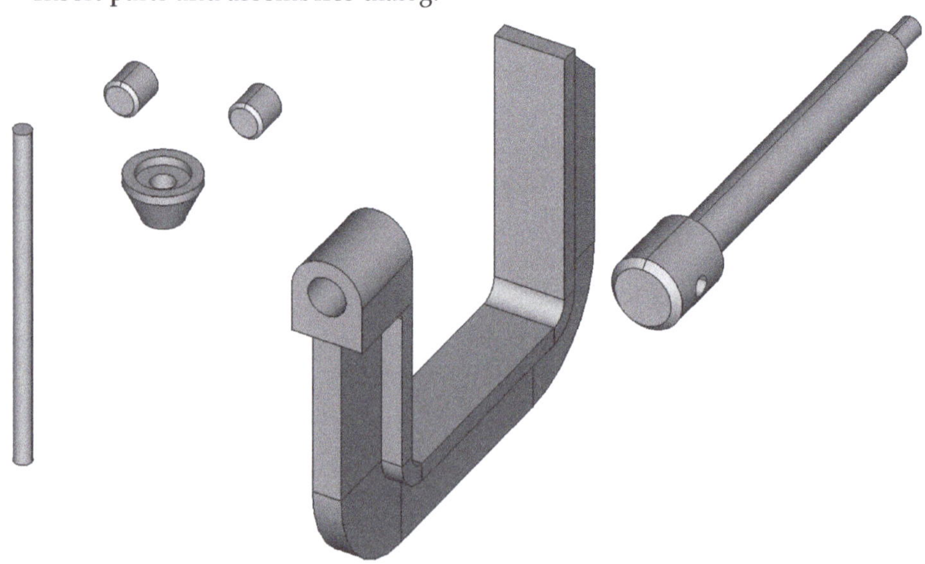

Defining Constraints

1. Press and hold the Ctrl key and select the flat face of the *Clamp Jaw*, as shown in the figure.
2. Rotate the model view and select the flat face of the model, as shown.
3. Click the **Add planeCoincident constraint**  icon on the **A2p_Constraints** toolbar (or) click **A2plus > Constraint > Add planeCoincident constraint** on the menu bar.
4. On the **Constraint Properties** dialog, select **Direction > opposed**. Next, type 31 in the **Offset** box, and then click **Flip sign**. Click **Accept** to create the planeCoincident constraint.

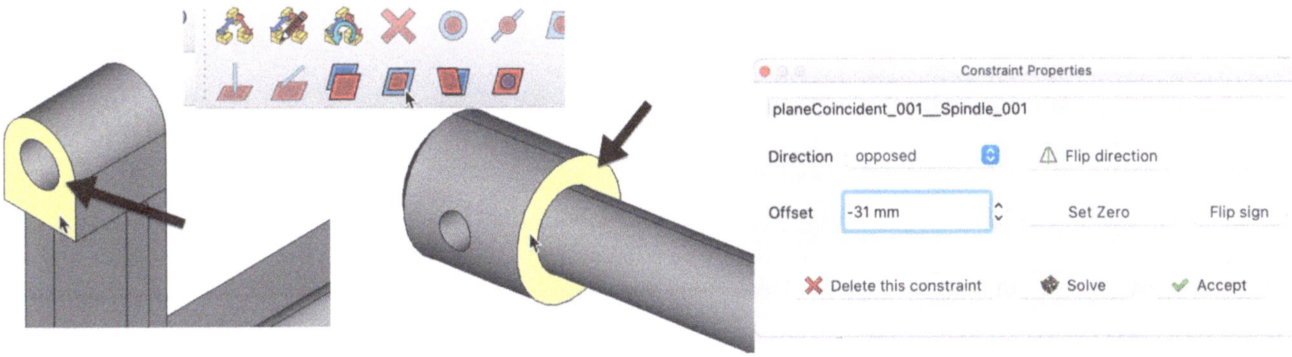

5. Click the **Define constraints**  icon on the **A2p_Constraint** toolbar (or) click **A2plus > Constraint > Define constraints** on the menu bar.
6. Press and hold the Ctrl key and select the cylindrical face of the *Spindle* and hole of the *Clamp Jaw*.
7. Click the **Add axis Coincident constraint**  icon on the **Constraint Tools** dialog.

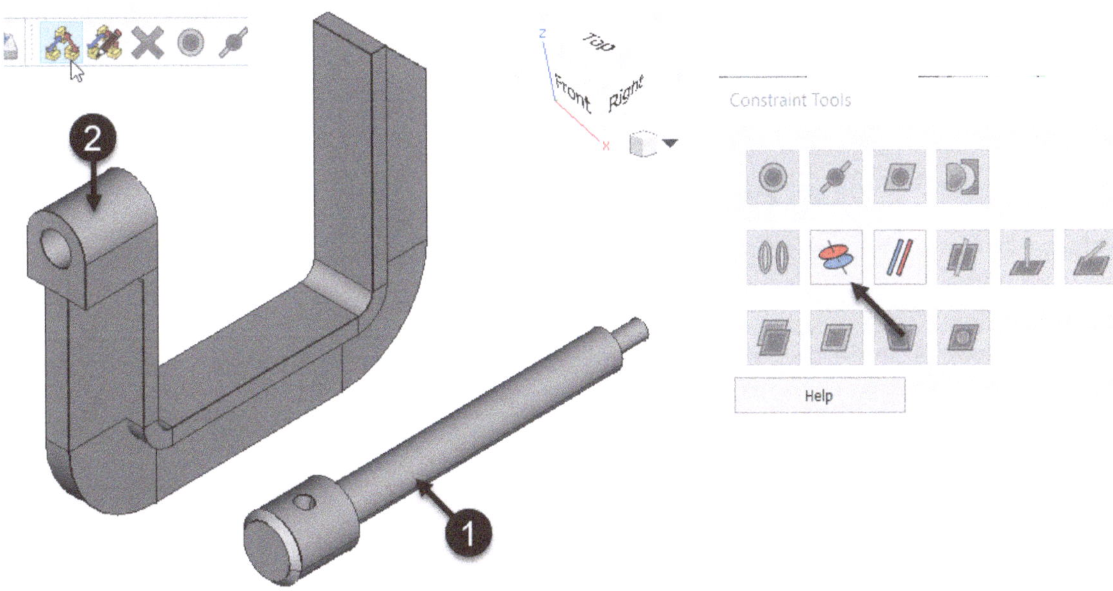

8. On the **Constraint Properties** dialog, select **Lock Rotation > True**. Click **Accept**.

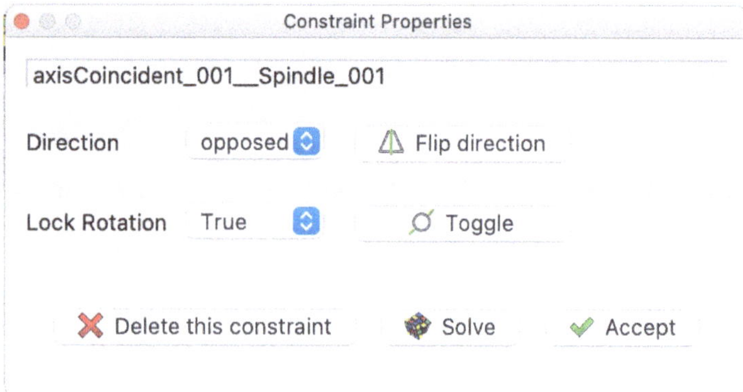

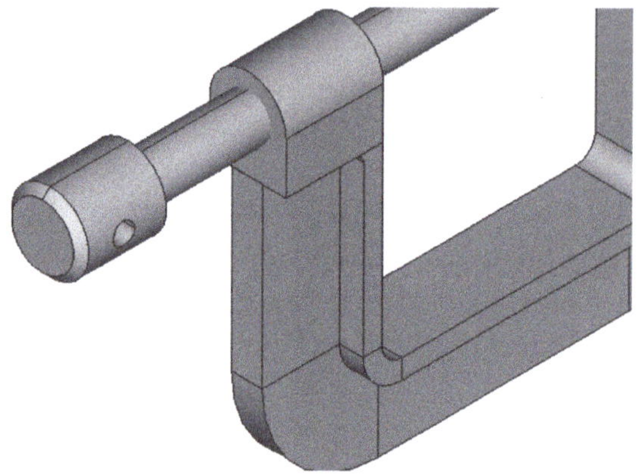

9. Click on the circular edge of the *Spindle Cap* hole, as shown.
10. Press and hold the Ctrl key and click on the circular edge of the *Spindle*, as shown.
11. Click the **Add circularEdge constraint**  icon on the **Constraint Tools** dialog.
12. Select **Direction > opposed** on the **Constraint Properties** dialog; the *Spindle* and *Spindle Cap* are axially aligned and positioned opposite to each other.

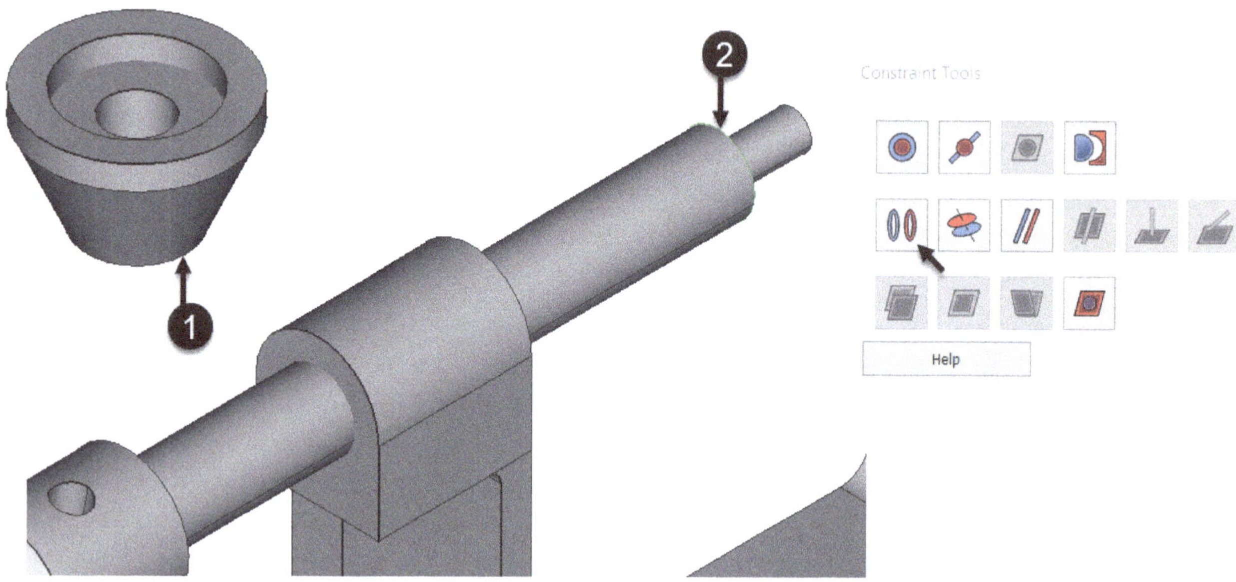

13. Select **Lock Rotation** > **True**, and then click **Accept**.

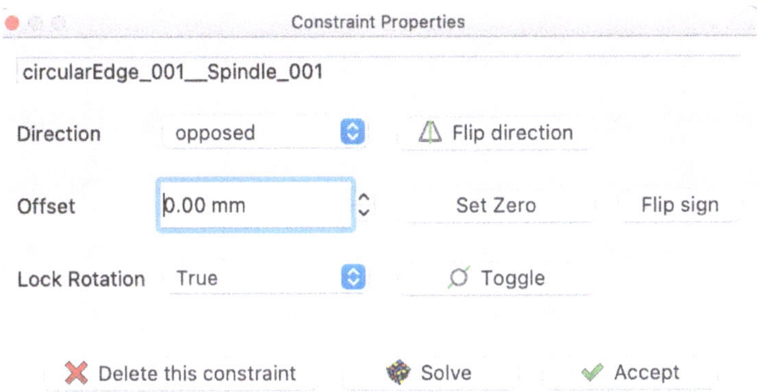

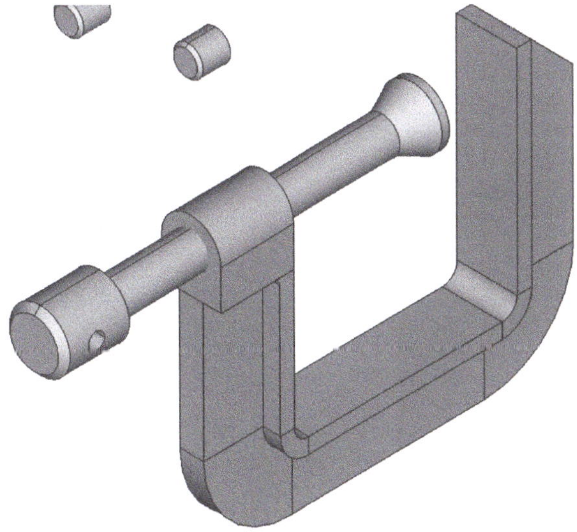

14. Press and hold the Ctrl key and select the cylindrical face of the *Handle* and the hole located on the *Spindle*.
15. Click the **Add axis Coincident constraint** icon on the **Constraint Tools** dialog.
16. Select **Lock Rotation** > **True**, and then click **Accept**.

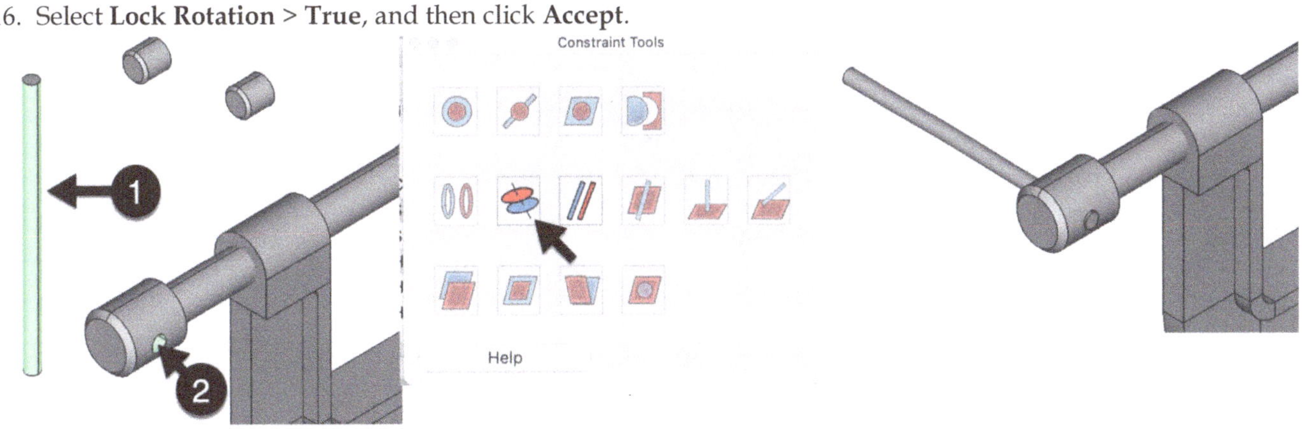

17. Close the **Constraint Tools** dialog.
18. Click the **Move the selected part under constraints** icon on the **A2p_Part** toolbar.
19. Select the handle, move the pointer toward right and click; the handle is moved along the constrained axis.

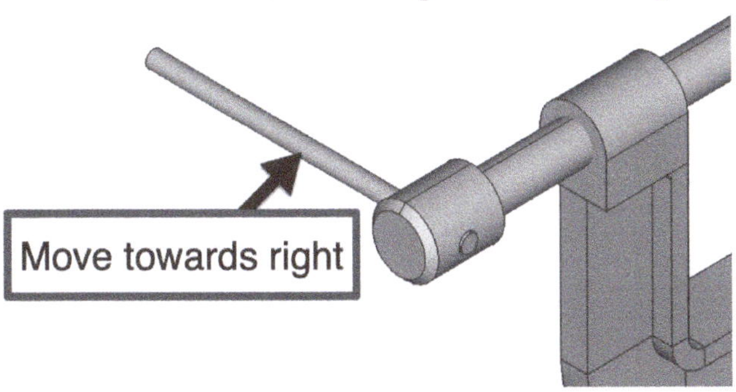

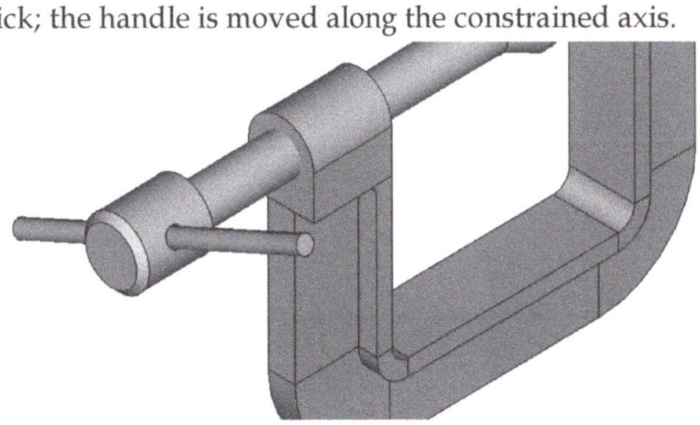

20. Press and hold the Ctrl key and click on the circular edge of the *Handle*, as shown.
21. Rotate the model and click on the inner circular edge of the *Handle cap*, as shown.
22. Click the **Add circularEdge constraint** icon on the **Constraint Tools** dialog.

23. Select **Direction > aligned** on the **Constraint Properties** dialog.
24. Select **Lock Rotation** > **True**, and then click **Accept**.

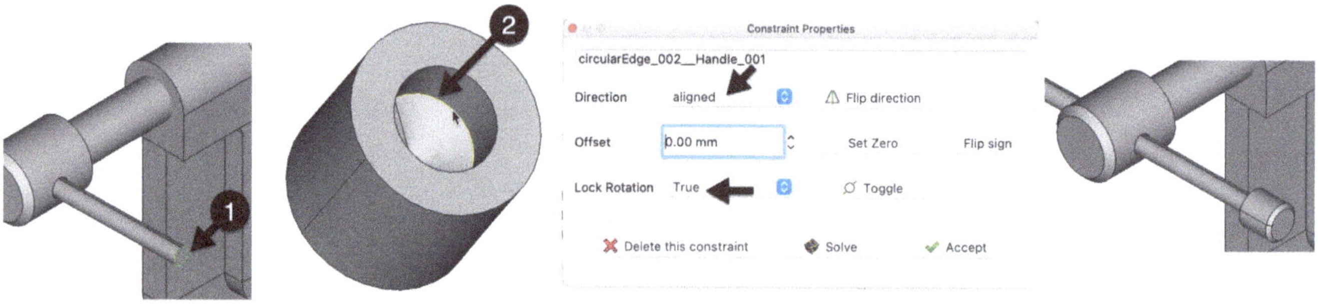

25. Press and hold the Ctrl key and click on the left circular edge of the *Handle* hole, as shown.
26. Rotate the model and click on the inner circular edge of the second *Handle cap*, as shown.
27. Click the **Add circularEdge constraint**  icon on the **Constraint Tools** dialog.
28. Select **Direction > opposed** on the **Constraint Properties** dialog.
29. Select **Lock Rotation** > **True**, and then click **Accept**.

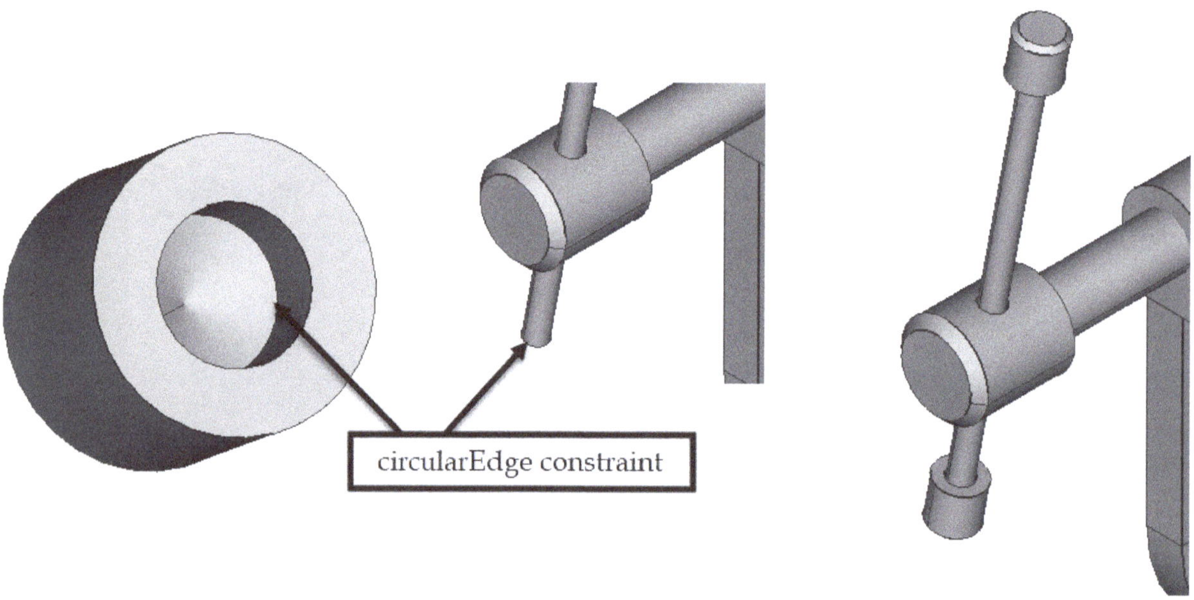

30. Click the **Print detailed DOF information**  icon on the **A2p_View** toolbar (or) **click A2plus > View > Print detailed DOF information** on the menu bar; the degrees of freedom of all the parts are displayed.

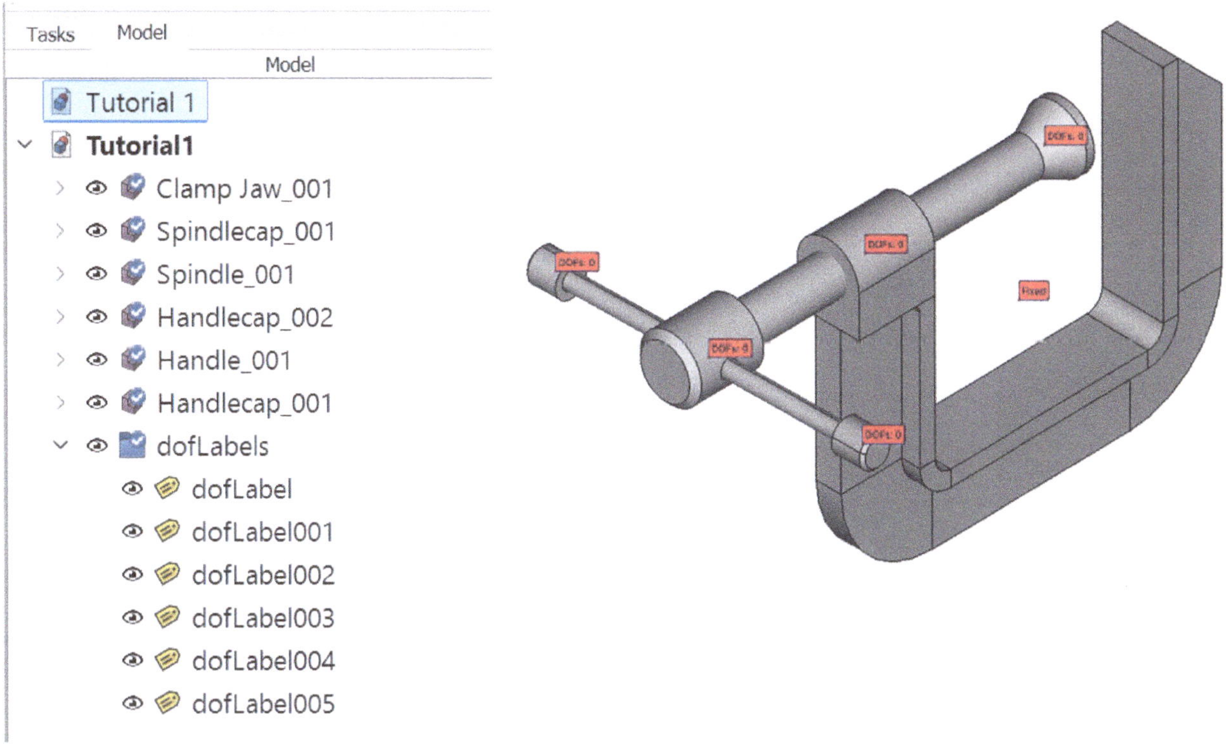

31. Click the **Print detailed DOF information**  icon on the **A2p_View** toolbar to hide the DOF labels.
32. Save and close the assembly file.

Questions

1. How do you start an assembly?
2. What is the use of the **Define Constraints** command?
3. What is the use of the **Angle Planes** command?
4. How to create a sub-assembly?

Exercises

Exercise 1

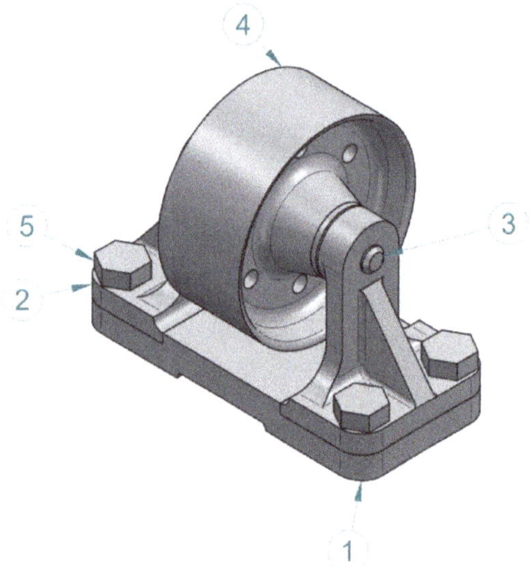

Item Number	File Name (no extension)	Quantity
1	Base	1
2	Bracket	2
3	Spindle	1
4	Roller-Bush assembly	1
5	Bolt	4

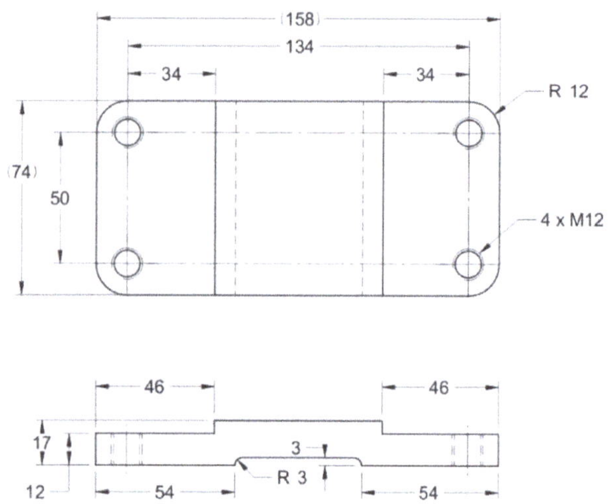

Base

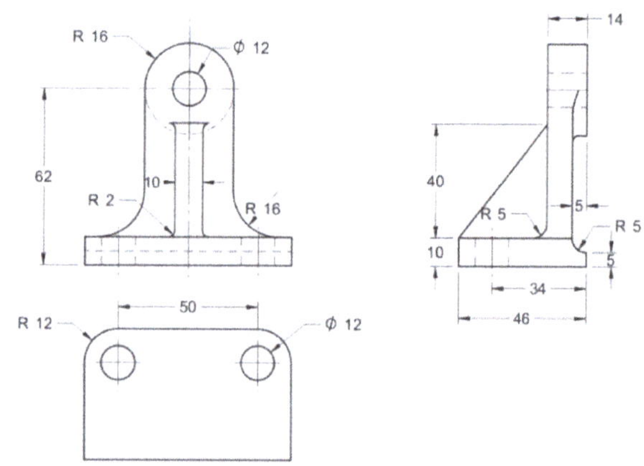

Bracket

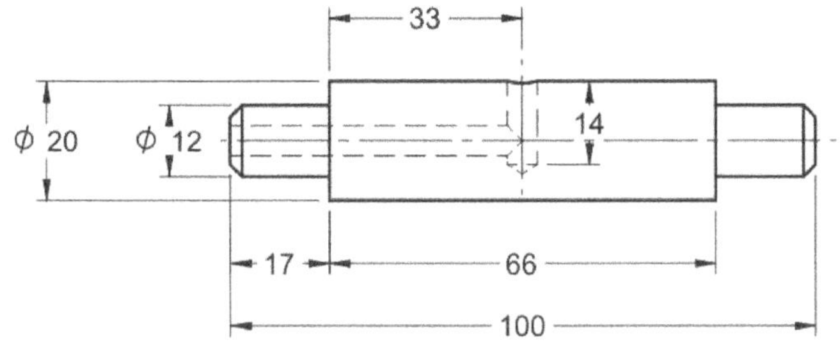

SPINDLE

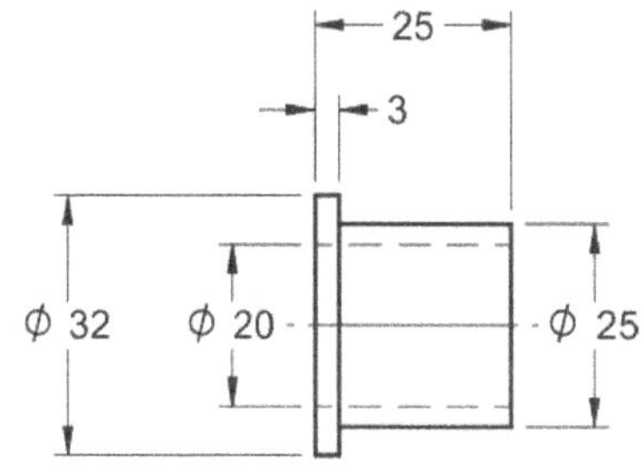

BUSH

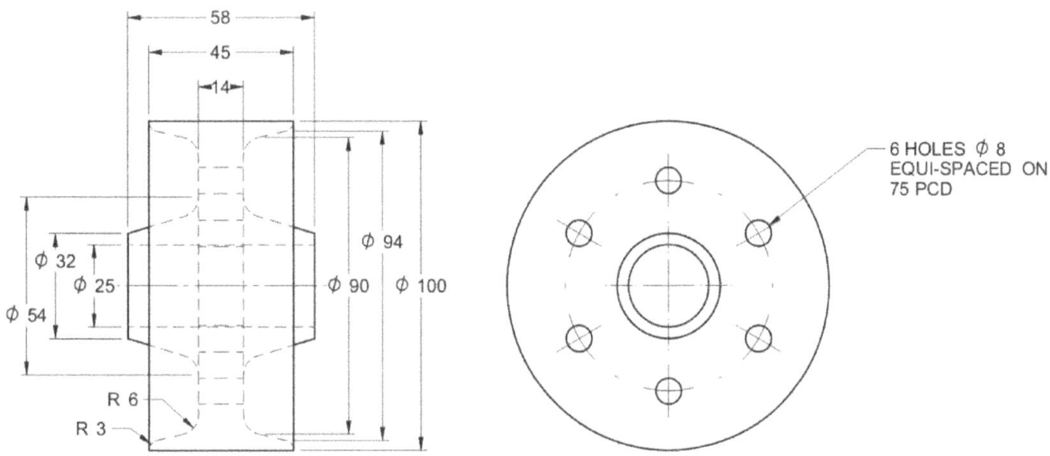

Roller

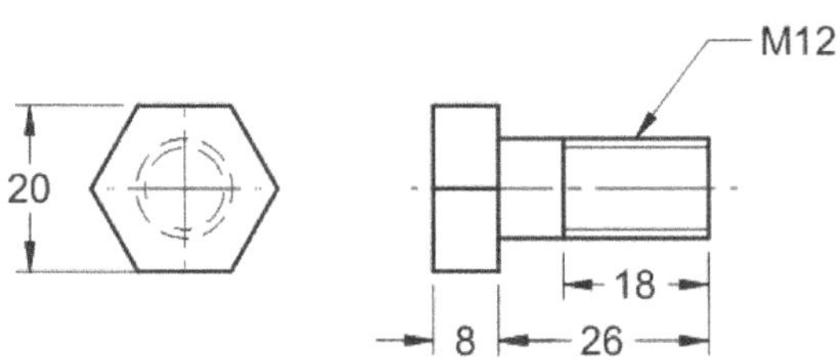

Bolt

Chapter 10: Drawings

Drawings are used to document your 3D models in the traditional 2D format, including dimensions and other instructions useful for manufacturing purposes. In FreeCAD 1.0, you first create 3D models and assemblies and then use them to generate drawings. There is a direct association between the 3D model and the drawing. When changes are made to the model, every view in the drawing will be updated. This relationship between the 3D model and the drawing makes the drawing process fast and accurate. Because the 2D drawings are widely used in the mechanical industry, drawings are one of the three main file types you can create in FreeCAD 1.0.

The topics covered in this chapter are:

- *Insert Views*
- *Projected Group*
- *Section views*
- *Detail views*
- *Centerlines*
- *Dimensions*
- *Text*

Starting a Drawing

To initiate the process of creating a new drawing in FreeCAD, follow these steps with precision:

1. **Open the Part File:** Begin by opening the specific part file for which you intend to generate a drawing. This part file serves as the basis for your drawing.
2. **Access TechDraw:** After opening the part file, navigate to the Workbench drop-down menu and select "**TechDraw**." Alternatively, you can go to the menu bar, click "**View**," then "**Workbench**," and choose "**TechDraw**."
3. **Preferences Configuration:** Proceed by accessing the preferences settings. You can achieve this by clicking "**Edit**" on the menu bar or, in the case of MacOS, by clicking "**FreeCAD 1.0**" on the title bar, and then selecting "**Preferences**."
4. **TechDraw Preferences:** In the **Preferences** dialog, locate the "**TechDraw**" option on the left side. Click on it to access the **TechDraw** preferences.
5. **Conventions Configuration:** Within the **TechDraw** preferences, switch to the "**General**" tab on the **Preferences** dialog. Here, under the "**Conventions**" section, select "**Projection Group Angle**" and set it to "**Third-angle**."

Click the **Browse** button next to the **Default Template** drop-down in the **File** section. Select the required template from the **Templates** folder and click Open. Click **OK** on the **Preferences** dialog.

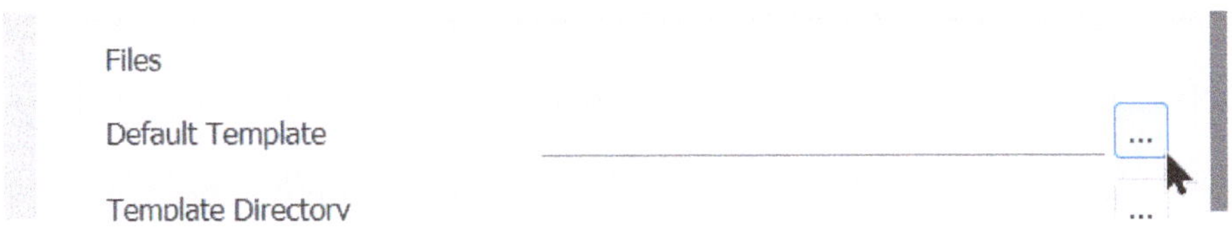

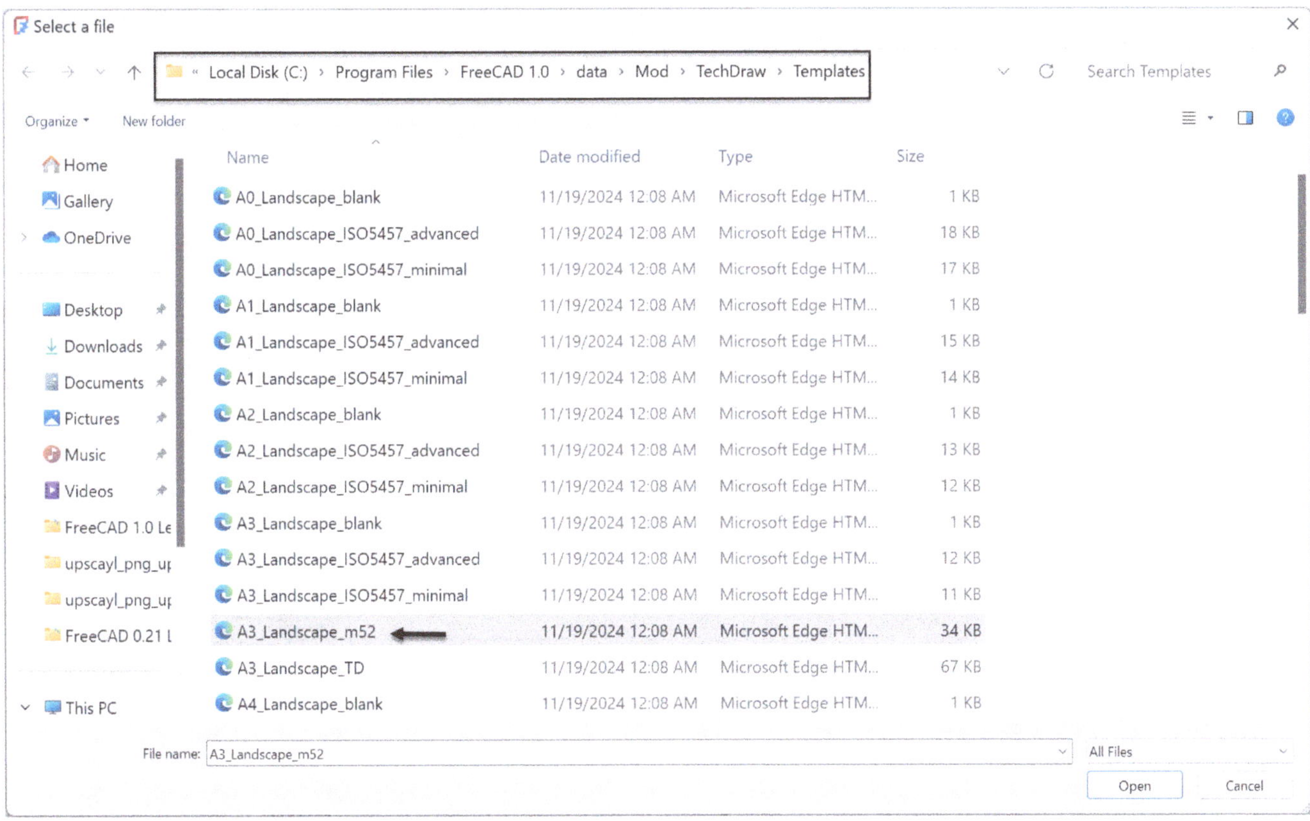

Inserting the Drawing page

Click **Insert Default Page** icon on the **TechDraw Pages** toolbar (or) click **TechDraw > Page > Insert Default Page** on the menu bar. The drawing page with the default template is inserted into the graphics window. Now, you can create drawing views and add annotations and dimensions.

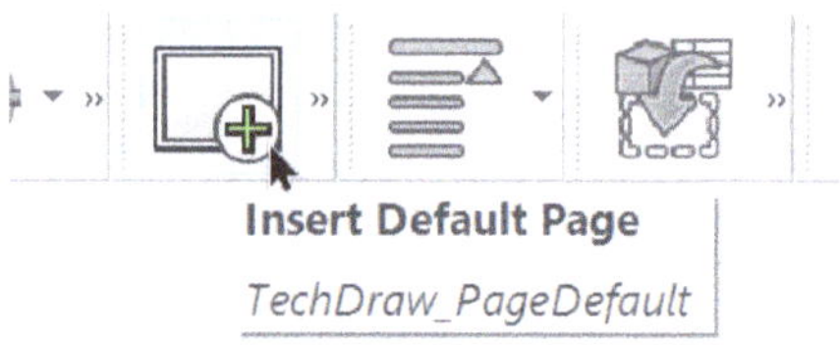

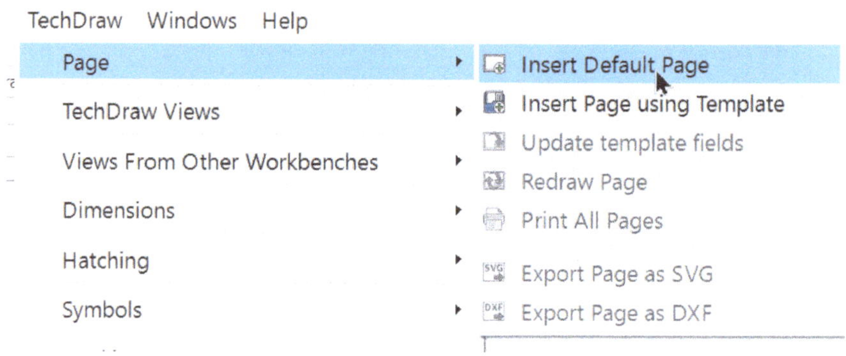

Insert View

To insert drawing views after adding a drawing page, follow these steps:

1. **Set the Model Orientation**: Switch to the 3D graphics window and adjust the model's orientation using the "**Standard View**" options on the **View** toolbar.
2. **Select a Face or Edge**: Choose a face or edge from the model. Then, click the "**Insert View**" icon on the **TechDraw Views toolbar** (or navigate to **TechDraw > TechDraw Views > Insert View** in the menu bar).

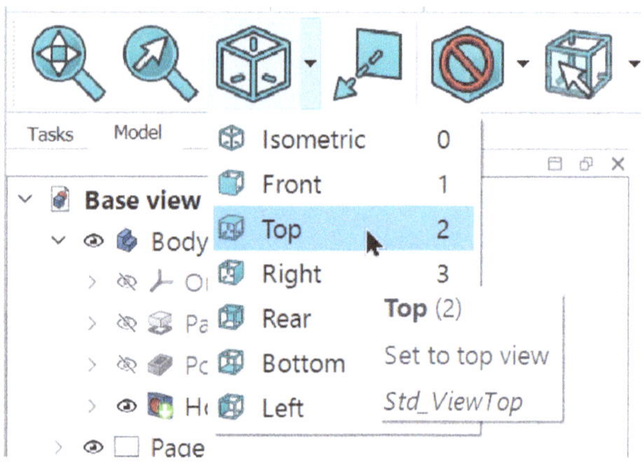

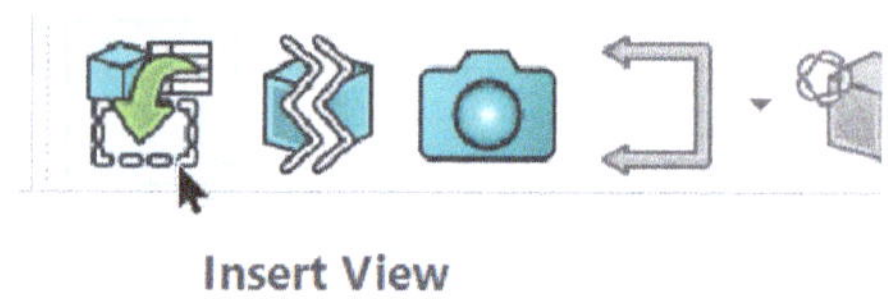

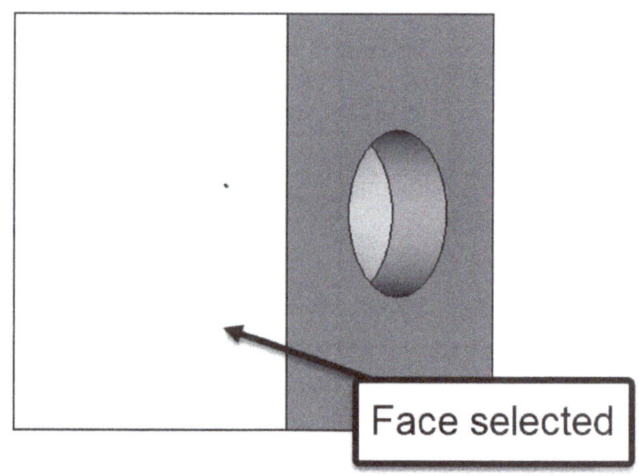

3. **Adjust the View Orientation**: The inserted view will appear on the drawing sheet in the **Page tab**. By default, the view orientation is set to the front view, regardless of the orientation selected in the 3D graphics window. This happens because the "**Set document front view as primary direction**" button is selected in the **Part view** section of the **Tasks panel**. To align the view with the selected face or edge, click the "**Set direction of camera, or selected face if any, as primary direction**" button.

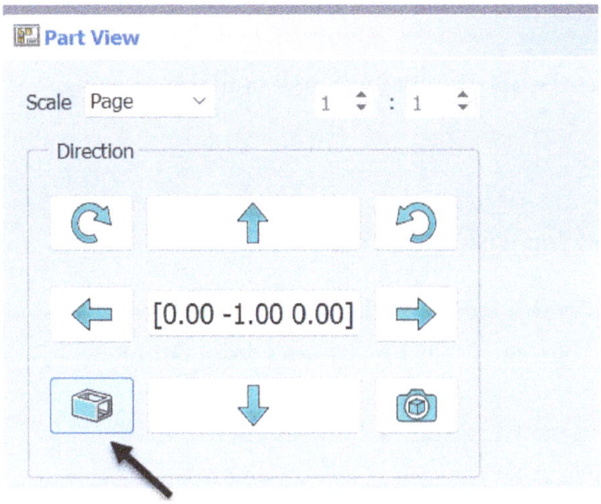

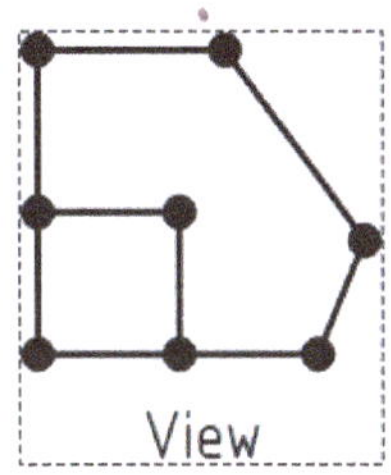

To adjust the size of the view to fit the sheet, change the scale factor using the **Scale** drop-down menu. You can select from the available options: **Page**, **Automatic**, or **Custom**. Choose **Page** for a direct scale, **Automatic** to let the software adjust the scale automatically, or **Custom** to manually input a specific scale factor that best fits your drawing sheet.

Use the arrow buttons in the **Direction** section on the **Part View** panel to change the orientation of the view.

Select the checkboxes in the **Secondary Projections** section. For example, select the **Top**, **Right**, and **RightFrontTop** checkboxes to create the top, right, and Isometric views.

Adjust the spacing between the views by entering values in the **X Spacing** and **Y Spacing** boxes. Next, click **OK** to create the projection group.

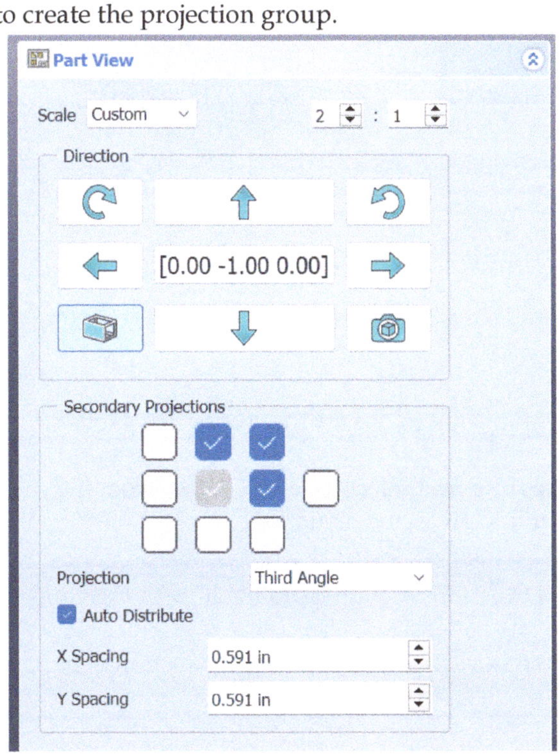

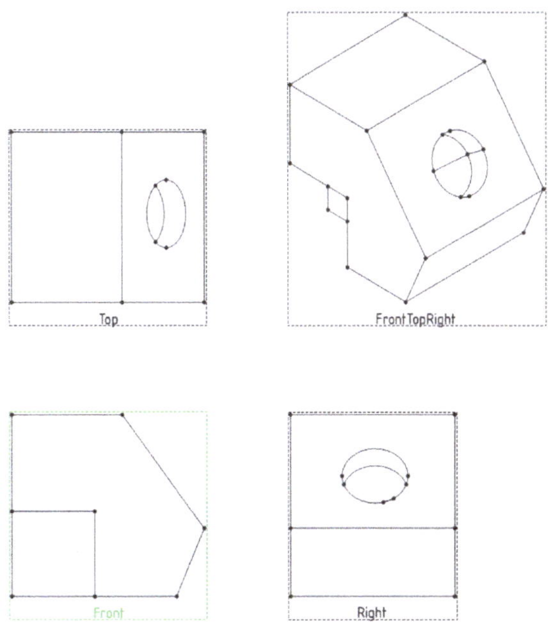

Insert Active View

This command serves to insert a snapshot of the model view from the 3D graphics window onto the drawing page. To execute this action, follow these steps:

1. Begin by switching to the 3D graphics window.
2. Within this window, select a face or edge from the model that you wish to capture.
3. Locate the "**Insert Active View**" icon on the **TechDraw Views** toolbar and click it. Alternatively, you can access this function by clicking "**TechDraw**" on the menu bar, then selecting "**Views from Other Workbenches**" > "**Insert Active View (3D View)**."
4. Once you've initiated the insertion process, proceed to specify the background using anyone of the background options within the **Active view to TD view** panel.
5. Finally, click "**OK**" to confirm and complete the insertion of the active view onto the drawing page.

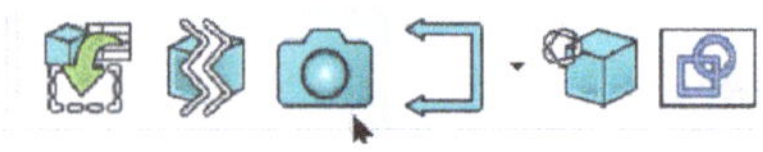

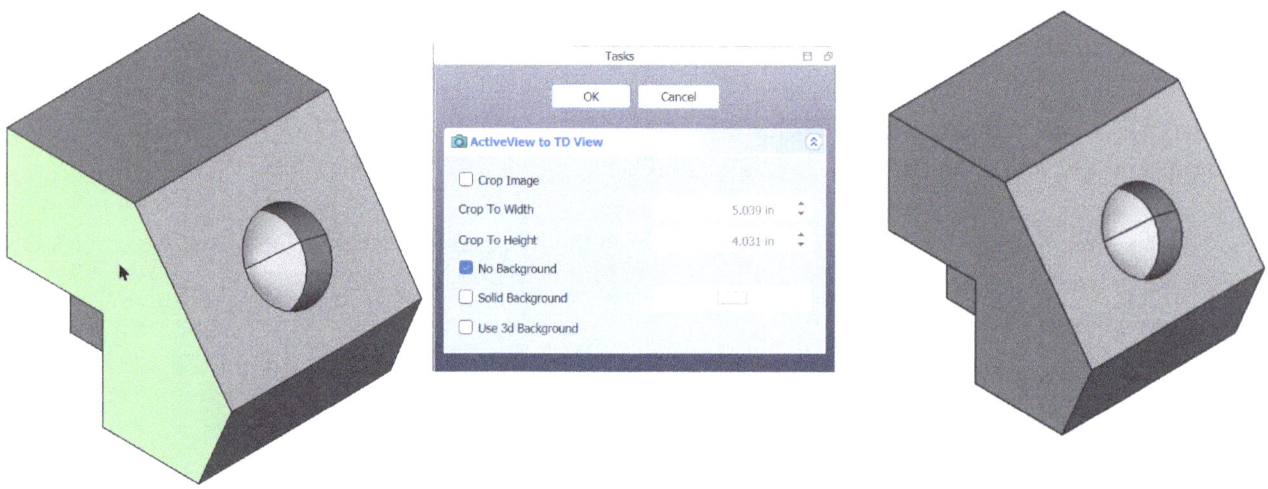

Section View

Section views are essential in 2D drawings to show the internal details of a 3D object. Here's how to create one in FreeCAD 1.0:

1. **Select the Base View**: Click on the frame of the base view you want to use for the section. This tells FreeCAD which view to work with.
2. **Access Section View Tools**: Go to the **TechDraw Views toolbar** and select "**Section View**" from the drop-down menu, or navigate to **TechDraw > Insert Section View** in the menu bar.
3. **Configure the Section View**: In the "**Create Section View**" panel:
    - Choose the **Section Orientation** in the "**Set View Direction**" section to define how the section plane cuts through the object.
    - Enable **Live Update** under the **Preview** section to see a real-time preview of the section view.

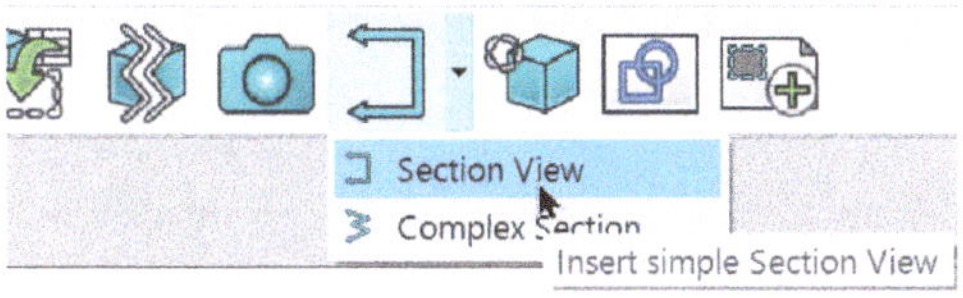

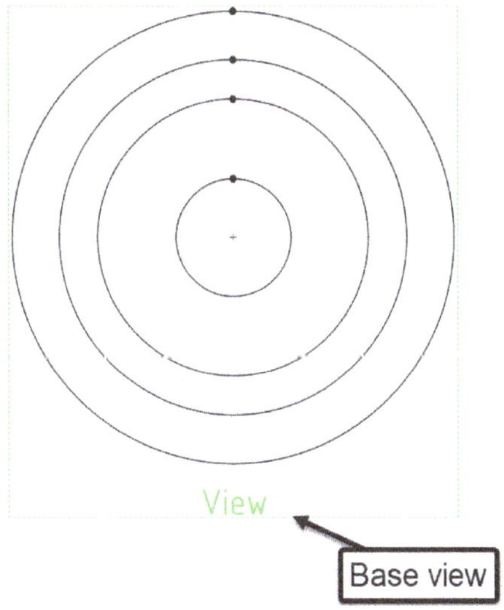

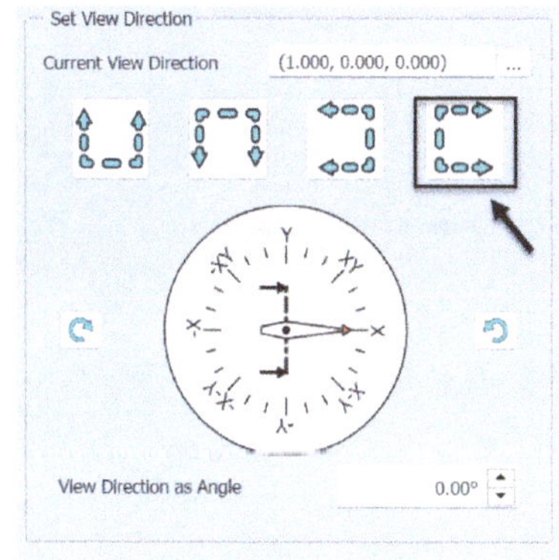

4. **Position the Section View:** Click and drag the section view to the desired location on your drawing. You also can position the section view horizontally and drag it, observing that it aligns horizontally with the base view.

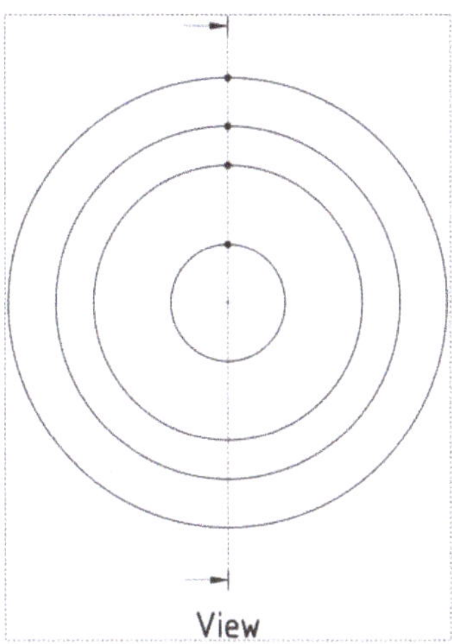

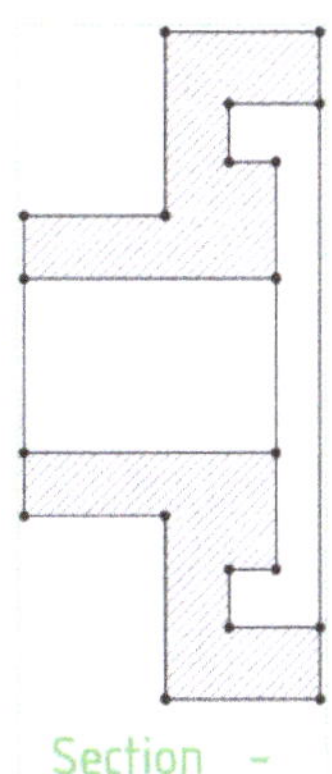

Enter a letter in the **Identifier** box to name the section view. You can change the section plane location by changing the X, Y or Z values. Next, click **OK** to create the section view.

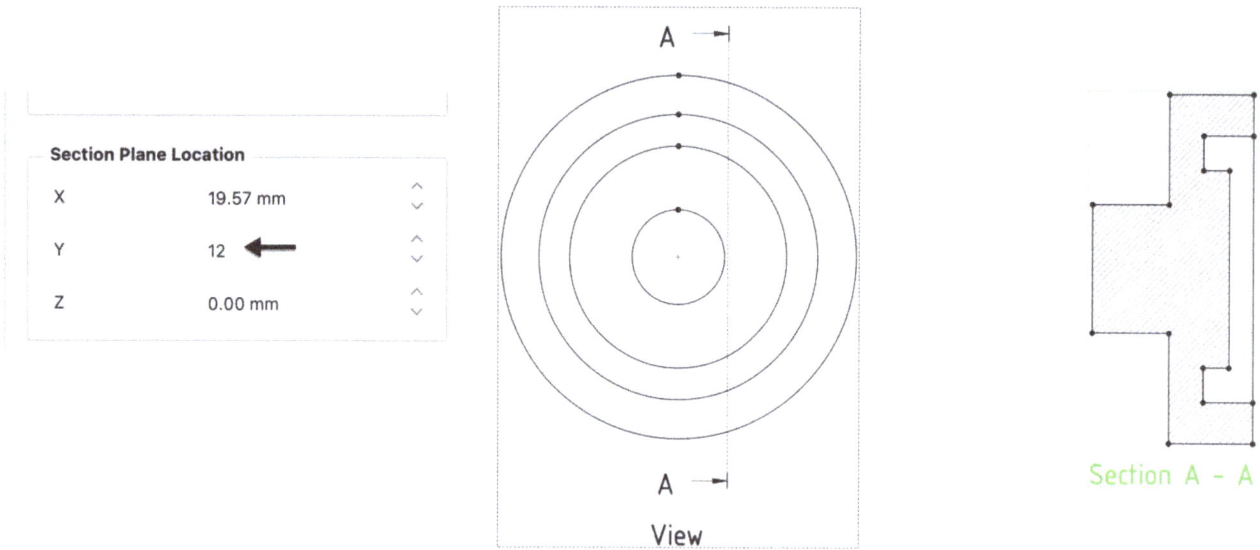

Section View alignment

By default, the section view is not aligned to the source view. You need align it manually. To do this, select the section view and click the **Position Section View**  command on the **TechDraw Attributes** toolbar aligns the selected view with the base view.

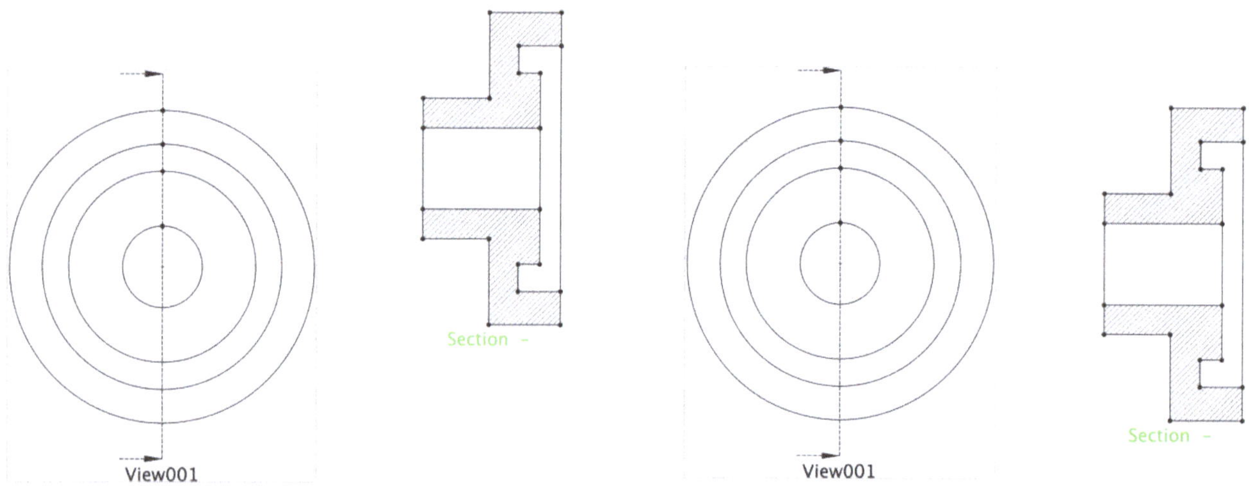

Creating an Offset view

Offset section views are a useful variation of standard section views in technical drawings. Unlike traditional section views that cut an object along a straight plane, offset section views shift the cutting plane away from the surface. This helps reveal internal features that might be hidden in a standard view, making it ideal for complex structures and highlighting specific details. Commonly used in mechanical, architectural, and electronic designs, offset section views improve communication and understanding by providing clearer depictions of an object's interior.

1. **Start with a Section Profile**:
    - Switch to the 3D model view.
    - Select the **Sketcher workbench** from the **Workbench drop-down menu**.
    - Choose the face of the model that should be perpendicular to the desired section view.
2. **Begin the Sketch**:
    - Click the "**Create Sketch**" icon on the **Sketcher toolbar**.
    - In the **Sketch attachment dialog**, select "**Plane face**" and click **OK**.

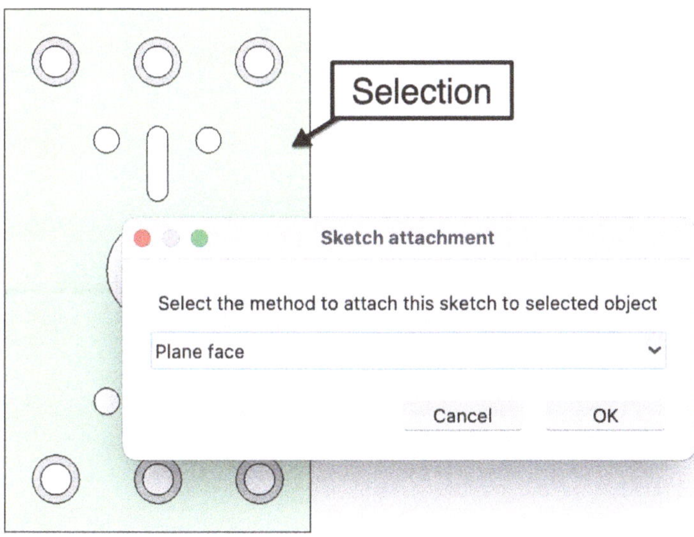

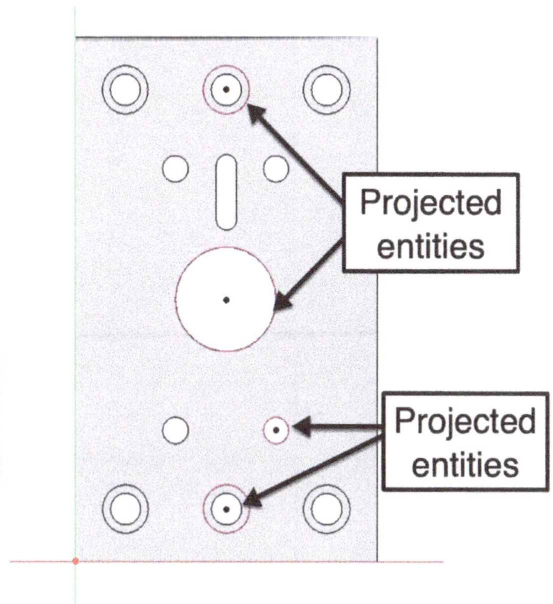

c. Click the "**Create external geometry**" icon on the **Sketcher tools** toolbar.
d. Select the vertices from the 3D model that your section line will pass through.
e. Sketch the section line, ensuring it intersects the features of the 3D geometry you want to include in the section view.
f. Use Sketcher constraint commands to align the section line with the projected geometry. Add dimensional constraints if needed.
g. Click the "**Close**" button on the **Tasks** panel.

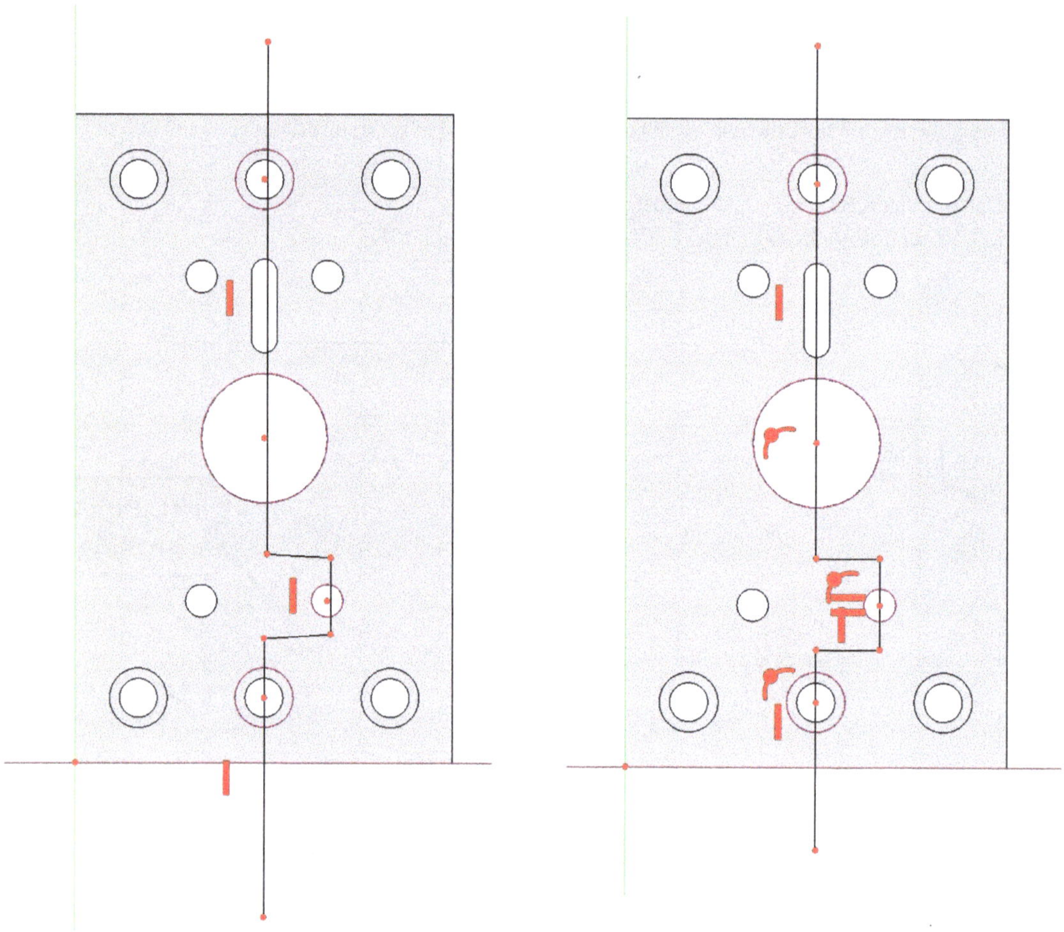

3. **Switch to TechDraw Workbench**:
    - Go to the **Page tab**.
    - Select the **TechDraw workbench** from the **Workbench drop-down menu**.
4. **Insert a Complex Section View**:
    - Hold the **CTRL key** (or **Command key** on Mac).
    - Select the **base view** and the **sketch** containing the section line from the **Model panel**.
    - On the **TechDraw Views toolbar**, click the "**Section View**" drop-down and choose "**Complex Section View**".
5. **Set Section Parameters**:
    - In the **New Complex Section panel**, under **Section Parameters**:
        - Set the **Projection Strategy** to "**Offset**".
        - Choose the **Scale Type** and enter an **Identifier**.
    - In the **Set View Direction** section, select the appropriate option to define how the section plane cuts through the object.

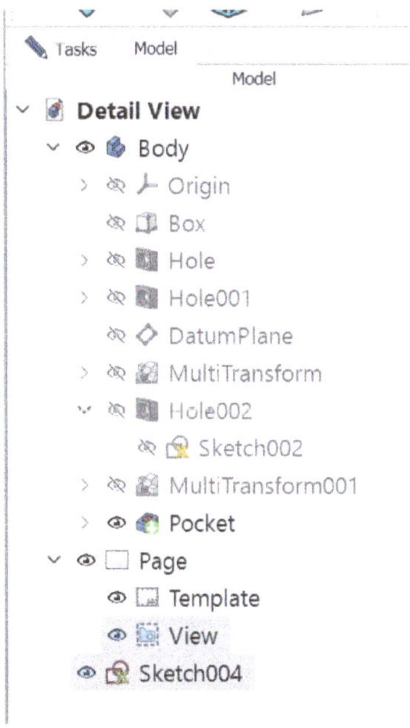

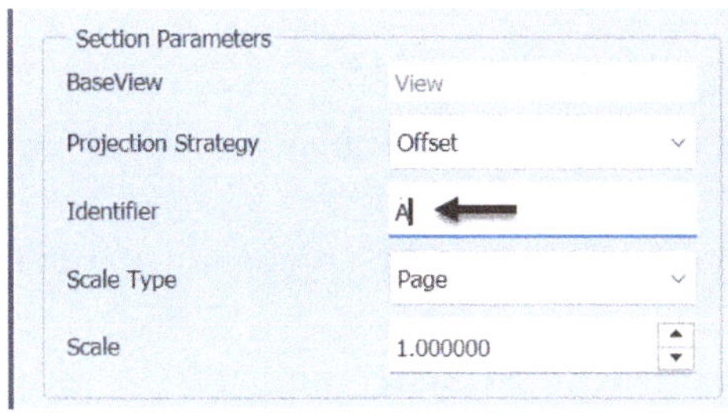

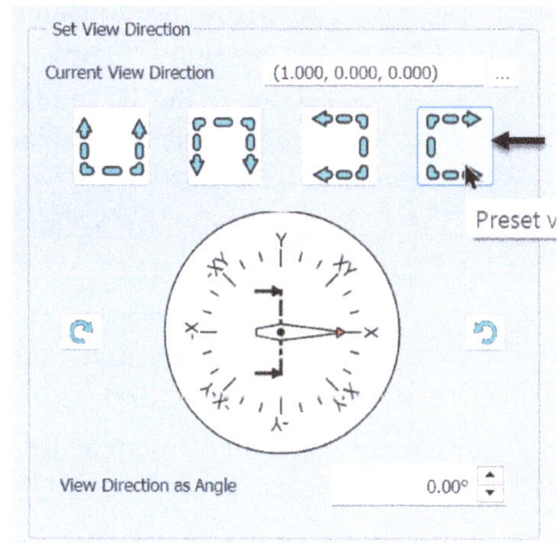

6. Finalize the Section View: Click "**OK**" to create the offset section view.

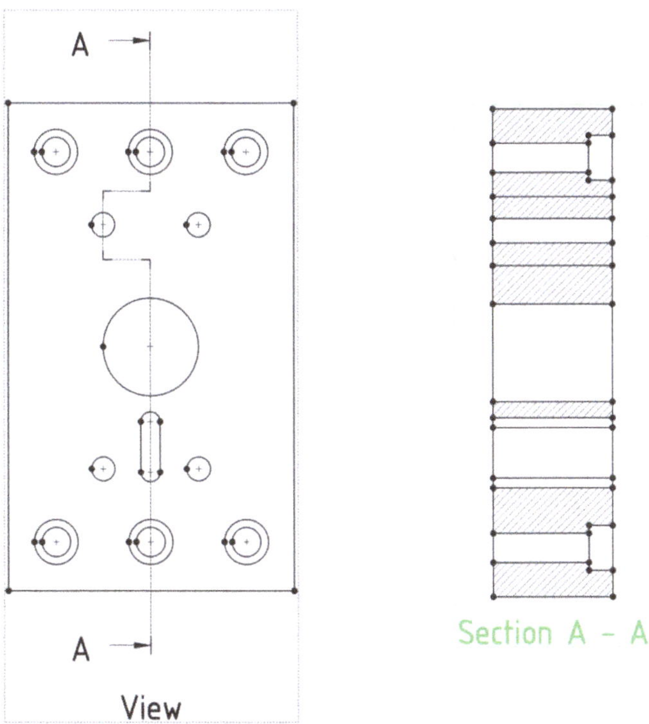

Creating a Revolved Section View

A revolved section view is a powerful technique in technical drawing that provides a detailed 2D representation of a mechanical part's internal features. By revolving a cutting plane around an axis, it reveals complex components like gears, pistons, and bearings. This method is essential in industries such as automotive design, helping visualize internal systems, identify issues, and improve designs.

Steps to Create a Revolved Section View

1. **Prepare the Section Profile**:
    - Switch to the **3D model view**.
    - Select the **Sketcher workbench** from the **Workbench drop-down menu**.
2. **Select the Base Face**:
    - Choose the face of the 3D model that should be perpendicular to the desired section view.
3. **Start the Sketch**:
    - Click the "**Create Sketch**" icon on the **Sketcher toolbar**.
    - In the **Sketch attachment dialog**, select "**Plane face**" and click **OK**.
4. **Define Sketch Boundaries**:
    - Click the "**Create external geometry**" icon on the **Sketcher tools toolbar**.
    - Select the vertices on the 3D model where the section line will pass.

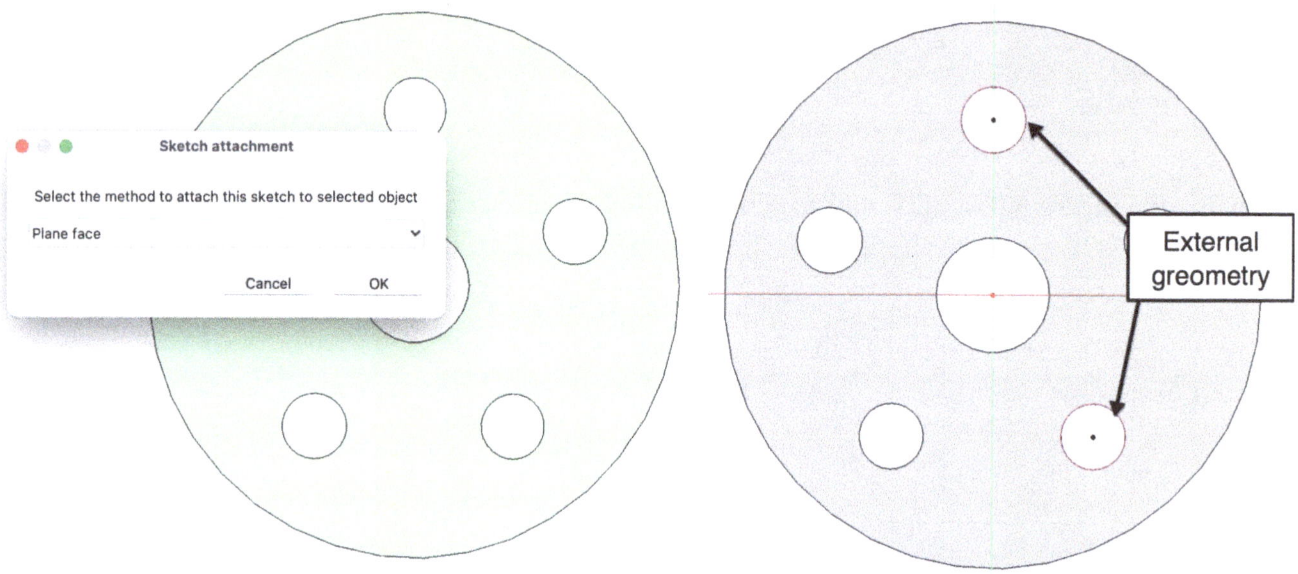

5. **Draw the Section Line**:
    - Sketch a section line that intersects the features you want to include.
    - Ensure the line has two or more angled linear elements.
    - Use **Sketcher constraints** to align the line with the geometry and add **dimensional constraints** if needed.

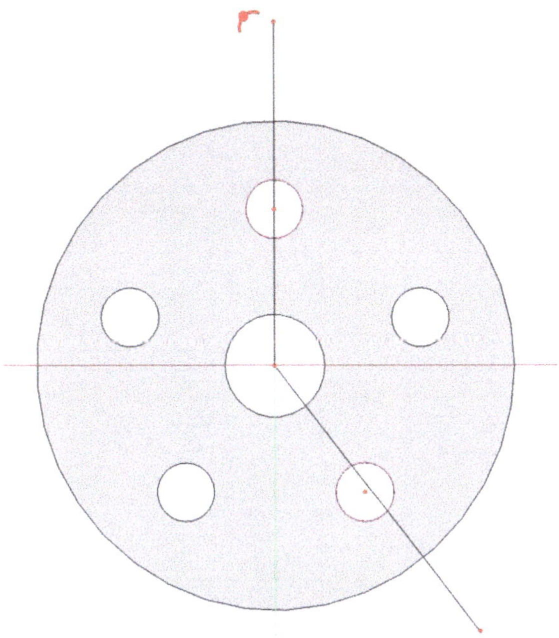

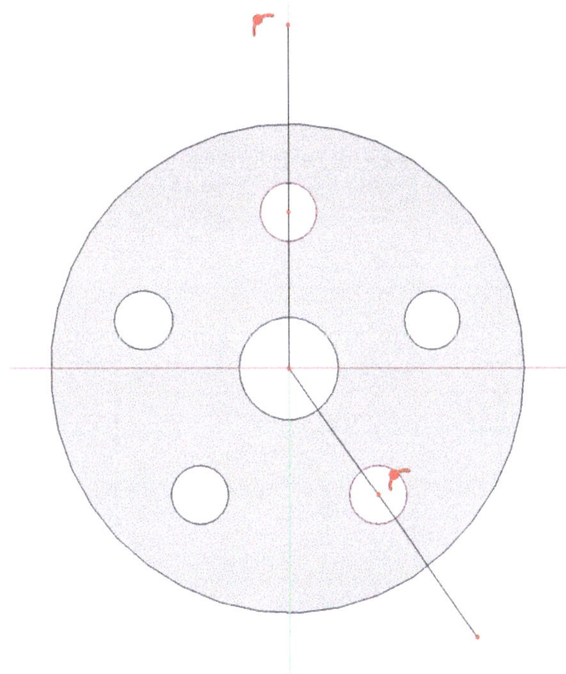

6. **Complete the Sketch**:
   - Click "**Close**" in the **Tasks panel**.
   - Switch to the **Page tab** and select the **TechDraw workbench**.
7. **Generate the Section View**:
   - Hold the **CTRL key** (or **Command key** on Mac) and select the **base view** and the **sketch** from the **Model tab**.
   - Go to the **TechDraw Views toolbar** and choose "**Section View**" > "**Complex Section View** ", or select **TechDraw > TechDraw Views > Insert Complex Section Views** from the menu bar.
8. **Configure Section Parameters**:
   - In the **New Complex Section panel**, set the **Projection Strategy** to "**Aligned**".
   - Define the **Scale Type** and enter an **Identifier**.

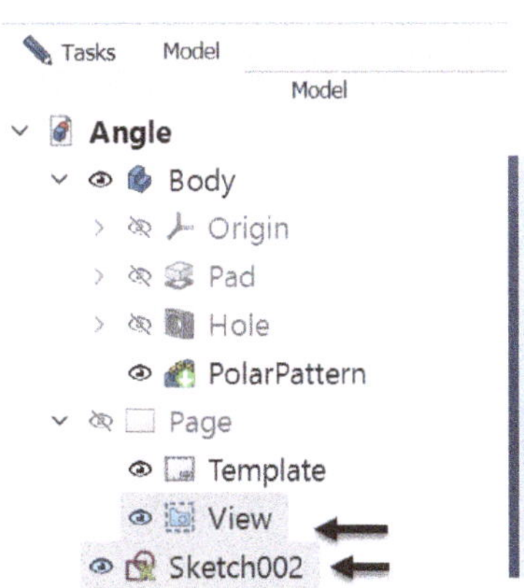

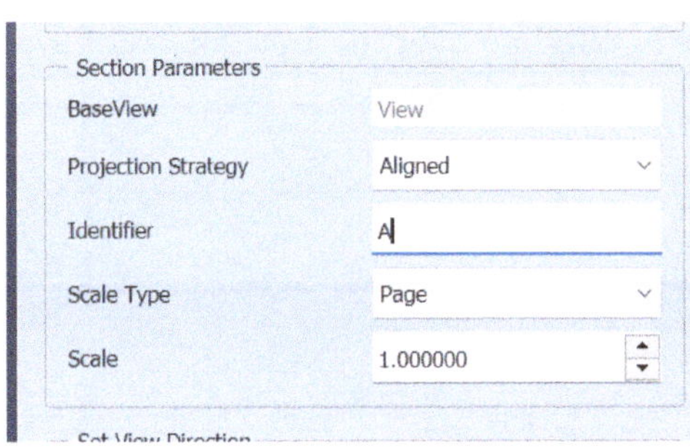

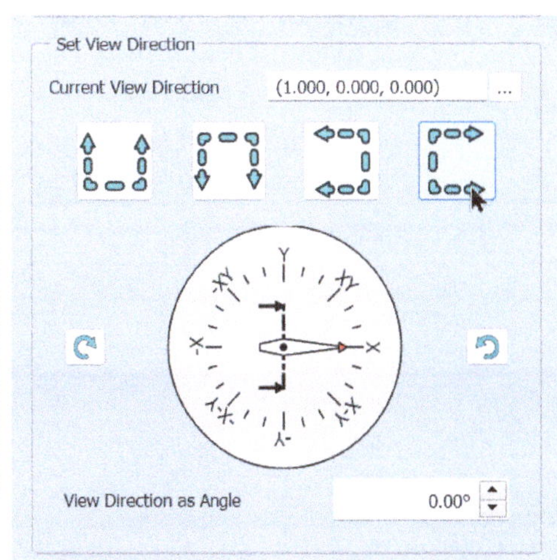

9. **Set View Direction**:

- Choose the appropriate option in the **Set View Direction** section to define the cutting plane's orientation.

10. **Preview and Create**:
    - Enable **Live Update** in the **Preview section** to see a real-time preview.
    - Click **OK** to generate the revolved section view.

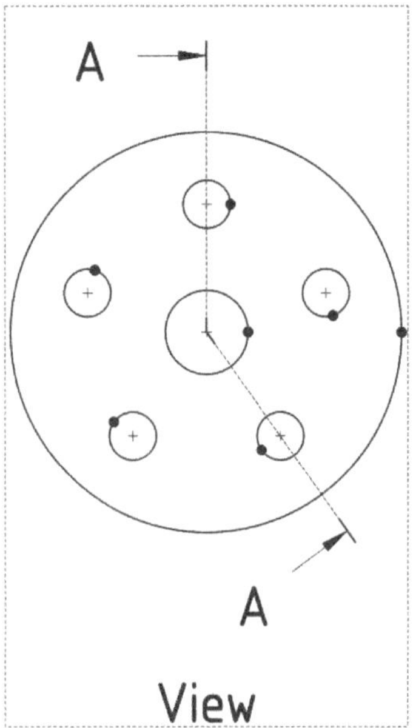

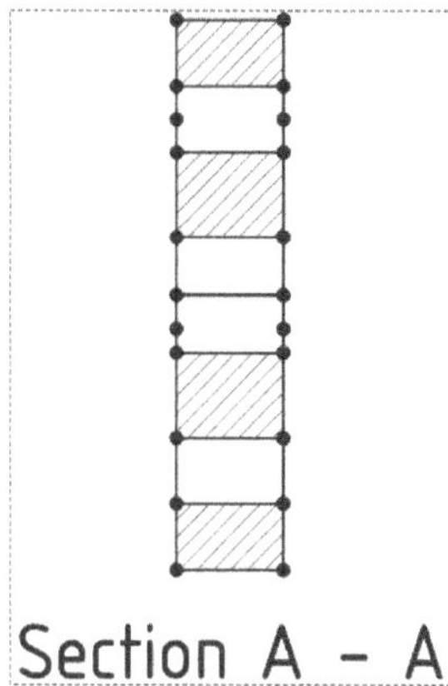

Detail View

When a drawing view contains small or intricate features that are hard to see, a detailed view can help zoom in and improve clarity. Follow these steps to create one:

1. **Select the Base View**: Choose the base view where you want to create the detailed view.
2. **Access Detail View Tools**:
    - Click the "**Insert Detail View**" icon on the **TechDraw Views toolbar**, or
    - Go to **TechDraw > TechDraw Views > Insert Detail View** in the menu bar.
3. **Highlight the Area**:
    - In the **New Detail View** panel, click the "**Drag Highlight**" button.
    - Use your cursor to drag the highlighter over the area you want to zoom in on.

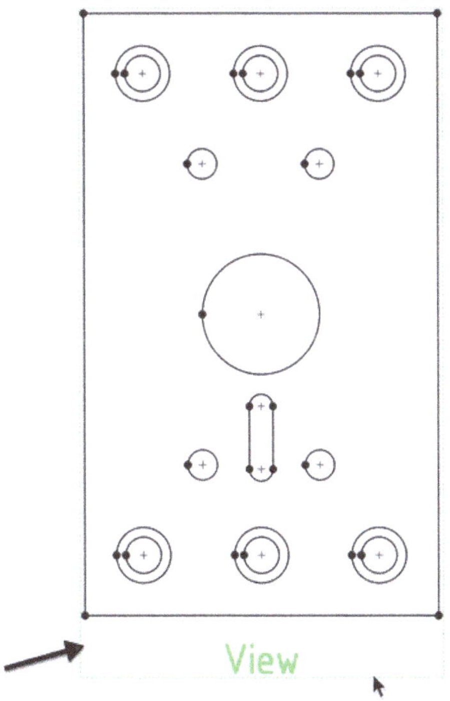

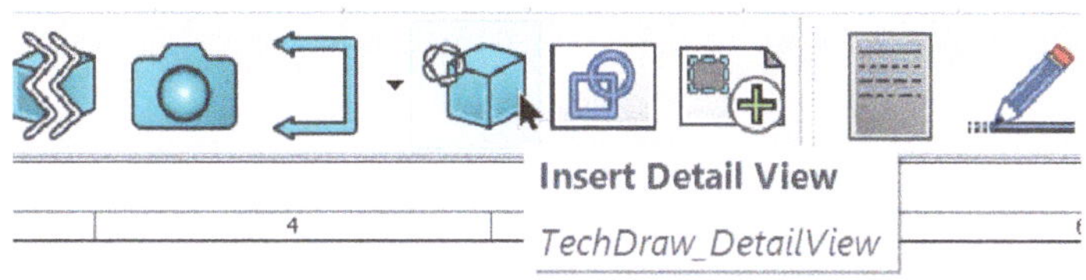

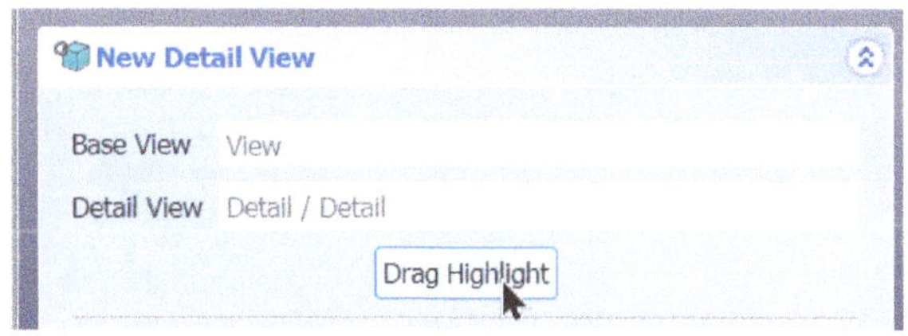

4. **Adjust Radius and Magnification**:
   - Set the **Radius** to control the size of the highlighted area.
   - Enter a **Scale factor** to determine the magnification level of the detailed view.

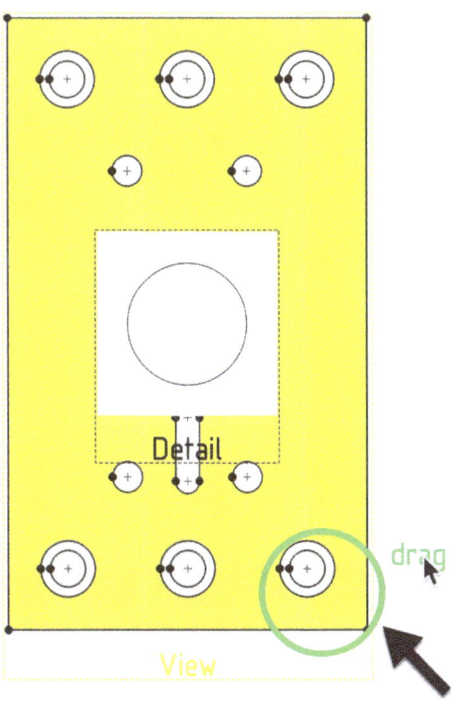

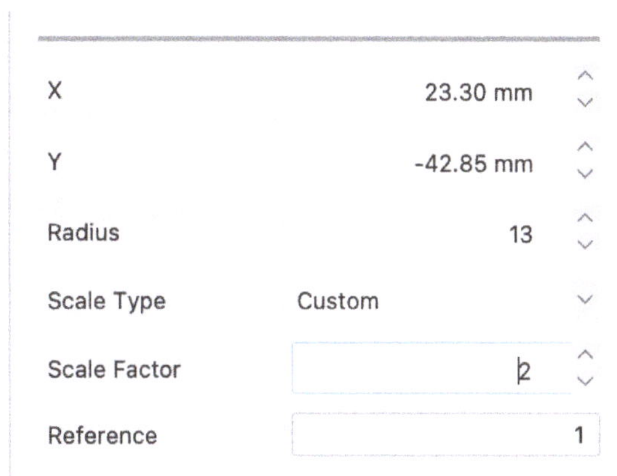

5. **Position the Detailed View**: Click and drag the detailed view to place it where you want in the drawing.

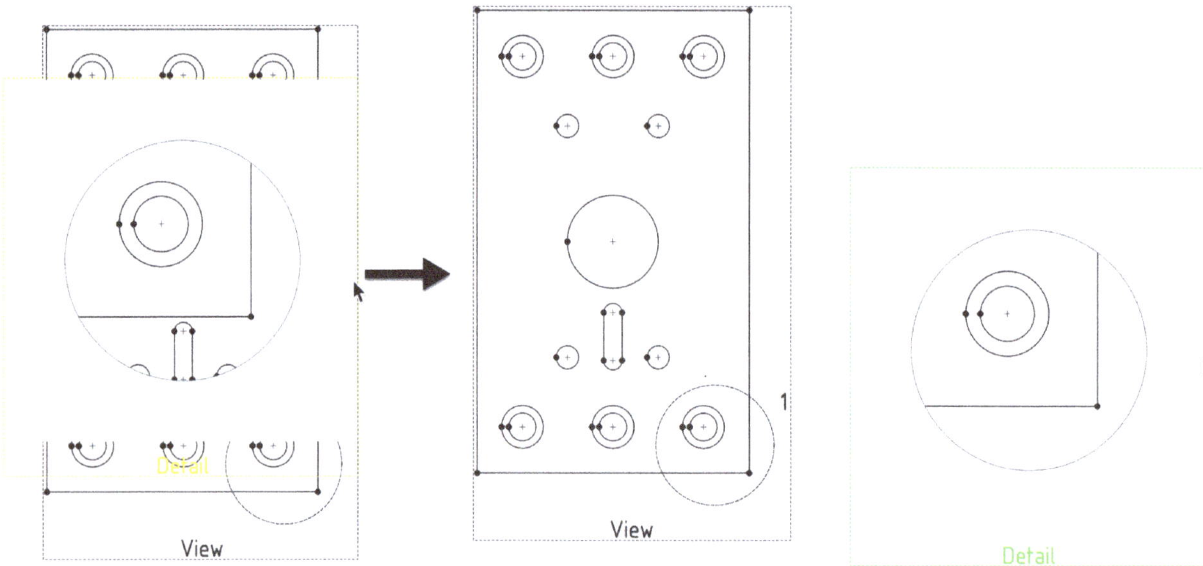

6. **Finalize**: Click **OK** to confirm and create the detailed view.

Add Centerlines to Faces

To include centerlines in your drawing, follow these steps:

1. **Select a Cylindrical Face**: Choose the cylindrical face in the drawing view where you want to add centerlines.
2. **Access Centerline Tools**:
   - On the **TechDraw Annotations toolbar**, click "**Add Lines**" in the drop-down menu and select "**Add Centerlines to Faces**  ", or
   - Go to **TechDraw > Add Lines > Add Centerlines to Faces** in the menu bar.
3. **Configure Line Properties**:
   - In the **Create Center Line** panel, adjust the **Weight** and **Style** settings to define the appearance of the centerlines.
4. **Apply Centerlines**: Click **OK** to confirm and add the centerlines to the selected cylindrical face.

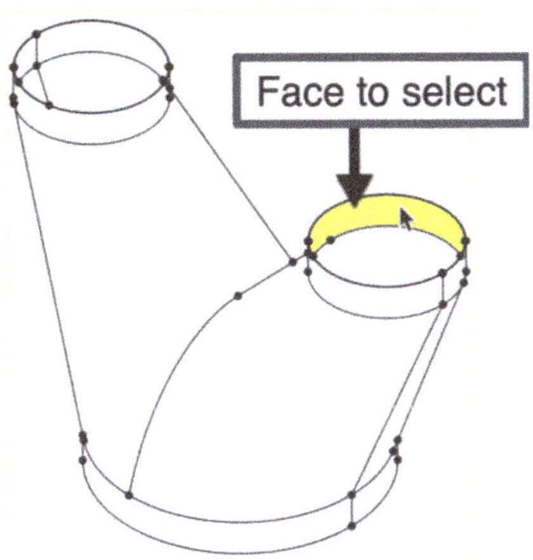

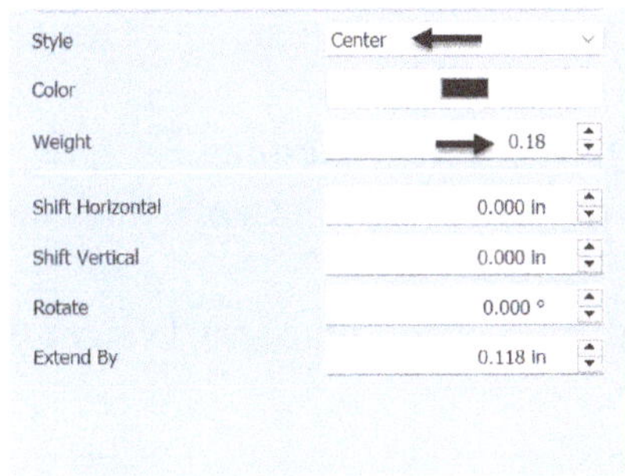

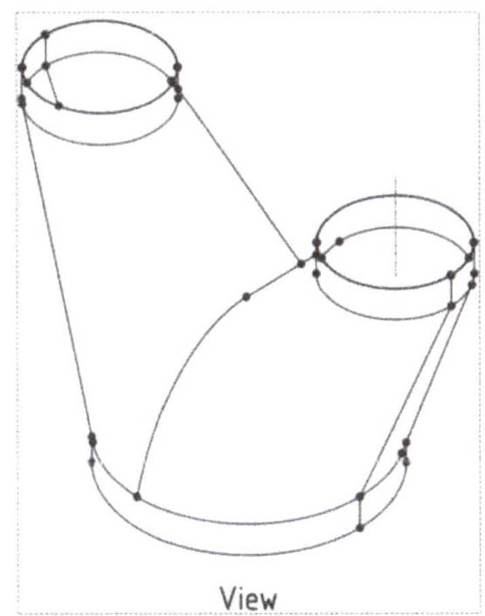

Add Centerline between 2 Lines

The "**Add Centerline between 2 Lines**" command is useful for creating a centerline that bisects two lines, especially in section or projected views. Here's how to use it:

1. **Select the Lines**: Hold the **CTRL key** (or **COMMAND key** on Mac) and click the two edges you want to bisect with the centerline.
2. **Access the Command**:
    - On the **TechDraw Annotations toolbar**, click "**Add Lines** " in the drop-down menu and select "**Add Centerlines between 2 Lines**", or
    - Go to **TechDraw > Add Lines > Add Centerlines between 2 Lines** in the menu bar.
3. **Customize the Centerline**:
    - In the **Create Center Line** panel, adjust the **Weight** and **Style** settings to suit your needs.
4. **Apply the Centerline**: Click **OK** to generate the centerline between the selected lines.

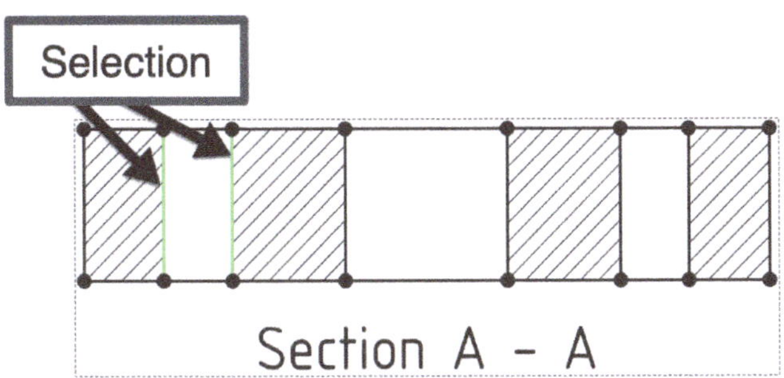

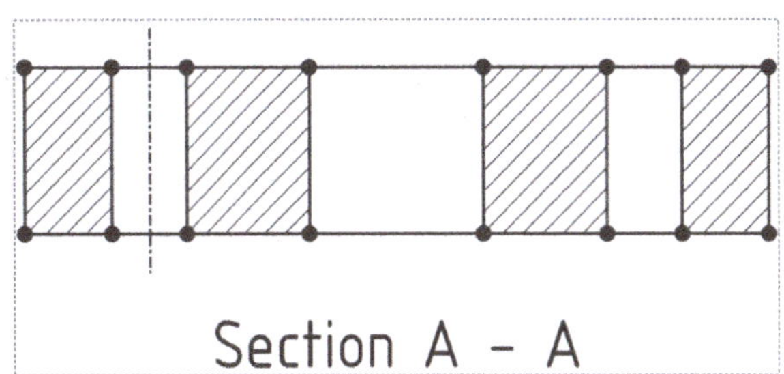

Add Centerline between 2 Points

The "**Add Centerline between 2 Points**" command allows you to draw a centerline between two specified points. Follow these steps:

1. **Select the Points**: Hold the **CTRL key** (or **COMMAND key** on Mac) and click the two vertices or points where you want the centerline to run.
2. **Access the Tool**:

- On the **TechDraw Annotations toolbar**, click "**Add Lines**" in the drop-down menu and select "**Add Centerlines between 2 Points** ", or
- Go to **TechDraw > Add Lines > Add Centerlines between 2 Points** in the menu bar.

3. **Set Line Properties**:
   - In the **Create Center Line** panel, adjust the **Weight** (thickness) and **Style** (appearance) of the centerline.
4. **Create the Centerline**: Click **OK** to generate the centerline between the selected points.

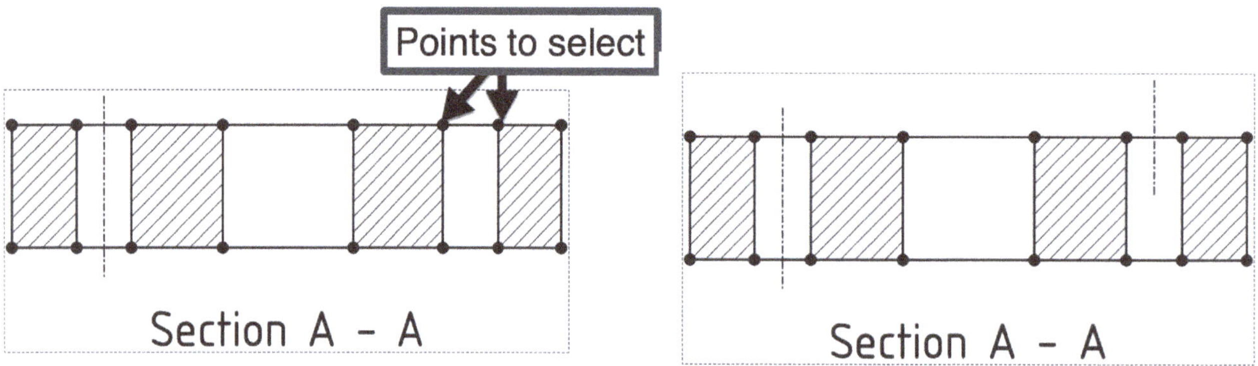

Add Circle Centerlines

To include centerlines in a circle, follow these steps:

1. **Select the Circular Edge**: Choose the circular edge in the drawing view where you want to add centerlines.
2. **Access Circle Centerlines Options**:
   - On the **TechDraw Centerlines toolbar**, click the **Circle Centerlines** drop-down, or
   - Go to **TechDraw > Extensions: Centerlines/Threading > Add Circle Centerlines** in the menu bar.

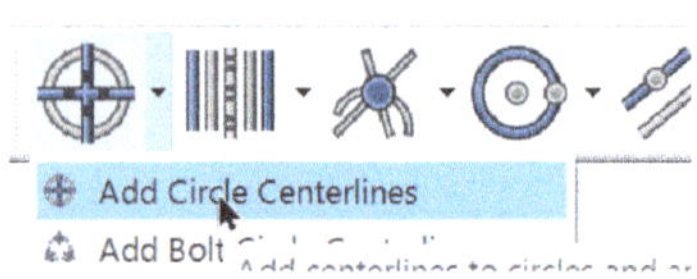

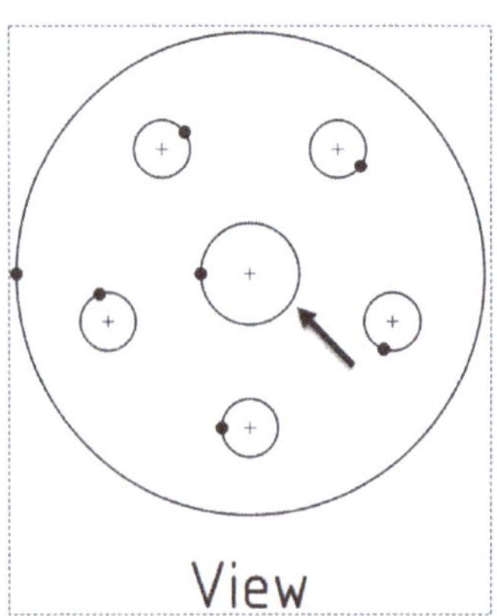

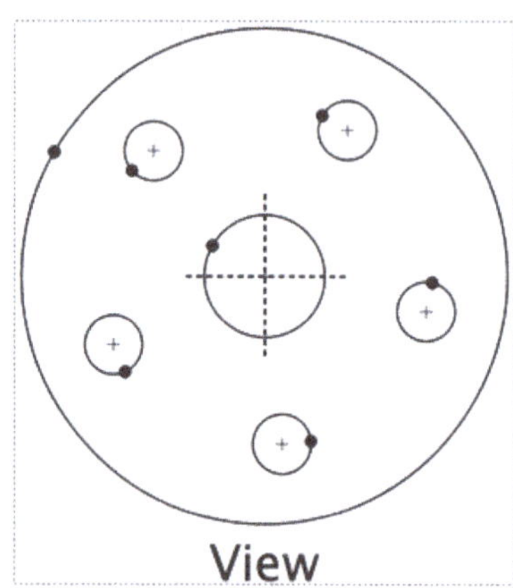

Add Bolt Circle Centerlines

A bolt circle centerline is essential in engineering for components with multiple holes arranged in a circular pattern, such as wheel rims, flanges, or mounting plates. It serves several purposes:

- **Alignment**: Ensures precise hole alignment for proper assembly and secure fastening.
- **Measurement**: Simplifies measuring distances between holes for accurate placement.
- **Visual Reference**: Provides a clear visual guide for understanding hole positioning and geometry.

1. **Select Holes**: Hold the **CTRL key** (or **COMMAND key** on Mac) and select all the holes in the circular pattern.
2. **Access the Command**:
   - On the **TechDraw Centerlines toolbar**, click the **Circle Centerlines** drop-down and choose "**Add Bolt Circle Centerlines**", or
   - Go to **TechDraw > Extensions: Centerlines/Threading > Add Bolt Circle Centerlines** in the menu bar.

3. **Create the Centerline**: FreeCAD will automatically generate a bolt circle centerline through the selected holes.

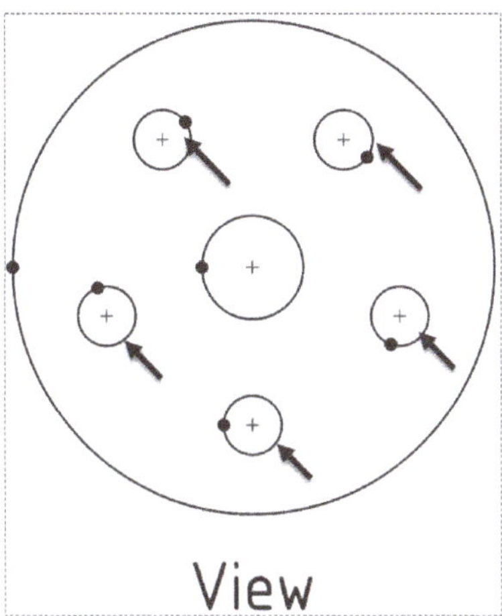

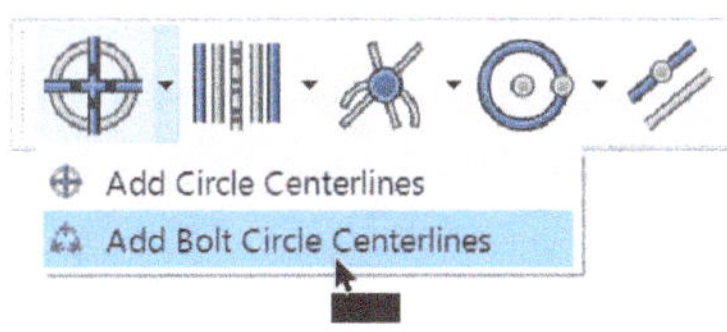

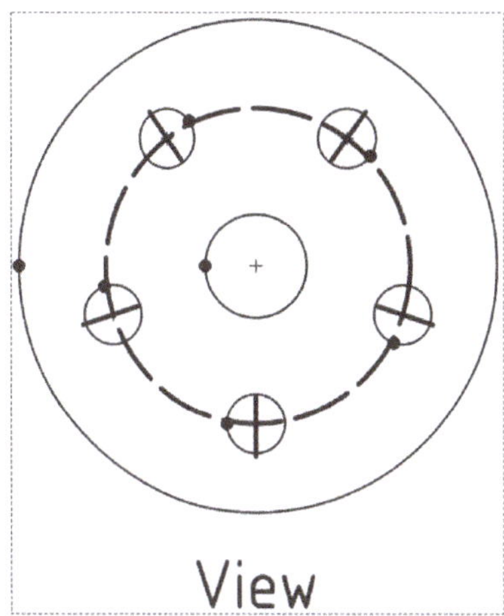

Add Cosmetic Thread Hole Bottom View

The "**Add Cosmetic Thread Hole Bottom View**" command allows you to add a cosmetic thread to a hole, visible from either the top or bottom view of your drawing. Here's how to use it:

1. **Select the Hole Edge**: Click on the edge of the hole where you want to add the cosmetic thread.
2. **Access the Command**:
   - On the **TechDraw Centerlines toolbar**, click the **Cosmetic Thread** drop-down and select "**Add Cosmetic Thread Hole Bottom View**", or
   - Go to **TechDraw > Extensions: Centerlines/Threading > Add Cosmetic Thread Hole Bottom View** in the menu bar.

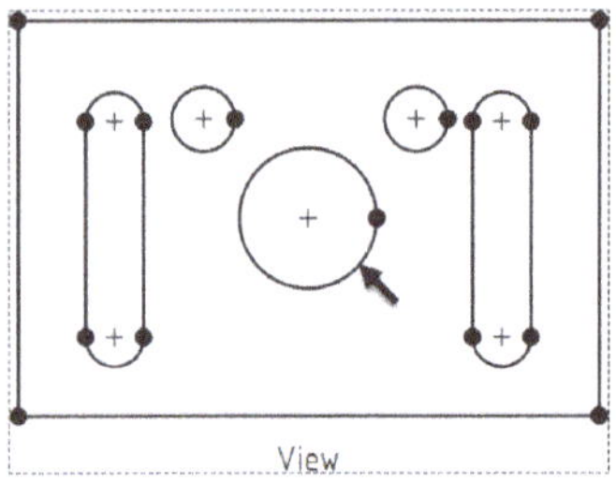

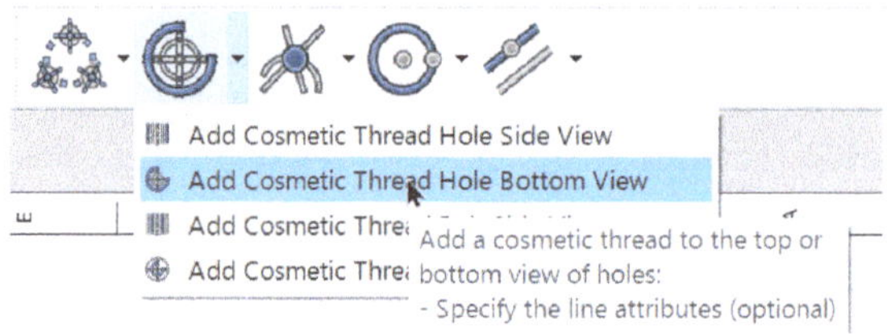

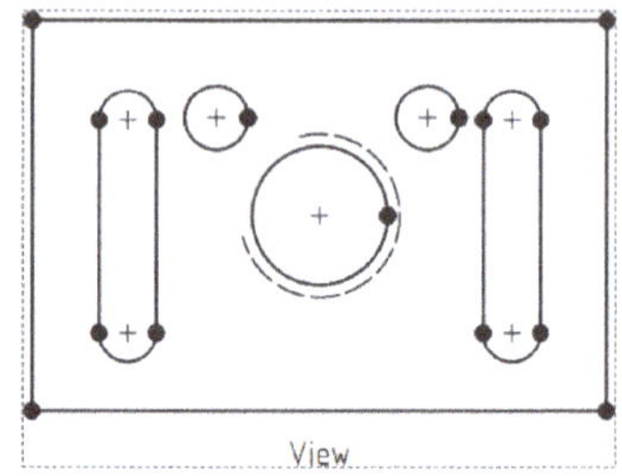

Add Cosmetic Thread Hole Side View

The **Add Cosmetic Thread Hole Side View** command lets you add a cosmetic thread to a hole in the side or section view of your design. Cosmetic threads provide a visual representation of threads without detailed modeling, enhancing the clarity of your technical drawings.

Steps to Use the Command

1. **Select the Hole Edges**: Hold the **CTRL key** (or **COMMAND key** on Mac) and select the edges of the hole where you want to add the thread.
2. **Access the Cosmetic Thread Option**:
    - On the **TechDraw Centerlines toolbar**, click the **Cosmetic Thread** drop-down, or
    - Go to **TechDraw > Extensions: Centerlines/Threading** in the menu bar.
3. **Choose 'Add Cosmetic Thread Hole Side View'**: Select this option from the drop-down menu to apply the cosmetic thread.

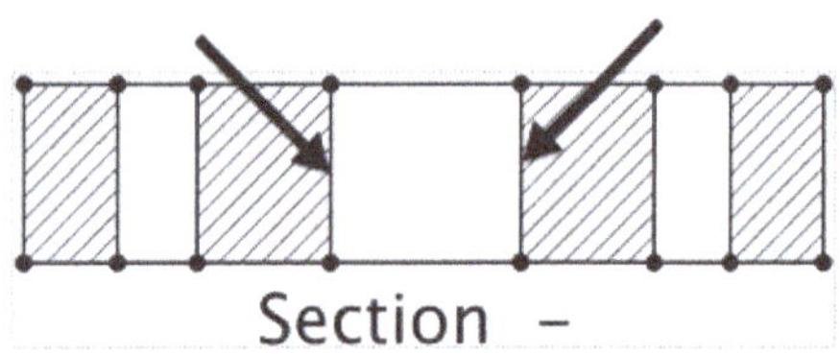

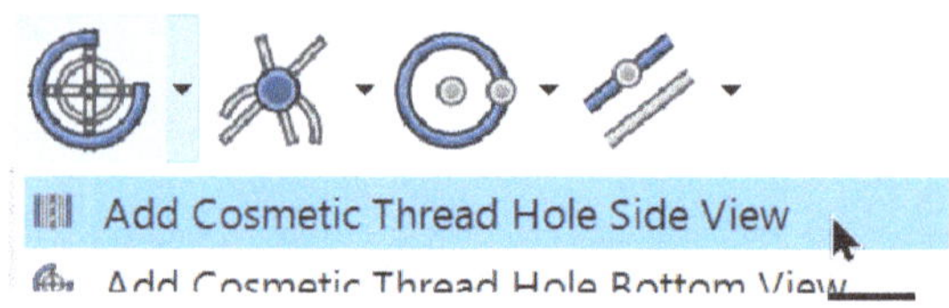

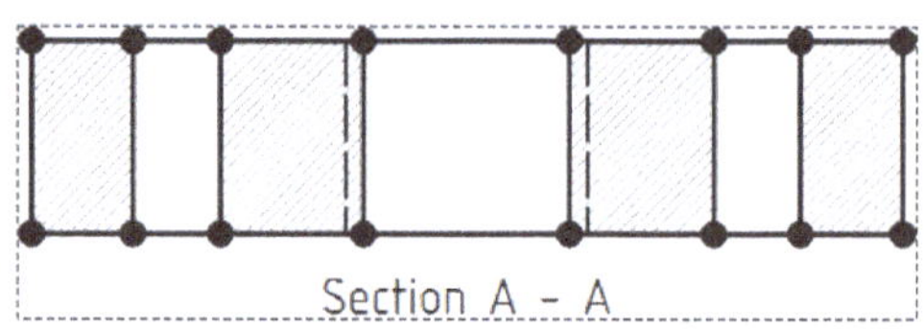

Add Cosmetic Thread Bolt Side View

The "**Add Cosmetic Thread Bolt Side View"** tool allows you to add cosmetic threads to bolts in side or section views, enhancing the clarity and precision of your technical drawings.

Steps to Use the Tool

1. **Select the Bolt Edges**:
    - Hold the **CTRL key** (or **COMMAND key** on Mac) and click on the edges of the bolt in your side or section view.
2. **Access the Command**:
    - On the **TechDraw Centerlines toolbar**, click the **Cosmetic Thread** drop-down, or

- Go to **TechDraw > Extensions: Centerlines/Threading > Add Cosmetic Thread Bolt Side View** in the menu bar.

Add Cosmetic Thread Bolt Bottom View

The **Add Cosmetic Thread Bolt Bottom View** command lets you add a cosmetic thread to the circular edge of a bolt. Here's how to use it:

1. **Select the Circular Edge**: Click on the circular edge of the bolt where you want to add the thread.
2. **Access the Command**:
   - On the **TechDraw Centerlines toolbar**, click the **Cosmetic Thread** drop-down and select **Add Cosmetic Thread Bolt Bottom View**, or
   - Go to **TechDraw > Extensions: Centerlines/Threading > Add Cosmetic Thread Bolt Bottom View** in the menu bar.

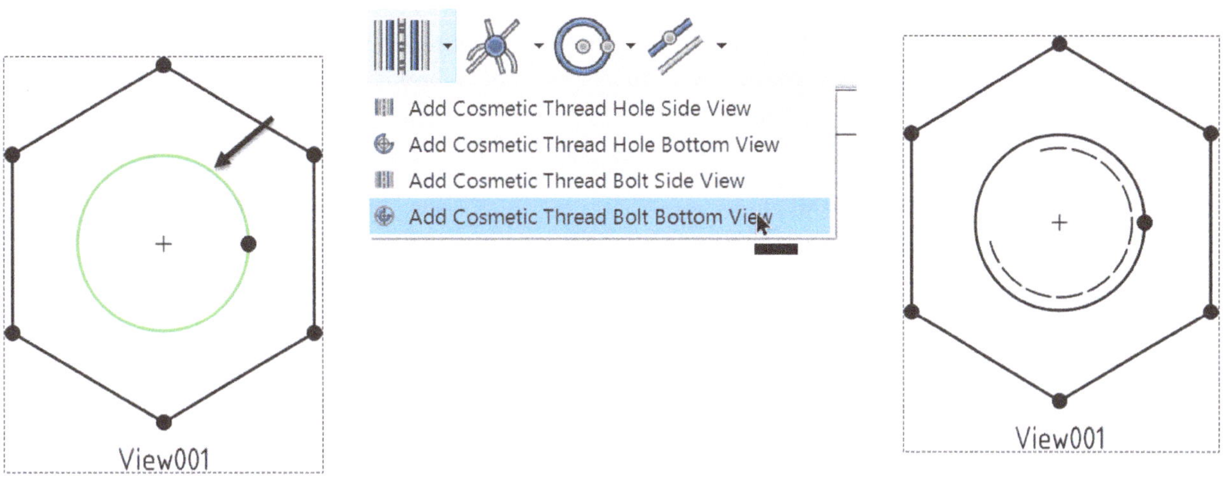

Add Cosmetic Intersection Vertex

Cosmetic intersection points are useful in complex drawings to clearly mark where edges or lines intersect, reducing ambiguity and aiding in accurate dimensioning, especially with filleted edges.

Benefits of Cosmetic Intersection Points

- **Clarity**: They explicitly mark intersections, making it clear where lines or edges meet.
- **Precision**: Helpful for adding dimensions to filleted edges, ensuring accurate measurements.
- **Avoid Misinterpretation**: Eliminate confusion in complex designs.

Adding Cosmetic Intersection Points

1. **Select Edges**: Hold the **CTRL key** (or **COMMAND key** on Mac) and select two non-parallel edges in the drawing view.
2. **Access the Command**:
    - On the **TechDraw Centerlines toolbar**, click the **Add Cosmetic Intersection Vertex** tool, or
    - Go to **TechDraw > Extensions: Centerlines/Threading > Add Cosmetic Intersection Vertex** in the menu bar.

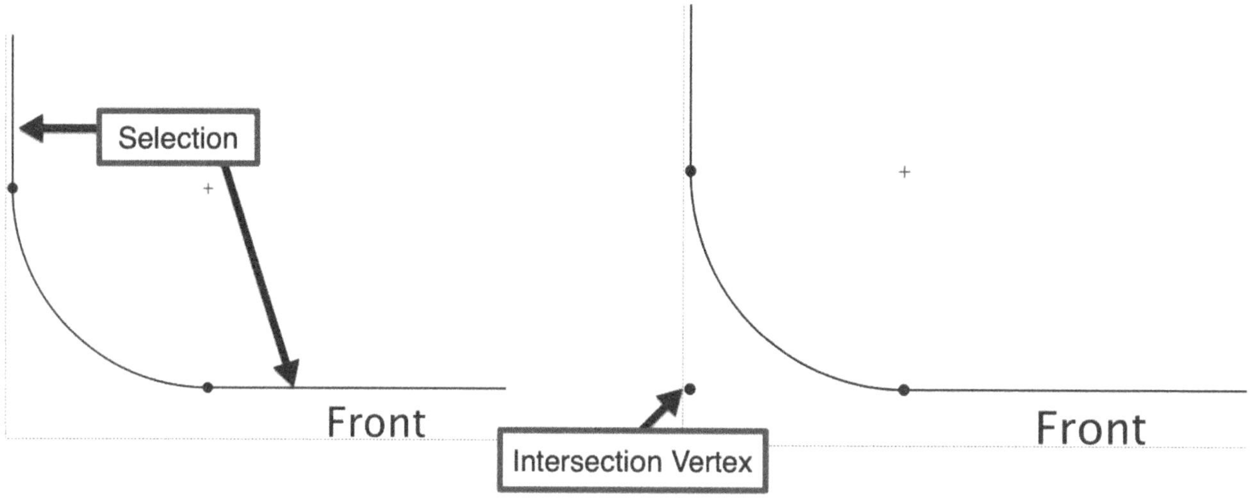

Dimensions

In FreeCAD, you have several options to add dimensions to your drawings. These dimensions play a crucial role in specifying the size, scale, and proportions of your design. To do this, you'll utilize the commands conveniently located on the **TechDraw Dimensions** toolbar.

Insert Horizontal Dimension

The **Insert Horizontal Dimension** command is a simple tool for adding horizontal measurements to your drawings, useful for specifying the width or horizontal extent of an object. Here's how to use it:

1. **Select a Line or Two Points**:
    - Choose an existing line, or hold the **CTRL key** and click two points to define the horizontal distance you want to measure.
2. **Access the Tool**:
    - On the **TechDraw Dimensions toolbar**, click the **Insert Dimensions** drop-down > **Insert Horizontal Dimension** icon, or
    - Go to **TechDraw > Dimensions > Insert Horizontal Dimension** in the menu bar.
3. **Place the Dimension**: Click and drag to position the dimension in your drawing, clearly indicating the horizontal measurement.

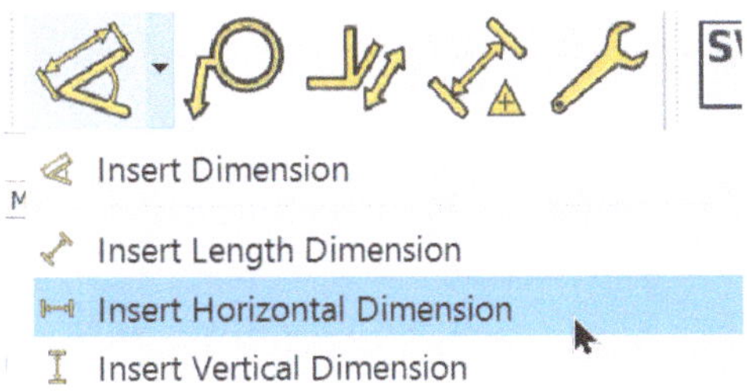

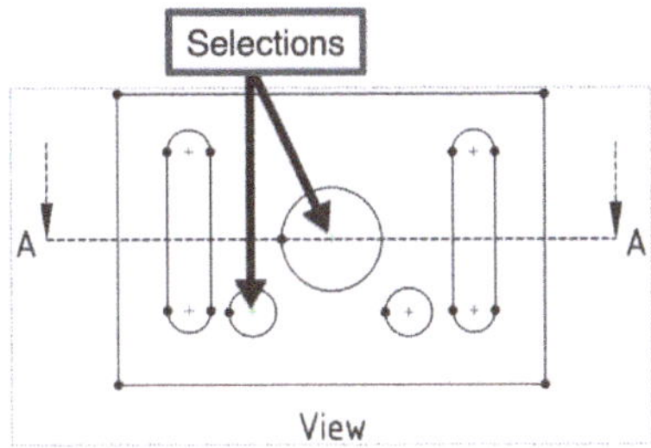

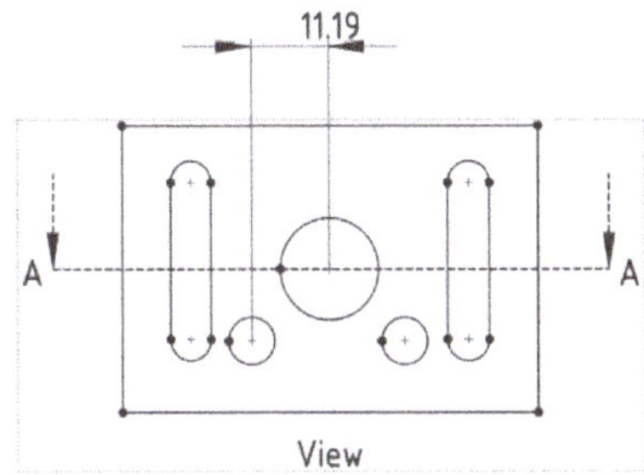

Insert Vertical Dimension

The **Insert Vertical Dimension** command allows you to add vertical measurements to your design, either between two points or along a selected line. Follow these steps:

1. **Select the Element**:
    - Choose the line for the vertical dimension, or hold the **CTRL key** and select two points to measure the vertical distance between them.
2. **Access the Tool**:
    - On the **TechDraw Dimensions toolbar**, click the **Insert Dimension** drop-down and select **Insert Vertical Dimension** , or
    - Go to **TechDraw > Dimensions > Insert Vertical Dimension** in the menu bar.
3. **Place the Dimension**: Click and drag to position the dimension in your drawing, ensuring it is clear and visually aligned.

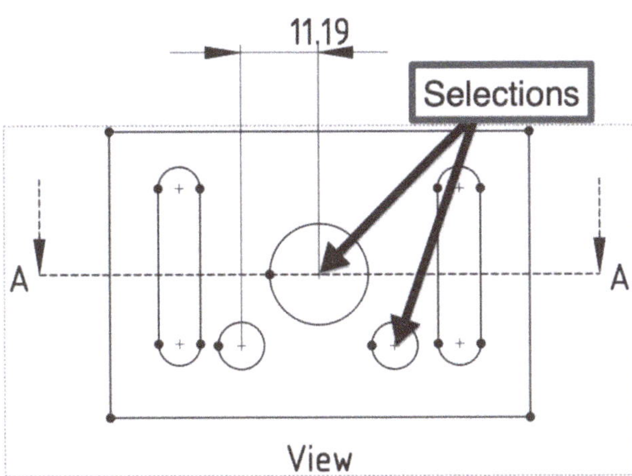

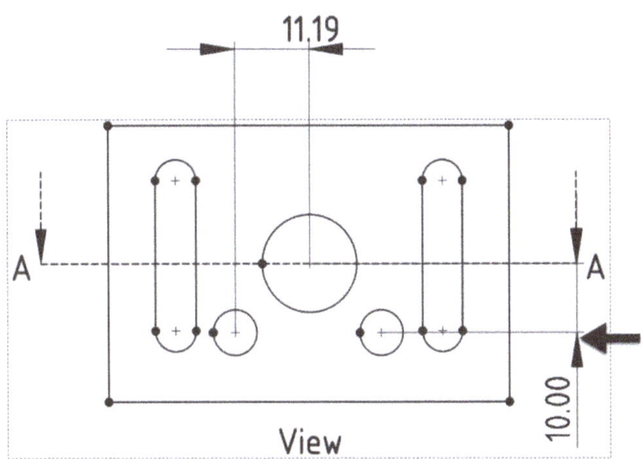

Insert Radius Dimension

To include a radius dimension for an arc or circle in your technical drawing, follow these steps:

1. **Select the Circular Edge**: Click on the circular edge you want to dimension.
2. **Insert the Radius Dimension**:
    - On the **TechDraw Dimensions toolbar**, click the **Insert Dimension** drop-down > **Insert Radius Dimension**  icon, or
    - Go to **TechDraw > Dimensions > Insert Radius Dimension** in the menu bar.

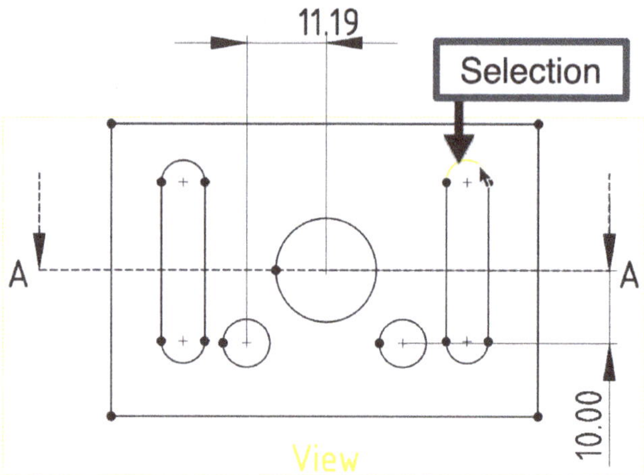

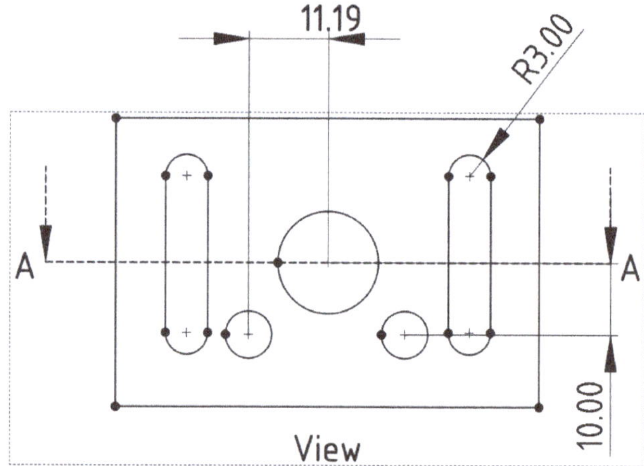

Insert Diameter Dimension

To add a diameter dimension to an arc or circle in FreeCAD, follow these simple steps:

1. **Select the Circular Edge**: Click on the arc or circle you want to measure.
2. **Insert the Diameter Dimension**:
   - On the **TechDraw Dimensions toolbar**, click the **Insert Dimension** drop-down > **Insert Diameter Dimension**  icon, or
   - Go to **TechDraw > Dimensions > Insert Diameter Dimension** in the menu bar.

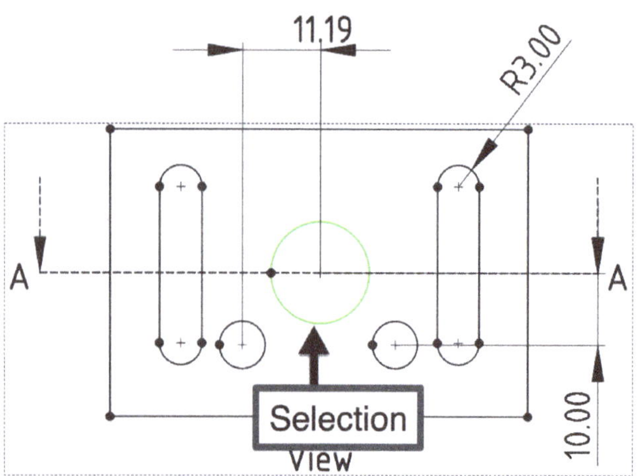

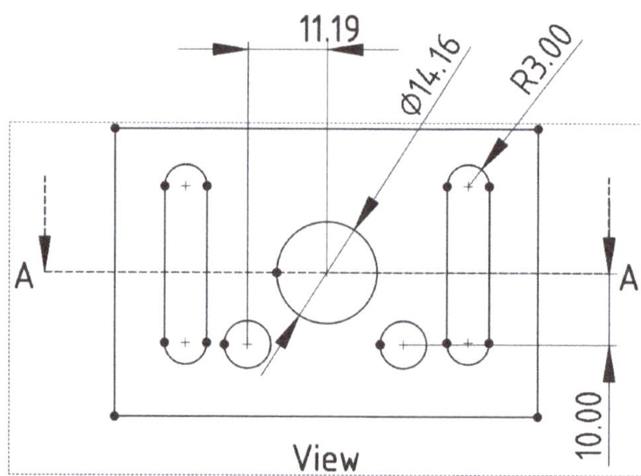

Insert Length Dimension

This command adds a linear dimension between two selected points. To do this, select linear edge (or) press and hold the CTRL key and select two points. Next, click the **Insert Dimension** drop-down > **Insert Length Dimension**  icon on the **TechDraw Dimensions** toolbar (or) click **TechDraw > Dimensions > Insert Length Dimension** on the menu bar.

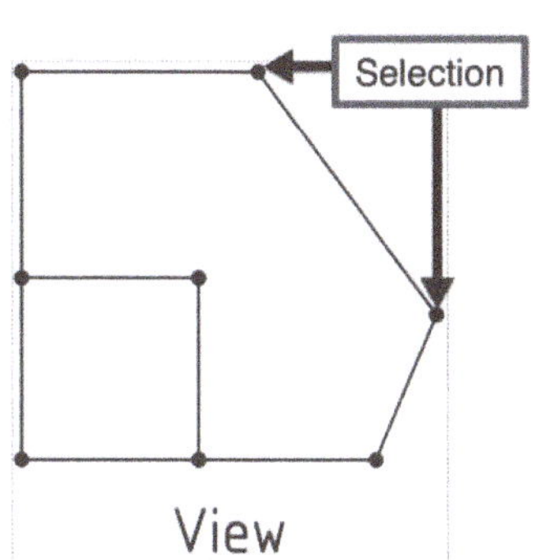

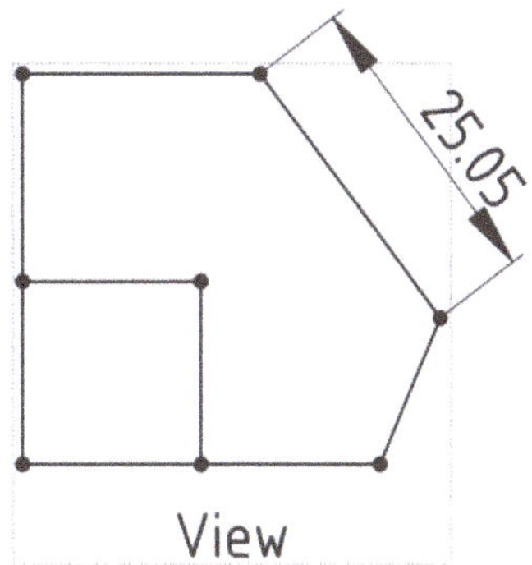

Insert Angle Dimension

This command adds an angular dimension between two selected lines. To do this, press and hold the CTRL key and select two lines. Next, click the **Insert Dimension** drop-down > **Insert Angle Dimension** icon on the **TechDraw Dimensions** toolbar (or) click **TechDraw > Dimensions > Insert Angle Dimension** on the menu bar.

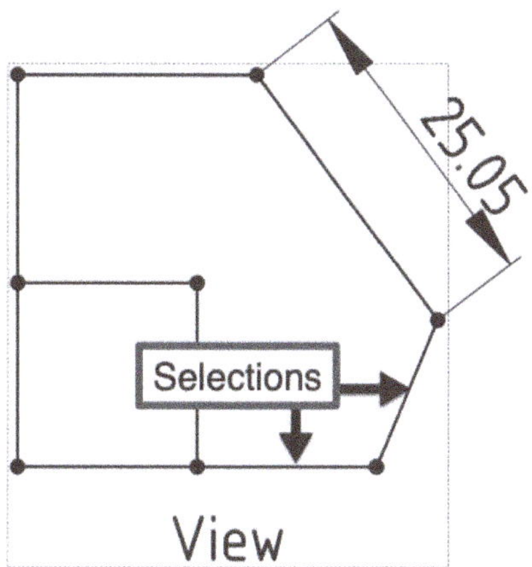

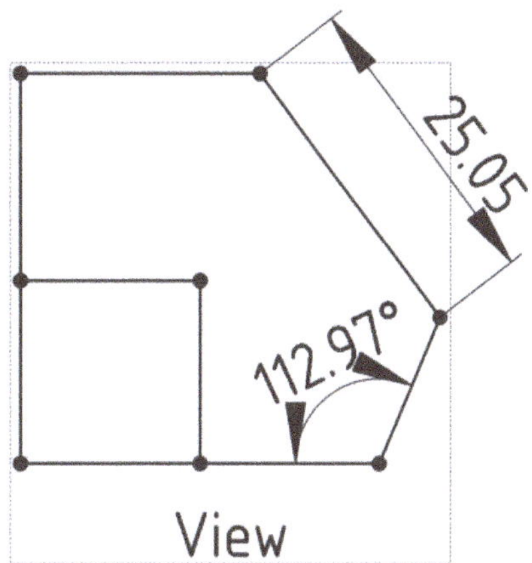

Insert 3-Point Angle Dimension

This command adds an angular dimension between two points. To do this, press and hold the CTRL key and select first point, centerpoint, and the second point. Next, click the **Insert Dimension** drop-down > **Insert 3-Point Angle Dimension** icon on the **TechDraw Dimensions** toolbar (or) click **TechDraw > Dimensions > Insert 3-Point Angle Dimension** on the menu bar.

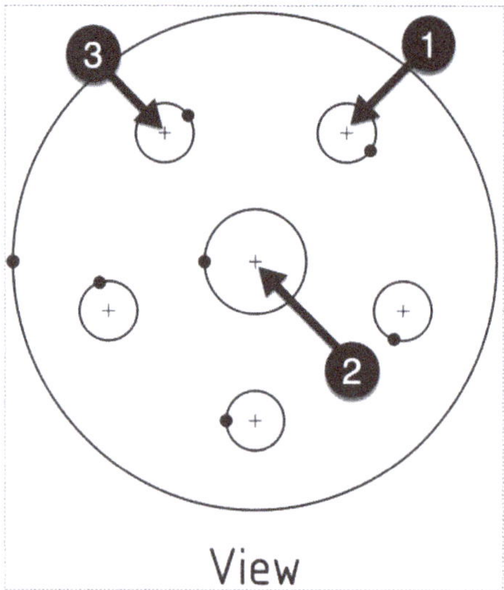

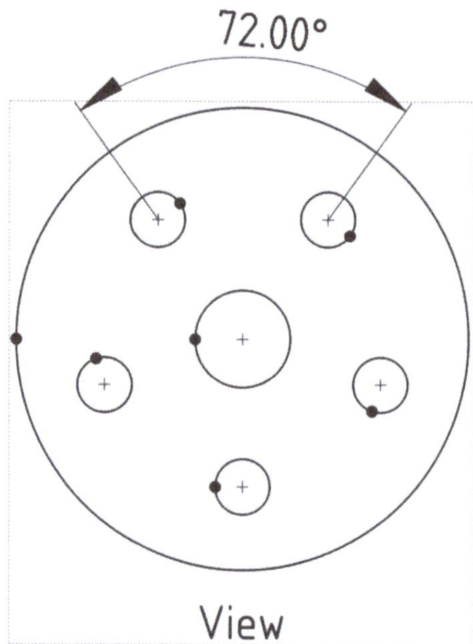

Insert Horizontal Extent Dimension

This command adds a horizontal extent dimension to the view. To do this, select the view and click the **Insert Dimensions** drop-down > **Insert Horizontal Extent Dimension** on the **TechDraw Dimensions** toolbar (or) click **TechDraw > Dimensions > Insert Horizontal Extent Dimension** on the menu bar.

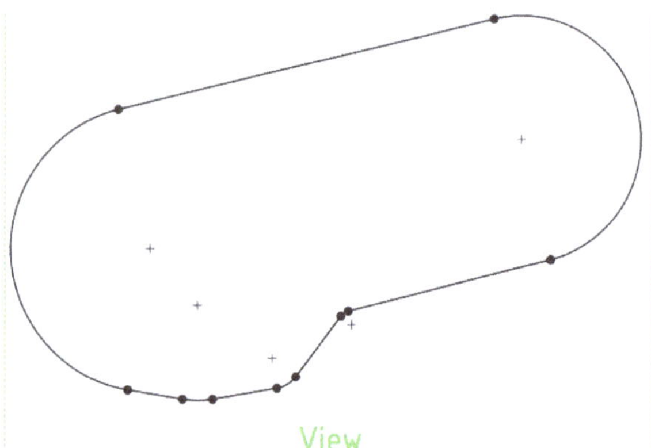

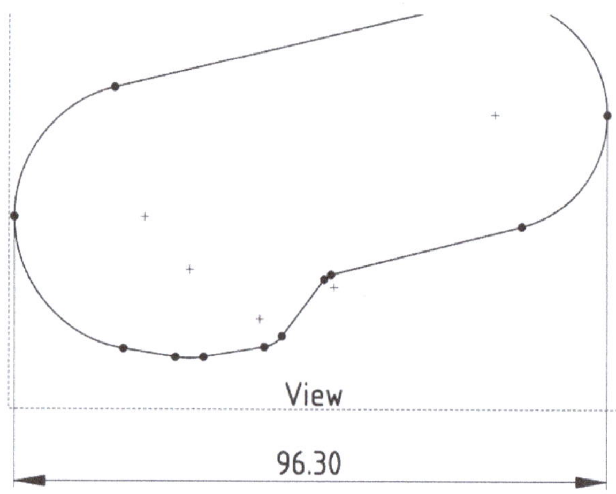

Insert Vertical Extent Dimension

This command adds a vertical extent dimension to the view. To do this, select the view and click the **Insert Dimensions** drop-down > **Insert Vertical Extent Dimension** on the **TechDraw Dimensions** toolbar (or) click **TechDraw > Dimensions > Insert Vertical Extent Dimension** on the menu bar.

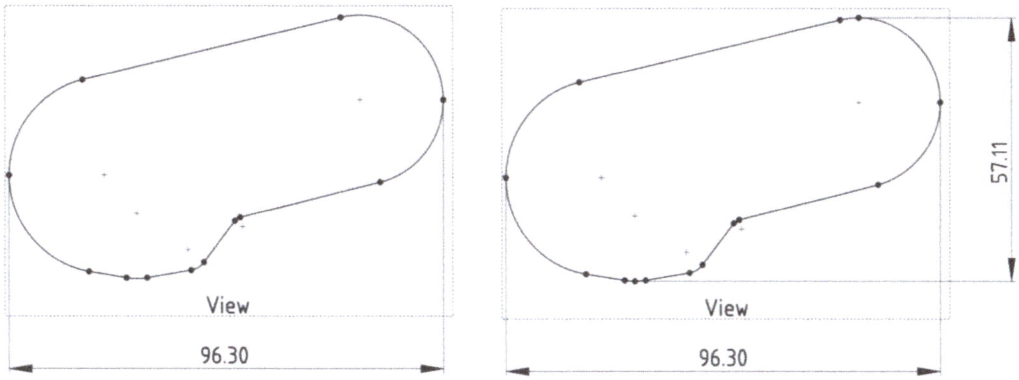

Add Axonometric length dimension

The **Axonometric Length Dimension** command is essential for adding precise length measurements to axonometric views, commonly used in technical drawings. This tool is particularly useful in isometric projections, where three-dimensional objects are represented on a two-dimensional surface with parallel lines and equal axis angles (120 degrees). It helps quantify edge lengths or distances between points, enhancing accuracy and clarity in designs.

Steps to Use the Command

1. **Select Edges**:
    - Hold the **CTRL key** (or **COMMAND key** on Mac) and select two non-parallel edges in the drawing view. The first edge sets the dimension line's direction, and the second determines the extension lines' direction.
2. **Activate the Tool**:
    - On the **TechDraw Dimensions toolbar**, click the **Axonometric Length Dimension** button, or
    - Go to **TechDraw > Dimensions > Axonometric Length Dimension** in the menu bar.
3. **Add and Adjust the Dimension**:
    - The dimension will be added to your view. Click and drag it to position it as needed.

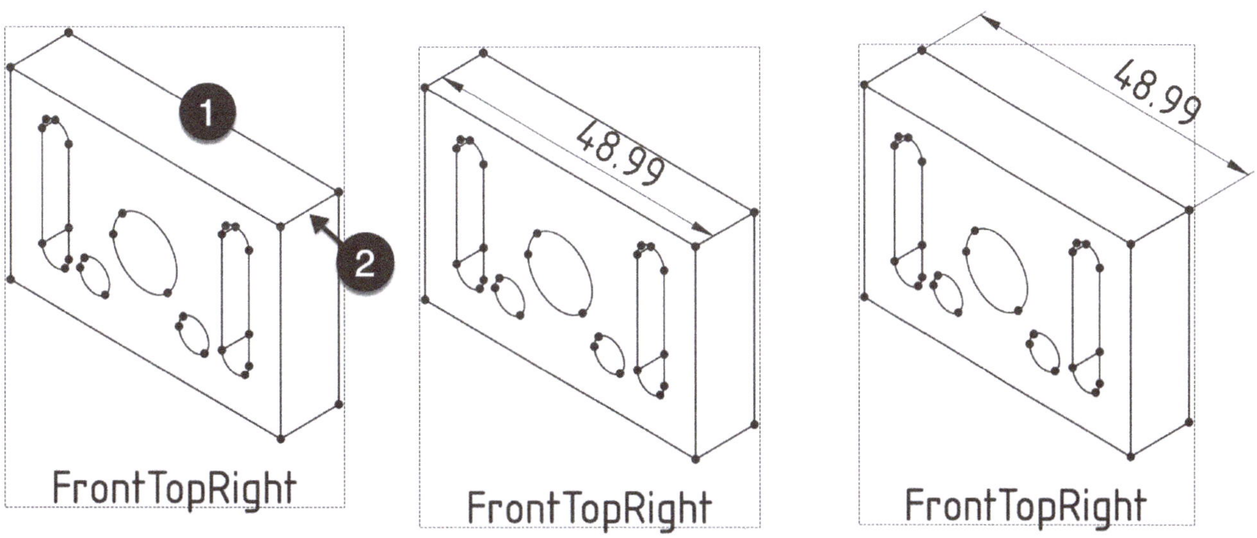

Create Arc Length Dimension

Select an arc and click **Insert Dimension** drop-down > **Create Arc Length Dimension** icon on the **TechDraw Extend Dimensions** toolbar (or) click **TechDraw > Extensions: Dimensions > Create Arc Length Dimension** on the menu bar.

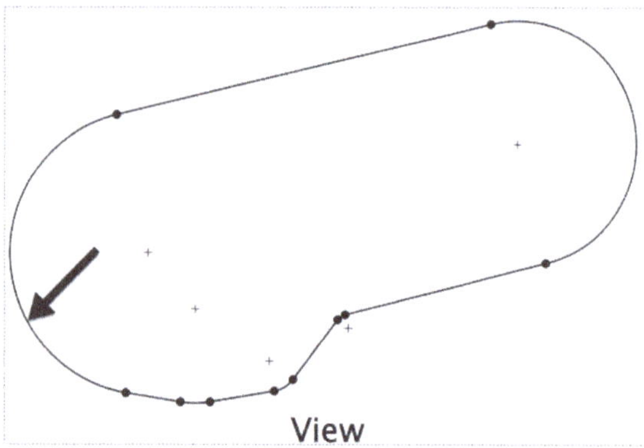

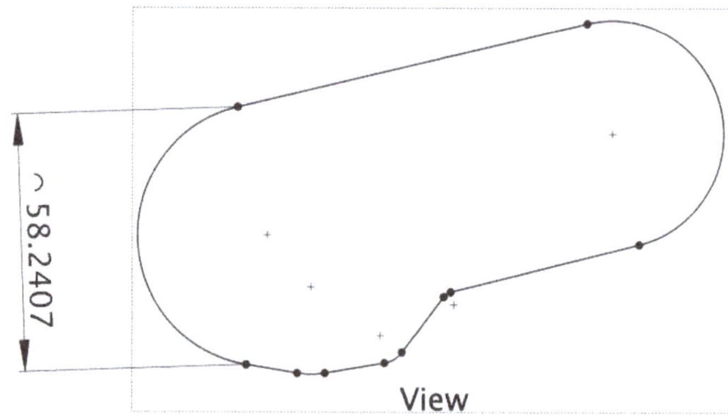

Create Coordinate Dimensions

The commands in the **Coordinate Dimensions** drop-down allow you to create dimensions between an origin point and multiple vertices. Select a vertex from the drawing view to define the origin of the coordinate dimensions. Next, press and hold the CTRL key and select two or more vertices from the drawing view. Click **Insert Dimensions** drop-down > **Create Horizontal Coordinate Dimensions** on the **TechDraw Dimensions** toolbar (or) click **TechDraw > Extensions: Dimensions > Create Horizontal Coordinate Dimensions** on the menu bar.

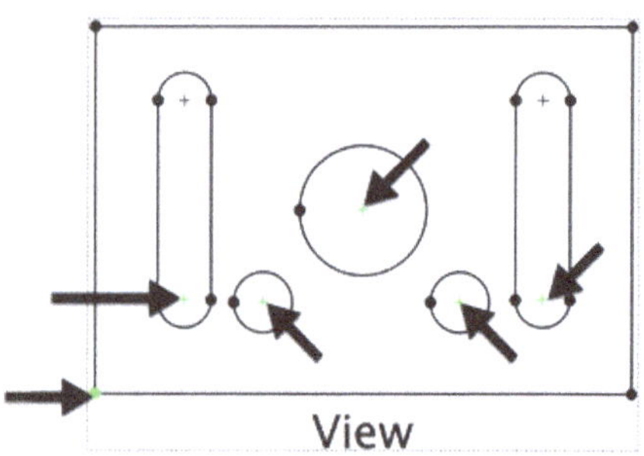

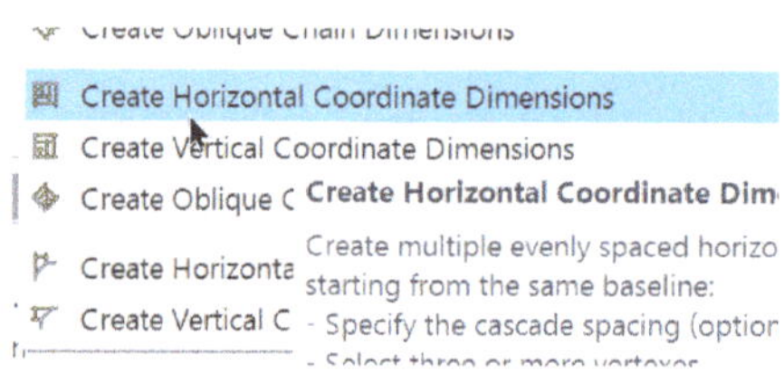

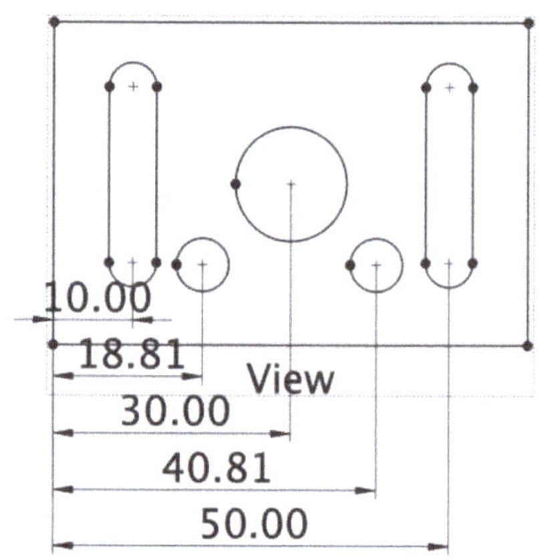

Likewise, you can create the vertical coordinate dimensions using the **Create Vertical Coordinate Dimensions** command.

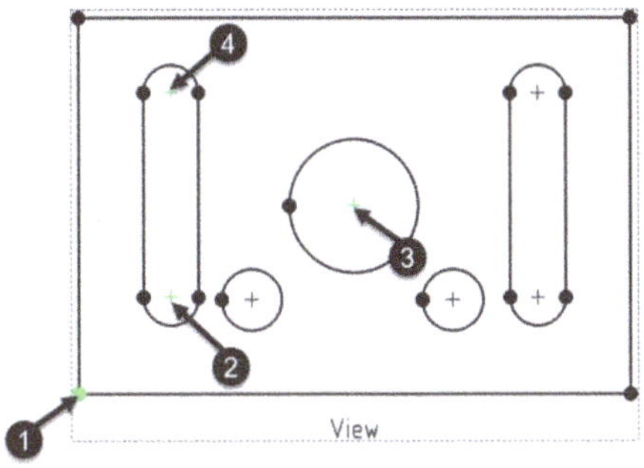

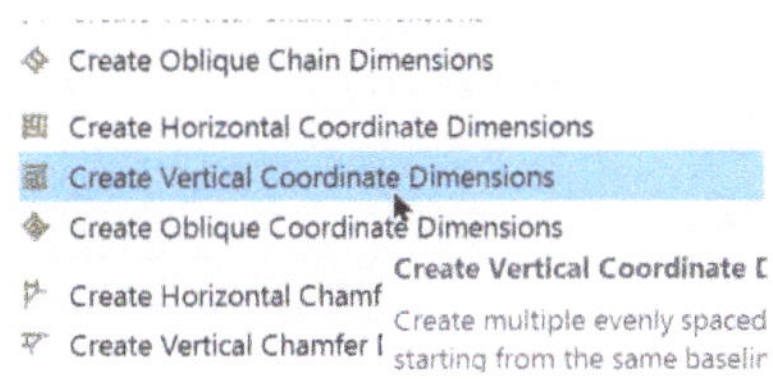

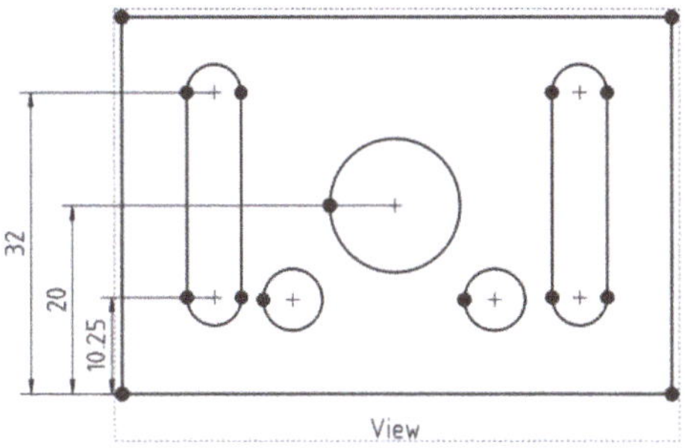

Likewise, you can create the oblique coordinate dimensions using the **Create Oblique Coordinate Dimensions** command.

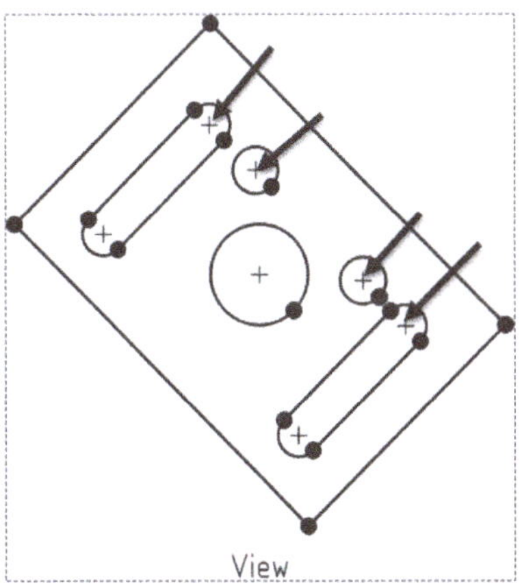

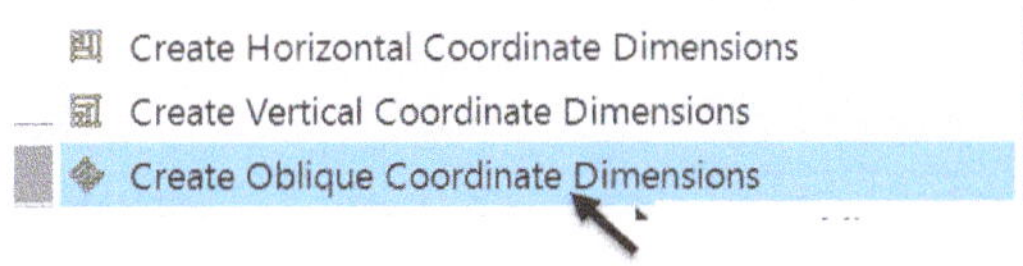

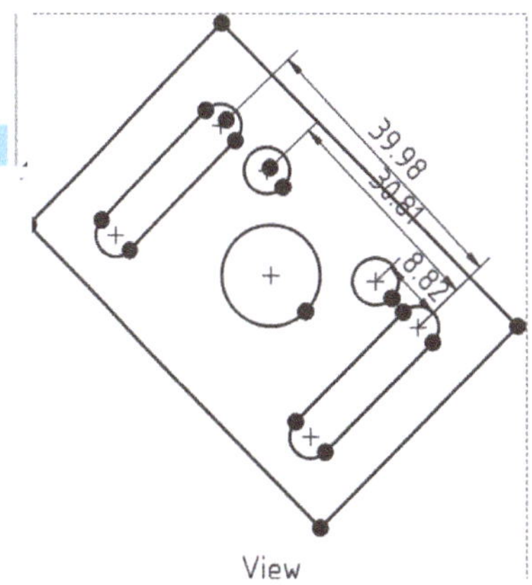

Cascade Dimensions

The commands in the **Cascade Dimensions** drop-down allow you to arrange the coordinate dimensions by equally spacing them. To do this, first you need to define the space between the dimension. Click and drag the first dimension of the coordinate dimensions up to the required distance. Next, press and hold the CTRL key and select the first and rest of dimensions of the coordinate dimension set. Click **TecchDraw** > **Extension: Attributes/Modifications > Cascade Horizontal Dimensions** on the menu bar.

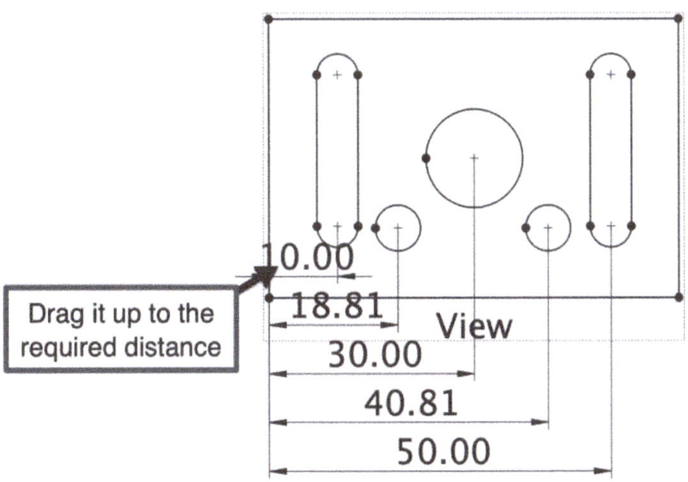

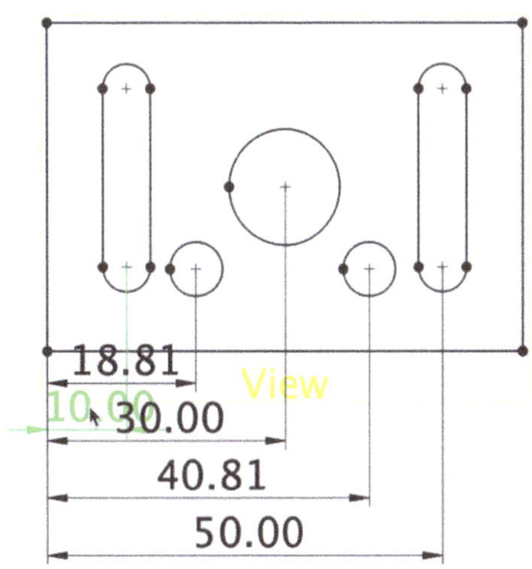

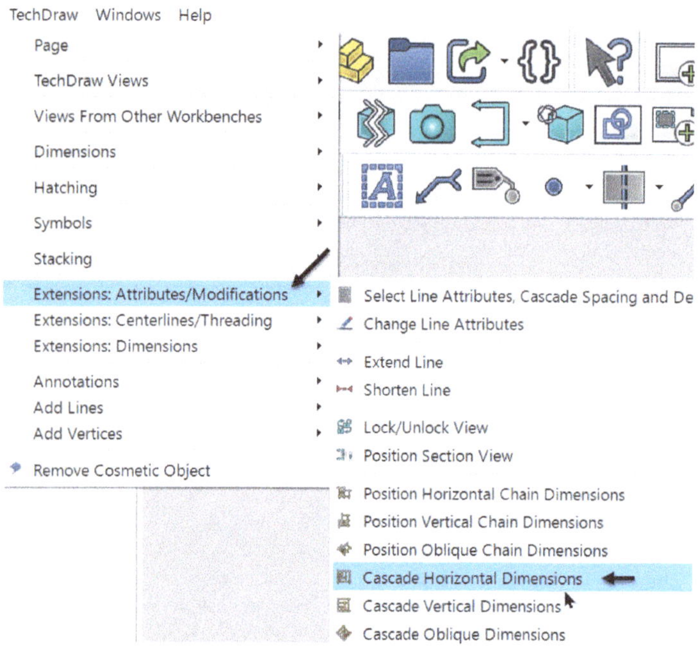

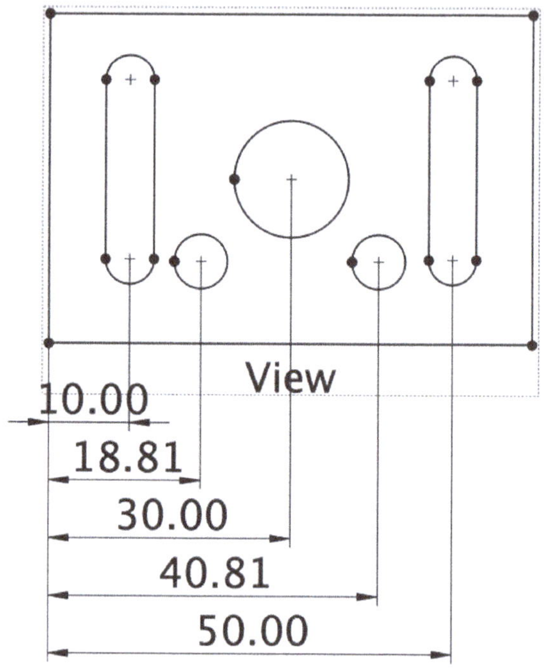

Likewise, you can cascade the vertical and oblique dimensions using the **Cascade Vertical Dimensions** and **Cascade Oblique Dimensions** commands, respectively.

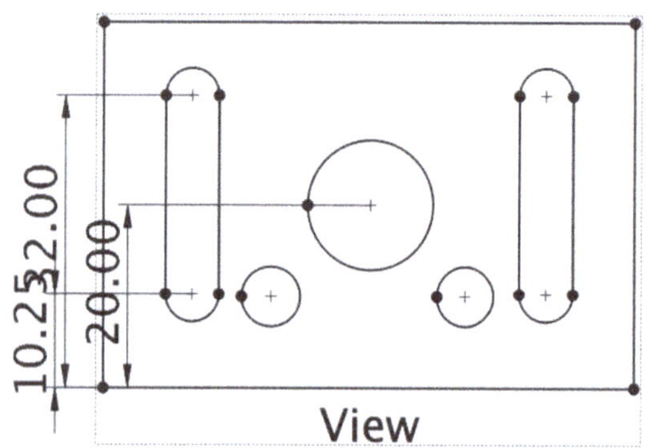

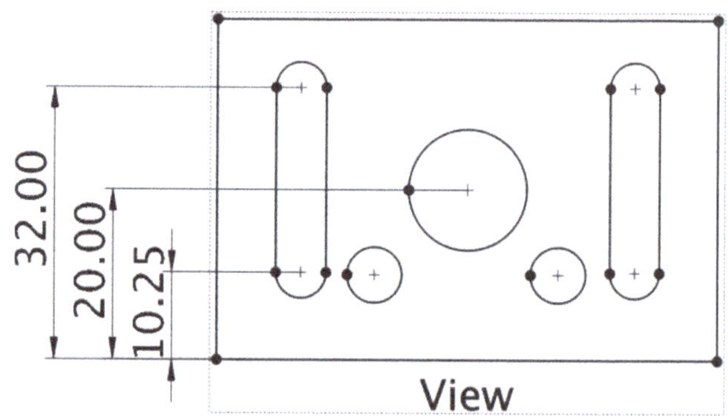

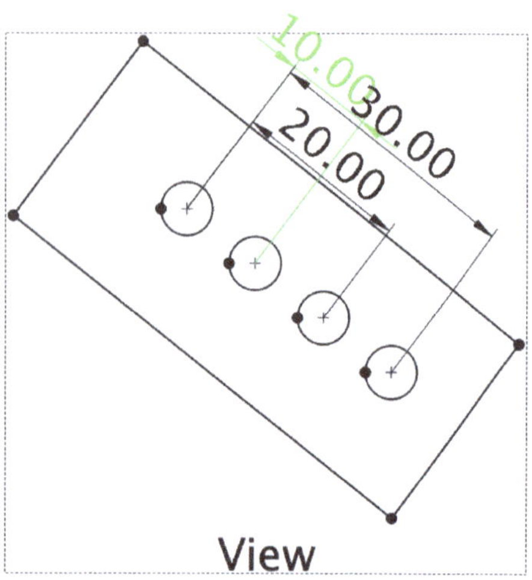

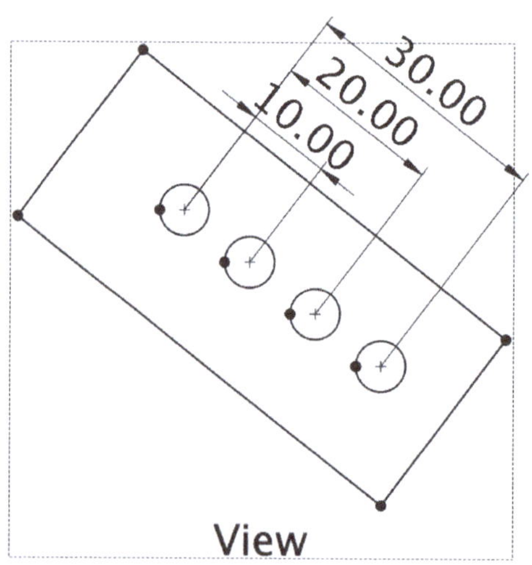

Chain Dimensions

Chain dimensions are continuous dimensions between multiple vertices of a drawing view. Select a vertex from the drawing view to define the origin of the chain dimensions. Next, press and hold the CTRL key and select two or more vertices from the drawing view. Click **Insert Dimensions** drop-down > **Create Horizontal Chain Dimensions** on the **TechDraw Dimensions** toolbar (or) click **TechDraw > Extensions: Dimensions > Create Horizontal Chain Dimensions** on the menu bar.

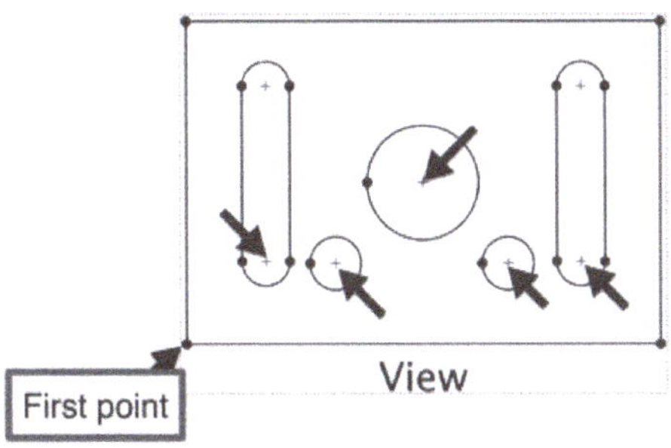

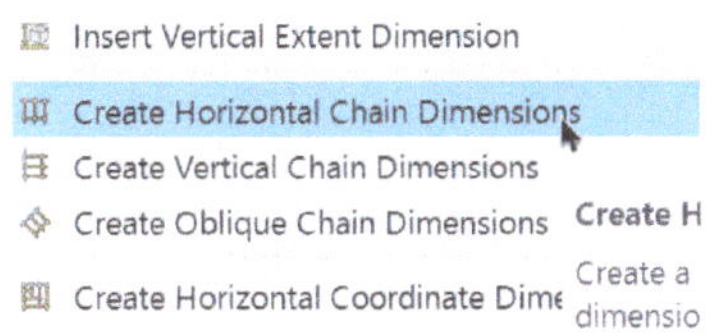

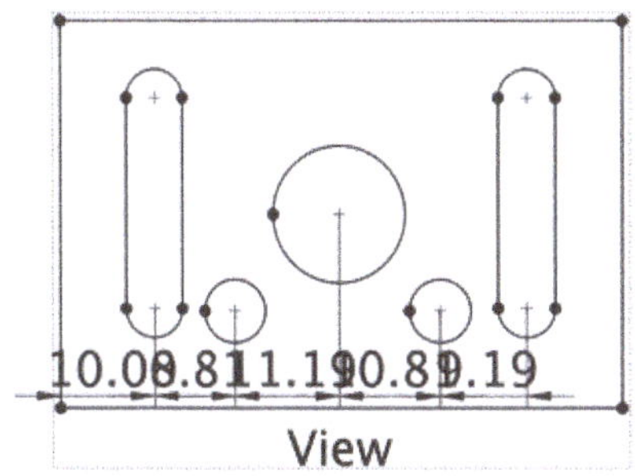

Likewise, you can create the vertical and oblique chain dimensions using the **Create Vertical Chain Dimensions** and **Create Oblique Chain Dimensions** command, respectively.

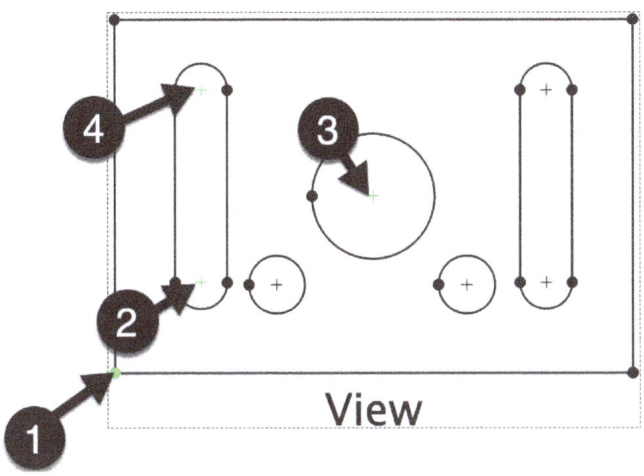

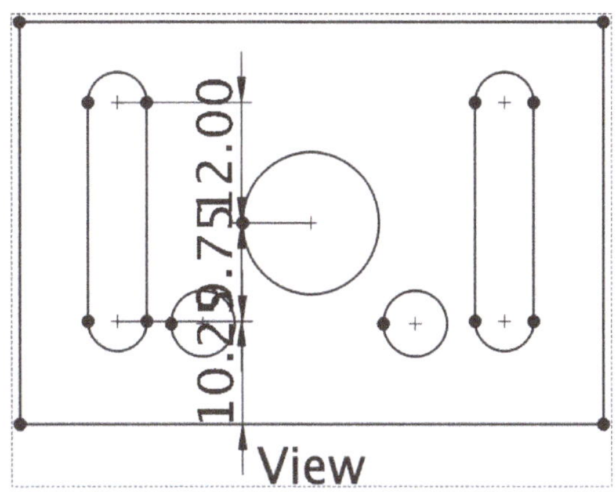

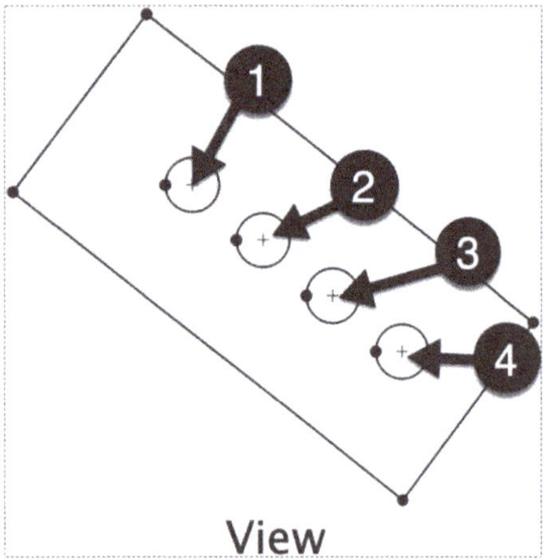

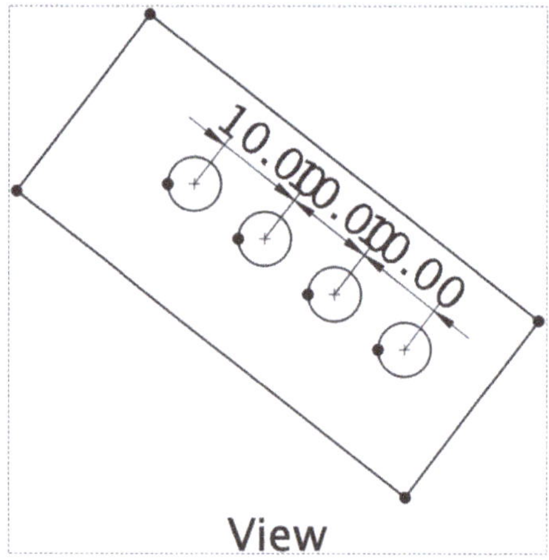

Position Chain Dimensions

The commands in the **Position Chain Dimensions** drop-down allow you to align the chain dimensions horizontally, vertically, or obliquely. To do this, first you need to drag the first dimension of the chain dimensions set up to the required distance. Next, press and hold the CTRL key and select the first and rest of dimensions of the chain dimension set. Click **TecchDraw > Extension: Attributes/Modifications >Position Horizontal Chain Dimensions** on the menu bar.

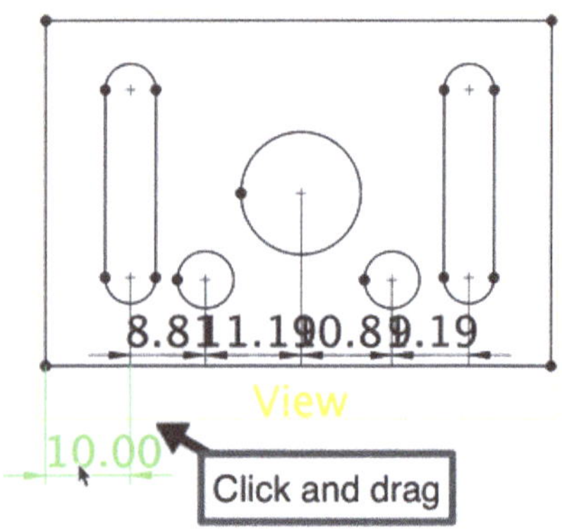

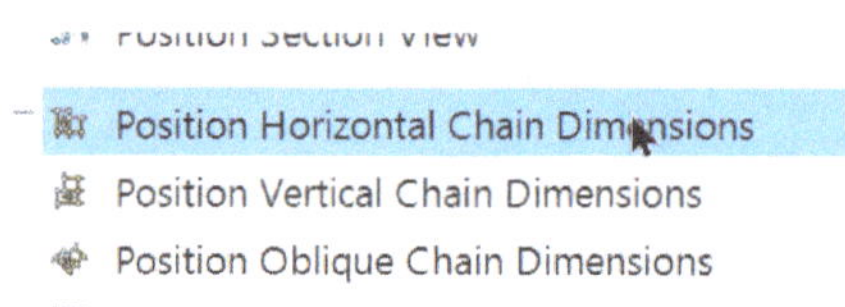

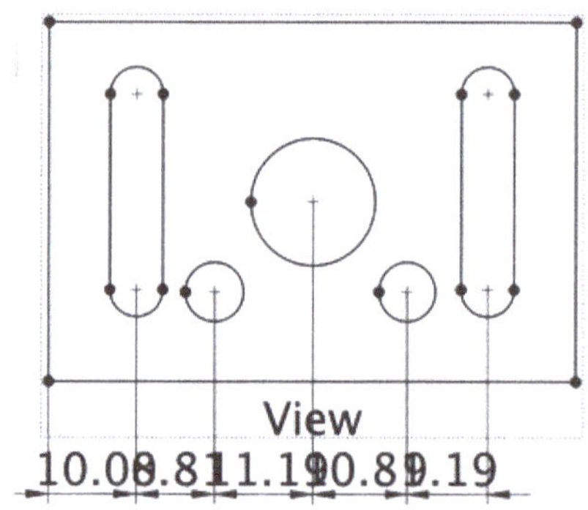

Likewise, you can align the vertical and oblique chain dimensions using the **Position Vertical Chain Dimensions** 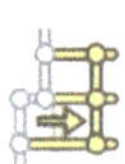 and **Position Oblique Chain Dimensions** 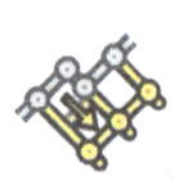 commands, respectively.

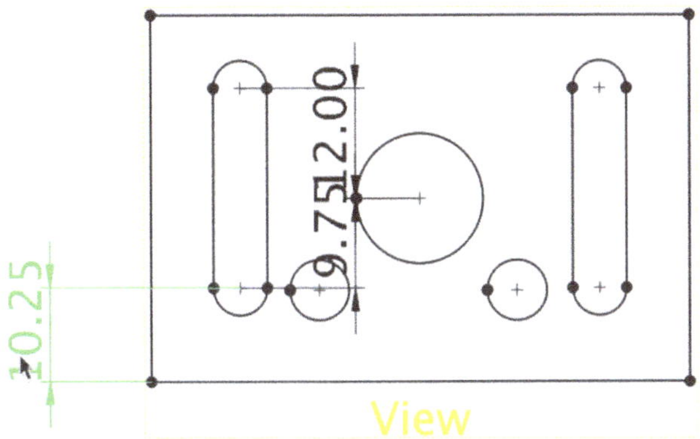

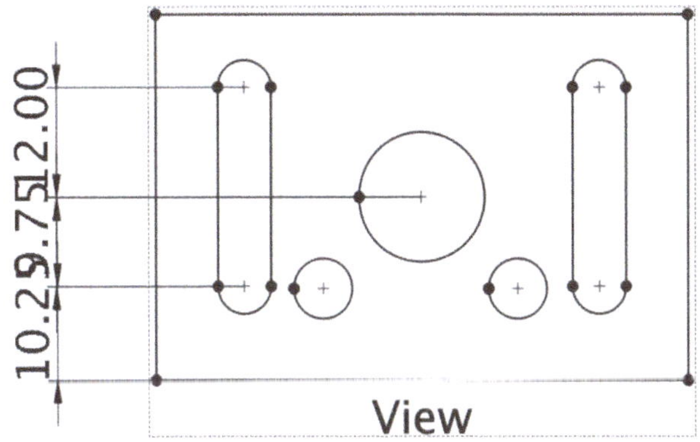

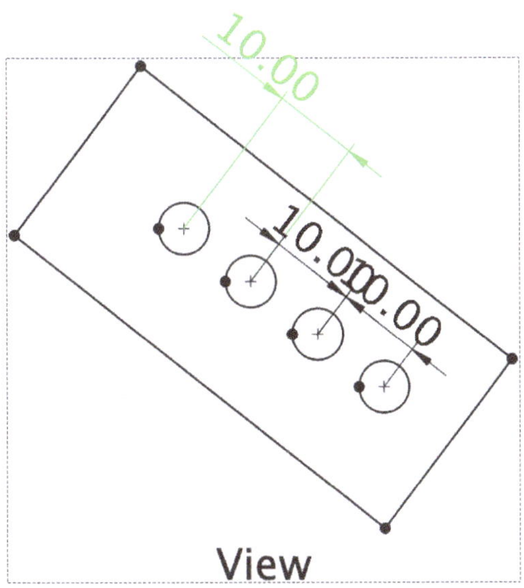

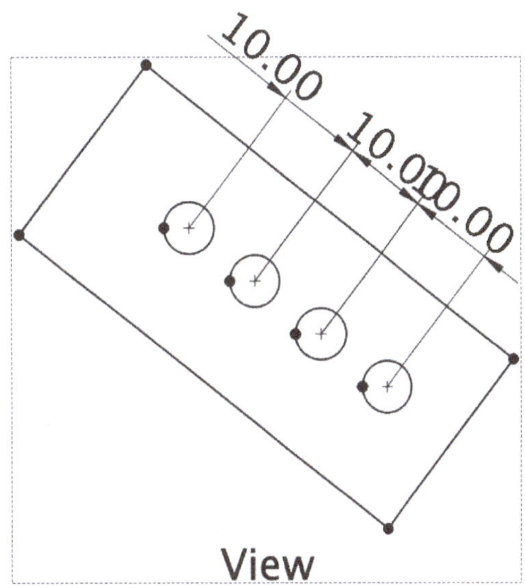

Calculate the area of selected faces

To determine the area of specific faces within your design, you can utilize the "**Calculate the area of selected faces**" tool. This tool computes the area of the chosen faces and adds an area annotation for your reference. It's important to note that this tool is best suited for faces with straight edges; it may not accurately handle faces with curved edges.

You can access the "**Calculate the area of selected faces**" tool from the menu bar. Navigate to the "TechDraw" menu, then proceed to "Extensions: Attributes/Modifications," and select the "Calculate the area of selected faces" option.

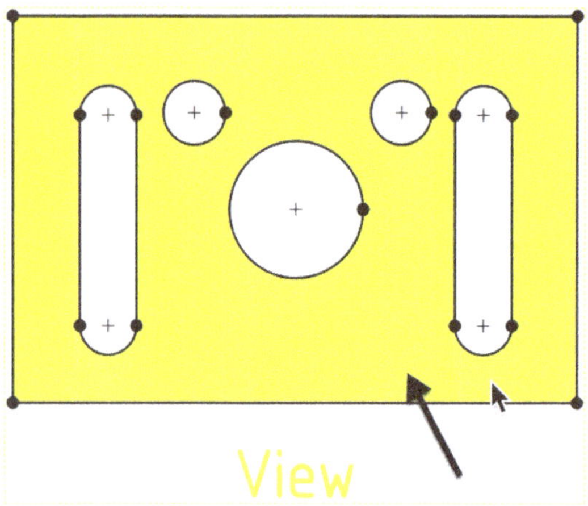

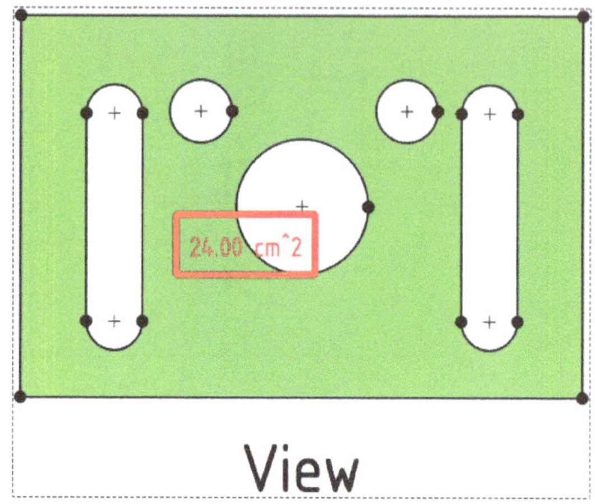

The ability to calculate the area of selected faces is particularly valuable in various design and engineering scenarios. For instance, it helps in assessing material requirements for manufacturing, estimating surface paint or coating quantities, and verifying compliance with design specifications. This tool is a practical asset for those who require precise area measurements.

Add Leaderline to View

Leader lines are essential in technical drawings for effectively conveying information. They connect notes or labels to specific elements, dimensions, or parts of the drawing, ensuring clarity and understanding. Typically, leader lines are straight and feature an arrow or dot at the end, pointing directly to the relevant area. This visual cue helps viewers quickly identify which part of the drawing the note or label refers to.

The main purpose of leader lines is to provide additional context, such as dimensions, annotations, or callouts, which are crucial for interpreting the drawing accurately. Whether in engineering schematics, architectural plans, or other technical illustrations, leader lines enhance communication by linking labels and notes to specific features, eliminating ambiguity and ensuring the drawing is easily understood. In summary, leader lines are vital tools in technical illustrations, promoting clarity and effective communication.

To add a leaderline to a specific view in FreeCAD, follow these steps:

1. **Select a View**: Choose the view where you want to add the leaderline.
2. **Access the Tool**:
    - Click the "**Add Leaderline to View**" button on the **TechDraw Annotation** toolbar.
    - Or, go to the menu: **TechDraw > Add Lines > Add Leaderline to View**.
3. **Task Panel**: A task panel will open.
4. **Pick Points**: Click "**Pick points**" to define the leaderline.

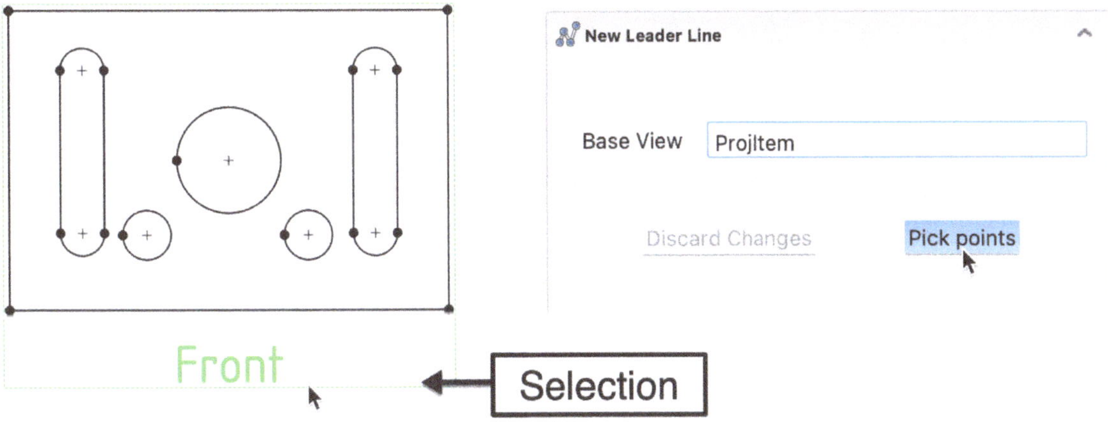

- **First Point**: Click to set the starting point.
- **Second Point**: Click to set the next point. Hold **Ctrl** to align at 22.5° angles, or double-click to confirm.

5. **Add More Points**: Add additional points if needed to shape the leaderline.
6. **Save Points**: If not double-clicked, press "Save Points" to confirm.

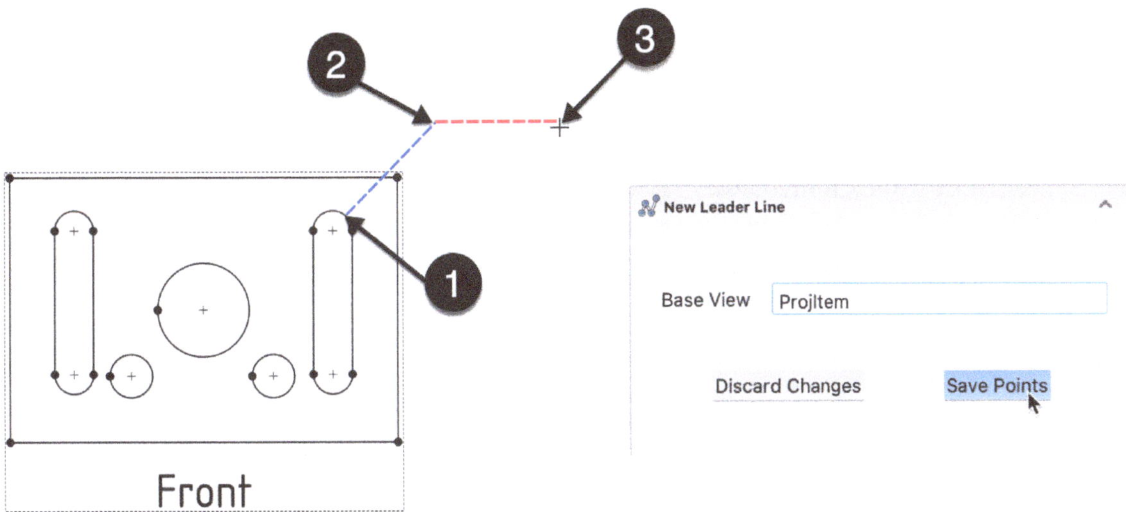

7. **Customize (Optional)**: Adjust the leaderline's appearance (e.g., Start/End Symbol, Color, Width, Style) in the task panel.
8. **Finalize**: Click "**OK**" to complete the process.

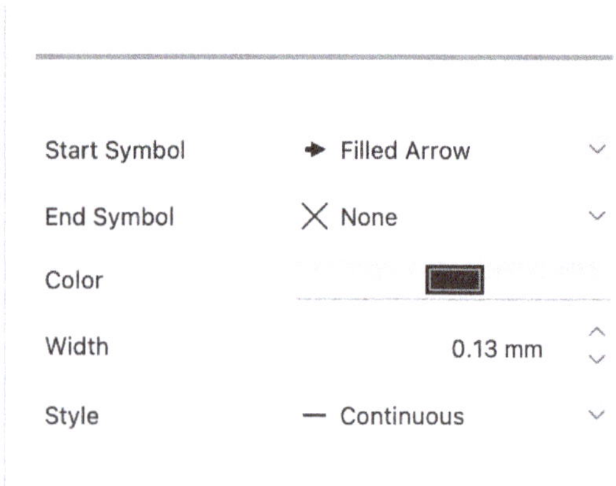

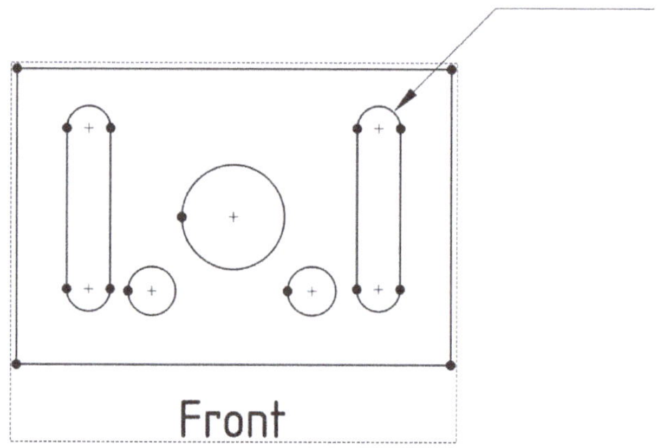

Insert Rich Text Annotation

The "**Insert Rich Text Annotation**" tool is a useful feature in FreeCAD that allows you to add a neatly formatted annotation block to either a Leaderline or a View in your project. To attach a Rich Text Annotation to a Leaderline, you can follow these steps:

1. **Select the Line:** Begin by selecting the desired line either in the Tree view or directly on the page where you want to add the annotation.
2. **Activate the Tool:** There are two ways to activate the "**Insert Rich Text Annotation**" tool:
    - **Method 1:** You can simply click on the "**Insert Rich Text Annotation**"  button found on the **TechDraw Annotation** toolbar.
    - **Method 2:** Alternatively, you can access it through the menu bar by going to "**TechDraw**," then selecting "**Annotations**," and finally choosing "**Insert Rich Text Annotation**." This will open a task panel for your convenience.
3. **Using the Task Panel:** The task panel is a user-friendly interface that makes it easy to enter your text. You can input your annotation quickly and effortlessly.
4. **Accessing the Rich Text Editor:** If you need more advanced formatting and editing options, you can press the "**Start Rich Text Editor**" button. This opens a comprehensive text editor, providing you with a wide range of tools for text formatting and customization.

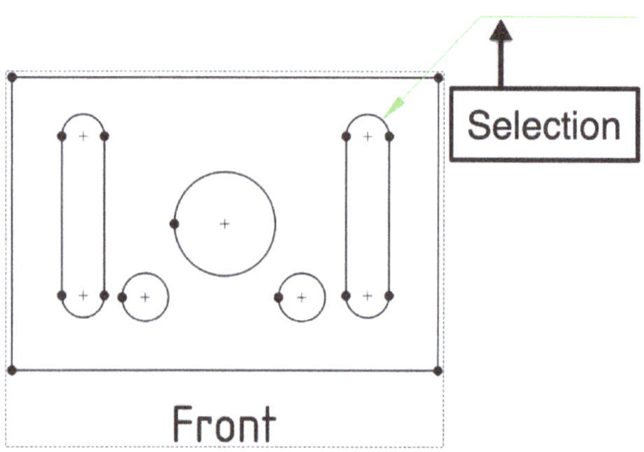

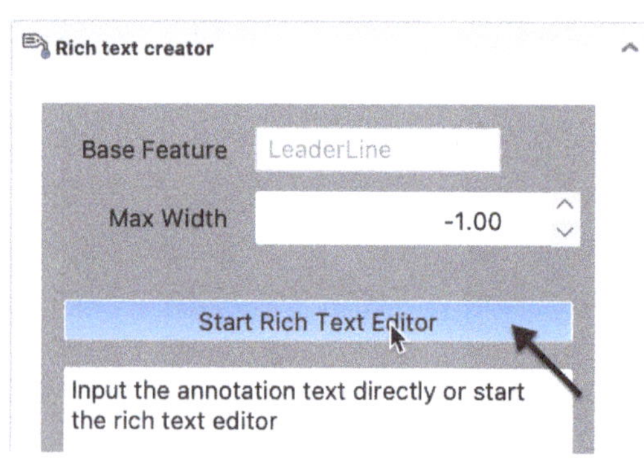

5. **Saving Your Changes:** Once you've added or edited the text to your satisfaction, be sure to press the "**Save**"  button within the Rich Text Editor. This ensures that your changes are retained, and then you can close the editor.

6. **Finalizing Your Annotation:** To complete the process, press the "**OK**" button within the task panel. This will close the panel and your Rich Text Annotation will be attached to the selected Leaderline.

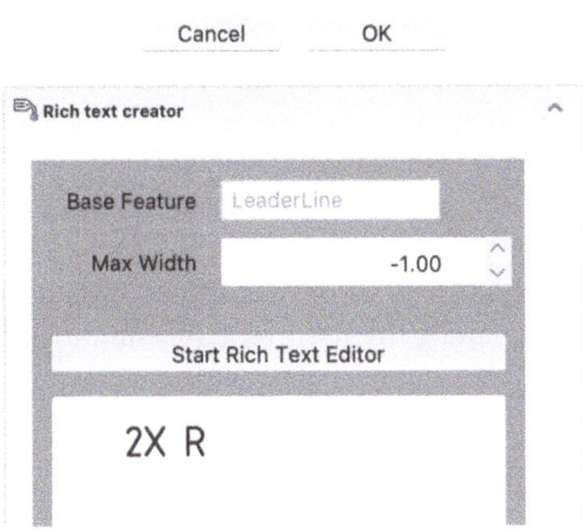

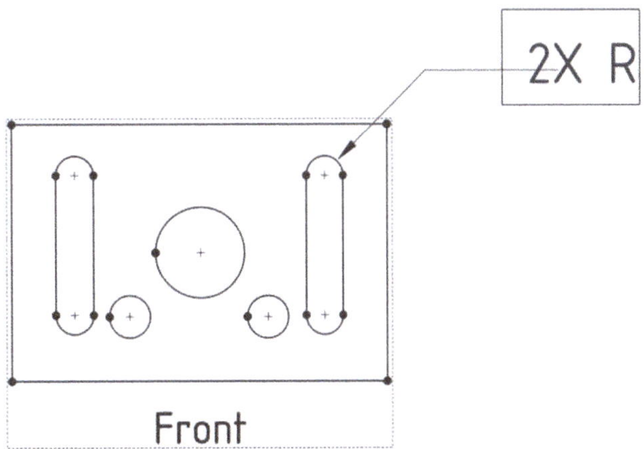

Insert Annotation

Annotation is an important part of a drawing. You add annotation to provide additional details, which cannot be done using dimensions and annotations. To add an annotation, click the **Insert Annotation**  icon on the **TechDraw Annotation** toolbar (or) click **TechDraw > Annotations > Insert Annotation** on the menu bar. Next, click and drag the annotation frame to the desired location. Place the pointer in the **Text** box of the **Properties** panel. Next, click the **Annotation text** icon displayed next to it. Type the annotation text in the **List** dialog and click **OK**.

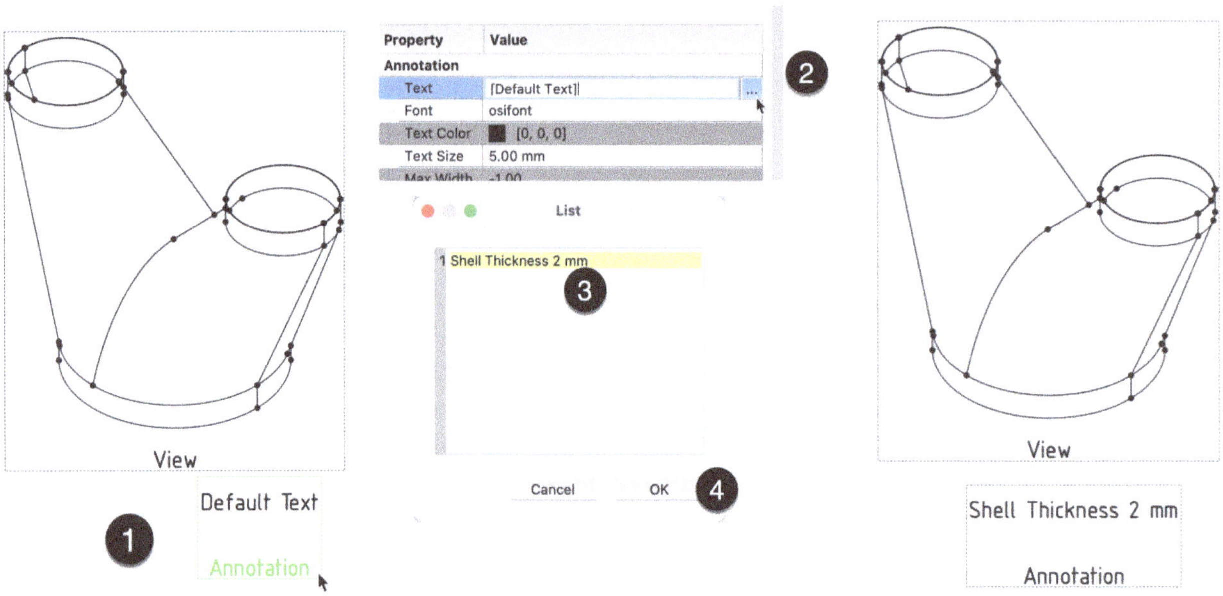

Add Welding Information to Leaderline

Weld symbols are a visual code used in construction and design to specify how a weld should be done. They prevent confusion by providing clear, standardized instructions through lines, arrows, and letters. This universal language ensures everyone – welders, engineers, and inspectors – understands the requirements, helping to build things correctly and safely.

A typical weld symbol includes:

- A **reference line** and **arrow** pointing to the weld location.
- Details like weld size, length, type, process, and sometimes position.

How to Add a Weld Symbol in FreeCAD:

1. **Select a Leaderline**: Choose an existing leaderline pointing to the weld area.
2. **Activate the Tool**:
   - Click the "**Add Welding Information to Leaderline**"  button in the **TechDraw Annotation** toolbar.
   - Or, go to **TechDraw → Symbols → Add Welding Information to Leaderline**.

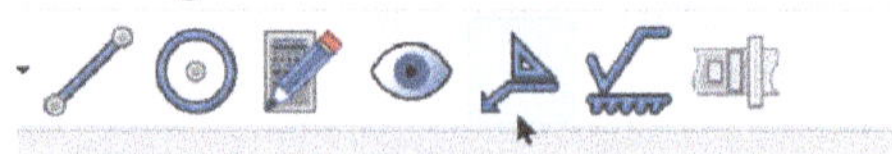

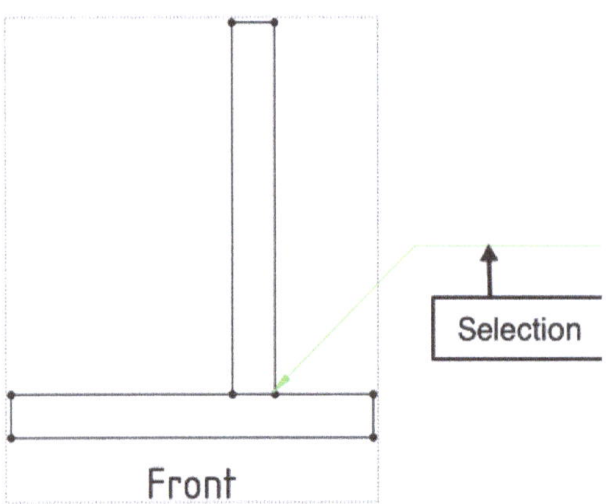

3. **Customize the Welding Information**:
   - **Weld Symbol Type**: Choose the weld type (e.g., fillet or groove) by clicking the **Symbol** button on the near side (lower side of the leaderline).

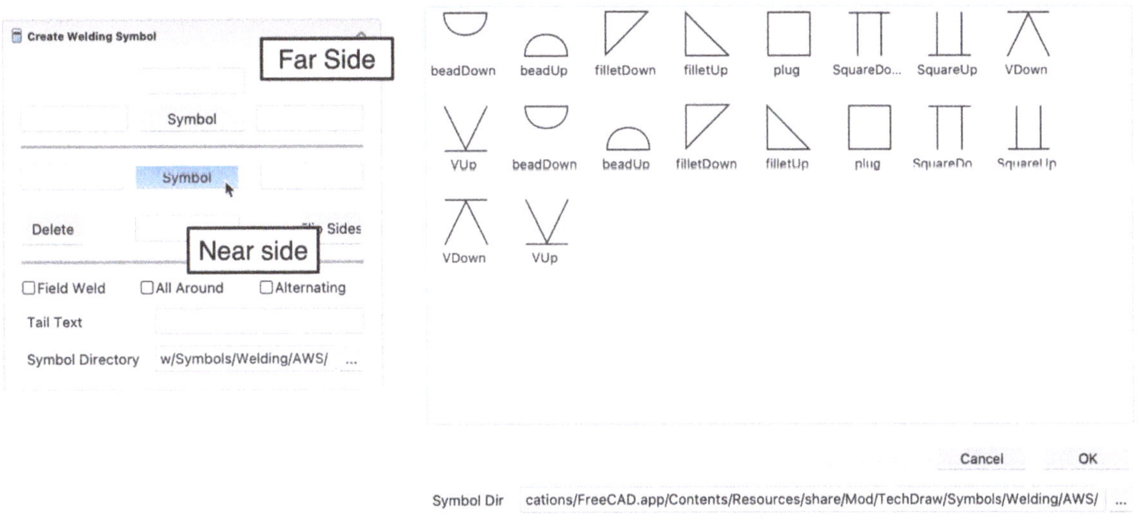

   - **Symbol Size**: Enter the weld dimensions in the box to the left of the Symbol button.
   - **Weld Length**: Specify the weld length in the box to the right of the Symbol button.
   - Repeat these steps for the far side (upper side of the leaderline) if needed.
   - **All Around**: Check this if the weld goes around the entire joint. A circle will appear at the intersection of the leaderline and reference line.
   - **Field Weld**: Check this for on-site welding. A flag symbol will appear opposite the arrow.

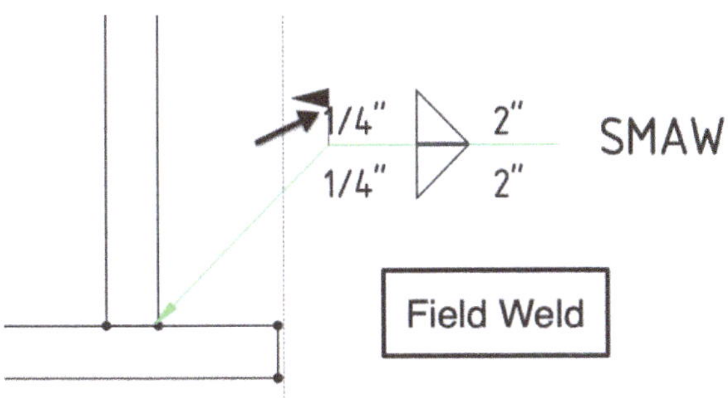

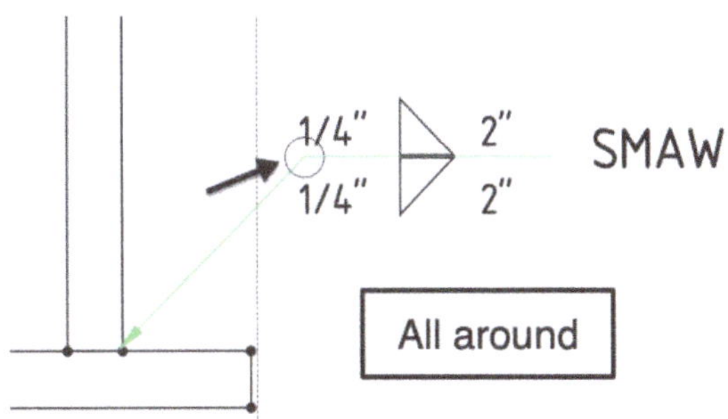

   - **Alternating**: Check this for alternating weld directions to ensure even heat distribution.

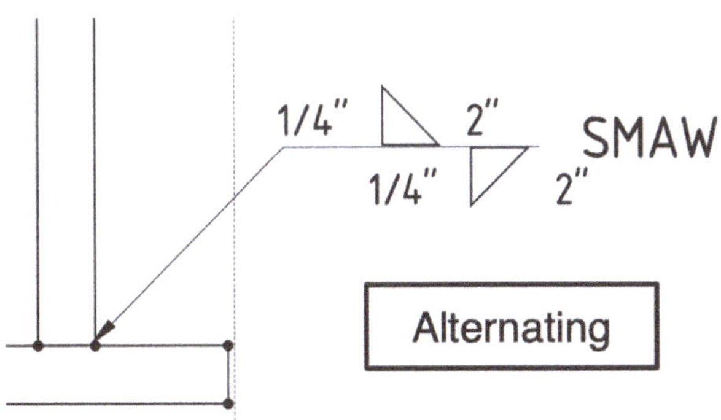

   - **Tail Text**: Add details like welding process, size, joint type, position, material, and special requirements (e.g., preheat, standards, or WPS references).
4. **Confirm**: Click **OK** to save your changes and close the task panel.

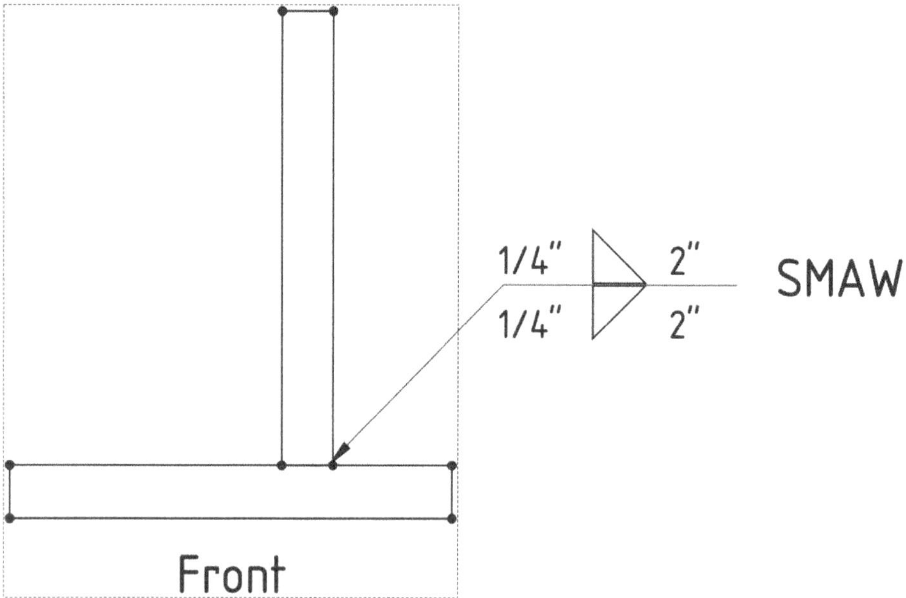

Create a Surface Finish Symbol

When it comes to engineering and manufacturing, a surface finish symbol, often referred to as a surface finish callout, plays a pivotal role. This graphical symbol or notation is an essential component of engineering and manufacturing drawings. Its purpose is straightforward: to specify the desired surface texture or finish for a particular part or component.

So, what does a typical surface finish symbol comprise? Let's break it down:

1. Symbol: The symbol itself is a unique combination of letters, numbers, and graphical symbols. It's like a coded message, conveying precise information about the surface finish. You might come across symbols like Ra, Rz, N, and others, each with its own significance.

2. Value: Next comes the numerical value, and this is where things get specific. The value attached to the symbol represents the desired roughness or smoothness of the surface. It's typically expressed in units such as micrometers (μm) or microinches (μin). This number sets the target for how finely finished the surface should be.

3. Additional Specifications: Surface finish symbols can get even more detailed. In some cases, you'll find extra notations. These could specify the method used to achieve the desired finish, whether it's grinding, polishing, or some other technique. Additionally, they might describe specific surface characteristics, like directional roughness or particular lay patterns.

But why are these symbols so important? Well, they're like a shared language among professionals in manufacturing and quality control. They help machinists, inspectors, and anyone else involved in the process understand precisely what's expected. It's a critical tool for maintaining quality standards and ensuring that parts or components meet their functional requirements.

Step 1: Select an Existing View

- Begin by selecting an existing view in your drawing where you want to add the surface finish symbol. This view represents the part or component you're working on.

Step 2: Access the Surface Finish Symbol Tool

There are two methods to access the Surface Finish Symbol tool:

- **Method 1:** Click on the "**Create a Surface Finish Symbol**" button. You can find this button on the **TechDraw Annotation** toolbar.
- **Method 2:** Alternatively, go to the menu bar and select "**TechDraw**," then choose "**Symbols**," and finally pick "**Create a Surface Finish Symbol**." This will open a task panel to assist you in the process.

Step 3: Define the Symbol and Style

Within the task panel, you will have several options:

- **Select the Symbol:** Choose the appropriate symbol that best represents the required surface finish from the six available symbol buttons.
- **Adjust the Symbol Angle (Optional):** You can optionally modify the angle of the symbol to align it precisely with your drawing, ensuring clarity and accuracy.
- **Choose ISO or ASME Style:** Depending on your industry or standards, select either the ISO or the ASME style for the symbol. This selection ensures that the symbol conforms to the applicable standards.

Step 4: Specify Attributes

- In this step, you can either select attributes from the provided list or enter custom attributes that describe the desired surface finish. These attributes should provide detailed information about the surface texture, such as roughness values, lay patterns, or any other relevant characteristics.

Step 5: Confirm and Add the Symbol

- Once you've set all the symbol details and attributes, press the "**OK**" button. This action will finalize the process and add the surface finish symbol to your selected view in the drawing.

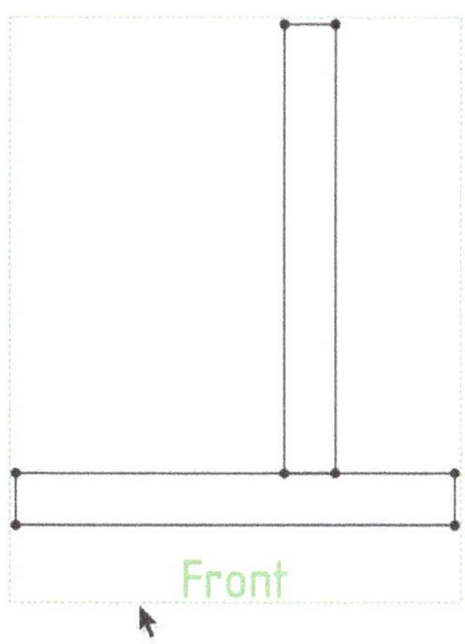

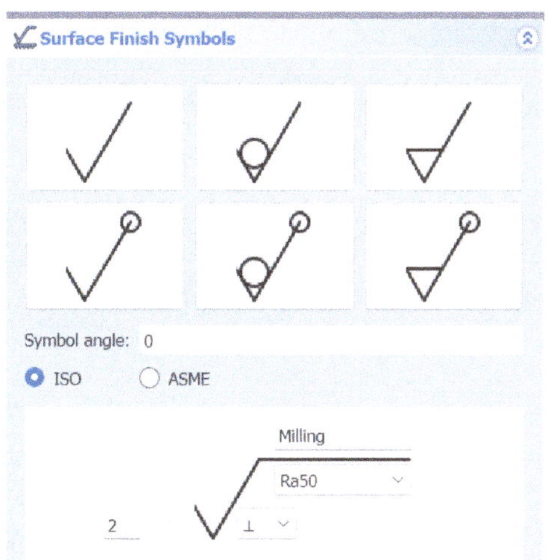

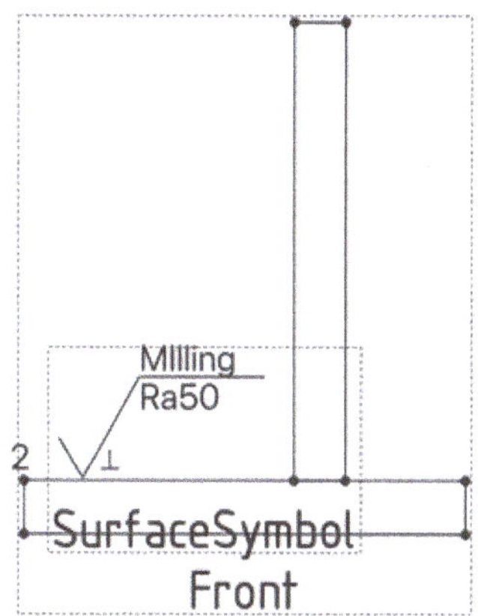

Adding hole Fit or Shat Fit

In the world of mechanical engineering and manufacturing, the concept of hole and shaft fits holds paramount importance. These fits define the relationship between two mating components - a hole (a cylindrical opening) and a shaft (a cylindrical projection). Their role is fundamental, ensuring that parts come together seamlessly and function precisely as intended. To gain a deeper insight into hole and shaft fits, let's break it down step by step:

1. Types of Fits

There are three primary types of fits, each characterized by the degree of interference or the tightness of fit between the hole and shaft:

- **Clearance Fit:** In this scenario, the shaft is slightly smaller than the hole, leaving a gap or clearance between them. This type of fit is ideal when relative motion between the parts is needed, such as in applications requiring regular assembly and disassembly.
- **Interference Fit:** Here, the shaft is slightly larger than the hole, creating a press or force fit. Interference fits are employed for non-separable assemblies, where a permanent, solid connection is essential.
- **Transition Fit:** Transition fits offer a compromise between clearance and interference fits. They strike a balance, ensuring that the fit isn't too tight or too loose. These are the go-to choice when a modest level of interference is required but not enough to necessitate a press fit.

2. Standardization
To maintain consistency and compatibility in manufacturing, hole and shaft fits are standardized. Leading organizations such as the International Organization for Standardization (ISO) and the American National Standards Institute (ANSI) provide guidelines and tables specifying dimensions and tolerances for different fits. These standards assist engineers in selecting the appropriate fit for their designs.

3. Design Considerations
When engineers opt for a particular hole and shaft fit, several crucial factors come into play:

- **Functionality:** The chosen fit must align with the intended function of the assembly. For instance, a rotating shaft might require a different fit compared to a stationary one.
- **Materials:** The material properties of the components play a significant role. Factors like coefficient of thermal expansion and wear resistance influence the fit selection.
- **Temperature and Environment:** Environmental conditions and temperature variations can influence fit selection. Materials can expand or contract under different circumstances, impacting the choice of fit.

4. Tolerances
Tolerances are essential to specify allowable variations in hole and shaft dimensions. These parameters are pivotal in ensuring manufacturability and correct assembly. ISO standards offer a range of tolerance classes, known as "IT grades," allowing engineers to define the desired level of precision.

5. Preferred Fits
Certain hole and shaft fits have earned recognition as "preferred fits." These are widely accepted and strike a balance between ease of assembly and performance. For example, H7/g6 represents a clearance fit, while H7/p6 signifies a transition fit, with "H7" and "g6" representing the tolerance classes of the hole and shaft, respectively.

6. Calculation and Analysis
Engineers employ mathematical calculations and Finite Element Analysis (FEA) to evaluate the stresses and clearances in various fits. This analytical approach guarantees that the selected fit can endure expected loads and environmental conditions.

The "**Add a hole or Shaft fit**" tool is a valuable feature in FreeCAD that facilitates the application of hole or shaft tolerances based on the ISO 286 standard. This tool is particularly useful when you need to define tolerances for linear dimensions or diameter dimensions in your engineering drawings.

Here's a simple step-step procedure on how to add hole or shaft fit to a linear or diameter dimension

Step 1: Select a Dimension
Begin by selecting a single linear dimension (this could represent length, a horizontal measurement, or a vertical measurement) or a single diameter dimension on your drawing.

Step 2: Invoking the Tool
There are a couple of ways to access the hole or shaft fit tool:

- **Method 1:** Click the "**Add hole or shaft fit**"  button on the **TechDraw Annotation** toolbar. This will activate the tool for you.
- **Method 2:** Alternatively, you can go to the menu by selecting "TechDraw," then choose "Symbols," and finally, pick "Add hole or shaft fit." This action opens a task panel where you can input your specifications.

Step 3: Specifying the Fit
Within the task panel, specify whether you are dealing with a **shaft fit** or a **hole fit**, depending on your design requirements.

Step 4: Choosing ISO 286 Fit
In the same task panel, you can now select the desired fit option from the provided dropdown menu. This selection will determine the tolerances and fits applicable to your dimension.

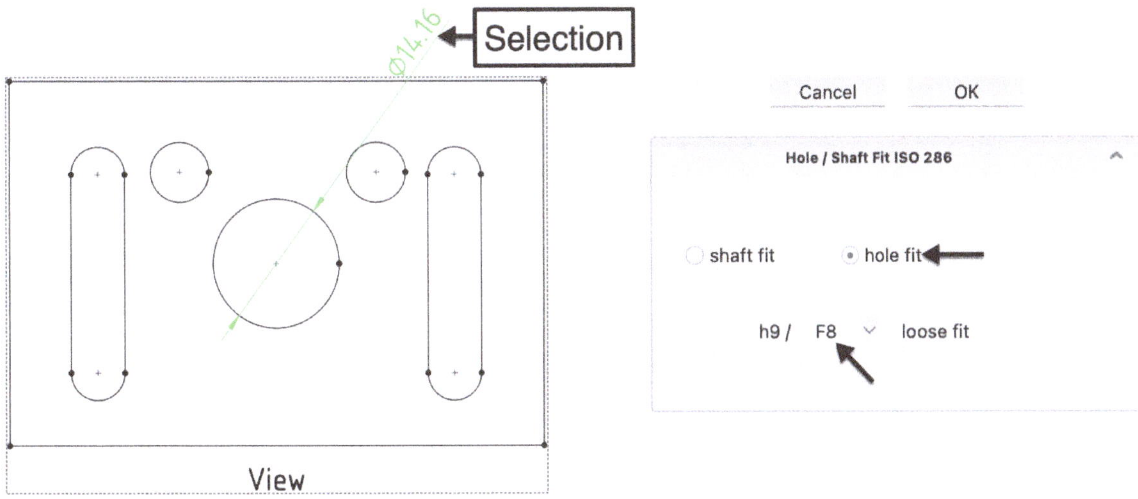

Step 5: Confirmation
Once you've set your fit preferences, press the "**OK**" button in the task panel to confirm your selections.

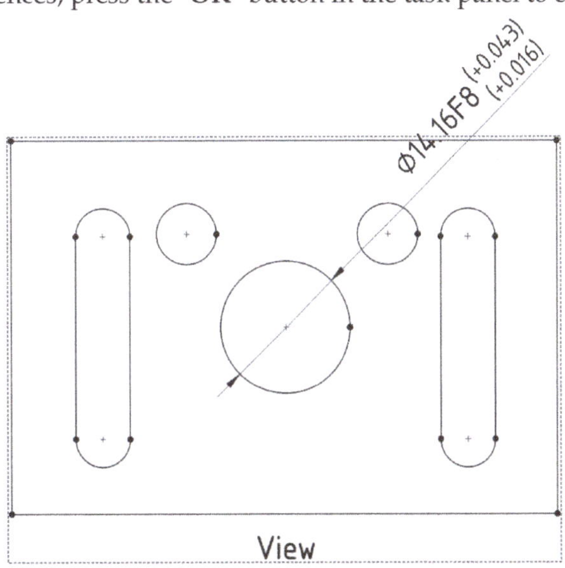

The selected fit option and the calculated tolerance values are now added to the chosen dimension on your drawing.

Chamfer Dimensions

You can create two types of chamfer dimensions in FreeCAD: Horizontal Chamfer Dimension and Vertical Chamfer Dimension. To create a horizontal chamfer dimension, first press and hold the CTRL key (Command Key for Mac users) and select the two vertices of a chamfer. Next, click **Insert Dimension** drop-down > **Create Horizontal Chamfer Dimension** on the **TechDraw Extend Dimensions** toolbar (or) click **TechDraw > Extensions: Dimensions > Create Horizontal Chamfer Dimension** on the menu bar.

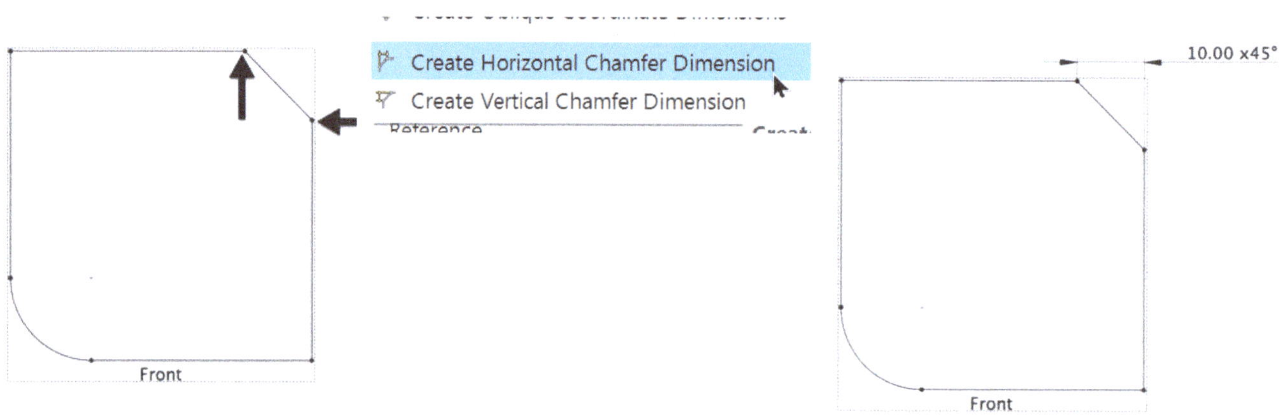

Likewise, you can create a vertical chamfer dimension using the **Create Vertical Chamfer Dimension** command.

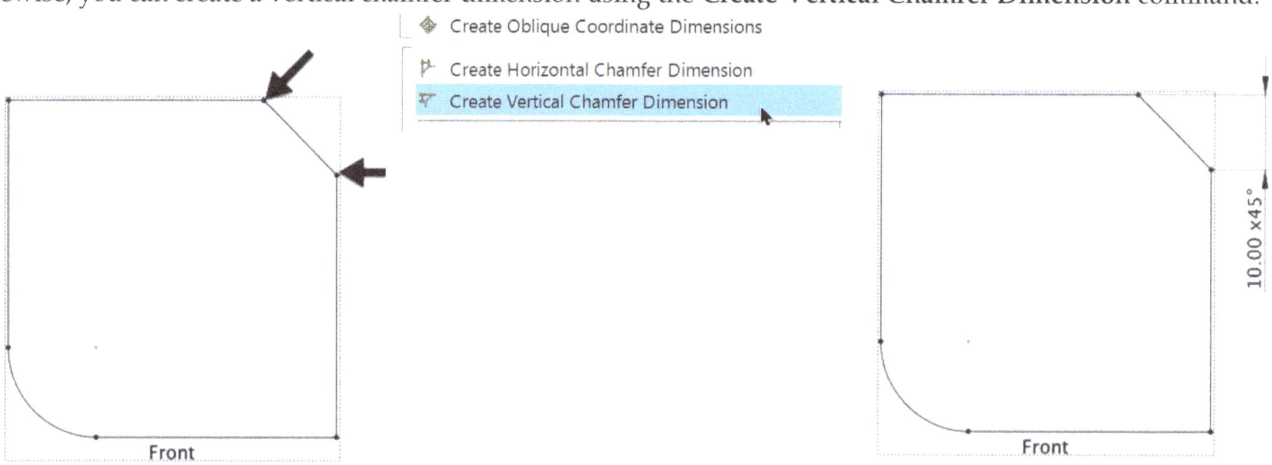

Best Practices for Generating Drawings in FreeCAD

- **Standards and Templates**: Start by selecting the appropriate industry and international drawing standards, such as ISO, ASME, or ANSI. Customize your FreeCAD templates to include essential information like title blocks and company logos.
- **Document Properties**: Configure document properties according to your project's needs, setting units (metric or imperial), dimensioning standards, and tolerancing standards.
- **Orthographic Views**: Utilize standard orthographic views (front, top, right, etc.) to accurately represent the part's geometry. This approach is typical in manufacturing and inspection.
- **Projection Views**: When required, include projected views, auxiliary views, or section views to represent complex geometry or hidden features.

- **Geometric Dimensioning and Tolerancing (GD&T)**: Implement GD&T symbols to specify tolerances and define critical dimensions.
- **Bill of Materials (BOM)**: Create a comprehensive BOM with part numbers, descriptions, quantities, and materials when producing assembly drawings.
- **Finish and Material Specifications**: Clearly specify surface finish requirements and the material used for each component.
- **Annotations**: Employ annotations like notes and labels to provide supplementary information, cautions, or special instructions.

Specific Considerations for Different Types of Parts

- **Plastic Parts**: Highlight draft angles and wall thickness to support mold design. Specify material properties, including modulus and shrinkage factors. Call out critical features for injection molding, such as gate locations.
- **Casted Parts**: Identify parting lines and draft angles to assist in the casting process. Include allowances for machining and surface finish requirements. Indicate potential defects and inspection points.
- **Forged Parts**: Highlight the grain flow direction for strength considerations. Specify any necessary heat treatment processes. Clearly define fillet radii, blends, and flash dimensions.
- **Machined Parts**: Specify machining processes, tool selections, and toolpath information. Detail surface finishes, tolerances, and fits for critical dimensions. Highlight datum references for CNC programming.

Precautions

- Avoid over-dimensioning: Include only necessary dimensions and annotations to prevent clutter and confusion.
- Ensure consistency: Double-check units, tolerances, and symbols to maintain uniformity within the drawing.
- Minimize ambiguities: Be clear and unambiguous in your language, especially when using notes and GD&T symbols.
- Proofread and review: Carefully review your drawings to identify errors, typos, and inaccuracies.
- Document revisions: Maintain a comprehensive record of revisions and changes made to the drawing.

In summary, creating drawings in FreeCAD requires meticulous attention to detail and adherence to industry standards. By following these best practices and keeping potential pitfalls in mind, you can effectively communicate your design intent to manufacturers, leading to a smoother manufacturing process and a higher-quality end product.

Tutorial 1

In this example, you create the 2D drawing of the part shown below.

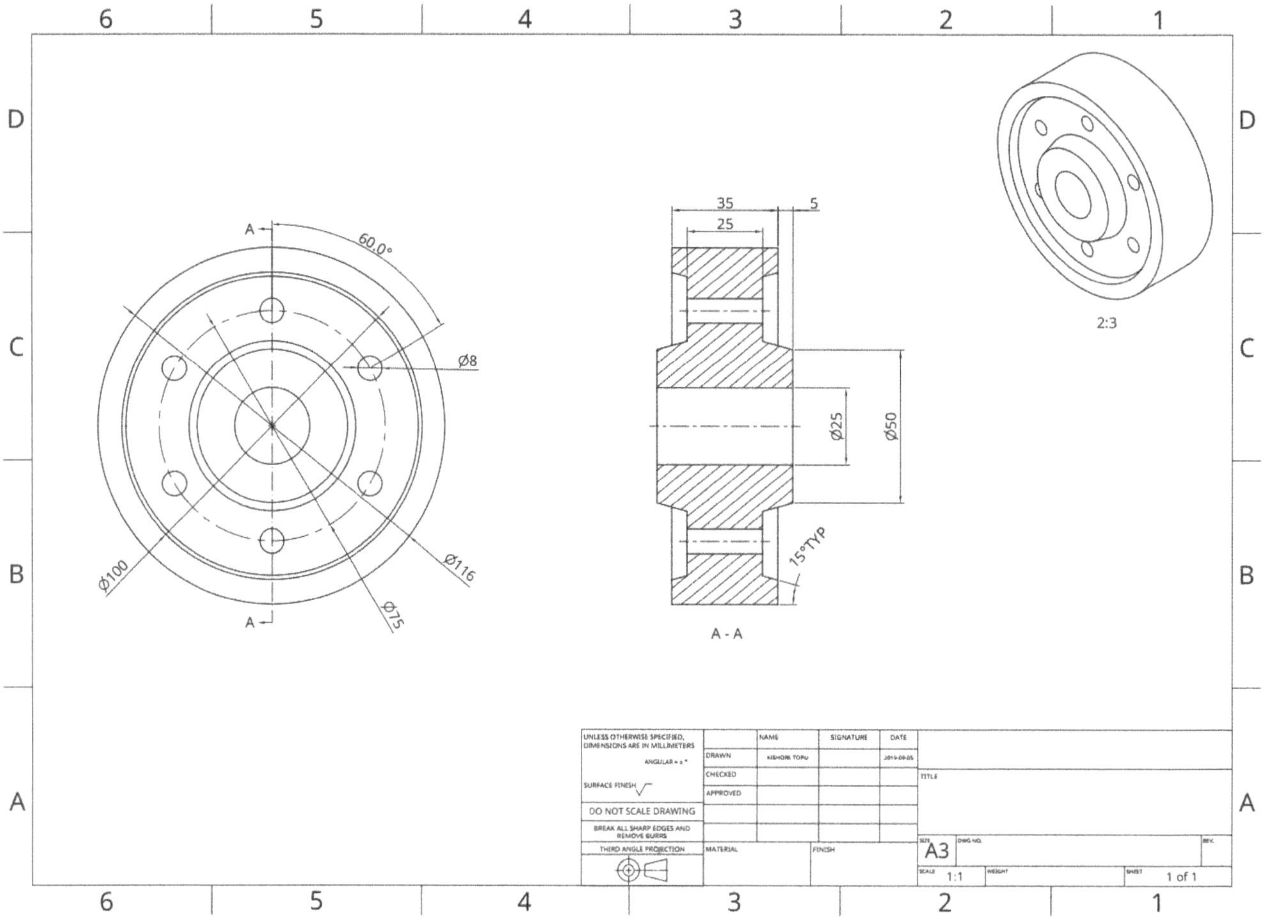

Creating a New Drawing

1. Download the **Chapter 10** part files from the companion website. Next, extract the zip file.
2. Click the **FreeCAD** icon on the Desktop.
3. Click **File > Open** on the Menu bar. Next, go to the location of the download files and double-click on the Tutorial1 file.
4. Select the **TechDraw** option from the **Workbench** drop-down (or) click **View > Workbench > TechDraw** on the menu bar.
5. Click **Edit > Preferences** on the menu bar (or) click **FreeCAD 1.0 > Preferences** on title bar, if you are working on MacOS. Next, select the **TechDraw** option from the left side of the **Preferences** dialog.
6. Select **Projection Group Angle > Third-angle**.
7. Click the **Annotation** tab, and then select **Center Line Style > Symmetry**. Next, click **OK**.

Lines	
Line Standard	ASME.Y14.2.2008
Line Width Group	FC 0.70mm
Hidden Line Style	---- Hidden
Section Line Style	— - Center
Detail Highlight Style	---- Hidden
Center Line Style	— - Symmetry
Break Line Style	—— Visible
Line End Cap Shape	Round

8. Click the **Insert Page using Template** icon on the **TechDraw Pages** toolbar (or) click **TechDraw > Insert Page using Template** on the menu bar.
9. Go to the Templates folder and select the **A3_LandscapeTD** template. Next, click **Open**.

Inserting the Base View

1. Click the **Tutorial 1** tab on the bottom of the window. Next, select the front face of the model.

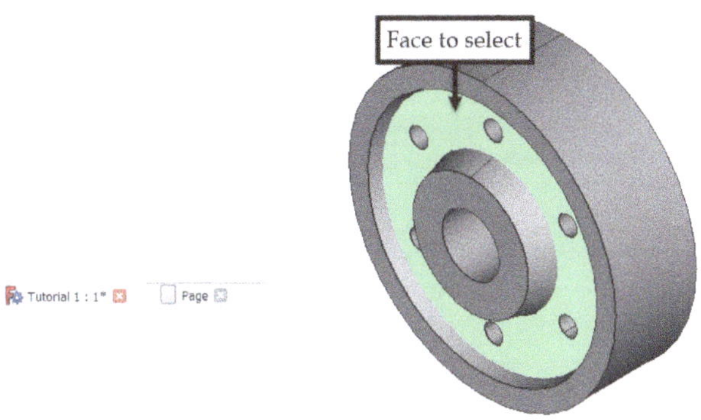

2. Click the **Align to selection** button on the **View** toolbar.
3. To generate the base view, click the **Insert View** icon on the **TechDraw Views** toolbar.
4. On the Part View section of the Tasks panel, click the Set direction of camera, or selected face if any, as primary direction button.
5. Click the **Spin counter clock wise** button and click **OK**.
6. Click on the dotted borderline of the view. Next, press and hold the left mouse and drag the view to left.

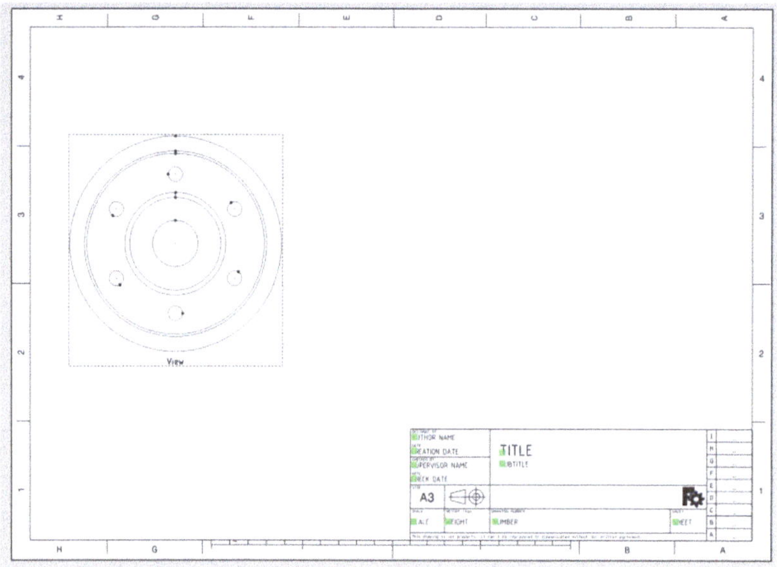

Generating the Section View

1. Select the base view.
2. Click the **Section View** drop-down > **Insert simple section view** icon on the **TechDraw Views** toolbar.
3. Click the **Preset view direction looking left** icon on the **Set View Direction** section.
4. Type **0** in the **X**, **Y**, and **Z** boxes, respectively. These values define the location of the section plane.
5. Type **A** in the **Identifier** box and click **OK** to create the section view.
6. Select the section view and click the **Position Section View** icon on the **TechDraw Attributes** toolbar; the section view is aligned with the base view.

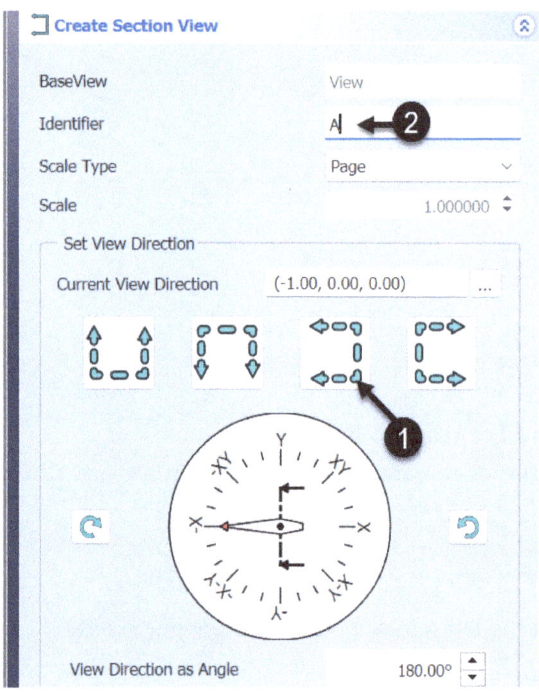

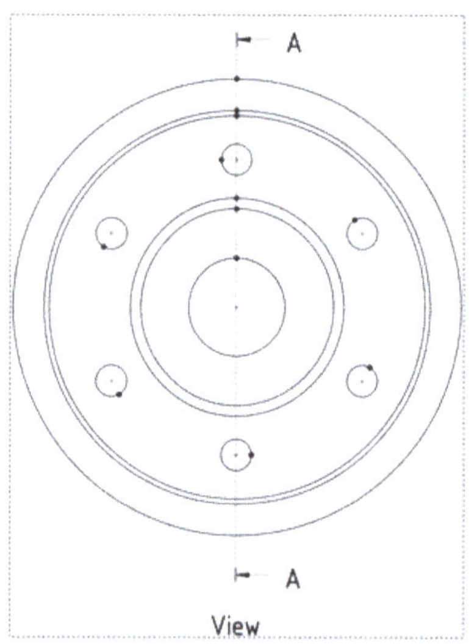

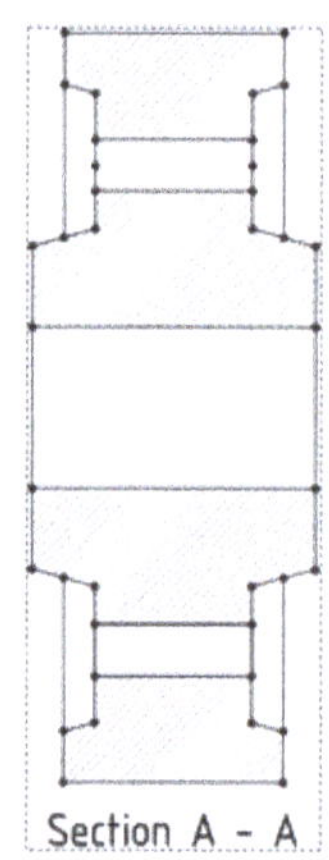

Inserting the Isometric View

1. In the **Model** panel, select the **Body**.
2. On the menu bar, click **View > Standard Views > Isometric**; the isometric view of the model is displayed on the drawing page.
3. Click the **Insert View**  icon on the **TechDraw Views** toolbar.
4. Select the isometric view and click the **Data** tab on the **Property** panel.
5. Scroll to the **Base** section and select **Scale Type > Custom**. Next, change the **Scale** value to 0.5.
6. Click **Edit > Refresh** on the menu bar.
7. Click and drag the isometric view to the top-right corner.

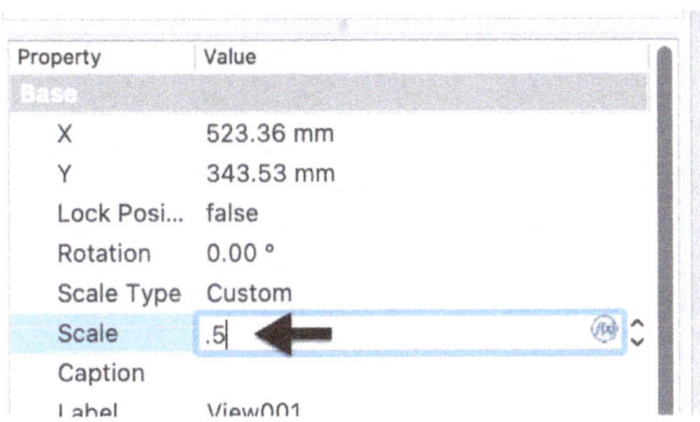

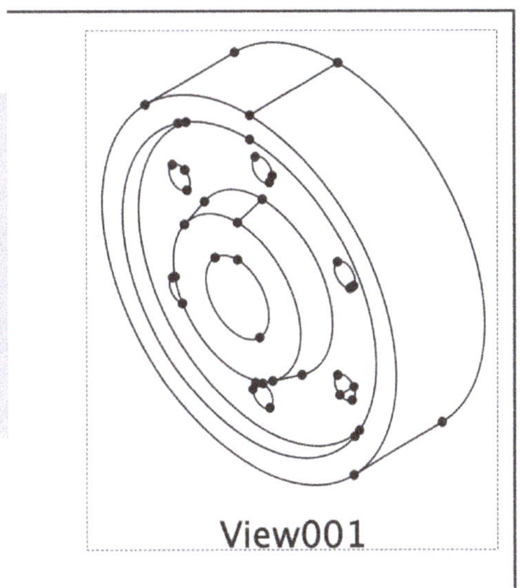

Adding the center lines to the drawing view

1. Select the outer circular edge of the base view from the drawing page. Next, click **Centerlines** drop-down > **Add Circle Centerlines** on the **TechDraw Centerlines** toolbar.

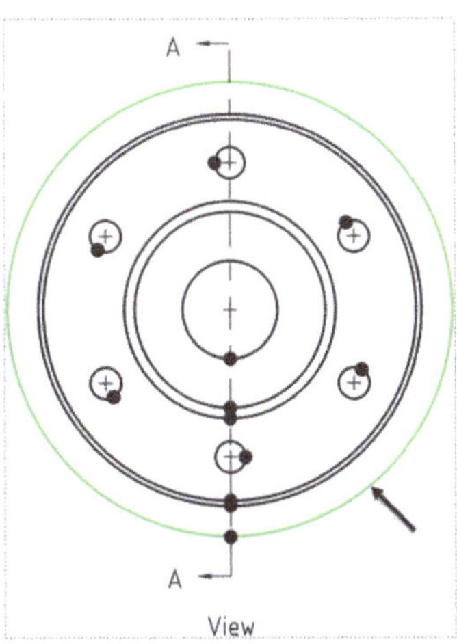

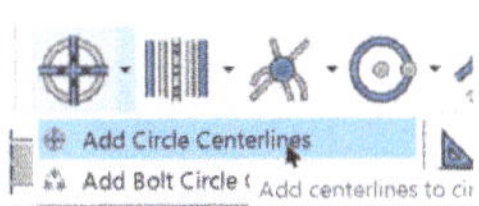

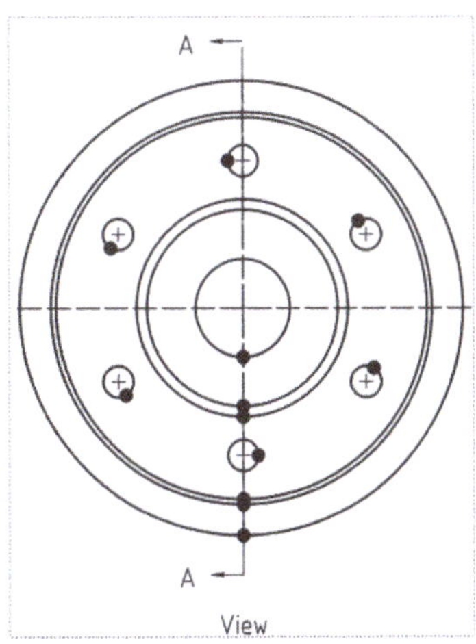

2. Press and hold the CTRL key (Command key for Mac users) and select all the circular edges of the polar pattern.
3. Click **Centerlines** drop-down > **Add Bolt Circle Centerlines** on the **TechDraw Centerlines** toolbar.

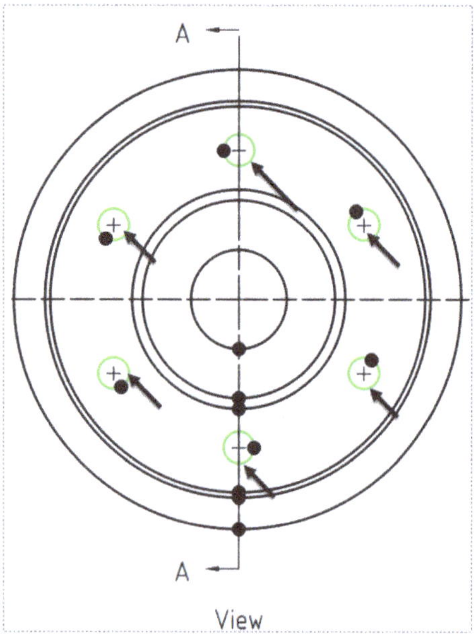

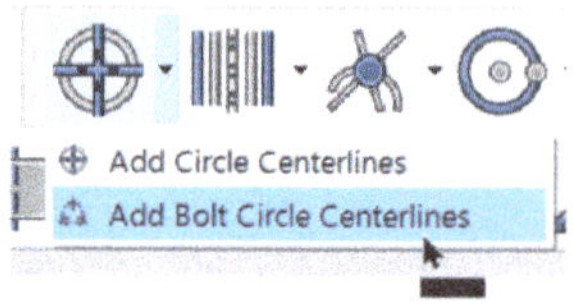

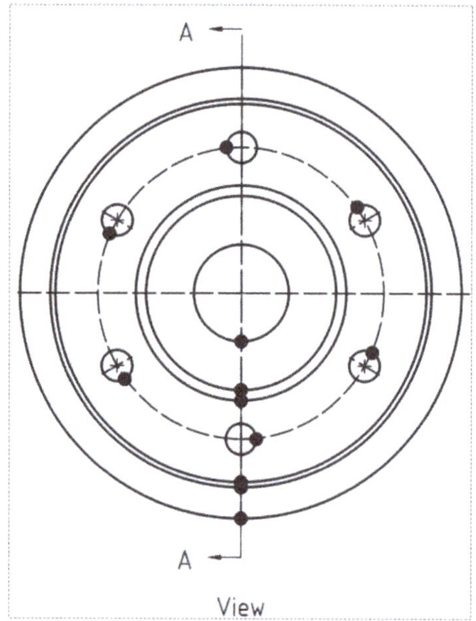

4. Select the two horizontal edges of section view, a shown.
5. Click **Add Lines** drop-down > **Add Centerlines Between 2 Lines** on the **TechDraw Annotations** toolbar.
6. Click **OK** on the **Tasks** panel.

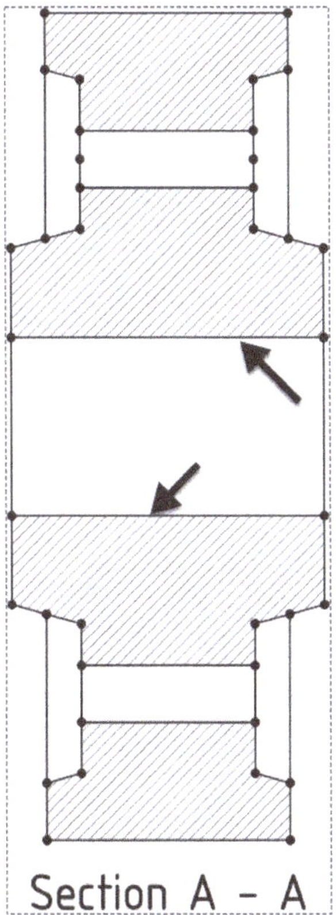

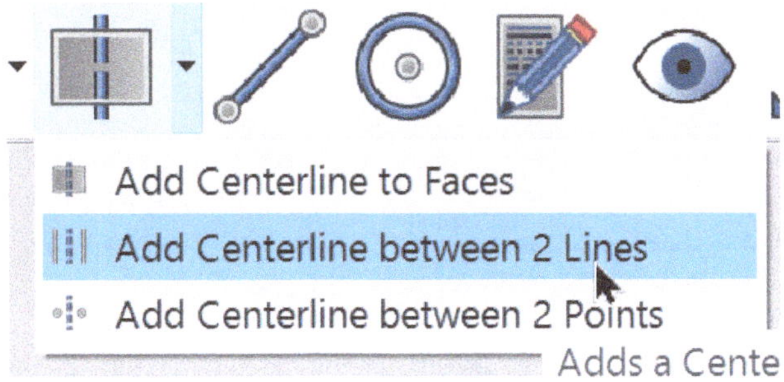

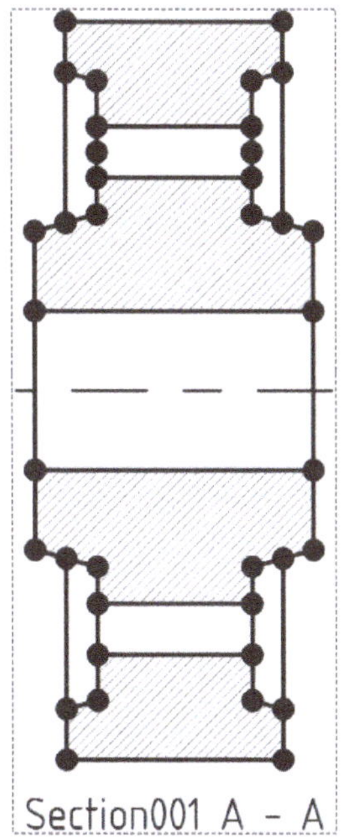

7. Likewise, create centerlines for the two holes on the section view, as shown.

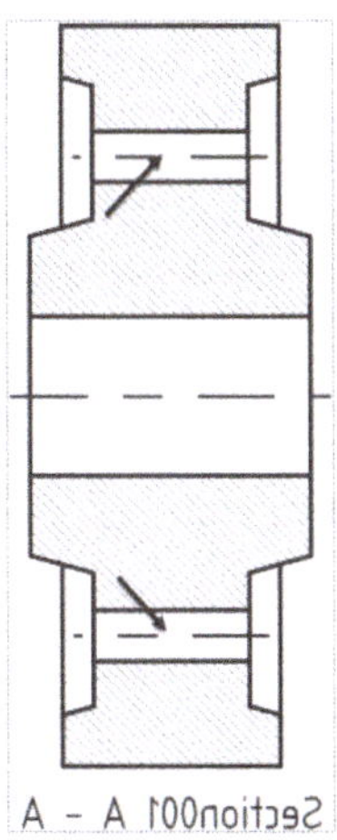

Adding Dimensions

Now, you add dimensions to the drawing.

1. Select the outer circular edge of the base view. Next, click the **Insert Dimensions** drop-down > **Insert Diameter Dimension**  icon on the **TechDraw Dimensions** toolbar (or) click **TechDraw > Dimensions > Insert Diameter Dimension** on the menu bar.

2. Click and drag the dimension outside the view.

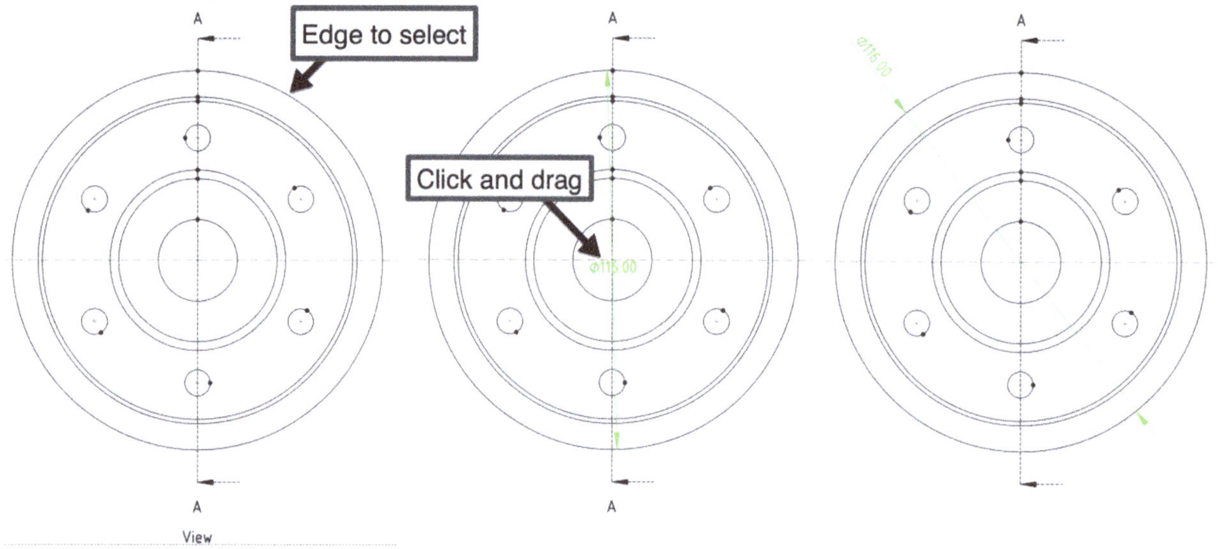

3. Likewise, add remaining dimensions to the base view, as shown.

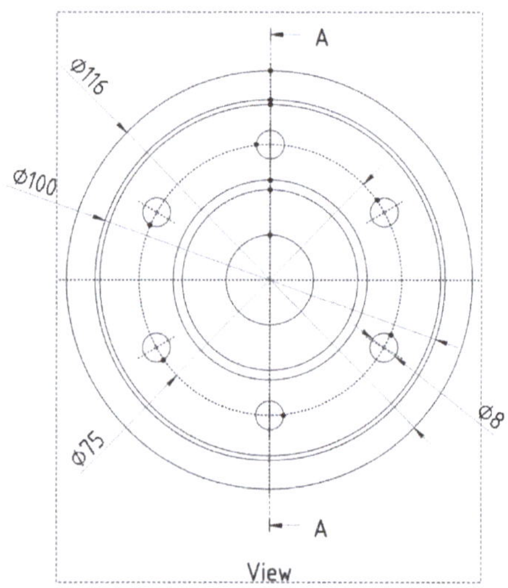

4. Press and the CTRL key (COMMAND key for Mac users) and select the four diameter dimensions.
5. Click the **View** tab on the **Property** panel. Next, select **Standard and Style > ASME Referencing**.
6. Select **Rendering Extent > Minimal**.

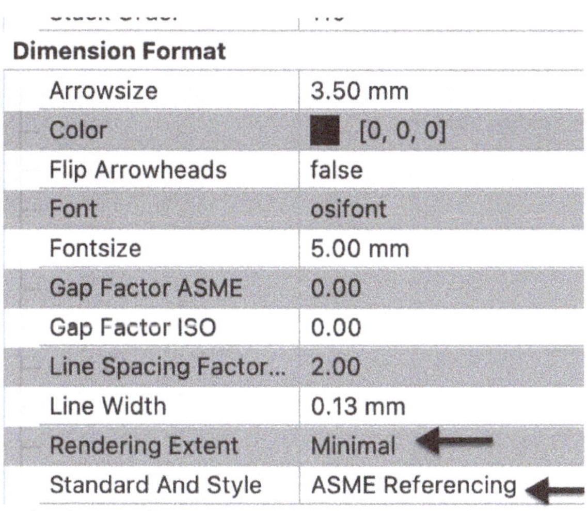

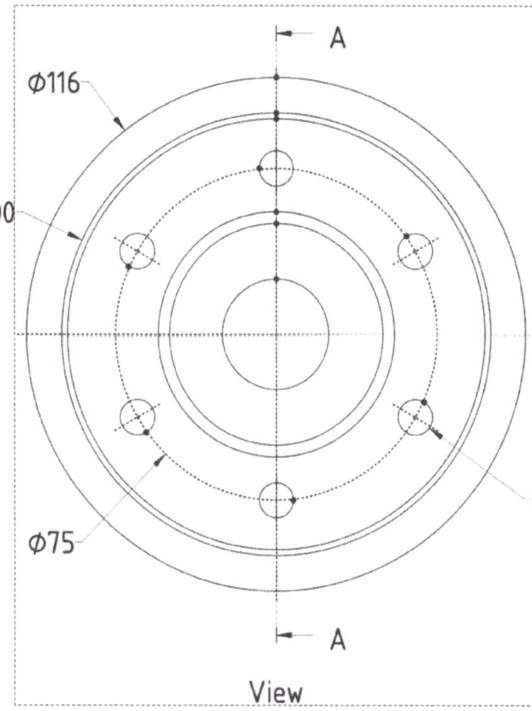

7. Select the diameter dimension of the small hole. Next, click the **Customize Format Label** icon on the **TechDraw Attributes** toolbar.
8. Click in the **Format Spec** box, as shown. Next, type **6 X** and press the SPACEBAR.
9. Click **OK**. On the drawing sheet, click and drag the dimension.

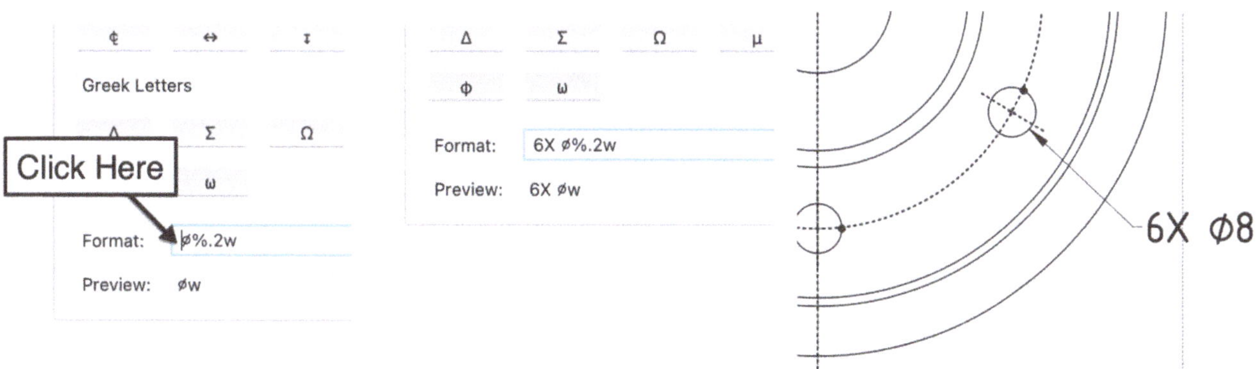

10. Press and hold the Ctrl key and select the vertices of the section view, as shown.
11. Click the **Insert Dimensions** drop-down > **Insert Horizontal Dimension** icon on the **TechDraw Dimensions** toolbar.
12. Click and drag the dimension upward.

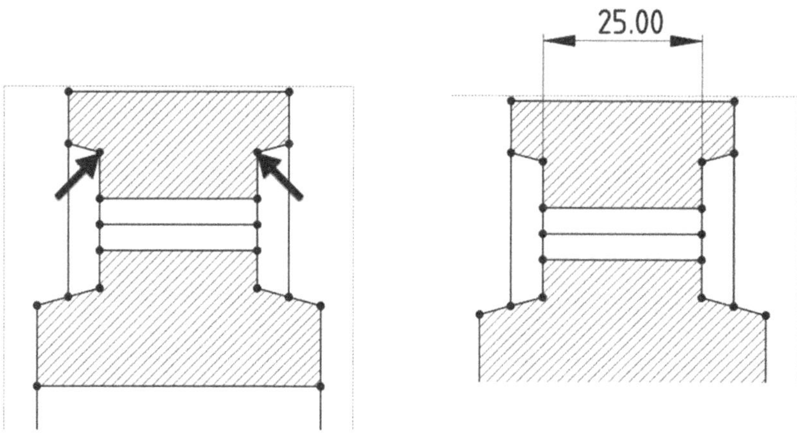

13. Press and hold the Ctrl key and select the vertices of the section view, as shown.
14. Click the **Insert Dimensions** drop-down > **Insert Horizontal Dimension** icon on the **TechDraw Dimensions** toolbar.
15. Likewise, create another horizontal dimension.
16. Drag the dimensions upward, as shown.

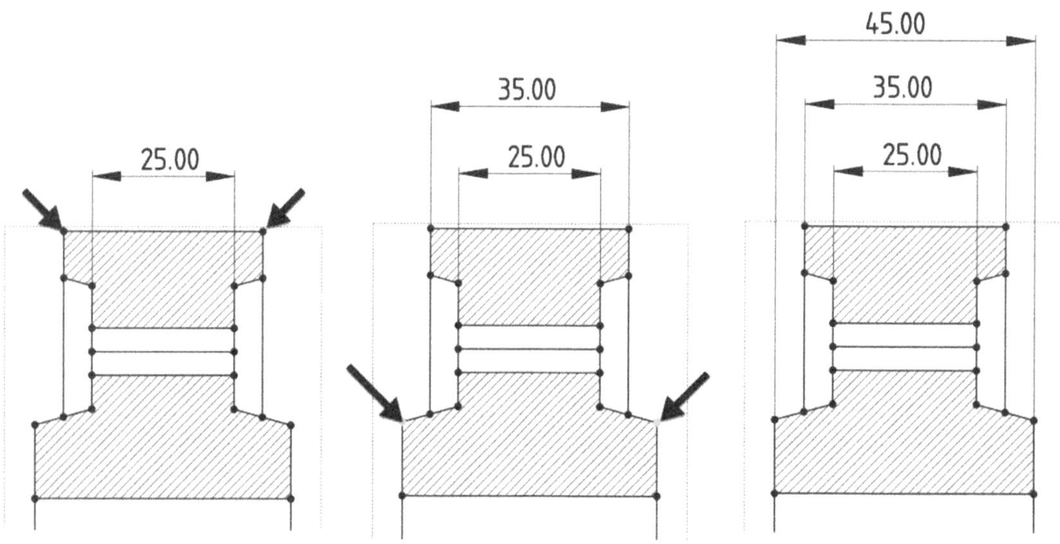

17. Press and hold the Ctrl key and select the two points of the section view, as shown.
18. Click the **Insert Vertical Dimension** icon on the **TechDraw Dimensions** toolbar.
19. Likewise, create another horizontal dimension.
20. Drag the dimensions toward the right, as shown.

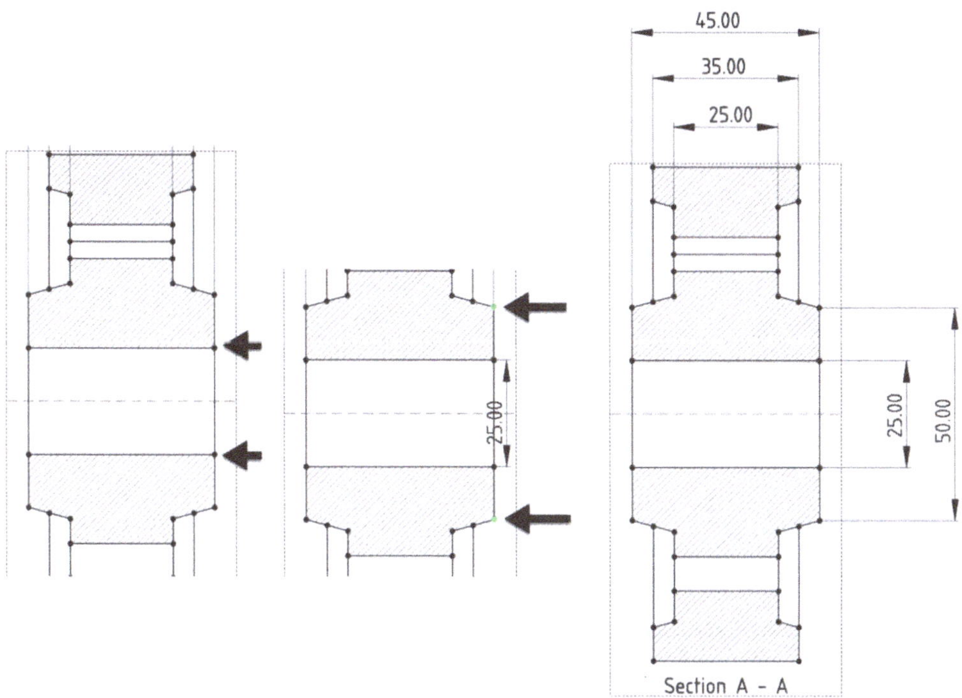

21. Press and hold the Ctrl key and select the inclined and horizontal edges of the section view, as shown.
22. Click the **Insert Dimensions** drop-down > **Angle Dimension** icon on the **TechDraw Dimensions** toolbar.
23. Select the angular dimension value. Press and hold the left mouse button and drag the pointer toward left. Position the dimension, as shown.

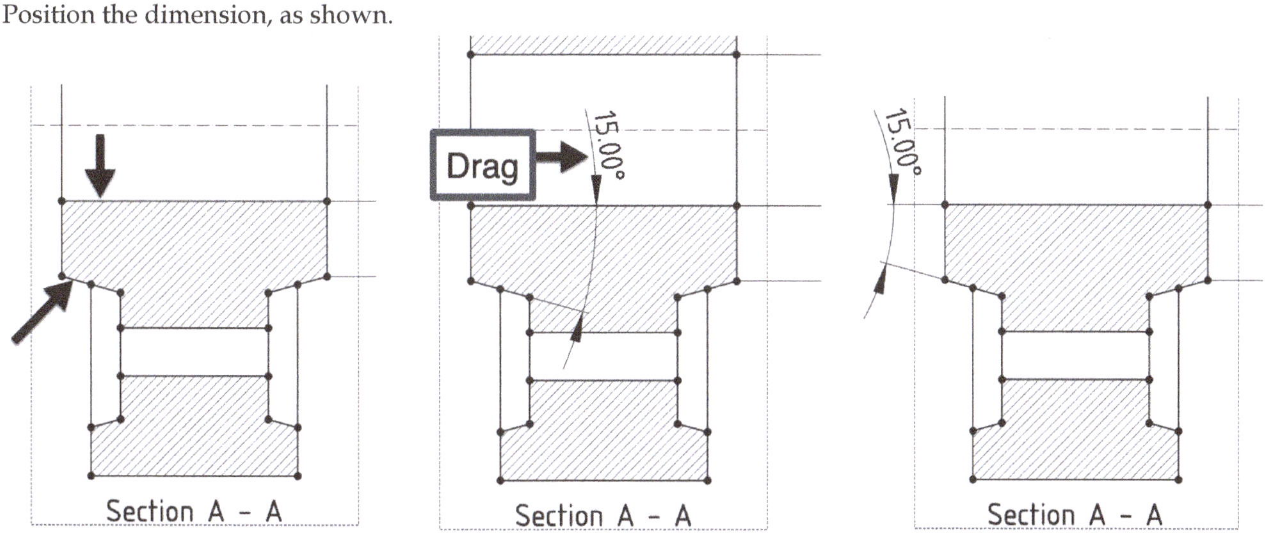

24. Select the angular dimension from the section view. Next, click the **Data** tab on the **Property** panel.
25. In the **Format Spec** box, click next to the dimension value and press the SPACEBAR. Next, type **TYP**.

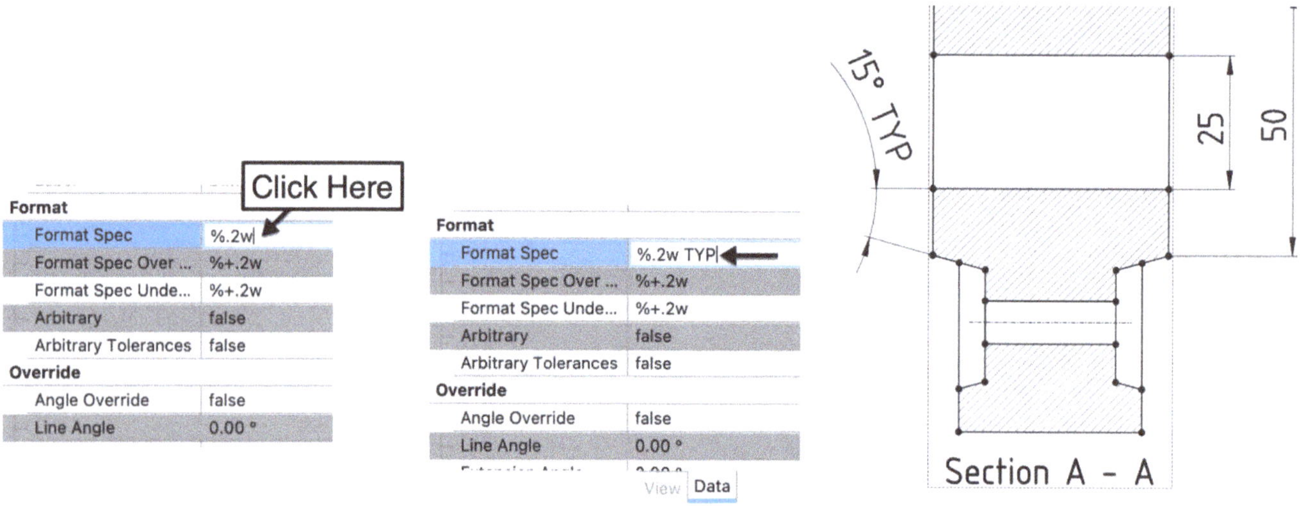

26. Select the vertical dimension from the section view. Next, click the **Insert Prefix**  icon on the **TechDraw Extend Dimensions** toolbar.
27. Likewise, add the diameter symbol to the vertical dimension with the value 50.

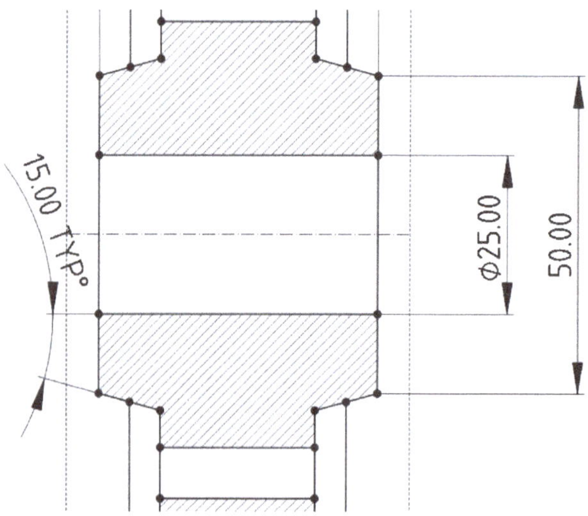

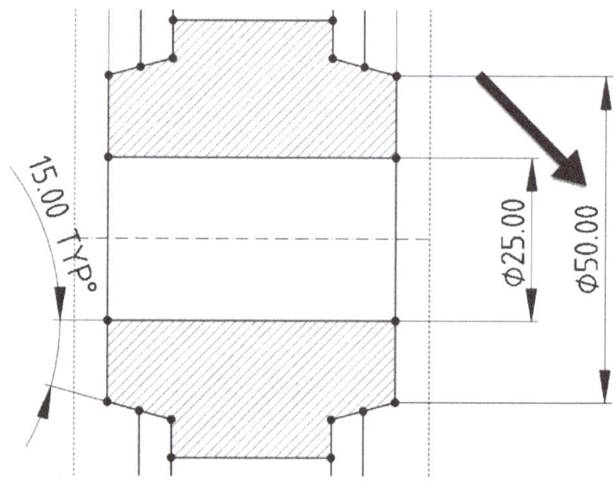

28. Save and close the file.

Questions

1. How to create drawing views from an existing part or assembly file?
2. List the commands used to create centerlines and center marks.
3. How to add symbols and texts to a dimension?
4. How to create section views?

Exercises

Exercise 1

Create orthographic views of the part model shown below. Add dimensions and annotations to the drawing.

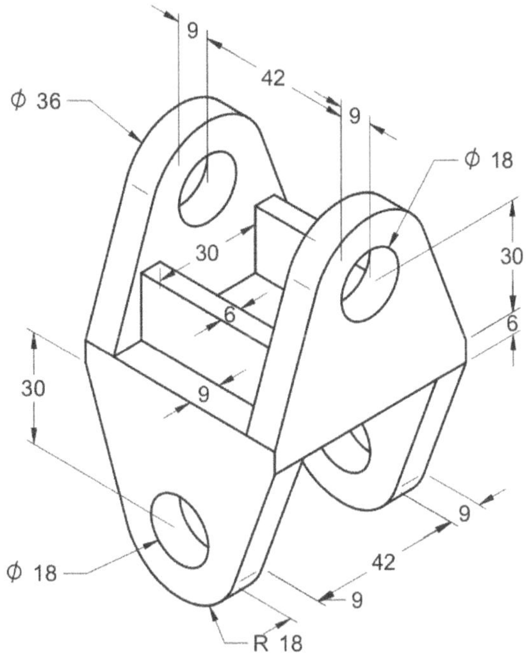

Exercise 2

Create orthographic views and an auxiliary view of the part model shown below. Add dimensions and annotations to the drawing.

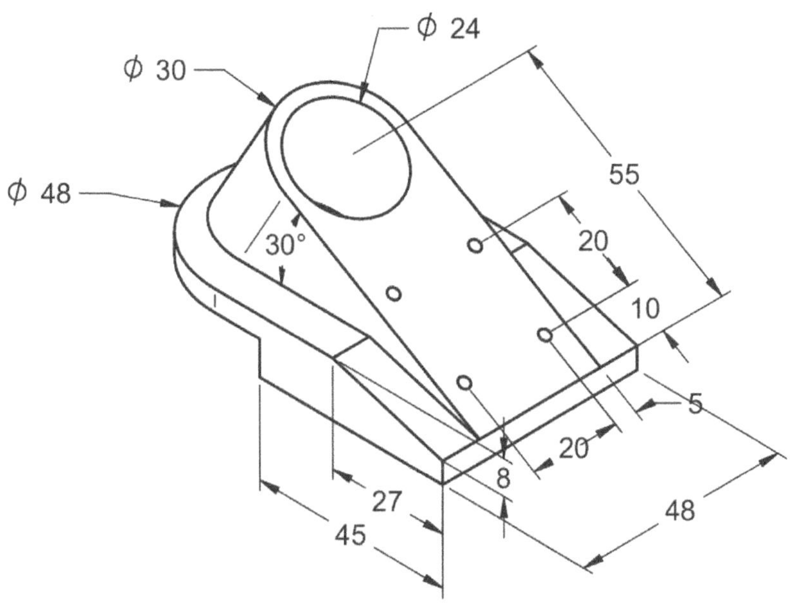

Index

3

3 rim points, 28
3-Point Angle Dimension, 326

A

Additive helix, 239
Additive Loft, 256
Additive Pipe, 231, 233
Aligned Section View, 312
Angle Constraint, 39
Angle Dimension, 326
Arc Length Dimension, 329

B

Block Constraint, 48
Bolt Circle Centerlines, 320
Box Zoom, 112
B-spline by control points, 60, 61

C

Center and end points, 26
Center and rim point, 27
Centered Rectangle, 28
Centerline between 2 Lines, 318
Centerline between 2 Points, 318
Chamfer, 140
Circle Centerlines, 319
Circular Edge Constraint, 286
Coincident, 42
Constrain auto radius/diameter, 41
Constrain radius, 40
Cosmetic Intersection Vertex, 322, 328
Cosmetic Thread Bolt Bottom View, 322
Cosmetic Thread Bolt Side View, 321
Cosmetic Thread Hole Bottom View, 320
Cosmetic Thread Hole Side View, 321
Counterbored Hole, 132
Countersink Hole, 133
Create Rectangle, 28
Create Sketch, 20

D

Datum Line, 103
Datum Point, 105
Delete all Constraints, 56
Delete all geometry, 56
Detail View, 315
Diameter Constraint, 39
Diameter Dimension, 325
Distance Constraint, 39
Draft, 142
Drill Point, 131

E

Edit Background, 16
Equal, 45
Extend edge, 51
Extent, 106
External Geometry, 96

F

File Toolbar, 9
Fillet, 137
Fit all, 112
Flat Lines, 113
Free Orbit, 112
FreeCAD Help, 18

G

Graphics Window, 7
Groove, 98

H

Heptagon, 32
Hexagon, 32
Hidden line, 113
Hole, 129
hole Fit or Shat Fit, 342
Horizontal Chain Dimensions, 332
Horizontal Chamfer Dimension, 345
Horizontal Constraint, 43
Horizontal Coordinate Dimensions, 329
Horizontal Distance, 37
Horizontal Extent Dimension, 327
Horizontal/Vertical, 45

I

Insert Annotation, 338
Insert Default Page, 304
Insert Rich Text Annotation, 337

L

Length Dimension, 325
Line, 23
Linear Pattern, 180
Lock, 41

M

Macro, 10
Menu, 14
Mirror Sketch, 59
Mirrored, 178
Mouse Functions, 15
Multi Transform, 183

N

No Shading, 114

O

Oblique Coordinate Dimensions, 330
Octagon, 32
Over-constrained Sketch, 42

P

Pad, 90
Pan, 112
Parallel Constraint, 46
Part Design Helper, 11
Part Design Modeling, 11
Pentagon, 31
Periodic B-spline by control points, 61, 62
Perpendicular Constraint, 47
Planes, 99
Planes Parallelism Constraint, 288
Pocket, 98
Points, 114
Polar Pattern, 181
Polygon, 30
Polyline, 24
Position Horizontal Chain Dimensions, 333
Position Section View, 309

R

Regular Polygon, 33
Remove axes alignment, 57
Removing Redundant Constraints, 57
Revolution, 92
Rotate Left, 112
Rotate right, 112
Rounded Rectangle, 29

S

Section View, 307
Select unconstrained DOF, 52
Shaded, 113
Simple Hole, 130
Sketch Fillet, 49, 50
Sketch Tools, 11
Sketcher, 10
Sketcher B-spline tools, 11
Sketcher constraints, 10
Sketcher geometries, 10
Sketcher Virtual Space, 11
Slot, 29, 30
Smart Dimension, 35
Sphere to Sphere constraint, 288
Split Edge, 52
Square, 31
Starting FreeCAD, 6
Status bar, 14
Structure, 10
Sub-assemblies, 291
Subtractive helix, 243
Subtractive Loft, 259
Subtractive pipe, 236
Surface Finish Symbol, 341
Symmetric to plane, 90
Symmetrical Constraint, 47

T

Tangent, 46
Taper, 109
Tasks tab, 15
TechDraw Attributes, 13
TechDraw Centerlines, 13
TechDraw Decoration, 13
TechDraw Dimensions, 13
TechDraw Extend Dimensions, 13
TechDraw File Access, 13
TechDraw Pages, 12
TechDraw Views, 12
Thickness, 145
Toggle Construction geometry, 35
Toolbars, 9
Triangle, 30
Trim Edge, 51

U

User Interface, 6

V

Vertical Chamfer Dimension, 345
Vertical Constraint, 44
Vertical Coordinate Dimensions, 329
Vertical Distance, 38
Vertical Extent Dimension, 327
View toolbar, 10

W

Welding Information, 339
Wireframe, 113
Workbench Toolbar, 10

Z

Zoom In, 112
Zoom Out, 112

9 788198 378309

Printed at Repro India Ltd.